A Bibliography of Female Economic Thought to 1940

Historians of economic thought have rarely given much attention to writings by women. This volume is intended to help remedy that situation. It presents a wide-ranging collection of references to women's writings on economic issues from the 1770s to 1940. Among the more than 1,700 writers included are prolific scholars, leading social reformers, economic journalists and government officials, along with many women who contributed only one or two works to the field. The topics addressed include principles of political economy, poverty, trade unions, women's employment, child labor, women's property rights, imperialism, and slavery. Most of the references are to writings in English, but some works are in other languages.

This bibliography will serve as a major reference work for inquiries concerning gender and economic thought. It will help illuminate the history and sociology of economics, the lives of female social scientists and activists, and the histories of labor, feminism, and social reform.

Kirsten K. Madden is Associate Professor of Economics at Millersville University, USA.

Janet A. Seiz is Associate Professor of Economics at Grinnell College, USA.

Michèle Pujol taught Women's Studies at the University of Victoria, Canada. Her 1992 book *Feminism and Antifeminism in Early Economic Thought* was a path-breaking study of women and gender in economics. She died in 1997 at the age of 46.

Routledge Studies in the History of Economics

1 **Economics as Literature**
Willie Henderson

2 **Socialism and Marginalism in Economics 1870–1930**
Edited by Ian Steedman

3 **Hayek's Political Economy**
The socio-economics of order
Steve Fleetwood

4 **On the Origins of Classical Economics**
Distribution and value from William Petty to Adam Smith
Tony Aspromourgos

5 **The Economics of Joan Robinson**
Edited by Maria Cristina Marcuzzo, Luigi Pasinetti and Alesandro Roncaglia

6 **The Evolutionist Economics of Léon Walras**
Albert Jolink

7 **Keynes and the 'Classics'**
A study in language, epistemology and mistaken identities
Michel Verdon

8 **The History of Game Theory, Vol. 1**
From the beginnings to 1945
Robert W. Dimand and Mary Ann Dimand

9 **The Economics of W. S. Jevons**
Sandra Peart

10 **Gandhi's Economic Thought**
Ajit K. Dasgupta

11 **Equilibrium and Economic Theory**
Edited by Giovanni Caravale

12 **Austrian Economics in Debate**
Edited by Willem Keizer, Bert Tieben and Rudy van Zijp

13 **Ancient Economic Thought**
Edited by B. B. Price

14 **The Political Economy of Social Credit and Guild Socialism**
Frances Hutchinson and Brian Burkitt

15 **Economic Careers**
Economics and economists in Britain 1930–1970
Keith Tribe

16 **Understanding 'Classical' Economics**
Studies in the long-period theory
Heinz Kurz and Neri Salvadori

17 **History of Environmental Economic Thought**
E. Kula

18 Economic Thought in Communist and Post-Communist Europe
Edited by Hans-Jürgen Wagener

19 Studies in the History of French Political Economy
From Bodin to Walras
Edited by Gilbert Faccarello

20 The Economics of John Rae
Edited by O. F. Hamouda, C. Lee and D. Mair

21 Keynes and the Neoclassical Synthesis
Einsteinian versus Newtonian macroeconomics
Teodoro Dario Togati

22 Historical Perspectives on Macroeconomics
Sixty years after the 'General Theory'
Edited by Philippe Fontaine and Albert Jolink

23 The Founding of Institutional Economics
The leisure class and sovereignty
Edited by Warren J. Samuels

24 Evolution of Austrian Economics
From Menger to Lachmann
Sandye Gloria

25 Concept of Money
The god of commodities
Anitra Nelson

26 The Economics of James Steuart
Edited by Ramón Tortajada

27 The Development of Economics in Europe since 1945
Edited by A. W. Bob Coats

28 The Canon in the History of Economics
Critical essays
Edited by Michalis Psalidopoulos

29 Money and Growth
Selected papers of Allyn Abbott Young
Edited by Perry G. Mehrling and Roger J. Sandilands

30 The Social Economics of Jean-Baptiste Say
Markets & virtue
Evelyn L. Forget

31 The Foundations of Laissez-Faire
The economics of Pierre de Boisguilbert
Gilbert Faccarello

32 John Ruskin's Political Economy
Willie Henderson

33 Contributions to the History of Economic Thought
Essays in honour of R. D. C. Black
Edited by Antoin E. Murphy and Renee Prendergast

34 Towards an Unknown Marx
A commentary on the manuscripts of 1861–63
Enrique Dussel

35 Economics and Interdisciplinary Exchange
Edited by Guido Erreygers

36 **Economics as the Art of Thought**
Essays in memory of G. L. S. Shackle
Edited by Stephen F. Frowen and Peter Earl

37 **The Decline of Ricardian Economics**
Politics and economics in post-Ricardian theory
Susan Pashkoff

38 **Piero Sraffa**
His life, thought and cultural heritage
Alessandro Roncaglia

39 **Equilibrium and Disequilibrium in Economic Theory**
The Marshall–Walras divide
Edited by Michel de Vroey

40 **The German Historical School**
The historical and ethical approach to economics
Edited by Yuichi Shionoya

41 **Reflections on the Classical Canon in Economics**
Essays in honor of Samuel Hollander
Edited by Sandra Peart and Evelyn Forget

42 **Piero Sraffa's Political Economy**
A centenary estimate
Edited by Terenzio Cozzi and Roberto Marchionatti

43 **The Contribution of Joseph Schumpeter to Economics**
Economic development and institutional change
Richard Arena and Cecile Dangel

44 **On the Development of Long-Run Neo-Classical Theory**
Tom Kompas

45 **F. A. Hayek as a Political Economist**
Economic analysis and values
Edited by Jack Birner, Pierre Garrouste and Thierry Aimar

46 **Pareto, Economics and Society**
The mechanical analogy
Michael McLure

47 **The Cambridge Controversies in Capital Theory**
A study in the logic of theory development
Jack Birner

48 **Economics Broadly Considered**
Essays in honor of Warren J. Samuels
Edited by Steven G. Medema, Jeff Biddle and John B. Davis

49 **Physicians and Political Economy**
Six studies of the work of doctor-economists
Edited by Peter Groenewegen

50 The Spread of Political Economy and the Professionalisation of Economists
Economic societies in Europe, America and Japan in the nineteenth century
Massimo Augello and Marco Guidi

51 Historians of Economics & Economic Thought
The construction of disciplinary memory
Steven G. Medema and Warren J. Samuels

52 Competing Economic Theories
Essays in memory of Giovanni Caravale
Sergio Nisticò and Domenico Tosato

53 Economic Thought and Policy in Less Developed Europe
The 19th century
Edited by Michalis Psalidopoulos and Maria-Eugenia Almedia Mata

54 Family Fictions and Family Facts
Harriet Martineau, Adolphe Quetelet and the population question in England 1798–1859
Brian Cooper

55. Eighteenth-Century Economics
Peter Groenewegen

56 The Rise of Political Economy in the Scottish Enlightenment
Edited by Tatsuya Sakamoto and Hideo Tanaka

57 Classics and Moderns in Economics Vol. I
Essays on nineteenth and twentieth century economic thought
Peter Groenewegen

58 Classics and Moderns in Economics Vol. II
Essays on nineteenth and twentieth century economic thought
Peter Groenewegen

59 Marshall's Evolutionary Economics
Tiziano Raffaelli

60 Money, Time and Rationality in Max Weber
Austrian connections
Stephen D. Parsons

61 Classical Macroeconomics
Some modern variations and distortions
James C. W. Ahiakpor

62 The Historical School of Economics in England and Japan
Tamotsu Nishizawa

63 Classical Economics and Modern Theory
Studies in long-period analysis
Heinz D. Kurz and Neri Salvadori

64 A Bibliography of Female Economic Thought to 1940
Kirsten K. Madden, Janet A. Sietz and Michele Pujol

A Bibliography of Female Economic Thought to 1940

Kirsten K. Madden, Janet A. Seiz
and Michèle Pujol

Routledge
Taylor & Francis Group
LONDON AND NEW YORK

First published 2004
by Routledge
2 Park Square, Milton Park, Abingdon, Oxon OX14 4RN

Simultaneously published in the USA and Canada
by Routledge
711 Third Avenue, New York, NY 10017

Routledge is an imprint of the Taylor & Francis Group, an informa business

First issued in paperback 2012

Typeset in Baskerville by Taylor & Francis Books

British Library Cataloguing in Publication Data
A catalogue record for this book is available from the British Library

Library of Congress Cataloging in Publication Data
A catalog record for this book has been requested

978-0-415-23817-5 (hb)

978-0-415-64607-9 (pb)

Contents

Abbreviations

coauth.	coauthor
n.s.	new series
o.s.	old series
pseud.	pseudonym
s.n.	sine nomine
s.l.	sine loco

Introduction

Kirsten Madden and Janet Seiz

A decade ago when work on this project began, it was fair to say that historians lacked even the "raw materials" for an assessment of women's contributions to economic thought. The pioneering works in the effort of recovery and evaluation (Pujol 1992; Groenewegen 1994; and M. A. Dimand *et al.* 1995) brought to light long-neglected writings by dozens of women. Since then the literature on women and economics has grown considerably, with M. A. Dimand *et al.* (2000) being a particularly vital contribution. We hope that this book will facilitate further research into this fascinating history.

This bibliography contains references to over 10,000 articles, books, and pamphlets on economic issues, written by more than 1,700 women, published between 1770 and 1940. It includes more than 400 doctoral dissertations and masters' theses, which have not to our knowledge been listed together before; it also lists many reports issued by national, state, and local governments in the U.K. and the U.S. There are works from academic journals and from popular magazines, treatises on public finance and on the "science" of household management, and even a few works of fiction and poetry. Browsing the titles listed here, one learns about not only intellectual history but social history as well.

In this introduction we provide some background information about the writings, describe our methods and sources, note some of the limitations of the collection, and reflect on uses we hope readers will make of the material.

The writers and their times

The women who appear here are remarkably varied in social origin, education, occupation, and political orientation. English aristocrats like Baroness Jeune rub shoulders with working-class activists such as Ada Nield Chew. Ph.D. recipients are present alongside women with only a few years' formal education. There are civil servants and trade unionists, feminists and antifeminists. One finds professors, novelists, journalists and poets, communists, conservatives and anarchists. There are several nineteenth-century authors, all largely self-educated – Jane Marcet, Harriet Martineau, and Millicent Garrett Fawcett – who wrote widely read books seeking to make the new insights of political economy available to the reading public. Far less well known, there is a mountain climber, Annie Smith Peck, who "climbed higher in the Western Hemisphere than any other American, man or woman" and was awarded a gold medal by the Peruvian government (James *et al.* 1971: 41). (We list one of several books she wrote seeking to improve relations between the Americas, a statistical handbook of South America.) And there is one of Karl Marx's daughters, Eleanor Marx Aveling, who wrote and edited many works of socialist political economy and also translated into English *Madame Bovary* and the plays of Henrik Ibsen.

While the majority of these women published only a few works on economics, some were remarkably prolific. Carol Aronovici had approximately fifty publications, Sophonisba Breckinridge, Anna Louise Strong, Mary Van Kleeck, and Beatrice Webb about seventy, and Edith Abbott nearly 100. Vera Anstey contributed over seventy book reviews to economics journals as well as writing books and articles on the economics of India.

Several contributors had path-breaking careers as journalists. Flora Shaw (later Lady Lugard) was Colonial Editor for *The Times* of London in the 1890s and wrote some 500 articles on colonial affairs. She influenced imperial policy as well as public opinion, "vigorously supporting British expansion, by military force if necessary" (Callaway and Helly 1992: 79). Ida M. Tarbell is described as "perhaps the most outstanding female investigative journalist that America has ever produced. Her exposé of Standard Oil's ruthlessness and other national ills made her a leader in the early muckraking movement" (Garraty and Carnes 1999: 322). Concerning her publications on tariffs (1911), U.S. President Woodrow Wilson said "she has written more good sense, good plain common sense, about the tariff than any man I know of" (James *et al.* 1971: 429). Sylvia Porter won "every economics prize awarded to undergraduates" at Hunter College in New York in the 1920s (Garraty and Carnes 1999: 715), and became a journalist after a stint with a New York investment firm. Writing as S. F. Porter to conceal the fact that she was a woman, she was a "pioneer in making the inner workings of the business and financial communities understandable for the general public, translating what she called 'bafflegab' into simple, understandable English" (ibid.: 716). Her articles were "quick to point out abuse and injustice, and she soon became known as both a watchdog and a champion of the small investor" (ibid.: 716).

Many important social investigators and social reformers are represented here. A description of one writer on working women, Elizabeth Beardsley Butler, says that she, like "other college-educated social reformers of the early twentieth century…believed that well-publicized research would galvanize American businessmen, civic leaders, and legislators to improve the living and working conditions of the working class" (Garraty and Carnes 1999: 95). Similar hopes animated many others. Clementina Black, Florence Kelley, and Josephine Goldmark were prolific writers on women's employment, child labor, and labor legislation. Clara Collet conducted many studies of women's work and other labor issues for the British government from the 1890s through the 1920s. Physician Alice Hamilton was a reform activist and a pioneer in industrial toxicology. Less famous, Catherine Krouse Bauer, an "urban-planning educator," wrote on the economics and politics of providing low-cost modern housing in northern Europe, noting the association between European housing reforms and the political power of labor unions. "There will never be any realistic housing movement" in the U.S., she argued, "until the workers and consumers – and the unemployed – themselves take a hand in the solution" (Garraty and Carnes 1999: 346). Margaret Bondfield developed from shop clerk to labor activist and eventually became the first woman to occupy a post in the British Cabinet, serving as Labour Secretary from 1929 to 1931. Frances Perkins achieved a comparable distinction a few years later, becoming U.S. Labor Secretary under President Franklin Roosevelt. Other well-known women reformers with works listed here include Jane Addams, Helen Bosanquet, Josephine Butler, Octavia Hill, Josephine Shaw Lowell, Florence Nightingale, Louisa Twining, and Frances Wright.

A number of the women who appear in this volume used fiction to address economic issues. Early in the nineteenth century, stories by Hannah More and Maria Edgeworth sought to instruct working- and middle-class readers on proper behavior in capitalist society. Later, economic problems inspired many fiction writers. Marie van Vorst's novel *Philip Longstreth* centered on "a young man who devotes himself to ameliorating the conditions of the poor" (James *et al.* 1971: 514). Van Vorst worked in a Lynn, Massachusetts, shoe factory to obtain firsthand experience of labor conditions for another book, *The Woman Who Toils*. Others who wrote about the hardships of industrial workers include Elizabeth Gaskell, Rebecca Harding Davis, Margaret Harkness, and Frances Trollope. And the economic situations of women were addressed in novels by Louisa May Alcott, Mary Cholmondeley, Isabella Ford, Elizabeth Stuart Phelps, and Mary Anne Sadlier, among others.

A handful of the authors appearing here were Catholic nuns. The earliest of them, Margaret Anna Cusack, was born in Ireland in 1829 and wrote on Irish poverty. Six other Catholic nuns have Ph.D. theses listed, on topics including "The Significance of a Changing Concept of Ownership to Current Economic and Social Planning" and "The Problem of Hours and Wages in American Organized Labor."

Some of the writing cited in these pages was honored with prestigious awards. Victorine Jeans wrote the Cobden Prize Essay for 1891, *Factory Act Legislation, Its Industrial and Commercial Effects, Actual and Prospective.* Helen Stuart Campbell's *Women Wage-earners* won an award from the American Economic Association and was published in 1893 with an introduction by Richard Ely (R. Dimand 1995). In 1924 Dorothy Swaine Thomas won the Hutchinson Silver Medal for excellence in research by a student at the London School of Economics for her Ph.D. thesis "Social Aspects of the Business Cycle." (Thomas is remembered as a sociologist because she ultimately received tenure in the University of California–Berkeley Sociology Department.) Eveline Burns received the same prize in 1926 for work on problems of wage regulation ("School Notes,"

Economica, March 1927: 274). Three women received the Hart, Schaffner and Marx Prize for their writing in economics: Yetta Scheftel in 1916 for *The Taxation of Land Value*; Hazel Kyrk for her University of Chicago Ph.D. thesis in 1920; and Caroline Ware for her thesis on the New England cotton industry in 1929.

During the 170 years spanned by this project, the world was transformed in many ways that are clearly reflected in this bibliography. In the early nineteenth century it was far from widely accepted that women would write at all, and female authors commonly had their work published anonymously or under male pseudonyms. By the twentieth century female authorship *per se* was no longer controversial in many societies – but still women's authority to define knowledge on economic, social and political matters was far from secure.

The period saw the emergence of feminist movements in many countries, which were intertwined in complex ways with other social movements. In the nineteenth-century U.S., Britain, and Ireland thousands of middle-class and wealthy women became involved in philanthropic and charitable work. Often this was portrayed as an extension of "mothering" beyond the home, to help the poor, the old, the sick, disadvantaged children, and – more controversially – natives of Britain's colonies. Many women also participated in antislavery and trade union and socialist struggles.

Among the writers appearing here are several leading abolitionists (Elizabeth Heyrick, Lydia Maria Child, Harriet Beecher Stowe), but also at least one prominent apologist for slavery (Louisa McCord). There are leaders in the battles for women's suffrage, property rights, and wider educational and employment opportunities, such as Barbara Bodichon, Eleanor Rathbone, and Harriot Stanton Blatch; and there are others who argued that women should not have the vote (Catharine Beecher). Quite a few contributors were socialists of various sorts (from the Fabian Beatrice Webb to Annie Besant and the revolutionaries Anna Louise Strong and Rosa Luxemburg) and several were anarchists (Louisa Bevington, Emma Goldman, Voltairine de Cleyre). Other writers, most notably Harriet Martineau and Millicent Garrett Fawcett, were staunch proponents of free markets.

The period covered by this bibliography also saw the creation of "social science" and then of the separate "social sciences" as academic disciplines. As a number of scholars have shown (see especially Yeo 1996 and Silverberg 1998), this process was a highly "gendered" one.

In both Britain and the U.S., "social science" was initially closely connected with social reform. Britain's National Association for the Promotion of Social Science (NAPSS) and the United States' American Social Science Association (ASSA) were created (in 1857 and 1865, respectively) in the hope that scientific inquiry would lead to wiser policies for the amelioration of social ills. Members of these organizations came from many walks of life, including the clergy, medicine, charitable work, business, teaching, and the civil service, and the papers they presented at conferences discussed housing, capital–labor conflicts, women's employment, poverty, public health, education, prisons, and law, as well as foreign trade and banking policy. Both the NAPSS and the ASSA included substantial numbers of women.

Near the turn of the century, for reasons we will not attempt to summarize here, the social world began to be carved into discrete pieces covered by separate bodies of "experts." In the U.S, groups broke away from the ASSA to form professional associations for historians in 1884, economists in 1885, political scientists in 1903, and sociologists in 1905. In Britain, similarly, the Royal Economic Society was founded in 1890. University departments in social science disciplines began to be established in the U.S. in the 1870s and 1880s, and Ph.D. programs were created. Specialized journals were developed to serve and to delimit the emerging professions. In economics the first academic journals were *Publications of the American Economic Association* and the *Quarterly Journal of Economics* (both started in 1886), the *Economic Journal* (1891), and the *Journal of Political Economy* (1892).

In the professionalization process the "impartial pursuit of knowledge" was elevated above advocacy. Over time, reformers and activists were either ejected from the "community" or more or less silenced within it. Authority was linked to formal credentials, and access to these credentials was limited. Not coincidentally, among those who were no longer welcome in the community of inquirers were most of the women.

Academic institutions became the dominant sites for the creation and dissemination of knowledge, and in academic institutions women were marginalized, either excluded altogether or relegated to niches related to traditional female roles. The gap between women's and men's formal schooling narrowed slowly: women made up about one-fifth of undergraduate students in the U.S. in 1870 and just over one-third in 1900. Admission to graduate study was very rare for women. In both the U.S. and Britain, some of the most prestigious universities allowed women to take courses but not to receive degrees. The first major British institution to allow women to take degrees was the University of London in 1878. By 1900 most British universities had been opened to women, but Oxford and Cambridge remained largely closed. Economics Ph.D. programs in the U.S. admitted a few women beginning in the 1890s. Even when women succeeded in acquiring impeccable "credentials," however, they found their prospects for employment as economists rather limited.

In the U.S. universities studied by Nancy Folbre, prior to 1900 men wrote eighty-four dissertations in political economy and women wrote five (about 6 percent); between 1906 and 1920, women's share of the dissertations rose to about 10 percent (Folbre 1998: 41). Evelyn Forget found that women's share of U.S. Ph.D. dissertations in economics peaked at 19 percent in 1920, then hovered between 10 and 15 percent through most of the 1920s and 1930s (Forget 1995: 26–7). As Helene Silverberg points out, figures on degrees awarded understate the extent of women's involvement in economic study. In the Department of Political Economy at Johns Hopkins University, for instance, "of the 252 people who completed at least one year of graduate work between 1876 and 1926..., nearly 35 percent (seventy-seven) were women" (Silverberg 1998: 11).

In this bibliography are over 350 women known to have received doctorates in some field. Of these, approximately 300 wrote Ph.D. theses with an obvious economics focus. Most of the doctorates were earned in economics departments, but many were in other disciplines, especially history, sociology, and political science. Nine institutions granted Ph.D's to ten or more of the women whose works are listed here: Columbia University, University of Chicago, Radcliffe College, University of Wisconsin at Madison, London School of Economics, Bryn Mawr College, University of Pennsylvania, University of California at Berkeley, and the Brookings Institution. There are also well over 130 master's theses cited in these pages. Approximately 40 women here earned both master's and Ph.D. degrees.

Many of the women who received advanced degrees in economics found employment as economists, though rarely on university faculties. Helen Frances Page Bates, the first woman to earn an economics Ph.D. (Wisconsin, 1896), became the Economics Department librarian at the University of California, Berkeley. Hannah Robie Sewall, whose 1898 Ph.D. dissertation on theories of value before Adam Smith became a standard work in the field, was hired by Carroll Wright at the U.S. Bureau of Labor. She wrote an important study of child labor in 1904 and then apparently stopped publishing (M. A. Dimand *et al.* 2000: 395). The prolific Edith Abbott received her Ph.D. in 1905 and taught briefly at Wellesley College before joining Sophonisba Breckinridge (who had Chicago doctorates in economics, politics, and law) in establishing a graduate school of social administration and social work in Chicago. Jessica Blanche Peixotto was "the only woman who received a Ph.D. before 1910 and managed to hold a faculty position in economics at a major research institution before 1920" (Folbre 1998: 43). Peixotto became the first female full-time faculty member at Berkeley, teaching courses on socialism and "social economy" in the Economics Department from 1904 to 1935 (Garraty and Carnes 1999: 258). She served as a vice-president of the American Economic Association in 1928.

Most of the economists represented here have received little scholarly attention, but it appears their careers were often quite interesting. Theresa Wolfson studied economics at Columbia University and earned her Ph.D. from the Brookings Institution in 1926. She taught economics and labor history in union-sponsored workers' schools and at Brooklyn College. Persia Campbell, an Australian, studied at the London School of Economics and worked as a research economist with the government of New South Wales. She later moved to the U.S., taught at Queens College, and was active in the consumers' movement (Garraty and Carnes 1999: 295–7). Helen Sumner did graduate work at Wisconsin with Richard Ely and John Commons. Unable to find a permanent academic position, she did research under contract for U.S. government agencies and was later employed by the Children's Bureau of the Department of Labor and the Brookings Institution (Garraty and Carnes 1999: 144). Elizabeth Waterman Gilboy did graduate work at Harvard/Radcliffe and the London School of Economics in the 1920s and held administrative and research posts at Harvard/Radcliffe from 1929 through the

1960s. She made significant contributions to English economic history, the study of consumer demand, and input–output analysis (M. A. Dimand *et al.* 2000: 168–72).

Quite a few of the writers cited in this study were academics from fields other than economics but made noteworthy contributions to the discipline. Lucy Salmon, who was trained as an historian, with the support of U.S. Bureau of Labor commissioner Carroll D. Wright "made a pioneering application of statistical method to this field" in her 1897 book *Domestic Service* (James *et al.* 1971: 224). Another historian, Constance McLaughlin Green, wrote a doctoral thesis on American industrial history that was awarded Yale University's prestigious Edward Eggleston Prize. Susan Kingsbury earned a history Ph.D. from Columbia University in 1905 and wrote extensively in economics thereafter. Kingsbury served as a vice-president for the American Economic Association in 1919.

Some women who were trained in economics migrated to other fields of teaching and scholarship. Barbara Nachtrieb Grimes Armstrong worked as assistant in the University of California–Berkeley Economics Department from 1914 to 1919 and received a Ph.D. in economics there. Armstrong is remembered as a law professor in the *American National Biography*, doing interdisciplinary research and teaching in law and economics (Garraty and Carnes 1999: 607). Sadie Tanner Mossell Alexander earned a Ph.D. in economics from the University of Pennsylvania in 1921, but then moved into law and soon ceased to publish in economics.

There was an interesting overlap between economics and the new discipline of home economics in the early twentieth century. Some women with economics Ph.D.s found jobs in university departments of home economics; and some home economists trained in other fields did research on households and consumption that is cited in this bibliography. Sophonisba Breckinridge, who wrote her Ph.D. dissertation on the history of monetary theory, held a faculty position in the University of Chicago's Department of Household Administration. Mary Schenk Woolman was a home economist who studied at Harvard with economist Thomas Nixon Carver and coauthored with him a book about the textile industry. Ellen Henrietta Richards, trained as a chemist, founded the American Home Economics Association and was its first president. Hazel Kyrk earned her Ph.D. in Economics at Chicago and ultimately became a full professor there in 1941, with joint appointments in the Departments of Economics and Home Economics (R. Dimand 1999). Kyrk is remembered for broadening "the economics curriculum to include consumer topics and establish[ing] Chicago as the premier university for the study of family and consumer economics" (Sicherman and Green 1980: 405, quoted in M. A. Dimand 1995: 47–8). The field of "social work" was also undergoing professionalization early in the century, as governments took more responsibility for helping disadvantaged individuals who earlier had depended on families and private charity. Social work provided careers for many of the growing population of educated women, and women involved in social work contributed many writings to the literature covered here.

Even more women who were trained in economics pursued careers outside the academy, often in government or in advocacy and research organizations. Frieda Miller did graduate research in labor economics, political science, law, and sociology from 1911 to 1915 at the University of Chicago. She later became a labor reformer and state and federal official (Garraty and Carnes 1999: 485). Emily Wayland Dinwiddie took graduate courses in economics at the University of Pennsylvania and worked in housing reform. Katharine Bement Davis had one of the most unusual stories: having completed an economics Ph.D. at the University of Chicago, she went on to an illustrious career in prison administration.

Subject matter

The definitions of "economist" and the "economic" were in considerable flux in the nineteenth century and well into the twentieth. This made our decisions about which writings and writers to include quite complex, and because the "professionalization" movement was at its most intense just before and after the beginning of the twentieth century, our pre-1900 collection looks rather different from the post-1900 one.

The boundaries between the social sciences, as mentioned earlier, were non-existent before the late nineteenth century and remained hazy well into the twentieth. Prior to the professionalization and "academicization" of the social sciences, writers tended to be broadly educated and to move between topics and approaches with relative ease. Women who wrote on political economy might pen novels and philosophical tracts as well, and any individual text on economic issues might also be laden with religious or other non-economic content. By 1940, in contrast, writers on economics were less likely to be contributing to other unrelated fields, and their writing conformed more clearly to currently recognized disciplinary norms.

Relatedly, for most of the nineteenth century the professional journals did not yet exist, and writers on economics published their work in non-specialist periodicals such as the *Westminster Review*, the *Edinburgh Review*, *Nineteenth Century*, the *Contemporary Review*, the *Arena*, and the *Forum* (see Coats 1993). Most writers – certainly most women – continued to find such publications the primary outlets open to them as the professionalization of economics proceeded. Still, if one could reorder this bibliography by chronology rather than by author, the transformation of the literature from generalist to specialist would be quite apparent.

The editors of the *Biographical Dictionary of Women Economists* dealt with the "whom to include" problem, they wrote, by deciding to concentrate on "individuals who were intentionally working in what would at the time they wrote, have been considered economics" (M. A. Dimand *et al.* 2000: xvii). This admirable rule is of course not easily applied in practice. And we have opted to cast a somewhat wider net: our authors need not have been economists, but merely have published some interesting (or interesting-sounding) writing on economic issues.

We believe we have identified most of what would be considered "contributions to the literature of the discipline" in the narrow sense – books and articles that were written primarily for and read by other economists. But we have also included many writings for much wider audiences, particularly for the period before 1900. We do this not to exaggerate the extent of women's presence "in economics," but to provide a fuller and (we hope) more vivid picture of the writers and the "economic discourse" of the times.

The writers who appear here are better understood, we believe, when one has a sense of the range of their interests and involvements. While we have excluded an enormous number of the writers' works focusing on subjects such as religion, art history, and literature, we have intentionally included a select few non-economic writings. We find it interesting that, for example, Frances Power Cobbe and other prominent British feminists writing in economics were also involved in the turn-of-the-century campaign against vivisection, which would now be called an "animal rights" movement.

Deciding which subject areas should be considered "economic" was far from simple, again especially for the earlier period. There are many social phenomena that are centrally "economic" but might be written about from non-economic angles: poverty, prostitution, and slavery are obvious examples. We include here a great deal of women's writing on poverty. Some pieces are analytical, some are descriptive, and some serve mostly to reveal the range of "middle-class" attitudes toward the poor. The writings on prostitution that we list are similarly varied: writers such as Josephine Butler and Annie Besant noted that many women became prostitutes because few other livelihoods were open to them, discussed ways the state should and should not regulate the sex trade, addressed moral issues, often in religious terms, and sometimes brought in public health and eugenics. On slavery, we cite some works with interesting economic emphases. Lydia Maria Child's *An Appeal in Favor of that Class of Americans Called Africans* (1833) was a pioneering scholarly study "addressing all aspects of the slavery controversy – moral, legal, economic, political, and racial" (Karcher 1996: xxiii). Elizabeth Heyrick's *Immediate, Not Gradual Abolition* (1824) called for radical changes in both the objective and the tactics of the antislavery movement, urging women to organize boycotts of West Indian sugar and other products of slave labor. On the other side of the debate, in defense of slavery, Louisa McCord (1851, 1856) drew on pseudoscientific "knowledge" about racial difference but also described the plight of the poor wage laborer in language that would have been at home in any socialist tract.

Feminist economists – including many whose work appears here – often argue that the fundamental fact shaping women's economic lives is the gender division of labor. Thus we have included many writings from the period's energetic debates about women's domestic roles and education. We have tried to choose mostly works that focus on economic, legal, and political issues, but religious and biological arguments are present as well. We have also included some writings on women's suffrage, in part because the writers so often stressed that the vote would give women a voice in shaping policies to improve their economic lives.

Most of our decisions about whether to list a piece of writing were necessarily based simply on the work's title. Sometimes an ambiguous or seemingly non-economic title was kept in because the author had other writings that were clearly economic in nature, or because her education or work experience focused on economic issues. We have generally not included memoirs or biographies, with a few exceptions. We have listed some books recounting travel experiences for the insights they might provide into the writers' attitudes about colonialism, race, and culture. Finally, we have included some works of fiction and poetry in which economic themes were central, especially if they were written by women who published significant nonfiction writings on economics or who were widely read and influential in shaping popular attitudes about the economy and social reform.

Procedures

This bibliography represents the melding of two separate research projects. In 1994 Michèle Pujol was commissioned by Routledge/Thoemmes to compile a multi-volume anthology of economic writing by women prior to 1900. By 1996 she had managed – painstakingly, without the aid of the electronic databases available to scholars now – to identify several hundred articles and books which she was beginning to evaluate for inclusion. Before Michèle's tragically premature death in 1997 she asked Janet Seiz to finish that work. Around the same time, Kirsten Madden began collecting references to works by women economists from 1900 to 1940 (for a discussion of this research, see her article in *History of Political Economy*, Madden 2002). Kirsten and Janet began to collaborate in the summer of 2000, with Kirsten keeping primary responsibility for writings published after 1900 and Janet focusing on earlier works. Although our searches were mostly conducted separately and our methods differed in some ways, the following account will describe what "we" did, neglecting the differences for simplicity's sake. We hope that sharing the procedures we followed will help others to identify ways in which the limitations of this collection may be overcome and the documentation of women's economic writing made much more complete.

We (including Michèle) began by extracting names and references from the initially small secondary literature on women and economics. We also searched the author indices of the *Index of Economic Journals* (*IEJ*), volumes I–III. The pre-1941 issues of the *American Economic Review*, *Quarterly Journal of Economics*, *Economic Journal*, *Journal of Political Economy*, and *Econometrica* were examined for female authors of articles and reviews, and the book reviews were checked for references to books by women. The journals' professional notes, thesis lists, and advertisements were perused as well.

Each female name found in these searches was entered into the online version of the FirstSearch *World Catalogue*, which lists books, pamphlets, and government documents catalogued in libraries around the world. The WorldCat provided hundreds of new references and also new names, as many women coauthored works with other women. Also very useful was Chadwyck Healey's online database *The Nineteenth Century*, which includes a large collection of works on economics.

We conducted similar searches with several electronic databases covering periodical literature. *Nineteenth Century Masterfile* (or "Poole's Plus") provides online access to Poole's Index (covering 1802–1906), Stead's Index (1890–1906), Jones and Chipman's Index to Legal Periodical Literature (1786–1922), and the Cumulative Index to a Selected List of Periodicals (1890–1906). The *Periodicals Contents Index* (from Chadwyck Healey) covers hundreds of journals and magazines published from the late eighteenth through the twentieth century. The *Wellesley Index to Victorian Periodicals* (on CD-ROM), covering the nineteenth century, makes a particularly valuable contribution because it identifies many authors of articles that were published without attribution or signed with initials or pseudonyms. We also were thankful for JSTOR, an electronic archive of full-text articles from hundreds of scholarly journals across many disciplines, which enabled us to verify information in many references, find new references, and in some cases examine the contents of articles to determine whether to include them in the bibliography.

To locate graduate theses, women's names were entered through FirstSearch into the *Dissertation Abstracts* database, which covers U.S., Canadian, and some British and European institutions. Each time a school was found to have approved a thesis by a woman before 1941, its complete thesis records between 1880 and 1940 were searched for additional women degree recipients. Several of the major economics journals during the pre-1940 period published dissertation lists, sometimes including works in progress. If completion of a woman's thesis could not be verified through *Dissertation Abstracts*, the institution's library catalogue was searched via the Internet. In addition, librarians at the Brookings Institution, Radcliffe College, Columbia University, and the London School of Economics were very helpful in responding to direct queries for information concerning women earning Ph.D.s through their economics departments.

We often used biographical reference books to learn more about authors' education and work lives and to obtain additional references. Particularly helpful sources included *Notable American Women* (James *et al.* 1971; Sicherman and Green 1980), *American National Biography* (Garraty and Carnes 1999), *The Dictionary of National Biography* (Stephen and Lee 1959–60; Nicholls 1993), *The Biographical Dictionary of British Feminists* (Banks 1985), and the *Encyclopedia of the American Left* (Buhle *et al.* 1990). We also consulted secondary works on the history of the social sciences, social reforms, feminism, the labor movement, and socialism; our coverage of this literature was unsystematic and, needless to say, far from complete. Finally, Internet searches using search engines such as Google often yielded treasures (as well as trash).

Problems

The reader will by now have discerned that our research proceeded wonderfully smoothly and provided consistent excitement and pleasure. Would that it were so. In fact, we encountered a multitude of difficulties. Searching databases (and often even journal issues) by name is problematic, as many references provide only the initials of authors' first names. Having writers' first names is often not sufficient for determining gender; some, such as Carroll, Marion, and Evelyn, could refer to either. For example, Alba Edwards was one individual we considered including, as "Alba" has been used by both women and men. Through email queries with the Census Bureau, where Edwards published some work, a record was uncovered referring to Edwards as "Mister," and so he was excluded. We generally assumed that a gender-indeterminate name (or initials) referred to a male unless we found evidence that the writer was a woman. It may be, however, that there are still a few men listed here whose names misled us.

Women's name changes due to changes in marital status also create uncertainty. As this volume goes to print, we discovered that Sarah Whittelsey married a man named Walden in 1905, and thus the 1900–3 Whittelsey references should be consolidated with the Walden references from 1916–17 (Hammond 1993). We have consolidated the references for those women whose name changes we were aware of – Beatrice Potter Webb, for instance, and Helen Dendy Bosanquet – and we have provided some cross-references. Most likely there are still women who make appearances under more than one name in the bibliography.

Although electronic databases such as the *WorldCat* and *Nineteenth Century Masterfile* make projects like this one vastly easier than they used to be, they remain in some ways cumbersome to use. A single book might have, say, twenty or forty separate WorldCat records, because the libraries holding it recorded the information slightly differently or because the book was reprinted many times. For prolific authors, a name search may yield over 1,000 entries, and we no doubt failed to catch some references in such situations. Different indexes often provide conflicting information about dates, places of publication, and page numbers. An author's name may be in the records in several different forms, some writings attributed to "Mary E. Kelley" and some to "M. E. J. Kelley," or some to "Phillipps, Evelyn March" and others to "March-Phillipps, Evelyn." We encountered many misspellings and strange electronic glitches. In light of all this, we would be grateful if readers would assume, when finding errors in this bibliography, that they are someone else's fault, not ours.

Limitations of the collection

As we see it, this collection has two rather major limitations and a host of more minor ones. The major limitations are its geographic restrictions and the exclusion of most works coauthored with men.

The vast majority of our writers lived and published in Great Britain and the United States. Some others who wrote in English were based in Ireland, Canada, Australia, New Zealand, and South Africa. Almost all of the remaining authors were European, writing in German, French, Dutch, Spanish, Italian, Danish, Swedish, Finnish, Polish, Czech, and Russian. There are hardly any voices from South or East Asia, Africa, or Latin America. There are two contributors known from Japan (Setsu Tanino and Kikue Yamakawa, both first noted in the *Biographical Dictionary of Women Economists*); and one female recipient of a Ph.D. from Columbia University has an East Asian name (Mabel Ping-Hua Lee).

The work's limited geographic variety is in part the product of the uneven distribution of opportunities to publish. Few countries before 1940 had the income, education, and literacy levels needed to support large publishing industries and research activity. The limitation is also in part a reflection of the sources available to us. The scholarly literature in English on women and economics does not often discuss writings in other languages (the *Biographical Dictionary of Women Economists* is an exception, and we benefited from it). The *Dissertation Abstracts* database includes mostly degrees from North American institutions (thus we were unable to find complete references to the doctoral theses of women who we know received Ph.D.s from European institutions). The periodicals databases include relatively few journals not in English.

The main constraint, however, was our meager knowledge of other languages and histories. In some languages we could not identify writers' genders from their names. (We sometimes consulted colleagues – Professor Bina Agarwal looked over a list of Indian economists for us, for example.) Often we could not fully translate a work's title. Knowing little about countries' social and intellectual histories made it difficult to search for and to evaluate references. Knowing that we could not do a competent job in literature not in English, we chose not to attempt it. We include some references in other languages to stimulate interest and we look forward to learning from other researchers about these literatures.

We have also included very little work that women wrote with male coauthors. Without substantial biographical or textual evidence, one cannot discern the relative contributions of multiple authors to a piece. The search for references for 1900–40 initially focused exclusively on works written by women in order to be "conservative" in representing women's contributions to the discipline. The pre-1900 search included male/female coauthored works, but there were not very many of them. In the end, because there were so many references produced by women only, we decided that works written with men would be included for only a few particularly significant "teams," Beatrice and Sidney Webb being the most prolific. The bibliography therefore undercounts the output of some of the women it includes, while women who wrote on economics only as coauthors with men are not represented at all.

Our coverage of government publications is also rather limited. As noted earlier, many women with training in economics found employment in government agencies beginning in the late nineteenth century, and some contributed substantially to publications of the British Board of Trade, U.S. Labor Department, Women's Bureau, Children's Bureau, Census Bureau, etc. Most of our government references were uncovered through WorldCat searches by author. Almost all of them are from government bodies in the U.S. and Britain. We were unaware of any convenient search tool with which to perform more systematic searches of government documents. The *United Kingdom Official*

Publications online database (BOPCRIS) is quite promising; the U.S. government provides no comparable index to documents that are not recent.

For ease of use, in this bibliography we typically present each woman's name only once at the beginning of her entries. In our research, we frequently encountered multiple name variations for a given contributor for many different reasons, including the author's use of various signatures across publications (e.g. first initials in some cases and full first names in others), the use of pseudonyms, marital name changes, as well as publication and electronic database naming procedure variations and misspellings. In this volume, brackets around portions of a woman's name are intended to alert the reader to the existence of name variations across publications and reference sources. When a researcher inquires further into the work and lives of these women, it is strongly recommended that all variations of a given woman's name are searched.

Although we have spent years on this project, it is still the case that we are able every day to discover new references. For example, our most recent discovery of personal information about Sarah Whittelsey also finally turned up a complete citation to her 1898 Yale University Ph.D. thesis entitled *In How Far has Massachusetts Labor Legislation Been in Accordance with Teachings of Economic Theory?* The tools and databases available to researchers are expanding at a dizzying rate. The World Catalogue and most of the periodicals indexes are updated daily. Many institutions are building online collections of full texts of articles and books. We trust that future researchers will take advantage of this electronic wealth and that our knowledge of female contributions to economics will grow rapidly.

Questions for future research

This bibliography excludes many references that we would like to have included; and it no doubt includes quite a few references that have less relation to economics than we imagined. We hope, however, that it will be a valuable resource for many kinds of research on gender and the history of economic thought. Among the inquiries we think of are the following.

Biographies and the sociology of economics

Some of the writers covered here have had their careers described in the *Biographical Dictionary of Women Economists* or elsewhere. But even for those "familiar" authors this bibliography includes many writings on economic issues that are not mentioned elsewhere. More significantly, most of the authors here have not been discussed at all by economists, and so this study introduces many women whose work lives and contributions to the literature might usefully be investigated and compared.

Many interesting questions can be asked about individuals' circumstances and outlooks. What psychological, familial, educational, and other social/cultural factors were important as girls matured to stimulate their interest in economics and their ability to pursue writing careers in such a male-dominated area? How important was it for women to have personal male, female, or parental support systems? Where did women obtain the economic resources to finance their training and/or to subsidize their participation in unpaid work? How did class, nationality, and racial/ethnic identity affect women's interests and perspectives? Many of the authors were deeply involved in work in areas such as literature and social reform. How did these other interests shape their economic questions and analyses? For women with strong religious backgrounds, how did religion affect their careers and how did it shape their contributions? Were some religious traditions more conducive to female contributions in the discipline than others?

Study of these less-known economists should add a great deal to our understanding of how women related to the economics profession. What obstacles did female academics in economics face, such as limited employment opportunities at research universities, low pay, and high teaching and service loads? How important were these problems, relative to other factors, in determining how prolific women were? How did women balance the demands of career and family? For those women who did not marry or raise children, what were the benefits and drawbacks of these personal choices for their work? For the women who earned advanced degrees but only briefly contributed to economics, was it mainly domestic responsibilities that shortened their careers, or discrimination, or disappointment? Did some women give up on economics as a field for pursuing their interests as the discipline narrowed in scope? When women economists pursued careers in government and reform organizations, was that their genuine preference or would some have chosen academic careers if they had not faced discrimination there? What role did their economics training play for those women who became leaders in the professionalization of home economics and social work?

There is a great deal we do not know about why some institutions granted so many more advanced economics degrees to women than others. How much was due to differences in the attitudes of administrators and of male economics professors? How much was due to differences in the programs' curricula and other factors that might affect their appeal for women? In which institutions were there professors willing to mentor female students?

Women economists often established extensive networks within academic settings, government agencies and advocacy organizations (M. A. Dimand 1995). Some networks may be detected here in the institutions chosen for graduate training and in patterns of coauthorship. What was the role of such networking among women, and between women and men, in nurturing and sustaining female contributions to the discipline? How did these networks function? Are there ways in which the networks limited female development in economics? Are there substantial differences in content, methodology, or quality of coauthored works compared to independently authored pieces?

As mentioned earlier, many female economists made substantial contributions to the writing of government reports for agencies such as the U.S. Women's Bureau, Children's Bureau, Department of Agriculture, and Census Bureau.

These women's writings and careers are ripe for investigation. What explains the availability of government employment to female economists, and how did the situation in the U.S. compare to that in other countries? Were women in government positions more easily able to excel in their research than in academia, where teaching and service loads may have limited research time? Did women define and lead their agencies' investigations or did they typically work under male authority? How did government employment affect the subject matter, methodology, and findings of women's economic research?

Finally, how was the economic writing of women received? Was it ignored, or treated in a paternalistic, derisive way? Or were women treated as equals, with as much chance as their male counterparts to be read, cited, and given awards? How did women perceive the reception of their work, and how did this affect their contributions?

Gender differences in economic thought?

Do women's perspectives on economic life and approaches to its study differ notably from those of men? One important question that has received scholarly attention concerns gender differences in topics of research. Studies of pre-1940 Ph.D. dissertations (Forget 1995) and journal publications (Folbre 1998) have found that research areas were distributed differently among women than among men, although Forget found that the differences diminished over time. Having compiled and examined a large list of women's publications in economics from 1900 to 1940, Madden (2002) proposed a new subject classification scheme arguably more appropriate for characterizing the range of women's writing than the conventional classification developed by the American Economic Association. What remains uncertain, of course, is how far the differences in focus represent gender differences in interests or inclinations rather than differences in opportunity. This bibliography provides material for further studies along these lines.

It is clear from this work that female contributions to economic thought spanned all ideologies and research areas, and the listings here can facilitate systematic inquiry into female contributions to fields such as international trade, public finance, and monetary economics. That said, it also appears that a very large proportion of women focused on labor studies and the welfare of the working class, including gender-, age-, and race-specific analyses.

A considerable fraction of the writings listed here are about the participation of women in the economy. Serious scrutiny of what women wrote on women's economic activity through 1940 would be a valuable contribution to the history of economic thought, economic history, and gender studies. Studies of women's contributions to and impact on the labor movement could also be undertaken from the references consolidated in this volume.

The work of women listed here might be compared to that of contemporaneous male economists along many dimensions, in both quantitative and qualitative studies. For instance, did adherence to particular economic theories differ between women and men? Can different patterns be identified in women's and men's choices of analytical methodologies and empirical techniques? If there are differences, why do they exist? Does the history of economics support the assertion that there are differences between women's and men's worldviews and/or modes of inquiry, emanating from the socially constructed differences in their life experiences? Similarly, examining more disaggregated groups, are there differences among women's perspectives on economics associated with other dimensions of identity such as class and ethnicity?

We hope that perusal of this bibliography will also inspire reflection on how economics evolved. The professionalization of the field involved explicit exclusions of women in some times and places – as when women were categorically denied admission to graduate programs or employment as university economics professors. But the process must also be seen as a move to exclude certain ways of thinking and communicating which might have been particularly attractive to women (though not exclusive to women or universal among them). One description of the American social reformer Jane Addams says that

> [her] mind was not the skilled instrument of the scholar or the logician, but one of intuitive wisdom. She was a mystic possessed of a devastating common sense who viewed everyday experience from a new angle of vision, distilling from it compelling insights into the human and social cost of industrial capitalism and international conflict.
>
> (James *et al.* 1971: 21)

The physician and social reformer Alice Hamilton is described in a similar way, as "[v]ery much a part of the humanitarian sector of the progressive movement" in occupational medicine (Garraty and Carnes 1999: 912). These thinkers would have fit in quite well with the "social science" practitioners of the late nineteenth century, but they probably found only a small audience among "economists."

Female contributors to economic thought through 1940 appear remarkably interdisciplinary. There are writers representing numerous disciplines and backgrounds, including social work, economic geography, sociology, history, political science, psychology, home economics, journalism, public health, and nutrition. Many devoted their energies to efforts to reduce gender inequality and rectify injustices associated with exploitation of the labor force (especially women and children). Exploration of the multi- and inter-disciplinary character of women's economic writing could offer timely insights related to the questioning of the narrow scope of economics today.

Women's participation in economic discourse prior to 1940 was clearly far more extensive than has been previously recognized. We hope that exploration of the female contributions to economics listed here will yield new insights into economic history and theory as well as more broadly informed assessments of the history and methodology of economics. The discipline's evolution has entailed both gains and losses. We hope that women's role in that development will be better understood. We also hope that gender-centered study of the history of economic thought will encourage some useful rethinking of the question "what is economics?"

Acknowledgments

Robert Langham, the economics editor at Routledge, was instrumental in motivating this project, and his consistent support, patience, and professionalism warrant thanks. Alfred Symons assumed editorial responsibilities during the last year of the work, and his thoughtfulness and flexibility contributed a great deal to the book's final form. Our copy editor, Lisa Williams, was truly superb: dedicated, scrupulous, communicative, and possessed of a fine sense of humor.

This project was completed in large part due to the incredible support provided by Beth Crumling Colvin, the Millersville University (MU) Economics Department Secretary. Much gratitude goes also to Cindy Groff and Kelly Urbanik, MU students who provided research assistance. Kirsten Madden received grant support from the MU Faculty Professional Development Committee, Released-Time Grants Committee, and Women's Endowment Grant. Janet Seiz benefited from the generous support of Grinnell College, including two invaluable sabbatical leaves. Professor Eliza Willis of Grinnell College offered very helpful comments on this introduction, along with crucial moral support.

We are also grateful to the International Association for Feminist Economics (IAFFE). For over a decade, its conferences and its journal *Feminist Economics* have provided sustenance for scholars, teachers, policymakers, and activists interested in gender and economic life. All royalties for this book will go to IAFFE, in celebration of the memory of Michèle Pujol.

References

Books and articles

Banks, Olive, ed. 1985. *The Biographical Dictionary of British Feminists*, vol. 1: *1800–1930*. New York: New York University Press.

Buhle, Mari Jo, Paul Buhle, and Dan Georgakas, eds. 1990. *Encyclopedia of the American Left*. New York: Garland Publishing.

Callaway, Helen and Dorothy O. Helly. 1992. Crusader for Empire: Flora Shaw/Lady Lugard. In Nupur Chaudhuri and Margaret Strobel, eds., *Western Women and Imperialism: Complicity and Resistance*. Bloomington, Ind.: Indiana University Press.

Coats, A. W. 1993. *The Sociology and Professionalization of Economics: British and American Economic Essays*, vol II. London and New York: Routledge.

Dimand, Mary Ann. 1995. Networks of Women Economists before 1940. In Mary Ann Dimand, Robert W. Dimand, and Evelyn L. Forget, eds., *Women of Value: Feminist Essays on the History of Economics*. Aldershot, UK, and Brookfield, Vt.: Edward Elgar.

Dimand, Mary Ann, Robert W. Dimand, and Evelyn L. Forget, eds. 1995. *Women of Value: Feminist Essays on the History of Economics*. Aldershot, UK, and Brookfield, Vt.: Edward Elgar.

——. 2000. *Biographical Dictionary of Women Economists.* Aldershot, UK, and Northampton, Mass.: Edward Elgar.

Dimand, Robert. 1995. The Neglect of Women's Contributions to Economics. In Mary Ann Dimand, Robert W. Dimand, and Evelyn L. Forget, eds., *Women of Value: Feminist Essays on the History of Economics.* Aldershot, UK, and Brookfield, Vt.: Edward Elgar.

——. 1999. Women Economists in the 1890s: Journals, Books and the Old Palgrave. Paper prepared for presentation at the Allied Social Science Association Meetings, New York City, January.

Folbre, Nancy. 1998. The "Sphere of Women" in Early Twentieth Century Economics. In Helene Silverberg, ed., *Gender and American Social Science: The Formative Years.* Princeton: Princeton University Press.

Forget, Evelyn. 1995. American Women Economists, 1900–1940: Doctoral Dissertations and Research Specialization. In Mary Ann Dimand, Robert W. Dimand, and Evelyn L. Forget, eds., *Women of Value: Feminist Essays on the History of Economics.* Aldershot, UK, and Brookfield, Vt.: Edward Elgar.

Garraty, John A. and Mark C. Carnes, eds. 1999. *American National Biography.* Oxford and New York: Oxford University Press.

Groenewegen, Peter, ed. 1994. *Feminism and Political Economy in Victorian England.* Aldershot, UK, and Brookfield, Vt.: Edward Elgar.

Hammond, Claire H. 1993. American Women and the Professionalization of Economics. *Review of Social Economy* 51 (fall): 347–70.

James, Edward J., Janet Wilson James, and Paul S. Boyer, eds. 1971. *Notable American Women 1607–1950.* Cambridge, Mass.: Belknap Press of Harvard University Press.

Karcher, Carolyn. 1996. Introduction to Lydia Maria Child, *An Appeal in Favor of that Class of Americans Called Africans.* Amherst, Mass.: University of Massachusetts Press.

Lewis, Margaret. 1999. History of Economic Thought. In Janice Peterson and Margaret Lewis, eds., *The Elgar Companion to Feminist Economics.* Aldershot, UK, and Northampton, Mass.: Edward Elgar.

Madden, Kirsten. 2002. Female Contributions to Economic Thought, 1900–1940. *History of Political Economy* 34(1): 1–30.

Nicholls, C. S., ed. 1993. *The Dictionary of National Biography. Missing Persons.* Oxford and New York: Oxford University Press.

Pujol, Michèle A. 1992. *Feminism and Anti-Feminism in Early Economic Thought.* Aldershot, UK, and Brookfield, Vt.: Edward Elgar.

——. 1996. Nineteenth Century Economic Writing by Women. Paper presented at the History of Economics Society meeting, June 1996, Vancouver, B.C.

Sicherman, Barbara and Carol Hurd Green, with Ilene Kantrov and Harriette Walker. 1980. *Notable American Women: The Modern Period. A Biographical Dictionary.* Cambridge, Mass.: Harvard University Press.

Silverberg, Helene, ed. 1998. *Gender and American Social Science: The Formative Years.* Princeton: Princeton University Press.

Stephen, Sir Leslie and Sir Sidney Lee, eds. 1959–60. *The Dictionary of National Biography, from the Earliest Times to 1900.* 22 vols. London: Oxford University Press.

Yeo, Eileen Janes. 1996. *The Contest for Social Science: Relations and Representations of Gender and Class.* London: Rivers Oram Press.

Electronic resources

BOPCRIS (British Official Publications Collaborative Reader Information Service) – online database of information on (and some full-text) British official documents: http://www.bopcris.ac.uk.

Chadwyck-Healey, online databases mentioned are:

- The Nineteenth Century – books and pamphlets: access available at http://c19.chadwyck.co.uk.
- Periodicals Contents Index (PCI) – covers wide variety of periodicals from eighteenth century to present: online access available through subscribing libraries; information at http://www.chadwyck.com.

Feminist Economics – for information on the International Association for Feminist Economics (IAFFE) and its journal *Feminist Economics*, see its website at http://www.iaffe.org.

JSTOR – full-text articles from scholarly journals in the social sciences and humanities, New York: JSTOR, 1995–: online access available through subscribing libraries at http://www.jstor.org.

Nineteenth Century Masterfile ("Poole's Plus") – online index to periodicals, Reston, VA: Paratext, Inc., 1999–: online access available through subscribing libraries at http://poolesplus.odyssi.com.

OCLC (Online Computer Library Center) FirstSearch: http://www.oclc.org/firstsearch.

Online databases, with access available through subscribing libraries, include:

- FirstSearch Dissertation Abstracts
- FirstSearch EconLit
- FirstSearch World Catalogue (WorldCat)

Victorian Women Writers Project – online texts of books and pamphlets. University of Indiana Library Electronic Text Resource Service (LETRS): http://www.indiana.edu/~letrs/vwwp/index.html

Wellesley Index to Victorian Periodicals, 1824–1900 – index to British publications; print version: ed. Walter Edwards Houghton. Toronto: University of Toronto Press, 1966–87; CD-ROM version: London and New York: Routledge, 1999.

A

Abbott, Edith. 1904. Book Review of "Elements of Political Economy" by J. Shield Nicholson. *School Review* 12 (December): 754–.

——. 1904. Wage Statistics in the Twelfth Census. *Journal of Political Economy* 12 (June): 339–61.

——. 1905. A Statistical Study of the Wages of Unskilled Labor in the United States, 1830–1900. Ph.D. thesis, University of Chicago (economics).

——. 1905. The Wages of Unskilled Labor in the United States 1850–1900. *Journal of Political Economy* 13 (June): 321–67.

——. 1906. *Co-operators and the Labour Party*. Manchester, UK: Women's Co-operative Guild.

——. 1906. Harriet Martineau and the Employment of Women in 1836. *Journal of Political Economy* 14 (December): 614–26.

——. 1906. The History of Industrial Employment of Women in the United States: An Introductory Study. *Journal of Political Economy* 14 (October): 461–501.

——. 1906. Woman Suffrage Militant. *Independent* 61 (November 29): 1,276–8.

——. 1907. Employment of Women in Industries: Cigar-Making – Its History and Present Tendencies. *Journal of Political Economy* 15 (January): 1–25.

——. 1907. The History of Industrial Employment of Women in the United States: A Supplemental Note. *Journal of Political Economy* 15 (December): 619–24.

——. 1907. Municipal Employment of Unemployed Women in London. *Journal of Political Economy* 15 (November): 513–30.

——. 1908. The English Working-woman and the Franchise. *Atlantic Monthly* 102: 343.

——. 1908. History of the Employment of Women in the American Cotton Mills. Part I: Statistics of Employment. Displacement of Women by Men. *Journal of Political Economy* 16 (November): 602–21.

——. 1908. History of the Employment of Women in the American Cotton Mills. Part II: Early Mill Operatives. Conditions of Life and Work. *Journal of Political Economy* 16 (December): 680–92.

——. 1908. Study of the Early History of Child Labor in America. *American Journal of Sociology* 14(1) (July): 15–37.

——. 1908. The Working Woman and the Public Moralist. *Association of Collegiate Alumnae, Publications* 3(18) (December): 12–.
——. 1909. *The Early Days of a Co-operative Society*. Manchester: Co-operative Union, Ltd.
——. 1909/1924. *Women in Industry. A Study in American Economic History*. New York: D. Appleton and Company. Reprinted New York: Arno Press, 1969.
——. 1909. History of the Employment of Women in the American Cotton Mills. Part III: Early Mill Operatives (continued.) the Period of Transition. *Journal of Political Economy* 17 (January): 19–35.
——. 1909. Women in Industry: The Manufacture of Boots and Shoes. *American Journal of Sociology* 15(3) (November): 335–60.
——. 1910. Book Review of "Women in Industry: A Study in American Economic History." *Economic Journal* 20(77) (March): 73–80.
——. 1910. Women in Industry, Library Shelf. *Chautauquan* 59 (June/August): 148–.
——. 1910/11. Book Review of "The Homelessness of the Woman Worker" by Mary Higgs and Edward E. Hay. *American Journal of Sociology* 16(1/6): 272.
——. 1911. English Poor Law Reform. *Journal of Political Economy* 19 (January): 47–59.
——. 1913. Massachusetts Report on Widows' Pensions. In the Documents and Reports section of *American Economic Review* 3 (September): 739–45.
——. 1913. Public Pensions to Widows with Children. In the Documents and Reports section of *American Economic Review* 3 (June): 473–8.
——. 1913. Women's Wages in Chicago: Some Notes of Available Data. *Journal of Political Economy* 21 (February): 143–58.
——. 1914. Book Review of "The American Girl in the Stockyards District" by Montgomery. *American Economic Review* 4(1) (March): 164–6.
——. 1914. Review of "Artificial Flower Makers" by Van Kleeck. *American Economic Review* 4(1) (March): 164–6.
——. 1914. Review of "Women in Trade Unions in San Francisco" by Matthews. *American Economic Review* 4(1) (March): 164–6.
——. 1915. *The Real Jail Problem*. Chicago: Juvenile Protective Association.
——. 1915. Are Women a Force for Good Government? *National Municipal Review* 4(3): 437–47.
——. 1915. Field Work and the Training of the Social Worker. *Proceedings of the National Conference of Charities and Corrections*. Chicago: s.n.
——. 1915. A Forgotten Minimum Wage Bill. *Life and Labor* 5 (January): 13–16.
——. 1915. Progress of the Minimum Wage in England. *Journal of Political Economy* 23 (March): 268–77.
——. 1915. Statistics in Chicago Suffrage. *New Republic* 3 (June): 151.
——. 1916. Book Review of "The Trade Union Woman." *American Economic Review* 6 (March): 148.
——. 1916. Review of "Summary of the Report on Condition of Woman and Child Wage Earners in the U.S." *American Economic Review* 6(3) (September): 662–4.

——. 1916. Review of "Women in Modern Industry". *American Economic Review* 6 (June): 399–400.

——. 1916. The Woman Voter and the Spoils System in Chicago. *National Municipal Review* 5(3): 460.

——. 1916/17. Book Review of "Old Age Pensions" by H. J. Hoare. *American Journal of Sociology* 22(1/6): 277.

——. 1917. *The Experimental Period of Widows' Pension Legislation.* Chicago: National Conference of Social Work.

——. 1917. Charles Booth, 1840–1916. *Journal of Political Economy* 25 (February): 195–200.

——. 1917. Organized Charity. *Dial* 62 (January 11/June 14): 478–.

——. 1917. War as a Crisis in Social Control. Discussion. *American Sociological Society, Papers and Proceedings* 12 (December): 41.

——. 1917. The War and Women's Work in England. *Journal of Political Economy* 25(7) (July): 641–78.

——. 1917/18. Book Review of "Munition Workers in England and France" by Henrietta R. Walter. *American Journal of Sociology* 23(1/6): 551.

——. 1917/18. Book Review of "A Seasonal Industry. A Study of the Millinery Trade in New York" by Mary Van Kleeck. *American Journal of Sociology* 23(1/6): 551.

——. 1917/18. Book Review of "A Study of Conditions in Bridgeport, Connecticut" by Amy Hewes. *American Journal of Sociology* 23(1/6): 551.

——. 1918. *Democracy and Social Progress in England.* University of Chicago War Papers, no. 8. Chicago: University of Chicago Press.

——. 1918. Crime and the War. *Journal of the American Institute of Criminal Law and Criminology* 9 (May): 32–45.

——. 1918. Review of Books Concerning Labor and Labor Organizations. *American Economic Review* 8 (December): 819–24.

——. 1918. The Social Case Worker and the Enforcement of Industrial Legislation. *Proceedings of the National Conference of Social Work.*

——. 1919. *Health Insurance in Great Britain, Report of the Health Insurance Commission of the State of Illinois* (May).

——. 1920. Book Review of "Report of the War Cabinet Committee on Women in Industry." *American Economic Review* 10 (June): 358–62.

——. 1920. Book Review of "Women's Wages: A Study of the Wages of Industrial Women and Measures Suggested to Increase Them." *American Economic Review* 10 (September): 609–10.

——. 1922. The English Census of 1921. *Journal of Political Economy* 30 (December): 827–40.

——. 1922. Recent Statistics Relating to Crime in Chicago. *Journal of the American Institute of Criminal Law and Criminology* 13 (November): 329–58.

——. 1922. Tragedy of the Excess Quota. *New Republic* 30 (March 9).

——. 1922/3. Book Review of "The History of Public Poor Relief in Massachusetts" by R. W. Kelso. *American Journal of Sociology* 28(1/6): 364.

——. 1924. *Immigration: Select Documents and Case Records*. Chicago: University of Chicago Press.
——. 1924. Federal Immigration Policies, 1864–1924. *The University Business Journal* 2(2) (March): 133–56.
——. 1924. Federal Immigration Policies, 1864–1924, II. *The University Business Journal* 2(3) (June): 347–67.
——. 1924. Federal Immigration Policies, 1864–1924, III. *The University Business Journal* 2(4) (September): 455–80.
——. 1925. English Statistics of Pauperism During the War. *Journal of Political Economy* 33 (February): 1–32.
——. 1926. *Historical Aspects of the Immigration Problem: Select Documents*. Chicago: University of Chicago Press.
——. 1927. The Civil War and the Crime Wave of 1865–70. *Social Service Review* I: 212–34.
——. 1927. Immigration Restriction – Economic Results and Prospects (in Round Table Conferences). *The American Economic Review* 17(1), Supplement, *Papers and Proceedings of the Thirty-ninth Annual Meeting of the American Economic Association* (March): 127–32.
——. 1928/9. Book Review of "Migration and Business Cycles." *Personnel Journal* 7: 483–.
——. 1929. The Webbs on the English Poor Law. *Social Service Review* 3(June): 252–69.
——. 1931/1983. *Social Welfare and Professional Education*. Chicago: University of Chicago Press.
——. 1932. Fallacy of Local Relief. *New Republic* 72 (November 9): 348–50.
——. 1932. Poor People in Chicago. *New Republic* 72 (October 5): 209.
——. 1933. *The Avatars: A Futurist Fantasy*. New York: Macmillan.
——. 1934. Abolish the Pauper Laws. *Social Service Review*, 8 March: 1–16.
——. 1933/4. Book Review of "The Administrative Control of Aliens" by Van Vleck. *Yale Law Journal* 43: 1,358–.
——. 1935. The Pauper Laws Still Go On. *Social Service Review* 9(1/4) (March/December): 731–.
——. 1936. Public Welfare and Politics. *Social Service Review* 10(1/4) (March/December): 395–.
——. 1938. Is There a Legal Right to Relief? *Social Science Review* 12(1/4) (March/December): 260–.
——. 1938. Poor Law Provision for Family Responsibility. *Social Service Review* 12(1/4) (March/December): 598–.
——. 1938. The University and Social Welfare. *Alabama Social Welfare* 3(2) (February): 15–.
——. 1939. Grace Abbott: A Sister's Memories. *Social Service Review* 13 (September): 351–408.
——. 1940. *Public Assistance*. Chicago: University of Chicago Press.
——. 1940. Unemployment Relief a Federal Responsibility. *Social Service Review* 14(1/4) (September): 438–52.

Abbott, Edith and S[ophonisba]. P[reston]. Breckenridge. 1906. Employment of Women in Industries: Twelfth Census Statistics. *Journal of Political Economy* 14 (January): 14–40.

——. 1910/1915. *The Housing Problem in Chicago*. Chicago: University of Chicago Press.

——. 1910/1919. *The Wage-earning Woman and the State, a Reply to Miss Minnie Bronson*. Pamphlets in American History. Boston: Boston Equal Suffrage Association for Good Government.

——. 1911. Women in Industry: The Chicago Stockyards. *Journal of Political Economy* 19(8) (October): 632–54.

——. 1912. *The Delinquent Child and the Home*. New York: Charities Publication Committee. Reprinted New York: Arno Press, 1970.

——. 1917. *Truancy and Non-attendance in the Chicago Schools: A Study of the Social Aspects of the Compulsory Education and Child Labor Legislation of Illinois*. Chicago: University of Chicago Press. Reprinted New York: Arno Press, 1970.

——. 1921. *The Administration of the Aid-to-Mothers Law in Illinois*. United States Children's Bureau, Legal series, no. 7: Bureau publication, no. 82. Washington: U.S. Government Printing Office.

Abbott, Edith and Katherine Kiesling. 1935. Evictions during the Chicago Rent Moratorium Established by the Relief Agencies, 1931–33. *Social Service Review* 9 (March): 34–57.

Abbott, Edith and O. Alsager MacIver. 1937. Tenements of Chicago. *Charity Organisation Quarterly* 11(4) (October): 249–.

Abbott, Edith, Mabel Gillespie, and Anne Withington. 1906. *The History of Trade Unionism among Women in Boston*. Boston: Women's Trade Union League of Massachusetts.

Abbott, Edith, Sophonisba Preston Breckinridge, and Grace Browning. 1935. *The Development of Poor Relief Legislation in Kansas*. Social Service Monographs, no. 35. Chicago: University of Chicago Press.

Abbott, Edith, Sophonisba P. Breckinridge and others. 1936. *The Tenements of Chicago: 1908–1935*. Chicago: University of Chicago Press. Reprinted New York: Arno Press, 1970.

Abbott, Edith. Coauth. *See* Breckinridge, Sophonisba Preston.

Abbott, Edith. Edith Abbott Papers, Regenstein Library, University of Chicago.

Abbott, Frances Matilda. 1893. How to Solve the Housekeeping Problem. *Forum* 14 (February): 778–88.

——. 1895. A Generation of College Women [at Vassar]. *Forum* 20 (November): 377–84.

——. 1896. The Pay of College Women. *North American Review* 163 (September): 337–44.

——. 1896. College Women and Matrimony, Again. *Century Illustrated Monthly Magazine* 51 (March): 796–8.

——. 1897. Have Americans Any Social Standards? *Forum* 23 (July): 609–21.

——. 1898. A Comparative View of the Woman Suffrage Movement. *North American Review* 166 (February): 142–51.

Abbott, Grace. 1908/9. The Chicago Employment Agency and the Immigrant Worker. *American Journal of Sociology* 14(1/6): 289–.

——. 1917. The Immigrant as a Problem in Community Planning. *American Sociological Society, Papers and Proceedings* 12 (December): 166–.

——. 1922. *Federal Aid for the Protection of Maternity and Infancy*. Washington: U.S. Government Printing Office.

——. 1923. *Ten Years' Work for Children*. Washington: U.S. Children's Bureau.

——. 1929. Children's Bureau. *Childhood Education* 5: 363–.

——. 1929. The County or the Community. *American Sociological Society, Papers and Proceedings* 24: 251–.

——. 1930. The County Versus the Community as an Administrative Unit. *Social Service Review* 4(1/4) (March/December): 11–.

——. 1931. Developing and Protecting Professional Standards in Public Welfare Work. *Social Service Review* 5(1/4) (March/December): 384–.

——. 1932. Improvement in Rural Public Relief: The Lesson of the Coalmining Communities. Chicago: Preprinted for the U.S. Children's Bureau from the *Social Service Review* 6(2) (June).

——. 1932. Rural Public Relief in Coal-mining Communities. *Social Service Review* 6(1/4) (March/December): 183–.

——. 1933. Human Cost of Unemployment. *American Labor Legislation Review* 23: 29–35.

——. 1934. Recent Trends in Mothers' Aid. *Social Service Review* 8(1/4) (March/December): 191–.

——. 1935. The United States at the Nineteenth International Labor Conference. *American Labor Legislation Review* 25: 107–14.

——. 1936. *The Social Security Act and Relief.* Chicago: s.n.

——. 1936/7. The Social Security Act and Relief. *University of Chicago Law Review* 4: 45–.

——. 1938. *The Child and the State. Vol. I: Legal Status in the Family. Apprenticeship and Child Labor. Select Documents, with Introductory Notes*. Chicago: University of Chicago Press.

——. 1939. Federal Regulation of Child Labor, 1906–38. *Social Service Review* 13(1/4) (March/December): 409–.

Abbott, Grace and S. P. Breckinridge. 1936. New Chapters in the History of the Courts and Social Legislation. *Social Service Review* 10(1/4) (March/December): 482–.

Abbott, Grace. Coauth. *See* Breckinridge, Sophonisba Preston.

Abel, Mary [W.] Hinman. 1890. Kitchen Experiment Stations. *Chautauquan* 12 (October): 84–.

——. 1900. *Food of Children and Some Remarks on Household Management*, Rochester: American Public Health Association.

——. 1903. Co-operative Housekeeping. *House Beautiful* 13 (April).

——. 1903. Labor Problems in the Household. *Lake Placid Conference on Home Economics, Proceedings*: 29–37.

——. 1920. For the Homemaker: Public Kitchens. *Journal of Home Economics* 12 (June).

——. 1921. *Successful Family Life on the Moderate Income: Its Foundation in a Fair State; the Man's Earnings; the Woman's Contribution; the Cooperation of the Community*. Philadelphia and London: Lippincott Company. Revised 2nd ed., 1927.

Abel, Mary Hinman and Ellen H. Richards. 1890–3. *The Story of the New England Kitchen. Part II, A Study in Social Economics*. Boston: Press of Rockwell and Churchill.

Abels, Margaret Hutton. 1917. *From School to Work: A Study of Children Leaving School under 16 Years of Age to Go to Work in Waltham, Mass.* Washington: U.S. Children's Bureau.

Aberdeen, Countess of [Ishbel Maria Marjoribanks Gordon]. 1892. Household Clubs: An Experiment. *Nineteenth Century* 31 (January/June): 391–8.

——. 1899. The International Council of Women in Congress. *Nineteenth Century* 46 (July): 18–25.

——. 1899. The Woman's International Parliament. *North American Review* 169 (August): 145–53.

Abraham, May Edith. *See* Tennant, May Edith Abraham.

Abram, Annie. 1909. *Social England in the Fifteenth Century*. London: G. Routledge and Sons.

——. 1909. Social England in the Fifteenth Century. Ph.D. thesis, University of London (economics).

——. 1916. Women Traders in Medieval London. *Economic Journal* 26 (June): 276–85.

[Adam,] Juliette Lambert. 1858. *Idées anti-proudhoniennes sur l'amour, la femme et le mariage*. Paris: A. Taride.

——. 1887. Paul Bert's Science in Politics. *Contemporary Review* 51 (January/June): 32–44.

——. 1891. The Dowries of Women in France. *North American Review* 152 (January): 37–46.

——. 1892. Woman's Place in Modern Life. *Fortnightly Review*, n.s. 51 (April): 522–9.

——. 1893. Criminal Law in France. *North American Review* 156 (January/June): 160.

——. 1893. England and France in Siam. *North American Review* 157 (September): 278–86.

——. 1894. France and England in Egypt. *North American Review* 159 (July/December): 34–46.

——. 1897. The Position of Woman in France. *Humanitarian* 10 (February): 81–.

Adams, Charlotte. 1888. Life at a Working-woman's Home. *Lippincott's* 41 (January/June): 235.

Adams, Elizabeth Kemper. 1910. Book Review of "Vocations for the Trained Woman" by Agnes F. Perkins. *School Review* 18: 642–.

——. 1910. The Psychological Gains and Losses of College Women. *Association of Collegiate Alumnae, Publications* 3(21) (April): 11–.

——. 1912. The Vocational Opportunities of the College of Liberal Arts. *Association of Collegiate Alumnae, Journal* 5(3) (April): 256–.

——. 1920. Some New Professional Standards for College. *Educational Record* 1(2) (April).

——. 1921. *Women Professional Workers: A Study Made for the Women's Educational and Industrial Union.* Chautauqua, N.Y.: The Chautauqua Press.

——. 1922. Agencies Other than Academic Appointment Bureaus Concerned with the Vocational Guidance and Placement of Professional Women. *Educational Record* 3(1) (January).

Adams, Grace Kinckle. 1939. *Workers on Relief.* New Haven, Conn.: Yale University Press.

Adams, Jane Elizabeth. 1925. The Abolition of the Brazilian Slave Trade. *Journal of Negro History* 10(4) (October): 607–37.

Adams, Marilla. 1898. The Women of Mexico. *Chautauquan* 27 (April/September) 622–.

Addams, Jane. 1892. Hull House, Chicago: An Effort toward Social Democracy. *Forum* 14 (October): 226–41. Reprinted as The Objective Value of a Social Settlement, in [Henry C. Adams, ed.] *Philanthropy and Social Progress: Seven Essays by Miss Jane Addams and Others.* New York and Boston: T. Y. Crowell, 1893. Book reprinted 1969, New York: Books for Libraries Press. Article included in Jean Bethke Elshtain, ed., *The Jane Addams Reader.* New York: Basic Books, 2002.

——. 1892. A New Impulse to an Old Gospel. *Forum* 14 (November): 345–58. Reprinted as The Subjective Necessity for Social Settlements, in [Henry C. Adams, ed.] *Philanthropy and Social Progress: Seven Essays by Miss Jane Addams and Others.* New York and Boston: T. Y. Crowell, 1893. Book reprinted 1969, New York: Books for Libraries Press. Article included in Jean Bethke Elshtain, ed., *The Jane Addams Reader.* New York: Basic Books, 2002.

——. 1895. The Settlement as a Factor in the Labor Movement. In [Residents of Hull House,] *Hull-House Maps and Papers.* New York, T. Y. Crowell. Reprinted New York: Arno Press, 1970. Essay included in Jean Bethke Elshtain, ed., *The Jane Addams Reader.* New York: Basic Books, 2002.

——. 1896. A Belated Industry [Domestic Labor]. *American Journal of Sociology* 1 (March): 536–50.

——. 1896. The Problem of Domestic Service. *Review of Reviews* 13 (May): 604.

——. 1898. The College Woman and the Family Claim. *The Commons* III (September): 3–7.

——. 1898. Ethical Survivals in Municipal Corruption. *International Journal of Ethics* 8 (April): 273–91.

——. 1898. Why the Ward Boss Rules. [Excerpted from Ethical Survivals…] *Outlook* 57 (April 2): 879–82. Included in Jean Bethke Elshtain, ed., *The Jane Addams Reader.* New York: Basic Books, 2002.

——. 1898. Working Women's Need of the Ballot. *Public Opinion* 23 (December 9): 749–.

——. 1899. A Function of the Social Settlement, *Annals of the American Academy of Political and Social Science* 13 (May): 323–45.

——. 1899. The Subtle Problems of Charity. *Atlantic Monthly* 83 (February): 163–78. Included in Jean Bethke Elshtain, ed., *The Jane Addams Reader.* New York: Basic Books, 2002.

——. 1899. Trades Unions and Public Duty. *American Journal of Sociology* 4(4) (January): 448–62.

——. 1901. *Democracy and Social Ethics.* New York: Macmillan Co.

——. 1902. The Housing Problem in Chicago. *Annals of the American Academy* 20 (July): 99–.

——. 1903. Child Labor and Pauperism. *Charities; a Weekly Review of Local and General Philanthropy* 11: 300.

——. 1904. Humanizing Tendency of Industrial Education. *Chautauquan. A Monthly Magazine Devoted to the Promotion of True Culture* 39: 266.

——. 1904. The Present Crisis in Morals of Trade. *North American Review* 179: 17.

——. 1905. Child Labor Legislation, a Requisite for Industrial Efficiency. *Annals of the American Academy of Political and Social Science* 25: 542.

——. 1905/6. Work and Play as Factors in Education. *Chautauquan* 42 (September/February): 251–.

——. 1906. Operation of the Illinois Law on Child Labor. *Annals of the American Academy of Political and Social Science* 27: 327.

——. 1907. *Newer Ideals of Peace.* New York: Macmillan Co.

——. 1907. Discussion of Professor Commons' Paper. *American Sociological Society, Papers and Proceedings* 2 (December): 152–.

——. 1907/8. Class Conflict in America. *American Journal of Sociology* 13(1/6): 770–.

——. 1910. *The Modern City and the Municipal Franchise for Women.* New York: National American Woman Suffrage Association.

——. 1910. Charity and Social Justice. *American Federationist* 17(8) (August): 673–.

——. 1911. *Symposium – Child Labor of the Stage.* Pamphlet/National Child Labor Committee, no. 165. New York: National Child Labor Committee.

——. 1911. Recreation as a Public Function in Urban Communities. *American Sociological Society, Papers and Proceedings* 6 (December): 35–.

——. 1911. Social Control. *Crisis* 1 (January): 22–.

——. 1911. Symposium – Child Labor of the Stage. *Proceedings of the Seventh Annual Conference on Child Labor*, Supplement, *Annals of the Academy of Political and Social Science* (July). Philadelphia: American Academy of Political and Social Science.

——. 1912. *A New Conscience and an Ancient Evil.* New York: Macmillan Co.

——. 1912. The Progressive Party and the Negro. *Crisis* 5 (November): 30–.

——. 1914. *A Plea for More Play, More Pay and More Education for Our Factory Girls and Boys.* Chicago: Chicago Association of Commerce.

——. 1914. The Larger Aspects of the Woman's Movement. *American Academy of Political and Social Science, Annals* 56 (November): 1–.

——. 1917. Labor as a Factor in the Newer Conception of International Relationships. *Academy of Political Science, Proceedings* 7(2) (July): 90–.

——. 1921. The Potential Advantage of the Mandate System. *American Academy of Political and Social Science, Annals* 96 (July): 70–.

——. 1922/1983. *Peace and Bread in Time of War*. New York: Macmillan Company.

——. 1929. Safety in the Home. *American Labor Legislation Review* 19: 409–.

——. 1931. *Social Consequences of Business Depressions*. Chicago: University of Chicago Press.

——. 1932. The Education of Negroes. *Opportunity* 10(12) (December): 370–.

——. 1932. A Great Public Servant, Julia C. Lathrop. *Social Service Review* 6(1/4) (March/December): 280–.

——. 1935. Julia Lathrop and Outdoor Relief in Chicago, 1893–94. *Social Service Review* 9(1/4) (March/December): 24–.

——. 1935. Julia Lathrop's Services to the State of Illinois. *Social Service Review* 9(1/4) (March/December): 191–.

——. Coauth. *See* Nicholes, Anna E.

Adler, Nettie. 1902. *Wage Earning Children in England*. London: Hazell.

——. 1903. Children as Wage-earners. *Fortnightly Review* (May): 918–.

——. 1907/8. Child Workers and Wage Earners. *Royal Society of Arts, Journal* 56 (November 22/November 13): 738–.

——. 1908. Child Employment and Juvenile Delinquency. In G. Tuckwell, ed., *Woman in Industry from Seven Points of View*. London: Duckworth.

——. 1915. Women's Industry During and after the War. *Contemporary Review* (December).

Aguirre, Mme. Gertrude G. de. 1894. *Women in the Business World, or, Hints and Helps to Prosperity*. Boston: Arena Publishing Company.

Alberdingk Thijm, Catherina. 1884. *Lucratieve betrekkingen voor vrouwen uit den beschaafden stand*. Gouda: G. B. van Goor Zonen.

Albertson, Mary. 1928. London Merchants and Their Landed Property During the Reigns of the Yorkists. Ph.D. thesis, Bryn Mawr College (economics).

——. 1932. *London Merchants and Their Landed Property during the Reigns of the Yorkists*, Philadelphia: John C. Winston Company.

Alcott, Louisa May. 1873. *Work: A Story of Experience*. Boston: Roberts Brothers. Reprinted with introduction by Sarah Elbert, New York: Schocken Books, 1977. [*novel*]

Alden, Cynthia M[ay]. Westover. 1898. Women in Journalism. *Frank Leslie's Popular Monthly* XLVII (December): 208–.

——.1904. *Women's Ways of Earning Money*. New York: A. S. Barnes.

Alden, Margaret. 1908/1909/1913. *Child Life and Labour*. London: Headley.

Aldrich, Mrs. 1900. The Management of a Modern Household. *National Union of Women Workers of GB and Ireland, Annual Report*. Papers read at the conference held in Brighton, October 23–26. P. S. King & Sons.

Alec-Tweedie, Mrs. Ethel [née Harley]. 1895. *Danish Versus English Butter Making*, London: Horace Cox.

——. 1906. *The Maker of Modern Mexico: Porfirio Diaz*. London: Hurst and Blackett.
——. 1914/1915. *Women the World Over; a Sketch Both Light and Gay, Perchance Both Dull and Stupid*. New York: G. H. Doran Company.
——. 1916. A Woman's Night in Furnaceland. *English Review* 22 (January/June): 463.
——. 1916. Women and War Economy. *English Review* 22 (January/June): 353–.
——. 1917. *Mexico, from Diaz to the Kaiser*. London: Hutchinson & Co.
——. 1917. Co-operative Homes. *English Review* 25 (July/December): 442–.
——. 1917. The Woman's Army. *English Review* 24 (January/June): 439–.
——. 1918. *Women and Soldiers*. London and New York: John Lane, Co.
[Alexander,] Sadie Tanner Mossell. 1921. Living Standards of One Hundred Southern Negro Families Migrated to Philadelphia. Ph.D. thesis, University of Pennsylvania (economics).
——. 1921. The Standard of Living among One Hundred Negro Migrant Families in Philadelphia. *Annals of the American Academy of Political and Social Sciences* 98 (November).
——. 1930. Negro Women in Our Economic Life. *Opportunity* 8(7) (July): 201–.
Allen, Barbara. 1886. Notes of a Workhouse Visitor. *Charity Organisation Review* 24 (December): 428–.
Allen, Edith C. Coauth. *See* Broughton, Gladys Mary.
Allen, Edith Louise. 1928. American Housing as Affected by Social and Economic Conditions. Ph.D. thesis, the American University (economics).
Allen, Jane. 1932. You May Have My Job: A Feminist Discovers Her Home. *Forum* 87 (April): 228–31.
Allen, Nellie Burnham. 1910. *Industrial Studies: United States.* Boston and New York: Ginn.
——. 1913. *Industrial Studies: Europe*. Boston and New York: Ginn.
——. 1916. *Geographical and Industrial Studies: Asia*. Boston and New York: Ginn. Revised edns. 1929, 1934.
——. 1918. *Geographical and Industrial Studies: South America.* Boston and New York: Ginn. Revised edn. 1934.
——. 1920. *Geographical and Industrial Studies: The New Europe*. Boston and New York: Ginn.
——. 1922. *Geographical and Industrial Studies: North America*. Boston: Ginn. Revised edn. 1935.
——. 1924. *Geographical and Industrial Studies: Africa, Australia and The Islands of the Pacific*. Boston: Ginn. Revised edn. 1938.
——. 1924. *How and Where We Live: An Open Door to Geography*. Boston and New York: Ginn.
——. 1925. *Geographical and Industrial Studies: United States.* Boston and New York: Ginn.
——. 1928. *Geographical and Industrial Studies: Europe*. Boston and New York: Ginn.
——. 1928. *Our Cereal Grains*. Boston and New York: Ginn.
——. 1929. *Cotton and Other Useful Fibers*. Boston: Ginn.

Allen, Ruth Alice. 1912. *Chapters in the History of Organized Labor in Texas.* Texas: University of Texas.

——. 1923. The Theory and Practice of a Minimum Wage. M.S. thesis, University of Texas at Austin.

——. 1931. *The Labor of Women in the Production of Cotton.* Austin: University of Texas. Reprinted New York: Arno Press, 1975.

——. 1931. The Labor of Women in the Production of Cotton. Ph.D. thesis, University of Chicago (economics).

——. 1931/2. Mexican Peon Women in Texas. *Sociology and Social Research* 16: 131–.

——. 1934. Review of "Economics of Household Production". *American Economic Review* 24(4) (December): 761–2.

——. 1938/9. The Capitol Boycott: A Study in Peaceful Labor Tactics. *Southwestern Historical Quarterly* 42: 316–.

——. 1940/1. Book Review of "One Thousand Strikes of Government Employees" by David Ziskind. *Southwestern Social Sciences Quarterly* 21: 184–.

——. Papers; and Labor Movement in Texas Papers. Located at Barker Texas History Center, University of Texas at Austin.

Allinson, May. 1914. *The Public Schools and Women in Office Service.* Boston: Women's Educational and Industrial Union.

——. 1914. Book Review of "La Vie tragique des travailleurs" by Bonneff. *American Economic Review* 4(1/2): 923–.

——. 1915. Book Review of "Working Girls in Evening Schools: A Statistical Study." *American Economic Review* 5 (September): 630–2.

——. 1916. *Dressmaking as a Trade for Women in Massachusetts.* Washington: U.S. Government Printing Office and New York: Federal Bureau of Labor Statistics.

——. 1916. Dressmaking as a Trade for Women in Massachusetts. Ph.D. thesis, Columbia University (economics).

Allinson, May and Susan Myra Kingsbury. 1917. *Industrial Experience of Trade-school Girls in Massachusetts.* Washington: U.S. Government Printing Office; Boston: Women's Educational and Industrial Union.

Allison, Frances Ekin. 1885. *Men, Women, and Money.* Chicago: Jansen, McClurg, and Co.

Alsop, Marjorie Hosken. 1938. *The Marketing of the World's Wheat Crop.* Ph.D. thesis, London School of Economics.

Amberley, Viscountess. 1871. The Claims of Women. *Fortnightly Review*, n.s. 9 (January): 95–110.

Ames, Mrs. Fanny B. 1886. Adequate Relief vs. Dole Giving. *Lend a Hand* 1(4) (April): 226–.

——. 1891. Child Labor. In *Proceedings of the Fifth Annual Convention of Factory Inspectors.* Cleveland, Ohio: International Association of Factory Inspectors.

Ames, Susie May. 1931. A Typical Virginia Business Man of the Revolutionary Era: Nathaniel Littleton Savage and his Account Book. *Journal of Economic and Business History* 3 (May): 407–23.

Amidon, Beulah. 1938. *Why Women Work.* New York: National Federation of Business and Professional Women's Clubs.

——. 1939. *Jobs after Forty.* New York: Public Affairs Committee, Inc.

Amidon, Jeannette Marie. 1937. Effect of the United States Silver Purchase Act upon Trade between the Pacific Northwest and the Orient. M.A. thesis, College of Puget Sound.

Anderson, Adelaide M[ary]. 1895. Joint Associations of Employers and Employed in France and Belgium. *Economic Journal* 5(20) (December): 641–50.

——. 1898/9. Factory Life and Legislation in England. *Chautauquan* 28 (October/March): 243–.

——. 1899. Truck Legislation in England and on the Continent. *Journal of the Society of Comparative Legislation* 1: 395–406.

——. 1908. Factory and Workshop Law. In Gertrude M. Tuckwell, Constance Smith [*et al.*], *Woman in Industry from Seven Points of View.* London: Duckworth.

——. 1913. Women in Public Administration. *New Statesman* 2, Supplement (November 1): xix–.

——. 1918. *Memorandum on Subsidiary Health and Kindred Service for Women.* London: H.M. Stationery Office. Darling and Son, Limited, printers for the Ministry of Reconstruction, Women's Employment Committee.

——. 1922. *Women in the Factory; An Administrative Adventure, 1893 to 1921.* New York: E. P. Dutton and Co.

——. 1925. The Recommendations of the Shanghai Child Labour Commission. *International Labour Review* (Geneva) 11 (May): 665–81.

——. 1928. *Humanity and Labour in China: An Industrial Visit and Its Sequel. 1923 to 1926.* London: Student Christian Movement.

——. 1930. The Employment of Children in Egyptian Industry. *International Labour Review* 22 (December): 723–51.

——.?/1964. *Brief History of Factory Legislation in the United Kingdom.* Labour Legislation Series, no. 2. Shanghai: National Christian Council of China, Industrial Committee.

——. ?/1964. *The Factory System and the Regulation of Labour Conditions by National and International Law.* Labour Legislation Series, no. 1. Shanghai: National Christian Council of China, Industrial Committee.

Anderson, Cornelia M. 1937. A View of the British Employment Exchanges. *Harvard Business Review* 16(1): 93–104.

Anderson, Elin Lilja. 1937. *We Americans: A Study of Cleave in an American City.* Cambridge, Mass.: Harvard University Press.

——. 1940. *Do We Want Health?* Lincoln: University of Nebraska.

[Anderson,] Elizabeth Garrett. 1866. Hospital Nursing. Paper read at the National Association for the Promotion of Social Science. Reprinted in Candida Ann Lacey, ed., *Barbara Leigh Smith Bodichon and the Langham Place Group.* New York and London: Routledge & Kegan Paul, 1987.

——. 1866/7. Volunteer Hospital Nursing. *Macmillan's Magazine* 15 (November/April): 494–.

——. 1874. Sex in Mind and in Education – A Reply. *Fortnightly Review* 21 (May): 582–94.

Anderson, Esther Sanfreida. 1917. *Geography of the Beet Sugar Industry*. M.A. thesis, University of Nebraska (Lincoln campus).

——. 1920. Beet Sugar Production in Nebraska. *Journal of Geography* 19 (January/December): 121–.

——. 1925. The Beet Sugar Industry of Nebraska as a Response to Geographic Environment. *Economic Geography* 1(3) (October): 373–86.

——. 1930. The Potato Industry in Nebraska. *Economic Geography* 6(1) (January): 37–53.

——. 1932. The Sugar Beet Industry in the Intermontane and the Great Plains Regions of the United States. Ph.D. thesis, Clark University.

——. 1935. *The Sugar Beet Industry of Nebraska.* Conservation Department of the Conservation and Survey Division, Bulletin 9. Lincoln, Nebr.: University of Nebraska.

Anderson, Harriet E. and Margaret E. Rich. 1931. *Care of the Homeless in Unemployment Emergencies: Suggestions for a Community Program.* New York: Family Welfare Association of America.

Anderson, Mary. 1918. Woman in Industry Service. *American Federationist* 25(8/12) (August/December): 798–.

——. 1919. Wages for Women Workers. *American Academy of Political and Social Science, Annals* 81 (January): 123–.

——. 1919. Will Women Retire from Industry with Return of Peace? *Academy of Political Science, Proceedings* 8(2) (February): 13–.

——. 1923. The Growing Army of Women Workers. *Current History (New York)* 17(6) (March): 1,003–.

——. 1924. Personnel Equipment in Factory Inspection. *American Academy of Political and Social Science, Annals* 113 (May): 321–.

——. 1924. Unemployed Women and Public Works. *American Labor Legislation Review* 24: 38–40.

——. 1925. The Federal Government Recognizes the Problems of Women in Industry. *American Federationist* 32(1/6) (January/June): 452–.

——. 1925. Hours of Work. *American Federationist* 32(7/12) (July/December): 769–.

——. 1925. Industrial Standards for Women. *American Federationist* 32 (July): 564–.

——. 1925. Should There Be Labor Laws for Women? Yes. *Good Housekeeping* (September): 53–.

——. 1925. Women in Industry. *American Federationist* 32(1/6) (January/June): 333–.

——. 1925. The Women Workers. *American Federationist* 32(7/12) (July/December): 1,073–.

——. 1925. Women's Wages. *American Federationist* 32(7/12) (July/December): 681–.

——. 1925. Working Conditions. *American Federationist* 32(7/12) (July/December): 946–.
——. 1927/8. The Importance of Women in Industry. *Personnel Journal* 6 (June/April): 329–.
——. 1928. Summer Schools for Women in Industry. *Journal of the American Association of University Women* 21(3) (April): 77–.
——. 1928. Women Work Long Hours in Southern Mills. *American Labor Legislation Review* 18: 35–.
——. 1929. What Use is the Women's Bureau to the Woman Worker? *American Federationist* 36(8) (August): 939–.
——. 1929. Women Workers in Textiles. *American Federationist* 36(6) (June): 696–.
——. 1930. Eighteen Years with the Minimum Wage Experiment. *State Government* 3(7) (October): 9–.
——. 1930. Labor's Attitude Toward Peace. *American Teacher* 14(8) (April): 13–.
——. 1931. *Women's Place in Industry in 10 Southern States*. Washington: U.S. Women's Bureau.
——. 1932. Behind the Counters in the "Five and Tens." *American Federationist* 39(3) (March): 283–.
——. 1932. The Clerical Worker and Industrial Change. *American Federationist* 39(9) (September): 1,024–.
——. 1932. Housekeepers for the Public. *American Federationist* 39(11) (November): 1,270–.
——. 1932. King Cotton and the Woman Worker. *American Federationist* 39(4) (April): 429.
——. 1932. The Negro Woman Worker. *American Federationist* 39(10) (October): 1,114–.
——. 1932. On the Trail of the Migrant. *American Federationist* 39(7) (July): 775–.
——. 1932. The Radio Worker and Unemployment. *American Federationist* 39(8) (August): 894–.
——. 1932. What Canneries Mean to Women. *American Federationist* 39(6) (June): 652–.
——. 1932. When Machines Make Cigars. *American Federationist* 39(12) (December): 1,375–.
——. 1932. With Women Workers in the Stockyards. *American Federationist* 39(5) (May): 556–.
——. 1932. Women in Laundries. *American Federationist* 39(2) (February): 182–.
——. 1932. Women and Their Jobs. Some Lessons of the Depression. *Journal of the American Association of University Women* 26(1) (October): 9–.
——. 1933. Women Who Enamel Stoves. *American Federationist* 40(1) (January): 49–.
——. 1934. The Sex Differential in Minimum Rates under N.R.A. Codes. *Women Lawyers' Journal* 21(2) (November): 29–.
——. 1934. Unemployed Women and Public Works. *American Labor Legislation Review* 24: 38–40.

——. 1935. Inside the Doors of Beauty Shops. *American Federationist* 42(11) (November): 1,213–.

——. 1935. Occupational Diseases and Women Workers. *American Federationist* 42(8) (August): 823–.

——. 1935. What's Wrong with the Shoe Industry. *American Federationist* 42(5) (May): 485–.

——. 1935. The Woman Office Worker. *American Federationist* 42(3) (March): 267–.

——. 1936. Factory Workers' Stake in Elimination of Industrial Home Work. *American Federationist* 43(2) (February): 183–.

——. 1936. The Plight of Negro Domestic Labor. *Journal of Negro Education* 5(1) (January): 66–.

——. 1938. Women and Their Jobs. Some Lessons of the Depression. *American Association of University Women, Journal* 26(1) (October): 9–.

——. 1938. A Year of the Minimum Wage. *American Federationist* 45(4) (April): 369–.

——. Coauth. *See* Smith, Florence Patteson.

[Andrews,] Irene Osgood. 1909. *Review of Labor Legislation of 1909.* American Association for Labor Legislation. Legislative Review no. 1. Madison: Parsons Printery.

——. 1909. Women Workers in Milwaukee Tanneries. *13th Biennial Report,* Part vii. Madison, Wisc.: Wisconsin Bureau of Labor and Industrial Statistics.

——. 1910. *Review of Labor Legislation of 1910.* Princeton: Princeton University Press.

——. 1911. Tendencies of the Labor Legislation of 1910. *American Political Science Review* 5(1/4): 224–.

——. 1914. *Minimum Wage Legislation.* Albany: New York State Factory Investigation Commission: J. B. Lyon, Printers.

——. 1915. *The Relation of Irregular Employment to the Living Wage for Women.* New York: New York State Factory Investigating Commission in cooperation with the American Association on Unemployment. Reprinted from the *American Labor Legislation Review* 5 (1915).

——. 1915. Relation of Irregular Employment to the Living Wage for Women. *American Labor Legislation Review* 5: 291.

——. 1918. Maternity Protection. *American Labor Legislation Review* 8: 365.

——. 1920. Legislation for Maternity Protection. *American Labor Legislation Review* 10: 131.

——. 1920. The Protection of Maternity, an Urgent Need. *American Labor Legislation Review* 10: 47.

——. 1920. A Tentative Outline for Maternity Protection Legislation. *American Labor Legislation Review* 10: 250.

——. 1921. State Legislation for Maternity Protection. *American Labor Legislation Review* 11: 80.

——. 1923. Maternity and Infancy Act Standards. *American Labor Legislation Review* 13: 194–.

——. 1924. Report of Work. *American Labor Legislation Review* 14: 100–.

——. 1925. Status of Minimum Wage Legislation in the United States. *American Labor Legislation Review* 15: 298–.

——. 1933. Minimum Wage Comes Back. *American Labor Legislation Review* 23: 103–5.

Andrews, Irene Osgood and Margaret A. Hobbs. 1918/1921. *Economic Effects of the War upon Women and Children in Great Britain.* Carnegie Endowment for International Peace. Preliminary Economic Studies of the War, ed. David Kinley. New York: Oxford University Press.

Angus, Eliza Young. 1931. The Higher Education of Girls and the Employment of Women. Ph.D. thesis, London School of Economics.

Anneke, Mathilde Franziska. 1847. *Das Weib im Conflict mit den socialen Verhältnissen* [Woman in Conflict with Social Conditions]. Cologne: s.n.

Anstey, Vera. 1923. Some Recent Literature on Finance and Politics in India. *Economica* 8 (June): 133–8.

——. 1923/4. Book Review of "Constitutional Developments in Mysore" by Mysore Committee Appointed to Work Out the Scheme. *Economica* 3/4(9): 265.

——. 1923/4. Book Review of "Democracies of the East" by Rudhakamal Mookerjee. *Economica* 3/4(12): 373.

——. 1923/4. Book Review of "The East India Trade in the Seventeenth Century" by Shafaat Ahmad Khan. *Economica* 3/4(10): 121.

——. 1923/4. Book Review of "Economic History of the United States" by Ernest Ludlow Bogard. *Economica* 3/4(8): 162.

——. 1923/4. Book Review of "From Akbar to Aurangzeb" by W. H. Moreland. *Economica* 3/4(10): 121.

——. 1923/4. Book Review of "India: A Bird's-eye View" by Lord Ronaldshay. *Economica* 3/4(12): 373.

——. 1923/4. Book Review of "Labour in Indian Industries" by G. M. Broughton. *Economica* 3/4(12): 373.

——. 1923/4. Book Review of "Report of an Enquiry into Agricultural Wages in the Bombay Presidency" by G. Findlay Shirras. *Economica* 3/4(12): 373.

——. 1923/4. Book Review of "The Springs of Lavenham and the Suffolk Cloth Trade in the Fifteenth and Sixteenth Centuries" by Barbara McClenaghan. *Economica* 3/4(11): 253.

——. 1923/4. Recent Literature on Finance and Politics in India. *Economica* 3/4(8): 133.

——. 1925. Book Review of "Financial Developments in Modern India" by C. N. Vakil. *Economica* 5: 232.

——. 1925. Book Review of "The Wealth of India" by P. A. Wadia and G. N. Joshi. *Economica* 5: 359.

——. 1926. Book Review of "The Punjab Peasant in Prosperity and Debt" by M. L. Darling. *Economica* 6: 109.

——. 1926. Book Review of "Then and Now: Economic Problems after the War a Hundred Years Ago" by Mrs. H. A. L. Fisher. *Economica* 6: 114.

——. 1928. Book Review of "Comparative Colonial Policy" by V. Shiva Ram. *Economica* 8: 125.

——. 1929/1931/1936. *The Economic Development of India.* New York: Longmans, Green, and Co.

——. 1929. Book Review of "Indigenous Banking in India" by L. C. Jain. *Economica* 9: 378.

——. 1929. Book Review of "Industrial Welfare in India" by P. S. Lokanathan. *Economica* 9: 377.

——. 1929. Book Review of "The New British Empire" by L. Haden Guest. *Economica* 9: 232.

——. 1929. *The Trade of the Indian Ocean.* London and New York: Longmans, Green, and Co.

——. 1930. Book Review of "Emigration from the British Isles" by W. A. Carrothers. *Economica* 10: 318.

——. 1932. Book Review of "The Indian Currency System, 1833–1926" by Sir J. C. Coyajee. *Economica* 12: 253.

——. 1932. Book Review of "Labour and Housing in India" by R. B. Gupta. *Economica* 12: 253.

——. 1932. Book Review of "Lancashire and the Far East" by Freda Utley. *Economica* 12: 256.

——. 1932. Book Review of "Taxation of Income in India" by V. K. R. V. Rao. *Economica* 12: 253.

——. 1933. Book Review of "The Co-operative Movement in India" by Eleanor M. Hough. *Economica* 13: 97.

——. 1933. Book Review of "Growth of Trade and Industry in Modern India" by C. N. Vakil, S. C. Bose, and P. V. Deolalkar. *Economica* 13: 97.

——. 1933. Book Review of "Indian Railways" by Nalimaksha Sanyal. *Economica* 13: 97.

——. 1933. Book Review of "The Indian Tariff Problem" by H. L. Dey. *Economica* 13: 335.

——. 1933. Book Review of "Purdah" by Frieda Hanswirth. *Economica* 13: 335.

——. 1933. Book Review of "Some Aspects of Indian Foreign Trade" by L. Durga Parshad. *Economica* 13: 97.

——. 1933. Book Review of "Some Bengal Villages" by N. C. Bhattachar Iyyar and L. A. Natesan. *Economica* 13: 335.

——. 1934. Book Review of "Child Marriage: The Indian Minotaur" by E. F. Rathbone. *Sociological Review* 26: 316.

——. 1934. Book Review of "Industrial Labour in India" by S. C. Panandikar. *Economica,* n.s. 1: 492.

——. 1934. Book Review of "Land Problems of India" by R. Mukerjee. *Economica* 1: 492.

——. 1934. Book Review of "Problems of Rural Reconstruction in India" by F. M. De Mello. *Economica* 1: 492.

——. 1935. Book Review of "Child Labour in India" by R. K. Das. *Economica,* n.s. 2: 485.

——. 1935. Book Review of "Communications in the Far East" by F. V. de Fellner. *Economica* 2: 483.
——. 1935. Book Review of "Cotton Industry and Trade in China, Grain Trade in Tientsin, Terminal Marketing of Tientsin Cotton" by H. D. Fong. *Economica* 2: 483.
——. 1935. Book Review of "Economic and Social Aspects of Crime in India" by B. S. Haikerwal. *Sociological Review* 27: 240.
——. 1935. Book Review of "Facing Labor Issues in China" by L. Chuan-Hua. *Economic Journal* 45: 752.
——. 1935. Book Review of "India's Foreign Trade since 1870" by P. Ray. *Economica* 2: 485.
——. 1935. Book Review of "Industrial Policy of India" by C. N. Vakil and M. C. Munshi. *Economic Journal* 45: 360.
——. 1935. Book Review of "Industrial Policy in India" by C. N. Vakil and M. C. Munshi. *Economica* 2: 485.
——. 1935. Book Review of "The Population Problem in India" by P. K. Wattal. *Economic Journal* 45: 360.
——. 1935. Book Review of "Problems of Transport Co-ordination in India" by S. K. Guha. *Economic Journal* 45: 360.
——. 1936. Book Review of "Industrial Organization in India" by P. S. Lokonathan. *Economica,* n.s. 3: 104.
——. 1936. Book Review of "Trade Unionism and Labour Disputes in India" by A. Mukhtar. *Economica* 3: 104.
——. 1936. India's Economic Position and Policy in Relation to the New Constitution. *Economica* 3(11) (August): 235–56.
——. 1937. Book Review of "The Cacao Industry of Trinidad" by C. Y. Shephard. *Economica,* n.s. 4: 359.
——. 1937. Book Review of "India's Balance of Indebtedness, 1898–1913" by Y.S. Pandit. *Economica* 4: 467.
——. 1937. Book Review of "India's Mineral Wealth" by J. Coggin Brown. *Economic Journal* 47: 146.
——. 1937. Book Review of "Southern India: Its Political and Economic Problems" by G. Slater. *Economica* 4: 358.
——. 1937. Book Review of "Der Tee im Britischen Weltreich" by F. Klopstock. *Economica* 4: 235.
——. 1937. The Indian Companies (Amendment) Act, 1936. *Asiatic Review* 33(115) (July): 642.
——. 1938. Book Review of "General Wage Census, Part II: Perennial Factories." *Economica,* n.s. 5: 482.
——. 1938. Book Review of "Industrial Enterprise in India" by N. Das. *Economica* 5: 482.
——. 1938. Book Review of "International Control in the Non-ferrous Metals" by W. Y. Elliott and others. *Economica* 5: 98.
——. 1938. Book Review of "Life and Labour in a Gujerat Taluka" by J. B. Shukla. *Economica* 5: 482.

——. 1938. Book Review of "Organisation and Finance of Industries in India" by D. R. Samant and M. A. Mulky. *Economica* 5: 482.

——. 1938. Book Review of "Railway Rates in Relation to Trade and Industry in India" by R. D. Tiwari. *Economica* 5: 482.

——. 1938. Book Review of "Studies in Indian Economics" by C. N. Vakil. *Economica* 5: 482.

——. 1938. Book Review of "Trade in the Eastern Seas, 1793–1813" by C. N. Parkinson. *Economic History* 4(13) (February): 152–.

——. 1938. Book Review of "Urban Handicrafts of the Bombay Deccan" by N. M. Joshi. *Economica* 5: 482.

——. 1939. Book Review of "Agrarian China." *Economic Journal* 49: 768.

——. 1939. Book Review of "The Central Problem of Indian Economy" by P. J. Thomas. *Economica* 6: 227.

——. 1939. Book Review of "Food Planning for Four Hundred Millions" by Radhakamal Mukerjee. *Sociological Review* 31: 334.

——. 1939. Book Review of "Indian Currency Problems in the Last Decade. 1926–1936" by J. C. Sinha. *Economica* 6: 469.

——. 1939. Book Review of "Industrial Labour in India." *Economic Journal* 49: 348.

——. 1939. Book Review of "The Industrial Worker in India" by B. Shiva Rao. *Economic Journal* 49: 348.

——. 1939. Book Review of "Kakao: Wandlungen in der Erzeugung und der Verwendung des Kakaos nach dem Weltkrieg" by F. Klopstock. *Economica* 6: 102.

——. 1939. Book Review of "Labour Conditions in Indo-China." *Economic Journal* 49: 348.

——. 1939. Book Review of "Marketing of Raw Cotton in India" by M. L. Dantwala. *Economica* 6: 357.

——. 1939. Book Review of "The Regional Balance of Man." *Sociological Review* 31: 334.

——. 1939. Book Review of "Trends of Agriculture and Population in the Ganges Valley" by Birendranath Ganguli. *Sociological Review* 31: 334.

——. 1940. Book Review of "India and Imperial Preference" by B. Madan. *Economica* 7: 347.

——. 1940. Book Review of "Indian Agricultural Statistics" by P. J. Thomas. *Economica* 7: 217.

——. 1940. Book Review of "Industrial Finance in India" by S. K. Basu. *Economica* 7: 346.

——. 1940. Book Review of "Japan's Economic Offensive in China" by Lowe Chuan-Hua. *Economica* 7: 97.

——. 1940. Book Review of "The National Income of British India, 1931–32" by V. K. R. V. Rao. *Economica* 7: 344.

——. 1940. Book Review of "State Banks for India" by A. I. Qureshi. *Economica* 7: 97.

Anthony, Helen Sylvia. 1932. *Women's Place in Industry and Home*. London: G. Routledge & Sons.

Anthony, Katharine Susan. 1914. *Mothers Who Must Earn*. New York: Survey Associates.

——. 1915. *Feminism in Germany and Scandinavia*. New York: H. Holt and Co.

——, comp. 1917. *Labor Laws of New York: A Handbook*. Brooklyn, N.Y.: Press of Hunter Collins, Inc. for the Consumers' League of the City of New York.

——, ed. 1920. *The Endowment of Motherhood*. New York: B. W. Huebach.

Anthony, Susan B. 1897. The Status of Woman, Past, Present, and Future. *Arena* 17 (May): 901–8.

Apolant, Jenny. 1910. *Stellung und Mitarbeit der Frau in der Gemeinde*. Leipzig and Berlin: B. G. Teubner.

——. 1918. *Das kommunale Wahlrecht der Frauen: in den deutschen Bundesstaaten*. Leipzig: B. G. Teubner.

Archer, Elizabeth. 1936. *The Assistance of the Poor in Paris and in the North-eastern French Provinces, 1614–1660, with Special Reference to the letters of St. Vincent de Paul.* Ph.D. thesis, London School of Economics.

——. 1938. Summaries of Theses: The Assistance of the Poor in Paris and the North-eastern French Provinces, 1614–60, with special reference to the Letters of St. Vincent de Paul. *Institute of Historical Research, Bulletin* 15(4) (February): 188–.

Arenal de García Carrasco, Concepción. 1861. *La beneficencia, la filantropia y la caridad. Memoria premiada por la Real academia de ciencias, morales y políticas, en el concurso de 1860*. Madrid: Imprenta del Colegio de Sordo-mudos y de Ciegos.

——. 1863. *Manual del visitador del pobre*. 2nd ed. Madrid: Imprenta de Tejado, á cargo de R. Ludeã.

——. 1869. *La mujer del porvenir*. Seville and Madrid: Perie.

——. 1879. *Ensayo sobre el derecho de gentes*. With an introduction by Gumersindo de Azcárate. Madrid: Imprenta de la Revista de legislación.

——. 1883. *La mujer de su casa*. Madrid: Gras y Compañía.

——. 1884. Spain. In Theodore Stanton, ed., *The Woman Question in Europe*. London: Sampson Low, Marston, Searle.

——. 1896. *El derecho de gracia ante la justicia. El reo, el pueblo y el verdugo. El delito colectivo*. Reprinted in *Obras completas*, Madrid: Victoriano Suárez.

——. 1896. *El visitador del preso*. Reprinted in *Obras completas*, Madrid: Victoriano Suárez.

——. 1897. *El pauperismo*. 2 vols. Reprinted in *Obras completas*, Madrid: Victoriano Suárez.

——. 1898. *La igualdad social y politica y sus relaciones con la libertad*. Reprinted in *Obras completas*, Madrid: Victoriano Suárez.

Arent, Leonora. 1919. Electric Franchises in New York City. Ph.D. thesis, Columbia University (economics). Also published New York: Longmans, Green & Co.

——. 1927. *The White Light*. Boston: Christopher Publishing House.

Armes, Ethel Marie. 1910. *The Story of Coal and Iron in Alabama*. Birmingham, Ala.: Chamber of Commerce.

Armold, Fay H. 1937. *A Woman's Approach to Business*. Los Angeles: Armold Sales Training Institute.

——. 1939. *Write Your Own Ticket*. Los Angeles: Armold Sales Training Institute.

Armstrong, Barbara Nachtrieb [Grimes]. 1915. Has a Public Utility the Right to Abandon Its Service to the Public in Toto or in Part? J.D. thesis, University of California Berkeley.

——. 1917. *Compulsory Health Insurance*. Berkeley: University of California.

——. 1921. Sickness as a Cause of Poverty in California and Consideration of Social Health Insurance as a Remedy. Ph.D. thesis, University of California Berkeley (economics).

——. 1929/30. Recent Legislation: Persons and Industrial Law. *California Law Review* 18: 267–.

——. 1932. *Insuring the Essentials: Social Insurance and Minimum Wage in Theory and Practice*. New York: Macmillan.

——. 1933. The Nature and Purpose of Social Insurance. *Annals of the American Academy of Political and Social Science* 170 (November): 1–6.

——. 1933. Trends in Workmen's Compensation Legislation. *Annals of the American Academy of Political and Social Science* 170 (November): 18–20.

——. 1934. Workmen's Compensation. *Encyclopedia of Social Science*.

——. 1935. The Federal Social Security Act. *American Bar Association Journal*, 21 December: 792–7.

——. 1935/1967. Rational Old Age Security System. In Ewald T. Grether, ed., *Essays in Social Economics in Honor of Jessica Blanche Peixotto*. Freeport, N.Y.: Books for Libraries Press.

——. 1935/6. The Federal Social Security Act and Its Constitutional Aspects. *California Law Review* 24: 247–.

——. 1936. Old Age Security Abroad: The Background of Titles II and VII of the Social Security Act. *Law and Contemporary Problems*, 3 April: 175–.

——. 1936. Social Insurance Abroad and at Home: The Background of Social Security Legislation. *National Municipal Review* 25(3) (March): 125–.

——. 1937/8. Recent Legislation: Community Property, Homesteads, Persons, Social Welfare. *California Law Review* 26: 329–.

——. 1939. *The Health Insurance Doctor: His Rôle in Great Britain, Denmark, and France*. Princeton: Princeton University Press.

——. 1939/1940. *Cases and Materials on Marriage, Annulment, Divorce, Community Property, Homesteads, Family Allowance*. Berkeley: School of Jurisprudence.

——. 1939/40. Recent California Legislation in the Law of Persons, Industrial Relations, and Social Welfare. *California Law Review* 28: 442–.

Armstrong, Louise Van Voorhis. 1938. *We Too Are the People*. Boston: Little, Brown and Co.

Arnold, Pauline. 1937. How Research Builds Sales. *Journal of Marketing* 2 (October): 134–40.

Arnold, Sarah L. 1910. Vocational Training for Women. In Helen Marot, ed., *The Economic Position of Women*. New York: Academy of Political Science.

——. 1910. Vocational Training for Women. *Proceedings of the Academy of Political Science* 1(1) (October): 129–39.

Arny, Clara Maude Brown and Agnes Larson. 1938. *A Survey of the Working Experience and Future Plans of the Girls in the Secondary Schools of St. Paul in Relation to Various Educational and Economic Factors*. St. Paul, Minn.: Saint Paul Department of Education.

Aronovici, Carol. 1908. *Annual Report of the Head Worker 1908*. Providence, R.I.: Providence Union Settlement.

——. 1910. *Some Nativity and Race Factors in Rhode Island*. Reprint from the *Annual Report of the Commissioner of Industrial Statistics of Rhode Island for 1909*. Providence, R.I.: State Printers.

——. 1911. *Municipal Street Cleaning: A Survey of the Problem of Street Cleaning in the City of Providence*. George H. Webb commissioner, Carol Aronovici special agent. Providence, R.I.: E. L. Freeman.

——. 1911. *Philanthropic Agencies in Rhode Island*, Part 8 of the Annual Report for 1910. Providence, R.I.: E. L. Freeman Company, State Printers.

——. 1911. Some Nativity and Race Factors in Rhode Island. Ph.D. thesis, Brown University (sociology).

——. 1912. *Housing Conditions in Fall River: Report Prepared for the Associated Charities Housing Committee*. Fall River, Mass.: Associated Charities Housing Committee.

——. 1912. *Housing Conditions in New Britain, Conn. Report Prepared for the Health Department*. New Britain, Conn.

——. 1912. *Knowing One's Small Own Community; Suggestions for Social Surveys of Small Cities or Towns*. Boston: American Unitarian Association.

——. 1912. *The Newport Survey of Social Problems*. Fall River, Mass.: Munroe Press.

——. 1912. *Report on Housing Conditions in Springfield, Massachusetts*. Springfield, Mass.: Bureau of Social Research of New England.

——. 1912. Housing Reform Through Legislation. *Academy of Political Science, Proceedings* 2(3) (April): 111–.

——. 1912. Municipal Street Cleaning and Its Problems *National Municipal Review* 1(2) (April): 218–.

——. 1912. Street Cleaning in Germany. *National Municipal Review* 1(2) (April): 225–.

——. 1913. *Housing Conditions in New Haven*. Committee on Tenement House Conditions Documents, no. 12. New Haven, Conn.: Civic Federation of New Haven.

——. 1913. Constructive Housing Reform. *National Municipal Review* 11(2): 210–20.

——. 1914. *Cost Factors in Housing Reform. Annals of the American Academy of Political and Social Science*, vol. LI [whole no. 140] (January). Philadelphia: American Academy of Political and Social Science.

——. 1914. *Housing and Town Planning. Annals of the American Academy of Political and Social Science*, vol. LI [whole no. 140]. Philadelphia: American Academy of Political and Social Science.

——. 1914. *A Housing Survey. Annals of the American Academy of Political and Social Science*, vol. LI [whole no. 140]. Philadelphia: American Academy of Political and Social Science.

——. 1914. *Introductory: Housing and the Housing Problem. Annals of the American Academy of Political and Social Science*, vol. LI [whole no. 140]. Philadelphia: American Academy of Political and Social Science.

——. 1914. The Cost of a Decent Home. *Forum* 51(1) (January).

——. 1914. The Garden City Idea in Urban Development. *American Institute of Architects Journal* 2(8) (August): 399–.

——. 1914. German Housing Reform. n.p.

——. 1914. Suburban Development. *American Academy of Political and Social Science, Annals* 51 (January): 234–.

——. 1915. *Unmarried Girls with Sex Experience.* Philadelphia: Seybert Institution/Bureau for Social Research.

——. 1915. Housing Reform in France. *American Institute of Architects Journal* 3(1) (January): 32–.

——. 1916. *The Social Survey*. Philadelphia: Harper Press.

——. 1917. *Housing Conditions in the City of Saint Paul: Report Presented to the Housing Commission of the St. Paul Association.* St. Paul, Minn.: Amherst H. Wilder Charity.

——. 1918/19. Book Review of "Welfare and Housing" by J. E. Hutton. *American Journal of Sociology* 24(1/6): 462.

——. 1918/19. Organized Leisure as a Factor in Conservation. *American Journal of Sociology* 24(1/6): 373–.

——. 1919. *Americanization.* St. Paul, Minn.: Keller.

——. 1919/20. Book Review of "The Housing of the Unskilled Wage-earner" by Edith Elmer Wood. *American Journal of Sociology* 25(1/6): 507–.

——. 1920. *Women in Industry in Minnesota in 1918*. Field Investigation Carried on by Women in Industry Committee, Council of National Defense, and Bureau of Women and Children. Minneapolis: Minnesota Department of Labor and Industry, Bureau of Women and Children.

——. 1920/1. *Housing and the Housing Problem.* The National Social Science Series. Chicago: A. C. McClurg & Co.

——. 1920/1. Book Review of "Defective Housing and the Growth of Children" by J. Lawsen Dick. *American Journal of Sociology* 26(1/6): 530–.

——. 1920/1. Book Review of "Industrial Housing" by Morris Knowles. *American Journal of Sociology* 26(1/6): 660.

——. 1920/1. Book Review of "United States Housing Corporation Report. Vol. I" by James Ford. *American Journal of Sociology* 26(1/6): 788.

——. 1920/1. Book Review of "What the Workers Want" by Arthur Gleason. *American Journal of Sociology* 26(1/6): 637.

——. 1930. Business Districts in Subdivision Planning. *National Municipal Review* XIX(7) (July): 464–70.

——. 1931. Zoning and the Home. *Annals of the American Academy of Political and Social Science* (May).

——. 1932. Urbanism – Its Coming of Age. *Columbia University Quarterly* 24(3) (September): 364–.

——. 1933/4. Housing the Poor: Mirage or Reality. *Law and Contemporary Problems* 1: 148–.

——. 1934. *America Can't Have Housing.* New York: Committee on the Housing Exhibition by the Museum of Modern Art.

——. 1934. *The Outlook for Low-cost Housing in America.* New York: Committee on the Housing Exhibition by the Museum of Modern Art.

——. 1936. Regionalism: A New National Economy. *Columbia University Quarterly* 28(4) (December): 268–.

——. 1938. Book Review of "Parkways and Land Values" by John Nolen and Henry V. Hubbard. *American Academy of Political and Social Science, Annals* 198 (July): 209–.

——. 1939. *Housing the Masses.* New York: J. Wiley and Sons, Inc.; London: Chapman and Hall Ltd.

——. 1939. Book Review of "Housing for the Machine Age" by Clarence Arthur Perry. *American Academy of Political and Social Science, Annals* 205 (September): 159–.

——. 1940. The Future of Negro Housing. *Opportunity* 18(12) (December): 378–.

Aronovici, Carol and Elizabeth McCalmont. 1936. *Catching up with Housing.* Newark: Beneficial Management Corporation.

Aronovici, Carol. Coauth. *See* Flint, Esther M.

Asch, Berta and A. R. Mangus. 1937. *Farmers on Relief and Rehabilitation.* Washington: Works Progress Administration.

Ashley, Annie [Anne]. 1912. *The Social Policy of Bismarck: A Critical Study, with a Comparison of German and English Insurance Legislation.* W. J. Ashley, ed. with a preface by Gustav von Schmoller. London: Longmans, Green.

——. 1914. Book Review of "Child Labour in United Kingdom" by F. Keeling. *Economic Journal* 24: 452–.

——. 1923. Book Review of "The Ministry of Health and the Poor Law" by Sir William Chance. *Economic Journal* 33: 238–.

——. 1923. Book Review of "Outspoken Essays" by W. R. Inge. *Economic Journal* 33: 214–.

——. 1923. Book Review of "Prevention and Relief of Distress." *Economic Journal* 33: 110–.

——. 1923. Book Review of "Social Administration, Including the Poor Laws" by J. J. Clarke. *Economic Journal* 33: 112–.

Ashley, Annie, Adam Wills Kirkaldy, Lynda Grier, and Charles G. Renold. 1921. *British Labour.* London and New York: I. Pitman & Sons.

Ashton, Bessie Leola. 1916. The Spring Wheat Industry in Minnesota and the Dakotas (North Dakota, South Dakota). M.S. thesis, University of Chicago (agriculture, agronomy).
——. 1926. The Geonomic Aspects of the Illinois Waterway. Ph.D. thesis, University of Wisconsin–Madison (economics).
Atherton, Sara Henry. 1915. *Survey of Wage-earning Girls below Sixteen Years of Age in Wilkes-Barre, Pennsylvania, 1915.* New York: National Child Labor Committee.
Atholl, Katharine Marjory Stewart-Murray, Duchess of. 1931. *The Conscription of a People.* New York: Columbia University Press.
——. 1932. *The Truth About Forced Labour in Russia.* [A summarised edition of *The Conscription of a People.*] London: P. Allan.
Atkinson, Ella S. 1893. Women and Money. *Canadian* 1: 27–.
Atkinson, Mabel. 1904. *Local Government in Scotland.* Edinburgh: W. Blackwood & Sons.
——. 1904. Trusts and Trade Unions, and Their Mutual Relations. *Political Science Quarterly* 19 (June): 193–.
——. 1910. The Feminist Movement and Eugenics. *Sociological Review* 3(1) (January).
——. 1911. *Economics, Descriptive and Theoretical, Part II: Theoretical.* London: Allman.
——. 1914. The Economic Foundations of the Women's Movement. Fabian Women's Group Series, no. 4. Fabian Tract, no. 175. London: Fabian Society. Reprinted in Sally Alexander, ed., *Women's Fabian Tracts.* London: Routledge, 1988.
——. 1930. Some Problems of the Transition from Subsistence to Money Economy. *South African Journal of Science* 27 (November).
Atwood, Alice May. 1930. Cyclical Fluctuations of Certain Activities of State Banks in Chicago. M.A. thesis, University of Chicago (business administration, banking).
Atwood, Jane Kellogg. 1915. Development of the Commerce of the Great Lakes. M.S. thesis, University of Chicago (economics).
Auclert, Hubertine. 1879. L'Égalité sociale et politique de la femme et de l'homme; discours prononcé au Congrès ouvrier socialiste de Marseille. Marseille: Imprimerie Commerciale A. Thomas.
——. 1900. *Les Femmes arabes en Algérie.* Paris: s.n.
——. 1904. *L'Argent de la femme* [on married women's property]. Paris: Pedone.
——. 1908. *Le Vote des femmes.* Paris: s.n.
Austin, Sarah. 1857. *Two Letters on Girls' Schools and on the Training of Working Women, with Additions.* London: Chapman and Hall.
Auten, Nellie Mason. 1901. Some Phases of the Sweating System in the Garment Trades of Chicago. A.M. thesis, University of Chicago.
——. 1901. Some Phases of the Sweating System in the Garment Trades of Chicago. *American Journal of Sociology* 6 (March): 602.
[Aveling,] Eleanor Marx. 1883. Karl Marx. *Progress* (May): 288–94.
——. 1883. Karl Marx II [Karl Marx's Theory of Value]. *Progress* (June).

——. 1884. The Irish Dynamiters. *Progress* (May).

——. 1885. Book Review of "Woman in the Past, Present and Future" by August Bebel. *Commonweal* [journal of the Socialist League] supplement (July).

——. 1885. The Pall Mall Gazette. *Commonweal* supplement (August): 69–70.

——, transl. 1886. *History of the Commune of 1871*, by Prosper Lissagaray. London: Reeves and Turner. Reprinted New York: Monthly Review Press, 1967.

——. 1890. The Trade Union Congress at Liverpool. *Time, A Monthly Miscellany* 23 (October): 1,088.

——, transl. 1893. *Ferdinand Lassalle as a Social Reformer*, by Eduard Bernstein. London: Swan Sonnenschein & Co.; New York: Charles Scribner's Sons.

——, transl. 1895. *Anarchism and Socialism*, by Georgii Valentinovich Plekhanov. London: Twentieth Century Press; Minneapolis, Minn.: New Times Socialist Publishing Co.

——, ed. 1896. *Revolution and Counter-revolution; or, Germany in 1848*, by Karl Marx and Friedrich Engels. London: Swan Sonnenschein; New York: C. Scribner's Sons.

——. 1896. *The Working Class Movement in England: Brief Historical Sketch.* Preface by Wilhelm Liebnecht, translated by Edward Aveling. London: Twentieth Century Press Ltd. Originally written in German for the *Volks Lexicon*, ed. Emmanuel Wurm.

——, ed. 1898. *Value, Price and Profit:...Addressed to Working Men*, by Karl Marx. London: Swan Sonnenschein.

——, ed. 1899. *Secret Diplomatic History of the Eighteenth Century*, by Karl Marx. London: Swan Sonnenschein.

——, ed. 1899. *The Story of the Life of Lord Palmerston*, by Karl Marx. London: Swan Sonnenschein.

Aveling, Eleanor Marx and Edward Bibbins Aveling. 1885. *The Factory Hell.* London: Socialist League. Reprinted Aberdeen: J. Leatham, 1891.

——. 1886. The Woman Question. *Westminster Review* 125 (January): 207–22. Published separately, London: Swan Sonnenschein, 1886. Reprinted in Marie Mulvey Roberts and Tamae Mizuta, eds., *Sources in British Feminism*, vol. 4: *The Reformers: Socialist Feminism.* London: Routledge/Thoemmes, 1993.

——. 1887. The Chicago Anarchists. *To-Day* (November). Reprinted London: W. Reeves, 1888.

——. 1888. *Shelley's Socialism: Two Lectures.* London: Printed for private circulation.

——. 1888. *The Working-class Movement in America.* London: Swan Sonnenschein & Co.

——, eds. 1897. *The Eastern Question*, by Karl Marx. London: Swan Sonnenschein.

Avery, Martha Moore. 1903. Boston Kitchen Help Organize. *American Federationist* 10 (April): 259–.

——. 1903. The Labor Problem Cannot Be Solved within the Political Arena. *American Federationist* 10(6) (June): 455–.

Ayers, Edith. 1933. Review of Economic Problems of the Family. *American Economic Review* 23(4) (December): 772–3.

Ayres, Ruth Wheelock [Mrs. Richard Givens]. 1929. The Study of the Problem Arriving out of American Ownership of Oil Properties in Mexico. Ph.D. thesis, Robert Brookings.

——. 1933. Book Review of "The Development of American Commerce" by John H. Frederick. *American Academy of Political and Social Science, Annals* 170 (November): 180–.

——. Papers, 1921–86. Located at the University of Wyoming American Heritage Center (http://www.uwyo.edu/ahc/).

B

Babcock, Lilian Hemans Whitney. 1912. *Pin-money Suggestion*. Boston: Little, Brown and Co.

Backus, Helen Hiscock, ed. 1887. *The Need and the Opportunity for College-trained Women in Philanthropic Work*. Papers presented to the New York Association of Collegiate Alumnae, March 19, 1887. New York: New York Association of Collegiate Alumnae.

Bacon, Alice M. 1896. *The Negro and the Atlanta Exposition*. Baltimore: John F. Slater Foundation.

Bacon, Dorothy Carolin. 1926. A Monthly Index of Commodity Prices, 1890–1900. *Review of Economics and Statistics* 8(4) (October): 177–83.

——. 1928. The Significance of Fixed-base and Link Relatives in Studies of Price Stability: A Comment on the Behavior of Prices. *Journal of the American Statistical Association* 23 (September): 274–81.

——. 1928. Price Maladjustment with Special Reference to Wholesale Commodity Price in the United States, 1890–1896. Ph.D. thesis, Radcliffe College (economics).

——. 1937. *Recent Economic History of Five Towns*. Northampton, Mass.: Smith College.

Bacon, Lois Bigelow. 1935. Institutional Factors Affecting the Marketing of Milk in Boston. Ph.D. thesis, Radcliffe College (economics).

——. 1937. The Milk Supply of Paris, Rome, and Berlin. *Quarterly Journal of Economics* 51(4) (August): 626–48.

Bacon-Foster, Corra. 1912. *Early Chapters in the Development of the Patomac Route to the West*. Washington: Colombia Historical Society.

Badham, Edith A. 1895. Women and Womanhood Suffrage. *Australian Economist* IV(14) (April 23): 479–84.

——. 1896. Private and Public School [System]s Compared. *Australian Economist* IV: 30–1, 607–10.

Bagwell, Lucile. 1929. Business Income and Profits. *Journal of Business* 2(4) (October): 345–60.

——. 1934. Book Review of "Debt and Production" by Bassett Jones. *American Academy of Political and Social Science, Annals* 172 (March): 166–.

——. 1934. Book Review of "Dollars" by Jionel D. Edie. *American Academy of Political and Social Science, Annals* 174 (July): 192–.

——. 1935. Book Review of "Money and Banking in the United States" by Louis Rufener. *American Academy of Political and Social Science, Annals* 179 (May): 258–.

——. 1935. Book Review of "Production Trends in the U.S. since 1870" by A. F. Burns. *Economica*, n.s. 2: 489–.

——. 1937. Book Review of "America's Experience as a Creditor Nation" by John T. Madden, *et al. American Academy of Political and Social Science, Annals* 193 (July): 229–.

——. 1937. Book Review of "Banking and the Business Cycle" by C. A. Phillips, *et al. American Academy of Political and Social Science, Annals* 193 (September): 172–.

——. 1937. Book Review of "Income Received in the Various States, 1929–1935" by John A. Slaughter. *American Academy of Political and Social Science, Annals* 194 (November): 244–.

——. 1938. Book Review of "The New York Bond Market 1920–1930" by Charles Cortez Abbott. *American Academy of Political and Social Science, Annals* 198 (July): 185–.

——. 1939. Book Review of "National Bank Failures and Non-failures" by Horace Secrist. *American Academy of Political and Social Science, Annals* 202 (March): 225–.

——. 1940. Book Review of "The Bank of Canada" by Milton L. Stokes. *American Academy of Political and Social Science, Annals* 212 (November): 261–.

——. 1940. Book Review of "English Theories of Central Banking Control, 1819–1858" by Elmer Wood. *American Academy of Political and Social Science, Annals* 212 (November): 261–.

Bailey, Margaret Burton. 1938. The Boston Elevated Railway: A Case Study of a Public Corporation (Massachusetts). M.A., University of Chicago (history).

Baird, Frieda. 1929. The Federal Reserve System and Brokers' Loans and The Evolution of Federal Reserve System Policies. Ph.D. thesis, Robert Brookings.

——. 1933. Reorganizing our Agricultural Credit Facilities. *Journal of Farm Economics* 15 (April): 319–30.

Baker, Elizabeth Faulkner. 1925. Protective Labor Legislation, with Special Reference to Women in the State of New York. Ph.D. thesis, Columbia University (sociology). Also published New York: Longmans, Green & Co., 1925.

——. 1929. At the Crossroads in the Legal Protection of Women in Industry. *American Academy of Political and Social Science, Annals* 143 (May): 265–.

——. 1930. Unemployment and Technical Progress in Commercial Printing. *American Economic Review* 20 (September): 442–66.

——. 1931. Machinery versus Trade Skill. *Journal of Adult Education* 3(1) (January): 26–.

——. 1932. Technological Change and Organized Labor in Commercial Printing. *American Economic Review* 22 (December): 669–90.

——. 1933. *Displacement of Men by Machines: Effects of Technological Change in Commercial Printing*. New York: Columbia University Press. Reprinted Arno Press, 1977.

Baker, Ella and Marvel Cooke. 1935. The Bronx Slave Market. *The Crisis* 42 (November): 330–2.

Baker, Helen. 1932. *Statistical Analysis of Twenty Employee Stock Purchase Plans, 1925–1932*. Princeton: Industrial Relations Section, Princeton University.

——. 1935. *Personnel Programs in Department Stores*. Princeton: Industrial Relations Section, Princeton University.

——. 1936/1939. *Social Security, Selected List of References on Unemployment, Old Age, and Health Insurance*. Princeton University Industrial Relations Section Report, no. 59. Princeton: Princeton University.

——. 1937. *Employee Savings Programs*. Princeton: Industrial Relations Section, Princeton University.

——. 1938. *The Office Library of an Industrial Relations Executive, 1938*. Princeton: Industrial Relations Section, Princeton University.

——. 1939. *Company Plans for Employee Promotions*. Princeton: Industrial Relations Section, Department of Economics and Social Institutions, Princeton University.

——. 1939. *The Determination and Administration of Industrial Relations Policy*. Princeton: Industrial Relations Section.

——. 1939. The Industrial Relations Executive and Collective Bargaining. *Society for the Advancement of Management, Journal* 4(4) (July): 105–.

——. 1940. *Current Policies in Personnel Relations in Banks*. Princeton: Industrial Relations Section, Princeton University.

——. 1940. *Problems and Policies in Industrial Relations in a War Economy, a Selected Annotated Bibliography*. Princeton: Industrial Relations Section, Princeton University.

Baker, Helen and Hazel Carolyn Benjamin, comp. 1935. *A Trade Union Library*. Princeton University Industrial Relations Section Report, no. 52. Princeton: Princeton University.

Balch, Emily Greene. 1891. Reform of Taxation in France. *The Nation* 52 (January 15): 47–8.

——. 1893. Public Assistance of the Poor in France. *Publications of the American Economic Association*, series I, VIII(4 and 5) (July and September): 3–179.

——. 1895. Book Review of "Hull House Maps and Papers" by Residents of Hull House. *Publications of the American Statistical Association* 4(30) (June): 201–3.

——. 1896. German Trades Union Congress. *American Federationist* 3: 86.

——. 1899. Book Review of "A Directory of the Charitable and Beneficent Organizations of Boston." *International Journal of Ethics* 9 (July): 532.

——. 1899. *Outline of Economics*. Cambridge: Co-operative Press.

——. 1903. *A Study of Conditions of City Life, with Special Reference to Boston*. Boston: Geo. H. Ellis Co., Printers.

——. 1904. Shepherd of Immigrants. *Charities and the Commons* 13 (December 3): 193–4.

——. 1906. Slave Emigration at Its Source. *Charities* (January 6).

——. 1907. Western Civilization and the Birth-rate. *American Journal of Sociology* 12 (March): 623–6.

——. 1907/8. The True Story of a Bohemian Pioneer. *Chautauquan* 49 (December/February): 397–.

——. 1910. *Our Slavic Fellow Citizens.* New York: Charity Publication Committee. Reprinted New York: Arno Press, 1969.

——. 1910. The Education and Efficiency of Women. In Helen Marot, ed., *The Economic Position of Women.* New York. Also published in Henry Raymond Mussey, ed., *Proceedings of the Academy of Political Science in the City of New York.* New York: Columbia University.

——. 1913. What the Poor Need Is Income. *Survey* (American Association for Labor Legislation), September 30: 755–6.

——. 1914. The Economic Role of the Housewife. *Home Progress* 4 (September): 620–4.

——. 1914. Housework, English and Immigrants. *Journal of Home Economics* 6 (December): 447–9.

——. 1915. The Effects of War and Militarism on the Status of Women. *Publications of the American Sociological Society*: 39–55.

——. 1915. Racial Contacts and Cohesions. *Survey* 33 (March 6): 610–11.

——. 1917. Developing the Sense of Social Justice and Responsibility. *Intercollegiate Community Service Quarterly* 2(4) (July): 9–.

——. 1917. War in Its Relation to Democracy and World Order. *Annals of the American Academy of Political and Social Science* 72 (July): 28–31.

——. 1918. *Approaches to the Great Settlement.* New York: B. W. Huebsch.

——. 1918. The White Man's Burden. *World Tomorrow (New World)* 1(2) (February): 37–.

——. 1922. Women's Work for Peace. *World Tomorrow* 5(11) (November): 355–.

——. 1924. Economic Aspects of a New International Order. *Report of the Fourth Congress of the Women's International League for Peace and Freedom*, Washington: Women's International League.

——. 1925. Why Cooperation Is Not Enough. *Co-operation* 11 (November): 208–10.

——, ed. 1927. *Occupied Haiti, Being the Report of a Committee of Six Disinterested Americans Representing Organizations Exclusively American, Who, Having Personally Studied Conditions in Haiti in 1926, Favor the Restoration of the Independence of the Negro Republic.* New York: Writers Publishing Company.

——. 1927. The Myth of Military Security. *World Tomorrow* 10(12) (December): 496–.

——. 1939. *Refugees as Assets.* Women's International League for Peace and Freedom. Revised 1940. Leaflet reprinted in Balch, *Beyond Nationalism: The Social Thought of Emily Greene Balch*, ed. Mercedes M. Randall. New York: Twayne Publishers, 1972.

Balch, Emily, Harlow S. Person, William Kent, C. W. Mixter, William E. Hotchkiss, Rudolph Seubert, and F. L. Hutchins. 1912. Industrial Efficiency and the Interest of Labor: Round Table Discussion. *American Economic Review* 2(1) (March): 117–30.

Balch, Emily Greene, W. F. Willcox, Jeremiah W. Jenks, Max J. Kohler, and J. W. Jenks. 1912. Restriction of Immigration: Discussion. *American Economic Review*, Supplement, 2(1) (March): 63–78.

Balch, Emily Green. Also published in the *Nation*, *Four Lights*. Her papers can be found in the Swarthmore College Peace Collection.

Ball, Katharine Frances. Coauth. *See* West, Miriam E.

Ballard, Margaret. 1931. The History of the Coal Mining Industry in the Mount Diablo Region, 1859–1885. M.A. thesis, University of California.

Ballard, Margaret Louisa. 1939. The Federal Trade Commission and Misrepresentation. Ph.D. thesis, Radcliffe College (economics).

Bancroft, Gertrude. 1940. Consistency of Information from Records and Interviews. Note in *Journal of the American Statistical Association* (June).

Banister, Marion [Glass]. 1924. *The Tariff as a Tax on Women: What Women Pay the Profiteers*. Washington: Democratic National Committee.

——. 1929. *The Lands Ye Possess: Who Shall Administer Them?* Washington D.C.: Democratic National Committee.

Banks, Elizabeth L. 1894. New Paid Occupations for Women. *Cassell's Family Magazine* 21 (July): 585.

——. 1895. My Trials as a Housekeeper. *Cassell's Family Magazine* 22 (November): 903.

——. 1896. Paying Occupations for Gentlewomen. *Cassell's Family Magazine* 23 (April): 422; (September): 821.

——. 1896. Self-help Among American College Girls. *Nineteenth Century* 39 (January/June): 502–13.

——. 1898. American "Yellow Journalism." *Nineteenth Century* 44 (August): 328–40.

——. 1899. The American Negro and His Place. *Nineteenth Century* 46 (September): 459–74.

Barbour, Anna Violet. 1914. Henry Bennet, Earl of Arlington, Secretary of State to Charles II, Ph.D. thesis, Cornell University (history).

Barbour, Violet. 1929. Marine Risks and Insurance in the Seventeenth Century. *Journal of Economic and Business History* 1 (August): 561–96.

——. 1930. Dutch and English Merchant Shipping in the Seventeenth Century. *Economic History Review* 2 (January): 261–90.

Barker, Corinne M. 1925. Connecticut's Share in Furnishing Munitions for the World War. M.A. thesis, Columbia University.

Barker, Lady [Mary Anne]. 1877. *A Year's Housekeeping in South Africa*. London: Macmillan.

Barlee, Ellen. 1860. *Our Homeless Poor; and What We Can Do to Help Them*. London: James Nisbet and Co.

——. 1860. Institution for the Employment of Needlewomen. *English Woman's Journal* 5 (June): 255–9.

——. 1862. Annals of the Needlewomen. *English Woman's Journal* 9 (April): 73–80; (June): 217–26.

——. 1863. *Friendless and Helpless.* London: Emily Faithfull, Victoria Press.

——. 1863. *A Visit to Lancashire in December 1862.* London: Seeley, Jackson and Halliday.

——. 1871. *Sketches of Working Women.* London: Seeley and Co.

——. 1874. *Locked Out, a Tale of the Strike.* London: Henry S. King & Co.

——. 1884. *Pantomime Waifs; or, a Plea for our City Children.* With an introduction by the Earl of Shaftesbury. London: S. W. Partridge.

Barmby, Catherine Watkins [as "Kate"]. 1839. The Condition of Women. *The New Moral World* (June 29).

——. 1843. The Demand for the Emancipation of Women Politically and Socially. In Goodwyn Barmby and Catherine Barmby, *The Communist Miscellany: A Collection of Tracts, Religious, Political, and Domestic.* London: B. D. Cousins. Reprinted in Marie Mulvey Roberts and Tamae Mizuta, eds., *Sources in British Feminism,* vol. 4: *The Reformers: Socialist Feminism.* London: Routledge/Thoemmes, 1993.

——. 1844. Reply to Anne Knight. *Some Account of the Progress of the Thought as It Is in Jesus* 31.

——. 1848. Women's Industrial Independence. *The Apostle and Chronicle of the Communist Church* 1: 1. Reprinted in Marie Mulvey Roberts and Tamae Mizuta, eds., *Sources in British Feminism*, vol. 3: *The Exploited: Women and Work.* London: Routledge/Thoemmes, 1993.

Barnes, Kathleen. 1934. Eastward Migration Within the Soviet Union. *Pacific Affairs* 7(4) December): 395–.

——. 1935. Another Perspective. *Pacific Affairs* 8(4) (December): 477–.

——. 1935. Book Review of "Soviet Journey" by Louis Fischer. *Pacific Affairs* 8(2) (June): 254–.

——. 1935. Japanese–Soviet Friction. *Far Eastern Survey* 4(19) (September 25): 148–.

——. 1935. The Soviet Union and the Far East. *Soviet Russia Today* 4(9) (November): 61–.

——. 1936. Book Review of "Soviet Communism: A New Civilization?" by Sidney and Beatrice Webb. *Pacific Affairs* 9(2) (June): 294–.

——. 1936. The Clash of Fishing Interests in the Pacific. *Far Eastern Survey* 5(1/25): 243–.

——. 1936. Siberia – From Mongolia to the Arctic. *Far Eastern Survey* 5(1/25): 93–.

——. 1936. The Soviet "Economic Stake" in the Orient. *Far Eastern Survey* 5(1/25): 19–.

——. 1937. The Agricultural Foundation of Siberia's Economy. *Far Eastern Survey* 6(1/25): 37–.

——. 1937. The New Soviet Constitution. *Social Work Today* 4(5) (February): 9–.

——. 1937. Overcoming Obstacles to Rubber Control. *Far Eastern Survey* 6(1/25): 177–.

——. 1938. Alaska Salmon in World Politics. *Far Eastern Survey* 7(1/25): 47–.

——. 1938. Asiatic Russia – Storehouse of Mineral Wealth. *Far Eastern Survey* 7(1/25): 157–.

——. 1938. Book Review of "Over the North Pole" by George Baidukov. *Pacific Affairs* 11(2) (June): 274–.

——. 1938. Book Review of "The Soviets" by Albert Rhys Williams. *Pacific Affairs* 10(4) (December): 490–.

——. 1938. Japanese Government Given Blank Check. *Far Eastern Survey* 7(1/25): 79.

——. 1938. Soviet Democracy at Work. *Soviet Russia Today* 7(8) (November): 22–.

——. 1938. USSR's Position in the Far East – What It Means to the United States. *Amerasia* 2(3) (May): 143–.

——. 1939. Outer Mongolia on the World Stage. *Far Eastern Survey* 8(1/25): 207–.

——. 1939. Soviet–Japanese Relations Still Hanging Fire. *Far Eastern Survey* 8(1/25): 1–.

——. 1940. Book Review of "Great Soviet World Atlas, Vol. I." *Pacific Affairs* 13(3) (September): 354–.

——. 1940. Fisheries, Mainstay of Soviet–Japanese Friction. *Far Eastern Survey* 9(1/25): 75–.

——. 1940. Seeing Red in the Far East. *Amerasia* 4(3) (May): 116–.

Barnes, Kathleen and Harriet Moore. 1936. *The Soviet Constitution of 1936*. New York: American Russian Institute for Cultural Relations with the Soviet Union, Inc.

Barnes, Mary Clark. 1898. The Science of Home Management. *North American Review* 167 (November): 633–8.

[Barnes,] Mary D. Sheldon. 1882. Poor White Trash. *Cornhill Magazine* 45 (May): 579–84.

Barnett, Edith A. 1894. *The Training of Girls for Work: An Expression of Opinions*. London and New York: Macmillan.

——. 1899. *Sunningham and the Curate: A Study of Creeds and Commerce*. London: Chapman and Hall Ltd.

Barnett, Edith A. and H. C. O'Neill. 1894. *Primer of Domestic Economy*. London and New York: Macmillan.

Barnett, Edith A. Coauth. *See* O'Neill, H. C.

Barnett, Henrietta O. [Rowland] [Mrs. Samuel A. Barnett.] 1879. The Young Women in our Workhouses. *Macmillan's* 40 (June): 133–9.

——. 1881. *The Work of Lady Visitors*. London: Metropolitan Association for Befriending Young Servants.

——. 1881. "At Home" to the Poor. *Cornhill Magazine* 43 (May): 579–89.

——. 1884. What Has the C.O.S. to Do with Social Reform? *Charity Organization Reporter* 528 (April 19): 128–.

——. 1885. *The Making of the Home: A Reading Book of Domestic Economy for School and Home Use*. London: Cassell.

——. 1886. National Enemies and National Defenses. *National Review* 7 (July): 652–67.

——. 1888. East London and Crime. *National Review* 12 (December): 433–43.

——. 1894. The Home or the Barrack for the Children of the State. *Contemporary Review* 66 (August): 243–58.

——. 1897. The Verdict on the Barrack Schools. *Nineteenth Century* 41 (January): 56–68.

——. 1898. The State as a Parent. *St George* 1 (January): 29–.

Barnett, Henrietta Octavia [Rowland] and Samuel Augustus Barnett. 1888. *Practicable Socialism: Essays on Social Reform.* 2nd ed., rev. and enlarged, London: Longmans, Green, and Co., 1894.

——. 1909. *Towards Social Reform.* London: T. Fisher Unwin.

Barnum, Gertrude. 1911. Button, Button, Who's Got the Button? The Strike at Muscatine, Iowa. *Survey* 26 (May): 253–5.

Barr, Amelia E. 1879. Housekeeping in Texas. *Lippincott's* 23 (January/June): 686.

——. 1889. Are Women to Blame [for unhappy marriages]? *North American Review* 148 (May): 638–42.

——. 1890. Shall Our Daughters Have Dowries? *North American Review* 151(6) (December): 755–9.

——. 1892. The Servant-girl's Point of View. *North American Review* 154(6) (June): 729–32.

Barrett, Rosa M. 1884. *Guide to Dublin Charities.* Dublin: Hodges and Co.

——. 1896. *Foreign Legislation on Behalf of Destitute and Neglected Children.* Paper read before the Statistical and Social Inquiry Society of Ireland. Dublin: Sealy and Co.

Barrett, Ruth Whitney. 1924. A Comparative Study of the British and American Foreign Services. M.A. thesis, University of California Berkeley.

——. 1934/1978. Administrative Responsiveness to Interest Groups: A Study in Labor Legislation Protecting Women and Children in Massachusetts. Ph.D. thesis, Radcliffe College (political science). Cambridge, Mass.: Harvard University Library.

Barrington, Mrs. Russell. 1914. *The Life of Walter Bagehot.* London: Longmans.

Barron, Mary Louise. 1913. California's Interest in Reciprocity with Canada. M.S. thesis, University of California Berkeley.

——. 1917. State Regulation of the Securities of Railroads and Public Service Companies. Ph.D. thesis, University of Pennsylvania (economics).

——. 1918. State Regulation of the Securities of Railroads and Public Service Companies. *Annals of the American Academy of Political and Social Science* LXXVI.

Barrows, Alice P. 1910. The Training of Millinery Workers. In Helen Marot, ed., *The Economic Position of Women.* New York: Academy of Political Science. Also published in Henry Raymond Mussey, ed., *Proceedings of the Academy of Political Science in the City of New York.* New York: Columbia University, 1910.

Bartlett, Harriett Moulton. 1927. The Injured Workman: A Sociological Study. M.A. thesis, University of Chicago (sociology, industrial and labor relations).

——. 1928. The Social Survey and the Charity Organization Movement. *American Journal of Sociology* 34(2) (September): 330–46.

Barton, Clara. 1889. Philanthropy at Johnstown. *North American Review* 149 (July/December): 142–.

——. 1898. Our Work and Observations in Cuba. *North American Review* 166(5) (May): 552–9.

Barton, Dorothea M. 1919. The Course of Women's Wages. *Journal of the Royal Statistical Society* 82(4) (July): 508–44.

——. 1921. Women's Minimum Wages. *Journal of the Royal Statistical Society* 84(4) (July): 538–75.

Barton, Eleanor. 1919. Women as Co-operators. In Margaret Grace Bondfield, *et al.*, *English Women in the Labor and Co-operative Movements: Three Speeches Delivered before the Seventh Biennial Convention of the National Women's Trade Union League, Philadelphia, June 2–7, 1919.* Chicago: Women's Trade Union League of America.

——. 1931. In Workshop and Home. *Listener* 6(152) (December 9): 1,015–.

Barus, Annie Howes. 1898. The College Woman's Opportunity in Co-operative Work. *Publications of the Association of Collegiate Alumnae*, series 3(1) (December): 78–83.

Bary, Helen Valeska. 1923. *Child Welfare in the Insular Possessions of the United States.* Washington: U.S. Children's Bureau.

Bary, Helen Valeska and Frances Cahn. 1936. *Welfare Activities of Federal, State, and Local Governments in California, 1850–1934.* Berkeley: University of California Press.

Bary, Helen Valeska. Coauth. *See* Obenauer, Marie Louise.

Baskerville, Beatrice C. 1906. *The Polish Jew: His Social and Economic Value.* New York: Macmillan Co.

——. 1906. Present Condition of Poland and Finland. *Fortnightly Review* 86 (ns80): 649.

——. 1907. The Land Famine in Russia and M. Stolypin's Scheme. *Fortnightly Review*, n.s 81 (January/June): 611.

——. 1910. The Late Shah. *Contemporary Review* 97 (January/June): 742–.

Bass, Bertha. 1895. Co-operative Housekeeping. *New England Kitchen Magazine* 2 (January): 159–63.

Bassett, Lucy Antoinett. 1934. *Transient and Homeless Persons: A Bibliography.* Jacksonville, Fla.: Florida Emergency Relief Administration.

Batchelder Stone, Ursula Chase. 1929. The Baking Industry with Special Reference to the Bread-making Industry in Chicago. Ph.D. thesis, University of Chicago (business administration).

Batchelder Stone, Ursula Chase and Raleigh Webster Stone. 1936. *The Baking Industry under N.R.A.* Chicago: University of Chicago Press.

Batchelder Stone, Ursula Chase. Coauth. *See* Goetz, Rachel Marshall; Kyrk, Hazel; Monroe, Day.

Bateman, Mary E. and Ellen Kristiane Jensen Newman. 1940. *Trends in Public Assistance, 1933–1939.* Washington: Social Security Board, Bureau of Research and Statistics.

Bates, Helen Frances Page. 1896. State Irrigation in the Australian Colonies. Ph.D. thesis, University of Wisconsin.

——. 1898. Australian Experiments in Industry. *Annals of the American Academy of Political and Social Science* 12(2) (September): 193–213.

——. 1907. *Employment of Blind; A Partial List of Material in the N.Y. State Library Relating to Industrial Training and Employment of the Adult Blind*. Albany: Legislative Reference Lists.

Bateson, Margaret. 1895. *Professional Women Upon Their Professions: Conversations Recorded by Margaret Bateson*. London: Horace Cox.

——. 1896. A Pound a Week – Why Girls Should Earn It. *A Girl's Own Paper* 18 (October): 14–; (November): 91–.

Bateson, Mary. 1903. *Cambridge Gild Records, with a Preface by Wm. Cunningham*. London: Bell.

——. 1903. Irish Exchequer Memoranda of the Reign of Edward I. *English Historical Review* 18: 497–.

——. 1904/1906/1996. *Borough Customs*. London: B. Quaritch; Buffalo, N.Y.: W. S. Hein. The Publications of the Selden Society, vols. 18 and 21.

Batson, Mrs. Stephen [Henrietta]. 1899. Town and Country Labourers. *Nineteenth Century* 46 (October): 570–82.

Baudouin, Eve. 1931. *La Mère au travail et le retour au foyer.* Paris: Bloud & Gay.

——. 1933. *Comment Envisager le Retour de la mère au foyer?* Paris: Spes.

Bauer-Mengelberg, Käthe. 1919. Die Finanzpolitik der sozialdemokratischen Partei in ihren Zusammenhängen mit dem sozialistischen Staatsgedanken. Ph.D. thesis, Mannheim-Berlin-Leipzig.

——. 1923. Die Liebknechtsche Marxkritik in ihrer Bedeutung für die sozialökonomische Theorie. *Archiv für Sozialwissenschaft und Sozialpolitik* 50: 486–.

——. 1926. Die liberalen Tendenzen in der ökonomischen Theorie des Sozialismus. *Archiv für die Geschichte des Sozialismus und der Arbeiterbewegung* 12: 199–212.

——. 1926. Zur Theorie der Arbeitsbewertung. *Archiv für Sozialwissenschaft und Sozialpolitik* 55: 680–719.

——. 1926. Zur Theorie der Arbeitsbewertung II. *Archiv für Sozialwissenschaft und Sozialpolitik* 56: 129–59.

——. 1931. *Agrarpolitik in Theorie, Geschichte und aktueller Problematik*. Leipzig and Berlin: B. G. Teubner.

——. 1934. De Duitsche graanpolitiek. *Economisch-statistische Berichten* 19(975) (September 5): 794–.

——. 1934. De Duitsche landbouw in het kader der standen. *Economisch-statistische Berichten* 19(970) (August 1): 704–.

Baugh, Ruth Emily. 1929. The Geography of the Los Angeles Water Supply. Ph.D. thesis, Clark University.

——. 1937. Land Use Changes in the Bishop Area of Owens Valley, California. *Economic Geography* 13(1) (January): 17–34.

Baumgartner, Grace. 1925. Effecta repartitio. M.A. thesis, University of Washington.

——. 1928. Rent as Cost and Rent as Surplus in Merchandising in Seattle. Ph.D. thesis, University of Washington (economics).

Baxter, Georgia Louise. 1917. A Statistical Investigation into the Shape of Demand Curves. M.A. thesis, University of California Berkeley.

Bayard, Mary Temple. 1896. Communistic Celibates of Economy. *Canadian* 7: 199–.

Beard, Mary Ritter. 1914. The Legislative Influence of Unenfranchised Women. *American Academy of Political and Social Science, Annals* 56 (November): 54–.

——. 1915. *Women's Work in Municipalities*. New York: D. Appleton and Co.

——. 1915. Woman's Work for the City. *National Municipal Review* 4(2) (April): 204–.

——. 1920. *A Short History of the American Labor Movement*. New York: Harcourt, Brace, & Howe.

——. 1921. Progress Toward Maternity Benefits in Massachusetts. *American Labor Legislation Review* 11: 66.

——. 1929. American Women and the Printing Press. *American Academy of Political and Social Science, Annals* 143 (May): 195–.

——. 1931. *On Understanding Women*. New York: Longmans, Green.

——. 1932. A Test for the Modern Woman. *Current History (New York)* 37(2) (November): 179–.

——. 1932. University Discipline for Women – Asset or Handicap? *American Association of University Women, Journal* 25(3) (April): 129.

——. 1933. Lucretia Mott. *American Scholar* 2(1) (January): 5–.

——. 1934. *A Changing Political Economy as It Affects Women*. Washington: American Association of University Women.

——. 1934. Book Review of "Women in Soviet Russia" by Fannina W. Halle. *Political Science Quarterly* 49: 615.

——. 1934. Book Review of "Women Who Work" by Grace Hutchins. *Political Science Quarterly* 49: 615.

——. 1935. The New Feminism. *Aryan Path* 6(5) May): 293–.

——. 1936. Books By and About Women. *American Association of University Women, Journal* 29(3) (April): 148–.

——. 1936. The Home and the State. *Aryan Path* 7(1) (January): 15–.

——. 1937. Book Review of "Feminine Attitudes in the 19th Century" by C. Willett Cunnington. *American Sociological Review* 2(1/6): 138–.

——. 1938. Book Review of "Feminisme et positivisme" by Louise-Marie Ferre. *American Sociological Review* 3(1/6): 897–.

——. 1938. Society's Interest in Human Resources. *Harvard Educational Review* 8 (January/December): 157–.

——. 1938/9. Book Review of "Women's Life and Work in the Southern Colonies" by Spruill. *Social Forces* 17(1/4): 449–.

Beard, Mary Ritter and Charles A. Beard. 1927. *The Rise of American Civilization*, 2 vols. New York: Macmillan.

——. 1939. *America in Mid-Passage*, 2 vols. New York: Macmillan.

Beard, Mary Ritter and Florence Kelley. 1916. *Why Women Demand a Federal Suffrage Amendment, Difficulties in Amending State Constitutions: A Study of the Constitutions of Non-suffrage States.* Washington: Congressional Union for Woman Suffrage.

Beard, Mary Ritter. The largest holdings of her papers are in the DePauw University Library; the Schlesinger Library, Radcliffe College; and the Sophia Smith Collection, Smith College.

Beardwood, Alice. 1930. Alien Merchants and the English Crown in the Later Fourteenth Century. *Economic History Review* 2 (January): 229–60.

——. ed. 1939. *The Statute Merchant Roll of Coventry, 1392–1416.* Publications of the Dugdale Society, vol. 17. London: H. Milford/Oxford University Press.

Beasley, Delilah L. 1918. Slavery in California. *Journal of Negro History* 3(1) (January): 33–44.

Beauchamp, Joan. 1931. *Agriculture in Soviet Russia.* London: V. Gollancz.

——. 1934. *British Imperialism in India.* London: Labor Research Department.

——. 1935. Asia – Body and Soul: Exploitation in India. *Living Age* 348 (July): 436.

——. 1937. *Women Who Work.* London: Lawrence and Wishart.

Beck, Dorothy Fahs. 1932. *The Cost of Equipping a Dental Office: A Study of the Initial Expenditures of Dental Graduates When Equipping an Office for Practice.* American Dental Association. Committee on the Study of Dental Practice. Publications, no. 2. Chicago: University of Chicago Press.

——. 1932. The Development of the Dental Profession in the United States: A Study in the Natural History of a Profession. M.A. thesis, University of Chicago (history).

——. 1938. Problems in the Compilation of Data on Total Relief and Work Program Expenditures. *Journal of the American Statistical Association* 33 (June): 353–62.

Becker, Lydia E[rnestine]. 1867. Female Suffrage. *Contemporary Review* 4 (March): 307–16.

——. 1868. Is There Any Specific Distinction between Male and Female Intellect? *English Woman's Journal* 8 (July): 483–91.

——. 1869. On the Study of Science by Women. *Contemporary Review* 10 (March): 386–404.

——. 1872. Political Disabilities of Women. *Westminster Review*, n.s. 41 [o.s. 97] (January): 50–70.

——. 1874. *Liberty, Equality, Fraternity: A Reply to Mr. Fitzjames Stephen's Strictures on Mr. J. S. Mill's "Subjection of Women."* Manchester: A. Ireland.

——. 1879. *The Rights and Duties of Women in Local Government.* Manchester: A. Ireland.

——. 1889. *A Reply to the [anti-suffrage] Protest Which Appeared in the "Nineteenth Century".* Manchester: Guardian Printing Works.

——. Edited the *Women's Suffrage Journal*, 1870–90.

Beckett, Grace L. 1939. *Reciprocal Trade Agreements Programs of the United States.* New York: Columbia University Press.

——. 1939. Reciprocal Trade Agreements Programs of the United States. Ph.D. thesis, Ohio State University.

——. 1939. Reciprocal Trade Agreements. *Pi Lambda Theta Journal* 18(2), Part I (December): 59–.

——. 1940. Effect of the Reciprocal Trade Agreements upon the Foreign Trade of the U.S. *Quarterly Journal of Economics* 55 (November): 80–4.

——. 1940. On Trade Agreements. *American Scholar* 9(3) (Summer): 379–.

——. 1940. The Problem of Reclassification in the Reciprocal Trade Agreements. *Journal of Political Economy* 48 (April): 199–209.

Beckwith, Ethelwynn. 1925. *Inequalities in the Distribution of Income, Their Meaning and Measurement.* Ph.D. thesis, Radcliffe College.

Beecher, Catharine E[sther]. 1835. *Essay on the Education of Female Teachers.* New York: Van Nostrand & Dwight.

——. 1837. *An Essay on Slavery and Abolitionism, with Reference to the Duty of American Females.* Philadelphia: Henry Perkins; Boston: Perkins & Marvin.

——. 1841. *A Treatise on Domestic Economy for the Use of Young Ladies at Home and at School.* Boston: Marsh, Capen, Lyon & Webb. Reprinted New York: Sourcebook Press, 1970.

——. 1842. *Letters to Persons Who Are Engaged in Domestic Service.* New York: Leavitt & Trow.

——. 1851. *The True Remedy for the Wrongs of Woman; with a History of an Enterprise Having that for Its Object.* Boston: Phillips, Sampson, & Co.

——. 1865. How to Redeem Woman's Profession from Dishonor. *Harper's* 31 (November): 710–.

——. 1872. *Woman's Profession as Mother and Educator with Views in Opposition to Women's Suffrage.* Philadelphia and Boston: George MacLean.

Beecher, Catherine and Harriet Beecher Stowe. 1869. *The American Woman's Home, or Principles of Domestic Science, Being a Guide to the Formation and Maintenance of Economical, Healthful, Beautiful and Christian Homes.* New York: J. B. Ford. Later published as *Principles of Domestic Science; as Applied to the Duties and Pleasures of the Home. A Textbook for the Use of Young Ladies in Schools....* New York: J. B. Ford, 1871–. Reprinted, with introduction by Nicole Tonkovich, New Brunswick, N.J.: Rutgers University Press, 2002.

Beecher, Mrs. Henry Ward [Eunice Ballard]. 1890. Shall Our Daughters Have Dowries? *North American Review* 151(6) (December): 759–.

Beer, Margrieta. 1901. Book Review of "Le Développement économique et social du Japon. From Chronique du musée social." *Economic Journal* 11: 397–.

——. 1901. Book Review of "Die gesellschaftliche und wirtschaftliche Entwickelung in Japan" by Tokuzo Fukuda. *Economic Journal* 11: 393–.

——. 1901. Book Review of "Die Zukunft der sozialen Frage" by Dr. Georg Adler. *Economic Journal* 11: 392–.

——. 1906. Book Review of "L'Assistance par le travail, et les jardins ouvriers en France" by Marcel Lecoq. *Economic Journal* 16: 259–.

——. 1908. Book Review of "Maternita e lavoro." *Economic Journal* 18(70) (June): 306–8.

——. 1910. Book Review of "A Bibliography of Unemployment and the Unemployed" by F. Isabel Taylor. *Economic Journal* 20: 83–.

——. 1910. Book Review of "How the Casual Labourer Lives. Report of the Liverpool Joint Research Committee on the Domestic Condition and Expenditure of the Families of Certain Liverpool Labourers." *Economic Journal* 20: 83–.

Beeton, Mrs. [Isabella Mary.] 1861. *The Book of Household Management…also, Sanitary, Medical, and Legal Memoranda; with a History of the Origin, Properties, and Uses of All Things Connected with Home Life and Comfort.* London: S. O. Beeton. 2nd ed., London and New York: Ward, Lock and Co., 1880. 1st ed. reprinted London: Jonathan Cape, 1968; New York: Farrar, Straus, and Giroux, 1969. Abridged ed., ed. with an introduction and notes by Nicola Humble, New York: Oxford University Press, 2000.

Behrens, Kathryn Laura. 1921. Paper Money in Maryland, 1727–1789. Ph.D. thesis, Johns Hopkins University (economics, political science).

——. 1923/1966/1975. *Paper Money in Maryland, 1727–89.* Baltimore: Johns Hopkins Press.

Belden, Wilma. 1936. Northern Nigeria – A Study in Political Geography. *Economic Geography* 12(4) (October): 325–39.

Bell, Miss. 1892. How Women May Keep Their Money. *Englishwoman's Review*, n.s. 214 (April): 85–; n.s. 215 (July): 159–; and n.s. 216 (October): 239–43.

Bell, Lady [Florence E.]. 1907. *At the Works: A Study of a Manufacturing Town.* Edward Arnold. Reprinted London: Virago, 1985.

——. 1908. *Down with the Tariff: A Tale of Free Trade.* London: A. L. Humphreys.

——. 1919. Women at the Works – and Elsewhere. *Fortnightly Review*, n.s. 106 (July/December): 909–.

Bell, Florence Seymour. 1934. Status of Women Lawyers in Canada. *Women Lawyers' Journal* 21(1) (August): 14–.

[Belloc,] Bessie Rayner Parkes. 1854. *Remarks on the Education of Girls, with Reference to the Social, Legal and Industrial Position of Women in the Present Day.* London: J. Chapman.

——. 1858. Domestic Life. *English Woman's Journal* II (October): 73–82.

——. 1858. The Profession of the Teacher. *English Woman's Journal* I (March).

——. 1859. The Market for Educated Female Labour. Paper read at the conference of the National Association for Promotion of Social Science and published in *English Woman's Journal* (November). Reprinted in Candida Ann Lacey, ed., *Barbara Leigh Smith Bodichon and the Langham Place Group.* London and New York: Routledge, 1987.

——. 1859. What Can Educated Women Do? (I). *English Woman's Journal* 4(22) (December): 217–26. Reprinted in Candida Ann Lacey, ed., *Barbara Leigh Smith Bodichon and the Langham Place Group.* London and New York: Routledge, 1987.

——. 1860. The Opinions of John Stuart Mill. *English Woman's Journal* 6 (September): 1–11; (November): 193–202.

—— [unsigned]. 1860. Outline of a Plan for the Formation of Industrial Associations Amongst Women. *English Woman's Journal* 6 (October): 73–6.

——. 1860. Statistics as to the Employment of the Female Population of Great Britain. *English Woman's Journal* 5 (March). Reprinted in Candida Ann Lacey, ed., *Barbara Leigh Smith Bodichon and the Langham Place Group*. London and New York: Routledge, 1987.

——. 1860. What Can Educated Women Do? (II). *English Woman's Journal* 4 (January). Reprinted in Candida Ann Lacey, ed., *Barbara Leigh Smith Bodichon and the Langham Place Group*. London and New York: Routledge, 1987.

——. 1860. A Year's Experience in Woman's Work. Paper read at the conference of the National Association for Promotion of Social Science and published in *English Woman's Journal* 6 (October). Reprinted in Candida Ann Lacey, ed., *Barbara Leigh Smith Bodichon and the Langham Place Group*. London and New York: Routledge, 1987.

——. 1861. The Condition of Working Women in England and France. Paper read at the conference of the National Association for Promotion of Social Science and published in *English Woman's Journal* 8 (September). Reprinted in Candida Ann Lacey, ed., *Barbara Leigh Smith Bodichon and the Langham Place Group*. London and New York: Routledge, 1987.

——. 1862. The Balance of Public Opinion in Regard to Woman's Work. Paper read at the conference of the National Association for Promotion of Social Science and published in *English Woman's Journal* 9(53) (July): 340–4. Reprinted in Candida Ann Lacey, ed., *Barbara Leigh Smith Bodichon and the Langham Place Group*. London and New York: Routledge, 1987.

——. 1862. Female Life in Prison. *English Woman's Journal* 10 (September). Reprinted in Candida Ann Lacey, ed., *Barbara Leigh Smith Bodichon and the Langham Place Group*. London and New York: Routledge, 1987.

——. 1864. Needlewomen at New York. *English Woman's Journal* 12 (January): 318–25.

——. 1864. A Review of the Last Six Years. *English Woman's Journal* 12 (February). Reprinted in Candida Ann Lacey, ed., *Barbara Leigh Smith Bodichon and the Langham Place Group*. London and New York: Routledge, 1987.

——. 1864. Women and Co-operation. *English Woman's Journal* 12 (February): 368–76.

——. 1865. *Essays on Women's Work*. London: Alexander Strachan.

——. 1865. Educated Destitution. *Essays on Women's Work*. London: Alexander Strachan. Reprinted in Marie Mulvey Roberts and Tamae Mizuta, eds., *Controversies in the History of British Feminism*, vol. 2: *The Workers, Women and Labour.* London: Routledge/Thoemmes, 1995.

Belloc [Lowndes], Marie A. 1896. The Women's Movement in Germany and France. *Humanitarian* 9 (November): 321–.

——. 1899. Women Millionaires. *Woman at Home* 7 (August): 1,049–.

Beney, Margarete Ada. 1936. *The Cost of Living in 54 Communities, March, 1936*. Conference Board Information Service. Domestic Affairs Series. Memorandum no. 54. New York: National Industrial Conference Board, Inc.

——. 1936. *Cost of Living in the United States, 1914–1936.* New York: National Industrial Conference Board, Inc.

——. 1936. *Wages, Hours, and Employment in the United States, 1914–1936.* New York: National Industrial Conference Board, Inc.

——. 1938. *Differentials in Industrial Wages and Hours in the United States.* National Industrial Conference Board Studies, no. 238 [i.e. 239]. New York: National Industrial Conference Board, Inc.

Benham, Elisabeth Dewel. 1939. *The Woman Wage Earner, Her Situation Today.* United States. Women's Bureau Bulletin no. 172. Washington: U.S. Government Printing Office.

Bennett, Helen Christine. 1915. *American Women in Civic Work.* New York: Dodd, Mead and Co.

Bennett, Helen Marie. 1917. *Women and Work: The Economic Value of College Training.* New York: D. Appleton.

Bennett, Louie. 1915. Women and the War. *Nation* 17(14) (July 3): 451–.

——. 1922. With Irish Women Workers. *Irish Economist* (August).

Bennett, Sarah R. I. 1877. *Woman's Work among the Lowly. Memorial Volume of the First Forty Years of the American Female Guardian Society and Home for the Friendless.* New York: American Female Guardian Society.

Benson, Miss [Mary Eleanor]. 1890. In Defence of Domestic Service. *Nineteenth Century* 28 (October): 616–26.

Benson, Margaret. 1891. *Capital, Labour, and Trade, and the Outlook. Plain Papers.* London: Society for Promoting Christian Knowledge; New York: E. & J. B. Young.

Bentham, Lady. 1853. On Certain Statements Contained in a Communication to the Statistical Section at Belfast, in September, 1852, Entitled "Statistics of Portsea and Portsmouth Dockyard." *Journal of the Statistical Society of London* 16(4) (December): 356–62.

Benton, Mildred Catherine. 1935. *Financing American Cotton Production and Marketing in the United States.* Washington: U.S. Bureau of Agricultural Economics.

——. 1940. *Social Aspects of Soil Conservation, Reference to Literature on the Subject.* Washington: U.S. Soil Conservation Service.

Benton, Mildred Catherine and Emily L. Day. 1932. *Uses for Cotton: Selected References in the English Language.* Washington: U.S. Bureau of Agricultural Economics Library.

Bercaw, Louise Oldham. 1925. *The Peach Industry in the United States: A Selected List of References on the Economic Aspects of the Industry Including Some References Relating to Canada.* Washington: U.S. Department of Agriculture, Bureau of Agricultural Economics.

——. 1925. *Price Spreads: A Selected List of References Relating to Analyses of the Portion of the Consumer's Price Accruing to Various Agencies.* Washington: U.S. Department of Agriculture, Bureau of Agricultural Economics.

——. 1925. *Refrigeration and Cold Storage: A Selected List of References Covering the Years 1915–1924 and the Early Part of 1925.* Washington: U.S. Department of Agriculture, Bureau of Agricultural Economics.

——. 1926. *Economic Periodicals of Foreign Countries Published in the English Language: A Selected List.* Washington: U.S. Department of Agriculture, Bureau of Agricultural Economics.

——. 1926. *Factors Affecting Prices: A Selected Bibliography, Including Some References on the Theory and Practice of Price Analysis.* Washington: U.S. Department of Agriculture, Bureau of Agricultural Economics.

——. 1932. The Department of Commerce Publications of Interest to Agricultural Librarians. *Agricultural Library Notes* 7(6/10) (June/October): 80.

——. 1934. Price Analysis: Selected References on the Theoretical Aspects of Supply and Demand Curves and Related Subjects. *Econometrica* 2(4) (October): 399–421.

——. 1935. *Price Studies of the U.S. Department of Agriculture Showing Demand–Price, Supply–Price and Price–Production Relationships.* Agricultural Economics Bibliography, no. 58. Washington: U.S. Department of Agriculture, Bureau of Agricultural Economics.

——. 1936. Methodology Used in Compiling a Bibliography in the Field of Agricultural Economics. *Agricultural Library Notes* 11(5) (May).

——. 1937. *Farm Tenancy in the United States, 1918–1936: A Selected List of References.* Washington: U.S. Department of Agriculture, Bureau of Agricultural Economics.

——. 1940. *State Trade Barriers: Selected References.* Washington: Department of Agriculture, Bureau of Agricultural Economics.

Bercaw, Louise Oldham and Mary Jessamine Abbott. 1930–1. *California: An Index to the State Sources of Agricultural Statistics.* Washington: U.S. Department of Agriculture, Bureau of Agricultural Economics.

Bercaw, Louise Oldham and Annie M. Hannay, comp. 1938. *Bibliography on Land Utilization, 1918–1936.* Compiled under the direction of Mary G. Lacy. Washington: U.S. Government Printing Office.

Bercaw, Louise Oldham and Mamie Idella Herb, comp. 1929. *Olives and Olive Oil; Selected References on the Culture of Olives and the Economic Aspects of the Industry.* Washington: U.S. Department of Agriculture Library.

Bercaw, Louise Oldham and Mary G. Lacy. 1927. *The Apple Industry in the United States: A Selected List of References on the Economic Aspects of the Industry Together with Some References on Varieties.* Washington: U.S. Department of Agriculture, Bureau of Agricultural Economics.

——. 1928. *The Poultry Industry: A Selected List of References on the Economic Aspects of the Industry, 1920–1927.* Washington: U.S. Department of Agriculture, Bureau of Agricultural Economics.

——. 1929. *Labor Requirements of Farm Products in the United States: A List of References to Material Published since 1922.* Washington: U.S. Department of Agriculture, Bureau of Agricultural Economics.

——. 1930. *Rural Standards of Living: A Selected Bibliography.* Washington: U.S. Department of Agriculture, Bureau of Agricultural Economics.

——. 1931. *Rural Standards of Living: A Selected Bibliography.* Washington: U.S. Government Printing Office.

——. 1931. *Wheat: Cost of Production, 1923–1930: References Relating to the United States and Some Foreign Countries*. Washington: U.S. Department of Agriculture, Bureau of Agricultural Economics.

——. 1932. *Advantages and Disadvantages of Country Life: Selected References*. Washington: U.S. Department of Agriculture, Bureau of Agricultural Economics.

——. 1933. *Domestic Allotment Plans for the Relief of Agriculture: Selected References*. Washington: U.S. Department of Agriculture, Bureau of Agricultural Economics.

——. 1933. *Price Analysis: Selected References on Supply and Demand Curves and Related Subjects*. Washington: U.S. Department of Agriculture, Bureau of Agricultural Economics.

——. 1937. *Incidences of the Processing Taxes under the Agricultural Adjustment Act: A Selected List of References*. Agricultural Economics Bibliography, no. 68. Washington: U.S. Department of Agriculture, Bureau of Agricultural Economics.

——. 1938. *The Tobacco Industry: A Selected List of References on the Economic Aspects of the Industry, 1932–June 1938*. Washington: U.S. Department of Agriculture, Bureau of Agricultural Economics.

——. 1939. *Price Fixing by Government in the United States, 1926–1939: A List of Selected References on Direct Price Fixing of Agricultural Products by the Federal and State Governments*. Agricultural Economics Bibliography, no. 79. Washington: U.S. Department of Agriculture, Bureau of Agricultural Economics.

Bercaw, Louise Oldham and Margaret Thompson Olcott. 1926. *Farm Youth*. Washington: s.n.

Bercaw, Louise Oldham, Esther M. Colvin, and Mary G. Lacy. 1932. *Bibliography on the Marketing of Agricultural Products*. Washington: U.S. Government Printing Office.

Bercaw, Louise Oldham, Vajen Eilleen Hitz Fischer, Marion Etta Wheeler, and Mamie Idella Herb. 1927. *Agricultural Relief Measures Relating to the Raising of Farm Prices*. Washington: Bureau of Agricultural Economics.

Bercaw, Louise Oldham, A. M. Hannay, Esther M. Colvin, and Mary G. Lacy. 1934. *Bibliography on Land Settlement, with Particular Reference to Small Holdings and Subsistence Homesteads*. Washington: U.S. Government Printing Office.

Bercaw, Louise Oldham, Annie M. Hannay, Nellie G. Larsen, and Mary G. Lacy. 1940. *Corn in the Development of the Civilization of the Americas: A Selected and Annotated Bibliography*. Agricultural Economics Bibliography, no. 87. Washington: U.S. Department of Agriculture, Bureau of Agricultural Economics.

Bercaw, Louise Oldham, Helen E. Hennefrund, and Mary G. Lacy. 1935. *Farm Tenancy in the United States, 1925–1935: A Beginning of a Bibliography*. Washington: s.n.

Bercaw, Louise Oldham, Margaret T. Olcott, and Mary G. Lacy. 1934. *State Measures for the Relief of Agricultural Indebtedness in the United States 1933 and 1934*. Washington: U.S. Department of Agriculture, Bureau of Agricultural Economics.

Bercaw, Louise Oldham. Coauth. *See* Herb, Mamie Idella; Olcott, Margaret Thompson.

Bergin, Mary Cecelia. 1927. *Markets for Prepared Medicines.* Washington: U.S. Bureau of Foreign and Domestic Commerce.

Bernard, Mrs. [William] Bayle. 1867. The Position of Women in America. *Englishwoman's Review* 4 (July): 208–18.

——. 1868. The Position of Women in India. *Englishwoman's Review* 8 (July): 471–82.

——. 1869. The Women of Brazil. *Englishwoman's Review* 10 (January): 89–99.

Bernays, Doris Fleischman. 1928/1931/1935. *An Outline of Careers for Women: A Practical Guide to Achievement.* New York: Doubleday, Doran, and Co.

——. 1939. *Careers for Women: A Practical Guide to Opportunity for Women in American Business.* New York: Garden City Publishing.

Bernstein, Blanche. 1940. *The Pattern of Consumer Debt, 1935–36: A Statistical Analysis.* New York: National Bureau of Economic Research.

——. 1940. The Pattern of Consumer Debt, 1935–36: A Statistical Analysis. Ph.D. thesis, Columbia University.

[Berry,] Gwendolyn Salisbury Hughes. 1925/1977. *Mothers in Industry: Wage-earning by Mothers in Philadelphia.* New York: New Republic, Inc. Reprinted New York: Arno Press, 1977.

——. 1925. Mothers in Industry: Wage-earning by Mothers in Philadelphia. Ph.D. thesis, Bryn Mawr College.

——. 1929. Mothers in Industry. *American Academy of Political and Social Science, Annals* 143 (May): 315–.

——. 1933. *Idleness and the Health of a Neighborhood.* New York: New York Association for Improving the Condition of the Poor.

Besant, Annie W[ood]. 1874. *The Political Status of Women.* London: Freethought Publishing. Reprinted in John Saville, ed., *A Selection of the Social and Political Pamphlets of Annie Besant.* New York: Augustus M. Kelley, 1970.

——. 1875. Liberty, Equality, Fraternity. Originally published in *Essays by Mrs. Besant.* Pamphlet 3rd ed. reprinted in John Saville, ed., *A Selection of the Social and Political Pamphlets of Annie Besant.* New York: Augustus M. Kelley, 1970.

——. 1876. *History of the Great French Revolution: A Course of Six Lectures Delivered at South Place Institute, Finsbury.* London: Watts.

——. 1876/1885. *The Legalisation of Female Slavery in England.* Originally published in the *National Reformer*, June 4, 1876. Pamphlet (1885) reprinted in John Saville, ed., *A Selection of the Social and Political Pamphlets of Annie Besant.* New York: Augustus M. Kelley, 1970.

—— [as "Ajax"]. 1877/1880. *Landlords, Tenant Farmers, and Laborers.* Originally serialized in *National Reformer*, September 20 and 27 and October 4. Pamphlet 4th ed. reprinted in John Saville, ed., *A Selection of the Social and Political Pamphlets of Annie Besant.* New York: Augustus M. Kelley, 1970.

——. 1877. *The Law of Population: Its Consequences, and Its Bearing upon Human Conduct and Morals.* Originally serialized in *National Reformer*, October 7, 14, 21 and 28, and November 4, 1877. Pamphlet London: Freethought Publishers,

1889. Reprinted in Maria Mulvey Roberts and Tamae Mizuta, eds., *Perspectives on the History of British Feminism*, vol. 3: *The Mothers: Controversies of Motherhood.* London: Routledge/Thoemmes, 1994. Pamphlet final version (1891) reprinted in John Saville, ed., *A Selection of the Social and Political Pamphlets of Annie Besant.* New York: Augustus M. Kelley, 1970.

——. 1878/1882. *Marriage as It Was, as It Is and as It Should Be: A Plea for Reform.* Originally serialized in *National Reformer* (February 17, March 10, 17, 24 and 31, and April 7 and 14, 1878). Reprinted in Maria Mulvey Roberts and Tamae Mizuta, eds., *Perspectives on the History of British Feminism*, vol. 2: *The Wives: The Rights of Married Women.* London: Routledge/Thoemmes, 1994. Pamphlet London: Freethought Publishing. 2nd ed. of pamphlet (1892) reprinted in John Saville, ed., *A Selection of the Social and Political Pamphlets of Annie Besant.* New York: Augustus M. Kelley, 1970.

——. 1879. *England, India, and Afghanistan.* London: Freethought Publishing.

——. 1880. The English Land System. *National Reformer* (January 11 and 18). Pamphlet London: Freethought Publishing. Reprinted in John Saville, ed., *A Selection of the Social and Political Pamphlets of Annie Besant.* New York: Augustus M. Kelley, 1970.

——. 1880 or 1881. *The Social Aspects of Malthusianism.* London: Freethought Publishing. Reprinted in John Saville, ed., *A Selection of the Social and Political Pamphlets of Annie Besant.* New York: Augustus M. Kelley, 1970.

——. 1881. *The Transvaal.* London: Freethought Publishing. Reprinted in John Saville, ed., *A Selection of the Social and Political Pamphlets of Annie Besant.* New York: Augustus M. Kelley, 1970.

——. 1882. Egypt. *National Reformer* (August 27 and September 3). Pamphlet London: Freethought Publishing. 2nd ed. of pamphlet (1885) reprinted in John Saville, ed., *A Selection of the Social and Political Pamphlets of Annie Besant.* New York: Augustus M. Kelley, 1970.

——. 1884. *The Story of the Soudan.* London: Freethought Publishing Co. Reprinted in John Saville, ed., *A Selection of the Social and Political Pamphlets of Annie Besant.* New York: Augustus M. Kelley, 1970.

——. 1885. *The Redistribution of Political Power. Our Corner.* (March). London: Freethought Publishing. Reprinted in John Saville, ed., *A Selection of the Social and Political Pamphlets of Annie Besant.* New York: Augustus M. Kelley, 1970.

——. 1885/1886. The Evolution of Society. Serialized in *Our Corner* (July–October). Pamphlet London: Freethought Publishing, 1886. Reprinted in John Saville, ed., *A Selection of the Social and Political Pamphlets of Annie Besant.* New York: Augustus M. Kelley, 1970.

——. 1885. Gordon Judged out of His Own Mouth. *National Reformer* (April 26 and May 3). Pamphlet London: Freethought Publishing. Reprinted in John Saville, ed., *A Selection of the Social and Political Pamphlets of Annie Besant.* New York: Augustus M. Kelley, 1970.

——. 1886/1890. *Modern Socialism.* First serialized in *Our Corner* (February–May). Pamphlet 2nd ed. (1890) London: Freethought Publishing Co. Reprinted in

John Saville, ed., *A Selection of the Social and Political Pamphlets of Annie Besant.* New York: Augustus M. Kelley, 1970.

——. 1886/1887. Radicalism and Socialism. First published in *Our Corner*, November and December 1886. Pamphlet (1887) reprinted in John Saville, ed., *A Selection of the Social and Political Pamphlets of Annie Besant.* New York: Augustus M. Kelley, 1970.

——. 1886. The Socialist Movement. *Westminster Review* 126 (July): 212–30. Pamphlet reprinted in John Saville, ed., *A Selection of the Social and Political Pamphlets of Annie Besant.* New York: Augustus M. Kelley, 1970.

——. 1886. Why I am a Socialist. *Our Corner* (September). Pamphlet London: Freethought Publishing. Reprinted in John Saville, ed., *A Selection of the Social and Political Pamphlets of Annie Besant.* New York: Augustus M. Kelley, 1970.

——. 1887. *England's Jubilee Gift to Ireland.* Originally published in the *National Reformer* (May 8). Pamphlet London: Freethought Publishing. Reprinted in John Saville, ed., *A Selection of the Social and Political Pamphlets of Annie Besant.* New York: Augustus M. Kelley, 1970.

——. 1887. *Essays on Socialism.* London: Freethought Publishing.

——. 1887. The Economic Position of Women; Lecture to the Fabian Society. *Our Corner* 10 (August): 95–99.

——. 1887. White Slavery in London. *The Link* (Summer).

——. 1888. *Free Trade versus Fair Trade:...Being the Substance of Five Lectures Delivered at the Hall of Science, London in October 1881.* London: Freethought Publishing.

——. 1888. *Political Essays.* London: Freethought Publishing Co.

——. 1889. Pourquoi je suis socialiste. *Revue socialiste* 10(59) (November): 539–.

——. 1889–90. The Trades Union Movement. Originally published in *National Reformer*, December 22 and 29, 1889, and January 5 and 12, 1890. Pamphlet London: Freethought Publishing Co., 1890. Reprinted in John Saville, ed., *A Selection of the Social and Political Pamphlets of Annie Besant.* New York: Augustus M. Kelley, 1970.

——. 1891. Industry under Socialism. In H. G. Wilshire, ed., *Fabian Essays in Socialism.* New York: Humboldt Publishing Co.

——. 1906/1921. *England and India.* Adyar, Madras, India: Theosophical Publishing House.

——. 1908. Industry under Socialism. In Bernard Shaw, ed., *Fabian Essays in Socialism.* London and Felling-on-Tyne: Walter Scott Publishing Co. Reprinted Boston: Ball Publishing Co., 1909; London: Fabian Society, 1931.

——. 1911. The Emperor of India. *Nash's Magazine* 4(4) (July): 401–.

——. 1912. *The Future Socialism.* Adyar pamphlets, no. 18, Adyar, Madras, India: Theosophist Office.

——. 1914. Forcible Feeding. *Nation* 15(15) (July 11): 567–.

——. 1914. India and the Empire. *Living Age* 7(282) (July/September): 118–.

——. 1914. India and the Empire. *Nation* 15(9) (May 30): 336–.

——. 1917. *The Case for India: The Presidential Address.* Address delivered at the 32nd Indian National Congress, Calcutta, December 26, 1917. London: The Home Rule for India League (British Section).

——. 1921. *Karma and Social Improvement.* Madras, India: Theosophical Publishing House.

——. 1925. *World problems of To-day.* London: Theosophical Publishing House.

Besant, Annie and Charles Bradlaugh. 1887. Socialism: For and Against. *Our Corner* (March, April and June). Pamphlet London: Freethought Publishing. Reprinted in John Saville, ed., *A Selection of the Social and Political Pamphlets of Annie Besant.* New York: Augustus M. Kelley, 1970.

Besant, Annie and G. W. Foote. 1887. *Is Socialism Sound?: Verbatim Report of a Four Nights' Public Debate Between Annie Besant and G. W. Foote, at the Hall of Science, Old St., London, Feb 2, 9, 16 & 23, 1887.* London: Progressive Publishing Co.

Besant, Annie and Frederick Millar. 1890. *Socialism v. Individualism. Public Debate in the Mechanics' Hall, Nottingham…, 1890, between Mrs. Annie Besant of the Fabian Society, and Mr. Frederick Millar of the Liberty and Property Defence League.* Nottingham: Welton.

Besant, Annie Wood and W. J. Nairn. 1888/1892. *What Is Socialism? A Discussion between Mrs. Annie Besant and Mr. W. J. Nairn.* Glasgow: Glasgow Branch of the Social Democratic Federation. Originally published in *Justice*, 1888.

Best, Ethel Lombard. 1923. *Women in Arkansas Industries: A Study of Hours, Wages, and Working Conditions.* Washington: U.S. Women's Bureau.

——. 1926. *Lost Time and Labor Turnover in Cotton Mills.* Washington: U.S. Women's Bureau.

——. 1929. *Causes of Absence for Men and for Women in Four Cotton Mills.* Bulletin of the U.S. Women's Bureau, no. 69. Washington: U.S. Government Printing Office.

——. 1929. *Conditions of Work in Spin Rooms.* Bulletin of the U.S. Women's Bureau, no. 72. Washington: U.S. Government Printing Office.

——. 1929. *Women Workers in Flint, Mich.* Bulletin of the U.S. Women's Bureau, no. 67. Washington: U.S. Government Printing Office.

——. 1930. *A Survey of Laundries and Their Women Workers in 23 Cities.* Bulletin of the U.S. Women's Bureau, no. 78. Washington: U.S. Government Printing Office.

——. 1932. *The Employment of Women in Vitreous Enameling.* Washington: U.S. Government Printing Office.

——. 1933. *The Change from Manual to Dial Operation in the Telephone Industry.* Bulletin of the Women's Bureau, no. 110. Washington: U.S. Government Printing Office.

——. 1933. *Hours, Earnings, and Employment in Cotton Mills.* Bulletin of the U.S. Women's Bureau, no. 111. Washington: U.S. Government Printing Office.

——. 1933. *Memorandum on the Practicability of Setting Maximum Standards of Work in Cotton Mills Operating under the Stretchout System.* Washington: U.S. Government Printing Office.

——. 1933. *A Study of a Change from 8 to 6 Hours of Work.* Bulletin of the United States Women's Bureau, no. 105. Washington: U.S. Government Printing Office.

——. 1934. *A Study of a Change from one Shift of 9 Hours to Two Shifts of 6 Hours Each*. Bulletin of the United States Women's Bureau, no. 116. Washington: U.S. Government Printing Office.

——. 1935. *Technological Changes in Relation to Women's Employment*. Bulletin of the United States Department of Labor, Women's Bureau, no 107. Washington: U.S. Government Printing Office.

——. 1936. *The Economic Problem of the Women of the Virgin Islands of the United States*. Washington: United States Department of Labor, Women's Bureau.

——. 1936. *Piecework in the Silk-dress Industry; Earnings, Hours, and Production*. Bulletin of the U.S. Women's Bureau, no. 141. Washington: U.S. Government Printing Office.

——. 1938. *Women in Kentucky Industries, 1937*. Bulletin of the United States Women's Bureau, no. 162. Washington: U.S. Government Printing Office.

Best, Ethel Lombard and Helen Bryan. 1922. *Women in Georgia Industries: A Study of Hours, Wages, and Working Conditions*. Bulletin of the U.S. Women's Bureau, no. 22. Washington: U.S. Government Printing Office.

Best, Ethel Lombard and Mildred Larcom Jones Gordon. 1918–19. *20th-Century Legal Treatises*. Bulletin of the Woman in Industry Service, no. 4. Washington: U.S. Government Printing Office.

——. 1919. *Wages of Candy Makers in Philadelphia in 1919*. Bulletin of the Woman in Industry Service. Washington: U.S. Government Printing Office.

Best, Ethel Lombard and Mary Elizabeth Pidgeon. 1930. *Women in Florida Industries*. Bulletin of the Women's Bureau, no. 80. Washington: U.S. Government Printing Office.

Best, Ethel Lombard and Mary Viola Robinson. 1922. *Women in Rhode Island Industries: A Study of Hours, Wages, and Working Conditions*. Bulletin of the U.S. Women's Bureau, no. 21. Washington: U.S. Government Printing Office.

Best, Ethel Lombard and Ruth I. Voris. 1926. *Women in Illinois Industries: A Study of Hours and Working Conditions*. Washington: U.S. Women's Bureau.

——. 1927. *Women in Tennessee Industries: A Study of Hours, Wages, and Working Conditions*. Washington: U.S. Women's Bureau.

Best, Ethel Lombard, Elisabeth Adshead Hyde, and Mary Viola Robinson. 1923. *Women in South Carolina Industries: A Study of Hours, Wages, and Working Conditions*. Bulletin of the U.S. Women's Bureau, no. 32. Washington: U.S. Government Printing Office.

Best, Ethel Lombard. Coauth. *See* Peterson, Agnes Lydia; Voris, Ruth Irene.

Bethem-Edwards, Matilda. 1870. Cottage Homes for Workhouse Children; or, The Boarding-out System. *Good Words* (1 March).

——. 1875. The International Working Men's Association,. *Fraser's*, n.s. 12 [o.s. 92] (July): 72–87; (August) 181–94; (September): 300–11.

——. 1875. Three Experiments in Cooperative Agriculture. *Fraser's*, n.s. 11 [o.s. 91] (April): 529–39.

——. 1877. The Progress of Colonisation in Algeria. *Fraser's*, n.s. 15 [o.s. 95] (October): 422–41.

——. 1887. French Peasant Proprietors. *Fortnightly Review* 46 (August): 223–36.

Betts, Lillian W. 1892/3. Some Tenement-house Evils. *Century Magazine* 45 (November/April): 314–16.
——. 1900. The Tenement House Exhibit. *Outlook* LXIV: 589–92.
——. 1903. *The Leaven in a Great City*. New York: Dodd, Mead and Company.
Bevington, Louisa S. 1881. How to Eat Bread. *Nineteenth Century* 10 (September): 341–56.
——. 1881. The Moral Colour of Rationalism. *Fortnightly Review*, n.s. 30 (August): 179–94.
——. 1890. *Common-sense Country*. London: James Tochatti, "Liberty" Press. Online in University of Indiana's LETRS.
——. 1891. *Dame Nature's Dumb Sermon*. London: Gee & Co. Online in University of Indiana's LETRS.
——. 1894. *Why I Am an Expropriationist*. London: James Tochatti, "Liberty" Press. Online in University of Indiana's LETRS.
——. 1895. *An Anarchist Manifesto*, London: Metropolitan Printing Works. Online in University of Indiana's LETRS.
——. 1895. *Chiefly a Dialogue. Concerning Some Difficulties of a Dunce*. London: "Freedom" Office. Online in University of Indiana's LETRS.
——. 1896. *Anarchism and Violence*. London: James Tochatti. Online in University of Indiana's LETRS.
Bevington, Sheila. 1924. The Analysis of Factory "Atmosphere." *National Institute of Industrial Psychology, Journal* 2(2) (April): 84–.
——. 1925. International Industrial Welfare Congress. *National Institute of Industrial Psychology, Journal* 2(8) (October): 384–.
——. 1928. The Psychologist's Contribution to Factory Planning. *National Institute of Industrial Psychology, Journal* 4(1) (January): 39–.
——. 1933. *Occupational Misfits: A Comparative Study of North London Boys, Employed and Unemployed*. London: George Allen & Unwin.
——. 1934. Occupational Misfits. *Charity Organisation Quarterly* 8(3) (July): 126–.
Bevington, Sheila and G. H. Miles. 1928. Some Improvements Effected by the Institute. *National Institute of Industrial Psychology, Journal* 4(2) (April): 86–.
Bevington, Sheila, G. H. Miles, and Gladys Roberts. 1928. An Investigation in a Tapestry Factory. *National Institute of Industrial Psychology, Journal* 4(3) (July): 160–.
[Beyer,] Clara [E.] Mortenson. 1916. Organized Labor in San Francisco, from 1892–1902. M.S. thesis, University of California–Berkeley (economics).
——. 1921. What is Equality? *Nation* 31 (January).
——. 1921. A Minimum Wage Conference at Work: Award for District of Columbia Laundry Workers. *Monthly Labor Review* 12 (January/June): 109–11.
——. 1923. Why Investigate Further? *American Labor Legislation Review* 13: 83–.
——. 1932. Review of "Frank Roney, Irish Rebel and California Labor Leader: An Autobiography". *American Economic Review* 22(1) (March): 188–9.
——. 1933. Child Labor Ruling. *School Life* 19(3) (November): 46–.
——. 1933. Depression's Children: A Friend of Children Discusses the Effects of Economic Adversity on the Employment of Children. *State Government* 6(4) (April): 14–.

——. 1937. Facing the Apprenticeship Problem. *Child* 2(2) (August): 27–.

——. 1939. I.L.O. Recommendations Concerning Vocational and Technical Education and Apprenticeship. *Child* 4(3) (September): 82–.

Beyer, Clara E. Mortenson and Mary Elizabeth Skinner. 1931. *Children of Working Mothers in Philadelphia*, part 1: *The Working Mothers*. United States Children's Bureau. Publication no. 204. Washington: U.S. Government Printing Office.

Beyer, Clara Mortenson and Florence Patteson Smith. 1929/1932. *History of Labor Legislation for Women in Three States*. U.S. Department of Labor Women's Bureau. Bulletin no. 66. Washington: U.S. Government Printing Office.

Beynon, Abi Elizabeth. 1920. The City-manager Plan in the United States. M.A. thesis, University of Nebraska (Lincoln campus).

——. 1930. The Land Problems of Mexico. Ph.D. thesis, University of Washington (political science).

Bezanson, Anne. 1921. Promotion from Without. *Quarterly Journal of Economics* 36(1) (November): 154–61.

——. 1922. *A Study in Labor Mobility*. Philadelphia: University of Pennsylvania, Wharton School of Finance and Commerce, Industrial Research Department Publication no. 16571.

——. 1922. The Early Use of the Term Industrial Revolution. *Quarterly Journal of Economics* 36(2) (February): 343–9.

——. 1922. Skill. *Quarterly Journal of Economics* 36(4) (August): 626–45.

——. 1923. Local Factors in Connection with Labor Turnover. *American Economic Review* 13(1) (March): 90–104.

——. 1924. Earnings of Coal Miners. *American Academy of Political and Social Science, Annals* 111 (January): 1–.

——. 1926/7. Labor Market Comparisons. Turnover Rates in Four Metal Manufacturing Centers. *Journal of Personnel Research* 5 (May/April): 387.

——. 1928. *Earnings and Working Opportunity in the Upholstery Weavers' Trade in 25 Plants in Philadelphia*. Philadelphia: University of Pennsylvania Press.

——. 1928. The Advantages of Labor Turnover: An Illustrative Case. *Quarterly Journal of Economics* 42(3) (May): 450–64.

——. 1929. *Help-wanted Advertising as an Indicator of the Demand for Labor*. Philadelphia: University of Pennsylvania Press.

——. 1929. Earnings and Working Opportunity in the Upholstery Weavers' Trade in Twenty-five Plants in Philadelphia: An Experiment in Co-operative Research. Ph.D. thesis, Radcliffe College (economics).

——. 1935. *Prices in Colonial Pennsylvania*. Philadelphia: University of Pennsylvania Press.

——. 1936/1937. *Wholesale Prices in Philadelphia, 1784–1861*. Philadelphia: University of Pennsylvania Press.

Bezanson, Anne and Miriam Hussey. 1930. *Wage Methods and Selling Costs*. Philadelphia: University of Pennsylvania Press.

——. 1931. *Wage Methods and Selling Costs; Compensation of Sales Clerks in Four Major Departments in 31 Stores, Pennsylvania*. Wharton School of Finance and

Commerce, Industrial Research Unit. Major Industrial Research Unit Studies, no. 10. Philadelphia: University of Pennsylvania Press.

Bezanson, Anne and Margaret Schoenfeld. 1925/6. Labor Turnover in the Coal Industry. *Journal of Personnel Research* 4: 268–.

Bezanson, Anne, Joseph H. Willits, Miriam Hussey, and Leda F. White. 1925. *Four Years of Labor Mobility: A Study of Labor Turnover in a Group of Selected Plants in Philadelphia. Annals of the American Academy of Political and Social Science* 119 (supplement) (May) Philadelphia: University of Pennsylvania.

Biaujeaud, Huguette. 1933. Essai sur la théorie ricardienne de la valeur. Ph.D. thesis, Université de Paris.

——. 1934/1988. *Essai sur la théorie ricardienne de la valeur.* Paris: Librairie du Receuil Sirey.

Biggs, Caroline A[shurst]. 1869. Women's Share in Social Science. *Englishwoman's Review* 10 (January): 77–88.

——. 1887. *Some Notes upon the Election of Guardians of the Poor.* London: Society for Promoting the Return of Women as Poor Law Guardians. Reprinted from the *Englishwoman's Review*, n.s. 167 (March, 1887): 97–107.

Biggs, Miss M[aude]. A. 1892. The Woman's Movement in Bohemia. *Englishwoman's Review*, n.s. 214 (April): 79–.

——. 1892. What Women Are Doing in the Kingdom of Poland. *Englishwoman's Review*, n.s. 216 (October): 230–.

——. 1893. The Woman's Movement in Galicia. *Englishwoman's Review* XXIV, n.s. 217 (January): 12–.

——. 1895. Poor Gentlewomen: A Suggestion. *Englishwoman's Review* XXVI, n.s. 227 (July): 151–.

——. 1898. Women as Public Librarians. *Englishwoman's Review*, n.s. 239 (July): 154–.

Billington, Mary Frances. 1895. *Women in India.* London: Chapman & Hall.

——. 1895. Tailor Made in Germany. *New Review* 12 (June): 631–40.

——. 1914. *The Red Cross in War: Woman's Part in the Relief of Suffering.* London: Hodder & Stoughton.

——. 1916. Women's Share in the War's Work. *London Quarterly Review* 5(11) (January/April): 70–.

——. Coauth. *See* Kendal, Madge.

Billington-Grieg, Teresa. 1912. *The Consumer in Revolt.* London: Steven Swift.

Birdsall, Katharine Newbold. 1903. *How to Make Money: Eighty Novel and Practical Suggestions for Untrained Women's Work, Based on Experience.* New York: Doubleday.

Bisland, Elizabeth. 1889. Co-operative Housekeeping in Tenements. *Cosmopolitan* 8 (November).

Biss [Spry], Irene M. 1930/1. The Dressmakers' Strike. *Canadian Forum* 11: 367.

——. 1933. *The Industrial Revolution in Canada.* The Machine Age Series, no. 1. Toronto: Social Service Council of Canada.

——. 1934. Book Review of "New Deal in Canada" by Harris. *American Economic Review* 24: 708.

——. 1934. Book Review of "Recovery by Control: Solution for Canada" by Hankin and Macdermott. *American Economic Review* 24: 493.

——. 1936. The Contracts of the Hydro-Electric Power Commission. *Economic Journal* 46(183) (September): 549–54.

——. 1936. Recent Power Legislation in Ontario. *Canadian Journal of Economics and Political Science* 2(2) (May): 212–15.

——. 1937. Recent Power Legislation in Quebec. *Canadian Journal of Economics and Political Science* 3(4) (November): 550–8.

——. 1938. Economic Aspects of National Unity. *Annual Review, The Commerce Journal* (March): 36–40.

Black, Anne. Coauth. *See* Hammond, Barbara Bradby.

Black, Clementina. 1883. Harriet Martineau. *Encyclopaedia Britannica,* 9th ed., vol XV.: 583–4. Edinburgh: A. and C. Black.

——. 1887. Caveat Emptor. *Longman's* 10(58) (August): 409–20.

——. 1888. Something about Needle-women. In *The Woman's World* (serial), ed. Oscar Wilde: 300–4.

——. 1889. *The Women's Trade Union Provident League.* Manchester: s.n. Reprinted from the *Women's Gazette and Weekly News.*

——. 1889. The Organization of Working Women. *Fortnightly Review* 52 (n.s. 46) (November): 695–704.

——. 1889. Some East End Workwomen. *National Review* 13 (August): 788–93.

——. 1889. What High Wages Mean. *Longman's Magazine* 14(81) (July): 283–7.

——. 1890. The Chocolate-makers' Strike. *Fortnightly Review* n.s. 48 (August): 305–14.

——. 1890. On Marriage: A Criticism. *Fortnightly Review,* n.s. 47 (April): 586–94.

——. 1890. The Trades Union Congress. *Universal Review* 8 (October): 182–.

——. 1891. Book Review of "Labour and Life in London" by Charles Booth. *Contemporary Review* 60 (August): 207–19.

——. 1891. The Coming Factory Act. *Contemporary Review* 59 (April): 710–17.

——. 1891. Matchbox Making in the Home. *English Illustrated Magazine* (August): 629–.

——. 1891. Women and Work. *New Review* 5 (September): 213–21.

——. 1892. The Coercion of Trade Unions. *Contemporary Review* 62 (October): 547–54. Reprinted in Andrea Broomfield and Sally Mitchell, eds., *Prose by Victorian Women: An Anthology*. New York: Garland Publishing, 1995.

——. 1892. Thrift for the Poor. *New Review* 7 (December): 666–9.

——. 1893. The Dislike to Domestic Service. *Nineteenth Century* 33(193) (March): 454–6. Reprinted in Andrea Broomfield and Sally Mitchell, eds., *Prose by Victorian Women: An Anthology*. New York: Garland Publishing, 1995.

——. 1893. What is a Fair Wage? *New Review* 8 (May): 587–92. Reprinted in *Prose by Victorian Women.*

——. 1894. *An Agitator: A Novel.* London: Bliss, Sands & Foster.

——. 1894. The Condition of Working Women. *Young Woman* 11 (May): 265–.

——. 1895. The Women's Industrial Council. *Monthly Packet* 10 (December): 648–.

——. 1897. A Voice in a Million. Story. *Werner's Magazine* 19(3) (March): 264–.
——. 1897. Who Should Emigrate? *Osborne* 1 (April): 278–.
——. 1897. Women Workers in Confectionery. *Osborne* 1 (January): 113–.
——. 1901. Some Current Objections. In Mrs. Sidney Webb, ed., *The Case for the Factory Acts*. London: Grant Richards.
——. 1902. *Frederic Walker*. London, Duckworth and Co.
——. 1903. Old-fashioned Accomplishments. *Longman's Magazine* 43(253) (November): 45–.
——. 1904. A Bill to Regulate Home Work. *Journal of the Royal Sanitary Institute* 25: 749.
——. 1904. London's Tailoresses. *Economic Journal* 14(56) (December): 555–67.
——. 1906. Book Review of "The Clothing Industry in New York" by Jesse Eliphalet Pope. *Economic Journal* 16: 398.
——. 1906. Book Review of "Le Développement de la fabrique et le travail à domicile dans les industries de l'habillement" by Albert Aftalion. *Economic Journal* 16: 595.
——. 1906. Trade Schools for Girls in London. *Economic Journal* 16(63) (September): 449–54.
——. 1907. *Sweated Industry and the Minimum Wage*. With an introduction by A. G. Gardiner. London: Duckworth.
——. 1908/1970. Legislative Proposals. In Gertrude Tuckwell, Constance Smith, Mary MacArthur, May Tennant, Nettie Adler, Adelaide Anderson, and Clementina Black. *Woman in Industry from Seven Points of View*. London: Duckworth and Co. Reprinted Washington: NCR Microcard Editions, 1970.
——. 1909. Report of the Department Committee on the Truck Acts. *Economic Journal* 19(74) (June): 315–19.
——. 1910. Book Review of "Les Sociétés co-operatives de consommation" by Charles Gide. *Economic Journal* 20: 69.
——. 1911. *The Linleys of Bath*. London: Martin Seeker.
——. 1913. The Police and Social Reform. *Nation* 13(21) (August 23): 780.
——. 1914. Assistants in Sub-Post-Offices. *Nation* 15(8) (May 23): 305–.
——. 1914. Book Review of "Conflicting Ideals" by B. L. Hutchins. *Sociological Review* 7: 165.
——. 1914. Book Review of "Ellen Key" by L. Nyström-Hamilton. *Sociological Review* 7: 165.
——. 1914. Book Review of "The Future of the Woman's Movement" by H. M. Swanwick. *Sociological Review* 7: 165.
——. 1914. Book Review of "War and Women" by A. St. Clair Stobart. *Sociological Review* 7: 165.
——. 1914. Book Review of "Woman, Marriage and Motherhood" by E. S. Chesser. *Sociological Review* 7: 165.
——. 1914. Book Review of "Woman's Place in Rural Economy" by P. de Vuyst. *Sociological Review* 7: 165.
——. 1915. *Married Women's Work: Report of an Enquiry Undertaken by the Women's Industrial Council*. London: Bell.

——. 1918. *A New Way of Housekeeping*. London: W. Collins and Sons.

——. 1919. Domestic Idiocies. *Contemporary Review* 115 (January): 67.

——. 1919. Hopes of Better Housing. *Contemporary Review* 115 (May): 536.

Black, Clementina and "Mrs. Briant." 1889. A Working Woman's Speech. *Nineteenth Century* 25(147) (May): 667–71. Reprinted in Maria Mulvey Roberts and Tamae Mizuta, eds., *Controversies in the History of British Feminism*, vol 2: *The Workers: Women and Labour*. London: Routledge/Thoemmes, 1995. Reprinted in Harriet Devine Jump, ed., *Women's Writing of the Victorian Period 1837–1901, An Anthology*. New York and London: Palgrave-Macmillan, 1999.

Black, Clementina and Margaret Llewelyn Davies. 1908. Suffragist Tactics [letter to the editor]. *Nation* 4(13) (December 26): 509.

Black, Clementina and Stephen N. Fox. 1894. *The Truck Acts: What They Do, and What They Ought to Do*. London: Women's Trade Union Association.

Black, Clementina and F. Melian Stawell. 1909. The Logic of Woman's Suffrage [letter to the editor]. *Nation* 4(26) (March 27): 967.

Black, Clementina, S. A. Byles, and H. N. Brailsford. 1909. The Set-back to Women's Suffrage. *Nation* 5(26) (September 25): 917–.

Black, Clementina, A. Grimshaw Haywood, and Emily Tomlinson. 1908. Votes for Women [letter to the editor]. *Nation* 3(11) (June 13): 381.

Black, Clementina, Winifred Holiday, and W. R. Snow. 1910. The Next Step in Women's Suffrage [letter to the editor]. *Nation* 6(22) (February 26): 846.

Black, Clementina. Coauth. *See* Davies, Margaret Llewelyn; Meyer, Adele Levis [Mrs. Carl].

——. Also published in *The Englishwoman*.

Blackburn, Helen. 1877. Law and Women Earners. *Englishwoman's Review* 50 (June): 251–6.

——. 1878. The Night Cometh When No "Woman" Can Work. *Englishwoman's Review* 59 (March): 97–102.

——. 1881. *A Hand-book for Women Engaged in Social and Political Work*. Bristol: J. W. Arrowsmith.

——. 1886. The Relation of Women to the State in Past Times. *National Review* 8 (November): 392–9.

——. 1887. Irish Industries. *Englishwoman's Review*, n.s. 175 (November): 492–.

——. 1888. *A Handy Book of Reference for Irishwomen*. London: Irish Exposition.

Blackburn, Helen and Jessie Boucherett. 1898. The Fall in Women's Wages. *Englishwoman's Review*, n.s. 238 (April 15): 73–87.

Blackburn, Helen. Coauth. *See* Boucherett, Emilia Jessie.

Blacker, Mrs. 1892. A Voice for Women from Germany. *Englishwoman's Review*, n.s. 215 (July): 155–.

Blackwell, Antoinette Brown. 1856. *Shadows of Our Social System*.

——. 1869. Industrial Reconstruction. *Woman's Advocate* 1(1) (January): 41–2.

——. 1871. *The Island Neighbors: A Novel of American Life*. New York: Harper. [*utopian novel*]

——. 1874. The Relation of Woman's Work in the Household to the Work Outside. In *Papers and Letters Presented at the First Woman's Congress of the Association for the Advancement of Woman, New York, October 1873.* New York: Mrs. William Ballard. Reprinted (abridged) in Aileen Kraditor, ed., *Up from the Pedestal: Landmark Writings in the American Woman's Struggle for Equality.* Chicago: Quadrangle Books, 1968.

——. 1875. *The Sexes Throughout Nature.* New York: G. P. Putnam's Sons.

Blackwell, [Dr.] Elizabeth. 1856. *Address on the Medical Education of Women, Dec 27th, 1855.* New York: Baker & Duyckinck.

——. 1870. *How to Keep a Household in Health: An Address Delivered before the Working Woman's College.* London: Printed by W. W. Head.

——. 1881/1882. *Rescue Work in Relation to Prostitution and Disease.* Read before the Association for the Advancement of Women at its annual congress, Buffalo, N.Y., October 1881. London: T. Danks. Reprinted New York: Fowler, 1882.

——. 1881. Morality and Medicine. *Modern Review* 2 (October): 750–61.

——. 1882. *Christian Socialism; Thoughts Suggested by the Easter Season.* Hastings: sold by D. Williams, The Library.

——. 1883. *Wrong and Right Methods of Dealing with Social Evil, as Shown by English Parliamentary Evidence.* New York, A. Brentano.

——. 1887. *Purchase of Women: The Great Economic Blunder. Part I.* London: John Kensit.

——. 1888. *A Medical Address on the Benevolence of Malthus, Contrasted with the Corruptions of Neo-Malthusianism.* London: T. W. Danks.

——. 1888. *On the Decay of Municipal Representative Government: A Chapter of Personal Experience.* London: Moral Reform Union.

——. 1889. *The Influence of Women in the Profession of Medicine.* Address given at the London School of Medicine for Women. London: G. Bell.

——. 1902. *Essays in Medical Sociology.* 2 vols. London: G. Bell. Reprinted New York: Arno Press, 1972.

Blackwell, Elizabeth and Emily Blackwell. 1860. Medicine as a Profession for Women. *English Woman's Journal* (May). Reprinted as pamphlet, New York: W. H. Tinson. Reprinted in Candida Ann Lacey, ed., *Barbara Leigh Smith Bodichon and the Langham Place Group.* London and New York: Routledge, 1987.

Blackwell, Dr. Emily. 1883. The Industrial Position of Women. *Popular Science Monthly* 23: 388–99.

——. 1890s. The Need of Combination among Women for Self-protection. New York: The Philanthropist.

——. 1895. Age of Consent Legislation. *Philanthropist* 10 (February): 1–2.

Blaine, Louisa Hubbard. 1928. A Problem in the Chicago Milk Market. Ph.D. thesis, University of Chicago (economics, agricultural).

Blair, Bertha and Ethel Erickson. 1935. *Women in Arkansas Industries.* Bulletin of the U.S. Women's Bureau, no. 124. Washington: U.S. Government Printing Office.

Blair, Bertha. Coauth. *See* Byrne, Harriet Anne; Nienburg, Bertha Marie; Sullivan, Mary Loretta.

Blair, Emily Newell. 1929. Books for the Business Woman. *Good Housekeeping* (1929): 104, 214–19.

Blake, Lillie Devereux [Umsted]. 1883. *Woman's Place Today*. New York: J. W. Lovell.

——. 1886. Are Women Fairly Paid? *Forum* 2 (October): 201–2.

Blake, Matilda M. 1892. Are Women Protected? *Westminster Review* 137 (January): 43–8.

——. 1892. The Lady and the Law. *Westminster Review* 137 (April): 364–70.

——. 1893. Women as Poor Law Guardians. *Westminster Review* 139 (January): 12–21.

Blakey, Gladys Campbell. 1934. *A History of Taxation in Minnesota*. Minneapolis: University of Minnesota Press.

Blakey, Gladys Campbell and Roy G. Blakey. 1919. The Revenue Act of 1918. *American Economic Review* 9(2) (June): 213–43.

——. 1932. The Revenue Act of 1932. *American Economic Review* 22(4) (December): 620–40.

——. 1934. Minnesota Income Tax and Homestead Exemption. *National Tax Association, Bulletin* 19(8) (May): 240–.

——. 1934. The Revenue Act of 1934. *American Economic Review* 24(3) (September): 450–61.

——. 1935. The Revenue Act of 1935. *American Economic Review* 25(4) (December): 673–90.

——. 1936. The Revenue Act of 1936. *American Economic Review* 26(3) (September): 466–82.

——. 1937. The Revenue Act of 1937. *American Economic Review* 27(4) (December): 698–704.

——. 1938. The Revenue Act of 1938. *American Economic Review* 28(3) (September): 447–58.

——. 1939. Federal Tax Legislation. *American Economic Review* 29(4) (December): 695–707.

——. 1939. Revenue Act of 1938: A Correction. *American Economic Review* 29(1) (March): 112.

——. 1940. Founders and Builders of the Income Tax. *Taxes* 18(3) (March): 139–.

——. 1940. Founders and Builders of the Income Tax. *Taxes* 18(4) (April): 206–.

——. 1940. Founders and Builders of the Income Tax. *Taxes* 18(5) (May): 271–.

——. 1940. Reorganization in Minnesota, 1939. *National Tax Association, Bulletin* 25(9) (June): 278–.

——. 1940. The Two Federal Revenue Acts of 1940. *American Economic Review* 30(4) (December): 724–35.

Blanc, Elise Terry. 1924. *The Cooperative Movement in Russia*. New York: Macmillan.

Blanc, Mme. Marie-Therese [as "Th. Bentzon"]. 1896. *The Condition of Woman in the United States*. Boston: Roberts Bros. Reprinted New York: Arno Press, 1972.

Blanchard, Elizabeth Rowell. 1918. *A Comparison of the Cereal Crop with the Political Votes in Wisconsin, Iowa, and Minnesota since 1880*, B.A. thesis, University of Wisconsin.

Blanchard, Elizabeth R. and W. O. Blanchard. 1929. The Grape Industry of Spain and Portugal. *Economic Geography* 5(2) (April): 183–93.

Blanchard, Marie. 1923. *Mariée ou non, la Femme doit être indépendante.* Paris: Nilsson.

Blankenhorn, Mary Dewson. 1927. Do Working Women Want It? *Survey* 58 (February 15).

Blascoer, Frances. 1912. *The Industrial Condition of Women and Girls in Honolulu: A Social Study*. Honolulu: Kaiulani Home for Girls.

Blatch, Harriot Stanton. 1891. Free Education in the United States. *Westminster Review* 136 (October): 367–75.

——. 1891. Married Women and Municipal Elections. London: Women's Franchise League.

——. 1893. Another View of Village Life. *Westminster Review* 140 (September): 318–24.

——. 1894. Collectivism and the Economic Freedom of Women. Lecture to the Fabian Society. Unpublished.

——. 1894. Problems of Village Life in England. M.A. thesis, Vassar College.

——. 1896. Specialization of Function in Women. *Gunton's Magazine* 10 (May): 349–56.

——. 1899. Fall River, Massachusetts: A Typical New England Factory Town. *Humanitarian* 14 (April): 253–.

——. 1914. The Race Has Two Parents. *Women's Political World* (July 15).

——. 1918. *Mobilizing Woman-power*. New York: Woman's Press.

——. 1920/1921. *Why I Joined the Socialist Party*. Chicago: Socialist Party.

——. 1920. *A Woman's Point of View; Some Roads to Peace*. New York: Woman's Press.

Blaze de Bury, Mme. Marie. 1892. The Problem of Crime in France. *Contemporary Review* 62 (July/December): 183–209.

Blaze de Bury, Yetta. 1898 French Women in French Industry. *Fortnightly Review*, n.s. 64 (July): 127–40.

Blomefield, A[delaide]. H. 1897. Book Review of "Neue Beitrage zur Frage der Arbeitslosen-Versicherung" by Georg Schanz. *Economic Journal* 7(28) (December): 583–5.

——. 1900. Book Review of "Bei Krupp, eine socialpolitische Reiseskizze" by Dr. W. Kley. *Economic Journal* 10(37) (March): 78–80.

——. 1900. Book Review of "Die heutige Grundlage der Deutschen Wehrkraft" by Prof. Lujo Brentano and Dr. Robert Kuezynski. *Economic Journal* 10: 216.

——. 1900. Book Review of "Eine socialpolitische Reiseskizze" by Dr. W. Kley and Bei Krupp. *Economic Journal* 10: 78.

——. 1901. Book Review of "Der Arbeiterschutz bei Vergebung öffentlicher Arbeiten und Lieferungen. Bericht des k. arbeitsstatistischen Amtes über die auf diesem Gebiete in den europäischen und überseeischen Industriestaaten unternommenen Versuche und bestehenden Vorschriften" by Dr. O. von Zwiedineck-Südenhorst. *Economic Journal* 11: 205.

——. 1901. Book Review of "Das Aufsteigen des Arbeiterstandes in England. Ein Beitrag zur socialen Geschichte der Gegenwart" by Hans von Nostitz. *Economic Journal* 11: 203–.

——. 1901. Book Review of "Lohnpolitik und Lohntheorie mit besonderer Berücksichtigung des Minimallohnes" by Dr. O. von Zwiedineck-Südenhorst. *Economic Journal* 11: 205.

——. 1902. Book Review of "Beiträge zur Geschichte des Handwerks in Preussen" by Dr. Otto Thissen. *Economic Journal* 12: 246–.

Blood, Pearle. 1937. Factors in the Economic Development of Baltimore, Maryland. *Economic Geography* 13(2) (April): 187–208.

Bloor, Ella Reeve. 1938. *Women in the Soviet Union.* New York: Workers Library Publishers.

Blos, Anna. 1928. *Frauen der deutschen Revolution 1848: zehn Lebensbilder und ein Vorwort.* Dresden: Kaden & Co.

——, ed. 1930. *Die Frauenfrage im Lichte des Sozialismus.* Dresden: Kaden.

Bloss, E[sther]. 1938. *Labor Legislation in Czechoslovakia, with Special Reference to the Standards of the International Labor Organization.* New York: Columbia University Press.

——. 1939. Labor Legislation in Czechoslovakia, with Special Reference to the Standards of the International Labor Organization. Ph.D. thesis, Columbia University (economics).

Bly, Nellie. Pseud. *See* Seaman, Elizabeth C.

[Bodichon,] Barbara Leigh Smith. 1854. *A Brief Summary, in Plain Language, of the Most Important Laws Concerning Women, Together with a Few Observations Thereon.* London: John Chapman. 2nd ed. 1856. Reprinted in Candida Ann Lacey, ed., *Barbara Leigh Smith Bodichon and the Langham Place Group.* London and New York: Routledge, 1987.

——. 1857/1859. *Women and Work.* London: Bosworth and Harrison. Reprinted in Candida Ann Lacey, ed., *Barbara Leigh Smith Bodichon and the Langham Place Group.* London and New York: Routledge, 1987. Reprinted also in Marie Mulvey Roberts and Tamae Mizuta, eds., *Sources in British Feminism*, vol. 3: *The Exploited: Women and Work.* London: Routledge/Thoemmes, 1993. U.S. edition, with introduction by Catharine M. Sedgwick, New York: C. M. Francis & Co., 1859.

Bodichon, Barbara Leigh Smith. 1860. Middle-class Schools for Girls. Paper read at the conference of the National Association for Promotion of Social Science (October) and published in the *English Woman's Journal* (November). Reprinted in Candida Ann Lacey, ed., *Barbara Leigh Smith Bodichon and the Langham Place Group.* London and New York: Routledge, 1987.

——. 1863. Of Those Who are the Property of Others, and of the Great Power that Holds Others as Property. *English Woman's Journal* (February). Reprinted in Candida Ann Lacey, ed., *Barbara Leigh Smith Bodichon and the Langham Place Group.* London and New York: Routledge, 1987.

——. 1864. Accomplices. *English Woman's Journal* (February). Reprinted in Candida Ann Lacey, ed., *Barbara Leigh Smith Bodichon and the Langham Place Group.* London and New York: Routledge, 1987.

——. 1866. *Objections to the Enfranchisement of Women Considered.* London: J. Bale, printer. Reprinted in Candida Ann Lacey, ed., *Barbara Leigh Smith Bodichon and the Langham Place Group*. London and New York: Routledge, 1987.

——. 1866. *Reasons for the Enfranchisement of Women.* Paper read at the conference of the National Association for Promotion of Social Science (October). Published as a pamphlet, London: J. Bale, printer. Reprinted in Candida Ann Lacey, ed., *Barbara Leigh Smith Bodichon and the Langham Place Group*. London and New York: Routledge, 1987.

——. 1867. Authorities and Precedents for Giving the Suffrage to Qualified Women. *Englishwoman's Review* 2 (January): 63–74.

——. 1869/1872. *Reasons for and against the Enfranchisement of Women*, London: London National Society for Women's Suffrage.

——. 1873. A Conversation on the Enfranchisement of Female Freeholders and Householders. *Englishwoman's Review* (April). Reprinted in Candida Ann Lacey, ed., *Barbara Leigh Smith Bodichon and the Langham Place Group*. London and New York: Routledge, 1987.

Boehmer, Florence Elsie. 1932. Vocational Continuity of College Women: A Study Based on Data Secured from 6466 Women Who Matriculated in Land-Grant Colleges between 1889 and 1922. Ph.D. thesis, Columbia University (economics, history).

Boehmer, Florence Elsie, Chase Going Woodhouse, and Ruth Frances Yeomans Schiffman. 1932. *After College – What?* Greensboro, N.C.: North Carolina College for Women.

Bölte, Amalie Charlotte Elise Mariane. 1877. *Nieuw vrouwen-brevier.* Arnhem: J. Rinkes, Jr.

Bolton, Mrs. 1884. Relations Between Employers and Employed. *Journal of Social Science* 18 (May): 279–88.

Bolton, Henrietta Irving. 1898. Women in Science. *Popular Science Monthly*: 506–11.

Bolton, Sarah K. 1885. *Lives of Poor Boys Who Became Famous.* New York: Thomas Y. Crowell.

Bond, Beverly Waugh. 1905. State Government in Maryland, 1777–1781. Ph.D. thesis, Johns Hopkins University (history).

——. 1907. *The Monroe Mission to France, 1?74–6.* Baltimore: Johns Hopkins Press.

——. 1919/1959. *The Quit-rent System in the American Colonies.* New Haven, Conn.: Yale University Press.

——. 1934/1970. *The Civilization of the Old Northwest: A Study of Political, Social, and Economic Development, 1788–1812.* Freeport, N.Y.: Books for Libraries Press.

Bondfield, Margaret G[race]. 1899. Conditions Under Which Shop Assistants Work. *Economic Journal* 9(34) (June): 277–86.

——. 1904. The Effects on Health of Women's Employment in Shops. *Journal of the Royal Sanitary Institute* 25: 738.

——. 1909. *Socialism for Shop Assistants.* London: Pass on Pamphlets, no 10.

——. 1911. The Government and Adult Suffrage [letters to the editor]. *Nation* 8(16) (January 14): 648–.

——. 1912. An Essay in Scientific Management [letters to the editor]. *Nation* 11(20) (August 17): 732–.

——. 1914. *The National Care of Maternity. Sectional Conference, March 1914.* London: Women's Co-operative Guild.

——. 1914. The National Care of Maternity. *New Statesman* 3, Supplement (May 6): 5.

——. 1918. Women as Domestic Workers. In M. Phillips, ed., *Women and the Labour Party*. London: F. Matthews.

——. 1919. Some Lessons of the British Health Insurance Act. *American Labor Legislation Review* 9: 202.

——. 1919. Woman and the Labor World. In Eleanor Barton, Mary Reid MacArthur, and Margaret Grace Bondfield, *English Women in the Labor and Co-operative Movements: Three Speeches Delivered before the Seventh Biennial Convention of the National Women's Trade Union League, Philadelphia, June 2–7, 1919*. Chicago: Women's Trade Union League of America.

——. 1927. Public Opinion – Women in Industry. *American Federationist* 37(7/12) (July/December): 836.

——. 1927. Women in Industry in Great Britain. *American Federationist* 34(1/6) (January/June): 567–.

——. 1927. Women Within the Trade Union. *American Federationist* 37(7/12) (July/December): 1,340.

——. 1928. The Meaning of Trade. In P. Redfein, ed., *Self and Society. First Twelve Essays: Social and Economic Problems from the Hitherto Neglected Point of View of the Consumer*. London: Ernest Benn Ltd.

——. 1929. A Labour Address. *Listener* 1(19) (May 22): 735.

——. 1930. Labour and International Affairs I. *Listener* 3(75) (June 18): 1,068.

——. 1930. Unemployment Insurance in Great Britain. *American Labor Legislation Review* 20: 237–48.

——. 1932. Rungs of the Ladder V. *Listener* 7(179) (June 15): 869–.

——. 1933. America's Approach to Job Insurance. *American Labor Legislation Review* 23: 121–2.

——. 1937. Birth of the Labour Party. *Listener* 18(451) (September 1): 429.

——. 1937. Why Trade Unions? Why Strikes? *Listener* 18(464) (December 1): 1,175.

Bondfield, Margaret Grace and Kathlyn Oliver. 1911. *Shop Worker and the Vote.* London: People's Suffrage Federation.

Bondfield, Margaret, Gertrude M. Tuckwell, Madeline J. Symons, and A. Susan Lawrence. 1926. Mary Macarthur [letters to the editor]. *Nation and the Athenaeum* 38(24) (March 13): 804–.

Bone, Lucy and Marie E. Lane. 1923. *Child Training through Occupation.* With an introduction by Alice Woods. London: Methuen & Co. Ltd.

Bonnevial, Marie. 1901. Le Mouvement syndical féminin en France. *Revue de morale sociale* II: 251–67.

Bontecou, Eleanor. 1928. Outline for Period 1789–1829. Ph.D. thesis, Robert Brookings.

——. 1931. Recent Court Decisions Relating to Social Welfare. *Social Service Review* 5(1/4) (March/December): 94–.

Boody, Elizabeth. *See* Schumpeter, Elizabeth Boody.

Booth, Eva Gore. *See* Gore-Booth, Eva.

Booth, Maud Ballington. 1895. Salvation Army Work in the Slums. *Scribner's Magazine* 17(1) (January): 102–14.

Boothe, Viva B[elle]. 1926. Criminality and the Home. *American Academy of Political and Social Science, Annals* 125 (May): 192–.

——, ed. 1929. *Women in the Modern World.* Philadelphia: American Academy of Political and Social Science.

——. 1932. *Salaries and the Cost of Living in Twenty-seven State Universities and Colleges, 1913–1932.* Columbus, Ohio: Ohio State University Press.

——. 1932. Gainfully Employed Women in the Family. *American Academy of Political and Social Science, Annals* 160 (March): 75–.

Borchers, Irma. 1925. Legislation Against the Oriental Farmer. *Land Economics* 1 (October): 509–12.

[Bosanquet,] Helen Dendy. 1891. The Causes of Poverty. *Economic Journal* 1/4 (December): 808–10.

——. 1893. The Industrial Residuum. *Economic Journal* 3(12) (December): 600–16. Reprinted in Bernard Bosanquet, ed. (1895), *Aspects of the Social Problem.* London and New York: Macmillan.

——. 1893. Thorough Charity. *Charity Organisation Review* 101 (June): 206–12.

——.1894. The Force of the Fabians. *Charity Organisation Review* 113 (June): 268

——. 1894/5. Marriage in East London. *Contemporary Review* 65 (March): 427–32. Reprinted in Bernard Bosanquet, ed. *Aspects of the Social Problem.*

——. 1894/5. The Position of Women in Industry. *National Review* 23 (August): 806–14. Included in Bernard Bosanquet, ed., *Aspects of the Social Problem.*

——. 1895. Book Review of "La Loi des pauvres et la société anglaise" by Émile Chevalier. *Economic Journal* 5(20) (December): 596–7.

——. 1895. Book Review of "Natural Rights" by David G. Ritchie. *International Journal of Ethics* 5(4) (July): 521–3.

——. 1895. The Children of Working London. In Bernard Bosanquet, ed., *Aspects of the Social Problem.* London and New York: Macmillan.

——. 1895. Dr Brentano on English Trade Unionism. *Economic Journal* 5(19) (September): 488–90.

——. 1895. The Meaning and Methods of True Charity. In Bernard Bosanquet, ed., *Aspects of the Social Problem.* London and New York: Macmillan.

——. 1895. Old Pensioners. In Bernard Bosanquet, ed., *Aspects of the Social Problem.* London and New York: Macmillan.

——. 1895. Origin and History of the English Poor Law. In Bernard Bosanquet, ed., *Aspects of the Social Problem.* London and New York: Macmillan.

——. 1895. The Socialist Propaganda. *National Review* 26 (September): 108–20.

Bosanquet, Helen Dendy. 1896. *Rich and Poor.* London and New York: Macmillan.

——. 1896. Book Review of "Poor Laws of Massachusetts and New York" by John Cummings. *Economic Journal* 6(21) (March): 94–5.

——. 1896. The Burden of Small Debts. *Economic Journal* 6(22) (June): 212–25.

——. 1896. The Moral Aspects of Socialism: Reply. *International Journal of Ethics* 6 (July): 509.

——. 1897. Book Review of "A Child of the Jago" by Arthur Morrison. *Charity Organisation Review*, n.s. 1 (January): 40–2.

——. 1897. Book Review of "German Social Democracy" by Bertrand Russell. *International Journal of Ethics* 8 (October): 130–1.

——. 1897. Book Review of "Juvenile Offenders" by W. D. Morrison. *International Journal of Ethics* 8 (October): 119–21.

——. 1897. Book Review of "Life in West London: A Study and a Contrast" by Arthur Sherwell. *Economic Journal* 7(25) (March): 85–7.

——. 1897. The Lines of Industrial Conflict. *Economic Journal* 7(28) (December): 503–10.

——. 1897. The Psychology of Social Progress. *International Journal of Ethics* 7 (April): 265–81.

——. 1898. *The Administration of Charitable Relief.* London: National Union of Women Workers.

——. 1898. *The Standard of Life and Other Studies*. London and New York: Macmillan.

——. 1898. Book Review of "Children Under the Poor Law" by W. Chance. *Economic Journal* 8(29) (March): 86–8.

——. 1898. Book Review of "The State and Charity" by Thomas Mackay. *Economic Journal* 8(30) (June): 216–18.

——. 1899. Book Review of "The Children's Labour Question." Reprinted from the *Daily News*, *Economic Journal* 9(34) (June): 228–9.

——. 1899. Book Review of "The Crowd" and "The Psychology of Peoples" by Gustave Le Bon. *International Journal of Ethics* 9 (July): 521–3.

——. 1899. Book Review of "The Development of Thrift" by Mary Willcox Brown. *Economic Journal* 9(34) (June): 229.

——. 1899. Book Review of "The Economic Foundations of Society" by Achille Loria. *International Journal of Ethics* 10 (October): 109–13.

——. 1899. Book Review of "Friendly Visiting among the Poor; A Handbook for Charity Workers" by Mary E. Richmond. *Economic Journal* 9(34) (June): 226–7.

——. 1899. Book Review of "Our Treatment of the Poor" by W. Chance. *Economic Journal* 9(36) (December): 563–4.

——. 1899. Book Review of "Problems of Modern Industry" by Sidney and Beatrice Webb. *International Journal of Ethics* 9(2) (January): 250–1.

——. 1900. People and Houses. *Economic Journal* 10 (March): 47–59.

——. 1900/1964. *The "Poverty Line."* London: Charity Organisation Society.

——. 1900. Methods of Training. *Charity Organisation Review* 44 (August): 103.

——. 1900/1. Book Review of "Chalmers on Charity" by N. Masterman, ed. *International Journal of Ethics* 11: 519.

——. 1900/1. Book Review of "The New Democracy" by Jethro Brown. *International Journal of Ethics* 11: 106.
——. 1901. Book Review of "The Case for the Factory Acts" by Mrs. Sidney Webb. *Economic Journal* 11(44) (December): 545–9.
——. 1901/2. Book Review of "Charity and the Poor Law" by S. D. Fuller. *International Journal of Ethics* 12: 530.
——. 1901/2. Book Review of "Public Relief of the Poor" by Thomas Mackay. *International Journal of Ethics* 12: 528.
——. 1902. *The Strength of the People: A Study in Social Economics*. London: Macmillan & Co.
——. 1902. Book Review of "Charity and the Poor Law" by S. D. Fuller. *Economic Journal* 12: 62.
——. 1902. A Study in Women's Wages. *Economic Journal* 12 (March): 42–9.
——. 1902. Women and Work in England. *International Monthly* 5 (January/June): 34.
——. 1903. The Administration of Charity in England. *International Quarterly* 7 (March/September): 392–.
——. 1903. Book Review of "Life and Labour of the People in London" by Charles Booth. *Economic Journal* 13: 409.
——. 1903. The "Poverty Line." *Charity Organisation Review* (January): 8–23.
——. 1903. Report of the Proceedings of the Third International Congress for the Welfare and Protection of Children. *Economic Journal* 13: 413.
——. 1904. *Wages and Housekeeping*. In C.S. Loch, ed., *Methods of Social Advance*. London: Macmillan.
——. 1904. Book Review of "Subdivision and Education in Charity" by Jeffrey Richardson Brackett. *Economic Journal* 14: 105.
——. 1904. Physical Deterioration and the Poverty Line. *Contemporary Review* (January).
——. 1905. *Home and School in the Life of the Child*. A lecture by Mrs. Bosanquet, delivered October 1905 under the joint auspices of the Carnegie Dunferline Trust and the school board of the burg of Dunfermline. Dunfermline: A. Romanes and Son.
——. 1905. Book Review of "The Danish Poor Relief System: An Example for England" by Edith Sellers. *Economic Journal* 15: 94.
——. 1905. Book Review of "Modern Methods of Charity" by Charles Richmond Henderson. *Economic Journal* 15: 97.
——. 1905. Book Review of "Poverty" by Robert Hunter. *Economic Journal* 15: 97.
——. 1905. Review of the Danish Poor Relief System: An Example for England. *Economic Journal* 15(57) (March): 94–6.
——. 1905/6. Book Review of "The Duties of Women" by Frances Power Cobbe. *International Journal of Ethics* 16: 398.
——. 1905/6. The Intellectual Influence of Women. *International Journal of Ethics* 16: 15.
——. 1906. *The Family*. London and New York: Macmillan.

——. 1906. Book Review of "Die Errichtung eines Institutes für Soziale Arbeit und die Organisation der Wohltätigkeit in München" by Dr. Karl von Singer. *Charity Organisation Review* 113 (May): 263–.

——. 1906. Book Review of "A History of English Philanthropy. From the Dissolution of the Monasteries to the Taking of the First Census" by B. Kirkman Gray. *Economic Journal* 16: 398.

——. 1906. Book Review of "Women's Work and Wages" by Edward Cadbury. *Charity Organisation Review* 118 (October): 221.

——. 1907. Book Review of "The Infant, the Parent, and the State" by H. Llewellyn Heath. *Economic Journal* 17: 383.

——. 1909. *The Poor Law Report of 1909*. London: Macmillan.

——. 1910. Book Review of "Social Forces" by Edward T. Devine. *Economic Journal* 20: 84.

——. 1910. Book Review of "Where Shall She Live?" by Mary Higgs and Edward E. Hayward. *Economic Journal* 20: 419.

——. 1910. The Historical Basis of English Poor-Law Policy. *Economic Journal* 20(78) (June): 182–94.

——. 1910. Old Age Pensions under the Act of 1908. *Cornhill Magazine* 3(28): 658.

——. 1911. Book Review of "The Child Labour Policy of New Jersey" by Arthur Sargent Field. *Economic Journal* 21: 249.

——. 1911. Book Review of "Child Problems" by George B. Mangold. *Economic Journal* 21: 248.

——. 1911. Book Review of "National Conference on the Prevention of Destitution (Report of the Proceedings)". *Economic Journal* 21: 585.

——. 1911. Book Review of "Die Psychologie der Frauen" by G. Heymans. *Mind* 20: 419–.

——. 1911. Book Review of "Women and Labour" by Olive Schreiner. *Economic Journal* 21(82) (June): 250–3.

——. 1911. The Claim of Married Women under the State Insurance Bill. *Academy* 80 (January/June): 769.

——, ed. 1912. *Social Conditions in Provincial Towns (First Series)*. London: Macmillan.

——. 1912/13. English Divorce Law and the Report of the Royal Commission. *International Journal of Ethics* 23: 443.

——. 1913/14. The Divorce Laws of England and Wales: Discussion. *International Journal of Ethics* 24: 451.

——. 1914. *Social Work in London, 1869–1912. A History of the Charity Organisation Society*. London: John Murray. Reprinted New York: A. M. Kelley, 1970.

——. 1914. Review of "Round about a Pound a Week". *Economic Journal* 24(93) (March): 109–12.

——. 1916. Review of Memoranda issued by the Health of Munition Works Committee. *Economic Journal* 26(102) (June): 209–18.

——. 1916. Review of "Women in Modern Industry". *Economic Journal* 26(102) (June): 209–18.

——. 1916/17. Reconstruction – Of What? *Hibbert Journal* 15 (October/July): 542–.

——. 1917. Housing Conditions in London. *Economic Journal* 27 (September): 330–45.

——. 1920. The Race for the Chinaman's Nightcap. *Economic Journal* 30 (September): 308–20.

——. 1921. Book Review of "The Slippery Slope" by William Amias Bailward. *Economic Journal* 31: 104–.

——. 1924. *Free Trade and Peace in the Nineteenth Century*. London: Williams and Norgate; Kristiania, Oslo: H. Aschehoug & Co. (W. Nygaard); New York: G. P. Putnam's Sons.

——. 1924. Book Review of "Bernard Bosanquet: A Short Account of His Life by M.J." *International Journal of Ethics* 35: 196–.

Bosanquet, Helen and Bernard Bosanquet. 1897. Charity Organisation: A Reply. *Contemporary Review* 71 (January): 112–16.

Bosanquet, Helen, Louise Creighton, and Beatrice Webb. 1897. Law and the Laundry: Commercial Laundries. *Nineteenth Century* 41 (February): 224–31.

Boserup, Ester. 1936. Nogle centrale okonomiske Sporgsmaal i Lys af den marxistiske Terori [Some central economic problems in the light of Marxian theory]. *Nationalokonomisk Tidsskrift* 74: 421–35.

Bostick, Mary Lenore. 1940. The Shade Tobacco Industry of Gadsden County, Florida. S.M. thesis, University of Chicago (economics, agricultural).

Boswell, Louise. 1932. The Apple Industry of the Ontario Plain. M.S. thesis, University of Chicago (economics, agricultural).

Bosworth, Louise Marion. 1910/1919. *Housing Conditions in Main Line Towns: An Investigation Made under the Direction of the Committee on Investigation, Main Line Housing Association*. Philadelphia: Harper.

——. 1911. The Living Wage of Women Workers. *Annals of the American Academy of Political and Social Science* 37, Supplement (May).

——. 1911. *The Living Wage of Women Workers. A Study of Incomes and Expenditures of 450 Women Workers in the City of Boston*. New York: Longmans, Green and Company.

Botte, Camille J. 1935. Recent Developments in Urban Transportation. Ph.D. thesis, Harvard University (economics).

Boucherett, [Emilia] Jessie. 1860. On the Obstacles to the Employment of Women. *English Woman's Journal* IV (February): 361–75. Reprinted in Candida Ann Lacey, ed., *Barbara Leigh Smith Bodichon and the Langham Place Group*. New York and London: Routledge & Kegan Paul, 1987.

——. 1860. On the Education of Girls, with Reference to their Future Position. Paper read at the conference of the National Association for Promotion of Social Science. *English Woman's Journal* VI (December): 217–24. Reprinted in Candida Ann Lacey, ed., *Barbara Leigh Smith Bodichon and the Langham Place Group*. London and New York: Routledge, 1987.

——. 1861. Local Societies [for promoting the employment of women]. Paper read at the conference of the National Association for Promotion of Social

Science. *English Woman's Journal* VIII (December). Reprinted in Candida Ann Lacey, ed., *Barbara Leigh Smith Bodichon and the Langham Place Group*. London and New York: Routledge, 1987.
——. 1862. Endowed Schools, Their Uses and their Shortcomings. *English Woman's Journal* IX (March): 20–9.
——. 1862. On the Choice of a Business. *English Woman's Journal* X (November): 145. Reprinted in Candida Ann Lacey, ed., *Barbara Leigh Smith Bodichon and the Langham Place Group*. London: Routledge, 1987.
——. 1863. *Hints on Self-Help: A Book for Young Women*. London, S. W. Partridge.
——. 1863. The Temperance Movement and Working Women. *English Woman's Journal* XI (May): 176–80.
——. 1864. On the Cause of the Distress Prevalent among Single Women. Paper read at the conference of the National Association for Promotion of Social Science. *English Woman's Journal*, XII (February): 300–9. Reprinted in Candida Ann Lacey, ed., *Barbara Leigh Smith Bodichon and the Langham Place Group*. London and New York: Routledge, 1987.
——. 1866. The Work We Have to Do. *Englishwoman's Review of Social and Industrial Questions* I (October): 1–5.
——. 1867. The Condition of Women in France, *Contemporary Review* 5 (May): 98–113.
——. 1869. How to Provide for Superfluous Women. In Josephine Butler, ed., *Woman's Work and Woman's Culture, a Series of Essays*. London: Macmillan.
——. 1870. The Probable Use Women Would Make of the Political Franchise. Paper read at the annual meeting of the National Association for the Promotion of Social Science.
——. 1873. Legislative Restrictions on Woman's Labour. *Englishwoman's Review*, n.s. 16 (October): 249–58. Reprinted London: Frederick Bell & Co.
——. 1874. Occupations of Women. *Englishwoman's Review*, n.s. 18 (April): 85–90.
——. 1878. The Agar–Ellis Case. *Englishwoman's Review*, n.s. 68 (December): 537–.
——. 1879. Agriculture as an Employment for Women. *Englishwoman's Review*, n.s. 79 (November): 481–4.
——. 1884. The Industrial Movement. In Theodore Stanton, ed., *The Woman Question in Europe*. New York: G. P. Putnam's Sons.
——. 1887. The Primrose League and Women. *Englishwoman's Review*, n.s. 176 (December 15): 537–.
——. 1894. Lead Works and Some Other Unhealthy Industries. *Englishwoman's Review* 221 (January): 11–12.
——. 1894–5. The Report on the Employment of Women by the Lady Assistant Commissioners. *Englishwoman's Review* 221 [(25) (January)]: 1–9; 222 [(25) (April)]: 73–9; 223 [(25) (July)]: 149–56; 225 [(26) (January)]: 10–17; 226 [(26) (April)]: 77–90.
——. 1899. Lead Poison in Pottery Work. *Englishwoman's Review* 30 [n.s. 242] (April): 98–102.

Boucherett, Emilia Jessie and Helen Blackburn. 1896. *The Condition of Working Women and the Factory Acts.* London: Elliot Stock.

Boucherett, Emilia Jessie. Coauth. *See* Blackburn, Helen.

Boughner, Genevieve. 1926. *Women in Journalism.* New York: D. Appleton and Co.

Bouvier, Jeanne. 1930. *Histoire des dames employées dans les postes, télégraphes, et téléphones de 1714–1929.* Paris: s.n.

Bowen, Louise De Koven. 1911. *The Department Store Girl: Based upon Interviews with Two Hundred Girls.* Chicago: s.n.

——. 1913. *The Colored People of Chicago.* Chicago: s.n.

——. 1914. *Safeguards for City Youth at Work and at Play.* New York: Macmillan.

Bowen, Margaret. 1929. $10.64 a Week: First Hand Testimony by A Textile Striker at Elizabethton, Tennessee. *New Republic* 59 (May 29): 41–3.

Bowley, Marian. 1936. Nassau Senior's Contribution to the Methodology of Economics. *Economica*, n.s. 3(11) (August): 281–305.

——. 1937. *Nassau Senior and Classical Economics.* London: Allen & Unwin.

——. 1937. Book Review of "Prezzie Mercati" by P. Jannaccone. *Economica* 4: 229.

——. 1937. Fluctuations in Housebuilding and the Trade Cycle. *Review of Economic Studies* 4(3) (June): 167–81.

——. 1938. Book Review of "Saving and Investment" by W. E. Armstrong. *Economica* 5: 251.

——. 1938. Some Regional Aspects of the Building Boom, 1924–36. *Review of Economic Studies* 5(3) (June): 172–86.

——. 1939. Book Review of "A History of Economic Thought" by E. Roll. *Economica* 6: 98–.

——. 1939. Book Review of "De la Nature de la richesse et de l'origine de la valeur" by A. Walras. *Economica* 6: 367–.

——. 1939. Book Review of "An Outline of the Science of Political Economy" by N. W. Senior. *Economica* 6: 368–.

——. 1939. Book Review of "Les Théories de l'équilibre économique: L. Walras et V. Pareto" by G. Pirou. *Economica* 6: 365–.

——. 1940. Book Review of "The Economics of Building" by H. W. Robinson. *Economica* 7: 98.

——. 1940. Local Rates and Housing Subsidies. *Review of Economic Studies* 6(1) (October): 33–43.

Bowley, Ruth. 1933. How the Workless Spend their Money. *Listener* 10(246) (September 27): 462–.

——. 1934. The Cost of Living of Girls Professionally Employed in the County of London. *Economic Journal* 44 (June): 328–34.

Bowman, Mary Jean. 1938. Economic Aspects of the Histories of Reformatory Women: A Study of Women Committed to the Massachusetts State Reformatory. Ph.D. thesis, Radcliffe College (economics).

——. 1939. Considerations in Developing a General Course in Consumption. *Journal of Marketing* 4(1) (July): 20.

——. 1939/40. Causes of Arrests of Women Committed to the Massachusetts State Reformatory. *Journal of Criminal Law and Criminology and Police Science* 30: 77–.

——. 1940. The Educational Equipment of Delinquent Women. *Harvard Educational Review* 10 (January/December): 60–.

Boyce, Helen. 1917. The Mines of the Upper Harz from 1514 to 1589. Ph.D. thesis, University of Chicago (economics, history).

Boyd, M. C. 1931. *Alabama in the Fifties: A Social Study*. New York: Columbia University Press.

Boyer, Helen M. 1939. Distribution of Sugar Cane Production in Cuba. *Economic Geography* 15(3) (July): 311–25.

Boyle, Ruth. 1929. A Business Girl's Investments. *Good Housekeeping* (July): 108.

——. 1929. Is this Stock High? *Good Housekeeping* (August): 112.

Brackett, Anna C. 1890. The Strange Tale of a Type-writer. *Harper's* 81 (October): 679–82.

Bradbury, Harriet B. 1899. War as a Necessity of Evolution. *Arena* 21 (January): 94–6.

Bradby, L. Barbara. *See* Hammond, Barbara Bradby.

Bradley, Edith. 1898. Agricultural Brigade of the Monstrous Regiment of Women. *Review of Reviews* 17 (March): 346.

——. 1898. Correspondence: The Agricultural Brigade of the Monstrous Regiment of Women. *Fortnightly Review* 69 [n.s. 63] (February): 334–7.

Bradley, Edith and Bertha La Mothe. 1903. *The Lighter Branches of Agriculture*. London: Chapman & Hall.

Bradley, Harriett. 1915. Book Review of "Croce's Historical Materialism and the Economics of Karl Marx." *Journal of Philosophy, Psychology and Scientific Methods* 12(26) (December 23): 718–.

——. 1916. Book Review of "English Field Systems" by H. L. Gray. *Political Science Quarterly* 31: 453–.

——. 1917. English Enclosures in England: An Economic Reconstruction. Ph.D. thesis, Columbia University.

——. 1918. *The Enclosures in England: An Economic Reconstruction*. New York: Longmans, Green & Co.

Bradley, Virginia. 1939. The Petroleum Industry of the Gulf Coast Sal Dome Area. *Economic Geography* 15(4) (October): 395–407.

Brady, Dorothy Stahl. 1933. On the Solution of the Homogeneous Linear Integral Equation. Ph.D. thesis, University of California–Berkeley (mathematics).

——. 1938. Variations in Family Living Expenditures. *Journal of the American Statistical Assocation* 33 (June): 385–9.

Brady, Dorothy S., Day Monroe, Janet Murray, Yetta A. Carmel, and Marjorie W. Ellsworth. 1940/1941. *Changes in Assets and Liabilities of Families, Five Regions*. Consumer Purchases Study: Urban, Village, and Farm, U.S. Dept. of Agriculture, Miscellaneous Publication no. 399. Washington: U.S. Government Printing Office.

Brady, Dorothy S., Day Monroe, Elizabeth Phelps, and Edith Rainboth. 1940. Family Expenditures, Five Regions. In *Family Income and Expenditures*. United States Department of Agriculture, Miscellaneous Publication no. 339. Washington: U.S. Government Printing Office.

Brady, Dorothy S., Day Monroe, Gertrude S. Weiss, and Thelma Dreis. 1940. Family Income. Southeast Region. In *Family Income and Expenditures*. United States Department of Agriculture, Miscellaneous Publication no. 339. Washington: U.S. Government Printing Office.

Brady, Dorothy S. Coauth. *See* Monroe, Day.

Braithwaite, Constance. 1938. *The Voluntary Citizen: An Enquiry into the Place of Philanthrophy in the Community*. London: Methuen.

Braithwaite, Dorothea Cotter Morison. 1924. The Recent History of the Copper Trade. *Economica* 4 (November): 353–68.

——. 1928. The Economic Effects of Advertisement. *Economic Journal* 38 (March): 16–37.

——. 1932. *The Distribution of Consumable Goods: An Economic Study*. London: G. Routledge.

Branch, Mary Sydney. 1934. *Women and Wealth, a Study of the Economic Status of American Women*. Chicago: University of Chicago Press.

Brandeis, Elizabeth [Mrs. Paul Rauschenbush]. 1922. Mercantile Wages in the District of Columbia. *Monthly Labor Review* 15 (July/December): 113–14.

——. 1928. The Wage Earner and the Common Rule – A Study of the Employer–Employee Relation. Ph.D. thesis, University of Wisconsin.

——. 1933. Official Challenge to Fatalism in Industry. *American Labor Legislation Review* 23: 137–41.

——. 1935. Economic and Administrative Criteria for a Social Insurance Program. *American Labor Legislation Review* 25: 19–29.

——. 1935. Economic and Administrative Criteria for a Social Insurance Program [summary]. *American Sociological Society, Proceedings* 29(3) (August): 165–.

——. 1935–6. Labor Legislation. In John R. Commons *et al.*, *History of Labor in the United States*, vol. 3 (of 4). New York: Macmillan.

——. 1936. The Employment Reserve Type of Unemployment Compensation Law. *Law and Contemporary Problems* 3: 54–.

——. 1937. A Progress Report from Wisconsin. *American Labor Legislation Review* 27: 61–70.

——. 1937. Unemployment Compensation in Action. *American Labor Legislation Review* 27: 61–70.

——. 1940. Federal Threat to State Progress in Unemployment Compensation. *American Labor Legislation Review* 30: 151–8.

——. Coauth. *See* True, Ruth Smiley.

Brandt, Gladys Lillian. 1928. The San Fernando Valley: A Study in Changing Adjustment between Its Economic Life and Its Natural Environment. M.S. thesis, University of Chicago (geography).

Brandt, Lilian. 1899. The Massachusetts Slave Trade. *New England Magazine* 21 (September): 83–96.

——. 1902–3. Negroes in St. Louis. *Publications of the American Statistical Association* 8: 203.

——. 1903. Social Aspects of Tuberculosis. *American Academy of Political and Social Science, Annals* 21 (January/June): 407.

——. 1905. *Five Hundred and Seventy-four Deserters and Their Families*. New York: Charity Organization Society.

——. 1908. The Causes of Poverty. *Political Science Quarterly* (December).

——. 1910. Characteristics of Social Work in the United States. *Chautauquan* 60 (September/November): 102.

——. 1915. *Facts about the Death Rate*. New York: New York School of Philanthropy.

——. 1916. *Facts about Tuberculosis*. New York: New York School of Philanthropy.

——. 1921. *How Much Shall I Give?* New York: Frontier Press.

——. 1932. *An Impressionistic View of the Winter of 1930–31 in New York City, Based on Statements from Some 900 Social Workers and Public Health Nurses*. New York: Welfare Council of New York City.

——. 1933. *Glimpses of New York in Previous Depressions: An Interim Report Made as a Feature of the Study of Social Welfare during the Business Depression*. New York: Welfare Council of New York City Research Bureau.

Braun, Lily. 1895. *Die Bürgerpflicht der Frau*. Lecture held in Dresden, Breslau, and Berlin. Berlin: F. Dümmler.

——. 1895. *Die Stellung der Frau in der Gegenwart*. Lecture held by the Berlin Department of the German Society for Ethical Culture and the Leipzig Society for Ethical Culture. Berlin: F. Dümmler.

——. 1896. *Frauenfrage und Sozialdemokratie; Reden anlässlich des Internationalen Frauenkongresses zu Berlin*. Berlin: Expedition der Bucchandlung Vorwärts.

——. 1901. *Frauenarbeit und Hauswirtschaft*. Berlin: Expedition der Buchhandlung Vorwärts (Th. Glocke in Berlin).

——. 1901. *Die Frauenfrage: ihre geschichtliche Entwicklung und wirtschaftliche Seite*. Leipzig: S. Hirzel.

——. 1903. *Die Frauen und die Politik*. Berlin: Verlag Vorwärts.

Braun, Stefanie and Carla Zaglitz. 1930. *Frauenbewegung, Frauenbildung und Frauenarbeit in Österreich*. Vienna: s.n.

Bray, Caroline [Hennell]. 1863. *The British Empire: A Sketch of the Geography, Growth, Natural and Political Features of the United Kingdom, Its Colonies and Dependencies*. London: Longman, Green, Longman, Roberts and Green.

Breckinridge, Sophonisba Preston. 1901. Legal Tender: A Study in English and American Monetary History. Ph.D. thesis, University of Chicago (political science).

——. 1901. Specie Contracts. *Journal of Political Economy* 9(3) (June): 437–9.

——. 1901/2. Book Review of "Domestic Service" by Lucy M. Salmon. *American Journal of Sociology* 7(1/6): 282.

——. 1903. *Legal Tender: A Study in English and American Monetary History*. Chicago: University of Chicago Press.

——. 1905. Two Decisions Relating to Organized Labor. *Journal of Political Economy* 13(4) (September): 593–7.

——. 1906. Legislative Control of Women's Work. *Journal of Political Economy* 14(2) (February): 107–9.

——. 1907. The Proper Attitude of Women's Trade Unions Toward the Marriage of Women Workers. *Public* 10(489) (August 17): 474.

——. 1907/8. Book Review of "Women's Work and Wages" by Edward Cadbury. *American Journal of Sociology* 13(1/6): 411.

——. 1908/9. Child-labor Legislation. *Elementary School Journal* 9(1/10): 511–.

——. 1910. *Concerning the Garment Workers Strike*. Chicago: Report of the Sub-Committee to the Citizen's Committee, November 5, 1910. Microfilm. Woodbridge, Conn., Research Publications, 1977. History of Women; reel 944, no. 8605.

——. 1910. The Illinois Ten-hour Law. *Journal of Political Economy* 18(6) (June): 465–70.

——. 1910. Neglected Widowhood in the Juvenile Court. *American Journal of Sociology* 16(1) (July): 53–87.

——. 1911. Beginnings of Child Labor Legislation. *Survey* 27 (21 October).

——. ed. 1912. *The Child in the City*. Chicago: Hollister Press.

Breckinridge, S. P. 1911/12. Book Review of "Half a Man. The Status of the Negro in New York" by M. W. Ovington. *American Journal of Sociology* 17(1/6): 414.

——. 1913. The Color Line in the Housing Problem. *Survey* 29 (February): 575–6.

——. 1913/14. Book Review of "The Charity Visitor: A Practical Handbook for Beginners" by Amelia Sears. *American Journal of Sociology* 19(1/6): 269.

——. 1914. The Family in the Community, but Not Yet of the Community. *Proceedings of the National Conference of Charities and Corrections* 41 (May): 69–75.

——. 1914. Political Equality for Women and Women's Wages. *Annals of the American Academy of Political and Social Science* 56 (November): 122–33.

——. 1914/15. Book Review of "Round about a Pound a Week" by Mrs. Pember Reeves. *American Journal of Sociology* 20(1/6): 831.

——. 1915. Book Review of "Problems of Child Welfare" by Mangold. *American Economic Review* 5(1/2): 384.

——. 1915. A Recent English Case on Women and the Legal Profession. Note in *Journal of Political Economy* 23(1) (January): 64–70.

——. 1917. Social Control Of Child Welfare. *American Sociological Society, Papers and Proceedings* 12 (December): 11–.

——. 1919. Book Review of "Italian Women in Industry: A Study of Conditions in New York City" by Odencrantz. *Journal of Political Economy* 27: 518.

——. 1921. *New Homes for Old*. New York and London: Harper.

——. 1923. The Home Responsibilities of Women Workers and the "Equal Wage." *Journal of Political Economy* 31(4): 521–43.

——. 1923. Summary of the Present State Systems for the Organization and Administration of Public Welfare. *Annals of the American Academy of Political and Social Science* 105 (January): 3–103.

——. 1924/1932/1934. *Family Welfare Work in a Metropolitan Community: Selected Case Records*. University of Chicago Social Service Series. Chicago: University of Chicago Press.

——. 1924. Introductory Note. In Edith Abott, *Women in Industry. A Study in American Economic History*. New York: D. Appleton and Company.

——. 1925. The Family and the Law. *Proceedings of the National Conference of Social Work* 52 (June): 290–7.

——. 1927. *Public Welfare Administration of the U.S.* Chicago: University of Chicago Press. Revised 1938.

——. 1927. Frontiers of Control in Public Welfare Administration. *Social Service Review* 1(1) (March): 84–99.

——. 1927. Widows' and Orphans' Pensions in Great Britain. *Social Service Review* 1 (June): 249–57.

——. 1930. Public Welfare Organization with Reference to Child Welfare Activities. *Social Service Review* (September): 376–422.

——. 1930. Separate Domicil for Married Women. *Social Service Review* 4 (March): 37–52.

——. 1931. *Marriage and the Civil Rights of Women*. Chicago: University of Chicago Press.

——. 1932. Children and the Depression. *Proceedings of the National Conference of Social Work* 59 (May): 126–35.

——. 1933. *Women in the Twentieth Century. A Study of Their Political, Social, and Economic Activities*. New York and London: McGraw Hill Book Company, Inc. Reprinted in the American Women: Image and Realities Series, New York: Arno Press, 1972.

——. 1933. The Activities of Women Outside the Home. In Wesley Mitchell, ed., *Recent Social Trends*, vol. 1. New York: McGraw-Hill.

——. 1933. University Women in the New Order. *American Association of University Women, Journal* 26(4) (June): 195–.

——. 1933/4. Book Review of "James Stansfeld, a Victorian Champion of Sex Equality" by J. L. Hammond and Barbara Hammond. *American Journal of Sociology* 39(1/6): 266.

——. 1934. *The Family and the State*. Chicago: University of Chicago Press.

——. 1934/5. Book Review of "The Courts and the Public Schools: The Legal Basis of School Organization and Administration" by Newton Edwards. *American Journal of Sociology* 40(1/6): 686.

——. 1934/5. Book Review of "An Introduction to Homemaking and Its Relation to the Community" by Willie Melmoth Bomar. *American Journal of Sociology* 40(1/6): 387.

——. 1935. *Public Welfare Administration in the United States: Select Documents*. University of Chicago Social Services Series, 3rd impression. Chicago: University of Chicago Press.

——. 1936. Book Review of "The Family and the State." *Charity Organisation Quarterly* 10(1) (January): 47.

——. 1936. Book Review of "Social Work and the Courts." *Charity Organisation Quarterly* 10(1) (January): 45.

——. 1936. The New Horizons of Professional Education for Social Work. *Social Service Review* 10(1/4) (March/December): 437–.

——. 1937. *Social Security and Public Welfare: A Comprehensive Program.* Address delivered at Rockefeller Memorial Chapel, University of Chicago, October 24, 1937. Chicago: s.n.

——. 1938. Social Workers in the Courts of Cook County. *Social Service Review* 12(1/4) (March/December): 230–.

——. 1938/9. Book Review of "American Family Laws, 1938, Supplement". *American Journal of Sociology* 44(1/6): 757.

——. 1939. *The Illinois Poor Law and Its Administration.* Chicago: University of Chicago Press.

——. 1939. Grace Abbott and Education for Social Work. *Child* 4(2) (August): 50–.

——. 1939. Statutory Provision for the Commitment of Insane Persons. *Social Service Review* 13(1/4) (March/December): 221–.

——. 1940. Government's Role in Child Welfare. *American Academy of Political and Social Science, Annals* 212 (November): 42–.

Breckinridge, Sophonisba Preston and Edith Abbott. 1910. Chicago's Housing Problem: Families in Furnished Rooms. *American Journal of Sociology* 16(3) (November): 289–308.

——. 1910/1915. Families in Furnished Rooms. In Edith Abbott and Sophonisba Preston Breckinridge, *The Housing Problem in Chicago.* Chicago: University of Chicago Press.

——. 1910/1915. South Chicago at the Gates of the Steel Mills. In Edith Abbott and Sophonisba Preston Breckinridge, *The Housing Problem in Chicago.* Chicago: University of Chicago Press.

——. 1910/1915. The Twenty-Ninth Ward Back of the Yards. In Edith Abbott and Sophonisba Preston Breckinridge, *The Housing Problem in Chicago.* Chicago: University of Chicago Press.

——. 1911. *Chicago Housing Conditions; V. South Chicago at the Gates of the Steel Mills.* Chicago: University of Chicago Press. Reprinted in *American Journal of Sociology* 17 (September 1911).

——. 1911. Chicago Housing Conditions, IV: The West Side Revisited. *American Journal of Sociology* 17(1) (July): 1–34.

——. 1911. Chicago Housing Conditions, V: South Chicago at the Gates of the Steel Mills. *American Journal of Sociology* 17(2) (September): 145–76.

——. 1911. Housing Conditions in Chicago, III: Back of the Yards. *American Journal of Sociology* 16(4) (January): 433–68.

——. 1924. The Graduate School of Social Service Administration: Material Submitted to Dean Tufts. *The University Presidents' Papers 1889–1925,* University of Chicago Archives, Box 61, Folder 13.

Breckinridge, Sophonisba and Grace Abbott. 1936. New Chapters in the History of the Courts and Social Legislation. *Social Service Review* 10 (December): 483–99.

Breckinridge, Sophonisba Preston and Marion Talbot. 1912/1919. *The Modern Household.* Boston: Whitcomb & Barrows.

Breckenridge, Sophonisba Preston, Edith Abbott, and Anne Sophia Davis. 1911. *Finding Employment for Children Who Leave the Grade Schools to Go to Work: Report to the Chicago Woman's Club, the Chicago Association of Collegiate Alumnae and the Woman's City Club.* Chicago: Manz Engraving Co., Hollister Press, for the Chicago School of Civics and Philanthropy, Department of Social Investigation.

Breckinridge, S. P., Alice Shaffer, and Mary Wysor Keefer. 1936/7 Book Review of "The Indiana Poor Law" by Carl M. Rosenquist. *International Journal of Ethics* 47: 127.

Breckinridge, Sophonisba Preston. Coauth. *See* Abbott, Grace; Bruce, Isabel Campbell; Kennedy, Aileen Elizabeth; Milchrist, Elizabeth Hayward; Shaffer, Alice; Wright, Helen Russell.

——. Papers located in the Breckinridge Family Papers at the Library of Congress.

Bremer, Fredrika. 1854/1856. *Hertha: eller, En Sjals Historia.* English edition, *Hertha*, transl. Mary Howitt. New York: Putnam; London: Arthur Hall. [*feminist novel*]

Bremner, Christina S[inclair]. 1888. Women in the Labour Market. *National Review* 11 (June): 458–70.

——. 1894. The Financial Dependence of Women. *North American Review* 158(3) (March): 382–4.

——. 1894. Hadleigh Farm Colony. *Lend a Hand* 13(4) (October): 285–.

——. 1897. *Education of Girls and Women in Great Britain.* London: Swan Sonnenschein & Co., Ltd.

——. 1898. American Women – Some Results of Their Education. *Journal of Education*, n.s. 20: 667–.

Brewer, Mrs. Emma. 1898. Gentlewomen Who Devote Their Lives to the Poor. *A Girl's Own Paper* 19 (February): 241–; (May): 500–; (June): 614–; (July): 638–; (August): 708–; (September): 781–.

Brewington, Ann Elizabeth. 1922. Prognostic Tests for Typewriting. M.A. thesis, University of Chicago (education).

——. 1926. Measurement and Testing of Commercial Achievements. *School and Society* 24(611) (September 11): 334–.

——. 1928. The National Association of Commercial Teacher-training Institutions. *Journal of Business of the University of Chicago* 1(3) (July): 388–9.

——. 1930. *Occupational Survey of Women Graduates of the School of Commerce and Administration, the University of Chicago.* Chicago: s.n.

——. 1931. Commercial Teacher Training. *School and Society* 33(856) (May 23): 702–.

——. 1937. *Direct-method Materials for Gregg Shorthand: Teacher's Manual.* New York: Gregg Publishing Company.

——. 1938. Money Management in the Public Schools. *National Business Education Quarterly* 8(2) (December): 9–.

——. 1938. What Children Think Money Is. *Banking* 30(10) (April): 32–.

——. 1939. *State Certification of Teachers of Business Education.* National Association of Commercial Teacher-training Institutions Bulletin, no. 16. Muncie, Ind.: National Association of Commercial Teacher-training Institutions.

——. 1939. Bibliography on Money Management for High School and Junior College. *National Business Education Quarterly* 8(2) (December): 41–.

Brewington, Ann and Verona B. Knisely. 1935. *The Social Concept of Money: A Bibliography.* Chicago: University of Chicago Press.

Brewington, Ann and Frances Nies Schrampfer. 1935. *Student's Shorthand Work Book for Use with Direct-method Materials for Gregg Shorthand.* New York: Gregg Publishing Co.

Brewington, Ann and Helen Ida Soutter. 1933. *Key to Direct-method Materials for Gregg Shorthand.* New York: Gregg Publishing Co.

Brewster, Alice Rollins. 1895. Early Experiments with the Unemployed. *Quarterly Journal of Economics* 9 (October): 88–95.

Brewster, Ethel Hampson. 1915. Roman Craftsmen and Tradesmen of the Early Empire. Ph.D. thesis, University of Pennsylvania (history).

——. 1926. Cambridgeshire and Its Lunitic [*sic*] Paupers and Criminals. M.A. thesis, University of Liverpool.

——. 1934/1984. *The Treatment of Poverty in Cambridgeshire, 1597–1834.* Cambridge, UK: Cambridge University Press.

Brewster, Margaret Maria. 1858. *Household Economy: A Manual Intended for Female Training Colleges and Senior Classes of Girls' Schools.* Edinburgh: Thomas Constable and Co.; London: Hamilton, Adams, and Co.

Briggs, Amelia C. 1898. A Tramp's Experience: A True Story. *Arena* 20 (August): 278–83.

Bright, Joanna. 1935. *Housewives and Downing Street: An Average Woman Looks at the Work of the National Government.* London: Ivor Nicholson and Watson.

Brion, Hélène. 1916. *La Voie féministe.* Paris: s.n.

Britton, Virginia. 1938. Iowa Incomes as Reported in Income Tax Returns. *Iowa Agricultural Experiment State Bulletin* 236 (June): 224–41.

——. 1938. Personal-loan Credit Versus Installment-store Credit from the Viewpoint of the Borrower. Ph.D. thesis, University of Chicago (business administration, banking).

——. 1940. *Housing of 299 Vermont Village Families.* Burlington: Vermont Agricultural Experiment Station.

Brodie, Emily. 1881. *Uncle Fred's Shilling: Its Travels and Adventures.* London: John F. Shaw. [*juvenile fiction*]

Brokaw, Estella Bachman. 1896. Representative Women on Social Problems: Is the Single Tax Enough? (Symposium). *Arena* 15 (January): 201–6.

Brokaw, Estella Bachman *et al.* 1894. The Land Question: A Woman's Symposium. *Arena* 10: 622–47.

Bromley, Dorothy Dunbar. 1926/7. The Ethics of Alimony. *Harper's Magazine* 154 (December/May): 305.

——. 1926/7. The Market Value of a Paris Divorce. *Harper's Magazine* 154 (December/May): 669–.

——. 1928. Are Women a Success in Business? *Harper's Magazine* 156(933) (February): 299–.

——. 1929. This Question of Birth Control. *Harper's Magazine* 160(955) (December): 34–.

——. 1930. The Crisis in Nursing. *Harper's Magazine* 161(962) (July): 159–.

——. 1933. New Move to End Child Labor. *Current History* 38(5) (August): 564.

——. 1934. Birth Control and the Depression, *Harper's* 169 (October): 563–.

——. 1934. Have the Veterans a Case? *Today* 1(23) (March 31): 10.

Bronson, Minnie. 1910/1912/1914. *Wage-earning Woman and the State: A Comparison of the Laws for Her Protection in Various States of the Union.* Boston: Massachusetts Association Opposed to the Further Extension of Suffrage to Women.

——. 1912. *The Wage-earning Woman and the State: A Reply to Miss Goldmark and Mrs. Kelley*. Boston: Massachusetts Association Opposed to the Further Extension of Suffrage to Women.

——. 1914. *Woman Suffrage and Child Labor Legislation.* New York: National Association Opposed to Woman Suffrage.

——. Coauth. *See* Goldmark, Pauline Dorothea.

Brook, Elizabeth. 1937/8. Federalist Jeremiahs. *American Historical Review* 43: 74–.

Brook, Elizabeth Cable. 1925. The Struggle for the Adoption of the Interstate Commerce Commission, 1872–1887. Ph.D. thesis, University of Chicago (history).

Brooke, Emma. 1898. *A Tabulation of the Factory Laws of European Countries, in So Far as They Relate to the Hours of Labor and to Special Legislation for Women, Young Persons, and Children.* London: Grant Richards.

——. 1909. *A Summary of Six Papers and Discussions upon the Disabilities of Women as Workers.* London: Fabian Women's Group.

Brophy, Loire. 1936. *If Women Must Work.* New York and London: D. Appleton-Century, Co.

——. 1938. *Men Must Work.* New York and London: D. Appleton-Century, Co.

Broughton, Gladys M. 1912. Report on Women and Child Wage-Earners in United States, Vols. VI, VII, and VIII. *Economic Journal* 22: 147.

——. 1912. Report on Women and Child Wage-earners in United States, Vols. IX, X, XV, and XVI. *Economic Journal* 22: 627.

——. 1924. *Labour in Indian Industries.* London, Bombay and Calcutta, Madras: Humphrey Milford, Oxford University Press.

——. 1924. Maternity and Infant Welfare Work in India. *Indian Journal of Economics* 5(1/16) (July): 20.

Broughton, Gladys Mary, Ethel M. Newbold, and Edith C. Allen. 1921. *A Statistical Study of Labour Turnover in Munition and Other Factories*. Great Britain. Industrial Fatigue Research Board. Reports, no. 13. London: H.M. Stationery Office.

Brower, F. Beatrice. 1929. *Employee Thrift and Investment Plans*. New York: National Industrial Conference Board.

——. 1940. Structure of Annual Wage Plans, Elements of Success or Failure. *Advanced Management* 5(3) (July/September): 110–.

——. 1940. Liquidity and Instability. Ph.D. thesis, Columbia University.

Brown, Dorothy Miles. 1922. The Theory of a Normal Rate of Profit. Ph.D. thesis, University of Michigan (economics).

Brown, Elizabeth Stow, M.D. 1888. The Working-women of New York: Their Health and Occupations. *Journal of Social Science* 25 (December): 78–89.

Brown, Emily Clark. 1923. A Labor Survey of the Book and Job Printing Industry in 1920. M.A. thesis, University of Chicago (economics, labor).

——. 1924. *Changes in Union Wage Scales in the Book and Job Printing Industry, 1914 to 1924*. Chicago: United Typothetae of America.

——. 1927. The Book and Job Printers of Chicago. A Study of Organizations of Employers and Their Relations with Labor. Ph.D. thesis, University of Chicago (economics).

——. 1928. *Joint Industrial Control in the Book and Job Printing Industry*. Washington: U.S. Government Printing Office.

——. 1929. *Selected References on the Health of Women in Industry*. Washington: U.S. Women's Bureau.

——. 1929. *A Study of Two Groups of Denver Married Women Applying for Jobs*. Washington: U.S. Government Printing Office.

——. 1930. *Industrial Accidents to Men and Women*. Washington: U.S. Government Printing Office.

——. 1930. *Industrial Home Work*. Washington: U.S. Government Printing Office.

——. 1930. Price Competition in the Commercial Printing Industry of Chicago. *Journal of Political Economy* 38(2) (April): 194–212.

——. 1931. *Book and Job Printing in Chicago*. Chicago: University of Chicago Press.

——. 1935. Book Review of "Current Economic Policies" by Joseph B. Hubbard *et al. American Academy of Political and Social Science, Annals* 178 (March): 202–.

——. 1935. Selection of Employees' Representatives. *Monthly Labor Review* 40(1) (January): 1–.

——. 1939. The New Collective Bargaining in Mass Production: Methods, Results, Problems. *Journal of Political Economy* 47(1) (February): 30–66.

——. 1939/40. Book Review of "Labour Courts: An International Survey of Judicial Systems for the Settlement of Disputes" by International Labour Office. *American Journal of Sociology* 45(1/6): 491–.

Brown, Emma Elizabeth. 1878. *The Child Toilers of Boston Streets*. With illustrations by Katherine Peirson. Boston: D. Lothrop & Co.

——. 1880. Children's Labor: A Problem. *Atlantic Monthly* 46 (December): 787–92.

Brown, Jean Collier. 1938. *The Negro Woman Worker.* Washington: U.S. Women's Bureau.

——. 1938. Domestic Workers and Unions. *American Federationist* 45(5) (May): 477–.

Brown, Jean Collier and Elizabeth Batson. 1936/7. *Reading List of References on Household Employment.* Washington: U.S. Women's Bureau.

Brown, Josephine Chapin. 1933. *The Rural Community and Social Case Work.* New York: Family Welfare Association of America.

——. 1940. *Public Relief, 1929–1939.* New York: H. Holt.

Brown, Lucy Williams. Coauth. *See* Stevenson, Marietta.

Brown, Mary Gertrude. *See* Working, Hazel Gertrude Brown.

Brown, Mary Margaret. 1940. [The] Economic Theory of the Business Cycle. M.A. thesis, Boston University.

Brown, Mary Willcox. 1899. *The Development of Thrift.* New York: Macmillan.

Brown, Miss R. E. 1900. *Women as Co-operators and Citizens: The Present Position of Working Women as Co-operators and Citizens with an Indication of Their Future Position.* Women's Co-operative Guild.

Browne, Charlotte Fielding. 1866. Wastes and Commons. *Temple Bar* 17 (May): 231–43.

Browne, Martha Stephanie. 1923–34. Contributions to *Mitteilungen des Verbandes österreichischer Banken und Bankiers.* Vol. 1 published Vienna: Holzhausen, 1918.

Browne, Ruth J. 1922. A Statistical Analysis of Labor Turnover. M.A. thesis, University of Chicago (economics, labor).

Browning, Grace A. 1935. The Development of Poor Relief Legislation in Kansas. Chicago: University of Chicago Press.

——. Coauth. *See* Abbott, Edith.

Brownlow, Jane M. E. 1896. *Women and Factory Legislation.* London: Women's Printing Society.

——. 1911. *Women's Work in Local Government (England and Wales).* London: D. Nutt.

Bruce, Isabel Campbell and Edith Eickhoff. 1936/7. Book Review of "The Michigan Poor Law" by Carl M. Rosenquist. *International Journal of Ethics* 47: 127–.

Bruce, Isabel Campbell, Edith Eickhoff, and Sophonisba Preston Breckinridge. 1936. *The Michigan Poor Law: Its Development and Administration with Special Reference to State Provision for Medical Care of the Indigent.* Social Service Monographs. no. 23. Chicago: University of Chicago Press.

Bruce, Kathleen. 1924. Virginia Iron Manufacture in the Slave Era. Ph.D. thesis, Radcliffe College (history).

——. 1926. *Economic Factors in the Manufacture of Confederate Ordnance.* Washington: Confederate States of America Army Ordnance.

——. 1926. Slave Labor in the Virginia Iron Industry. *William and Mary Quarterly,* 2nd series, 6(4) (October): 289–302.

——. 1927. Slave Labor in the Virginia Iron Industry. *William and Mary Quarterly,* 2nd series, 7(1) (January): 21–31.

——. 1930. *Virginia Iron Manufacture in the Slave Era*. New York and London: Century Co.

——. 1930. Materials for Virginia Agricultural History. *Agricultural History* IV(1) (January).

——. 1932. Virginian Agricultural Decline to 1860: A Fallacy. *Agricultural History* 6 (January): 3–13.

——. 1932. Virginia Iron Manufacture in the Slave Era. *South Atlantic Quarterly (SAMLA)* 31(1) (January).

Bruère, Martha [S.] Bensley. 1926. The Impossible Profession. *Century Monthly Magazine* 112 (May/October): 584–.

——. 1927. *Does Prohibition Work? A Study of the Operation of the Eighteenth Amendment Made By the National Federation of Settlements, Assisted by Social Workers in Different Parts of the United States*. New York and London: Harper & Brothers.

——. 1935. *The Lower One Third and the Forest Service*. Washington: Forest Service, U.S. Dept. of Agriculture.

——. 1936. *Here Are Forests*. Prepared for the Third World power conference, September 1936. Washington: U.S. Government Printing Office.

——. 1938/1940. *What Forests Give*. Washington: U.S. Forest Service.

——. 1939. *Taming Our Forests*. Washington: Forest Service, U.S. Dept. of Agriculture.

Bruère, Martha Bensley and Robert W. Bruère. 1911. *Increasing Home Efficiency*. New York: Macmillan.

Bryan, Helen. Coauth. *See* Best, Ethel Lombard; Peterson, Agnes Lydia.

Bryant, Sophie Willock, D.Sc. 1894. Educational Finance. *Economic Journal* 4(13) (March): 90–105.

Büchner, Louise. 1856. *Die Frauen und ihr Beruf. Ein Buch der weiblichen Erziehung*. Frankfurt a.M.: Meidinger Sohn & Co. English edition, *Women and Their Vocation: A Nineteenth-century View*, transl. with an introduction by Susan L. Piepke. New York: P. Lang, 1999.

——. 1870. *Practische Versuche zur Lösung der Frauenfrage*. Berlin: O. Janke.

—— [as "Mentor"]. 1872. *Ueber weibliche Berufsarten*. Darmstadt: C. Köhler.

——. 1878. *Die Frau: hinterlassene Aufsätze, Abhandlungen und Berichte zur Frauenfrage; Mit dem Portrait der Vesfasserin und einem Erinnerungsblatt an dieselbe*. Halle: H. Gesenius.

Buckmaster, Barbara. 1940. Bessarabia. *Fabian Quarterly* 24.

Buckstaff, Florence [Griswold]. 1888. A True Story. *Lend a Hand* 3(12) (December): 691–.

——. 1894. Married Women's Property in Anglo-Saxon and Anglo-Norman Law and the Origin of the Common-law Dower. *Annals of the American Academy of Political and Social Science* 4: 233–64.

Buer, Mabel C[raven]. 1915. Book Review of "Die Bank von England" by O. Hulftegger. *Economic Journal* 25: 414–.

——. 1921/1927/1935. *Economics for Beginners*. London: G. Routledge & Sons.

——. 1921. Book Review of "The Economics of Welfare" by A. C. Pigou. *Charity Organisation Review* 291 (March): 163–.

——. 1921. The Trade Depression Following the Napoleonic Wars. *Economica* 1 (May): 159–79.

——. 1926/1968. *Health, Wealth, and Population in the Early Days of the Industrial Revolution.* New York: H. Fertig.

——. 1928. England To-day and Yesterday. *Eugenics Review* 20(1) (April): 20–.

——. 1929. Health and Prosperity in the Nineteenth Century. *Eugenics Review* 21(3) (October): 189–.

——. 1930. The Reformed Parliament And Civil Registration Of Births And Deaths. *Public Administration (London, UK)* 8(3) (July): 323–.

——. 1932/3. Book Review of "Nottinghamshire in the Eighteenth Century" by J. D. Chambers. *Economic History Review* 4: 365–.

Buer, Mabel C. and W. T. J. Gun. 1931. The Kin of Genius III. *Eugenics Review* 22(4) (January): 253–.

Buisson, Suzanne. 1934. *Les Répercussions du travail féminin.* Paris: Librairie Populaire du Parti Socialiste.

Bulkley, Mildred E[mily]. 1914. *The Feeding of School Children.* London: G. Bell & Sons.

——. 1915. *The Establishment of Legal Minimum Rates in the Boxmaking Industry under the Trade Boards Act of 1909.* London: G. Bell & Sons.

——. 1922. *Bibliographical Survey of Contemporary Sources for the Economic and Social History of the War.* Carnegie Endowment for International Peace. Division of Economics and History. British Series, no. 6. Oxford: Clarendon Press; H. Milford.

Bull, Susan. 1938. An Historical and Critical Analysis of British Health Insurance. Ph.D. thesis, London School of Economics.

Bulley, A[gnes]. Amy. 1890. The Political Evolution of Women. *Westminster Review* 134 (July): 1–8.

——. 1891. Domestic Service. *Westminster Review* 135 (February): 177–86.

——. 1894. The Employment of Women, The Lady Assistant Commissioners' Report. *Fortnightly Review* cccxxv (January): 39–48.

——. 1896. The Rise of Women's Conferences. *Englishwoman* 4 (November): 213–.

Bulley, A[gnes]. Amy and Margaret Whitley. 1894. *Women's Work.* With a preface by Lady Dilke. London: Methuen; New York: Scribners.

Bullock, Edna Dean. 1911. *Selected Articles on Child Labor.* Minneapolis: H. W. Wilson. 2nd ed. New York: Wilson, 1915.

——. 1911/1920. *Selected Articles on the Employment of Women.* Minneapolis: H. W. Wilson.

——. 1912. *Selected Articles on Compulsory Insurance.* Minneapolis: H. W. Wilson Co.

——. 1913/1916. *Selected Articles on Trade Unions.* White Plains, N.Y.: H. W. Wilson.

——. 1915. *Agricultural Credit.* White Plains, N.Y., and New York: H. W. Wilson.

——. 1915. *Selected Articles on Mothers' Pensions.* White Plains, N.Y., and New York: H. W. Wilson.

——. 1915/1917. *Selected Articles on Single Tax.* White Plains, NY: H. W. Wilson.

——. 1932. Do Not Be Stampeded. *State Government* 5(3) (March): 7–.

——. Coauth. *See* Johnsen, Julia Emily; Morgan, Joy Elmer.

Bülow von Dennewitz, Gertrud, Gräfin. 1908. *Die Bevölkerungsfrage in weiblicher Beurteilung*. Gautzsch: Dietrich.

Burchard, Agnes. 1892/3. How Society in India Suffers from Woman's Position. *Chautauquan* 16 (October/March): 216–.

Burdett-Coutts, Angela, Baroness, ed. 1893. *Woman's Mission [to Women]: A Series of Congress Papers on the Philanthropic Work of Women by Eminent Writers*. Royal British Commission, Chicago Exhibition. London: Sampson Low, Marston & Company Ltd.; New York: Scribner's.

Burdick, Anna Lalor. 1920. Woman's Place in Industry. *Independent Woman* (March).

Burke, Dorothy Williams. 1927. Women at Work on Chicago Truck Farms. *Social Service Review* 1(1/4) (March/December): 194–.

Burke, Dorothy May Williams, Ellen Nathalie Matthews, and Mary Elizabeth Skinner. 1926. *Work of Children on Illinois Farms*. United States Children's Bureau. Bureau publication no. 168. Washington: U.S. Government Printing Office.

Burnham, Elizabeth Abbott. 1938. The Influence of Size of Business on Department Store Operating Results. *Harvard Business Review* 16(2): 211–25.

——. 1940. The Department Store in Its Community. *Harvard Business Review* 18(4): 455–71.

——. 1940. Expenses and Profits of Limited Price Variety Chains in 1939. *Harvard School of Business Administration Bulletin* 112.

Burnham, Grace Martha. 1930. *Work or Wages: The Challenge of Unemployment*. New York: International Pamphlets. 2nd ed. entitled *Unemployment*, 1932.

——. 1932. *Social Insurance*. International pamphlets, no. 11. New York: International Pamphlets. Political Pamphlets at the University of Buffalo, no. 471.

——. 1933. *Dangerous Jobs*. International pamphlets, no. 34. New York: International Pamphlets.

Burns, Eveline Mabel [Richardson]. 1922. Recent Contributions to Economic Theory. *Economica* 2 (October): 272–8.

——. 1923. The French Minimum Wage Act of 1915. *Economica* 3 (November): 236–44.

——. 1925. The Economics of Family Endowment. *Economica* 14 (June): 155–64.

——. 1926. *Wages and the State: A Comparative Study of the Problems of State Wage Regulation*. London: P. S. King & Son.

——. 1926. The Problems of State Regulation of Wages. Ph.D. thesis. London School of Economics.

——. 1929. Statistics and Economic Forecasting. *Journal of the American Statistical Association* 24 (June): 152–63.

——. 1931. Does Institutionalism Complement or Compete with "Orthodox Economics"? *American Economic Review* 21 (March): 80–7. Correction *American Economic Review* 21(2) (June): 287.

——. 1933. The Economics of Unemployment Relief. *American Economic Review* 23 (March): 31–43.

——. 1935. Germany Spends for Recovery. *Today* 3(16) (February 9): 14–.

——. 1936. *Memorandum on Wall Street Journal Articles.* Washington: U.S. Social Security Board.

——. 1936. *Toward Social Security: An Explanation of the Social Security Act and a Survey of the Larger Issues.* London: Whittelsey House; New York: McGraw-Hill.

——. 1936. The Financial Aspects of the Social Security Act. *American Economic Review* 26(1) (March): 12–22.

——. 1936. The Relation Of Unemployment Compensation to the Broader Problem of Relief. *Law and Contemporary Problems* 3: 150–.

——. 1938. *The Arguments for and against the Old-Age Reserve.* Washington: U.S. Social Security Board.

——. 1938. Administrative Integration of Unemployment Insurance and Relief in Great Britain. *Social Service Review* 12(1/4) (March/December): 374.

——. 1938. Impact of Social Security Act on Relief. *National Municipal Review* 27(1) (January): 13–.

——. 1938. Unemployment Compensation in the United States. *International Labour Review* 37 (May): 584–617.

——. 1939. An Appraisal of Services for the Unemployed. *American Academy of Political and Social Science, Annals* 202 (March): 45–.

——. 1939. Book Review of "Trends in Relief Expenditures" by Anne E. Geddes. *Journal of Political Economy* 47: 439–.

——. 1939. Common Sense and Unemployment Compensation. *American Federationist* 46(3) (March): 248–.

——. 1940. Economic Problems in the Provision of Security against Employment Hazards. *American Economic Review* 30(1) (March): 68–77.

Burns, Eveline Mabel Richardson, Paul T. Homan, M. A. Copeland, J. J. Spengler, O. H. Taylor, and William Jaffe. 1931. Economic Theory – Institutionalism: What It Is and What It Hopes to Become. *American Economic Review* 21(1) (March): 134–41.

Burr, Susan S. *See* Litchfield, Susan Sophia Burr.

Burroughs, Nannie Helen, 1915. Black Women and Reform. *Crisis* (August).

Burton, Margaret E[rnestine]. 1911. *The Education of Women in China.* New York and Chicago: Fleming H. Revell Company.

——. 1912. *Notable Women of Modern China.* New York and Chicago: Fleming H. Revell Company.

——. 1914. *The Education of Women in Japan.* New York and Chicago: Fleming H. Revell Company.

——. 1915. *Comrades in Service.* New York: Missionary Education Movement of the United States and Canada.

——. 1915. Oriental Women Students. *Women's International Quarterly* 3(4) (July): 197–.

——. 1917. Women Students. *International Review of Missions* 6(23) (July): 422–.

——. 1918. *Women Workers of the Orient.* West Medford, Mass.: Central Committee of the United Study of Foreign Missions.

——. 1940. *Toward International Organization.* New York: Woman's Press.

Burton, Miss Mary. 1875. Should the Labour of Women in Factories be Regulated by Legislation? *Transactions of the National Association for the Promotion of Social Science.* London: Victoria Press.

Busbey, Katherine Graves. 1909. *Women's Trade Union Movement in Great Britain.* Bulletin of the Bureau of Labor. Washington: U.S. Bureau of Labor.

Bush, Ada Lillian. 1924. *The Education of a Retail Sales Force.* Washington: U.S. Bureau of Foreign and Domestic Commerce.

——. 1924. *Retail Store Planning.* Bureau of Foreign and Domestic Commerce (Department of Commerce) Trade Information Bulletin, no. 291. Washington: U.S. Government Printing Office.

——. 1926. *Department Leasing in Retail Stores.* Washington: U.S. Bureau of Foreign and Domestic Commerce.

——. 1931. *Suggestions for an Outline of a City Survey (Industrial and Commercial).* Washington: U.S. Bureau of Foreign and Domestic Commerce.

——. 1934. *Consumer Viewpoint on Returned Goods.* Washington: U.S. Bureau of Foreign and Domestic Commerce.

——. 1935. *Consumer Use of Selected Goods and Services.* Washington: U.S. Bureau of Foreign and Domestic Commerce.

——. 1938. *Suggestions for Use in Making a City Survey (Industrial and Commercial).* Washington: U.S. Bureau of Foreign and Domestic Commerce.

Butler, C[hristina]. Violet. 1907. Book Review of "Capital. Vol. II. The Process of Circulation of Capital" by Karl Marx. Edited by Frederick Engels. Transl. from the 2nd German ed. by Ernest Untermann. *Economic Journal* 17: 558.

——. 1907. Book Review of "Pictures of the Socialistic Future" by Eugene Richter. *Economic Journal* 17: 558.

——. 1907. Book Review of "Socialism before the French Revolution" by William B. Guthrie. *Economic Journal* 17: 558.

——. 1908. Book Review of "Essai de solution du problème social par les magasins généraux" by L. Scansa-Lanza. *Economic Journal* 18: 82.

——. 1908. Book Review of "Political Socialism: A Remonstrance" by Mark H. Judge. *Economic Journal* 18: 565.

——. 1908. Book Review of "Socialism" by J. Macdonald and M. P. Ramsay. *Economic Journal* 18: 80.

——. 1908. Book Review of "Socialismus und sociale Bewegung" by Werner Sombart. *Economic Journal* 18: 440.

——. 1908. Book Review of "The Socialist Movement in England" by Brougham Villiers. *Economic Journal* 18: 566.

——. 1909. Book Review of "Ferdinand Lassalle und seine Bedeutung für die deutsche Sozialdemokratie" by Bernhard Harms. *Economic Journal* 19: 445.

——. 1909. Book Review of "Das Lebenswerk von Karl Marx" by Professor Werner Sombart. *Economic Journal* 19: 239.

——. 1909. Book Review of "Socialism in Theory and Practice" by Morris Hillquit. *Economic Journal* 19: 240.
——. 1910. Book Review of "Darwinism and Modern Socialism" by F. W. Headley. *Economic Journal* 20: 66.
——. 1910. Organised Charities in Oxford. *Economic Review* (October).
——. 1911. Book Review of "Il Capitale" by Umberto Ricci. *Economic Journal* 21: 257.
——. 1911. Book Review of "Contemporary Social Problems" by Achille Loria. Transl. John Leslie Gardner. *Economic Journal* 21: 257.
——. 1911. Book Review of "Della Emigrazione Europea" by Emilia de Luca Paolo. *Economic Journal* 21: 257.
——. 1911. Book Review of "Le dogane interne nel secolo XX. Il mercantilismo municipale" by Giuseppe Prato. *Economic Journal* 21: 591.
——. 1911. Book Review of "Il Protezionismo operaio. L'esclusione del lavoro straniero" by Giuseppe Prato. *Economic Journal* 21: 113.
——. 1911. Book Review of "La Rendita Edilizia nelle moderne metropolis" by Carlo Grilli. *Economic Journal* 21: 257.
——. 1911. Book Review of "Saggio di un inchiesta sul Lavoro a domicilio in Milano." *Economic Journal* 21: 587.
——. 1912. *Social Conditions in Oxford*. London: Sidgwick and Jackson.
——. 1912. Book Review of "Il banco di san Giorgio" by Emilio Marengo, *et al.* *Economic Journal* 22: 103–.
——. 1912. Book Review of "L'espansione commerciale inglese nel primo settecento" by Giuseppe Prato. *Economic Journal* 22: 301–.
——. 1912. Book Review of "Le forme del progresso economico in Capitanata" by A. Fraccacreta. *Economic Journal* 22: 480–.
——. 1912. Book Review of "La Moneta nei suoi rapporti quantitative" by D. Bearardi. *Economic Journal* 22: 105–.
——. 1912. Book Review of "Saggi economici e finanziari sull' Inghilterra" by R. Dalla Volta. *Economic Journal* 22: 480–.
——. 1914. Book Review of "La Navigazione" by C. Supin. *Economic Journal* 24: 119–.
——. 1915. Book Review of "La Concorrenza" by E. Sella. *Economic Journal* 25: 240–.
——. 1916. Book Review of "Old Age Pensions" by H. J. Hoare. *Economic Journal* 26: 254–.
——. 1917. Book Review of "La Concurrenza" vol. 2 by E. Sella. *Economic Journal* 27: 99–.
——. 1919. Book Review of "Women in the Engineering Trades" by Barbara Drake. *Economic Journal* 29(114) (June): 238–41.
——. 1919. Book Review of "Economics Effects of the War upon Women and Children in Great Britain" by Irene Andrews and Margaret A. Hobbs. *Economic Journal* 29(115) (September): 341–2.
——. 1922. Book Review of "Getting and Spending: An Introduction to Economics." *Economic Journal* 32(127) (September): 393–4.

——. 1922. Book Review of "Industrial and Commercial Geography" by A. Radford. *Economic Journal* 32: 518.

——. 1922. Book Review of "Physical Economics" by L. Southerns. *Economic Journal* 32: 518.

——. 1922. Book Review of "Précis d'économie politique" by M. Journé. *Economic Journal* 32: 518.

——. 1922. Book Review of "Premières Notions d'économie politique" by C. Gide. *Economic Journal* 32: 518.

——. 1922. Book Review of "Principles of Political Science" by R. N. Gilchrist. *Economic Journal* 32: 518.

——. 1922. Book Review of "A Text-book of Economics" by M. Briggs. *Economic Journal* 32: 518.

——. 1923. Book Review of "Settlements and their Outlook." *Economic Journal* 33: 408–.

——. 1924. Book Review of "Principii di sociologia e politica" by Amerigo Namias. *Sociological Review* 16: 360–.

——. 1928. *Village Survey-making: An Oxfordshire Experiment.* Great Britain. Board of Education Pamphlets, no. 61. London: H.M. Stationery Office.

Butler, Christina Violet and Baroness Marie Frances Lisette Hanbury Verney Willoughby de Broke. 1916. *Domestic Service; an Enquiry by the Women's Industrial Council.* London: G. Bell and Sons, Ltd.

Butler, Elizabeth Beardsley. 1907. New Jersey Children in the Trades. *Charities and the Commons* 17 (March 16): 1,062–4.

——. 1907. Sweated Trades in Hudson County. *Charities and the Commons* 19 (December 21): 1,257–64.

——. 1908. Women's Suffrage in England. *American Lawyer* 16: 268.

——. 1908. Women's Suffrage in England. *New Jersey Law Journal* 31: 202.

——. 1908. Working Women of Pittsburgh. *Charities* 20: 433–49, 549–63, 648–54; and 21: 34–47, 570–80, 1,117–42.

——. 1909. *Women and the Trades: Pittsburgh, 1907–1908.* New York: Charities Publication Committee. Reprinted, ed. and with an introduction by Maurine Weiner Greenwald, University of Pittsburgh Press, 1984.

——. 1909. Work of Women in the Mercantile Houses of Pittsburgh. *American Academy of Political and Social Science, Annals* 33 (January/June): 326–.

——. 1910. Training for Salesmanship. *Proceedings of the Academy of Political Science* 1(1) (October): 52–. Reprinted in Helen Marot, ed., *The Economic Position of Women.* New York. Also published in Henry Raymond Mussey, ed., *Proceedings of the Academy of Political Science in the City of New York.* New York: Columbia University.

——. 1912. *Saleswomen in Mercantile Stores: Baltimore, 1909.* New York: Charities Publication Committee.

Butler, Josephine Elizabeth Grey. 1868. *The Education and Employment of Women.* Liverpool: T. Brakell. Online in University of Indiana's LETRS.

——. 1869. *An Appeal to the People of England, on the Recognition and Superintendence of Prostitution by Governments. By an English Mother.* Banks, Nottingham: s.n.

——, ed. 1869. *Woman's Work and Woman's Culture: A Series of Essays.* London: Macmillan.

——. 1870. *The Duty of Women in Relation to our Great Social Evil.* Carlisle: Hudson Scott.

——. 1870. The Lovers of the Lost [women's refuges]. *Contemporary Review* 13 (January): 16–40.

——. 1871. *The Constitution Violated.* Edinburgh: Edmonston and Douglas.

——. 1872. *The New Era; Containing a Retrospect of the History of the Regulation System in Berlin, of the Repeated Opposition Directed against the System There, and the Causes of the Failure of that Opposition; with an Indication of the Lessons to Be Learned from Past Failure.* Liverpool: T. Brakell.

——. 1874. *Legislative Restrictions on the Industry of Women: Considered from the Women's Point of View.* London: Matthews and Sons, steam printers.

——. 1874. *Some Thoughts on the Present Aspect of the Crusade against the State Regulation of Vice.* Liverpool: T. Brakell. Online in University of Indiana's LETRS.

——. 1876. *The Hour before the Dawn. An Appeal to Men.* London: Trübner & Co.

——. 1876. *The New Abolitionists: A Narrative of a Year's Work: Being an Account of the Mission Undertaken to the Continent of Europe by Mrs. Josephine E. Butler, and of the Events Subsequent Thereupon.* London: Federation for the Abolition of Government Regulation of Prostitution.

——. 1878/9. The New Religious Movement in France. *Contemporary Review* 34 (March): 781–94.

——. 1879. *Government by Police.* London: Dyer Brothers.

——. 1886. *Our Christianity Tested by the Irish Question* [home rule]. London: T. Fisher Unwin.

——. 1886. *Simple Words for Simple Folk, about the Repeal of the Contagious Diseases Acts, which License Prostitution, and Place Women under the Arbitrary Power of Spy Police.* Bristol: J. W. Arrowsmith.

——. 1887. *The Revival and Extension of the Abolitionist Cause.* London: Dyer Brothers.

——. 1888. *Mrs. Butler's Appeal to the Women of America Addressed to the International Council of Women.* New York: The Philanthropist. Transcription online in University of Indiana's LETRS.

——. 1892. Woman's Place in Church Work. *Magazine of Christian Literature* 5 (April): 31–7.

——. 1897. *Truth Before Everything.* Liverpool: Pewtree & Co. Online in University of Indiana's LETRS.

——. 1909. *Souvenirs & pensées.* Saint-Blaise: Foyer Solidariste.

Butler, Selena S. 1897. *The Chain-gang System.* Read before the National Association of Colored Women at Nashville, Tenn., 16 September 1897. Tuskegee, Ala.: Normal School Steam Press Print.

Butlin, Frances M. 1895. Book Review of "Das Capital. Kritik der politischen Oekonomie" by Karl Marx. *Economic Journal* 5(18) (June): 249–51.

——. 1895. Book Review of "A Handbook of Socialism" by W. D. P. Bliss. *Economic Journal* 5(20) (December): 575–7.

——. 1895. Book Review of "How It Can Be Done; or, Constructive Socialism" by John Richardson. *Economic Journal* 5(18) (June): 248–9.

——. 1895. Book Review of "The Social Contract on Principles of Political Right" by Jean Jacques Rousseau. *Economic Journal* 5(20) (December): 575.

——. 1895. Book Review of "Socialism" by Prof. Robert Flint. *Economic Journal* 5(18) (June): 247–8.

——. 1895. Book Review of "Socialism" by Lord Norton. *Economic Journal* 5(20) (December): 574–5.

——. 1895. Book Review of "Socialism and Modern Thought" by M. Kaufmann. *Economic Journal* 5(20) (December): 577–8.

——. 1896. Book Review of "Economics and Socialism. A Demonstration of the Cause and Cure of Trade Depressions and National Poverty" by F. N. Laycock. *Economic Journal* 6(22) (June): 260–1.

——. 1896. Book Review of "Geschichte des Socialismus und Communismus im 19 Jahrhundert [on Louis Blanc]" by Prof. Dr. Otto Warschauer. *Economic Journal* 6(22) (June): 259–60.

——. 1897. Book Review of "Socialism and Catholicism" by Count Edward Sordoni. Transl. Richard Jenery-Shee. *Economic Journal* 7(27) (September): 411–13.

——. 1897. Book Review of "Socialism: Notes on a Political Tour" by Sir Henry Wrixon. *Economic Journal* 7(27) (September): 413–15.

——. 1897. Book Review of "Le Socialisme et la science sociale" by Gaston Richard. *Economic Journal* 7(27) (September): 415.

——. 1898. Book Review of "Karl Marx and the Close of His System: A Criticism" by Eugen von Böhm-Bawerk. *Economic Journal* 8(31) (September): 375–8.

——. 1898. Book Review of "Outlines of Sociology" by L. Ward. *Economic Journal* 8(31) (September): 373–4.

——. 1898. Book Review of "Sozialismus und soziale Bewegung im 19 Jahrhundert" by Prof. Werner Sombart. *Economic Journal* 8(29) (March): 103.

——. 1898. Book Review of "What is Socialism?" by Scotsburn. *Economic Journal* 8(31) (September): 375.

——. 1899. Book Review of "Communism in Central Europe in the Time of the Reformation" by Karl Kanbsky. *International Journal of Ethics* 9 (January): 265–6.

——. 1899. Book Review of "To-morrow: A Peaceful Path to Real Reform" by E. Howard. *Economic Journal* 9(33) (March): 71–2.

——. 1899. Book Review of "Über das Verhältnis von Wert und Preis im ökonomischen System von Karl Marx"' by Prof. Dr. Karl Diehl. *Economic Journal* 9(33) (March): 73–4.

——. 1899. Book Review of "Value, Price, and Profit" by Karl Marx. *Economic Journal* 9(33) (March): 72–3.

——. 1899. Book Review of "Women and Economics" by Charlotte Perkins Stetson. *Economic Journal* 9(35) (September): 439–40.

——. 1899. International Congress of Women. *Economic Journal* 9(35) (September): 450–5.

Byington, Margaret Frances. 1908/9. The Family in a Typical Mill Town. *American Journal of Sociology* 14(1/6): 648–.

——. 1909. The Family in a Typical Mill Town. *American Econonic Association Quarterly*, 3rd series 10(1) (April): 193–206.

——. 1910. *Homestead: The Households of a Mill Town.* New York: Charities Publication Committee.

——. 1911/1912/1916/1924/1929/. *What Social Workers Should Know about Their Own Communities*, an outline. Russell Sage Foundation. Charity Organization Department, Publication no. 7. New York: Charity Organization Department of the Russell Sage Foundation. 4th ed., revised and enlarged, Russell Sage Foundation, 1929. Charity Organization Department, Pamphlets, C. O. 66.

——. 1912. *Confidential Exchange: A Form of Social Co-operation.* New York: Russell Sage Foundation.

——. 1913. Some Unconsidered Elements in Household Expenditure. *American Academy of Political and Social Science, Annals* 48 (July): 112–.s

——. 1918. *Report on the Charities of Lexington, Kentucky: Made at the Request of the Mayor and the City Commission.* Lexington, Ky.: The City of Lexington.

——. 1918. The Normal Family. *American Academy of Political and Social Science, Annals* 77 (May): 13–.

——. 1918. Scope and Organization of the Department of Civilian Relief. *American Academy of Political and Social Science, Annals* 79 (September): 88–.

——. 1923. The Neighborhood as an Asset in Case Work. *Family* 4(8) (December): 201–.

——. 1939. Community Needs: The Focus. *Social Work Today* 6(8) (May): 15–.

Byington, Margaret Frances and Mary Sewall Gardner. ?1920/1993. *The Interdependence of the Nurse and the Social Worker.* New York: National Organization for Public Health Nursing.

Bynum, Mary L. 1926. *International Trade in Coffee.* Washington: U.S. Bureau of Foreign and Domestic Commerce.

——. 1930. *The World's Exports of Coffee.* Washington: U.S. Bureau of Foreign and Domestic Commerce.

Byrne, Harriet A[nne]. 1933. The Effects on Women of Changing Conditions in the Cigar and Cigarette Industries. M.A. thesis, University of Chicago (economics).

——. 1934. *The Age Factor as It Relates to Women in Business and the Professions.* Bulletin of the U.S. Women's Bureau, no. 117. Washington: U.S. Government Printing Office.

——. 1935. *The Health and Safety of Women in Industry.* Bulletin, United States Department of Labor, Women's Bureau, no. 136. Washington: U.S. Dept. of Labor, Women's Bureau.

——. 1936. *The Effects of the Depression on Wage Earners' Families: A Second Survey of South Bend.* United States Department of Labor, Women's Bureau Bulletin, no. 108. Washington: U.S. Government Printing Office.

——. 1936. *Employment in Hotels and Restaurants.* United States Women's Bureau Bulletin, no. 123. Washington: U.S. Government Printing Office.

——. 1936. *Women Unemployed Seeking Relief in 1933.* United States Department of Labor, Women's Bureau Bulletin, no. 139. Washington: U.S. Department of Labor, Women's Bureau.

——. 1937. *Women's Employment in West Virginia.* Washington: U.S. Department of Labor.

Byrne, Harriet A. and Bertha Blair. 1935. *Industrial Home Work in Rhode Island with Special Reference to the Lace Industry.* Department of Labor, Bulletin of the Women's Bureau, no. 131. Washington: U.S. Government Printing Office.

Byrne, Harriet A. and Ethel Erickson. 1932. *Women Office Workers in Philadelphia.* Washington: U.S. Government Printing Office.

——. 1935. *Women Who Work in Offices.* Bulletin of the Women's Bureau, no. 132. Washington: U.S. Government Printing Office.

Byrne, Harriet Anne and Cecile Hillyer. 1938. *Unattached Women on Relief in Chicago, 1937.* Bulletin of the U.S. Women's Bureau, no. 158. Washington: U.S. Government Printing Office.

Byrne, Harriet Anne and Caroline Manning. 1932. *The Effects on Women of Changing Conditions in the Cigar and Cigarette Industries.* Washington: U.S. Women's Bureau.

——. 1935. *The Employment of Women in the Sewing Trades of Connecticut.* Washington: U.S. Government Printing Office.

Byrne, Harriet Anne and Ellen Nathalie Matthews. 1928. *Child Labor in Representative Tobacco-growing Areas. United States.* Children's Bureau Publication, no. 155. Washington: U.S. Government Printing Office.

Byrne, Harriet Anne. Coauth. *See* Manning, Caroline; Springer, Ethel Maria.

Byrnes, Agnes Mary [Hadden]. 1920. Industrial Home-Work in Pennsylvania. Ph.D. thesis, Bryn Mawr College (economics, history).

——. 1921/1923. *Industrial Home Work in Pennsylvania: Data Collected in 1916–1917 with Preface Including Brief Survey in 1920.* Special bulletin, no. 3. Harrisburg, Pa.: Pennsylvania Department of Labor and Industry.

C

Cahill, Marion Cotter. 1932. *Shorter Hours: A Study of the Movement Since the Civil War*. New York: Columbia University Press.

——. 1932. Shorter Hours: A Study of the Movement Since the Civil War. Ph.D. thesis, Columbia University (economics, history).

——. 1934. Book Review of "Hours of Labor" by Lazare Teper. *Journal of Political Economy* 42: 568–.

Caird, Mona. 1888. Ideal Marriage. *Westminster Review* 130 (November): 617–36.

——. 1888. Marriage. *Westminster Review* 130 (August): 186–201.

——. 1890. The Emancipation of the Family. *North American Review* 150 (June): 692–705; 151 (July): 22–37.

——. 1890. The Morality of Marriage. *Fortnightly Review*, n.s. 7 (March): 310–30. Reprinted in Andrea Broomfield and Sally Mitchell, eds., *Prose by Victorian Women: An Anthology*. New York: Garland Publishing, 1995.

——. 1890. Results of the Non-enfranchisement of Women. *Westminster Review* 133 (March): 231–9.

——. 1892. A Defense of the So-called "Wild Women." *Nineteenth Century* 31 (May): 811–29.

——. 1897. *Beyond the Pale. An Appeal on Behalf of the Victims of Vivisection*. London: William Reeves. Online in University of Indiana's LETRS.

——. 1897. *The Morality of Marriage and other Essays on the Status and Destiny of Women*, London: George Redway.

——. 1897. Political Enfranchisement for Women. *New Century Review* 11 (October): 280–.

Callaway, Alice Rhinehart. 1898. The Workman in Berlin. *Publications of the American Statistical Association* 6 (June): 102–6.

Callcott, Mary Stevenson. 1931. Child Labor Legislation in New York: The Historical Development and the Administrative Practices of Child Labor Laws in the State of New York, 1905–1930. Ph.D. thesis, Columbia University (economics, labor).

——. 1935. Russian Justice. New York: Macmillan.

Callcott, Mary Stevenson and W. C. Waterman. 1932. *Principles of Social Legislation*. New York: Macmillan.

Calverley, Mary. 1893. Thrift and Old-age Pensions. *Charity Organisation Review* 96 (January): 1–.

Calvin, Jeannette M. 1926. *International Trade in Toys*. Washington: Government Printing Office.

——. 1928. *International Trade in Clocks and Watches*. Washington: U.S. Bureau of Foreign and Domestic Commerce.

Camalier, Renah F. 1932. *Digest for Personal Finance Laws*. Washington: American Association of Personal Finance Companies.

——. 1938. *Personal Finance Laws*. American Association of Personal Finance Companies.

Cameron, Alice Mackenzie. 1934. *Civilisation and the Unemployed*. London: Student Christian Movement Press.

Cameron, Mary Effie. 1940. The Bituminous Coal Industry: The Emergence of a Social Problem. Ph.D. thesis, Cornell University (history).

Cammon, Miss H. M. 1868/9. Woman's Work and Wages. *Harper's New Monthly Magazine* 38 (December/May): 665–.

Campbell, Agnes Horne. 1935. *Consumers' Cooperation*. New York: Russell Sage Foundation.

——. 1937. *Costs, Content, or Levels and Standards of Living*. New York: Russell Sage Foundation.

——. 1937. *Negro Housing in Towns and Cities, 1927–1937*. New York: Russell Sage Foundation.

Campbell, Annie. 1894. Is the Employment of Minors in Tobacco Factories Injurious to Their Health? In *Proceedings of the 8th Annual Convention of Factory Inspectors*. Cleveland, Ohio: International Association of Factory Inspectors of North America.

Campbell, Mrs. [Bourne]. 1853. *The British West India Colonies in Connection with Slavery, Emancipation, etc. By a Resident in the West Indies for Thirteen Years*. London: T. Bosworth.

Campbell, Helen Stuart. 1880. Studies in the Slums – Diet and Its Doings. *Lippincott's Magazine* 26 (July/December): 362.

——. 1880. Studies in the Slums – Jack. *Lippincott's Magazine* 26 (July/December): 213.

——. 1880. Studies in the Slums – Jan of the North. *Lippincott's Magazine* 26 (July/December): 498.

——. 1880. Studies in the Slums – Jerry. *Lippincott's Magazine* 25 (January/June): 740.

——. 1880. Studies in the Slums – Nan; or, A Girl's Life. *Lippincott's Magazine* 26 (July/December): 103.

——. 1880. Studies in the Slums – Water Street and Its Work. *Lippincott's Magazine* 25 (January/June): 568.

——. 1881. *The Easiest Way in House-keeping and Cooking: Adapted to Domestic Use or Study in Classes*. New York: Fords, Howard & Hulbert. Revised ed. Boston: Little, Brown, 1893.

——. 1882. *The Problem of the Poor: A Record of Quiet Work in Unquiet Places*. New York: Fords, Howard, & Hulbert.

——. 1882. Bread or a Stone. *Lippincott's Magazine* 29 (January/June): 309.
——. 1882. New-Year's with the Ojibways. *Lippincott's Magazine* 29 (January/June): 390.
——. 1884/5. Wayside Homes. *Chautauquan* 5 (October/July): 567–.
——. 1885/6. Village Improvement Societies. *Chautauquan* 6 (October/July): 391.
——. 1886. *Miss Herndon's Income*. Boston: Roberts Bros.
——. 1886. *Miss Melinda's Opportunity: A Story*. Boston: Roberts Bros.
——. 1886. Criminal Geography. *Lend a Hand* 1(6) (June): 366.
——. 1886. Miss Marion's Difficulty. *Lend a Hand* 1(4) (April): 203.
——. 1886/7. Guilds for Working Women. *Chautauquan* 7 (October/July): 604.
——. 1886/7. Out-of-Door Employments for Women. *Chautauquan* 7 (October/July): 200.
——. 1887. *Prisoners of Poverty: Women Wage Workers, Their Trades and Their Lives.* Originally published in *New York Tribune*. Boston, Roberts Brothers. Reprinted Westport, Conn.: Greenwood Press, 1970.
——. 1887/8. Octavia Hill and Her Mission. *Chautauquan* 8 (October/July): 235.
——. 1888/9. The Child and the Community. *Chautauquan* 9 (October/July): 458.
——. 1889. *Prisoners of Poverty Abroad*. Boston: Roberts Brothers.
——. 1889. Certain Forms of Woman's Work for Woman. *Century Illustrated Monthly Magazine* 38 (June): 217–29.
——. 1889. Certain Convictions as to Poverty. *Arena* 1 (December): 101–13.
——. 1889. Child Labor and Some of Its Results. *Chautauquan* 10 (October): 21–4.
——. 1891. Domestic Service: A Voice from the Silent Side. *Chautauquan* 13 (April/September): 351–.
——. 1891. Association in Clubs, with its Bearings on Working-women. *Arena* 5 (December): 61–7.
——. 1891. The Working-women of To-day. *Arena* 4 (August): 329–39.
——. 1893. *Women Wage Earners, Their Past, Their Present and Their Future.* With an introduction by Richard T. Ely. Boston: Roberts Bros. Reprinted New York, Arno Press, 1972.
——. 1893. Women Wage-earners of America and Europe. Part I. *Arena* 7 (January): 153–72.
——. 1893. Women Wage-earners. Part II: Rise and Growth of Trades, Labor Bureaus and Their Work. *Arena* 7 (February): 321–36.
——. 1893. Women Wage-earners. Part III: Present Wage Rates in the United States. *Arena* 7 (March): 433–40.
——. 1893. Women Wage-earners. Part IV: General Conditions. *Arena* 7 (May): 668–79.
——. 1893. Women Wage-earners. Part V: In the Western States. *Arena* 8 (June): 32–8.
——. 1893. Women Wage-earners. Part VI: Specific Evils and Abuses. *Arena* 8 (July): 172–84.
——. 1896/1907. *Household Economics: A Course of Lectures in the School of Economics at the University of Wisconsin*. New York: G. P. Putnam's Sons.

——. 1896. Household Economics as a University Movement. *Review of Reviews* 13 (March): 204–9.
——. 1896. Household Furnishings. *Architectural Record* 6 (October): 97–104.
——. 1896. Is Woman Embodied Obstruction? *Arena* 15 (February): 371–5.
——. 1897. Household Economics. *Public Opinion* 22 (April 8): 440.
——. 1898. Is American Domesticity Decreasing, and If So, Why? *Arena* 19 (January): 86–96.
——. 1898. Social Settlements and the Civic Sense. *Arena* 20 (November/December): 589–603.
——. 1899. The Beginning of Liberation. *Arena* 22(3) (September): 350–60.
Campbell, Helen *et al.* 1890. White Child Slavery, A Symposium. *Arena* 1 (April): 589–603.
Campbell, Helen Stuart, with Col. Thomas W. Knox and Supt. Thomas Byrnes. 1891. *Darkness and Daylight, or Lights and Shadows of New York Life.* Hartford, Conn.: A. D. Worthington and Co.
Campbell, Helen Stuart. Also wrote column on Woman's Work and Wages for *Good Housekeeping.*
Campbell, Mrs. J. [Weston]. 1896. American Women from a Colonial Point of View. *Contemporary Review* 70 (October): 516–28.
—— [as "C. de Thierry"]. 1896. The Empire and Downing Street. *New Review* 15 (October): 396–409.
—— [as "A Colonial"]. 1897. Arbitration and the Colonies. *New Review* 16 (January): 29–40.
—— [as "C. de Thierry"]. 1897. Colonial Empires. *New Review* 17 (August): 151–62.
——[as "C. de Thierry"]. 1897. England and Her Colonies. *New Review* 16 (April): 436–52.
—— [as "C. de Thierry"]. 1897. Imperialism, Part I. *New Review* 17 (September): 316–33.
—— [as "C. de Thierry"]. 1897. Imperialism, Part II. *New Review* 17 (October): 382–97.
—— [as "C. de Thierry"]. 1898. *Imperialism.* London: Duckworth.
——. 1899. The Sons of Han [on Chinese immigration]. *Macmillan's* 80 (May): 58–66.
—— [as "C. De Thierry"]. 1900. The Empire and the War. *United Service Magazine* (March): 593–606.
Campbell, M. Edith. 1910. Employment Bureaus for Women. In Helen Marot, ed., *The Economic Position of Women.* New York: U.S. Academy of Political Science. Also in Henry Raymond Mussey, ed., *Proceedings of the Academy of Political Science in the City of New York.* New York: Columbia University.
Campbell, Mary Edith and Anne Sophia Davis. 1932. *Vocational Guidance: Report of the Subcommittee on Vocational Guidance.* New York and London: Century Co.
Campbell, Persia Crawford. 1921/2. Asiatic Immigration into Australia. *Economica* 1/2(1): 52–.

——. 1923. *Chinese Coolie Emigration to Countries in the British Empire.* London School of Economics and Political Science, Studies in Economics and Political Science series of monographs, no. 72. London: P. S. King & Son.

——. 1923. Chinese Coolie Emigration to Countries in the British Empire. M.Sc. thesis, London School of Economics.

——. 1925. Examination of Immigrants. *Australasian Journal of Psychology and Philosophy* 3: 290–.

——, ed. 1928. *Studies in Australian Affairs.* Melbourne: Macmillan in association with Melbourne University Press.

——. 1928. Australian Nationalism. *Royal Australian Historical Society, Journal and Proceedings* 14(6): 321–.

——. 1933. *American Agricultural Policy.* London: P. S. King.

——. 1934. The American Wheat Program. *Pacific Affairs* 7(3): (September): 279–.

——. 1939. Book Review of "Australia Advances" by David M. Dow. *Pacific Affairs* 12(1): (March): 98–.

——. 1940/1941. Consumer Representation in the New Deal. Ph.D. thesis, Columbia University.

——. Collection of Writings located at the Center for the Study of the Consumer Movement, Mount Vernon, New York; also in the Consumers' Union Archives in Yonkers, New York.

Campbell, Sybil. 1928. Usury and Annuities of the Eighteenth Century. *Law Quarterly Review* (October).

——. 1933. The Economic and Social Effect of the Usury Laws in the Eighteenth Century. In *Transactions of the Royal Historical Society*, vol. 16: 197–210. London: Royal Historical Society (Great Britain).

Candee, Helen Churchill [Hungerford]. 1896. Li Hung Chang's Kingdom in America. *Illustrated American* 20 (November 28): 715–27.

——. 1897. City Clubs for Household Economics. *Illustrated American* 22 (September 25): 409.

——. 1897. City Homes of Bachelor Women. *Illustrated American* 22 (July 3): 20.

——. 1897. Woman of the Middle West. *Harper's Bazar* 30 (February 13): 130.

——. 1898. Myth or a Reality? *Harper's Bazar* 30 (December): 1,064.

——. 1898. New Home for Invalid Working-girls. *Harper's Bazar* 30 (December 11): 1,042.

——. 1898. Oklahoma Claims. *Lippincott's Magazine* 62 (October): 557–61.

——. 1898. Social Conditions in our Newest Territory [Oklahoma]. *Forum* 25 (June): 426–37.

——. 1898. Training-schools for Domestic Service. *Harper's Bazar* 31 (July 23): 623.

——. 1898. Violet-growing as Woman's Trade. *Ladies' Home Journal* 15 (April): 36.

——. 1899. Housekeeping on an Ocean Steamship. *Ladies' Home Journal* 16 (June): 2.

——. 1900. Oklahoma. *Atlantic Monthly.* 86: 328.

——. 1900. *How Women May Earn a Living.* New York and London: Macmillan.

Canel, Eva. 1893. The Spanish Women. *North American Review* 157 (July/December): 566–.

Cannon, Poppy. 1930. Pin Money Slaves. *Forum and Century* 84 (August): 98–103.

Canon, Helen. 1930. The Family Finances of 195 Farm Families in Tompkins County. Ph.D. thesis, Cornell University (economics, agricultural).

——. 1931. *The Family Finances of 195 Farm Families in Tompkins County, New York, 1927–28.* Ithaca, N.Y.: Cornell University.

Canon, Helen and Mabel Alice Rollins. 1936. *Notes on the Construction of the Index of the Cost of Goods and Services Bought by Farm Families in New York State, 1920 to 1935.* Ithaca, N.Y.: Cornell University.

——. 1937. *Index Numbers of the Cost of Goods and Services Bought by Farm Families in New York, 1920 to 1935.* Ithaca, N.Y.: Cornell University.

Canoyer, Helen Gertrude. 1930. The Importance of Brand in Merchandising Policies. M.A. thesis, University of Minnestoa.

Canoyer, Helen Gertrude and Roland S. Vaile. 1938. *Income and Consumption.* New York: H. Hold & Co.

Cappe, Catharine. 1800. *An Account of Two Charity Schools for the Education of Girls, and of a Female Friendly Society in York, Interspersed with Reflections on Charity Schools and Friendly Societies in General.* London: Sold by J. Johnson; New York: William Blanchard.

——. 1805. *Observations on Charity Schools, Female Friendly Societies, and Other Subjects Connected with the Views of the Ladies Committee.* York, UK: Printed by W. Blanchard for J. Hatchard, J. Johnson, and J. Mawman.

——. 1816. *Thoughts on the Desirableness and Utility of Ladies Visiting the Female Wards of Hospitals and Lunatic Asylums.* London: The Pamphleteer, vol. 8.

Carmichael, Maude. 1935. The Plantation System in Arkansas, 1850–1876. Ph.D. thesis, Radcliffe College (economics).

Carne, Elizabeth C. T. 1868. *Country Towns, and the Place They Fill in Modern Civilization.* London: Bell and Daldy.

Carner, Lucy P. 1923. An Educational Opportunity for Industrial Girls. *Journal of Social Forces* 1(5) (September): 612–13.

——. 1928. Shorter Hours for Women Workers. *American Federationist* 35(10): (October): 1,246–.

——. 1939. Let's Do Something About It. *Social Work Today* 6(9) (June): 29–.

——. 1940. The Challenge to Social Workers. *Social Work Today* 7(9) (June): 20–.

Carnes, Kate. 1890. Homesteads for Women. *Chautauquan* 11 (April/September): 465–.

——. 1892. Our Indian Tribes. *Chautauquan* 15 (April): 83–.

Carpenter, Mary. 1849. *Ragged Schools: Their Principles and Modes of Operation.* London: Partridge and Oakley.

——. 1851. *Reformatory Schools for the Children of the Perishing and Dangerous Classes and for Juvenile Offenders.* London: C. Gilpin.

——. 1853. *Juvenile Delinquents: Their Condition and Treatment.* London: W. and F. G. Cash.

——. 1857. On the Importance of Statistics to the Reformatory Movement. *Journal of the Statistical Society of London* 20 (March): 33–40.

——. 1858. Women's Work in the Reformatory Movement. *English Woman's Journal* 1 (July).

——. 1859. *The Claims of Ragged Schools to Pecuniary Educational Aid from the Annual Parliamentary Grant, as an Integral Part of the Educational Movement of the Country.* London: Partridge and Co.

——. 1861. *What Shall We Do with Our Pauper Children?* Paper read before the Social Economy Section of the Social Science Association, Dublin, August 1861. Pamphlet. London: Longman Brown & Co.

——. 1861. On Educational Help from Government for the Destitute and Neglected Children of Great Britain. *Journal of the Statistical Society of London* 24(1) (March): 22–9.

——. 1863. On the Treatment of Female Convicts. *Fraser's* 67 (January): 31–46.

——. 1864. *Our Convicts.* 2 vols. London: Longman, Green, Longman, Roberts & Green.

——. 1865. Our Neglected and Destitute Children: Are They to Be Educated? *Journal of Social Science* 1(2).

——. 1867. *Addresses to the Hindoos, Delivered in India.* London: Newman and Co.; Calcutta: Longman's and Co.

——. 1867. *Suggestions on Prison Discipline and Female Education in India.* London: Longmans.

——. 1868. *Six Months in India.* 2 vols. London: Longmans, Green.

Carr, Elma B[ebee]. 1918. Comparison of Food Costs in 45 Cities, September, 1917, to August, 1918. *Monthly Labor Review* 7 (July/December): 1,243–53.

——. 1919. Average Retail Food Prices and Percentages of Increase in 39 Cities, 1918 Compared with 1913. *Monthly Labor Review* 8(3) (March): 103–10.

——. 1919. Trend in Retail Prices of Food in 39 Cities, 1913 to May, 1919. *Monthly Labor Review* 9(1) (July): 57–60.

——. 1920. Production, Cold Storage Holdings, and Wholesale and Retail Prices of Butter and Cheese. *Monthly Labor Review* 10(1) (January): 100–14.

——. 1924. Cost of Living Statistics at U.S. Bureau of Labor Statistics and the National Industrial Conference Board: Comparison of Methods Used in the Collection and Computation of Cost of Living Figures. *Journal of the American Statistical Association* 19(148) (December): 484–507.

——. 1925. *The Use of Cost-of-Living Figures in Wage Adjustments.* Washington: U.S. Government Printing Office.

——. 1925. Cost of Preparation for Teaching, and Salary Return. *Monthly Labor Review* 21 (July/December): 20–7.

Carroll, Mollie Ray. 1915. A Survey of the Paupers and Dependents in Cook County, Illinois. A.M. thesis, University of Chicago (sociology, public and social welfare).

——. 1920. Labor and Politics: The Attitude of the American Federation of Labor Toward Legislation and Politics. Ph.D. thesis, University of Chicago (economics, sociology).

——. 1922/3. Some Problems in the Training of Social Workers. *Social Forces* 1(1/5): 547–.

——. 1923. *Labor and Politics: The Attitude of the American Federation of Labor Toward Legislation and Politics.* Chicago: University of Chicago Libraries. Hart, Schaffner & Marx Prize Essay, no. 33.

——. 1923. *Women and the Labor Movement in America.* Pamphlets in American History. Women, WO 58. Washington: National League of Women Voters, Women in Industry Committee.

——. 1923/4. Centrifugal and Centripetal Forces in Social Work. *Social Forces* 2(1/5): 515–.

——. 1925. *The Federal Women's Bureau.* Washington: Committee on Women in Industry, National League of Women Voters.

——. 1925. *A Program for Unemployment.* Washington: Women in Industry Committee, National League of Women Voters.

——. 1925. Book Review of "Labor and Politics, the Attitude of the American Federation of Labor Toward Legislation and Politics." *Journal of Negro History* 10(2) (April): 312–13.

——. 1925. Developing Economic Tendencies. *American Federationist* 32(7/12) (July/December): 907–.

——. 1925. Pan-American Problems of Women in Industry. *American Federationist* 32(7/12) (July/December): 546–.

——. 1925. Women Workers and the Minimum Wage. *American Federationist* 32(7/12) (July/December): 1,155–.

——. 1926. The Right of the Worker to Education. *American Federationist* 33(7/12) (July/December): 810–.

——. 1928. German Unemployment Insurance. *American Federationist* 35(5) (May): 536–.

——. 1928. The Hedwig–Rudiger Homes. *American Federationist* 35(10) (October): 1,210–.

——. 1929/1930. *Unemployment Insurance in Germany.* Washington: Brookings Institution.

——. 1929. Germany's New Unemployment Insurance. *American Labor Legislation Review* 19: 97–.

——. 1929. Present-day Social Insurance in Germany. *Social Forces* 8(1) (September): 126–34.

——. 1929. Two Years of German Unemployment Insurance. *Social Service Review* 3(1/4) (March/December): 563–.

——. 1930. *Our Wants and How They Are Satisfied.* Boston: M. Barrows & Company.

——. 1930. Amending The German Unemployment Insurance Act. *Social Service Review* 4(1/4) (March/December): 452–.

——. 1930. The Burden of Unemployment. *American Labor Legislation Review* 20: 260–1.

——. 1931. Unemployment Insurance by Industry? *American Labor Legislation Review* 21(3) (September): 319–.

——. 1931/2. Book Review of "Wirtschaftsgemässe Gestaltung der Arbeitslosenversicherung" by Erich Haussermann. *American Journal of Sociology* 37(1/6): 156–.

——. 1932. *Unemployment Insurance in Austria.* Washington: Brookings Institution.

——. 1932. Book review of "The Real Meaning of Social Insurance" by Hugh H. Wolfenden. *American Journal of Sociology* 38(1/6): 811–12.

——. 1933. Special Legislation in Relation to Public Policies. *American Federationist* 40(8) (August): 849–.

——. 1933/4. Book Review of "Human Aspects of Unemployment and Relief" by James Nickel Williams. *American Journal of Sociology* 39(1/6): 433–.

——. 1933/4. Book Review of "State Aid in Several Forms of Public Relief" by James Fogarty. *American Journal of Sociology* 39(1/6): 557–.

——. 1933/4. Book Review of "Unemployment Insurance in Belgium: A National Development of the Ghent and Liege Systems" by Constance A. Kiehel. *American Journal of Sociology* 39(1/6): 253–.

——. 1934. Book Review of "Unemployment in Germany since the War" by Kenneth Ingram Wiggs. *Journal of Political Economy* 42: 422–.

——. 1934. The Emergency Education Program and Labor. *Journal of Adult Education* 6(4) (October): 493–.

——. 1934/5. Book Review of "The Scandinavian Unemployment Relief Program" by C. J. Ratzlafe. *American Journal of Sociology* 40(1/6): 697–.

——. 1934/5. Book Review of "Work Relief in Germany" by Hertha Kraus. *American Journal of Sociology* 40(1/6): 696–.

——. 1935. *The American Federation of Labor: A Discussion Outline for Trade Union Groups.* Syllabus series, no. 4. New York: Workers Education Bureau Press.

——. 1935. Rural Electrification. *American Federationist* 42(9) (September): 944–.

——. 1935/6. Book Review of "After the Shutdown" by Ewan Clague, Walter J. Couper, and E. Wight Bakke. *American Journal of Sociology* 41(1/6): 699–.

——. 1937. Cooperative Workers' Education. *Journal of Adult Education* 9(2) (April): 184–.

——. 1938. The Costs of Administering Unemployment Compensation. *American Federationist* 45(7) (July): 696–.

——. 1939. *What is Collective Bargaining?* New York: Longmans, Green.

——. 1940. The Nature and Purpose of Workers' Education. *Journal of Adult Education* 12(4) (October): 502–.

Carsel, Winifred. 1940. *A History of the Chicago Ladies' Garment Workers' Union.* Chicago: Normandie House.

Carter, Harriet. 1890/1. A Co-operative Experiment. *Chautauquan* 12 (October/March): 224–.

——. 1890/1. Training Boys and Girls in Housework. *Chautauquan* 12 (October/March): 515–.

Carter, Susan N. 1892. Women in the Field of Art Work. *North American Review* 155 (July/December): 381–.

Carus-Wilson, Eleanor Mary. 1927. Summaries of Theses: The Overseas Trade of Bristol in the Later Middle Ages, 1399–1485. *Institute of Historical Research, Bulletin* 5(14) (November): 106.

——. 1928. The Merchant Adventurers of Bristol in the Fifteenth Century. *Royal Historical Society, Transactions* 4(11): 61–.

——. 1929. The Aulnage Accounts: A Criticism. *Economic History Review* 2(1) (January): 114–23.

——. 1933. The Iceland Trade. In Eileen Edna Power, ed., *Studies in English Trade in the Fifteenth Century*. London: Routledge.

——. 1933. The Origins and Early Development of the Merchant Adventurers' Organization in London as Shown in Their Own Mediaeval Records. *Economic History Review* 4(2) (April): 147–76.

——. 1933. The Overseas Trade of Bristol. In Eileen Edna Power, ed., *Studies in English Trade in the Fifteenth Century*. London: Routledge.

——. 1935/6. Book Review of "The Great Red Book of Bristol." *Economic History Review* 6: 120–.

——. 1935/6. Book Review of "The Staple Court Books of Bristol" by E. E. Rich, ed. *Economic History Review* 6: 118–.

——. 1937. *The Overseas Trade of Bristol in the Later Middle Ages*. Bristol Record Society Publications, vol. VII. Bristol: Bristol Record Society.

——. 1937/8. Book Review of "Acts of Court of the Mercers' Company, 1453–1527" by L. Lyell and F. D. Watney. *Economic History Review* 8: 196–.

——. 1939/40. Book Review of "The Port Books or Local Customs Accounts of Southampton for the Reign of Edward IV" by D. B. Quinn and A. A. Ruddock. *Economic History Review* 10: 72–.

Casady, Lauren W. 1938. Labor Unrest and the Labor Movement in the Salmon Industry of the Pacific Coast. Ph.D. thesis, University of California–Berkeley (economics).

Catherwood, Mary Hartwell. 1880. The Career of a Prairie Farmer. *Lippincott's Magazine* 25 (January/June): 706.

——. 1884. A Western Industry. *Lippincott's* 34 (July/December): 617–.

——. 1890/1. The Housekeeping Student. *Chautauquan* 12 (October/March): 360.

——. 1896. A Little Domestic. *Atlantic Monthly* 77 (February): 217–22.

Cauer, Minna Schelle. 1893. *Die Frauen in den Vereinigten Staaten von Nord-Amerika*. Berlin: R. Lesser.

——. 1898. *Die Frau im 19. Jahrhundert*. Berlin: S. Cronbach.

Caulfeild, Sophie F. A. 1891. New Employments for Girls. *A Girl's Own Paper* 13 (October): 20.

Caunes, Magdeleine. 1938. *Des Mesures juridiques propres à faciliter la présence de la mère au foyer ouvrier*. Paris: A. Pedone.

——. 1938. Des Mesures juridiques propres à faciliter la présence de la mère au foyer ouvrier. Thesis, University of Paris, Faculty of Law.

Cavan, Ruth Shonle. 1926. Suicide – A Study of Personal Disorganization. Ph.D. thesis, University of Chicago (sociology).

——. 1929. *Business Girls: A Study of Their Interests and Problems*. Chicago: Religious Education Association.

——. 1929/30. Book Review of "An Outline of Careers for Women: A Practical Guide to Achievement" by Doris E. Fleischman. *American Journal of Sociology* 35(1/6): 678–.

——. 1929/30. Book Review of "The Saleslady" by Frances R. Donovan. *American Journal of Sociology* 35(1/6): 676–.

——. 1929/30. Education and the Business Girl. *Journal of Educational Sociology* 3: 83–.

——. 1929/30. Interviewing for Life-history Material. *American Journal of Sociology* 35(1/6): 100–.

——. 1930/1. Note on the Statistical Treatment of Life-history Material. *Social Forces* 9(1/4): 200–.

——. 1931/2. Book Review of "Post-war Progress in Child Welfare. Annals of the American Academy of Political and Social Science." *American Journal of Sociology* 37(1/6): 171–.

——. 1932/3. Book Review of "Influence of Social and Economic Factors on the Health of The School Child" by Raymond Franzen. *American Journal of Sociology* 38(1/6): 965–.

——. 1932/3. The Questionnaire in a Sociological Research Project. *American Journal of Sociology* 38(1/6): 721–.

——. 1938/9. Book Review of "Child Workers in America" by Katharine DuPre Lumpkin and Dorothy Wolff Douglas. *American Journal of Sociology* 44(1/6): 777–.

Cavan, Ruth Shonle and Katherine Howland Ranck. 1938/1969. *The Family and the Depression: A Study of One Hundred Chicago Families*. Chicago: University of Chicago Press.

Cavendish, Lady Lucy [Lyttelton]. 1890. What Is to Be Done with the Morally Deficient: An Appeal to All Christians, Philanthropists, and Political Economists. *New Review* (March): 212–20.

——. 1892. Thrift for the Poor. *New Review* 7 (December): 669–73.

——. 1897. Law and the Laundry II: Laundries in Religious Houses. *Nineteenth Century* 41 (February): 232–5.

Cers, Edna. *See* Macmahon, Edna Cers.

Chace, Elizabeth Buffum. 1881. *Factory Women and Girls of New England*. Providence, R.I.: Rhode Island Woman Suffrage Association.

Chandler, Lucinda B. 1891. The Woman Movement. *Arena* 4 (November): 704–11.

Channing, Alice. 1925. *Child Labor on Maryland Truck Farms*. Children's Bureau Publication, no. 123. Washington: U.S. Government Printing Office.

——. 1932. *Employed Boys and Girls in Milwaukee*. Children's Bureau Publication, no. 213. Washington: U.S. Government Printing Office.

——. 1932. *Employment of Mentally Deficient Boys and Girls*. Children's Bureau Publication, no. 210. Washington: U.S. Government Printing Office.

——. 1932. Employed Boys and Girls of Rochester and Utica, New York. Ph.D. thesis, University of Chicago (sociology).

——. 1933. *Employed Boys and Girls*. Washington: U.S. Government Printing Office.

——. 1933. *Employed Boys and Girls in Rochester and Utica, New York*. Children's Bureau Publication, no. 218. Washington: U.S. Government Printing Office.

Channing, Alice, Ellen Nathalie Matthews, and Mary E. Skinner. 1926. *Child Labor in Fruit and Hop Growing Districts of the Northern Pacific Coast*. Children's Bureau Publication, no. 151. Washington: U.S. Government Printing Office.

Channing, Alice, Katherine Walkley, Eunice Usher, and Carolyn Keller. 1940. *State Program for Crippled Children in Maine, Connecticut, and Ohio, 1939*. Boston: Simmons College.

Channing, Alice. Coauth. *See* Matthews, Ellen Nathalie.

Chapman, Altona A. 1895. Representative Women on Social Problems: Is the Single Tax Enough? (Symposium). *Arena* 13 (August): 413–18.

Chapman, Elizabeth Rachel. 1883. *The New Godiva: and Other Studies in Social Questions*. London: T. Fisher Unwin.

——. 1888. Marriage Rejection and Marriage Reform. *Westminster Review* 130 (September): 358–77.

——. 1890. The Decline of Divorce. *Westminster Review* 133 (April): 417–.

Chapman, Priscilla. 1839. *Hindoo Female Education*. London: R. B. Seeley and W. Burnside.

Charles, Enid. 1932. *The Practice of Birth Control: An Analysis of the Birth Control Experiences of Nine Hundred Women*. London: Williams & Norgate.

——. 1934. *The Twilight of Parenthood: A Biological Study of the Decline of Population Growth*. New York: Watts & Co.

——. 1935. *The Effect of Present Trends in Fertility and Mortality upon the Future Population of England and Wales and upon Its Age Composition*. London & Cambridge Economic Service Special Memorandum, no. 40. London: Executive Committee of London & Cambridge Economic Service.

——. 1936. *The Menace of Under-population: A Biological Study of the Decline of Population Growth*. London: Watts & Co.

——. 1937. The Changing Structure of the Family in Australia. *Economica*, n.s. 4(15) (August): 245–73.

——. 1937. Differential Fertility. *Sociological Review* 29: 243–.

Chase, Ellen and Octavia Hill. 1929. *Tenant Friends in Old Deptford*. London: Williams & Norgate.

Chauvin, Jeanne. 1892. *Étude historique sur les professions accessibles aux femmes; influence du sémitisme sur l'évolution de la position économique de la femme dans la société*. Paris: A. Giard & E. Brière.

——. 1892. *Des Professions accessibles aux femmes en droit romain et en droit français: Evolution historique de la position économique de la femme dans la société*. Thesis, Faculté de droit de Paris.

——. 1893. *Proposition de loi sur la capacité des femmes d'être témoin dans les actes publics ou privés*. Paris: Publications de l'Avant-courrière.

——. 1893. *Proposition de loi sur la capacité des femmes mariées de disposer du produit de leur travail ou de leur industrie personnels*. Paris: Publications de l'Avant-courrière.

——. 1895. *Cours de droit professé dans les lycées de jeunes filles de Paris*. Paris: V. Giard & E. Briére.

Cheney, Mrs. Ednah D. 1891. Shall Women Work for Pay? *Chautauquan* 13 (April/September): 215– and 356–.

Cheney, May S. 1905. Will Nature Eliminate the College Woman? *Association of Collegiate Alumnae, Publications*, series 3, 10 (January): 1–.

Chesney, Jane. 1879. New Vocation for Women. *Macmillan's* 40 (August): 341–6.

——. 1880. Poultry-keeping as National Industry. *Macmillan's* 42 (February): 315–21.

——. 1881. Poultry-keeping in Normandy. *Macmillan's* 43 (April): 476–80.

Chester, Eliza. 1892. *The Unmarried Woman*. New York: Dodd, Mead and Co.

Chew, Ada Nield. 1894. Letter to the Crewe, Cheshire, *Chronicle* (July 14). Reprinted in Doris Nield Chew, ed., *Ada Nield Chew: The Life and Writings of a Working Woman*. London: Virago Press, 1982.

——. 1894. Life in a Crewe Factory. Serialized in the *Crewe Chronicle* (June 9, 23, 30 and July 14, 1894). Reprinted in Doris Nield Chew, ed., *Ada Nield Chew: The Life and Writings of a Working Woman*. London: Virago Press, 1982.

——. 1894. A Living Wage for Factory Girls at Crewe. Originally published in *Crewe Chronicle* (May 19, 1894). Reprinted in Doris Nield Chew, ed., *Ada Nield Chew: The Life and Writings of a Working Woman*. London: Virago Press, 1982.

——. 1912. The Economic Freedom of Women. *Freewoman* 2(35) (July 13).

——. 1914. The Problem of the Married Working Woman. *Common Cause* 5(255) (February 27).

——. 1922. Family Endowment: Another View. *Woman's Leader* 14(33) (September 15).

Cheyney, Alice S[quires]. 1922. England's Verdict on Unemployment Insurance. *American Labor Legislation Review* 12: 175.

——. 1923. A Definition of Social Work. Ph.D. thesis, University of Pennsylvania (social work).

——. 1926. What Consumers Want of Bituminous Coal. *American Federationist* 33(7/12) (July/December): 1,366–.

——. 1926. What the Miners Want of the Coal Industry. *American Federationist* 33(7/12) (July/December): 1,226–.

——. 1926. What the Operators Want from the Coal Industry. *American Federationist* 33(7/12) (July/December): 1,085–.

——. 1926. Who Is to Blame for the Trouble of the Coal Mines? *American Federationist* 33(7/12) (July/December): 947–.

——. 1929/30. Ten Years of Disarmament Through Labor Legislation. *Social Forces* 8(1/4): 582–.

——. 1931. *International Labor Standards and American Legislation (A Comparison)*. Geneva Special Studies, vol. 2, no. 8 (August). Geneva: Geneva Research Information Committee.

——. 1931. An International Minimum Age For Employment. *Vocational Guidance Magazine* 10(3) (December): 114–.
——. 1933. The Character and Accessibility of Office Research Materials. *American Academy of Political and Social Science, Annals* 166 (March): 114–.
——. 1933. A Comparison of Convention Provisions with Labor Legislation in the United States. *American Academy of Political and Social Science, Annals* 166 (March): 176–.
——. 1933. The International Conference on Reduction of Hours of Work. *American Federationist* 40(5) (May): 501–.
——. 1934. *The International Labor Organization.* Foreign Policy Reports, vol. X, no. 9 (July 4). New York: Foreign Policy Association, Inc.
——. 1934. International Labor Conventions. *Monthly Labor Review* 38(4) (April): 759–.
——. 1935. Workers' Education in the United States. *International Labour Review, Geneva* 32 (July): 39–59.
——. 1938. The Course of Minimum Wage Legislation in the United States. *International Labour Review, Geneva* 38 (July): 26–43.
Chickering, Martha A[lexander]. 1934. Personnel For Public Welfare Service: Discussion. *Social Service Review* 8(1/4) (March/December): 470–.
——. 1936. Public Provisions for the Care of the Dependent Sick in Alameda County, California. Ph.D. thesis, University of California–Berkeley (economics).
——. 1938. An Early Experiment in State Aid to the Aged, California, 1883–95. *Social Service Review* 12(1/4) (March/December): 41–.
——. 1938. What a Visitor in a Public Agency Should Know. *Alabama Social Welfare* 3(12) (December): 13–.
[Child], Lydia Maria Francis. 1824. *Hobomok, A Tale of Early Times.* Boston: Cummings, Hilliard. [*novel*]. In Carolyn Karcher, ed., *Lydia Child, Hobomok and other writings on Indians.* New Brunswick, N.J.: Rutgers University Press, 1986.
Child, Lydia Maria Francis [Mrs. D. L. Child]. 1829. T*he First Settlers of New England: or, Conquest of the Pequods, Narragansets and Pokahokets, as Related By a Mother to Her Children, and Designed for the Instruction of Youth.* Boston: Munroe and Frances; New York: Charles S. Francis.
——. 1829. *The Frugal Housewife, Dedicated to Those Who Are Not Ashamed of Economy.* Boston: Marsh & Capen and Carter & Hendee. 14 eds. by 1834. From 1832 entitled *The American Frugal Housewife.* Reprinted Mineola, N.Y.: Dover Publications, 1999.
——. 1831. *The Mother's Book.* Boston: Carter, Hendee & Babcock. Revised and enlarged ed. Boston: Joseph H. Francis, 1844.
——. 1833. *An Appeal in Favor of that Class of Americans Called Africans.* Boston: Allen & Ticknor. Reprinted New York: Arno Press, 1968. Reprinted 1996, ed. Carolyn Karcher. Amherst: University of Massachusetts Press.
——. 1834. Conversation between the Editor and a Colonizationist. In L. M. Child, ed., *The Oasis.* Boston: Bejamin C. Bacon.

——. 1835. *The History of the Condition of Women, in Various Ages and Nations*, Vol. 1: Asia & Africa; Vol. 2: Europe, America & South Seas. Boston: John Allen & Co. Revised ed., retitled *Brief History of the Condition of Women, in Various Ages and Nations*. Boston: J. H. Francis, 1845.

——. 1836. *Anti-slavery Catechism*. Newburyport, Mass.: Charles Whipple.

——. 1836. *The Evils of Slavery, and the Cure of Slavery: The First Proved By the Opinions of Southerners Themselves, the Last Shown By Historical Evidence*. Newburyport, Mass.: Charles Whipple.

——. 1837. *The Family Nurse; or Companion of the Frugal Housewife*. Boston: Charles J. Hendee.

——, ed. 1843. *The American Anti-slavery Almanac for 1843*. New York: American Anti-slavery Society.

——. 1843. *Letters From New York. First Series*. New York: C. S. Francis; and London: Bentley.

——. 1844. *Letters From New York. Second Series*. New York: C. S. Francis.

——. 1860. *The Duty of Disobedience to the Fugitive Slave Act: An Appeal to the Legislators of Massachusetts*. Boston: American Anti-slavery Society.

——, ed. 1860. *The Patriarchal Institution, as Described By Members of Its Own Family*. New York: American Anti-Slavery Society.

——. 1860. *The Right Way, the Safe Way, Proved By Emancipation in the British West Indies, and Elsewhere*. New York: American Anti-Slavery Society.

——, ed. 1865. *The Freedmen's Book*. Boston: Ticknor and Fields.

——. 1868. *An Appeal for the Indians*. New York, W. P. Tomlinson. Reprinted in Carolyn L. Karcher, ed., *Lydia Child, Hobomok & Other Writings on Indians*. New Brunswick, N.J.: Rutgers University Press, 1986.

Chisholm, Caroline. 1842. *Female Immigration Considered, in a Brief Account of the Sydney Immigrant's Home*. Sydney: James Tegg.

——. 1847. *Comfort for the Poor! Meat Three Times a Day!! Voluntary Information from the People of New South Wales, Collected in that Colony by Mrs. Chisholm, in 1845–46*. London: John Ollivier.

——. 1847. *Emigration and Transportation Relatively Considered; in a Letter, Dedicated, By Permission, to Earl Grey*. London: John Ollivier.

——. 1850. *The A.B.C. of Colonization. In a Series of Letters*. London: John Ollivier.

Cholmondeley, Mary. 1899. *Red Pottage*. London: Edward Arnold. [*novel*]

Chudleigh, Elizabeth, Countess of Bristol. 1777. *The Laws Respecting Women as They Regard Their Natural Rights, or Their Connections and Conduct: in Which Their Interests and Duties as Daughters, Wards, Heiresses, Spinsters, Sisters, Wives, Widows, Mothers, Legatees, Executrixes, &c. Are Ascertained and Enumerated: Also, the Obligations of Parent and Child, and the Condition of Minors*. London: Printed for J. Johnson.

Church, Ella Rodman. 1882. *Money-making for Ladies*. New York: Harper.

Claflin, Tennessee. *See* Cook, Lady Tennessee Claflin.

Claghorn, Kate Holladay. 1896. The Ethics of Copyright. *Yale Review* 4 (February): 426–40.

——. 1897. *College Training for Women*. New York: Crowell

——. 1897. Edmund Burke: A Centenary Perspective. *Atlantic Monthly* 80: 84–95.

——. 1898. The Problem of Occupation for College Women. *Educational Review* 15 (March): 217–30.

——. 1900. Occupation for the College Graduate. *Association of Collegiate Alumnae, Publications* 3(3) (February): 62–.

——. 1900. Our Immigrants and Ourselves. *Atlantic Monthly. A Magazine of Literature, Art and Politics* 86: 535.

——. 1901. The Changing Character of Immigration (Twelve Illustrations). *World's Work* 1(4) (February): 381–.

——. 1904. Immigration and Dependence. *Charities; a Weekly Review of Local and General Philanthropy* 12: 135.

——. 1904. Immigration in Its Relation to Pauperism. *Annals of the American Academy of Political and Social Science* 24: 187.

——. 1904. Italian, under Economic Stress. *Charities; a Weekly Review of Local and General Philanthropy* 12: 501.

——. 1911. Book Review of "Woman and Labor" by Olive Schreiner. *American Economic Review* 1 (December): 812–13.

——. 1912. The Protection and Distribution of Immigrants. *Academy of Political Science, Proceedings* 2(4) (July): 199–.

——. 1913. Book Review of "I Fattori Demografici dell'Evoluzione delle Nazioni. The Contributions of Demography to Eugenics" by Gini. *American Economic Review* 3: 959–.

——. 1913. Book Review of "The Immigrant" by Haskin. *American Economic Review* 3: 686.

——. 1913. Book Review of "The Immigrant Invasion" by Warne. *American Economic Review* 3: 686.

——. 1913. Book Review of "Immigration" by Fairchild. *American Academy of Political and Social Science, Annals* 50 (November): 273–.

——. 1913. Book Review of "The New Immigration" by Roberts. *American Economic Review* 3: 686.

——. 1914. Record Keeping as an Aid to Enforcement. *American Academy of Political and Social Science, Annals* 51 (January): 117–.

——. 1918. *Juvenile Delinquency in Rural New York.* Washington: U.S. Children's Bureau.

——. 1918. Crime and Immigration (Report of Committee E of the Institute). *Journal of Criminal Law and Criminology and Police Science* 8(5) (January): 675–.

——. 1923. *The Immigrant's Day in Court.* New York: Harper.

——. 1923. Methods of Evaluating Our Immigrant Peoples. *Mental Hygiene* 7 (January/October): 20–31.

——. 1925. Book Review of "Immigration; Select Documents and Case Records" by Edith Abbott. *Mental Hygiene* 9 (January/October): 648–9.

——. 1927. The Problem of Measuring Social Treatment. *Social Service Review* 1(1/4) (March/December): 181–.

——. 1930. Book Review of "500 Criminal Careers" by Glueck and Glueck. *Harvard Law Review* 43(8) (June): 1,332–.

Clapperton, Jane Hume. 1877. *What Do We Women Want? For It Is Certain that Discontent or a Spirit of Unrest Has Taken Possession More or Less of Us All.* London: W. H. Reynolds.

——. 1885. *Scientific Meliorism and the Evolution of Happiness.* London: Kegan Paul, Trench & Co.

——. 1888. *Margaret Dunmore; or, A Socialist Home.* London: Sonnenschein, Lowrey & Co. [*novel*]

——. 1888. Miss Chapman's Marriage Reform: A Criticism. *Westminster Review* 130 (December): 707–17.

——. 1899. *Some Evolutional Aspects of the Woman Movement.* S.l.: s.n.

——. 1904. *A Vision of the Future: Based on the Application of Ethical Principles.* London: Swan Sonnenschein.

Clark, Alice. 1919. *Working Life of Women in the Seventeenth Century.* London and New York: G. Routledge & Sons, Ltd./E. P. Dutton & Co. Reprinted London: Cass, 1968; New York: A. M. Kelley, 1968; London and New York: Routledge, 1974, 1992; London and Boston: Routledge & Kegan Paul, 1982.

Clark, Alice Lee Hardenbergh. 1939. Union Responsibility in the Glass Container Industry. M.A. thesis, University of Minnesota.

Clark, Bertha W. 1924. The Huterian Communities. Part I. *Journal of Political Economy* 32 (June): 357–74.

——. 1924. The Huterian Communities. Part II. *Journal of Political Economy* 32 (August): 468–86.

Clark, Dorothy K. 1937. Thomas Osborne, Earl of Danby: Lord Treasurer, 1673–1679. Ph.D. thesis, Radcliffe College (history).

——. 1938. Edward Backwell as a Royal Agent. *Economic History Review* 9 (November): 45–55.

Clark, Florence E[lizabeth]. 1922. Industrial Studies and Their Relation to Placement and Counseling. *National Vocational Guidance Association Bulletin* 1(4) (June): 5–.

——. 1925. Occupational Research Meetings, National Vocational Guidance Conference, February 19 and 20, 1925. *Vocational Guidance Magazine* 3(7) (April): 240–.

——. 1926. The Content and Arrangement of Schedules for Occupational Investigation. *Vocational Guidance Magazine* 4(7) (April): 318–.

——. 1926. Survey of Research Carried on in the Field of Occupations and Industry by Persons and Bureaus Connected with the Public School System. *Vocational Guidance Magazine* 4(7) (April): 309–.

——. 1927. A Schedule and Instructions for Investigation. *Vocational Guidance Magazine* 6(1) (October): 9–.

——. 1929. The Use of Occupational Studies in the Classroom and in the Personal Interview. *Vocational Guidance Magazine* 7(7) (April): 296–.

——. 1937. Part I: Preparatory Steps. *Occupations: The Vocational Guidance Magazine* 16(2) (November): 117–.

——. 1937. Part II: Field Studies. *Occupations: The Vocational Guidance Magazine* 16(3) (December): 548–.

——. 1938. The Socio-economic Approach to Gathering Information about Occupations. *Occupations: The Vocational Guidance Magazine* 16(6) (March): 548–.

——. 1939. *The Printing Trades and Their Workers*, 2nd ed. Scranton: International Textbook Company.

Clark, Florence M. 1935. Unemployment Survey of Bridgeport, Conn., 1934. *Monthly Labor Review* 40(3) (March): 626–.

Clark, Jane Perry. 1931. *Deportation of Aliens from the United States to Europe*. Ph.D. thesis, Columbia University (political science) New York: Columbia University Press.

——. 1938. *The Rise of a New Federation*. New York: Columbia University Press.

Clark, Marjorie Ruth. 1925. The British Labour Government in Contemporary Opinion. M.A. thesis, University of California–Berkeley.

——. 1928. French Syndicalism (1910–1927). Ph.D. thesis, University of California–Berkeley (economics).

——. 1930. *A History of the French Labor Movement (1910–1928)*. Berkeley: University of California Press.

——. 1930. French Syndicalism of the Present. *Journal of Political Economy* 38 (June): 317–27.

——. 1931. *The Contribution of Nebraska Farm Women to Farm Income through Poultry and Dairy Products*. Bulletin, University of Nebraska, Agricultural Experiment Station, 258. Lincoln: University of Nebraska, College of Agriculture.

——. 1931. Organized Labor and the Family-Allowance System in France. *Journal of Poltical Economy* 39 (August): 526–37.

——. 1932. History of the French Labor Movement (1910–1928). *Diritto del lavoro* 6(1): 577–.

——. 1934. *Organized Labor in Mexico*. Chapel Hill, N.C.: University of North Carolina Press.

——. 1936. Recent History of Labor Organization. *American Academy of Political and Social Science, Annals* 184 (March): 161–.

Clark, Marjorie Ruth and Greta Gray. 1929. *Water Carried for Household Purposes on Nebraska Farms*. Bulletin, University of Nebraska. Agricultural Experiment Station, 234. Lincoln: University of Nebraska, College of Agriculture.

——. 1930. *The Routine and Seasonal Work of Nebraska Farm Women*. Bulletin, University of Nebraska. Agricultural Experiment Station, 238. Lincoln: University of Nebraska, College of Agriculture, Experiment Station.

Clark, Marjorie Ruth and S. Fanny Simon. 1938. *The Labor Movement in America*. New York: W. W. Norton.

Clark, Martha Louise. 1894. The Relation of Imbecility to Pauperism and Crime. *Arena* 10 (November): 788–94.

Clark, Sue Ainslie. 1933. Wellesley Summer Institute for Social Progress *School and Society* 37(965) (June 24): 815–.

Clark, Sue Ainslie and Edith Wyatt. 1911. *Making Both Ends Meet. The Income and Outlay of New York Working Girls*. New York: Macmillan.

Clark, Vida Mae. 1895. Conference on Agricultural Depression. *Charities Review* 5(2) (December): 105–9.

Clarke, Helen A. 1899. Mrs [Charlotte Perkins] Stetson as Social Philosopher and Poet. *Poet Lore* 11 (March): 124–.

Clauder, Anna Cornelia. 1930. American Commerce as Affected by the Wars of the French Revolution and Napoleon, 1793–1812. Ph.D. thesis, University of Pennsylvania (economics, commerce-business).

——. 1932/1972. *American Commerce as Affected by the Wars of the French Revolution and Napoleon, 1793–1812.* Clifton, N.J.: A. M. Kelley.

Clerke, Agnes M. 1884. The Future of the Congo. *Edinburgh Review* 160 (July): 151–88.

——. 1889. The Cape in 1888. *Dublin Review*, n.s. 21 [o.s. 104] (January): 106–13.

——. 1889. East Africa. *Edinburgh Review* 170 (October): 389–416.

——. 1895. Problems of the Far East. *Edinburgh Review* 182 (July): 132–55.

Clerke, E[llen]. M[ary]. 1883. Modern Mexico. *Dublin Review*, 3rd series, 10 [o.s. 93] (October): 260–91.

——. 1884. The Revolution in the Soudan. *Dublin Review*, 3rd series, 11 [o.s. 94] (April): 392–414.

——. 1885. The Commercial Future of West Africa. *Dublin Review*, 3rd series, 13 [o.s. 96] (January): 1–30.

——. 1885. The Destiny of Khartoum. *Dublin Review*, 3rd series, 13 [o.s. 96] (April): 355–81.

——. 1885. Maritime Canals. *Dublin Review*, 3rd series, 14 [o.s. 97] (July): 1–19.

——. 1886. Burma and the Farther East. *Dublin Review*, 3rd series, 15 [o.s. 98] (April): 309–40.

——. 1886. The Future of Petroleum. *Dublin Review*, 3rd series, 16 [o.s. 99] (July): 31–65.

——. 1886. The Present Position of China. *Dublin Review*, 3rd series, 16 [o.s. 99] (October): 364–91.

——. 1887. The Age of Steel. *Dublin Review*, 3rd series, 18 [o.s. 101] (July): 54–77.

——. 1887. The Portuguese in India. *Dublin Review*, 3rd series, 17 [o.s. 100] (January): 98–124.

——. 1887. Rural Life in Italy. *Edinburgh Review* 165 (January): 107–18.

——. 1888. Assam and the Indian Tea Trade. *Asiatic Quarterly Review* 5 (January/April): 362.

——. 1888. The Empire Route to the East. *Dublin Review*, 3rd series, 19 [o.s. 102] (April): 274–93.

——. 1888. Irish Industries. *Dublin Review*, 3rd series, 20 [o.s. 103] (October): 378–99.

——. 1889. The Dock Labourers' Strike. *Dublin Review*, 3rd series, 22 [o.s. 105] (October): 386–406.

——. 1889. The New Crusade [against the slave trade]. *Dublin Review*, 3rd series, 21 [o.s. 104] (January): 1–24.

——. 1889. Syndicates, Trusts, and Corners. *Dublin Review*, 3rd series, 21 [o.s. 104] (April): 353–77.

——. 1890. Medieval Guilds and Modern Competition. *Dublin Review*, 3rd series, 23 [o.s. 106] (July): 145–64.

——. 1891. The Insurrection in Chile. *Dublin Review*, 3rd series, 25 [o.s. 108] (April): 308–27.

——. 1891. The Teaching of Economic Geography. *Dublin Review*, 3rd series, 25 [o.s. 108] (January): 35–53.

——. 1894. Mashunaland and Its Neighbours. *Dublin Review*, 4th series, 5 [o.s. 114] (January): 145–66.

——. 1896. Crisis in Rhodesia. *Dublin Review*, 4th series, 10 [o.s. 119] (October): 256–70.

Clevenger, Clara Eulalie Howard. 1920. Americanization as a Social Problem. A.M. thesis, Leland Stanford Junior University.

——. 1934. Legislative Control of Banking in Missouri since 1889. Ph.D. thesis, Cornell University (economics).

Clifford, Mary. 1896. *Out-relief.* London: National Council of Women of Great Britain.

Cobbe, Frances Power. 1861. *Friendless Girls, and How to Help Them. Being an Account of the Preventive Mission at Bristol.* London: Emily Faithfull.

——. 1861. *The Sick in Workhouses: Who They Are and How They Should Be Treated.* London: J. Nisbet.

——. 1861. *The Workhouse as an Hospital.* London: Emily Faithfull.

——. 1861. The Preventative Branch of the Bristol Female Mission. Paper read at the meeting of the National Association for the Promotion of Social Science (August) and published in the *English Woman's Journal* (November 1861). Reprinted in Candida Ann Lacey, ed., *Barbara Leigh Smith Bodichon and the Langham Place Group*. London and New York: Routledge, 1987.

——. 1861. Social Science Congresses, and Women's Part in Them. *Macmillan's Magazine* 5 (December): 81–94.

——. 1861. Workhouse Sketches. *Macmillan's Magazine* 3 (April): 448–61.

——. 1862. *Female Education and How It Would Be Affected by University Examinations: A Paper Read at the Social Science Congress, London, 1862*. London: Emily Faithfull.

——. 1862. Celibacy v. Marriage. *Fraser's* 65 (February): 228–35.

——. 1862. Female Charity: Lay and Monastic. *Fraser's* 66 (December): 774–88.

——. 1862. What Shall We Do with Our Old Maids? *Fraser's Magazine* 66 (November): 594–605. Reprinted in Candida Ann Lacey, ed., *Barbara Leigh Smith Bodichon and the Langham Place Group*. London and New York: Routledge, 1987. Reprinted in Andrea Broomfield and Sally Mitchell, eds., *Prose by Victorian Women: An Anthology*. New York: Garland Publishing, 1995.

——. 1862. Women in Italy in 1862. *Macmillan's Magazine* 6: 363–75.

——. 1863. *Essays on the Pursuits of Women, Reprinted from Fraser's and Macmillan's Magazines, also, a Paper on Female Education Read before the Social Science Congress, at Guildhall.* London: Emily Faithfull.

——. 1863. *The Red Flag in John Bull's Eyes.* London: Emily Faithfull. Online in University of Indiana's LETRS.

——. 1863. *Rejoinder to Mrs. Stowe's Reply to the Address of the Women of England.* London: Emily Faithfull.

——. Philosophy of the Poor-Laws. *Fraser's* 70 (September): 373–94.

——. 1865. *Studies New and Old of Ethical and Social Subjects.* London: Trubner's. Boston: W. V. Spencer, 1866.

——. 1865. Ireland and Her Exhibition in 1865. *Fraser's* 72 (October): 403–22.

——. 1866. Indigent Classes, Their Schools and Dwellings. *Fraser's* 73 (February): 143–60.

——. 1867. *Hours of Work and Play. Essays and short stories reprinted from various periodicals.* London: Trübner.

——. 1867. The American Sanitary Commission and Its Lesson. *Fraser's* 75 (March): 401–14.

——. 1867. The Organisation of Charity. *Theological Review* 4 (October):553–72.

——. 1867. What Is Progress, and Are We Progressing? *Fortnightly Review*, n.s. 1 [o.s. 7] (March): 357–70.

——. 1868. Criminals, Idiots, Women and Minors: Is This Classification Sound? A discussion of the Laws Concerning the Property of Married Women. *Fraser's Magazine* 78 (December): 777–94. Reprinted in Candida Ann Lacey, ed., *Barbara Leigh Smith Bodichon and the Langham Place Group*. London and New York: Routledge, 1987. Also reprinted in Marie Mulvey Roberts and Tamae Mizuta, eds., *Sources of British Feminism*, vol. 2: *The Disempowered: Women and the Law*. London: Routledge/Thoemmes, 1993.

——. 1868. Household Service. *Fraser's* 77 (January): 121–34.

——. 1869. *Why Women Desire the Franchise.* London: National Society for Women's Suffrage, Spottiswoode & Co., Printers. Online in University of Indiana's LETRS.

——. 1869. The Defects of Women, and How to Remedy Them. *Putnam's Magazine*, n.s. 4 (July/December): 226–33.

——. 1869. The Final Cause of Women. In Josephine Butler, ed., *Woman's Work and Woman's Culture*. London: Macmillan.

——. 1869. The Subjection of Women, *Theological Review* 6 (July): 355–75. Reprinted in Andrew Pyle, ed., *The Subjection of Women, Contemporary Responses to John Stuart Mill*. Bristol: Thoemmes Press, 1995.

——. 1870. *Our Policy: An Address to Women Concerning the Suffrage.* London: National Society for Women's Suffrage. Online in Indiana University's LETRS.

——. 1872. *Darwinism in Morals, and Other Essays.* London and Edinburgh: Williams & Norgate.

——. 1878. The Little Health of Ladies. *Contemporary Review* 31 (January): 276–96.

——. 1878. Wife-torture in England. *Contemporary Review* 32 (April): 55–87.

——. 1881. *The Duties of Women: A Course of Lectures.* London: Williams & Norgate; Boston: G. H. Ellis.

——. 1881. The Medical Profession and Its Morality. *Modern Review* 2 (April): 296–326.

——. 1882. The Salvation Army. *Contemporary Review* 42 (August): 182–9.

——. 1882. Vivisection and Its Two-faced Advocates. *Contemporary Review* 41 (January/June): 610–26.

——. 1882/3. Social Duties in the Family. *Chautauquan* 3 (October/July): 342.

——. 1883/4. Duties of Women as Mistresses of Households. *Chautauquan* 4 (October/July): 473–.

——. 1884. Introduction. In Theodore Stanton, ed., *The Woman Question in Europe: A Series of Original Essays*. London: Sampson Low, Marston, Searle; New York: G. P. Putnam's Sons. Reprinted New York: Source Book Press, 1970.

——. 1888. The Scientific Spirit of the Age. *Contemporary Review* 54 (July): 126–39.

——. 1889. *The Modern Rack: Papers on Vivisection*. London: S. Sonnenschein.

——. 1889. The Excess of Widows Over Widowers. *Westminster Review* 131: 501–5.

——. 1892. *Public Money: An Enquiry Concerning an Item of Its Expenditure*. London: Victoria Street Society [Society for the Protection of Animals Liable to Vivisection].

——. 1895. The Ethics of Zoophily. *Contemporary Review* 68 (October): 497–508.

Cobbett, Anne. 1835. *The English Housekeeper: or, Manual of Domestic Management: Containing Advice on the Conduct of Household Affairs and Practical Instructions…Together with Remarks on the Best Means of Rendering Assistance to Poor Neighbours…The Whole Being Intended for the Use of Young Ladies Who Undertake the Superintendence of Their Own Housekeeping*. London: Anne Cobbett; Edinburgh: William Tait.

Cochman, Margaret. 1933. State Grants for Medical Service with Special Reference to State Aid to General Hospitals. M.A. thesis, University of Chicago (economics, finance).

Cochran, Mary Elizabeth. 1930. A History of Restriction of American Immigration, 1607–1820. Ph.D. thesis, University of Chicago (history).

Cochrane, Constance. 1900. *Labourers' Cottages: Three Letters Especially Addressed to Agricultural Labourers*. St. Neots: s.n. Microfiche reproduction available from Columbia University Libraries.

——. 1901. *Papers on Rural Housing: The Present Condition of the Cottage Home of the Agricultural Labourer*. St. Neots, UK: printed at the *Advertiser* Office.

——. 1901. Village Water Supplies. London: Sanitary Institute. Reprinted from *Journal of the Sanitary Institute* XXII(4).

——. 1908. *Rural Housing. Pan-Anglican Papers*. London: Society for Promoting Christian Knowledge.

Cohen, Miss Mary M. 1884. Hebrew Charities. *Journal of Social Science* 19 (December): 168–76.

Cohen, Ruth Louisa. 1930. *Factors Affecting the Price of Potatoes in Great Britain*. Cambridge, UK: W. Heffer & Sons.

——. 1933. *A Survey of Milk Marketing Schemes and Price Policies*. Cambridge, UK: University of Cambridge Department of Agriculture.

——. 1934. Agricultural Reorganization and Price Control. *Economic Journal* 44(175) (September): 424–52.
——. 1935. Book Review of "Agricultural Co-operation in Fascist Italy" by F. Cotta. *Economic Journal* 45: 561.
——. 1935. Book Review of "The American Vegetable Shortening Industry: Its Origin and Development" by G. M. Weber and C. L. Alsberg. *Economic Journal* 45: 357.
——. 1935. Book Review of "Annuaire international de legislation agricole." *Economic Journal* 45: 561.
——. 1935. Book Review of "Considerations on the Present Evolution of Agricultural Protectionism." *Economic Journal* 45: 561.
——. 1935. Book Review of "Economics of the Farm Business" by T. Brinkmann. *Economic Journal* 45: 562.
——. 1935. Book Review of "The Hop Industry" by H. H. Parker. *Economic Journal* 45: 559.
——. 1935. Book Review of "La Nouvelle Politique agricole britannique" by P. Chautemps. *Economic Journal* 45: 777.
——. 1935. Book Review of "Proceedings of the Third International Conference of Agricultural Economists." *Economic Journal* 45: 561.
——. 1936. *The History of Milk Prices: An Analysis of the Factors Affecting the Price of Milk and Milk Products*. Oxford: Agricultural Economics Research Institute.
——. 1936. Book Review of "Agricultural Credit" by A. I. Qureshi. *Economic Journal* 46: 741.
——. 1936. Book Review of "Agricultural Organisation in New Zealand." *Economic Journal* 46: 739.
——. 1936. Book Review of "Marketing Agreements under the A.A.A." by E. G. Nourse. *Economic Journal* 46: 343.
——. 1936. Book Review of "The World Agricultural Situation in 1934–35." *Economic Journal* 46: 737.
——. 1937. Book Review of "Regional Types of British Agriculture" by J. P. Maxton. *Economic Journal* 47: 360.
——. 1937. Book Review of "A Study of Fluid Milk Price" by J. M. Cassels. *Economic Journal* 47: 556.
——. 1937. Milk: Report of Reorganisation Commission for Great Britain. *Economic Journal* 47: 172.
——. 1938. Book Review of "The Dairy Industry in Canada" by H. A. Innis, ed. *Economic Journal* 48: 731.
——. 1939. Book Review of "Le Mouvement des grains dans le monde" by P. van Hissenhoven. *Economic Journal* 49: 524.
——. 1939. Book Review of "Public Regulation of Milk Marketing in California" by J. M. Tinley. *Economic Journal* 49: 345.
——. 1939. Book Review of "The Wheat Economy" by G. E. Britnell. *Economic Journal* 49: 524.
——. 1939. Milk Policy and Milk Prices. *Economic Journal* 49(193) (March): 79–90.

——. 1940/1983. *The Economics of Agriculture*. Cambridge Economic Handbooks, 10. London: Nisbet.

——. 1940. Book Review of "On Agricultural Policy, 1926–38" by J. S. Davis. *Economic Journal* 50: 127–.

Cohen, Ruth Louisa and J. D. Barker. 1935. The Pig Cycle: A Reply. *Economica* 2(8) (November): 408–22.

Cohn, Adele, Alice Hamilton, and Susan Myra Kingsbury. 1937. *Occupational Disease in Pennsylvania : A Study of Lead and Carbon Disulphide as Industrial Poisons in Storage Battery Manufacture, Paint Manufacture, and the Rayon Industry by the Viscose Process in the State of Pennsylvania*. Harrisburg, Pa.: Department of Labor and Industry, Commonwealth of Pennsylvania.

Cohn, Elsbeth. 1906. Die neuere Literatur über den französischen Sozialismus. *Archiv für Sozialwissenschaft und Sozialpolitik* 5(23): 596–.

——. 1906. Die politische Arbeiterbewegung Frankreichs in den letzten Jahren. *Archiv für Soziale Gesetzgebung und Statistik*: 575–.

Cohn, Fannia. 1917. Complete Equality between Men and Women. *Ladies Garment Worker* (December).

Colcord, Joanna Carver. 1918. Desertion and Non-support in Family Case Work. *American Academy of Political and Social Science, Annals* 77 (May): 91–.

——. 1919. *Broken Homes; a Study of Family Desertion and Its Social Treatment*. New York, Russell Sage Foundation.

——, ed. 1920s. *The Art of Helping: A Course of Lectures on Social Case Work*. New York: Association of Volunteers in Social Service.

——. 1920. From the Point of View of the Prospective Employer. *Family* 1(2) (April): 9–.

——. 1920. From the Point of View of the Worker. *Family* 1(3) (May): 6–.

——. 1923. Relief. *Family* 4(1) (March): 13–.

——. 1930. *Community Planning in Unemployment Emergencies: Recommendations Growing out of Experience*. New York: Russell Sage Foundation.

——. 1931. *Setting up a Program of Work Relief*. New York: Russell Sage Foundation.

——. 1931. Unemployment Insurance in Great Britain. *Family* 12(3) (May): 85–.

——. 1932. The Commissary System. *Family* 13(7) (November): 235–.

——. 1932. Remedial Agencies Dealing with the American Family. *American Academy of Political and Social Science, Annals* 160 (March): 124–.

——. 1932. Unemployment Relief, 1929–1932. *Family* 13(8) (December): 270–.

——. 1934. The Challenge of the Continuing Depression. *American Academy of Political and Social Science, Annals* 176 (November): 14–.

——. 1934. Civil Works and Beyond. *Today* 1(11) (January 6): 9–.

——. 1934. Co-operation and the New Leisure. *Family* 15(2) (April): 35–.

——. 1934. Helping the Jobless Help Themselves. *Today* 1(28) (May 5): 11–.

——. 1936. *Cash Relief*. New York: Russell Sage Foundation.

——. 1937. Cash Relief. *Charity Organisation Quarterly* 11(1) (January): 26–.

——. 1939. *Your Communnity: Its Provision for Health, Education, Safety, and Welfare*. New York: Russell Sage Foundation.

Colcord, Joanna Carver and Mary Johnston. 1933. *Community Programs for Subsistence Gardens*. New York: Russell Sage Foundation.

Colcord, Joanna Carver, William C. Koplovits, and Russell H. Kurtz. 1932. *Emergency Work Relief as Carried out in Twenty-six American Communities, 1930–1931*. New York: Russell Sage Foundation.

Colcord, Joanna Carver. Coauth. *See* Richmond, Mary Ellen.

Cole, Ester Waneta. 1929. Indian Tribal Claims against the Government and Some Historical Aspects of the Indian Problem. Ph.D. thesis, Robert Brookings.

Cole, Margaret I. 1921. *The Control of Industry*. London: Labour Publishing Co.

——, ed. 1933. *Twelve Studies in Soviet Russia*. London: V. Gollancz, Ltd.

——. 1936. *The Road to Success: Twenty Essays on the Choice of a Career for Women*. London: Methuen.

——. 1937. *The New Economic Revolution*. London: Gollancz.

——. 1938. *Women of Today*. London: Nelson.

——. 1938. *Marriage*. London: Dent.

——. 1938. *Books and the People*. London: Hogarth Press.

——. 1939. The Progress of Government Control. *Fabian Quarterly* 23.

[Cole,] Margaret Winslow Hall. 1933. Aspects of Mediaeval Credit Operations: A Study Based on the Genoese Notarial Records of the Late Twelfth and Early Thirteenth Centuries. Ph.D. thesis, University of Wisconsin–Madison (history).

Cole, Margaret Winslow Hall. 1935. Early Bankers in the Genoese Notarial Records. *Economic History Review* 6 (October): 73–9.

——. 1937/8. The Investment of Wealth in Thirteenth-Century Genoa. *Economic History Review* 8: 185–7.

Coleman, Louise Moore. 1929. *Tobacco Trade in the Netherlands and the Netherland East Indies*. Bureau of Foreign and Domestic Commerce, Trade promotion series, no. 89. Washington: U.S. Government Printing Office.

——. 1931. *United States Tobacco and Its Markets*. Bureau of Foreign and Domestic Commerce, Trade Information Bulletin, no. 757. Washington: U.S. Government Printing Office.

Coleman, Mary Winniett. 1895. Model Working Girls' Clubs from an American Point of View. *Charities Review* 4(6) (April): 307.

Colenso, Harriette E. 1892. *Mr. Commissioner Osborn as One Cause of Confusion in Zulu Affairs*. London: Burt and Sons.

——. 1893. *The Present Position among the Zulus, 1893; with Some Suggestions for the Future*. London: Burt and Sons.

——. 1897. The Problem of the Races in South Africa. *Imperial and Asiatic Quarterly Review and Oriental and Colonial Record*. ser. 3(4:7/8) (July/October): 43.

Colenso, Harriette E. and Alice Werner. 1892. Colonial Questions: White and Black in Natal. *Contemporary Review* 61 (February): 205–13.

Collet, Clara E[lizabeth]. 1886. M.A. thesis, University College, London (political economy).

—— [as C. E. C.] 1888. Women's Trade Unions. *Charity Organisation Review* 46 (October): 420–25.

——. 1889. Maria Edgeworth and Charity. *Charity Organisation Review* 59 (November): 418–24.

——. 1889. Women's Work. In Charles Booth, ed., *Labour and Life of the People of London*. London: Williams and Norgate.

——. 1890. *The Economic Position of Educated Working Women. A Discourse.* London: South Place Ethical Society Publications.

——. 1890. Foreign Competition. *Charity Organisation Review* 65 (May): 185–9; and 67 (July): 285–9.

——. 1890. Salaries of Women Teachers. *Journal of Education* (August).

——. 1891. Book Review of "West Barbary, or Notes on the System of Work and Wages in the Cornish Mines" by L. L. Price. *Charity Organisation Review* 80 (August): 323.

——. 1891. George Gissing's Novels. *Charity Organisation Review* 82 (October): 375.

——. 1891. Moral Tales. *International Journal of Ethics* 1 (April): 370–85.

——. 1891. Reports of the Massachusetts Bureau of Statistics of Labour on Working Women 1870–1889. *Economic Journal* 1(2) (June): 398–405.

——. 1891. Strikes and Lock-outs, 1889. *Charity Organisation Review* 74 (February): 74.

——. 1891. Wages and the Standard of Living. *Quarterly Journal of Economics* 5 (April): 365–8.

——. 1891. Women's Work in Leeds. *Economic Journal* 1(3) (September): 460–73.

——. 1892. Prospects of Marriage for Women. *Nineteenth Century* 31(182) (April): 537–52.

——. 1894. *Statistics of Employment of Women and Girls, Report.* Board of Trade, Great Britain. Parliamentary Papers, Cmnd 7564. London: H.M. Stationery Office.

——. 1894. Three Ideal COS Secretaries. *Charity Organisation Review* 110 (March): 119–28.

——. 1895. Industrial and Economic Position of Women: Extracts from Miss Collet's Report on the Statistics and Employment of Women. *Englishwoman's Review* 26 (July): 208–12; (October): 222–4.

——. 1895. Statistics of Employment of Women and Girls (excerpt). *Journal of the Royal Statistical Society* 58(3) (September): 518–28.

——. 1896. Book Review of "Family Budgets; Being the Income and Expenses of Twenty-eight British Households, 1891–1894" compiled for the Economic Club. *Economic Journal* 6(24) (December): 570–3.

——. 1898. *Changes in the Employment of Women and Girls in Industrial Centres, Part 1: Flax and Jute Centers.* Board of Trade, Great Britain. Parliamentary Papers, Cmnd 8794. London: H.M. Stationery Office.

——. 1898. The Collection and Utilisation of Official Statistics Bearing on the Extent and Effects of the Industrial Employment of Women. *Journal of the*

Royal Statistical Society 61(2) (June): 219–60, incl. appendix tables: 244–60; followed by discussion of paper: 261–70.

——. 1898. The Expenditure of Middle Class Working Women. *Economic Journal* 8(32) (December): 543–53.

——. 1899. *Money Wages of In-door Domestic Servants, Report.* Board of Trade, Great Britain. Parliamentary Papers, Cmnd 9346. London: H.M. Stationery Office.

——. 1899. The Age Limit for Women. *Contemporary Review* 76 (December): 868–77.

——. 1901. Wages Boards in Victoria. *Economic Journal* 11(44) (December): 557–65.

——. 1902. *Educated Working Women.* London: P. S. King & Sons.

——. 1902/1970. West End Tailoring (Women). In Charles Booth, ed., *Life and Labour of the People in London.* London: Macmillan & Co.

——. 1903. Book Review of "The Strength of the People" by Helen Bosanquet. *Economic Journal* 13(43) (March): 81–4.

——. 1908. The Social Status of Women Occupiers. *Journal of the Royal Statistical Society* 71(3) (September): 513–15.

——. 1910. Female Labour. In *Palgrave Dictionary of Political Economy*, Vol. 2. London: Macmillan.

——. 1910. Females and Children, Earnings of. In *Palgrave Dictionary of Political Economy*, Vol. 2. London: Macmillan.

——. 1911. *Women in Industry*. London: Women's Printing Society, Ltd.

——. 1915. The Professional Employment of Women. *Economic Journal* 25(100) (December): 627–30.

——. 1916. Cost of Food for an Adult Woman. *Royal Statistical Society Journal*, series A, 79 (May): 300–3.

——. 1919. Comment on Dorothea Barton. *Journal of the Royal Statistical Society* 82(4) (July): 547–9.

——. 1923. Book Review of "The Charity Organisation in the U.S." by F. D. Watson. *Economic Journal* 33: 410–.

——. 1923. Loch, Sir Charles. *Economic Journal* 33: 123–.

——. 1924. Book Review of "Labour in Indian Industries" by G. M. Broughton. *Economic Journal* 34(135) (September): 457–9.

——. 1924. Review of Welfare. *Economic Journal* 34(135) (September): 457–9.

——. 1926. The Development of Ruskin's Views on Interest. *Economic History* 1 (January): 23–33.

——. 1927. Some Recollections of Charles Booth. *Social Service Review* 1(1/4) (March/December): 384–.

——. 1931. Domestic Service. In Sir Hubert Llewellyn Smith, ed., *The New Survey of London Life and Labour.* London: P. S. King & Son.

——. 1933. Source Materials: Mrs. Sidney Webb before the Royal Commission on Unemployment Insurance. *Social Service Review* VII(2).

——. 1936. E. C. Price. *Charity Organisation Quarterly* 10(1) (January): 9–.

——. 1936. Professor Foxwell and University College. *Economic Journal* 46(184) (December): 614–19.

——. 1939. Book Review of "Women Servants of the State, 1870–1938, a History of Women in the Civil Service" by Hilda Martindale. *Economic Journal* 49(193) (March): 124–5.

Collet, Clara and J. M. Keynes. 1940. Obituary of Henry Higgs. *Economic Journal* 50(200) (December): 546–61.

Collet, Clara E. Coauth. *See* Orme, Eliza.

Collier, Frances. 1921. The Family Economy of the Working Classes in the Cotton Industry, 1784–1833. M.A. thesis. Published Manchester: Manchester University Press, 1965. Reprinted New York: A. M. Kelley, 1964, 1965, 1967, 1968.

——. 1930. An Early Factory Community. *Economic History* 2 (January): 117–24.

——. 1936. Workers in a Lancashire Factory at the Beginning of the Nineteenth Century. *Manchester School of Economics and Social Studies* 7(1): 50–4; 7(2): 126–31.

Collins, Jennie. 1871. *Nature's Aristocracy; or, Battles and Wounds in Time of Peace. A Plea for the Oppressed.* Boston: Lee and Shepard.

——. 1872. *A Plan for Future Work, in Behalf of the Working Women.* Boston: George L. Keyes,.

Collins, Mrs. Pattie L. 1884/5. Government Employment for Women. *Chautauquan* 5 (October/July): 27– and 467–.

Colmache, Mme. Georgina Alicia. 1895. How Cuba Might Have Belonged to France. *Fortnightly Review*, n.s. 58 (November): 747–52.

Colman, G. M. 1927. *Capitalist Combines.* London: Longmans, Green & Co. Ltd.

Colvin, Esther Marie. 1929. *Agricultural Relief.* Washington: U.S. Government Printing Office.

——. 1929. *The Strawberry Industry in the United States: A Selected List of References on the Economic Aspects of the Industry.* Washington: Department of Agriculture, Bureau of Agricultural Economics.

——. 1933. *Group and Chain Farming in the United States, 1930–March 1933, with Some References to Group Farming in Foreign Countries.* Washington: U.S. Government Printing Office.

——. 1933. *Part-time Farming: A Brief List of Recent References.* Washington: U.S. Government Printing Office.

——. 1937. *Large Scale and Corporation Farming: A Selected List of References.* Washington: U.S. Government Printing Office.

——. 1939. *Transportation of Agricultural Products in the United States, 1920–June 1939: A Selected List of References Relating to the Various Phases of Railway, Motor and Water Carrier Transportation.* Washington: U.S. Government Printing Office.

Colvin, Esther Marie and Mary G. Lacy. 1932. *List of State Official Serial Publications Containing Material on Agricultural Economics.* Washington: U.S. Government Printing Office.

——. 1935. *List of Periodicals Containing Prices and Other Statistical and Economic Information on Fruits, Vegetables and Nuts.* Washington: U.S. Government Printing Office.

——. 1937. *List of Periodicals Containing Prices and Other Statistical and Economic Information on Dairy Products.* Washington: U.S. Government Printing Office.

Colvin, Esther Marie and Margaret T. Olcott. 1936. *Crop and Livestock Insurance.* Washington: U.S. Government Printing Office.

Colvin, Esther Marie. Coauth. *See* Bercaw, Louise Oldham.

Coman, [Prof.] Katharine. 1891. The Tailoring Trade and the Sweating System. *Publications of the American Economic Association,* series I, vol. VI, no. 1/2 (January/March): 144–7.

——. 1892. *History of Industrial Development in England and America: Outlines and References for Class-work.* Wellesley, Mass.: The Author.

——. 1893. *Outline Study of Economic Theory.* Boston: Frank Wood.

——. 1893. *Outlines and References: The French Revolution and Its Influence in Europe during the Nineteenth Century.* Boston: Frank Wood.

——. 1893. Wages and Prices in England, 1261–1701. *Journal of Political Economy* 2(1) (December): 92–4.

——. 1898. The Problem of Domestic Service in Its Industrial Aspects. *Chautauquan* 26 (March): 651–3.

——. 1903. *History of Contract Labor in the Hawaiian Islands.* Publications of the American Economic Association, 3rd series, IV(3). New York: Macmillan Co. Reprinted New York: Arno Press, 1978.

——. 1903/1905/1914/1917. *The Industrial History of the United States.* New York: Macmillan. Reprinted 1975, New York: Arno Press.

——. 1904. Book Review of "The Woman Who Toils." *Economic Journal* 15(57) (March): 80–6.

——. 1904. The Negro as a Peasant Farmer. *Journal of the American Statistical Association* 9 (June): 39–54.

——. 1905. *The Industrial History of the United States for High Schools and Colleges.* New York: Macmillan Co.

——. 1906. The Ancoats Brotherhood (Illustrated). *Chautauquan* 44 (September/November): 369–.

——. 1906/7. The Camp of the Unemployed at Levenshulme, Manchester. *Chautauquan* 45 (December/February): 219.

——. 1908. The Railroads as an Advanced Agent of Prosperity. *Review of Reviews* 38 (November): 591–2.

——. 1908. The Supreme Court Decision on the Oregon Ten Hour Law. *Association of Collegiate Alumnae, Publications* 3(18) (December): 31–.

——. 1911. Book Review of "American Commercial Legislation Before 1789" by A. A. Giesecke. *American Academy of Political and Social Science, Annals* 37 (January/June): 777–.

——. 1911. Government Factories: An Attempt to Control Competition in the Fur Trade. *Bulletin of the American Economic Association*, 4th series, 1(2) (April): 368–88.

——. 1911. Some Unsettled Problems of Irrigation. *American Economic Review* 1(1) (March): 1–19.

——. 1912/1925. *Economic Beginnings of the Far West. How We Won the Land beyond the Mississippi*. New York: Macmillan. Reprinted New York: A. M. Kelley, 1969.

——. 1915. *Unemployment Insurance: A Summary of European Systems*. New York: Progressive National Service.

Coman, Katharine and Elizabeth Kimball Kendall. 1894. *The Growth of the English Nation*. Meadville, Pa.: Flood and Vincent.

Coman, Katharine. Published a series of articles in *Survey*, 1914–15.

Combs, Mable Van Able. Coauth. *See* Lumpkin, Katharine Du Pre.

Comegys, Eva. 1927. Protection of the Consumer under Section V of the Federal Trade Commission Act. M.A. thesis, University of Chicago (economics, commerce-business).

Comish, Alison. *See* Thorne, Alison Comish.

Common, Sarah. 1933. *The Economics of the Settlement of the Prairie Provinces of Canada, 1900–1931*. Ph.D. thesis, London School of Economics.

Compain, Louise-Marie. 1910. *Les Femmes dans les organisations ouvrières*. Paris: s.n.

——. 1913. Les Conséquences du travail de la femme. *La Grande revue* 10: 364–76.

Comstock, A[lzada]. P[eckham]. 1910/1915. The Problem of the Negro. In Edith Abbott and Sophonisba Preston Breckinridge, *The Housing Problem in Chicago*. Chicago: University of Chicago Press.

——. 1912/13. Chicago Housing Conditions, VI. *American Journal of Sociology* 18(1/6): 241–.

——. 1919. Book Review of "War Finance" by Nicholson. *Journal of Political Economy* 27: 412–.

——. 1920. British Income Tax Reform. *American Economic Review* 10(3) (September): 488–506.

——. 1920. Excess Profits and Corporation Taxes in Great Britain. *National Tax Association, Bulletin* 6(1) (October): 7–.

——. 1920. Fiscal Aspects of State Income Taxes. *American Economic Review* 10(2) (June): 259–71.

——. 1920. The Memoranda of the British Inland Revenue on a War Levy. *National Tax Association, Bulletin* 5(8) (May): 238–.

——. 1920. Proposals for the Taxation of Wealth in Great Britain. *Journal of Political Economy* 28(5) (May): 399–406.

——. 1920. The Turnover Tax in Great Britain. *National Tax Association, Bulletin* 6(3) (December): 71–.

——. 1921. *State Taxation of Personal Incomes*. New York: Longmans, Green & Co.

——. 1921. State Taxation of Personal Incomes. Ph.D. thesis, Columbia University (economics, finance).

——. 1923. The Inside of Germany's Purse. *Forum* 69 (January/June): 1,332–.

——. 1925. The Cost of Debating. *Educational Review* 70 (June/December): 24–.

——. 1926. Women Members of European Parliaments. *American Political Science Review* 20(1/4): 379–.

——. 1928. From Capital Levy to Surtax. *American Economic Review* 18(1) (March): 9–18.

——. 1929. *Taxation in the Modern State*. New York: Longmans Green.
——. 1929. Financing Soviet Russia. *Fortnightly Review* 126 (July/December): 545.
——. 1929. The Grain War in Soviet Russia. *Current History (New York)* 31(3) (December): 490–.
——. 1930. The Daily Struggle in Soviet Russia. *Current History (New York)* 33(3) (December): 346–.
——. 1930. Reparation Payments in Perspective. *American Economic Review* 20(2) (June): 199–209.
——. 1932. Pitfalls of Soviet Planning. *Current History (New York)* 35(6) (March): 799–.
——. 1933. The British Exchange Equalization Account. *American Economic Review* 23(4) (December): 608–21.
——. 1933. The College Girl: 1933 Model. *Current History (New York)* 39(2) (November): 180–.
——. 1934. The Defense of Sterlingaria. *Current History (New York)* 39(6) (March): 692–.
——. 1934. Inflation: Promise or Peril? *Current History (New York)* 41(2) (November): 136–.
——. 1934. Soviet Individualism. *Current History (New York)* 40(2) (May): 245–.
——. 1935. The British Go to Moscow. *Current History (New York)* 42(2) (May): 215–.
——. 1935. The British Way to Recovery. *Current History (New York)* 43(2) (November): 147–.
——. 1936. Excises in Modern Times. *American Academy of Political and Social Science, Annals* 183 (January): 111–.
——. 1937. Britain's Rearmament Boom. *Events* 1(2) (February): 105–.
——. 1937. Realism and the Tax Burden. *Events* 2(8) (August): 126–.
——. 1937. That Mysterious National Debt. *Events* 1(1) (January): 18–.
——. 1937. When Britain's Bankers Speak. *Events* 1(3) (March): 209–.
——. 1938. Review of the £ s. d. of National Defence. *American Economic Review* 28(1) (March): 174–5.
——. 1939. America's Warring Groups. *Events* 5(30) (June): 404–.
——. 1939. Book Review of "The Finance of British Government." *American Economic Review* 29(1) (March): 184–5.
——. 1939. Britain Again Muddling through. *Events* 6(36) (December): 426–.
——. 1939. Britain in Wartime. *Events* 6(34) (October): 282–.
——. 1939. British Home Front. *Events* 6(35) (November): 346–.
——. 1939. Congress and Economy. *Events* 5(29) (May): 366–.
——. 1939. The Congress Shall Have Power. *Events* 6(31) (July): 19–.
——. 1939. Economic and Social Conditions in New England. South Hadley, Mass.: Department of Economics and Sociology, Mount Holyoke College.
——. 1939. Fiscal New Year Party. *Events* 6(32) (August): 91–.
——. 1940. *The Canadian Economy*. South Hadley, Mass.: Department of Economics and Sociology, Mount Holyoke College.

——. 1940. Bombs on Britain's "Little Men." *Events* 8(47) (November): 367–.

——. 1940. Britain "Can Stand It." *Events* 8(46) (October): 285–.

——. 1940. Britain Goes It Alone. *Events* 8(44) (August): 129–.

——. 1940. Britain Grumbles Along. *Events* 7(37) (January): 34–.

——. 1940. Britain's Pace Quickens. *Events* 7(38) (February): 124–.

——. 1940. British Morale. *Events* 8(45) (September): 189–.

——. 1940. British War Burden. *Events* 7(41) (May): 346–.

——. 1940. British War-time Politics. *Events* 7(39) (March): 195–.

——. 1940. Churchill at Britain's Helm. *Events* 7(42) (June): 431–.

——. 1940. The Distant Drum. *American Association of University Women, Journal* 34(2) (December): 67–.

——. 1940. Grim Days in Britain. *Events* 8(43) (July): 46–.

——. 1940. New Perils Ahead for Britain. *Events* 8(48) (December): 434–.

——. 1940. On the British Home Front. *Events* 7(40) (April): 267–.

Comstock, Alzada P., Virginia C. Gildersleeve, and Mary E. Woolley. 1939. University Women and the World Crisis. *American Association of University Women, Journal* 33(1) (October): 7–.

Comstock, Sarah. 1932. Marriage or Career? *Good Housekeeping* 94 (June): 32–3, 159–62.

Cone, Ada. 1898. The Feminist Movement in France. *Humanitarian* 12 (January): 5–.

——. 1899. English-speaking Women and French Commerce. *Contemporary Review* 75 (May): 710–19.

——. 1900. French Women in Industry. *Contemporary Review* 77 (February).

Coney, Faye. 1938. The Potteries, Stoke-on-Trent (England). M.S. thesis, University of Chicago (economics, commerce-business).

Conklin, Mabel L. 1897. *How Women May Earn a Living One Hundred and Seventeen Ways.* New York: C. Francis.

Conolly, Violet. 1928. Two Months in Soviet Russia. *Studies* 17: 637–.

——. 1929. Two Months in Soviet Russia – Part II. *Studies* 18: 64–.

——. 1933. *Soviet Economic Policy in the East: Turkey, Persia, Afghanistan, Mongolia and Tana Tuva, Sin Kiang.* London: Oxford University Press. Reprinted Westport, Conn.: Hyperion Press, 1981.

——. 1934. Die Wirtschaftspolitik der Sowjets im Osten. *Zeitschrift für Politik* 24: 121–.

——. 1935. *Soviet Trade from the Pacific to the Levant, with an Economic Study of the Soviet Far Eastern Region.* New York: Oxford University Press. Reprinted Westport, Conn.: Hyperion Press, 1981.

——. 1935. The Industrialization of Persia. *Royal Central Asian Society, Journal* 22(3) (July): 454–.

——. 1936/7. The Soviet Union and the Industrialization of Asia. *Foreign Affairs; an American Quarterly Review* 15(1/4): 187–.

——. 1937. On Revisiting Soviet Russia. *Studies* 26: 297–.

——. 1938. Some Impressions of Sweden. *Studies* 27: 63–.

Conrad, Else. 1902. Vagabundiren mit Vagabunden. *Archiv für Kriminal-Anthropologie und Kriminalistik* 8(2) (February 6): 129.

——. 1903. Book Review of "Die Frauenfrage, ihre geschichtliche Entwicklung und ihre wirtschaftliche Seite" by Lily Braun. *Jahrbücher für Nationalökonomie und Statistik* 3(26:2) (August): 271.

——. 1906. *Der Verein für Sozialpolitik und seine Wirksamkeit auf dem Gebiet der gewerblichen Arbeiterfrage.* Jena: Fischer.

——. 1907. Book Review of "Amerikanisches Armenwesen" by E. Münsterberg. *Jahrbücher für Nationalökonomie und Statistik* 3(34:2) (August): 271.

——. 1907. Book Review of "Schule und Brot" by Helene Simon. *Jahrbücher für Nationalökonomie und Statistik* 3(34:2) (August): 272.

——. 1907. Book Review of "Untersuchung der Wohnungen der minder bemittelten Klassen in Bremen." *Jahrbücher für Nationalökonomie und Statistik* 3(34:4) (October): 566.

——. 1908. Book Review of "Dienstbotenfrage und Dienstbotenvereine" by Aug. Pieper. *Jahrbücher für Nationalökonomie und Statistik* 3(36:2) (August): 274.

——. 1908. Book Review of "Ein mittelbürgerliches Budget über einen zehnjährigen Zeitraum" by Henriette Fürth. *Jahrbücher für Nationalökonomie und Statistik* 3(36:4) (October): 565.

——. 1908. *Das Dienstbotenproblem in den Nordamerikanischen Staaten und was es uns lehrt.* Jena: G. Fischer.

——. 1909. Book Review of "Aus der sozialen Tätigkeit der preussischen Kreisverwaltungen" by Heinrich Sohnrey. *Jahrbücher für Nationalökonomie und Statistik* 3(37:1) (January): 135–.

——. 1909. Book Review of "Wegweiser für ländliche Wohlfahrts- und Heimatspflege" by Heinrich Sohnrey. *Jahrbücher für Nationalökonomie und Statistik* 3(37:1) (January): 135–.

——. 1910. Zur Dienstbotenfrage. Erhebungen der Arbeiterinnenschutzkommission des Bundes Deutscher Frauenvereine. *Archiv für Sozialwissenschaft und Sozialpolitik* 31: 520–.

——. 1911. Book Review of "Stiefkinder der Sozialpolitik. Bilder aus dem Berufsleben der Krankenpflegerinnen." *Jahrbücher für Nationalökonomie und Statistik* 3(41:4) (April): 567–.

——. 1911. Book Review of "Ueber Fabrikarbeit verheirateter Frauen. Münchener Volkswirtschaftliche Studien" by Rose Otto. *Jahrbücher für Nationalökonomie und Statistik* 3(41:5) (May): 716–.

——. 1911. Book Review of "Die Wohnungsinspektion, ein Beitrag zur Einführung derselben in Oesterreich" by Arthur Fuchs. *Jahrbücher für Nationalökonomie und Statistik* 3(41:4) (April): 566–.

——. 1912. Book Review of "Neuere Untersuchungen über Arbeitspsychologie." *Jahrbücher für Nationalökonomie und Statistik* 3(44:4) (October): 532–.

——. 1913. Book Review of "Die Lebenshaltung der arbeitenden Klassen in den bedeutenderen Industriestaaten" by Carl von Tyszka. *Jahrbücher für Nationalökonomie und Statistik* 3(46:3) (September): 411–.

——. 1913. Book Review of "Die Verteuerung der Lebensmittel in Berlin im Laufe der letzten 30 Jahre und ihre Bedeutung für den Berliner Arbeiterhaushalt" by Gustav Brutzer. *Jahrbücher für Nationalökonomie und Statistik* 3(46:3) (September): 409–.

——. 1914. Book Review of "Landrat des Unterwesterwaldkreises, die Sparpflicht für Minderjährige und die Wohnungsfrage" by Freih Marschall von Bieberstein. *Jahrbücher für Nationalökonomie und Statistik* 3(48:4103) (October): 565–.

——. 1914. Jahresbericht des Kgl. Württembergischen Landeswohnungsinspektors für die Jahre 1911 und 1912. *Jahrbücher für Nationalökonomie und Statistik* 3(48:6103) (December): 817–.

——. 1916. Book Review of "Ergebnisse einer Untersuchung über die Arbeits- und Lebensverhältnisse der Frauen in der Landwirtschaft. I. Teil: Die Einwirkung der wirtschaftlich-sozialen Verhältnisse auf das Frauenleben. Auf Grund einer vom ständigen Ausschuss zur Förderung der Arbeiterinneninteressen veranstalteten Erhebung, dargestellt von Gertrud Dyhrenfurth, mit Beiträgen von Freiin Elly zu Putlitz, Dr. Rosa Kempf und Elisabeth Boehm-Lamgarben." *Jahrbücher für Nationalökonomie und Statistik* 107(5) (November): 710–.

Conrad, Laetitia M. 1936. Some Effects of the Depression on Family Life. *Social Forces* 15(1) (October): 76–81.

——. 1939. Differential Depression Effects on Families of Laborers, Farmers and the Business Class: A Survey of an Iowa Town. *American Journal of Sociology* 44(4) (January): 526–33.

Conway, Katharine St. John. *See* Glasier, Katharine Bruce.

Conyngton, Mary K[atherine]. 1895. Review of Report by Miss Collet on the Statistics of Employment of Women and Girls. *Publications of the American Statistical Association* 4(32) (December): 366–8.

——. 1896. Book Review of "Compensation in Certain Occupations of Graduates of Colleges for Women" by H. Wadlin. *Publications of the American Statistical Association* 5(33) (March): 44–7.

——. 1896. Inquiries Concerning Poverty. [Review of two German studies]. *Publications of the American Statistical Association* 5(34) (June): 88–92.

——. 1906. *A Manual of Practical Charity: How to Get Help: Designed for the Use of Non-professional Workers among the Poor.* New York: Ronald Press.

——. 1909/1913. *How to Help: A Manual of Practical Charity.* New York: Macmillan.

——. 1911. *Report on Condition of Women and Child Wage-earners in the United States*, vol. 15: *Relation Between Occupation and Criminality of Women.* 61st Congress, 2nd sess. S. Doc. 645. Washington: U.S. Government Printing Office.

——. 1918. *Effect of Workmen's Compensation Laws in Diminishing the Necessity of Industrial Employment of Women and Children.* Bulletin of the United States Bureau of Labor Statistics, Whole No. 217. Washington: U.S. Bureau of Labor Statistics.

——. Coauth. *See* Parker, Florence Evelyn.

Cook, Edith Valet. 1936. *The Married Woman and Her Job*. Washington: National League of Women Voters.

Cook, Eliza. 1849. Our Women Servants. *Eliza Cook's Journal* 1(12) (July 21): 177–9. Reprinted in Harriet Devine Jump, ed., *Women's Writing of the Victorian Period 1837–1901, An Anthology*. New York and London: Palgrave Macmillan, 1999.

——. 1852. The Education of Women. *Eliza Cook's Journal* 8 (November 20): 57–9.

Cook, Helen E. Coauth. *See* Manson, Grace.

Cook, Lady Tennessee C[laflin]. 1893. Habits and Customs of Savage Life. *Westminster Review* 140 (November): 514–22.

——. 1894. Habits and Customs of Ancient Times. *Westminster Review* 141 (January): 19–32.

——. 1894. Habits and Customs of Medieval Times. *Westminster Review* 141 (February): 139–55.

——. 1894. Modern Habits and Customs. *Westminster Review* 141 (March): 271–88.

——. 1894. A Short History of Marriage. *Westminster Review* 141 (April): 380–95.

——. 1895. Wills and Inheritance. *Westminster Review* 143 (February): 187–203.

Cooke, Alice R. 1889. *Industrial Education for the Defective Classes* [Training insane women in domestic industry]. Papers of the Education Department, no. 2. New York: American Social Science Association. Reprinted in *Journal of Social Science* 26.

Cooke, Rose Terry. 1889. Are Women to Blame? *North American Review* 148 (May): 626–30.

——. 1889. Is Housekeeping a Failure? *North American Review* 148 (February): 246–50.

[Coolidge,] Mary E[lizabeth]. B[urroughs]. Roberts Smith. 1895. Almshouse Women: A Study of Two Hundred and Twenty Eight Women in the City and County Almshouse of San Francisco. *Publications of the American Statistical Association* IV(31) (September): 219–62.

——. 1896. Almshouse Women: A Study of 228 Women in the City and County Almshouse of San Fransisco. Ph.D. Thesis, Standford University (economics).

——. 1900. Statistics of College and Non-college Women. *Journal of the American Statistical Association* VII (March–June): 49–50: 1–26.

[Coolidge,] Mary E. B. Roberts Smith (1898—1900). 1898. Education for Domestic Life. *Popular Science Monthly* LIII(4) (August): 521–5.

——. 1899. What Degrades Domestic Service. *Werner's Magazine* 24(3) (November): 308–31.

——. 1899. Domestic Service: The Responsibility of Employers. *Forum* 27 (August): 678–89.

Coolidge, Mary Roberts [Smith] [Mrs. Dane Coolidge]. 1909. *Chinese Immigration*. New York: Henry Holt and Company.

——. 1909. Chinese Labor Competition on the Pacific Coast. *American Academy of Political and Social Science, Annals* 34 (July/December): 340–.

——. 1912. *Why Women Are So*. New York: Henry Holt. Reprinted New York: Arno Press, 1972.

——. 1916. *What the Women of California Have Done with the Ballot*. San Francisco: California Civic League.

Coon, Shirley Jay. 1926. The Economic Development of Missoula, Montana. Ph.D. thesis, University of Chicago (economics).

——. 1929. Collective Bargaining and Productivity. *American Economic Review* 19 (September): 419–27.

——. 1930. Influence of the Gold Camps on the Economic Development of Western Montana. *Journal of Poltical Economy* 38(5) (October): 580–99.

——. 1933. Factors Controlling Business Recovery. *World Affairs Interpreter* 3(4) (Winter): 65–.

——. 1933. The Technocracy Panacea. *World Affairs Interpreter* 4(1) (Spring): 51–.

——. 1935. Devaluation and Damages. *Accounting Review* 10(3) (September): 294–.

——. 1937. Business Education on the Four-year College Level. *National Business Education Quarterly* 6(2) (December): 38–.

Cooper, Anna Julia. 1892. Has America a Race Problem? *A Voice of the South, By a Black Woman from the South*. Xenia, Ohio: Aldine Printing House. Reprinted New York: Negro Universities Press, 1969. Reprinted in C. Lemert and E. Bhan, eds., *The Voice of Anna Julia Cooper*. New York and Oxford: Rowman and Littlefield, 1998.

——. 1892. The Higher Education of Women. *A Voice of the South, By a Black Woman from the South*. Xenia, Ohio: Aldine Printing House. Reprinted New York: Negro Universities Press, 1969. Reprinted in C. Lemert and E. Bhan, eds., *The Voice of Anna Julia Cooper*. New York and Oxford: Rowman and Littlefield, 1998.

——. 1892. The Status of Woman in America. *A Voice of the South, By a Black Woman from the South*. Xenia, Ohio: Aldine Printing House. Reprinted New York: Negro Universities Press, 1969. Reprinted in C. Lemert and E. Bhan, eds., *The Voice of Anna Julia Cooper*. New York and Oxford: Rowman and Littlefield, 1998.

——. 1892. What Are We Worth? *A Voice of the South, By a Black Woman from the South*. Xenia, Ohio: Aldine Printing House. Reprinted New York: Negro Universities Press, 1969. Reprinted in C. Lemert and E. Bhan, eds., *The Voice of Anna Julia Cooper*. New York and Oxford: Rowman and Littlefield, 1998.

——. 1892. "Woman Versus the Indian". *A Voice of the South, By a Black Woman from the South*. Xenia, Ohio: Aldine Printing House. Reprinted New York: Negro Universities Press, 1969. Reprinted in C. Lemert and E. Bhan, eds., *The Voice of Anna Julia Cooper*. New York and Oxford: Rowman and Littlefield, 1998.

——. 1899. Colored Women as Wage-earners. *Southern Workman and Hampton School Record* (August 28): 295–8. Reprinted in Shirley Wilson Logan, *We Are*

Coming: The Persuasive Discourse of Nineteenth-Century Black Women. Carbondale, Ill.: Southern Illinois University Press, 1999.

——. 1913. *The Social Settlement: What It Is and What It Does.* Washington: Murray Brothers.

——. 1925. L'Attitude de la France a l'égard de l'égalite des Races [The attitude of France regarding equality of the races]. Ph.D. thesis, University of the Sorbonne, Paris.

Cooper, Miss C. L. 1890. Some Curiosities of Irish Farming. *National Review* 15 (July): 697–707.

Copley, Esther. 1845. *The Young Women of the Factory: or, Friendly Hints on Their Duties and Dangers.* London: Religious Tract Society.

Copping, Victoria Page. 1937. *Expansion of Japan's Foreign Trade and Industry.* Washington: U.S. Bureau of Foreign and Domestic Commerce.

Corbert, Anita. 1896. Circulation of Money. *Publications of the American Statistical Association* 5(34) (June): 96–8.

Corbett, Elizabeth Burgoyne [Mrs George Corbett]. 1889. *New Amazonia: A Foretaste of the Future.* London: Lambert & Co. [*novel*]

Corbin, Caroline Fairfield. 1886. *One Woman's Experience of Emancipation.* 3rd ed., Chicago: Illinois Association Opposed to the Extension of Suffrage to Women.

——. 1893. *Are Women Citizens?* Chicago: Women's Anti Suffrage Association of America, Fergus Print. Co.

——. 1896. *The Home Versus Woman Suffrage: Extract from the Appendix to a Woman's Philosophy of Love.* Boston: s.n. Printed by permission of Messrs. Lee and Shepard.

——. 1898. *Socialism in Politics: Dangers which Menace the Republic – Woman Suffrage; Mrs. Corbin in Reply: Letter Defining and Proving Her Statements Regarding Socialism and Woman's Rights.* Chicago: Illinois Association Opposed to the Extension of Suffrage to Women. Letters reprinted from the *Chicago Times-Herald* (October 2 and November 7, 1898).

——. 1901/1902. *The Position of Women in the Socialistic Utopia.* Chicago: American Association Opposed to Socialism.

——. 1901. Suffrage and Industrial Independence [A letter dated Chicago, May 7, 1891]. Reprinted *Chicago Evening Post*, May 8, 1901.

——. 1902. *The Woman Movement in America.* Chicago: Illinois Association Opposed to the Extension of Suffrage to Women.

——. 1905. *Socialism and Christianity with Reference to the Woman Question.* Chicago: Illinois Association Opposed to the Extension of Suffrage to Women.

——. 1908. *The Antisuffrage Movement.* Chicago: Association Opposed to the Extension of Suffrage to Women. Reprinted from the *Chicago Daily News*, November 24, 1908.

——. 1908. *Woman's Rights in America: A Retrospect of Sixty Years, 1848–1908.* 5th ed. Chicago: Illinois Association Opposed to the Extension of Suffrage to Women.

——. 1910. *Equality*. Chicago: Illinois Association Opposed to Woman Suffrage.

——. 1910. *Socialism and Sex*. Bulletin no. 6. Chicago: Illinois Association Opposed to Woman Suffrage.

——. 1912. *Dignity of Womanhood*. Bulletin no. 11. Chicago: Illinois Association Opposed to Woman Suffrage.

——. 1912. *Woman's Best Work: The Making of Voters*. Bulletin no. 13. Chicago: Illinois Association Opposed to Woman Suffrage.

Corelli, Marie. 1897. *Jane, a Social Incident*. Philadelphia: J. B. Lippincott.

——. 1900. *Patriotism, or Self-Advertisement? A Social Note on the Present War*. Philadelphia: J. B. Lippincott Company.

——. 1905. *Free Opinions*. London: A. Constable.

——. 1907. *Woman, or Suffragette? A Question of National Choice*. London: C. Arthur Pearson, Limited.

——. 1917. *Is All Well with England, A Question*. London: Jarrolds.

——. 1917. *The World's Greatest Need: An Appeal to the Sanity of Governments*. Taunton: Wessex Press.

Corelli, Marie, Flora Annie W. Steel, Lady Susan Hamilton Ardagh, and Baroness Susan Mary St. Helier Jeune. 1898. *The Modern Marriage Market*. London: Hutchinson. U.S. ed. Philadelphia: J. B. Lippincott Company, 1900. Online at Indiana University's LETRS.

Cornwallis, Caroline F. 1846. *On the Principles of Criminal Law*. Philadelphia: Lea and Blanchard; London: Pickering.

——. 1851. *The Philosophy of Ragged Schools*. London: W. Pickering.

——. 1856. The Property of Married Women. *Westminster Review*, n.s. 10 [o.s. 66] (October): 331–60.

——. 1857. The Capabilities and Disabilities of Women. *Westminster Review*, n.s. 11 [o.s. 67] (January): 42–72.

Correll, Marie. 1932. *State Requirements for Industrial Lighting: A Handbook for the Protection of Women Workers, Showing Lighting Standards and Practices*. Washington: U.S. Government Printing Office.

——. 1934. *Standards of Placement Agencies for Household Employees*. Bulletin of the U.S. Women's Bureau, no. 112. Washington: U.S. Government Printing Office.

Correll, Marie and Janet Tucker Howell Clark. 1933. *Industrial Injuries to Women in 1928 and 1929 Compared with Injuries to Men*. Bulletin of the Women's Bureau, no. 102. Washington: U.S. Government Printing Office.

Costantino, Costanza. 1939. Sulle Fluttuazioni economiche di lunga durata [On long-term economic fluctuations]. *Rivista Internationale di Scienze Sociali*: 794–809.

Courtney, Janet E. 1915. The War and Women's Employment. *Fortnightly Review* 97 (January/June): 239–.

——. 1915. The War and Women's Employment. *Living Age* 7(285) (April/June): 3–.

Courtney, Janet Elizabeth Hogarth. 1933. *Countrywomen in Council; the English and Scottish Women's Institutes, with Chapters on the Movement in the Dominions and on Townswomen's Guilds.* London: Milford.

——. Coauth. *See* Kendal, Madge.

Cowper, Countess Katrine [Compton]. 1885. Some Experiences of Work in an East-End District. *Nineteenth Century* 18 (November): 783–93.

Coyle, Eunice S. 1920. The World's Industrial Consumption of Gold. *Review of Economics and Statistics* 2 (June): 147–54.

——. 1920. The World's Industrial Consumption of Gold. Error. *Review of Economics and Statistics* 2 (December): 368.

——. 1921. Physical Production in 1920. *Review of Economics and Statistics* 3: 37–9.

——. 1924. Raw Silk Prices and the Business Cycle. *Review of Economics and Statistics* 6 (January): 22–31.

——. 1932. Electric Power Data as Indexes of Business Fluctuations. *Review of Economics and Statistics* 14 (May): 88–96.

——. 1932. A Review of Recent Bank Failures. *Review of Economics and Statistics* 14 (February): 38–41.

Coyle, Eunice S. and Warren M. Persons. 1921. A Commodity Price Index of Business Cycles. *Review of Economic Statistics* 3(11) (November): 353–69.

Coyle, Grace Longwell. 1925. The Swing Toward Humanism. *World Tomorrow* 8(12) (December): 368–.

——. 1928. *Jobs and Marriage? Outlines for the Discussion of the Married Woman in Business.* New York: Woman's Press.

——. 1928. *Present Trends in the Clerical Occupations.* New York: Womans Press.

——. 1928. "White Collars" and Trade Unions. *American Federationist* 35(10) (October): 1,211–.

——. 1929. Women in the Clerical Occupations. *American Academy of Political and Social Science, Annals* 143 (May): 180–.

——. 1930. *Social Process in Organized Groups.* New York: R. R. Smith Inc.

——. 1931. Social Process in Organized Groups. Ph.D. thesis, Columbia University (sociology).

——. 1934. *Personal Significance and Social Action; an Address Given at the Thirteenth National Convention of the Young Women's Christian Associations, Philadelphia, May 1934.* New York: Womans Press.

——. 1935. The Limitations of Social Work in Relation to Social Reorganization. *American Sociological Society, Publication* 29(3) (August): 177–.

——. 1935/6. The Limitations of Social Work in Relation to Social Reorganization. *Social Forces* 14(1/4): 94–.

——. 1937. *Studies in Group Behavior.* New York and London: Harper.

——. 1937. Group Work and Social Action. *Social Work Today* 5(2) (November): 13–.

——. 1939/40. Book Review of "Supervision in Group Work" by Sidney J. Lindenberg. *American Journal of Sociology* 45(1/6): 632–.

——. 1940. An Invitation to the National Conference. *Alabama Social Welfare* 5(5) (May): 14–.

Coyle, Grace Longwell and Katharine C. Halsey. 1922. *College Women's Industrial Research Group under the Auspices of the Young Women's Christian Association, Cleveland, Summer 1922*. Cleveland, Ohio: Young Women's Christian Association (Cleveland, Ohio), National Industrial Committee.

Coyle, Grace Longwell *et al.* 1936. Political Action and Social Work, "A Symposium." *Social Work Today* 3(9) (June): 5–.

Coyle, Grace. Coauth. *See* Daniels, Harriet McDoual.

Craig, Isa. 1859. Emigration as a Preventive Agency. *English Woman's Journal* (January). Reprinted in Candida Ann Lacey, ed., *Barbara Leigh Smith Bodichon and the Langham Place Group*. London and New York: Routledge, 1987.

——. 1859. Insanity: Its Cause and Cure. *English Woman's Journal* (September). Reprinted in Candida Ann Lacey, ed., *Barbara Leigh Smith Bodichon and the Langham Place Group*. London and New York: Routledge, 1987.

Craik, Dinah Mulock. 1858. *A Woman's Thoughts about Women*. London: Hurst and Blackett; New York: Rudd & Carleton.

——. 1886. *About Money and Other Things*. London: Macmillan; New York: Harper's.

——. 1887. Concerning Men – By a Woman. *Cornhill Magazine* 9: 368–77.

Crampton, Ethel M. 1918. Administration of Jose Ballivian in Bolivia. *Hispanic American Historical Review* 1(4) (November): 403–.

——. 1920/1. The Executive Office in Latin-American Constitutions. *Southwestern Social Sciences Quarterly* 1: 380–.

——. 1921/2. The Judicial Department in the Latin-American Constitutions. *Southwestern Social Sciences Quarterly* 2: 239–.

——. 1921/2. The Legislative Department in the Latin-American Constitutions. *Southwestern Social Sciences Quarterly* 2: 161–.

——. 1922. *Foreign Periodicals on Trade and Economic Conditions*. Washington: U.S. Bureau of Foreign and Domestic Commerce.

——. 1922/3. Controversy over Tacna and Arica and the Washington Conference. *Southwestern Social Sciences Quarterly* 3: 126–.

Crandall, Ruth. 1927. Hidden Treasure in Old-time Taxes. *Business History Review* 1(9) (September): 11–15.

——. 1934. Wholesale Commodity Prices in Boston during the Eighteenth Century. *Review of Economics and Statistics* 16 (June): 117–28.

Crane, Alice Rollins. 1898. Why the Indians Break Out. *Arena* 20 (October): 491–7.

Crans, Lillian. Coauth. *See* Gill, Minna; Hannay, Annie Murray Macgregor.

Crary, Catherine S. 1935. The Free City of Danzig: Its Economic and Political Development since the Peace Treaty. Ph.D. thesis, Radcliffe College (history).

Craske, May. 1908. Girl Life in a Slum. *Economic Review*.

Craton, Ann W. 1927. Working the Women Workers. *Nation* 124 (March 23): 311–13.

Craven, Florence. 1883. Servants of the Sick Poor. *Nineteenth Century* 13 (April): 667–78.

Craven, Ida Sonntag. *See* Merriam, Ida Craven.

Crawford, Emily J. 1891. The Education and Status of Women. In William Wilson Hunter *et al.*, *State Education for the People*. London and New York: G. Routledge and Sons.

——. 1893. Journalism as a Profession for Women. *Contemporary Review* 64 (September): 362–71.

Crawford, Mabel Sharman. 1863. *Through Algeria*. London: R. Bentley.

——. 1887. Experiences of an Irish Landowner. *Contemporary Review* 52 (August): 263–74.

——. 1893. Maltreatment of Wives. *Westminster Review* 139 (March): 292–.

Crawford, Virginia M[ary]. 1891. Life in the London Slums: Extracts from the Diary of a District Nurse. *Temple Bar* 91 (February): 275–83.

——, transl. 1896. *A Key to Labour Problems, Being an Adapted Translation of the Catechisme du Patron by Leon Harmel*. London: Catholic Truth Society.

——. 1897. Cooperative Village Banks. *Dublin Review* 121 (October): 269–83.

——. 1897. Feminism in France. *Fortnightly Review*, n.s. 61 (April): 524–34.

——. 1898. Englishwomen and Agriculture. *Contemporary Review* 74 (September): 426–35.

——. 1899. Ideals of Charity. *Month, a Catholic Magazine* 93 (419) (May): 459–.

——. 1899. Within Workhouse Walls. *Contemporary Review* 75 (June): 831–42.

——. 1900. Social Work among the Paris Poor. *Month; a Catholic Magazine* 96(434) (August): 143–.

——. 1900. The Work of the Catholic Guardians' Association. *Month; a Catholic Magazine* 95(428) (February): 145–.

——. 1901. Aspects of Charity in Vienna. *Month; a Catholic Magazine* 98(449) (November): 465–.

——. 1901. Philanthropy and Wage-paying. *Economic Journal* 11 (March): 96–105.

——. 1902. Some Aspects of Charity in Canada. *Month; a Catholic Magazine* 100(460) (October): 337–.

——. 1906. A Paris Centre of Social Activity. *Month; a Catholic Magazine* 107(502) (April): 408–.

——. 1908. *Ideals of Charity*. St. Louis: Herder.

——. 1909. The Women's Industrial Council. *Month; a Catholic Magazine* 114(546) (December): 576–.

——. 1910. *Unemployment and Education: A Lesson from Switzerland*. Philadelphia: Dolphin Press. Also published in the *Dublin Review* (July), Educational briefs, no. 31 (October).

——. 1910. Labor Problems in Switzerland (Social Work in Switzerland). *Catholic World* 91(541/546) (April/September): 764–.

——. 1911. *Switzerland Today: A Study in Social Progress*. London and Edinburgh: Sands & Co.

——. 1911. The Ethics of Shopping. *Month; a Catholic Magazine* 118(570) (December): 577–.

——. 1912. The Catholic Social Guild. *Catholic World* 95(565/570) (April/September): 478–.

——. 1920. War's Disillusionment. *Studies* 9: 232–.
——. 1922. The Catholic Social Movement in France. *Studies* 11: 424–.
——. 1923. The Rise of Fascism. *Studies* 12: 539–.
——. 1925. A New Method of Wage Distribution. *Studies* 14: 218–.
——. 1933. *Catholic Social Doctrine, 1891–1931.* Oxford: Catholic Social Guild.
——. 1933. 'La Croix" and Its Founder. *Studies* 22: 233–.
——. 1934. Social Work in Belgium. *Studies* 23: 313–.
——. 1934. Social Work in Holland. *Studies* 23: 412–.
——. 1939. The Institute of the Assumption. *Studies* 28: 303–.
Crawshay, Rose-Mary. 1876. *Domestic Service for Gentlewomen: A Record of Experience and Success.* London: R. Crawshay.
Creighton, Louise von Glehn. 1876. *England a Continental Power: From the Conquest to Magna Charta, 1066–1216.* London: Longmans, Green & Co.
——. 1881. *A First History of England.* London: Rivingtons.
——. 1887. *Social History of England.* London: Rivingtons.
——. 1889. The Appeal Versus Female Suffrage: A Rejoinder. *Nineteenth Century* 26 (August): 347–54.
——. 1893. *A First History of France.* London and New York: Longmans, Green & Co.
——. 1901. *The Modern Home.* Paper read at the Brighton Conference of the National Union of Women Workers. London: Wells Gardner, Darton & Co.
——. 1907. *The Economics of the Household. Six Lectures Given at the London School of Economics.* London: Longmans, Green & Co.
——. 1908. Women's Settlements. *Nineteenth Century*, April.
——. 1914. *The Social Disease and How to Fight It: A Rejoinder.* London: Longmans, Green & Co.
——. Coauth. *See* Bosanquet, Helen Dendy.
Crepaz, Frau Adele. 1893. *The Emancipation of Women and Its Probable Consequences.* With a letter to the authoress by the Right Hon. W. E. Gladstone. London: Swan Sonnenschein & Co.; New York: Charles Scribner's Sons. Originally published in German as *Die gefahren der Frauen-emancipation.*
Creyke, Caroline. 1893. The Rothemsted Experiments [in fertilising crops]. *Nineteenth Century* 34 (July): 970–80.
Croffut, Bessie B. 1899. How Holland Helps the Helpless. *North American Review* 168(2) (February): 251–3.
Crofts, Maud L. 1925. *Women under English Law.* London: National Council of Women.
Croly, Jane Cunningham [Jennie]. 1889. Domestic Service. *Forum* 7 (July): 567–76.
——. 1891. *Thrown on Her Own Resources, or, What Girls Can Do.* New York: Thomas Y. Crowell.
——. 1898. *History of the Women's Club Movement in America.* New York: H. G. Allen.
Crook, Evelyn Buchan. 1922. The Delinquency of Girls. M.A. thesis, University of Chicago (sociology).
——. 1933/4. Book Review of "A Publication of the White House Conference on Child Health and Protection." *American Journal of Sociology* 39(1/6): 719–.

——. 1934/5. Book Review of "The Taxi-Dance Hall. A Sociological Study in Commercialized Recreation and City Life" by Paul G. Cressey. *American Journal of Sociology* 40(1/6): 123–.

——. 1940/1. Book Review of "State Administration of Child Welfare in Illinois" by Elizabeth Hayward Milchrist. *American Journal of Sociology* 46(1/6): 410–.

Crook, Evelyn Buchan and Elizabeth Ritts. 1939. *Leisure Time Needs and Resources in Swoyersville, Pennsylvania.* Ann Arbor, Mich.: Edwards Brothers, Inc.

Crowther, Phyllis M. 1929. The Reclamation of the Middle Level of the Fens. Ph.D. thesis, Reading.

Croy, Mae Savell. 1928. *How Women Can Make Money*. New York and London: Funk & Wagnalls Co.

Culp, Alice Bessie. 1921. A Case Study of the Living Conditions of Thirty-five Mexican Families with Special Reference to Mexican Children. Master's thesis, University of Southern California.

Cumming, C. F. Gordon. *See* Gordon-Cumming, Constance F.

Cummings, Edith Mae Cunliffe. 1929. *Pots, Pans and Millions: A Study of Women's Right to Be in Business.* Washington: National School of Business Science for Women.

Cunningham, Audrey. 1910. *British Credit in the Last Napoleonic War.* Cambridge, UK: Cambridge University Press.

Curry, Hannah Ida. 1927. *Public Child-caring Work in Certain Counties of Minnesota, North Carolina, and New York.* Washington: U.S. Children's Bureau.

Curtis, Isabel Gordon. 1906. *The Making of a Housewife.* New York: Frederick A. Stokes.

Curtis, Myra. 1932. American Office Management. *Public Administration (London, UK)* 10(2) (April): 179–.

——. 1934. Treatment of Suggestions from Staff. *Public Administration (London, UK)* 2(2) (April): 168–.

——. 1935. National Income and Expenditure and the Measurement of Savings [Notes and Memoranda]. *Economic Journal* 45 (September): 573–7.

——. 1936. Book Review of "General Theory of Employment, Interest and Money" by J. M. Keynes. *Public Administration (London, UK)* 14(2) (April): 206–.

——. 1937. Is Money Saving Equal to Investment? *Quarterly Journal of Economics* 15 (August): 604–25.

——. 1937. Measurement of Staff Output in Clerical Work. *Public Administration (London, UK)* 15(3) (July): 225–.

——. 1939. Savings and Investment: Saving and Savings. *Quarterly Journal of Economics* 53(4) (August): 623–6.

Cusack, Mary Francis. 1874. *Woman's Work in Modern Society*. Kenmare, Co. Kerry, Ireland: Kenmare Publications.

——. 1877. *A History of the Irish Nation, Social, Ecclesiastical, Biographical, Industrial, and Antiquarian.* London: John G. Murdoch.

——. 1881. *The Present Case of Ireland Plainly Stated: A Plea for My People and My Race.* New York: P. J. Kenedy.

——. 1887. *The Question of Today. Anti-poverty and Progress. Labor and Capital.* Chicago and New York: Belford, Clarke and Co.

Cusack, Sister Mary Thomasine. 1940. The Significance of a Changing Concept of Ownership to Current Economic and Social Planning. Ph.D. thesis, Catholic University of America.

Cushman, Susan. 1891. Bibliographical Note on Statistics of Immigration. *Publications of the American Statistical Association* 2(16) (December): 451–3.

D

Daggett, Mabel Potter. 1918. *Women Wanted.* New York: George H. Doran.

Dale, Marian K. 1928. Summaries of Theses: Women in the Textile Industries and Trade of Fifteenth-century England. *Institute of Historical Research, Bulletin* 6(17) (November): 111–.

——. 1933. The London Silkwomen of the Fifteenth Century. *Economic History Review* 4 (October): 324–35.

Dall, Caroline Wells Healey. 1847. *Sherry Williams, or, The Danger of Being Religious in a Land of Slavery.* London: C. Gilpin, M. Ross. Reprinted from the *Liberty Bell* of 1847. [*short story*]

——. 1860. *"Woman's Right to Labor"; or Low Wages and Hard Work: In Three Lectures Delivered in Boston, November, 1859.* Boston: Walker, Wise and Co. Reprinted in David Rothman and Sheila M. Rothman, eds., *Low Wages and Great Sins: Two Antebellum American Views on Prostitution and the Working Girl.* New York: Garland Publishing, 1987.

——. 1861. *Woman's Rights under the Law; in Three Lectures, Delivered in Boston, January, 1861*, Boston: Walker, Wise, and Company.

——. 1867. *The College, the Market and the Court, or Women's Relation to Education, Labor and Law.* Boston: Lee and Shepard. Memorial Edition Concord, N.H.: Rumford Press, 1914. Reprinted New York: Arno Press, 1972.

——. 1868/1872. Something about Women. *Putnam's*, n.s. 1 (June): 695–703. Reprinted in *Dublin University Magazine* 79 (April 1872): 447–57.

——. 1903. *Of "Lady Rose's Daughter." A Defense and an Analysis.* Boston: T. Todd.

——. A collection of her papers is located in the Massachusetts Historical Society, Boston, and in the Schlesinger Library, Radcliffe College.

Dallas, Helen Alex. 1897. Profit Sharing [Bryant and May's Works]. What Are the Interests of Shareholders? *Economic Review* 7 (April): 182–.

Daly, Kathryn W. 1938. The International Ladies' Garment Workers' Union in Chicago, 1930–1939 (Illinois). A.M. thesis, University of Chicago (economics, labor).

Damon, Dr. Mary B. 1893. Medical Women in Tenements. In Frances A. Goodale, ed., *The Literature of Philanthropy.* New York: Harper & Brothers.

Daniel, Dr. Anna S. 1892. Conditions of the Labor of Women and Children in New York. *Journal of Social Science* 30 (October): 73–85.

Daniels, Harriet McDoual. 1916. College Settlement Week. *College Settlements Association Quarterly* 1(3) (March): 9–.

Daniels, Harriet McDoual and Grace Coyle. 1914. *The Emergency Workshops*. New York: College Settlement.

Dare, Shirley. 1889. Is Housekeeping a Failure? *North American Review* 148 (February): 243–6.

Dart, Helen Marietta. 1921. *Maternity and Child Care in Selected Rural Areas of Mississippi*. Washington: U.S. Government Printing Office.

Dart, Helen Marietta, Ella A. Merritt, and E. J. Allett. 1923. *Minors in Automobile and Metal-manufacturing Industries in Michigan*. Washington: U.S. Children's Bureau.

Dart, Helen Marietta. Coauth. *See* Matthews, Ellen Nathalie; Springer, Ethel Maria.

Darwin, Ellen W. [Crofts] [Mrs. Francis Darwin]. 1890. Domestic Service. *Nineteenth Century* 28 (August): 286–96.

——. 1896. Is British Housekeeping a Success? *National Review* 26 (January): 619–27.

Darwin, Maud. 1914. Policewomen: Their Work in America. *Nineteenth Century* 75 (June): 1,371–7.

Daubié, Julie Victoire. 1862. Quel Moyens de subsistance ont les femmes? *Journal des économistes*, 2nd series, 34.

——. 1863. Travail manuel des femmes. *Journal des économistes*, 2nd series, 38 and 39.

——. 1865. De l'Enseignement secondaire pour les femmes. *Journal des économistes*, 2nd series (June): 382–402; (August): 384–403; (December): 408–27.

——. 1866. *La Femme pauvre au dix-neuvième siècle*. Paris: Guillaumin. Reprinted Paris: Côté-femmes, 1992. 2nd ed., revised and enlarged, Paris: E. Thorin, 1869, 1870.

——. 1870/1872. *French Morality under the Regulation System*. Excerpt from *La Femme pauvre…* Transl. and with a preface by Josephine Elizabeth Butler. London: Trübner & Co.; Liverpool: Thomas Brakell. Reprinted in Josephine Butler, ed., *The New Era: A Collection of 25 Pamphlets Relating to the Contagious Disease Acts of 1864, 1866 and 1869*. London: Th. Brakell, 1872.

——. 1871. *L'Emancipation de la femme en dix livraisons*. Paris: E. Thorin.

Davenport, Frances Gardiner. 1894. *A Classified List of Printed Original Materials for English Manorial and Agrarian History during the Middle Ages*. Radcliffe College monographs, no. 6. Boston: Ginn.

——. 1897. Agricultural Changes of the 15th Century. *Quarterly Journal of Economics* 11: 205–10.

——. 1898. Book Review of "Leadam's Domesday of Inclosures, 1517–18." *American Historical Review* 3 (January): 245–6.

——. 1899. Terra Soliata, a Phrase in the Court Rolls of Certain Norfolk Manors. *English Historical Review* 14 (July): 507–9.

——. 1900. Decay of Villeinage in East Anglia. *Transactions of the Royal Historical Society* 14: 123.

——. 1904. The Economic Development of a Norfolk Manor, 1086–1565. Ph.D. thesis, University of Chicago (history).

——. 1906. *The Economic Development of a Norfolk Manor, 1086–1565*. Cambridge, UK: Cambridge University Press.

——. 1920. Agreement Respecting the Town and Fortress of Lumbier, in Navarre. *Hispanic American Historical Review* 3: 41–.

Davidge, Clara Sidney. 1894. Working-girls' Clubs. *Scribner's Magazine* 15(5) (May): 619–28.

Davidson, E. H. 1939. *Child Labor Legislation in the Southern Textile States*. Chapel Hill, N.C.: University of North Carolina Press.

Davidson, J. E. [Mrs. Hugh Coleman Davidson.] 1894. *What Our Daughters Can Do for Themselves: A Handbook of Women's Employments*. London: Smith, Elder.

Davies, E. 1927. The Small Landowner, 1780–1832, in the Light of the Land Tax Assessments. *Economic History Review* 1 (January): 87–113.

Davies, Emily. 1862. Female Physicians. *English Woman's Journal* (May). Reprinted in Candida Ann Lacey, ed., *Barbara Leigh Smith Bodichon and the Langham Place Group*. London and New York: Routledge, 1987.

——. 1862. *Medicine as a Profession for Women*. Paper read at the conference of the National Association for the Promotion of Social Science, June. London: Emily Faithfull. Reprinted in Candida Ann Lacey, ed., *Barbara Leigh Smith Bodichon and the Langham Place Group*. London and New York: Routledge, 1987.

——. 1863. The Influence of University Degrees on the Education of Women. *Victoria Magazine* 1 (June): 260–71. Reprinted in Candida Ann Lacey, ed., *Barbara Leigh Smith Bodichon and the Langham Place Group*. London and New York: Routledge, 1987.

——. 1863. Needleworkers v. Society. *Victoria Magazine* 1: 348–60.

——. 1864. *On Secondary Instruction, as Relating to Girls*. Paper read at the conference of the National Association for the Promotion of Social Science. London: William Ridgway. Reprinted in Candida Ann Lacey, ed., *Barbara Leigh Smith Bodichon and the Langham Place Group*. London and New York: Routledge, 1987.

——. 1865. *The Application of Funds to the Education of Girls*. Paper read before the Education Department of the National Association for the Promotion of Social Science, May 3. London: Longman, Green, Longman, Roberts, & Green.

——. 1866. *The Higher Education of Women*. London and New York: A. Strahan. Reprinted with an introduction by Janet Howarth, London: Hambledon Press, 1988.

——. 1868. *Some Account of a Proposed New College for Women*. Paper read at the annual meeting of the National Association for the Promotion of Social

Science and published in *Contemporary Review* 9 (December): 540–57. Reprinted London: J. Bale.

——. 1868. *Special Systems of Education for Women.* London: Savill, Edwards and Co.

——. 1878. *Home and the Higher Education.* London: London Association of Schoolmistresses.

——. 1896. *Women in the Universities of England and Scotland.* Cambridge, UK: Macmillan and Bowes.

——. 1910. *Thoughts on Some Questions Relating to Women, 1860–1908.* Cambridge: Bowes and Bowes.

Davies, Harriette Brooke. 1887. A Kitchen College. *Nineteenth Century* 22 (July): 55–9.

Davies, Margaret Llewelyn. 1890. *The Relations between Co-operation and Socialistic Aspirations.* Manchester, UK: Women's Co-operative Guild.

——. 1892. *The Co-operative Movement.* Manchester, UK: Women's Co-operative Guild.

——. 1895. *Suggested Reforms in Co-operative Education.* Manchester, UK: Women's Co-operative Guild.

——. 1897. Why Working Women Need the Vote. In *Why Working Women Need the Vote: Four Papers Read by Members of the Women's Co-Operative Guild at the Sectional Conferences, 1897.* Manchester, UK: Women's Co-operative Guild (Kirkby Lonsdale, UK).

——. 1898. *Guild Work in Relation to Educational Committees of Co-operative Societies.* Manchester, UK: Women's Co-operative Guild.

——. 1899. *Co-operation in Poor Neighborhoods.* Kirkby Lonsdale, UK: Women's Co-operative Guild.

——. 1900. *A Co-operative Colony.* Papers reprinted from the *Co-operative News* dealing with a scheme of co-operation for poor neighborhoods. Manchester, UK: Women's Co-operative Guild.

——. 1904. *The Woman's Co-operative Guild, 1883–1904.* Kirkby Lonsdale, UK: Westmorland Women's Co-operative Guild.

——. 1906. *The Co-operative Store Abroad: A Comparison.* Women's Co-operative Guild.

——. 1907. Women in Council [letter to the editor]. *Nation* 1(25) (August 17): 898.

——. 1908. Militant and Constitutional Action: A Contrast [letter to the editor]. *Nation* 4(3) (October 17): 117.

——. 1908. Personal Service among the London Poor [letter to the editor]. *Nation* 4(8) (November 21): 307.

——. 1909. The Government and Women's Suffrage [letter to the editor]. *Nation* 6(10) (December 4): 400.

——. 1909. The New Suffrage Bill [letter to the editor]. *Nation* 4(22) (February 27): 824.

——. 1910. The Government and Adult Suffrage [letter to the editor]. *Nation* 8(14) (December 31): 574.

——. 1910. The Spirit of Equity [letter to the editor]. *Nation* 7(1) (April 2): 19.

——. 1910. Women and the Insurance Bill [letter to the editor]. *Nation* 9(11) (June 3): 363.

——. 1910. Women and the Insurance Bill [letter to the editor]. *Nation* 9(11) (June 10): 400.

——. 1911. Higher Popular Education [letter to the editor]. *Nation* 9(21) (August 19): 741.

——. 1911. Marriage and Divorce. *Nation* 8(23) (March 4): 908–.

——. 1913/14. Motherhood and the State. *Public Health* 27.

——. 1915. *Maternity: Letters from Working Women*. London: G. Bell & Sons. Reprinted Virago Reprint Library, no. 4. London: Virago Press, 1978.

——. 1918. The Claims of Mothers and Children. In M. Phillips, ed., *Women and the Labour Party*. London: F. Matthews.

——. 1918. *The Vote at Last! More Power to Co-operation*. Manchester, UK: Co-operative Union.

——. 1920. The Co-operative Movement as a Medium for Surmounting Economic Credit Difficulties. *International Co-operative Bulletin* 13: 27–.

——. 1921. *Women as Organised Consumers*. Manchester, UK: Co-operative Union.

——. 1921. England. *International Co-operative Bulletin* 14: 1–.

——. 1922. The Woman with the Basket. *Irish Economist* (February).

——. 1924. Death or Life? A Call to Co-operative Women. *International Co-operative Bulletin* 17: 353–.

——, ed. 1931. *Life as We Have Known It by Co-operative Working Women*. With an introduction by Virginia Woolf. London: Hogarth Press. Reprinted, with an introduction by Anna Davin, London: Virago Press, 1977.

Davies, Margaret Llewelyn and Clementina Black. 1908. Suffragist Tactics [letter to the editor]. *Nation* 4(13) (December 26): 509.

Davies, Margaret Llewelyn, Honora A. Enfield, and Lilian Harris. 1919. *Co-operation Versus Capitalism: Memorandum on the Co-operative Movement and the Menace of Capitalism*. London: Women's Co-operative Guild.

Davies, Margaret Llewelyn. Coauth. *See* Black, Clementina; MacArthur, Kathleen.

Davies, Mary. 1914. *Employments for Women: A Report*. Cardiff, Wales: Appointments Board for Wales.

Davies, Mary Emily. 1904. Study of the Negro in Lincoln. M.A. thesis, University of Nebraska–Lincoln.

Davis, Anna Mae Campbell/Anne Mabel C. 1927. Evolution of Trade Practices and Judicial Decisions. Ph.D. thesis, University of Wisconsin.

——. 1928. The Correlation of Law and Economics in the Commodity Transaction. Ph.D. thesis, University of Wisconsin–Madison (economics).

Davis, Anne Sophia. Coauth. *See* Breckinridge, Sophonisba Preston; Campbell, Mary Edith.

Davis, Eleanor. 1932. *The Use of Credit Unions in Company Programs for Employee Savings and Investment.* Princeton: Industrial Relations Section, Princeton University.

——. 1933. *Company Retraining Programs.* Princeton: Industrial Relations Section, Princeton University.

——. 1933. *Employee Stock Ownership and the Depression.* Ann Arbor, Mich.: Edwards Brothers, Inc. for Princeton University Industrial Relations Section.

——. 1933/1936. *Minimum Wage Legislation in the United States: A Summary of Fact and Opinion.* Princeton: Industrial Relations Section, Princeton University.

——. 1933/4. Book Review of "The Development of Social Insurance and Minimum Wage Legislation in Great Britain" by Hohman. *Personnel Journal* 12 (June/April): 233–.

——. 1934. *Company Plans for Employee Savings and Investment.* Ann Arbor, Mich.: Edwards Brothers, Inc. (for Princeton University Industrial Relations Section).

——. 1934. *Hours of Work and Recovery: Summary of Fact and Opinion.* Ann Arbor, Mich.: Edwards Brothers, Inc. (for Princeton University Industrial Relations Section).

——. 1934/1935. *The Use of Credit Unions in Company Programs for Employee Savings and Investment.* Princeton: Industrial Relations Section, Princeton University.

——. 1935. *Educational Refunds in Industry.* Princeton: Industrial Relations Section, Princeton University.

——. 1935. *Personnel Programs in Banks.* Princeton: Industrial Relations Section, Princeton University.

——. 1935. *Recent Trends in Vacation Policies for Wage Earners.* Princeton: Industrial Relations Section, Princeton University.

——. 1936. *Company Sickness Benefit Plans for Wage Earners.* Princeton: Industrial Relations Section, Princeton University.

Davis, Hilda Mary. 1911. *Irish Trade in the Time of Strafford.* Ph.D. thesis, London School of Economics.

Davis, Jean Scobie. 1929. Collective Bargaining in the Men's Ready Made Clothing Industry. Ph.D. thesis, University of Wisconsin.

——. 1929. The Development of Labor Management in Southern Cotton Mills. Ph.D. thesis, University of Wisconsin–Madison.

Davis, Katharine [Katherine] Bement. 1895. *Report on the Exhibit of the Workingman's Model Home as Exhibited by the State of New York at the World's Columbian Exposition.* Albany: James B. Lyon.

——. 1898. Tables Relating to the Price of Wheat and Other Farm Products since 1890. *Journal of Political Economy* 6(3) (June): 403–10.

——. 1899. An Error in Austrian Wages Statistics. *Journal of Political Economy* 8(1) (December): 102–6.

——. 1900. Causes Affecting the Standard of Living and Wages. Ph.D. thesis, University of Chicago (economics).

——. 1900. The Condition of the Negro in Philadelphia. *Journal of Political Economy* 8 (March): 248–60.

——. 1900. The Modern Condition of Agricultural Labor in Bohemia. *Journal of Political Economy* 8 (September): 491–523.

——. 1905. The Fresh Air Treatment for Moral Disease. *Proceedings of the Annual Congress of the National Prison Association of the U.S.*: 205–11.

——. 1906. Moral Imbeciles. *Proceedings of the Annual Congress of the National Prison Assoc. of the U.S.*

——. 1908. A Glimpse of Life in a State Reformatory. *Vassar Miscellany* (June).

——. 1909. Outdoor Work for Women Prisoners. *Proceedings of the National Conference of Charities and Corrections*: 289–94.

——. 1911. The New York State Reformatory for Women. *Survey* 25: 851–4.

——. 1912. Feeble Minded Women in Reformatory Institutions. *Survey* 27 (March).

——. 1913. A Study of Prostitutes Committed from New York City to the State Reformatory for Women at Bedford Hills. In George Kneeland, ed., *Commercialized Prostitution in New York City*. New York: Century Co.

——. 1913/14. A Plan of Rational Treatment for Women Offenders. *Journal of Criminal Law and Criminology* 4(3).

——. 1915. Charities and Correction. *Proceedings of the Academy of Political Science* 5(3) (April): 86–.

——. 1915. The Department of Corrections. *Proceedings of the Academy of Political Science* 5 (April): 564–80.

——. 1916. The Reformatory Method. *Proceedings of the National Conference of Charities and Corrections.*

——. 1916. Settlement Work as a Preparation for Civic Work. *College Settlements Association Quarterly* 2(1) (October): 6–.

——. 1917. Plan for the Rational Treatment of Women Convicted in the Courts of the County of New York (or City). In Burdette G. Lewis, ed., *The Offender and His Relation to Law and Society.* New York: Harper and Brothers.

——. 1918. Women's Education in Social Hygiene. *Annals of the American Academy of Political and Social Science* 79 (September): 167–77.

——. 1920. Introduction. In Mabel Ruth Fernald, Mary Holmes Stevens Hayes, and Almena Dawley, eds., *A Study of Women Delinquents in New York State.* With statistical chapter by Beardsley Ruml and preface by Katharine Bement Davis. Reprinted Montclair, N.J.: Paterson Smith, 1968.

——. 1922. *Housing Conditions of Employed Women in the Borough of Manhattan.* New York: Bureau of Social Hygiene.

——. 1928. Why They Failed to Marry. *Harper's Monthly Magazine* 156 (March): 460–9.

——. 1929. *Factors in the Sex Life of Twenty-two Hundred Women.* New York: Harper and Brothers. Reprinted New York: Arno Press and the *New York Times*, 1972.

——. 1933. Three Score Years and Ten. *University of Chicago Magazine* 26 (December): 58–61.

Davis, Katharine Bement and Clara Jean Weidensall. 1916. *The Mentality of the Criminal Woman: A Comparative Study of the Criminal Woman, the Working Girl, and the Efficient Working Woman in a Series of Mental and Physical Tests*. Baltimore: Warwick & York.

Davis, Maxine. 1936. *The Lost Generation: A Portrait of American Youth Today*. New York: Macmillan.

——. 1937. *They Shall Not Want*. New York: Macmillan.

——. 1937. Hungry Children. *Atlantic Monthly* 159 (January/June): 82–.

Davis, Rebecca Harding. 1861. Life in the Iron Mills. *Atlantic Monthly* 7 (April): 430–51. Reprinted in Tillie Olson, ed., *Life in the Iron Mills and Other Stories*. New York: Feminist Press, 1972.

——. 1861/2. Margret Howth: A Story of To-Day. Serialized in *Atlantic Monthly* (October/March). Reprinted Boston: Ticknor and Fields, 1862. Reprinted with afterword by Jean Fagan Yellin, New York: Feminist Press, 1990.

——. 1869. Men's Rights. *Putnam's* 13 (February): 212–25.

——. 1889. Are Women to Blame? *North American Review* 148 (May): 622–6.

——. 1899. The Curse in Education. *North American Review* 168(5) (May): 609–14.

Davydova, Sofiä Aleksandrovna. 1894. *Zapiska o zhenskikh rabotakh v Voronezhskoï i Nizhegorodskoï guberniiäkh: 1892–1893 g.* St Peterburg: Tip. I. N. Skorokhodova.

——. 1895. *La Dentelle russe; histoire technique statistique*. Leipzig: K. W. Hiersemann.

Dawes, Mary C. 1891. The Salaries of Women Teachers. *Education* [London] 2 (January): 20–.

Dawson, Julia. 1909. *Why Women Want Socialism*. London: Independent Labour Party.

Day, Mrs. 1899. *Women on Management Committees: A Few Reason Why Women Should Sit on Management Committees of Co-operative Societies*. Manchester, UK: Women's Co-operative Guild.

Day, Emily Louise. 1925. *Aids to Writers and Editors: A Selected List of Books on the Preparation of Manuscripts and the Mechanics of Writing for Use in the Bureau of Agricultural Economics*. Washington: U.S. Bureau of Agricultural Economics.

——. 1929. *Valuation of Real Estate with Special Reference to Farm Real Estate*. Washington: U.S. Bureau of Agricultural Economics Library.

——. 1936. *Government Control of Cotton Production in the United States, 1933–1935*. Washington: U.S. Government Printing Office.

——. 1940. *Cotton Linters*. Washington: U.S. Government Printing Office.

Day, Emily Louise and Rachel P. Lane. 1935. *Economic Development of the Cotton-textile Industry*. Washington: U.S. Government Printing Office.

Day, Emily Louise, Katharine Jacobs, and Margaret T. Olcott. 1924. *Bibliography on the Marketing of Agricultural Products*. Washington: U.S. Government Printing Office.

Day, Emily Louise. Coauth. *See* Benton, Mildred Catherine; Lacy, Mary Goodwin.

de Borring, Frances Mary. 1885. The Peasant Proprietor of the South [of France]. *National Review* 6 (November): 345–57.

——. 1888. Notes from a Prosperous Agricultural Country [Denmark]. *Fortnightly Review*, n.s. 43 [o.s. 49] (May): 707–18.

de Bovet, Marie A. 1892. The Marriage Market: French and English. *New Review* 7 (July): 80–91.

de Broke, Baroness Marie Frances Lisette Hanbury Verney Willoughby. Coauth. *See* Butler, Christina Violet.

de Burgos, Carmen. 1927. *La mujer moderna y sus derechos.* Valencia: s.n.

de Cleyre, Voltairine. 1894. *In Defence of Emma Goldman and the Right of Expropriation: A Lecture Delivered in New York, December 16, 1894.* London: James Tochatti, "Liberty" Press. Reprinted in Alexander Berkman, ed., *Selected Works of Voltairine de Cleyre.* New York: Mother Earth Publishing Association, 1914.

——. 1902. *A Catechism of Anarchy.* Philadelphia: Social Science Club.

——. 1903. *Crime and Punishment; a Lecture Delivered before the Social Science Club of Philadelphia, March 15th, 1903.* Philadelphia: Social Science Club.

——. 1909. *Anarchism and American Traditions.* New York: Mother Earth Publishing Association.

——. 1911. *The Mexican Revolt.* New York: Mother Earth Publishing Association.

——. 1912. *Direct Action. A Lecture Delivered in Chicago, January 21, 1912.* New York: Mother Earth Publishing Association.

de Grouchy, Sophie. 1798. *Lettres à C[abanis], sur la théorie des sentiments moraux.* In Adam Smith, *Théorie des sentiments moraux*, transl. from the 7th ed. (1792) by Sophie de Grouchy, Marquise de Condorcet. Paris: F. Buisson.

de Iongh, Jane. 1930. The International Economic-history Exhibition, Amsterdam, 1929. *Economic History Review* 2 (January): 314–19.

——. 1934. *Van Gelder Zonen, 1734–1934.* Haarlem: Erven F. Bohn.

de Lébédeff, Olga. 1899. *De l'Émancipation de la femme musulmane.* Lisieux: Morière.

de Lima, Agnes. 1921. How Nightwork of Women Is Menacing Maternity. *American Labor Legislation Review* 11: 85–.

——. 1922. Night Working Women in Textile Mills in Passaic, N.J. Passaic, N.J.: National Consumers' League and Consumers' League of New Jersey.

de Montaigu, Annie, Countess. 1890. Women in the Industrial Arts. *Chautauquan* 11 (April/September): 756–.

——. 1891. Perfumery-making as an Occupation for Women. *Chautauquan* 13 (July): 520–.

de Morgan, Mary. 1890. Cooperation in England in 1889. *Westminster Review* 133 (May): 532–40.

de Nyevelt, Baroness Suzette I. de Zuylen. 1892. The Dutch Peasantry. *National Review* 19 (June): 467–75.

de Pledge, Josephine L. 1894. History and Progress of Nursing in Poor Law Infirmaries. *Westminster Review* 142 (August): 173–82.

[De Roover,] Florence [Marguerite] Edler. 1931. *Glossary of Mediæval Terms of Business. Italian Series, 1200–1600.* Cambridge, Mass.: Mediæval Academy of America. New York: Kraus Reprint, 1970.

——. 1923. The English Poor Laws of the Eighteenth Century. M.A. thesis, University of Chicago (history).

——. 1930. The Silk Trade of Lucca during the Thirteenth and Fourteenth Centuries. Ph.D. thesis, University of Chicago (history).

——. 1936. Winchcombe Kerseys in Antwerp (1538–44). *Economic History Review* 7 (November): 57–62.

——. 1939/40. Book Review of "Cosimo de' Medici Pater patriae, 1389–1464" by Curt Gutkind. *Economic History Review* 10: 71–.

——. 1940. The Business Records of an Early Genoese Notary, 1190–92. *Business History Review* 14 (June): 41–6.

De Roover, Florence Edler *et al.* 1937/8. The Literature of Business History. *Harvard Business Review* 16 (Autumn/Summer): 105–.

de Thierry, C. Pseud. *See* Campbell, Mrs. J. Weston.

de Witt, Marguerite Schlumberger. *See* Schlumberger, Marguerite de Witt.

Deans, Mrs. 1898. *Credit and High Prices in Co-operative Stores.* Manchester, UK: Women's Co-operative Guild.

Deardorff, Neva Ruth. 1911. English Trade in the Baltic During the Reign of Elizabeth. Ph.D. thesis, University of Pennsylvania (economics, history).

——. 1912. *English Trade in the Baltic during the Reign of Elizabeth.* Philadelphia: University of Pennsylvania; New York: D. Appleton and Co.

——. 1914. Citizen Co-operation in the Administration of Health and Charities. *National Municipal Review* 3(4) (October): 760–.

——. 1914. Women in Municipal Activities. *American Academy of Political and Social Science, Annals* 56 (November): 71–.

——. 1924/5. Objectives of Social Work Education. *Social Forces* 3(1/4): 237–.

——. 1925. The Place of a Professional School in Training for Social Work. *American Academy of Political and Social Science, Annals* 121 (September): 172–.

——. 1927. *Child-welfare Conditions and Resources in Seven Pennsylvania Counties.* Washington: U.S. Government Printing Office.

——. 1927. *The Extent of Child Dependency and Delinquency in Seven Pennsylvania Counties.* Washington: U.S. Department of Labor, Children's Bureau.

——. 1927. Trend of Income and Expenditure of Eleven Family Welfare Agencies in New York. *American Sociological Society, Papers and Proceedings* 22 (December): 205–.

——. 1930. Research in the Field of Child Welfare since the War. *American Academy of Political and Social Science, Annals* 151 (September): 195–.

——. 1931/1932. *A Survey of Work for Boys in Brooklyn.* New York: Welfare Council of New York City.

——. 1931. The Social Studies of the Welfare Council of New York City. *Journal of Educational Sociology* 4(9) (May): 585–.

——. 1932/3. The Relation of Applied Sociology to Social Work. *Social Forces* 11(1/4): 190–.

——. 1933. Social Statistics – Whose Responsibility? *Family* 14(2) (April): 50–.

——. 1933/4. Book Review of "Economic Problems of the Family" by Hazel Kyrk. *American Journal of Sociology* 39(1/6): 706–.

——. 1935. Continuity in Research and Planning. *American Sociological Society, Publication* 29(3) (August): 178–.

——. 1937. Social Study by Councils of Social Agencies and Community Chests. *Social Service Review* 11(1/4) (March/December): 167–.

Deardorff, Neva Ruth, Edith G. Seltzer, and Kathleen Allen. 1937. *Medical Social Service*. New York: United Hospital Fund of New York.

Decouvelaere, Mathilde. 1934. *Le Travail industriel des femmes mariées*. Paris: Rousseau.

——. 1934. Le Travail industriel des femmes mariées. Thesis, University of Lille, Faculty of Law.

Del Plaine, Frances Kelley. 1920. *A History of Public-school Support in Minnesota, 1858 to 1917*. Minneapolis: University of Minnesota.

Delzell, Ruth. 1919. *The Early History of Women Trade Unionists of America*. Chicago: National Women's Trade Union League of America.

Delzell, Ruth, Dorothy Sears, and Frances Porter. 1914. *Articles on the Early History of Women Trade Unionists of America; Illustrated with Historical Industrial Charts*. Chicago: National Woman's Trade Union League of America.

DeMille, Anna George. 1924. *Henry George's Progress and Poverty: An Abridgement of the Economic Principles*. New York: Harcourt, Brace & Co.

Dempsey, Maria Veronica. 1919. *Infant Mortality*. Washington: U.S. Children's Bureau.

——. 1922. *The Occupational Progress of Women: An Interpretation of Census Statistics of Women in Gainful Occupations*. Washington: U.S. Government Printing Office.

——. 1933. *The Occupational Progress of Women, 1910–1930*. Washington: U.S. Women's Bureau.

Dendy, Helen. *See* Bosanquet, Helen Dendy.

Dendy, Mary. 1903. The Feeble-minded. *Economic Review* (July): 257–.

——. 1910. *Only a Business Man*. London: Sherratt & Hughes.

——. 1913. The Mental Deficiency Bill [letter to the editor]. *Nation* 13(14) (July 5): 531–.

Deraismes, Maria. 1891. *Eve dans l'humanité*. Paris: L. Sauvaitre.

Deroin, Jeanne. 1848. *Cours de droit social pour les femmes*. Paris: Imprimerie de Plon.

——. 1851. *Lettre aux associations sur l'organisation du crédit*. Paris: Gustave Sandré.

——. 1852. Le Travail des femmes. *Almanach des femmes*. Paris: self-published.

——, ed. 1853. *Almanach des femmes, seconde année. Women's Almanack for 1853, in the English and French Languages*. London: James Watson.

——, ed. 1854. *Almanach des Femmes pour 1854*. London: James Watson.

DeSchweinitz, D. 1932. *How Workers Find Jobs: A Study of Four Thousand Hosiery Workers in Philadelphia*. Philadelphia: University of Pennsylvania Press.

Despard, Charlotte. 1884. *A Voice from the Dim Millions; Being the True History of a Working-woman*. London: Griffith and Farran. [*novel*]

Dessauer[-Meinhardt], Marie. 1933. *Die Big Five: Zur Charakteristik der englischen Depositenbanken*. Stuttgart: C. E. Poeschel.

——. 1935. The German Bank Act of 1934. *Review of Economic Studies* 2 (June): 214–24.
——. 1936. The German Bank Act of 1934: A Correction. *Review of Economic Studies* 3(2) (February): 139.
——. 1940. Monthly Unemployment Records 1854–1892. *Economica* 7(27) (August): 322–6.
——. 1940. Unemployment Records, 1848–59. *Economic History Review* 10(1) (February): 38–43.
Deutche, Helene. 1909. *Die Entwicklung der Seidenindustrie in Österreich, 1160–1840.* Vienna: Konegen.
Deverell, Edith M. 1898. Shop Benefit Clubs. *Economic Journal* 8(30) (June) 243–54.
——. 1899. Slate Clubs. *Economic Journal* 9(34) (June): 266–77.
DeVilbiss, L. A. 1923. *Birth Control, What Is It?* Boston: Small, Maynard, & Co.
Dewey, Mary E. 1892. The Indian Need. *Lend a Hand* 9(2) (August): 77.
——. 1892. Present Status of the Indians. *Lend a Hand* 8(4) (April): 225.
——. 1893. Indian Schools Report. *Lend a Hand* 10(4) (April): 229.
Dewsbury, Ethel M. 1933. Control of Community Opinion: A Case Study of a Means of Averting a Bank Failure. *Social Forces* 11(3) (March): 385–91.
Dewson, Mary Williams. 1900. *Twentieth Century Expense Book.* Boston: School of Housekeeping.
——. 1910. *Conditions that Make Wayward Girls.* Lancaster, Mass.: s.n.
——. 1923. *The Cave Report on the British Trade Board Act, 1909–1922; the Success of Minimum Wage Legislation.* New York: Steinberg Press, Inc.
——. 1931. Book Review of "Oregon's Experiment with Minimum Wage Legislation" by Victor P. Morris. *Columbia Law Review* 31: 520–.
——. 1938. *Next Steps in Social-security Legislation.* Chicago: University of Chicago Press. Also published in *Social Service Review* 12(1) (March 1938): 21–.
Dewson, Mary Williams, Francis H. Stephens, and Felix Frankfurter. 1923. *District of Columbia Minimum Wage Cases.* New York: Steinberg Press, Inc.
Dexter, Elizabeth A. 1924/1931. *Colonial Women of Affairs: Women in Business and Affairs in America Before 1776.* Boston: Houghton Mifflin.
Diaz, Abby Morton. 1875. *A Domestic Problem: Work and Culture in the Household.* Boston: J. R. Osgood. Reprinted in *Liberating the Home*, New York: Arno Press, 1974.
——. 1893. *Only a Flock of Women.* Boston: D. Lothrop.
Dickins, Dorothy. 1928. *A Nutrition Investigation of Negro Tenants in the Yazoo Mississippi Delta.* State College, Miss.: Mississippi State University, Agricultural Experiment Station, A. & M. College.
——. 1937. *Occupations of Sons and Daughters of Mississippi Cotton Farmers.* State College, Miss.: Mississippi Agricultural Experiment Station.
——. 1937. The Normal White Share-cropper Family with Grown Children. *Journal of Farm Economics* 19 (August): 814–17.
——. 1937. Occupations of Sons and Daughters of Mississippi Cotton Farmers. Ph.D. thesis, University of Chicago (sociology).

——. 1937. Some Characteristics of White Owner and Tenant Cotton Farm Families with Children 19 to 34 Years of Age. *Rural Sociology* 2(4) (December): 409–.

——. 1939. Some Contrasts in Levels of Living in Industrial, Farm, and Part-time Farm Families in Rural Mississippi. *Social Forces* 18(2) (December): 247–55.

——. 1940. Book Review of "The Agrarian Revival" by Lord. *Rural Sociology* 5(1/4): 279–.

——. 1940. Some Contrasts in White Women Employees in Garment Plants Located in Three Types of Communities of Mississippi. *Rural Sociology* 5(1/4): 427–.

——. 1940/1. Some Contrasts in Women Employed in Two Types of Industries in Mississippi. *Social Forces* 19(1/4): 522–.

Dickinson, Anna Elizabeth. 1876. *A Paying Investment.* Boston: J. R. Osgood.

Dickinson, Mary Lowe. 1896. A Half Century of Progress. *Arena* 15 (February): 361–70.

Dickson, Marguerite. 1919. *Vocational Guidance for Girls.* New York: Rand McNally.

——. 1928. Book Review of "A Short History of Women" by John A. Langdon-Davies. *Journal of Educational Sociology* 2: 63.

Dietrich, Ethel Barbara. 1921. Standardization and Stabilization. Ph.D. thesis, University of Wisconsin–Madison (business administration).

——. 1924. The Administration of Unemployment Insurance. *American Labor Legislation Review* 14: 146–.

——. 1928. The Plight of the Lancashire Cotton Industry. *American Economic Review* 18 (September): 468–76.

——. 1929. National Arbitration in the Balance: The Newspaper Publishers Versus the Compositors. *Social Forces* 8(2) (December): 284–94.

——. 1930. The Present Status of the Wool Textile Industry. *International Labour Review, Geneva* 22 (November): 583–98.

——. 1933. French Import Quotas. *American Economic Review* 23 (December): 661–74.

——. 1934. The New Model Trade Agreements. *Journal of Political Economy* 42 (October): 595–612.

——. 1935. British Export Credit Insurance. *American Economic Review* 25 (June): 236–49.

——. 1938. British Commercial Policy at the Crossroads. *Far Eastern Survey* 7(1/25): 59–.

——. 1938. Closing Doors against Japan. *Far Eastern Survey* 7(1/25): 181–.

——. 1939. *World Trade.* New York: Holt.

——. 1940. *Far Eastern Trade of the United States.* New York: International Secretariat, Institute of Pacific Relations.

——. 1940. Foreign Trade Blocs. *American Academy of Political and Social Science, Annals* 211 (September): 85–.

Dietrick, Ellen Battelle. 1891. Restriction of Immigration. *Social Economist* 5: 21–.

——. 1891. Who Shall Prescribe the Sphere of Woman? *American Magazine of Civics* 3 (August): 154–.

——. 1891. Woman and Negro Suffrage. *Westminster Review* 135 (April): 364–72.

——. 1892. How to Abolish Poverty. Reply. *American Magazine of Civics* 4 (June): 635–.

——. 1892. Who Is Responsible for Poverty? *American Magazine of Civics* 4: 404–.

——. 1895. The Standard of Value. *American Magazine of Civics* 7: 243–.

Digby, Margaret. 1928/1938. *Producers and Consumers: A Study in Co-operative Relations.* London: G. Routledge. 2nd ed., revised and enlarged, London: P. S. King, 1938.

——. 1929. Book Review of "Producers and Consumers: A Study in Co-operative Relations." *Review of International Co-operation* 22: 38–.

——. 1929. Co-operation at the International Congress of Agriculture, Bucharest. *Review of International Co-operation* 22: 299–.

——. 1930. *Agricultural Co-operation in Czechoslovakia.* London: G. Routledge & Sons, Ltd.

——. 1930. *Co-operative Electrification of Czechoslovakia. Paper read on February 24th, 1930.* Dublin: Engineering and Scientific Association of Ireland.

——. 1933. *Digest of Co-operative Law at Home and Abroad.* London: P. S. King & Son, Ltd.

——. 1934. *Report on the Opportunities for Co-operative Organisation in Newfoundland and Labrador.* London: P. S. King & Son, Ltd.

——. 1934. Agricultural Co-operation in Scandinavia. *African Observer* 1(5) (September): 46–.

——. 1935. Agricultural Co-operation in Denmark. *African Observer* 2(3) (January): 29–.

——. 1937. Genossenschaftswesen und gegenwärtige Agrarpolitik in Grossbritannien. *Jahrbücher für Nationalökonomie und Statistik* 145(1) (January): 58–.

——. 1939. Book Review of "The Economics of Co-operative Marketing" by H. H. Bakken and M. A. Schaars. *Economic Journal* 49: 754–.

——. 1940. Agricultural Co-operation in the Eastern States of the U.S.A. *Annals of Collective Economy* 16(2) (May/July): 310–.

——. 1940. Book Review of "Britain's Food Supplies in Peace and War" by C. Smith. *Economic Journal* 50: 493.

——. 1940. Book Review of "Canadian Frontiers of Settlement, Vol. I" by A. S. Morten and C. Martin. *Economic History* 4(15) (February): 414.

——. 1940. Book Review of "Colin Robertson's Correspondence Book, 1817–22" by E. E. Rich and R. H. Fleming, eds. *Economic Journal* 50: 306–.

——. 1940. Book Review of "Feeding the Nation in Peace and War" by G. Walworth. *Economic Journal* 50: 493.

——. 1940. Book Review of "Food Production in Western Europe" by P. Lamartine Yates. *Economic Journal* 50: 493.

——. 1940. Book Review of "Journal of Occurrences in the Athabasca Department" by E. E. Rich, ed. *Economic History* 4(15) (February): 414.

Diggs, Annie L. 1892. The Farmers' Alliance and Some of Its Leaders. *Arena* 5 (April): 590–607.

——. 1892. The Women in the Alliance Movement (Illustrated). *Arena* 6 (July): 160–79.

——. 1894. A Captain of Industry. *Arena* 10 (June): 112–14.

Dilke, Lady Emilia F[rances]. S[trong]. [Pattison]. 1889. Benefit Societies and Trades Unions for Women. *Fortnightly Review*, n.s. 45 (June): 852–6.

——. 1890. The Seamy Side of Trade Unionism for Women. *New Review* 2 (May): 418–22.

——. 1890. Technical Schools in Austria. *Fortnightly Review*, n.s. 47: 231–.

——. 1890. Trade Unionism for Women. *New Review* 2 (January): 43–53.

——. 1891. The Starved Government Department [the Labour Statistical Department of the Board of Trade]. *New Review* 4 (January): 75–80.

——. 1891. Trades Unionism among Women, *Fortnightly Review* 55(ccxciii) [n.s. 49] (May): 741–6.

——. 1891. Trades-unions for Women. *North American Review* 153 (August): 227–39. Reprinted London: Women's Trade Union League, 1893.

——. 1891. Women and the Royal Commission on Labour. *Fortnightly Review* 56(ccxcviii) [n.s. 50] (October): 535–8.

——. 1893. The Industrial Position of Women. *Fortnightly Review* 60 [n.s. 54] (October): 499–508.

——. 1897. Woman Suffrage in England. *North American Review* 164 (February): 151–9.

Dill, Rosalie Jones. 1923. *The American Standard of Living and World Co-operation.* Boston and New York: Cornhill Publishing Company.

——. 1928. *Women's Influence through the Ballot.* Spokane, Wash.: s.n.

Dillenback, Mary Emily. 1926. A Study of the Wholesale Prices of Beef and Veal on the Chicago Market. M.S. thesis, University of Chicago (economics, agricultural).

Dinwiddie, Emily Wayland. 1903. Women Tenement Inspectors in New York. *American Academy of Political and Social Science, Annals* 22 (September): 394.

——. 1904. *Housing Conditions in Philadelphia.* Philadelphia: Octavia Hill Association.

——. 1904. Housing and Social Conditions in Philadelphia. *Charities; a Weekly Review of Local and General Philanthropy* 12: 490.

——. 1905/6. The Mills of Dundee. *Charities and the Commons* 15: 522.

——. 1906. The Work of New York's Tenement House Department. *Charities and the Commons* (October 6): 11–12.

——. 1909. *A Report on the Condition of All Residence Buildings Owned and Controlled by Trinity Church, as Found on Inspections from June 24th to October 12th.* Condensed report of the Charity Organization Society of the City of New York, Tenement House Committee. New York: Charity Organization Society of the City of New York.

——. 1909. Pittsburgh's Housing Laws. *Charities and the Commons* (February 6).
——. 1910. Good Tenements for a Million People (Illustrated). *World's Work* 20(5) (September).
——. 1910. The Truth about Trinity's Tenements. *Survey* (February 26): 797–809.
——. 1911. The Tenant's Responsibility. *National Housing Association Proceedings* I, 2(3): 52–60.
——. 1912. Tenement House Supervision. *Journal of Home Economics* (February).
——. 1915. Management of Wage-earners' Dwellings in England. *American City* (August).
——. 1916. Educating the Tenant. *National Housing Association Proceedings* V: 386–92.
——. 1916/17. Book Review of "Commission of Immigration and Housing of California. First Annual Report, January, 1915." *American Journal of Sociology* 22(1/6): 847–.
——. 1937. *Social Welfare in Kansas, 1936.* Topeka, Kans.: Kansas Emergency Relief Committee.
Director, Rose. *See* Friedman, Rose Director.
Dissard, Clotilde. 1900. La Protection du travail feminine. *La Fronde* (January 29).
Dittmar, Elisabeth Caroline Gunderloch. 1909. *Die Einwanderung gebildeter weiblicher Erwerbsbedürftiger nach den Vereinigten Staaten. Mit einem Anhang: Die Einwanderung junger Männer.* Bielefeld and Leipzig: Velhagen & Klasing
Dittmar, Louise. 1849. *Das Wesen der Ehe nebst einigen Aufsätzen über die soziale Reform der Frauen* [The essence of marriage along with some essays about women's social reform]. Leipzig: Otto Wiegand.
Dix, Gertrude [Lane]. 1893. Hard Labour in the Hospitals. *Westminster Review* 140 (December): 627–34.
Dixie, Lady Florence. 1882. *In the Land of Misfortune* [Zululand]. London: R. Bentley & Son.
——. 1890. *Gloriana; or The Revolution of 1900.* London: Henry and Co. [*novel*].
Dixon, E. 1895. Craftswomen in the *Livre des métiers. Economic Journal* 5(18) (June): 209–28.
——. 1896. Le Logement du pauvre à Londres. *Revue d'économie politique* 10: 972–.
Dodd, Agnes F. 1901. *A Short History of the English Colonies.* London: J. M. Dent & Co.
——. 1904. Taxation of Land Values in Australasia. *Economic Journal* 14 (September): 401–12.
——. 1911. *History of Money in the British Empire & the United States.* New York: Longmans, Green.
——. 1913. *Early English Social History from the Chronicles.* London: G. Bell.
——. 1925. *A Short History of the British Empire.* London: J. M. Dent.

Dodd, Anna Bowman. 1888. *The Republic of the Future, or Socialism and Reality, Letters from a Swedish Nobleman Living in the 21st Century to a friend in Christiana.* New York: Cassell and Co.

Dodge, Grace H[oadley]. 1886. Manual Training School of the Industrial Training Association of New York. *Lend a Hand* 1(11) (November): 666–8.

——. 1887. *A Bundle of Letters to Busy Girls on Practical Matters.* New York: Funk and Wagnalls. Reprinted New York: Arno Press, 1974.

——. 1888/9. Working Girls' Societies. *Chautauquan* 9 (October/July): 223–5.

——. 1891. What Country Girls Can Do. *Lippincott's Monthly Magazine* 47 (January/June): 631–5.

——. 1894. Glimpses into Working Girls' Club Life and Principles. *American Federationist* 1(4) (June): 68–.

——. 1899. *What Women Can Earn: Occupations of Women and their Compensation.* New York: Frederick A. Stokes.

Dodge, Mary A[bigail]. [as "Gail Hamilton"]. 1868. *Woman's Wrongs: A Counter-irritant.* Boston: Ticknor and Fields. Reprinted New York: Arno Press, 1972.

—— [as "Gail Hamilton"]. 1872. *Woman's Worth and Worthlessness.* New York: Harper and Brothers.

Dohm, Hedwig. 1874. *Die wissenschaftliche Emancipation der Frau.* Berlin: Wedekind & Schwieger.

——. 1876. *Der Frauen Natur und Recht: zur Frauenfrage zwei Abhandlungen über Eigenschaften und Stimmrecht der Frauen.* Berlin: Wedekind & Schweiger. English ed., *Women's Nature and Privilege,* transl. Constance Campbell, London: Women's Printing Society, 1896. Reprinted Westport, Conn.: Hyperion Press, 1976.

Dolan, Eleanor Frances. 1935. The Effect of Rapid Transit on Land Value and Building Construction in Boston, Cambridge, and Arlington, 1900–1930. Ph.D. thesis, Radcliffe College (economics).

Doman, Leila M. 1935. A Study of Price Variations in Retail Grocery Stores. Ph.D. thesis, Cornell University (economics).

Donahue, Alice Madorah. 1928. *Children of Illegitimate Birth Whose Mothers Have Kept Their Custody.* Washington: U.S. Children's Bureau.

——. 1930. Children Born out of Wedlock. *American Academy of Political and Social Science, Annals* 151 (September): 162–.

——. 1937. Child-welfare Services of the District of Columbia. *Child* 2(3) (September): 56–.

Donahue, Alice Madorah and Rena Rosenberg. 1925. *The Welfare of Infants of Illegitimate Birth in Baltimore as Affected by Maryland Law of 1916.* Washington: U.S. Children's Bureau.

Donlevy, Alice. 1890/1. Employments for Women. *Chautauquan* 12 (October/March): 372–.

Donnan, Elizabeth. 1926. Book Review of "A Legacy to Wage-Earning Women: A Survey of Gainfully Employed Women of Brattleboro, VT, and of Relief Which They Have Received from the Thomas Thompson Trust" by Eaves. *American Economic Review* 16(2) (June): 331–2.

——. 1928. The Slave Trade into South Carolina Before the Revolution. *The American Historical Review* XXXIII(4) (July): 804–.

——, ed. 1930–5. *Documents Illustrative of the History of the Slave Trade to America*. Vol. I: *1441–1700*; Vol. II: *The Eighteenth Century*; Vol. III: *New England and the Middle Colonies*; Vol. IV *The Border Colonies and the Southern Colonies*. Carnegie Institution of Washington Publication, no. 409. Washington: Carnegie Institution of Washington.

——. 1930. The Early Days of the South Sea Company, 1711–1718. *Journal of Economic and Business History* 2 (May): 419–50.

——. 1930. The New England Slave Trade. *New England Quarterly* 3(1/4): 251–.

——. 1931. Eighteenth-century English Merchants: Micajah Perry. *Journal of Economic and Business History* 4 (November): 70–98.

——. 1932. Book Review of "Economic and Social History of an English Village" by Gras and Gras. *American Economic Review* 22(2) (June): 287–.

——. 1935. Book Review of "The Caracas Company, 1728–1784" by Hussey. *American Economic Review* 25: 532–.

——. 1937. Book Review of "Cases Concerning…Slavery and the Negro" by Helen T. Catterall, ed. *New England Quarterly* 10(1/4): 396–.

Donovan, Mrs. Frances R. 1920. *The Woman Who Waits*. Boston: R. G. Badger.

——. 1929. *The Saleslady*. Chicago: University of Chicago Press.

——. 1938. *The Schoolma'am*. New York: Frederick A. Stokes Co.

Dooly, Myra A. 1893. The Industrial Schools of the Netherlands. *Arena* 7 (May): 714–20.

Dopp, Katharine Elizabeth. 1902. The Place of Industries in Elementary Education. Ph.D. thesis, University of Chicago (education).

——. 1902/3. New Factor in Elementary School Curriculum. *American Journal of Sociology* 8: 145.

——. 1902/3. Steps in the Evolution of Social Occupations – I. *Elementary School Journal* 3(1/10): 318–.

——. 1902/3. Steps in the Evolution of Social Occupations – II. *Elementary School Journal* 3(1/10): 219–.

——. 1902/3. Steps in the Evolution of Social Occupations – III. *Elementary School Journal* 3(1/10): 416–.

——. 1902/3. Steps in the Evolution of Social Occupations – IV. *Elementary School Journal* 3(1/10): 499–.

——. 1902/3. Steps in the Evolution of Social Occupations – V. *Elementary School Journal* 3(1/10): 625–.

——. 1903. *The Place of Industries in Elementary Education*. Chicago: Chicago University Press; London: P. S. King.

——. 1903/4. Relation of History and Industry. *Elementary School Journal* 4(1/10): 477–.

——. 1903/4. Steps in the Evolution of Social Occupations. *Elementary School Journal* 4(1/10): 73–.

——. 1904. Tree-dwellers. *Science* 20: 20.

——. 1907/8. A Report of the First Annual Meeting of the National Society for the Promotion of Industrial Education. *Elementary School Journal* 8(1/10): 393–.

——. 1927. *The Tree-dwellers.* Chicago: Rand-McNally.

Dorr, Rheta Louise Childe. 1909. *Women's Demand for Humane Treatment of Women Workers in Shop and Factory.* New York: Consumers' League of the City of New York.

——. 1910. *Breaking into the Human Race.* New York: National American Woman Suffrage Association.

——. 1910. *What Eight Million Women Want.* Boston: Small, Maynard & Co.

——. 1917. *Inside the Russian Revolution.* New York: Macmillan Co.

Dorsey, Ella Loraine. 1891. Women in the Patent Office. *Chautauquan* 13 (April/September): 366–.

——. 1891. Women in the Pension Office. *Chautauquan* 13 (April/September): 661–.

——. 1891/2. Women in the Land Office. *Chautauquan* 14 (October/March): 346–.

——. 1891/2. Women in the Pension Office. *Chautauquan* 14 (October/March): 475–.

Doughty, Frances Albert. 1897. Life in the Cotton Belt. *Lippincott's* 59 (May): 687–.

——. 1897. The Southern Side of the Industrial Question. *Lippincott's* 59 (January/June): 266–.

Douglas, Dorothy [Sybil] Wolff. 1919. American Minimum Wage Laws at Work. *American Economic Review* 9(4) (December): 701–38. Reprinted in John R. Commons, ed., *Trade Unionism and Labor Problems*, 2nd series. Boston: Ginn and Co.

——. 1920. The Cost of Living for Working Women: A Criticism of Current Theories. *Quarterly Journal of Economics* 34(2) (February): 225–59.

——. 1925. *Guillaume de Greef: The Social Theory of an Early Syndicalist.* London: P. S. King.

——. 1925. Guillaume de Greef: The Social Theory of an Early Syndicalist. Ph.D. thesis, Columbia University (political science).

——. 1925/6. The Social Purpose in the Sociology of DeGreef. *American Journal of Sociology* 31(1/6): 433–.

——. 1928/9. P. J. Proudhon: A Prophet of 1848, Part I: Life and Works. *American Journal of Sociology* 34(5): 781–803.

——. 1929/30. P. J. Proudhon: A Prophet of 1848, Part II. *American Journal of Sociology* 35(1): 35–59.

——. 1932. Ira Steward on Consumption and Unemployment. *Journal of Political Economy* 40(4) (August): 532–43.

——. 1932/3. The Effect of Unemployment and Short-time during 1931 in the Families of 200 Alabama Child Workers. *Social Forces* 11(1/4): 548–.

——. 1934. What Kind of Unemployment Insurance. *Social Work Today* 1(2) (May/June): 3–.

——. 1937. The Social Security Act. *American Teacher* 21(5) (May/June): 18–.
——. 1938. Book Review of "Industrial Unionism in Action" by J. Raymond Walsh. *Science & Society* 2: 549–.
——. 1938. Book Review of "The Post-War History of the British Working Class" by Allen Hutt. *Science & Society* 2: 549–.
——. 1939. *Mexican Labor: A Bulwark of Democracy*. New York: American League for Peace and Democracy.
——. 1939. Book Review of "Child Labor Legislation in the Southern Textile States" by Elizabeth H. Davidson. *American Sociological Review* 4(1/6): 766–.
——. 1940. British Wage Boards: A Study in Industrial Democracy. *American Economic Review* 30(3) (September): 636–7.
——. 1940. Land and Labor in Mexico. *Science & Society* 4(2): 127–52.
Douglas, Dorothy Wolff and Paul Douglas. 1921. What Can a Man Afford? *American Economic Review* 11(4), Supplement no. 2 (December).
Douglas, Dorothy Wolff. Coauth. *See* Lumpkin, Katharine Du Pre.
Douglas, Iris. 1931. The American Census of Distribution, 1930. *Royal Statistical Association Journal*, series A 94(3): 432–7.
——. 1935. Retail Trade Statistics in Different Countries. *Royal Statistical Association Journal*, series A 98(3): 455–96.
——. 1937. Irish Free State Census of Distribution, 1933. *Royal Statistical Association Journal*, series A 100(1): 98–9.
Dowe, Dorothy. 1932. A Comparison of Independent and Chain Store Prices. *Journal of Business* 5(2) (April) 130–44.
Drake, Barbara [Mrs. Bernard]. 1908. A Study of Infant Life in Westminster. *Journal of the Royal Statistical Society* 71(4) (December): 678–86.
——. 1913. The Case of the Sub-Postmaster's Assistant. *Women's Industrial News* (October).
——. 1913. Earnings of Tea-shop Waitresses [letter to the editor]. *Nation* 13(3) (April 19): 106–.
——. 1913. The Tea-Shop Girl. *Women's Industrial News* (April).
——. 1914. The Barmaid. *Women's Industrial News* (April).
——. 1914. The Girl-worker and the Opportunity of the Juvenile Advisory Committee. *Women's Industrial News* (July).
——. 1914. Government Contracts and the Disenfranchised Worker: A Study on the Brush-making Trade. *Women's Industrial News* (January).
——. 1914. The Waste of Life [letter to the editor]. *Nation* 15(7) (May 16): 270–.
——. 1915. The Shop Assistant. *Women's Industrial News* (April).
——. 1917. *Women in the Engineering Trades. A Problem, a Solution, and Some Criticisms. Being a Report Based on an Enquiry by a Joint Committee of the Fabian Research Department and the Fabian Women's Group*. Trade Union Series, No. 3. London: Fabian Research Department/George Allen and Unwin.
——. 1918. Women as Politicians [letter to the editor]. *Nation* 22(17) (January 26): 539.

——. 1920. *Women in Trade Unions*. London: Labour Research Department/G. Allen and Unwin.

——. 1929. This Tragedy of Milk [letter to the editor]. *Nation and Athenaeum* 46(2) (October 12): 44–6.

——. 1933. *Starvation in the Midst of Plenty: A New Plan for the State Feeding of School Children*. London: Fabian Society.

——. 1935/1936. *Nutrition: A Policy of National Health*. Fabian Society Research series, no. 31. London: New Fabian Research Bureau.

——. 1937. *State Education: An Immediate Programme for a Socialist Government*. Fabian Society Research series, no. 35. London: V. Gollancz.

——. 1939. The Spens Report. *Political Quarterly (1930-)* 10: 215–.

Drew, Catherine. 1890. Technical Training for Women. *Englishwoman's Review*, n.s. 201 (January): 2.

Du Bois, Florence. 1923. *Enrollment in Foreign Languages, Sciences and Commercial Subjects*. Washington: U.S. Bureau of Education.

——. 1923. *School Support and School Indebtedness in Cities*. Washington: U.S. Bureau of Education, Statistical Division.

——. 1930. *A Guide to Statistics of Social Welfare in New York City*. New York: Welfare Council of New York City.

——. 1931. *Bronx House Numbers in Health Areas*. Section 2 of Study 10 of the Research Bureau of the Welfare Council of New York City. New York: Research Bureau, Welfare Council of New York City.

——. 1931. *Population in Health Areas, New York City, 1930*. Section 7 of Study 10 of the Research Bureau of the Welfare Council. New York: Research Bureau, Welfare Council of New York City.

——. 1933. A Guide to the Statistics of Social Trends in the United States. In Florence Du Bois and Stuart Arthur Rice, eds., *Report to the President's Research Committee on Social Trends, on Social Statistics in the United States*. Ann Arbor, Mich.: Edwards Brothers, Inc.

Duclauk, Mrs. Mary Robinson. 1902. A Farm in the Cantal (Haute-Auvergne). *Contemporary Review* (November).

Dudley, Helena S. 1894. Relief Work Carried on in the Wells Memorial Institute. *Annals of the American Academy of Political and Social Science* 5 (November): 377–97.

——. 1898. Women's Work in Boston Settlements. *Municipal Affairs* 2 (September): 493–.

Duff Gordon, Lucie. 1865. *Letters from Egypt, 1863–65*. London: Macmillan.

——. 1875. *Last Letters from Egypt: To Which Are Added Letters from the Cape*. London: Macmillan.

Dufferin and Ava, Marchioness of [Blackwood, Harriot]. 1891. The Women of India. *Nineteenth Century* 29 (January/June): 359–66.

Dugdale, Harriet A. 1883. A Few Hours in a Far-off Age. Melbourne: McCarron, Bird. [*utopian novel*]

Duke, Emma and Beatrice Sheets Duncan. 1917. *Infant Mortality: Results of a Field Study in Manchester, N.H.* Washington: U.S. Government Printing Office.

Dulles, Eleanor Lansing. 1926. The French Franc 1918–1926. Ph.D. thesis, Radcliffe College (economics).
——. 1929. *The French Franc, 1914–1928*. New York: Macmillan.
——. 1932. *The Bank for International Settlements at Work*. New York: Macmillan.
——. 1932. *The Evolution of Reparation Ideas*. Monograph.
——. 1933. *The Dollar, the Franc and Inflation*. New York: Macmillan.
——. 1933. Book Review of "Walter Lippmann's Interpretations 1931–1932" by Allen Nevins, ed. *American Academy of Political and Social Science, Annals* 166 (March): 212–.
——. 1934. Book Review of "World Prosperity" by Wallace McClure. *American Academy of Political and Social Science, Annals* 171 (January): 277–.
——. 1936. *Depression and Reconstruction: A Study of Causes and Controls*. Philadelphia: University of Pennsylvania Press.
——. 1936/1937. *Financing the Social Security Act*. Washington: Bureau of Research and Statistics, Social Security Board, Bureau Memoranda nos. 4, 10.
——. 1936. The French Franc in 1935. *Harvard Business Review* 14(2): 146–60.
——. 1938. The Bank for International Settlements in Recent Years. *American Economic Review* 28(2) (June): 290–304.
——. 1939. Financing Old-age Insurance. *American Academy of Political and Social Science, Annals* 202 (March): 176–.
——. 1939. Financing Old-age Insurance. *Social Security Bulletin* 2(4) (April): 19–.
Dulles, Eleanor Lansing, William A. Berridge, Edison L. Bowers, and H. V. Roelse. 1938. Social Security Program: Discussion. *American Economic Review* Supplement 28 (March): 136–40.
Duncan, Sara Jeannette [Mrs. Everard Cotes]. 1893. *The Simple Adventures of a Memsahib*. London: Chatto & Windus
——. 1904. *The Imperialist*. Westminster: Archibald Constable & Co. [*novel*]
——. 1906. *Set in Authority*. London: Constable.
Dunlop, O. J[ocelyn]. 1911. Some Aspects of Early English Apprenticeship. *Royal Historical Society, Transactions* 3(5): 193–.
——. 1913. *The Farm Labourer: The History of a Modern Problem*. London: Fisher Unwin.
Durant, R. 1939. *Watling: A Survey of Social Life on a New Housing Estate*. London: P. S. King.
Dyhrenfurth, Gertrud. 1895. Die Berichte der weiblichen Fabrikinspektoren in England. *Jahrbücher für Nationalökonomie und Statistik*, series 3(9:64): 594.
——. 1896. Bericht von Mifs Collet über gewerbliche Frauenarbeit. *Jahrbücher für Nationalökonomie und Statistik*, series 3(12:67): 867.
——. 1898. *Die Hausindustriellen Arbeiterinnen in der Berliner Blusen-, Unterrock-, Schürzen- und Tricotkonfektion*. Leipzig: Duncker & Humblot. Reprinted Bad Feilnbach, Germany: Schmidt, 1990.
——. 1905. Die weibliche Heimarbeit. *Jahrbücher für Nationalökonomie und Statistik* 3(29:1) (January): 21–.

——. 1906/1990. *Ein Schlesisches Dorf und Rittergut: Geschichte und soziale Verfassung.* Bad Feilnbach, Germany: Schmidt.

——. 1908. *Tarifämter für die Hausindustrie.* Berlin: s.n.

——. 1910. Die Entwicklung der englischen Trade-Boards (Gewerkämter). *Jahrbücher für Nationalökonomie und Statistik* 3(40:6) (December): 791–.

——. 1916. *Ergebnisse einer Untersuchung über die Arbeits- und Lebensverhältnisse der Frauen in der Landwirtschaft.* Jena: Fischer.

——. Coauth. *See* Schmidt, Anna.

E

Eagle, Mary Kavanaugh Oldham, ed. 1894. *The Congress of Women Held in the Woman's Building, World's Columbian Exposition, Chicago, U.S.A., 1893*. 2 vols. Chicago: W. B. Conkey Co.

Earle, Alice Morse. 1894. New Chapters of African Discovery. *Dial* 16 (January 1/June 16): 269–.

——. 1897/8. Colonial Household Industries. *Chautauquan* 26 (October/March): 475–.

——. 1897/8. Indian Corn in Colonial Times. *Chautauquan* 26 (October/March): 586–.

——. 1898. *Home Life in Colonial Days*. New York and London: Macmillan.

——. 1899. *Child Life in Colonial Days*. New York and London: Macmillan.

Earle, Frances M. 1929. *Geographic Influences upon British Economic Policy in West Africa*. Ph.D. thesis, George Washington University (economics).

——. 1931. Mechanization of Agriculture in U.S.S.R. *Economic Geography* 7(3) (July): 297–307.

East, Emma Tolman. 1918–19. *Romance of Big Business Series*. Vol. 1: *Dreams that Came True* (1918); Vol. 2: *The Story of a Soap Bubble* (1919); Vol. 3: *The Story of Glue* (1919); Vol. 4: *Musical Strings and Pharmaceuticals* (1919); Vol. 5: *Feeding the Farm* (1919); Vol. 6: *The River of Food* (1919). Chicago: Armour's Bureau of Agricultural Research and Economics.

——. 1919. *Musical Strings and Pharmaceuticals*. Chicago: Armour's Bureau of Agricultural Research and Economics.

Eastlake, Lady Elizabeth [Rigby]. 1876. London Alms, London Pauperism. *Quarterly Review* 142 (October): 373–402.

——. 1879. Bastiat, an Apostle of Free Trade. *Edinburgh Review* 149 (April): 355–77.

Eastman, Crystal. 1909. *"Employers' Liability": A Criticism Based on Facts*. New York: New York Branch of the American Association for Labor Legislation.

——. 1909. The American Way of Distributing Industrial Accident Losses: A Criticism. *American Economic Association Quarterly* 10(1) (April): 119–34.

——. 1910–16. Work-accidents and the Law. In Paul Underwood Kellogg, ed., *The Pittsburgh Survey Findings in Six Volumes*. New York: Charities Publication Committee of Russell Sage Foundation.

——. 1911. The Three Essentials for Accident Prevention. *American Academy of Political and Social Science, Annals* 38(1) (July): 98–.

——. 1927. Women, Rights and Privileges. *Outlook* 59(1514) (February): 122–.

——. Articles in *New Republic*, *Survey* and *Liberator*.

[Eastman,] Elaine Goodale. 1889. The Future Indian School System. *Chautauquan* 10 (October): 51–.

——. 1890. How to Americanize the Indians. *New Englander and Yale Review* 52 (May): 452–5.

——. 1890/1. A Woman's View of the Indian Troubles. *Chautauquan* 12 (October/March): 786–.

——. 1891. Indian Girls in Indian Schools. *Home-maker* 6(3) (June): 199–205.

——. 1891. Wives and Property. *Indian's Friend* 4 (December): 1.

——. 1893. A Woman among the Indians. In Frances A. Goodale, ed., *The Literature of Philanthropy*. New York: Harper Bros.

Eaton, Isabel. 1895. Receipts and Expenditures of Certain Wage-earners in the Garment Trades. *Journal of the American Statistical Association* IV(30) (June): 135–80.

——. 1895. Receipts and Expenditures of Cloak Makers in Chicago. In [Residents of Hull House,] *Hull House Maps and Papers*. New York: T. Y. Crowell. Reprinted New York: Arno Press, 1970.

——. 1899. Special Report on Negro Domestic Service. In W. E. B. Du Bois, *The Philadelphia Negro: a Social Study*. Boston: Gian & Co. for the University of Pennsylvania. Reprinted Philadelphia: University of Pennsylvania Press (Centennial ed.), 1996.

Eaton, Jeanette. 1927. *The Story of Transportation*. New York: Harper.

——. 1935. *Behind the Show Window*. New York: Harcourt, Brace and Co.

——. 1939. Our Backward Farmers. *Forum and Century* 102(3) (September): 138–.

Eaton, Jeanette and Bertha M. Stevens. 1915. *Commercial Work and Training for Girls*. New York: Macmillan.

Eaton, Jeanette. Coauth. *See* Matthews, Ellen Nathalie.

Eaton, Mary Alice. 1936. Changes in Land Occupance in Puerto Rico, 1898–1930. S.M. thesis, University of Chicago (economics, agricultural).

——. 1939/40. Book Review of "White Settlers in the Tropics" by Price. *Social Forces* 18(1/4): 303–.

Eaton, Mary Alice and Margaret Jarman Hagood. 1938/9. An Examination of Regional Differentials in Fertility by Analysis of Variance and Co-variance. *Social Forces* 17(1/4): 495–.

Eaves, Lucile. 1906. San Francisco, Where It Was Sorest Stricken. *Charities and the Commons* 16: 161.

——. 1910. *A History of California Labor Legislation*. Berkeley: University of California Press.

——. 1910. A History of California Labor Legislation, with an Introductory Sketch of the San Francisco Labor Movement. Ph.D. thesis, Columbia University (sociology, industrial and labor relations).

——. 1912/13. Book Review of "Economic Beginnings of the Far West" by Katherine Coman. *American Journal of Sociology* 18(1/6): 819–.

——. 1913/14. Book Review of "Women in the Bookbinding Trade" by Mary Van Kleck. *American Journal of Sociology* 19(1/6): 247–.

——. 1914. Social Politics in California. *American Economic Review* 4 (June): 450–4.

——. 1916. Book Review of "Regularity of Employment in the Women's Ready-to-wear Garment Industries" by U.S. Bureau of Labor Statistics. *American Economic Review* 6(2) (June): 403–4.

——. 1916. Book Review of "The Relation of Irregular Employment to the Living Wage for Women" by Irene Osgood Andrews. *American Economic Review* 6(2) (June): 403–4.

——. 1916. Book Review of "Unemployment among Women in Department and Other Retail Stores of Boston" by U.S. Bureau of Labor Statistics. *American Economic Review* 6(2) (June): 403–4.

——. 1917. *The Food of Working Women in Boston: An Investigation by the Department of Research, Women's Educational and Industrial Union, Boston.* Women's Educational and Industrial Union. Department of Research. Studies in Economic Relations of Women, vol. 10. Boston: Wright & Potter.

——. 1917. War as a Crisis in Social Control. Discussion. *American Sociological Society, Papers and Proceedings* 12 (December): 34–.

——. 1918. The Social Education of Women. Discussion. *American Sociological Society, Papers and Proceedings* 13 (December): 28–.

——. 1919. Training Children for Work after the War. *American Labor Legislation Review* 9: 59.

——. 1919/20. Plans for Co-operative Research. *American Journal of Sociology* 25(1/6): 568–.

——. 1920. *Training for Store Service: The Vocational Experiences and Training of Juvenile Employees of Retail Department, Dry Goods, and Clothing Stores in Boston.* Boston: Badger.

——. 1921. *Gainful Employment for Handicapped Women.* Co-operative Social Research by Simmons College and the Women's Educational and Industrial Union, Report no. 1. Boston: Women's Education and Industrial Union.

——. 1921. *Old-age Support of Women Teachers: Provisions for Old Age Made by Women Teachers in the Public Schools of Massachusetts.* Women's Educational and Industrial Union. Department of Research. Studies in Economic Relations of Women, vol. 11. Boston: Spartan Press Inc.

——. 1922. *One Thousand Industrial Accidents Suffered by Massachusetts Children.* Boston: Women's Educational and Industrial Union.

——. 1922/3. Women in Conference on Industrial Problems. *Sociology and Social Research* 7: 201–.

——. 1923. *Children in Need of Special Care: Studies Based on Two Thousand Case Records of Social Agencies.* Co-operative Social Research by Simmons College School of Social Work, Boston Council of Social Agencies and the Women's

Educational and Industrial Union, Report no. 2. Boston: Women's Educational and Industrial Union.

——. 1923/4. Applied Sociology in Relation to Social Work. *Sociology and Social Research* 8: 26–.

——. 1923/4. The Social Worker's Clients. *Social Forces* 2(1/5): 497–.

——. 1923/4. Women's Education Union of Boston. *Social Forces* 2(1/5): 574–.

——, ed. 1925. *Aged Clients of Boston Social Agencies.* Boston: Women's Educational and Industrial Union.

——. 1925. *A Legacy to Wage-earning Women: A Survey of Gainfully Employed Women of Brattleboro, VT, and of Relief Which They Have Received from the Thomas Thompson Trust.* Boston: Women's Educational and Industrial Union.

——. 1926/7. Social Sciences in the Sixth International Congress of Philosophy. *Social Forces* 5(1/4): 407–.

——. 1929. Studies of Breakdowns in Family Income, Sickness, Children, and Sick Children in Dependent Families. *Family* 10(8) (December): 227–.

——. 1931. Book Review of "Earnings of Women in Business and the Professions" by Margaret Elliott and Grace E. Manson. *American Economic Review* 21(2) (June): 321–3.

——. 1931. Book Review of "La Généralisation des allocations familiales en Belgique" by Georges Heyman. *American Journal of Sociology* 37(3): 506–7.

Eccles, Charlotte O'Conor. 1893. Experiences of a Woman Journalist. *Blackwood's* 153 (June): 830–8.

——. 1897. The Girls of Today and Their Education. *Irish Monthly* 25.

Eck, Catharina W. 1898. *Een nieuw beroep voor vrouwen.* S'Gravenhage: J. L. Wéry.

Edgar, Mrs. J. D. 1896/7. Early History of Newfoundland. *Canadian* 8: 406–.

Edgeworth, Maria. 1796. *The Parent's Assistant, or Stories for Children.* 3 vols. London: Joseph Johnson. Expanded edition, 6 vols., 1800.

——. 1800. *Castle Rackrent.* London: printed for J. Johnson. Reprinted J. M. Dent & Sons, 1960.

——. 1804. *Popular Tales.* 3 vols. London: J. Johnson; and Philadelphia: James Humphreys.

——. 1808. *The Match Girl. A Novel.* 3 vols. London: printed by J. Dennett for J. F. Hughes.

——. 1809/1812. *Tales of Fashionable Life.* Vols. 1–3, 1809; 4–6, 1812. London: J. Johnson. [Includes "The Absentee" and "Ennui".]

Edler De Roover, Florence. *See* De Roover, Florence Edler.

Edmondson, Edna Elder Hatfield. 1914. State Aid to Mothers of Dependent Children. A.M. thesis, Indiana University.

——. 1917. Juvenile Delinquency and Adult Crime. Certain Associations of Juvenile Delinquency and Adult Crime in Gary, Indiana, with Special Reference to the Immigrant Population. Ph.D. thesis, Indiana University (sociology).

——. 1930. *Study Program of Child Welfare Laws in Indiana, with Special Emphasis on School Attendance and Child Labor.* Bulletin of the Extension Division, Indiana University. Bloomington, Ind.: Indiana University.

Edmondson, Edna Elder and Mabel Thacher Wellman. 1919. *Feeding Children at School: A Method of Meeting the Problem of Undernourished Children.* Bulletin of the Extension Division, Indiana University, vol. 4, no. 8. Bloomington, Ind.: Indiana University.

Edson, Katherine Philips [Mrs. Charles Farwell Edson]. 1912. *The Actual Operation of Woman's Suffrage in California.* Paper read at the convention of the National Municipal League held in Los Angeles, Cal., July, 1912. Los Angeles: National Municipal League.

——. 1915. Will Limited Hours of Work and the Minimum Wage Force Women out of Industrial Competition? *Association of Collegiate Alumnae, Journal* 8(4) (May): 94.

——. 1919. *A Study of the Cost of Living.* Sacramento, Calif.: California Industrial Welfare Commission.

Edwards, Henrietta Muir. 1908. *Legal Status of Canadian Women, as Shown by Extracts from Dominion and Provincial Laws Relating to Marriage, Property, Dower, Divorce, Descent of Land, Franchise, Crime and Other Subjects.* Calgary: National Council of Women of Canada.

Eickhoff, Edith. 1935. The Michigan Poor Law and Health Services. M.A. thesis, University of Chicago (sociology).

——. Coauth. *See* Bruce, Isabel Campbell.

Eisen, Edna Esther. 1929. *Commercial Utilization of the Rhine River.* S.M. thesis, University of Chicago (geography).

——. 1934. The Structure of Rhine Traffic. *Economic Geography* 10(3) (July): 254–67.

Elderton, Marion. 1931. *Case Studies of Unemployment.* Philadelphia: University of Pennsylvania.

——. 1931. Unemployment Consequences on the Home. *American Academy of Political and Social Science, Annals* 154 (March): 58–.

Eliot, Clara. 1926. The Farmers' Campaign for Credit. Ph.D. thesis, Columbia University (business administration, accounting).

——. 1927. *The Farmer's Campaign for Credit.* New York, London: D. Appleton and Company.

Eliot, T. D., ed. 1931. *American Standards and Planes of Living.* Boston: Ginn.

Eliot-James, Mrs. A. G. F. 1886. Tobacco Culture in England. *National Review* 7 (August): 816–22.

Elizabeth, Charlotte. *See* [Tonna,] Charlotte Elizabeth.

Ellet, Elizabeth Fries Lummis. 1857. *The Practical Housekeeper, a Cyclopaedia of Domestic Economy… Comprising Five Thousand Practical Receipts and Maxims.* New York: Stringer and Townsend. Later published as *The New Cyclopedia of Domestic Economy, and Practical Housekeeper: Adapted to all Classes of Society, and Comprising Subjects Connected with the Interest of Every Family.* Norwich, Conn.: H. Bill, 1872.

Elliot, Margaret. 1875. *Workhouse Girls: Notes of an Attempt to Help Them.* London: J. Nisbet.

Elliott, Mabel Agnes. 1928. *Correctional Education and the Delinquent Girl. A Follow-up Study of One Hundred and Ten Sleighton Farm Girls.* Harrisburg: s.n. Prepared through the cooperation of the Carola Woerishoffer Graduate Department of Social Economy and Social Research of Bryn Mawr College, Sleighton Farm and the Department of Welfare of the Commonwealth of Pennsylvania.

——. 1931. *Conflicting Penal Theories in Statutory Criminal Law.* Chicago: University of Chicago Press.

——. 1933/4. Child Labor is a Family Problem. *Sociology and Social Research* 18: 251–.

——. 1935/6. Book Review of "Development of Poor Relief Legislation in Kansas" by Grace A. Browning and S. P. Breckenridge. *Illinois Law Review* 30: 960–.

——. 1936. Book Review of "I was a Soviet Worker" by Andrew Smith and Maria Smith. *American Sociological Review* 1(1/6): 862.

——. 1936. Book Review of "This Soviet World" by Anna Louise Strong. *American Sociological Review* 1(1/6): 861.

——. 1936. Book Review of "We Soviet Women" by Tatiana Tchernavin. *American Sociological Review* 1(1/6): 864.

Elliott, Margaret. 1924. Occupational Statistics: A Study in Classification. Ph.D. thesis, Radcliffe College (economics).

——. 1934. Book Review of "College Women and the Social Sciences" by Robert Elmer Mills. *American Academy of Political and Social Science, Annals* 175 (September): 272–.

——. 1934. Book Review of "Women and Wealth" by Mary Sydney Branch. *American Academy of Political and Social Science, Annals* 175 (September): 271–.

Elliott, Margaret and Grace E. Manson. 1929. Some Factors Affecting Earnings of Business and Professional Women. *American Academy of Political and Social Science, Annals* 143 (May): 137–.

——. 1930. *Earnings of Women in Business and the Professions.* Ann Arbor, Mich.: University of Michigan.

Elliott, S. Maria. 1898. The Science of Keeping a House Clean. *Chautauquan* 27 (April/September): 662–.

Ellis, Ellen Deborah. 1905. *An Introduction to the History of Sugar as a Commodity.* Philadelphia: John C. Winston Co.

——. 1905. Introduction to the Study of Sugar as a Commodity. Ph.D. thesis, Bryn Mawr College (economics).

Ellis, Ellen D. 1914. The Feminist Movement in Turkey. *Contemporary Review* 105 (January/June): 857–.

——. 1920. The Pluralistic State. *American Political Science Review* 14(1/4): 393–.

——. 1923. Guild Socialism and Pluralism. *American Political Science Review* 17(1/4): 584–.

——. 1927. Political Science at the Crossroads. *American Political Science Review (1927–)* 21(4) (November): 773–.

——. 1933. Intervention as a Sanction of International Law. *American Society of International Law, Proceedings* 27: 78–.

——. 1935. National Parties and Local Politics. *American Political Science Review (1927–)* 29(1) (February): 60–.

Ellis, L[eonora]. B[eck]. 1899. Recent Developments in the South. *Forum* 28 (December): 442–50.

——. 1899. The State as a Farmer. *Review of Reviews* 19 (June): 706–9.

——. 1900. Cotton-mills in Cotton-fields. *Review of Reviews* 22: 61.

——. 1900. The United States in Cuba. *Arena* 24 (July/December): 57–.

——. 1901. Child Labor Legislation in the South. *Gunton's Magazine* 21: 45.

——. 1901. Child Operatives in Southern Mills. *Independent* 53: 2,637.

——. 1901. Industrial Awakening of the South. *Gunton's Magazine* 20: 527.

——. 1901. A Model Factory Town. *Forum* (September): 60.

——. 1901. Mill Operatives: A New Class of Labor in the South. *Forum* 31(May): 306.

——. 1901. Our Educational Responsibility in Cuba. *Gunton's Magazine* 20(3) (March): 250–.

——. 1902. The Movement to Restrict Child Labor. *Arena* 28: 370.

——. 1903. A Study of Southern Cotton-mill Communities. Child Labor. The Operatives in General. *American Journal of Sociology* (5) (March): 623–30.

——. 1903. Educating Southern Factory Children (Illustrated). *Gunton's Magazine* 24(5) (May): 459–.

——. 1903. The Georgia State Industrial College for Negroes. *Gunton's Magazine* 25(3) (September): 218–.

——. 1903. The Seminoles of Florida. *Gunton's Magazine* 25(6) (December): 495–.

——. 1904. Organization of Sugar-Cane Growers. *Gunton's Magazine* 27(5) (November): 478–.

——. 1910. The South's Greatest Genius. *Americana* 5 (January/December): 137–.

Ellis, Pearl Idella. 1929. *Americanization through Homemaking*. Los Angeles: Wetzel Publishing.

[Elmy,] E[lizabeth] C. Wolstenholme. 1869. The Education of Girls, Its Present and Its Future. In Josephine Butler, ed., *Woman's Work and Woman's Culture*. London: Macmillan.

——. 1874. *The New Factory Bill: Reasons Why Women Should Oppose the Nine Hours' Factory Bill, and any Others Like It.* London: Vigilance Association for the Defence of Personal Rights.

——. 1880. *The Criminal Code in Its Relation to Women, a Paper Read before the Dialectical Society, March 3rd, 1880.* Manchester: A. Ireland.

——. 1882. The Married Women's Property Act. *Englishwoman's Review*, n.s. 113 (September): 386–.

——. 1884. *The Custody and Guardianship of Children: Opinions of the Press on the Law Relating to the Custody and Guardianship of Children and on the Infants Bill.* Manchester: A. Ireland & Co.

——. 1884. The Custody & Guardianship of Children. *Englishwoman's Review*, n.s. 139 (November): 491–.

——. 1886. *A Woman's Plea to Women*. Paper read before the Congleton Fair Trade Lodge, November 8, 1886. London: Women's Printing Society.

——. 1888. *The Emancipation of Women.* London: Women's Printing Society.

——. 1888. *Foreign Investments and British Industry: A Series of Four Letters.* London: Wyman and Sons. Reprinted, with notes and appendix, from the *Manchester Courier* (December 1887).

——. 1888. *The Infants Act 1886. The Record of a Three Years' Effort for Legislative Reform, with Its Results.* London: Women's Printing Society.

——. 1891. *The Decision in the Clitheroe Case, and Its Consequences: A Series of Five Letters.* Manchester: Guardian Printing Works. Reprinted from the *Manchester Guardian* (April 1891).

——. 1892. *Modern Liberalism; the Enfranchisement of Women.* London: s.n.

——. 1896. *Woman and the Law: A Series of Four Letters.* Congleton, UK: Women's Printing Society. Reprinted from the *Western Daily Press.*

——. 1896. *Women and Legislation; a Series of Articles.* Revised and enlarged from *Shafts* of April, May, June, and July 1896. Congleton, UK: Women's Emancipation Union.

—— [as "Ignota"]. 1897. Women's Suffrage – The Need of the Hour. *Westminster Review* 148 (October): 357–72.

—— [as "Ignota"]. 1898. Judicial Sexual Bias. *Westminster Review* 149 (February): 147–60; (March): 279–88.

—— [as "Ignota"]. 1898/1899. Women in Local Administration. *Westminster Review* 150 (July 1898): 32–46; (September 1898): 248–60; (October 1898): 377–89; 151 (February 1899): 159–71.

——. 1899. *Women's Emancipation Union.* Congleton, UK: Women's Emancipation Union.

——. 1899. The Awakening of Women, by Mrs Frances Swiney. *Westminster Review* 152 (July): 69–72.

——. 1899. Privilege vs. Justice to Women. *Westminster Review* 152 (August): 128–41.

——. 1904. *Woman – The Communist.* London: Independent Labour Party.

——. 1906/1907/1908. *Woman's Franchise, the Need of the Hour.* London: Independent Labour Party.

Embree, Frances Buckley. 1900. The Housing of the Poor in Chicago. *Journal of Political Economy* 8(3) (June): 354–77.

——. 1900. Social Settlements in Chicago. *Gunton's Magazine* 19: 452.

Emery, Sarah E[lizabeth]. V[an de Vort]. 1887/1888. *Seven Financial Conspiracies Which Have Enslaved the American People.* Lansing, Mich.: L. Thompson. Revised ed. Lansing, Mich.: R. Smith, 1894. Reprinted Westport, Conn.: Hyperion, 1975.

——. 1893. *Imperialism in America, Its Rise and Progress.* Revised ed. Lansing, Mich.: Emery & Emery.

Enfield, A. Honora. 1920. *The Place of Co-operation in the New Social Order.* Women's Co-operative Guild.

——. 1922. *Unemployment and Co-operative Trade.* Women's Co-operative Guild.

——. 1927. *Co-operation, Its Problems and Possibilities.* London: Longmans, Green & Co.

——. 1928. Glimpses into the Co-operative Movement of Eastern Europe. *Review of International Co-operation* 21: 403–.

——. 1928. U.S.S.R. Women's Conference at Moscow. *Review of International Co-operation*, 21: 344–.

——. 1929. The Place of Women in the Agricultural Co-operative Movement. Summary of Report Prepared for the International Women's Guild. *Review of International Co-operation* 22: 265–.

——. 1929. Women's Work for Co-operation. *Review of International Co-operation* 22: 293–.

——. 1930. *The Legal Position of Women in Co-operative Societies*. International Co-operative Women's Guild.

——. Coauth. *See* Davies, Margaret Llewelyn.

——. Contributor to International Women's Notes. *Review of International Co-operation*, 1930–5.

England, Minnie Throop. 1906. On Speculation in Relation to the World's Prosperity 1897–1902. *University Studies* (University of Nebraska) 6(1) (January): 21–107.

——. 1906. Church Government and Church Control. Ph.D. thesis, University of Nebraska–Lincoln (religion).

——. 1907. Statistical Inquiry into the Influence of Credit upon the Level of Prices. *University Studies* (University of Nebraska) 7(1) (January): 41–123.

——. 1910. Trade and the Flag. *University Studies* (University of Nebraska) 10(3) (November): 177–234.

——. 1912. Fisher's Theory of Crises: A Criticism. *Quarterly Journal of Economics* 27(1) (November): 95–106.

——. 1913. An Analysis of the Crisis Cycle. *Journal of Political Economy* 21(8) (October): 712–34.

——. 1913. Economic Crises. *Journal of Political Economy* 21(4) (April): 345–54.

——. 1915. Promotion as the Cause of Crises. *Quarterly Journal of Economics* 29(4) (August): 748–67.

——. 1916. The Chinese Colonies. *Mid-West Quarterly* 4(1) (October): 42–62.

——. 1918. Race Contact and Mixture in Colonies. *Mid-West Quarterly* 5(3) (April): 163–81.

Engle, Bessie C. 1926. Sugar Production in Czechoslovakia. *Economic Geography* 2(2) (April): 213–29.

Engle, Ruth M. Hoffman. 1930. The Incidence of Advertising Cost. Ph.D. thesis, University of Michigan (economics).

Entrican, Sara. 1896. Married Women's Property in Anglo-Saxon Times. *Englishwoman's Review*, n.s. 232 (October): 229–35.

Erickson, Ethel Elvera. 1923. Workmen's Compensation in Illinois. M.A. thesis, University of Chicago (sociology, public and social welfare).

Erickson, Ethel. 1934. *The Employment of Women in Offices*. Bulletin of the U.S. Women's Bureau, no. 120. Washington: U.S. Government Printing Office.

——. 1935. *Employment Conditions in Beauty Shops: A Study of Four Cities*. Bulletin of the U.S. Women's Bureau, no. 133. Washington: U.S. Government Printing Office.

——. 1937. *Employment of Women in Tennessee Industries*. Washington: U.S. Department of Labor.

——. 1940. *Earnings and Hours in Hawaii Woman-employing Industries*. Bulletin of the U.S. Women's Bureau, no. 177. Washington: U.S. Government Printing Office.

——. Coauth. *See* Blair, Bertha; Byrne, Harriet Anne; Manning, Caroline; Sullivan, Mary Loretta.

Escombe, Jane. 1901. *The Housing Problem in Rural Districts*. S.l.: s.n.

——. 1901. *Powers of Councils to Promote Better Housing*. London: Women's Liberal Federation.

——. 1902. *Sanitary Work in Rural Districts: The Experience of a Woman Councillor....* London: Women's Local Government Society.

Espenshade, Esther Elizabeth. 1931. The Economic Development and History of Chicago, 1860–1865 (Illinois). M.A. thesis, University of Chicago.

Estey, Helen Grace. 1918. Cost of Living in the United States (Bibliography). *Special Libraries* 9(9) (November): 203–.

——. 1918. Cost of Living in the United States (Bibliography). *Special Libraries* 9(10) (December): 231–.

——. 1919. *Cost of Living in the United States: A Bibliography*. Boston, Mass.: s.n.

Etten, Ida Van. *See* Van Etten, Ida.

Evans, Elizabeth G[ardiner]. Glendower. 1893. Statement from the Trustees of the State Primary and Reform Schools. In Elizabeth Cabot Putnam, ed., *Massachusetts' Care of Dependent and Delinquent Children*. Boston: Massachusetts Board of Managers, World's Fair.

——. 1898. *Report of the Committee on Domestic Reform, no. 1: The Effort to Attract the Workers in Shops and Factories to Domestic Service*. Boston: Women's Educational and Industrial Union.

——. 1910. The Roxbury Carpet Factory Strike. *Survey* 24 (May 28): 337–8.

——. 1912. The Minimum Wage for Women: A Plea for Wage Boards. *Twentieth Century Magazine* 6(1) (May): 65–.

——. 1915. The Social Aspect of the Public Regulation of Wages. *American Economic Review*, supplement (March): 270–7.

——. 1923. Minimum Wage: The Massachusetts Law. *Catholic World* 117(697/702) (September): 210–.

Evans, Mary Sanger. 1891. Domestic Servants in Australia: A Rejoinder. *Westminster Review* 136 (July): 46–53.

Everett, Helen [Mrs. Alexander Meiklejohn]. 1924. The Reorganization of the British Coal Industry. Ph.D. thesis, Robert Brookings.

——. 1925. Book Review of "The Women's Garment Workers: A History of the International Ladies' Garment Workers' Union." *American Economic Review* 15(3) (September): 524–5.

——. 1936. *The Dress Industry: A Study of the Impact of Fashion on the Ways of Business.* The Price Study Report, no. 19. Washington: Consumers' Project, Under Supervision of the U.S. Department of Labor.

Everett, Helen Gould. 1936. A Study of Homemaking Activities in Florida. M.S. thesis, Florida State College for Women.

F

Fairbridge, Dorothea. 1918/1926/1939. *A History of South Africa.* London: Oxford University Press.

——. 1931. *Historic farms of South Africa.* London: Oxford University Press.

Fairchild, Mildred. 1929. Skill and Specialization: A Study in the Metal Trades. Ph.D. thesis, Bryn Mawr College (engineering, industrial).

——. 1930. Skill and Specialization, a Study in the Metal Trades. *Personnel Journal* IX, 1 (June); 2 (August).

——. 1932. Book Review of "Protection of Women and Children in Soviet Russia." *American Economic Review* 22(3) (September): 540.

——. 1932. Our Social and Economic Dilemma. *American Association of University Women, Journal* 25(4) (June): 193–.

——. 1934. The Analysis of Skill. *Occupations: The Vocational Guidance Magazine* 12(10) (June): 40–.

——. 1934. Book Review of "Women Who Work" by Grace Hutchins. *American Academy of Political and Social Science, Annals* 175 (September): 271–.

——. 1936. Organization for State Legislative Work. *American Association of University Women, Journal* 29(4) (June): 250–.

——. 1937. The Russian Family Today – Social and Economic Forces Change the Pattern, but the Family Group Endures. *American Association of University Women, Journal* 30(3) (April): 142–.

——. 1937. The Status of the Family in the Soviet Union Today. *American Sociological Review* 2(1/6): 619–.

——. 1937. Valery Mezhlauk. *Soviet Russia Today* 6(4) (June): 11–.

——. 1938. Book Review of "Intervention, Civil War and Communism in Russia" by James Bunyan. *Science & Society* 2: 278.

——. 1938. Book Review of "The New Soviet Constitution" by Anna Louise Strong. *Science & Society* 2: 278.

——. 1938. Book Review of "The Soviets" by Albert Rhys Williams. *Science & Society* 2: 278.

——. Coauth. *See* Kingsbury, Susan Myra.

Faithfull, Emily. 1860. The Victoria Press. Paper read at the meeting of the National Association for the Promotion of Social Science, August. Published in *Transactions of the NAPSS*: 819–22 and in *English Woman's Journal* (October).

Reprinted in Candida Ann Lacey, ed., *Barbara Leigh Smith Bodichon and the Langham Place Group*. London and New York: Routledge, 1987.

——. 1861. Women Compositors. Paper read at the meeting of the National Association for the Promotion of Social Science, August. Published in *English Woman's Journal* (September). Reprinted in Candida Ann Lacey, ed., *Barbara Leigh Smith Bodichon and the Langham Place Group*. London and New York: Routledge, 1987.

——. 1862. On Some of the Drawbacks Connected with the Present Employment of Women. Paper read before the National Association for the Promotion of Social Science in London, June 11, 1862. *Transactions of the National Association for the Promotion of Social Science,* 1863. London: Emily Faithfull/Victoria Press.

——. 1863. *How Shall I Educate My Daughter?* London: Victoria Press.

——. 1864. The Unfit Employments in which Women Are Now Engaged. Paper read at the National Association for the Promotion of Social Science, October 1863. *Transactions of the National Association for the Promotion of Social Science,* 1864. London: Emily Faithfull Victoria Press.

——. 1870/1. Woman's Work: With Special Reference to Industrial Employment: A Paper [read before the Society of Arts]. *Journal of the Society of Arts* 19: 378–83. Reprinted London: Victoria Press.

——. 1874. Employments of Women. *Victoria Magazine* 23: 191–.

——. 1884. *Three Visits to America.* New York. Fowler & Wells Co.; Edinburgh: Douglas.

——. 1891. Domestic Service in England. *North American Review* 153 (July): 23–31.

Falkner, Helen D. 1925. Variation and Correlation with the Credit Structure. *Journal of the American Statistical Association* 20 (December): 496–511.

Faraday, Ethel Richmond. 1898. Some Economic Aspects of the Imperial Idea. *Fortnightly Review*, n.s. 64 [o.s. 70] (December): 961–7.

Farley, Harriet. 1850. *Operatives' Reply to Hon Jere. Clemens: Being a Sketch of Factory Life and Factory Enterprise and a Brief History of Manufacturing by Machinery.* Lowell, Mass.: S. J. Varney.

Farley, Miriam S. 1934. Book Review of "Duranth Reports Russia" by Walter Duranty. *Political Science Quarterly* 49: 478–.

——. 1934. Russia Warms to the League. *Current History (New York)* 40(4) (July): 402–.

——. 1936. *Agricultural Adjustment under the New Deal.* New York: American Council, Institute of Pacific Relations.

——. 1936. America's Stake in the Far East – I: Trade. *Far Eastern Survey* 5(1/25): 161.

——. 1936. Philippine Independence and Agricultural Readjustment. *Far Eastern Survey* 5(1/25): 71–.

——. 1937. Book Review of "Japanese Trade and Industry, Present and Future" by Mitsubishi Economic Research Bureau. *Pacific Affairs* 10(1) (March): 99–.

——. 1937. Japan Moves Toward Wartime Economy. *Far Eastern Survey* 6(1/25): 183–.

——. 1937. Japan's Unsolved Tenancy Problem. *Far Eastern Survey* 6(1/25): 153–.

——. 1937. Pygmy Factories – The Backbone of Japanese Industry. *Far Eastern Survey* 6(1/25): 1–.

——. 1937. Railway Strategy in China, New Style. *Far Eastern Survey* 6(1/25): 165–.

——. 1938. War and the Japanese Budget. *Far Eastern Survey* 7(1/25): 85–.

——. 1939. *The Problem of Japanese Trade Expansion in the Post-war Situation*. New York: Institute of Pacific Relations.

——. 1939. The Impact of War on Japan's Foreign Trade. *Far Eastern Survey* 8(1/25): 123–.

——. 1939. Japan Between Two Wars. *Far Eastern Survey* 8(1/25): 243–.

——. 1939. Japan's Economic Dilemma. *Amerasia* 3(8) (October): 367–.

——. 1939. The National Mobilization Controversy in Japan. *Far Eastern Survey* 8(1/25): 25–.

——. 1940. Japanese Agriculture under War Pressure. *Far Eastern Survey* 9(1/25): 135–.

Farmer, Lydia Hoyt, ed. 1893. *The National Exposition Souvenir. What America Owes to Women*. Buffalo, N.Y.: C. W. Moulton.

Farnham, Eliza Woodson [Burhans]. 1856. *California, In-doors and Out, or, How We Farm, Mine, and Live Generally in the Golden State*. New York: Dix, Edwards.

——. 1864. *Eliza Woodson; or, The Early Days of One of the World's Workers. A Story of American Life*. New York: A. J. Davis & Co.

——. 1864. *Woman and her Era*. New York: A. J. Davis.

Farnham, Rebecca Tufts and Irene Link. 1938. *Effects of the Works Program on Rural Relief: A Survey of Rural Relief Cases Closed in Seven States, July through November, 1935*. Washington: Works Progress Administration. Reprinted New York: Da Capo Press, 1971.

Farnham, Rebecca Tufts. Coauth. *See* Nelson, Eleanor Crosby.

Farnsworth, Helen Elliott Cherington. 1930. Rate Structures of the Manufactured Gas Industry. Ph.D. thesis, Leland Stanford Junior University.

——. 1939. *"World" Wheat Stocks, 1890–1914 and 1922–39*. Wheat Studies of the Food Research Institute, vol. 16, no. 2. Stanford, Calif.: Food Research Institute, Stanford University.

Farquhar, Barbara H. 1849. *The Pearl of Days; or, The Advantages of the Sabbath to the Working Classes*. New York: S. Hueston.

——. 1851. *Female Education: Its Importance, Design, and Nature Considered. By a Labourer's Daughter*. London: Partridge and Oakey.

Fauchère, Germaine. 1934. *La Travail des femmes*. Paris: Librairie Populaire.

Fawcett, [Dame] Millicent Garrett [Mrs. Henry Fawcett]. 1868. The Education of Women of the Middle and Upper Classes. *Macmillan's Magazine* 17 (April): 511–17.

——. 1868. The Medical and General Education of Women. *Fortnightly Review*, n.s. 4 (November): 554–71. Revised version, The Schools' Inquiry Commissioners on the Education of Girls. In Henry Fawcett and Millicent Garrett Fawcett, *Essays and Lectures on Social and Political Subjects.* London: Macmillan, 1872. Reprinted in *Works of Henry Fawcett and Millicent Garrett Fawcett.* London: Routledge/Thoemmes, 1995.

——. 1870. *Political Economy for Beginners.* London: Macmillan. Reprinted in *Works of Henry & Millicent Fawcett.* London: Routledge/Thoemmes, 1995.

——. 1870. The Electoral Disabilities of Women, *Fortnightly Review* 13 (May): 622–32. Reprinted in Henry Fawcett and Millicent Garrett Fawcett, *Essays and Lectures on Social and Political Subjects.* London: Macmillan, 1872. Also reprinted in *Works of Henry & Millicent Fawcett.* London: Routledge/Thoemmes, 1995; and in Andrew Pyle, ed., *The Subjection of Women: Contemporary Responses to J. S. Mill.* Bristol: Thoemmes, 1995.

——. 1870. Free Education in its Economic Aspects. Originally published in *The Times* [letter to the editor] (December 1870). Reprinted in Henry Fawcett and Millicent Garrett Fawcett, *Essays and Lectures on Social and Political Subjects.* London: Macmillan, 1872. Also reprinted in *Works of Henry Fawcett and Millicent Garrett Fawcett.* London: Routledge/Thoemmes, 1995.

——. 1870. Proportional Representation. *Macmillan's Magazine* 22 (September): 376–82. Included in Henry and Millicent Fawcett, *Essays and Lectures on Social and Political Subjects* (1872).

——. 1871. A Short Explanation of Mr. Hare's Scheme of Representation. *Macmillan's Magazine* 23 (April): 481–7. Included in Henry and Millicent Fawcett, *Essays and Lectures on Social and Political Subjects* (1872).

——. 1872. *Mrs. Fawcett on Women's Suffrage. Speech delivered in the Town Hall, Birmingham, December 6th, 1872.* Birmingham: Birmingham Morning News.

——. 1872. The Education of Women. Lecture delivered in Newcastle, November 13, 1871. In Henry Fawcett and Millicent Garrett Fawcett, *Essays and Lectures on Social and Political Subjects.* London: Macmillan, 1872. Also reprinted in *Works of Henry Fawcett and Millicent Garrett Fawcett.* London: Routledge/Thoemmes, 1995.

——. 1872. National Debts and National Prosperity, *Macmillan's Magazine* 25 (January): 180–9. Reprinted in Henry Fawcett and Millicent Garrett Fawcett, *Essays and Lectures on Social and Political Subjects.* London: Macmillan, 1872. Also reprinted in *Works of Henry Fawcett and Millicent Garrett Fawcett.* London: Routledge/Thoemmes, 1995.

——. 1872. Why Women Require the Franchise. In Henry Fawcett and Millicent Garrett Fawcett, *Essays and Lectures on Social and Political Subjects.* London: Macmillan. Reprinted in *Works of Henry Fawcett and Millicent Garrett Fawcett.* London: Routledge/Thoemmes, 1995.

——. 1873. *Mr. Fitzjames Stephen on the Position of Women.* London: Macmillan.

——. 1873. Edmond About's Social Economy. *Congregationalist* (January): 15–20.

——. 1873. The Government and the Bank Act. *Examiner* (April 5): 351.

——. 1874. *Tales in Political Economy.* London: Macmillan. Reprinted in *Works of Henry & Millicent Fawcett.* London: Routledge/Thoemmes, 1995.

——. 1875. *Janet Doncaster*. London: Smith, Elder & Co. (Later U.S. editions retitled *Janet: A Novel* and *Friend or Lover: A Novel*.)
——. 1877. *The Martyrs of Turkish Misrule*. London: Cassell, Petter and Galpin.
——. 1877. Communism. *The Encyclopaedia Britannica*, 9th ed., vol. 6: 211–19. Edinburgh: A. and C. Black.
——. 1878. The Future of Englishwomen: A Reply. *Nineteenth Century* 6 (August): 347–57.
——. 1883. Women and Representative Government. *Nineteenth Century* 14 (August): 285–91.
——. 1884. Women's Suffrage and the Franchise Bill. *Pall Mall Gazette* (January 14).
——. 1884. The Women's Suffrage Movement. In Theodore Stanton, ed., *The Woman Question in Europe: A Series of Original Essays*. London: Sampson Low, Marston, Searle; New York: G. P. Putnam & Sons.
——. 1885. Speech or Silence: The Protection of Girls. *Contemporary Review* 48 (September): 326–31.
——. 1886. Women's Suffrage: A Reply. *Nineteenth Century* 19 (May): 740–8.
——. 1886. The Use of Higher Education to Women. *Contemporary Review* 50 (November): 719–27.
——. 1887. Holes in the Education Net. *Contemporary Review* 51 (May): 639–53. Reprinted London: National Vigilance Association.
——. 1888. How the Factory Acts and Education Acts Have Worked. *Echo* (10 December).
——. 1888. Women's Suffrage: A Reply. *National Review* 11 (March): 44–61.
——. 1889. The Appeal against Female Suffrage: A Reply. *Nineteenth Century* 26 (July): 86–96.
——. 1889. The Employment of Children in Theatres. *Contemporary Review* 56 (November): 822–9.
——. 1889. The Women's Suffrage Bill I: The Enfranchisement of Women. *Fortnightly Review*, n.s. 45 (April): 555–67.
——. 1890. Indian Child Marriages. *New Review* 3 (November): 450–4.
——. 1890. Infant Marriage in India. *Contemporary Review* 58 (November): 712–20.
——. 1891. The Emancipation of Women. *Fortnightly Review*, n.s. 50 (November): 673–85.
——. 1891. Introduction. In Mary Wollstonecraft, *A Vindication of the Rights of Women*, ed. Millicent Garrett Fawcett. London: Unwin.
——. 1892. Mr Sidney Webb's Article on Women's Wages. *Economic Journal* 2(5) (March): 173–6.
——. 1892. Women in English Politics. *Forum* 14 (December): 453–64.
——. 1892. The Women's Suffrage Question. *Contemporary Review* 61 (June): 761–8.
——. 1893. Politics in the Home. *Literary Digest* 7 (July 22): 310.
——. 1894. New Zealand under Female Franchise. *Contemporary Review* 65 (March): 433–7.

——. 1894. *Home and Politics. An Address Delivered at Toynbee Hall and Elsewhere.* London: London Society for Women's Suffrage.

——. 1895. "The Woman Who Did". *Contemporary Review* 67 (May): 625–31.

——. 1896. Degrees for Women at Oxford. *Contemporary Review* 69 (March): 347–56.

——. 1896. Old Ideals of Woman. *Woman's Signal* 7 (May).

——, 1897. *Speech to the General Committee of the National Union of Women Workers, October 1897, on the New Rules for Dealing with the Sanitary Condition of the British Army in India.* London: Women's Printing Society.

——. 1899. *Some Eminent Women of Our Times: Short Biographical Sketches* [Includes chapters on Harriet Martineau and Maria Edgeworth]. London: Macmillan.

——. 1899. The Vaccination Act of 1898. *Contemporary Review* 75 (March): 328–42.

——. 1899. The White Slave Trade: Its Causes, and the Best Means of Preventing It. *Transactions of the International Congress on the White Slave Trade.* London: National Vigilance Association/Wertheimer, Lee & Co.

——. 1903. Impressions of South Africa, 1901 and 1903. *Contemporary Review* 84 (July/December): 635–.

——. 1904. Book Review of "Women in the Printing Trades: A Sociological Study." *Economic Journal* 14(54) (June): 295–9.

——. 1907. Book Review of "Labour Ideal Series: The Woman Socialist" by Ethel Snowden. *Economic Journal* 17(67) (September): 376–8.

——. 1909. Book Review of "Women in Industry from Seven Points of View" by Gertrude Tuckwell, Constance Smith, Mary MacArthur, May Tennant, Nettie Adler, Adelaide Anderson, and Clementina Black (with a Preface by D. J. Shackleton, M.P.). *Economic Journal* 19(74) (June): 228–33.

——. 1911. *Political Economy for Beginners*, 10th ed. London: Macmillan and Co.

——. 1913. Local Option for Woman Suffrage [letter to the editor]. *Nation* 12(23) (March 8): 925.

——. 1913. The Remedy of Political Emancipation. In B. Webb, ed., *Special Supplement on the Awakening of Women, New Statesman* 2 (November).

——. 1914. Is the Labor Party a Suffrage Party? [letter to the editor]. *Nation* 15(11) (June 13): 418.

——. 1914. Women's Work in War Time. *Contemporary Review* 106 (July/December): 775–.

——. 1917. The Position of Women in Economic Life. In W. H. Dawson, ed., *After-War Problems, by the Earl of Cromer, Viscount Haldane, the Bishop of Exeter, Professor Alfred Marshall, and Others.* New York: Macmillan.

——. 1918. Equal Pay for Equal Value. *Contemporary Review* 114 (October): 387–.

——. 1918. Equal Pay for Equal Work. *Economic Journal* 28 (March): 1–6.

——. 1924. *What I Remember.* London: T. Fisher Unwin.

——. 1928. The Milan Outrage [letter to the editor]. *Nation and Athenaeum* 43(6) (May 12): 170–3.

Fawcett, Millicent Garrett and Frances M. Stirling. 1916. Women's Maternity Hospital for Refugees in Russia [letter to the editor]. *Nation* 18(21) (February 19): 731.

Fawcett, Millicent Garrett *et al.* 1910. Mr. Lloyd-George and Woman Suffrage [letter to the editor]. *Nation* 7(21) (August 20): 737.

Fawcett, Millicent Garrett *et al.* 1911. Woman Suffrage and Conscientious Objectors [letter to the editor]. *Nation* 9(16) (July 15): 574.

Fay, Frances Marion. 1918. English Trade between 1670 and 1700 with Special Reference to the West Indies. Ph.D. thesis, Radcliffe College (history).

Feder, Leah [Hannah]. 1931. The Relation of Private Case Working Agencies to Programs of Public Welfare. *Social Forces* 9(4) (June): 515–25.

——. 1935. Unemployment Relief in Periods of Depression: A Study of Measures Adopted in Certain American Cities, 1857–1929. Ph.D. thesis, Bryn Mawr College (sociology).

——. 1936. *Unemployment Relief in Periods of Depression: A Study of Measures Adopted in Certain American Cities, 1857 through 1922.* New York: Russell Sage Foundation.

——. 1937. Methods Used in Strike Statistics. *Journal of the American Statistical Society* 32(197) (March): 90–6.

——. 1937. Unemployment Relief in Periods of Depression. *Charity Organisation Quarterly* 11(4) (October): 227–.

Fellows, Mrs. 1886. Nova Scotia's Cry for Home Rule. *Nineteenth Century* 20 (July/December): 785–93.

Felton, Katharine. 1898. Rousiers's Theory of the Evolution of the Laborer. *Journal of Political Economy* 6 (June): 380–95.

Fergusson, Mary S. 1898. *Boarding Homes and Clubs for Working Women.* Bulletin of the U.S. Dept of Labor, no. 15. Washington: U.S. Government Printing Office.

Fern, Fanny. Pseud. *See* Parton, Sara Willis.

Field, A. W. 1932. *Protection of Women and Children in Soviet Russia.* New York: Dutton.

Fields, Mrs. Annie. 1884. *How to Help the Poor.* Boston, New York: Houghton Mifflin & Co.; Cambridge, UK: Riverside Press.

——. 1888/9. The Aged Poor. *Chautauquan* 9 (October/July): 517.

Filene, Catherine, ed. 1920. *Careers for Women: New Ideas, New Methods, New Opportunities – to Fit a New World.* Boston: Houghton Mifflin Company.

Fine, Ruth. 1940. *The National Health Program and Medical Care in the United States: Selected Recent References.* Washington: U.S. Department of Labor.

Fine, Ruth and Laura Amelia Thompson. 1939. *Profit-sharing: Selected References, 1923–1939 (Supplementary to "Profit-sharing and Labor Copartnership: A List of Recent References," in Monthly labor Review, April 1923).* Washington: U.S. Department of Labor.

Fine, Selma E. 1937. Production and the Excise in England, 1643–1825. Ph.D. thesis, Radcliffe College (economics).

Firuski, Elizabeth Boody. 1934. Trade Statistics and Cycles in England, 1697–1825. Ph.D. thesis, Radcliffe College (economics).

Fischer, Vajen Eilleen Hitz. 1930. *List of Publications on Agriculture Contained in the United States Department of Agriculture Library and in Part Those Contained in the Library of Congress.* Washington: U.S. Government Printing Office.

——. 1932. *The Grape Industry: A Selected List of References on the Economic Aspects of the Industry in the United States, 1920–1931.* Washington: U.S. Government Printing Office.

——. 1933. *Business and Agriculture, 1920–1933.* Washington: U.S. Government Printing Office.

——. 1934. *Measures of Major Importance Enacted by the 73rd Congress, March 9 to June 16, 1933 and January 3 to June 18, 1934.* U.S. Bureau of Agricultural Economics, no. 54. Washington: U.S. Department of Agriculture.

——. 1936. *Measures of Major Importance Enacted by the 74th Congress, January 3 to August 26, 1935 and January 3 to June 20, 1936.* U.S. Bureau of Agricultural Economics, no. 66. Washington: U.S. Department of Agriculture.

——. Coauth. *See* Herb, Mamie Idella.

Fish, Marion. 1932. A Statistical Analysis of Purchasing Practices of Farm Households. Ph.D. thesis, Cornell University (economics).

——. 1933. *Buying for the Household as Practiced by 368 Familes in New York, 1928–29.* Cornell University Agricultural Experiment Station Bulletin, no. 561. Ithaca: Cornell University.

——. 1940. The Economic Basis of Family Life. *Living* 2(4) (November): 108–.

Fisher, Katherine R. 1899. American Women and Their Work. *Humanitarian* 15 (December): 409–.

——. 1921. Women Workers and the A.F. of L. *New Republic 27* (August): 265–7.

[Fisher,] Lettice Ilbert [Mrs. H. A. L. Fisher]. 1897. Book Review of "Lo Stato al suo Posto, ossia delle opinioni di Raffaele Mariano, intorno all' Economia Politica e alla libertà" by Prof. Lorenzo Michelangelo Billia. *Economic Journal* 7(28) (December): 587–.

——. 1898. Book Review of "Lectures on the Principles of Local Government" by G. L. Gomme, F.S.A. *Economic Journal* 8(29) (March): 91.

——. 1899. Labourers' Dwellings. *Economic Journal* 9(36) (December): 605–11.

——. 1900. Elements of the Housing Problem. *Economic Review* (October): 434–445.

——. 1901. Book Review of "The Housing Question in London: Being an Account of the Housing Work Done by the Metropolitan Board of Works and the London County Council, 1855–1900" by C. J. Stewart. *Economic Journal* 11: 56–.

——. 1902. Local Authorities and the Housing Problem in 1901. *Economic Journal* 12(46) (June): 263–71.

——. 1905. Book Review of "Report upon Housing and Industrial Conditions and Medical Inspection of School Children" by Dundee Social Union. *Economic Journal* 15: 552–.

——. 1905. The Town Housing Problem. *The Economic Journal* 15(57) (March): 23–36.

——. 1922. *Getting and Spending: An Introduction to Economics*. London: Collins Clear Type Press.

——. 1924. *The Economic Problem of the Married Woman*. Oxford: Oxford University Press.

——. 1924. *Life and Work in England: A Sketch of Our Social and Economic History*. London: E. Arnold and Co.

——. 1924. Family Allowances. *Quarterly Review* (July).

——. 1925. *Then and Now: Economic Problems after the War a Hundred Years Ago*. London: Oxford University Press.

——. 1925. Book Review of "Wages and the Family" by P. H. Douglas. *Economic Journal* 35: 598–.

——. 1926. Book Review of "My Apprenticeship" by Beatrice Webb. *Economic Journal* 36(143) (September): 444–7.

Fisher, Ruth A. 1928. Extracts from the Records of the African Companies [Documents]. *Journal of Negro History* 13(3) (July): 286–394.

Fitz-Randolph, Helen Elizabeth. 1927. *Decorative Crafts and Rural Potteries*. Oxford: Clarendon Press.

Fitz-Randolph, Helen Elizabeth and M. Doriel Hay. 1926. *Osier-Growing and Basketry and Some Rural Factories*. Oxford: Clarendon Press.

——. 1926. *Timber and Underwood Industries and Some Village Workshops*. Oxford: Clarendon Press.

Fitzgerald, Rose Dorothy. 1928. The Geographical Distribution of Foreign Labor in Massachusetts. Ph.D. thesis, Yale University (economics).

Fledderus, Mary Lambertine. 1932. *International Unemployment: A Study of Fluctuations in Employment and Unemployment in Several Countries, 1910–1930*. The Hague: Industrial Relations Institute.

——. 1932. *World Social Economic Planning: The Necessity for Planned Adjustment of Productive Capacity and Standards of Living*. The Hague and New York: Industrial Relations Institute.

——. 1935. *Ten Years I.R.I. Report of the International Industrial Relations Institute since Its Inception in 1925*. The Hague and New York: Industrial Relations Institute.

——. 1939. Optimum Productivity. *Synthese* 4(5) (May): 255–.

Fletcher, Alice C[unningham]. 1883. On Indian Education and Self-Support. *Century Illustrated* 26 (May): 312–15.

——. 1884. *On the Lawlessness of the Indian Reservation System*. Massachusetts Indian Association. Boston: Frank Wood.

——. 1886. Economy of Justice. *Lend a Hand* 1(9) (September): 524–30.

——. 1888. *Indian Education and Civilization: A Report Prepared in Answer to Senate Resolution of Feb 23, 1885*. Washington: US Government Printing Office.

——. 1889. Allotting Lands. *Indian's Friend* 2(1) (September): 4–.

——. 1892. The Preparation of the Indian for Citizenship. *Lend a Hand* 9(3) (September): 190–8.

——. 1899. The Indian Woman and Her Problems. *Southern Workman* 28 (May): 172–6.

Fletcher, Mildred Stahl. 1930/1. Louisiana as a Factor in French Diplomacy from 1763 to 1800. *Mississippi Valley Historical Review* 17: 367–.

Flexner, Jean Atherton [Mrs. Paul Lewinson]. 1922. *Some Aspects, the British Workers Control Movement.* New York: s.n.

——. 1923. Some Aspects of Worker's Control in Industry. *Economica* 3 (January): 67–82.

——. 1924. Stabilized Employment in a Garment Factory. *American Labor Legislation Review* 14: 133–.

——. 1929. A Study of the Migration of the Cotton Industries. Ph.D. thesis, Robert Brookings.

——. 1935. A Federal Apprentice Program. *American Federationist* 42(1) (January): 40–.

——. 1936. When Wages Are Not Paid. *American Federationist* 43(7) (July): 687–.

——. 1939. *The Work of an Industrial Hygiene Division in a State Department of Labor.* U.S. Department of Labor, Division of Labor Standards, Bulletin no. 31. Washington: U.S. Government Printing Office.

——. 1940/1941. *Handbook of Federal Labor Legislation.* U.S. Department of Labor, Division of Labor Standards, Bulletin no. 39. Washington: U.S. Government Printing Office.

——. 1941. *Handbook of Federal Labor Legislation*, vol. II: *Labor Laws of General Application.* Washington: U.S. Government Printing Office.

Flexner, Jean Atherton and Esther Cole Franklin. 1938. *Fair Labor Standards: What Are They?* Social Studies Series, American Association of University Women. Washington: American Association of University Women.

Flexner, Jean Atherton and Lucy Manning. 1933. *Child Labor: Facts and Figures.* Children's Bureau Publication no. 197. Washington: U.S. Government Printing Office.

Flexner, Jean Atherton. Coauth. *See* Parker, Florence Evelyn.

Flint, Esther M. and Carol Aronovici. 1919. *Health Conditions and Health Service in Saint Paul.* Saint Paul: Amberst H. Wilder Charity.

Flood, Hulda. 1930. *Den Socialdemokratiska Kvinnorörelsen i Sverige.* Stockholm: Tiden.

Flügge, Eva. 1922. Die Bedeutung William Thompsons für die Wirtschaftswissenschaft. *Schmollers Jahrbuch für Gesetzgebung, Verwaltung und Volkswirtschaft im deutschen Reich* 46(2): 43-; 46(3/4): 349–.

——. 1923. Book Review of "William Thompson. (Beiträge zur Geschichte der Nationalökonomie)" by Marie Hasbach. *Jahrbücher für Nationalökonomie und Statistik* 121(2) (August): 182–.

——. 1929. Book Review of "The Economics of Instalment Selling, a Study in Consumers' Credit. With Special Reference to the Automobile" by Edwin R. A. Seligman. *Jahrbücher für Nationalökonomie und Statistik* 130(3) (March): 462–.

——. 1929. Possibilities and Problems of Integration in the Automobile Industry. *Journal of Political Economy* 37 (April): 150–74.

——. 1930. Book Review of "Amerikanische Wirtschaftsgeschichte" by H. U. Faulkner. *Jahrbücher für Nationalökonomie und Statistik* 133(1) (July): 133–.

——. 1930. Book Review of "Banking Standards under the Federal Reserve System. A Study of Norms, Trends, and Correlations of the Assets, Deposits, Expenses, and Earnings of Member Banks. Published for the Bureau of Business Research" by Horace Secrist. *Jahrbücher für Nationalökonomie und Statistik* 133(4) (September): 463–.

——. 1930. Book Review of "Foreign Investments (Lectures on the Harris Foundation 1928)" by Gustav Cassel, T. E. Gregory, R. E. Kuczynsky, and H. K. Norton. *Jahrbücher für Nationalökonomie und Statistik* 133(4) (October): 613–.

——. 1930. Book Review of "Die Verlendungstheorie. Studien und Untersuchungen zur internationalen Dogmengeschichte der Volkswirtschaft (Philosophischsoziologische Bücherei. Band XXXVII)" by Robert Michels. *Jahrbücher für Nationalökonomie und Statistik* 132(6) (June): 926–.

——. 1930. Neuerliche Wirtschaftsveränderungen in den Vereinigten Staaten. *Jahrbücher für Nationalökonomie und Statistik* 133(1) (July): 77–.

——. 1931. *Die Automobilindustrie der Vereinigten Staaten.* Jena: Gustav Fischer.

——. 1933. Book Review of "Die vormaxistische Arbeiterbewegung in den Vereinigten Staaten. Eine Darstellung ihrer Geschichte" by Arvid Harnack. *Jahrbücher für Nationalökonomie und Statistik* 139(6) (December): 958–.

——. 1936. *Kunstseidenindustrie; der Internationale Aufbau der Kunstseidenindustrie und Seine Folgen.* Wandlungen in der Weltwirtschaft, Heft 3. Leipzig: Bibliographisches Institut AG.

——. 1936. *Rohseide: Wandlungen in der Erzeugung und Verwendung der Rohseide nach dem Weltkrieg.* Leipzig: Bibliographisches Institut AG.

——. 1938. *Baumwolle: Wandlungen in der Erzeugung und der Verwendung der Baumwolle nach dem Weltkrieg.* Leipzig: Bibliographisches Institut AG.

——. 1938. Book Review of "L'Industria tessile italiana. Come è sorta, e come è oggi" by Roberto Tremelloni. *Jahrbücher für Nationalökonomie und Statistik* 147(3) (March): 373–.

——. 1938. Book Review of "Die Textilrohstoffversorgung Deutschlands" by Conrad Herrmann. *Jahrbücher für Nationalökonomie und Statistik* 147(3) (March): 374–.

——. 1938. Book Review of "World Cotton Production and Trade" by International Institute of Agriculture. *Jahrbücher für Nationalökonomie und Statistik* 147(2) (February): 249–.

Flynn, Eleanor Jeanne. 1936. Public Care of Dependent Children in Pennsylvania, 1676–1901. Ph.D. thesis, University of Chicago (sociology).

Flynn, Elizabeth Gurley. 1915/16. *Sabotage: The Conscious Withdrawal of the Workers' Industrial Efficiency*. Cleveland, Ohio, I.W.W. Pub. Bureau.

——. 1940. *I Didn't Raise My Boy to Be a Soldier – for Wall Street.* New York: Workers Library Publishers.

Fogg-Meade, Emily. *See* Meade, Emily Fogg.

Foley, Caroline A. *See* Rhys-Davids, Caroline A.

Foley, Ruth A. 1931. Cost of Railway Capital through June, 1931. *Land Economics* 7 (November): 439–42.

Ford, Amelia C. 1918. Book Review of "A Social History of the American Family from Colonial Times to the Present." *American Economic Review* 8 (September): 596.

——. 1928. Book Review of "Economic History of the United States." *American Economic Review* 18(2) (June): 286.

Ford, Isabella O[rmston]. 1893. *Women's Wages, and the Conditions under Which They Are Earned.* London: Humanitarian League/William Reeves. Reprinted in Marie Mulvey Roberts and Tamae Mizuta, eds., *Sources in British Feminism*, vol. 3: *The Exploited: Women and Work.* London: Routledge/Thoemmes, 1993.

——. 1894. Women in the Labour Movement. *Labour Prophet* (December).

——. 1895. *On the Threshold.* London and New York: Edward Arnold. [*feminist novel*]

——. 1898. *Women as Factory Inspectors and Certifying Surgeons.* Investigation Papers, no. 4. London: Women's Cooperative Guild.

——. 1900. *Industrial Women and How to Help Them.* London: Humanitarian League.

——. 1904. *Women and Socialism.* London: Independent Labour Party.

Forsyth, Louise. 1930. Forecasting Financial Progress for Going Concerns. *Journal of Business of the University of Chicago* 3(1) (January): 72–91.

Foster, Alice. 1921. Geography of the Industrial District of Orizaba, Mexico. S.M. thesis, University of Chicago (geography).

——. 1923. Barbados: A Geographical Study of a Densely Populated Island in Tropical America. *Journal of Geography* 22 (January/December): 205–.

——. 1924. A Geographical Interpretation of the Cotton-manufacturing Industry of Orizaba, Mexico. Paper read before the Association of American Geographers, Cincinnati, 1923. *Bulletin of the Geographical Society of Philadelphia* XXII(2) (April).

——. 1925. Orizaba – A Community in the Sierra Madre Oriental. *Economic Geography* 1(3) (October): 356–72.

——. 1930. Sisal Production of Semi-arid Karst Country of Yucatan. *Journal of Geography* 29 (January/December): 16–.

——. 1933. A Geographical Sketch of the World's Diamond Trade. *Journal of Geography* 32 (January/December): 290–.

——. 1936. The Geographic Structure of the Vega De Valencia. M.A. thesis, University of Chicago (physical geography).

Foster, Carol H. 1918. Growth of Commissioned Personnel of the United States Navy. *Current History (New York)* 9(1:3) (December): 484–.

——. 1923. *Austrian Trade in Rubber Products.* Washington: U.S. Bureau of Foreign and Domestic Commerce.

Foster, Mrs. E. P. 1895. Woman's Work in the Labor Movement. *American Federationist* 2(5) (July): 86–.

Foster, Mrs. F. M. 1889. Women as Social Reformers. *National Review* 13 (April): 220–5.

Foster, Florence J. 1893/4. The Grange and the Co-operative Enterprises in New England. *Annals of the American Academy of Political and Social Science* 4(5)(July/June): 798–805.

Foster, J[udith]. Ellen [Horton]. 1888. *The Crime Against Ireland.* Boston: D. Lothrop.

——. 1888. Repeal of the Internal Tax on Alcoholic Liquors. S.l.: s.n.

——. 1897. Woman's Political Evolution in the United States. *North American Review* 165 (November): 600–9.

Foulds, Margaret Hadley. 1930. The Massachusetts Bank, 1784–1865. *Journal of Economic and Business History* 2 (February): 256–70.

Fox, C. Ethel. 1895. The Annual Conference of the National Union of Women Workers at Nottingham. *Educational Review* (London) 11 (December): 381–.

Fox, Evelyn. 1904. Book Review of "The History of Contract Labour in the Hawaiian Islands." *Economic Journal* 14(53) (March): 95–7.

——. 1904. Labour Treaties. *Economic Journal* 14 (March): 115–18.

——. 1938. Modern Developments in Mental Welfare Work. *Eugenics Review* (July).

Fox, Myrtle Perrigo and Ethel Lendrum. 1919. Starting a Community Kitchen: Just How It Can Be Done with Little Outlay. *Ladies' Home Journal* 36 (June).

Francke, Marie and Susan Myra Kingsbury. 1916. *Opportunities for Women in Domestic Science.* Association of Collegiate Alumnae Bulletin no. 2, Pamphlets in American History. Philadelphia: Association of Collegiate Alumnae.

Fraser, Agnes [as "Frances MacNab"]. 1897. On Veldt and Farm in Bechuanaland – Cape Colony – the Transvaal – and Natal. London: Edward Arnold.

—— [as "Frances MacNab"]. 1898. British Columbia for Settlers: Its Mines, Trade, and Agriculture. London: Chapman & Hall.

Fraser, Helen. 1918. *The Protection of Women in Industry in Great Britain.* Toledo Consumers' League Pamphlet no. 7. Toledo: Toledo Consumers' League.

——. 1918. *Women and War Work.* New York: G. Arnold Shaw.

——. 1919. Women in Industry in England during the War. *Academy of Political Science, Proceedings* 8(2) (February): 36–.

——. 1926. What Came of Votes for Women? *Century Monthly Magazine* 112 (May/October): 48–.

Frederick, Christine. 1913. *The New Housekeeping: Efficiency Studies in Home Management.* Garden City, N.Y.: Doubleday, Page & Co.

——. 1919. *Household Engineering: Scientific Management in the Home. A Correspondence Course on the Application of the Principles of Efficiency Engineering and Scientific Management to the Every Day Tasks of Housekeeping.* Chicago: American School of Home Economics.

——. 1929. *Selling Mrs. Consumer.* New York: The Business Bourse.

French, Anna D. 1887. *A Report on Industrial Education.* Paper read before the Association for the Advancement of Women at Louisville, Kentucky, October 22, 1886. Buffalo, N.Y.: Peter Paul & Bro.

French, Frances Graham. 1899. *Status of Woman from the Educational and Industrial Standpoint.* U.S. Office of Education. Washington: U.S. Government Printing Office.

——. 1899. Brief Statement of Education in Finland. In *Report of the Commissioner of Education for 1893–94.* Washington: U.S. Government Printing Office.

——. 1899. Education in Russia. In *Report of the Commissioner of Education for 1893–94.* Washington: U.S. Government Printing Office.

French-Sheldon, Mrs. Mary. 1892. Customs among the Natives of East Africa, from Teita to Kilimegalia, with Special Reference to their Women and Children. *Journal of the Anthropological Institute of Great Britain and Ireland* 21: 358–90.

——. 1897. England's Commercial and Industrial Future in Central Africa. *Journal of the Tyneside Geographical Society* 3 (May): 415–18.

Frere, Margaret. 1909. *Children's Care Committees, How to Work Them in Public Elementary Schools.* London: P. S. King and Son.

——. 1911. *London County Council, Children's Care Committees, Board of Trade, Juvenile Labour Exchanges, Parent's Meetings.* Pimlico: S. Flutter.

Freund, Amelia Lewis. 1871. Benevolence and Pauperism. *Dark Blue* 2 (October): 205–10.

Freund, Miriam Kottler. 1936. Jewish Merchants in Colonial America: Their Achievements and Their Contributions to the Development of America. Ph.D. thesis, New York University (history).

——. 1939. *Jewish Merchants in Colonial America: Their Achievements and Their Contributions to the Development of America.* New York: Behrman's Jewish Book House.

Freundlich, Emmy. 1936. *Housewives Build a New World.* International Co-operative Women's Guild.

Fricker, Mary Hannah. 1930/1932/1936. *Preparing Shipments to Canada: Documentation and Customs Entry.* Washington: U.S. Bureau of Foreign and Domestic Commerce.

Friedlander, Etta. 1940. Education in the Workers' Schools of New York City. *Social Research* 7 (February): 92–101.

Friedlander, Lilian M. 1929. Labour Problems in Two Worlds. *Economica* 9 (April): 4–14.

Friedman, Rose Director. 1936. Fixed Capital in the Ricardian System. Mimeo, Box 48, Folder 18, Frank H. Knight Papers, Joseph Regenstein Library, University of Chicago.

Fries, Ellen. 1893. *Reports from the Swedish Ladies' Committee to the World's Columbian Exposition at Chicago 1893.* Stockholm: Printed by Central-Tryckeriet.

Friis, Astrid. 1925/6. Bemaerkninger til Vurdering af Øresundstoldregnskaberne og Principerne for deres Udgivelse. *Historisk tidsskrift (Kobenhavn)* 9(4): 109–82.

——. 1927. *Alderman Cockayne's Project and the Cloth Trade.* London: Oxford University Press.

——. 1932/3. Book Review of "Dänische Wirtschaftsgeschichte" by various authors. *Economic History Review* 4: 484–.

——. 1933. Kansler Johan Friis' første Aar. *Scandia* 6(2) (December): 231–.

——. 1934. Kansler Johan Friis' første Aar. *Scandia* 7(2) (December): 167–.

——. 1937/8. Book Review of "Sveriges Ekonomiska Historia fran Gustav Vasa. Vols. i and ii" by Eli F. Heckscher. *Economic History Review* 8: 194–.

——. 1939. Forbindelsen mellem det europaeiske og asiatiske kobbermarked. *Scandia* 12: 151–.

Frost, Beulah M. 1927. *Paper and Paper Products in Colombia, Venezuela, Ecuador and the Guianas*. Trade Information Bulletin, no. 477. Washington: U.S. Government Printing Office.

——. 1930. *Paper Trade and Industry of Japan*. Washington: U.S. Bureau of Foreign and Domestic Commerce.

Frost, Winifred Lillian [Mrs. Paul Kerschbaum]. 1930. The Consumer's Purchasing Problem. Ph.D. thesis, Robert Brookings.

Fuller, Fannie E. 1890. Practical Co-operation. *Good Housekeeping* 11 (July 19): 125–42.

Fuller, Margaret. 1845. *Woman in the Nineteenth Century*. New York: Greeley & McElrath. Reprinted New York: W. W. Norton, 1971.

G

Gadsby, Margaret. 1924. Steadying the Workers' Income – Trade-union and Joint Out-of-work Benefit Plans. *Monthly Labor Review* 19 (July/December): 8–32.

Gage, Matilda Joslyn. 1868. The Cotton Gin Invented by a Woman. *The Revolution* 1: 259–60.

——. 1873. On Woman and Work. In *Woman, Church and State: The Original Expose of Male Collaboration Against the Female Sex*. Chicago: Charles Kerr. Reprinted Salem, N.H.: Ayer Co., 1893. Reprinted, with an introduction by Sally Roesch Wagner, New York: Humanity Books, 2002.

——. 1883. Woman as an Inventor. *North American Review* 136 (May): 478–89.

Gale, Zona. 1919. Shall the Kitchen in Our Home Go? *Ladies' Home Journal* 36 (March).

Galloway, Countess of. 1886. Women and Politics. *Nineteenth Century* 19 (January/June): 896–901.

Galster, Augusta Emilie. 1922. The Labor Movement in the Shoe Industry, with Special Reference to Philadelphia. Ph.D. thesis, University of Illinois at Urbana–Champaign (economics).

——. 1924. *The Labor Movement in the Shoe Industry with Special Reference to Philadelphia*. New York: Ronald Press Company.

Galvin, Sister Eucharista. 1929. The Influences and Conditions Affecting the Settlement of Minnesota, 1837–1860. Ph.D. thesis, University of Chicago (history).

——. 1940. Book Review of "Catholic Immigrant Colonization Projects" by Kelly. *Minnesota History* 21: 73–.

Gardener, Helen H. 1892. The Danger of an Irresponsible Educated Class in a Republic. *Arena* 6 (August): 311–16.

Gardiner, Mrs. Ruth K. 1904. Household Budgets Abroad: II. Cost of Living in the United States of America. *Cornhill Magazine* series 3 (17): 181–.

Garnett, Lucy M. J. 1895. Women under Islam. *Nineteenth Century* 37 (January): 57–70.

——. 1898. The Philippine Islanders. *Fortnightly Review*, n.s. 64 [o.s. 70] (July): 72–87.

Garrett, Constance. 1937. The Poor Ye Have with You Always. *Social Forces* 15(4) (May): 519–24.

Gary Markey, Dorothy Page. 1928. Some Behavior Patterns of Carolina Textile Workers. Ph.D. thesis, University of Minnesota (sociology).

Gaskell, Lady Catherine Milnes. 1884. A Farm that Pays. *Nineteenth Century* 16 (October): 568–75.

——. 1885. Servants Old and New. *Longman's* 5 (January): 286–97.

——. 1889. Women of Today: What Is Expected of Them? *Nineteenth Century* 26: 776–84.

Gaskell, Elizabeth Cleghorn. 1848. *Mary Barton: A Tale of Manchester Life*. London: Chapman & Hall; New York: Harper. Reprinted New York: Oxford University Press, 1987. [*novel*]

——. 1852. *Ruth*. London: Chapman & Hall; Boston: Ticknor Reed and Fields. [*novel*]

——. 1855. *North and South*. London: Chapman & Hall; New York: Harper. Reprinted New York: Penguin Books, 1970. [*novel*]

——. 1859. A Fear for the Future that Women Will Cease to Be Womanly. *Fraser's* 59 (February): 243–8.

Gaskell, Ellen S. 1907. Women's Sphere of Work. *Westminster Review* (March).

Gasson, Mrs. 1907. *Wives' Savings*. Women's Co-operative Guild.

Gatti de Gamond, Mme. Zoe. 1838/1842. *Fourier et son système*. Paris: L. Desessart. English ed., *Fourier and His System*, transl. C. T. Wood, Jr. London: J. H. Young, 1842.

Gay, Sarah Mifflin. 1896. Representative Women on Social Problems: Is the Single Tax Enough to Solve the Labor Problem? (Symposium). *Arena* 15 (May): 956–9.

Gay, Sarah Mifflin and Frances E. Russell. 1895. Representative Women on Social Problems: Is the Single Tax Enough? (Symposium). *Arena* 13(2) (July): 284–91.

Geddes, Anne E[lizabeth]. 1937. *Trends in Relief Expenditures, 1910–1935*. Washington: U.S. Government Printing Office. Reprinted New York: De Capo Press, 1971.

——. 1938. *Preparation of Valid Statistics of the Cost of Relief Administration*. New York: Joint Committee on Relief Statistics of the American Public Welfare Association and the American Statistical Association.

——. 1938. Relief Trends in Cambridge, Massachusetts, 1929–37. *Social Security Bulletin* 1(8) (August): 17–.

——. 1939. The Concept of Administrative Expenses in Accounting for Public-assistance Expenditures. *Social Security Bulletin* 2(7) (July): 27–.

——. 1940. Book Review of "Applicants for Work Relief: A Study of Massachusetts Families under the FERA and WPA" by Gilboy. *American Economic Review* 30(4): 909–10.

——. 1940. Who are the People Receiving Aid to the Blind and How Much Assistance Are They Receiving? *Social Security Bulletin* 3(9) (September): 16–.

Geddes, Anne E. and Agnes Leisy. 1938. Relief Status of One Million Recipients Accepted for Old-age Assistance. *Social Security Bulletin* 1(12) (December): 3–.

Gemmell, Mrs Jean. 1923. *Trade and Still More Trade.* Scottish Co-operative Women's Guild.

George, Mary Dorothy. 1925. *London Life in the Eighteenth Century.* New York: A. A. Knopf.

——. 1927. The Combination Laws Reconsidered. *Economic History* (supplement to *Economic Journal*) 1 (May): 214–28.

——. 1927. The London Coal-Heavers: Attempts to Regulate Waterside Labour in the Eighteenth and Nineteenth Centuries. *Economic History* 1 (May): 229–48.

——. 1929. The Early History of Registry Offices: The Beginnings of Advertisement. *Economic History* 1 (January): 570–90.

——. 1931. *England in Transition Life and Work in the Eighteenth Century.* London: George Routledge & Sons, Ltd.

——. 1932. Some Causes of the Increase of Population in the Eighteenth Century as Illustrated by London. *Economic Journal* 32 (September): 325–52.

——. 1936. The Combination Laws. *Economic History Review* 6 (April): 172–8.

Georgi, Elsbeth. 1908. *Theorie und Praxis des Generalstreiches in der Modernen Arbeiterbewegung.* Jena: Fischer.

Gerrish, Catherine Ruggles. *See* Ruggles, Catherine G.

Gerritsen, Aletta Henrietta Jacobs. 1915. *Reisbrieven uit Afrika en Azië; benevens eenige brieven uit Zweden en Noorwegen.* Almelo: W. Hilarius.

Gibbs, Winifred Stuart. 1917. *The Minimum Cost of Living: A Study of Families of Limited Income in New York City.* New York: Macmillan.

——. 1921. New Trails in Employment Relationships. *Industrial Management* 61(5) (March 1): 173–.

——. 1926. The Sales and Advertising Value of the Home Economics Woman. *Printers' Ink Monthly* 13(3) (September): 31–.

Gilboy, Elizabeth [Lane] Waterman. 1928. Some New Evidence on Wage Assessments in the Eighteenth Century. *English Historical Review* 171 (July): 398–408.

——. 1929. Standard of Living of Eighteenth Century English Labor, 1700–1790. Ph.D. diss., Radcliffe College (economics).

——. 1930. Demand Curves in Theory and in Practice. *Quarterly Journal of Economics* 44 (August): 601–20.

——. 1930. Discussion: Methods Used in Price Forecasting. *Journal of Farm Economics* 12 (January): 133–6.

——. 1930. Wages in Eighteenth-century England. *Journal Economic and Business History* 2 (August): 603–29.

——. 1930/1. Labour at Thornborough: An Eighteenth-century Estate. *Economic History Review* 3: 388–.

——. 1931. The Leontief and Schultz Methods of Deriving "Demand" Curves. *Quarterly Journal of Economics* 45 (February): 218–61.

——. 1932. Demand as a Factor in the Industrial Revolution. In A. H. Cole, ed., *Facts and Factors in Economic History*. Cambridge, Mass.: Harvard University Press. Reprinted in R. M. Hartwell, ed., *The Causes of the Industrial Revolution*. London: Methuen, 1967.

——. 1932. Demand Curves by Personal Estimate. *Quarterly Journal of Economics* 46 (February): 376–84.

——. 1932. Labour at Thornborough: An Eighteenth-century Estate. *Economic History Review* 3 (April): 388–98.

——. 1932. Studies in Demand: Milk and Butter. *Quarterly Journal of Economics* 46 (August): 671–97.

——. 1934. *Wages in Eighteenth Century England*. Cambridge, Mass.: Harvard University Press, Harvard Economic Studies. Reprinted New York: Russell & Russell, 1969.

——. 1934. Time Series and the Derivation of Demand and Supply Curves; A Study of Coffee and Tea, 1850–1930. *Quarterly Journal of Economics* 48 (August): 667–85.

——. 1936. Book Review of "Prices in Colonial Pennsylvania" by Anne Bezanson, Robert D. Gray, and Miriam Hussey. *American Academy of Political and Social Science, Annals* 184 (March): 223–.

——. 1936. The Cost of Living and Real Wages in Eighteenth Century England. *Review of Economics and Statistics* 18 (August): 134–43.

——. 1937. The Unemployed: Their Income and Expenditure. *American Economic Review* 27 (June): 309–23.

——. 1938. The Expenditure of the Unemployed. *American Sociological Review* 3 (December): 801–14.

——. 1938. The Propensity to Consume. *Quarterly Journal of Economics* 53 (November): 120–40.

——. 1939. Methods of Measuring Demand or Consumption. *Review of Economics and Statistics* 21 (May): 69–74.

——. 1939. The Propensity to Consume: Reply. *Quarterly Journal of Economics* 53 (August): 633–8.

——. 1940. *Applicants for Work Relief. A Study of Massachusetts Families under the FERA and WPA*. Cambridge, Mass.: Harvard University Press.

——. 1940. Income–Expenditure Relations. *Review of Economics and Statistics* 22 (August): 115–21.

Gilboy, Elizabeth Waterman and Helen Laura Sorenson. 1937. The Economics of Low Income Diets. *Quarterly Journal of Economics 51* (August): 663–80.

Gilbreth, Lillian Moller. 1914. *The Psychology of Management: The Function of the Mind in Determining, Teaching and Installing Methods of Least Waste*. London: Sir I. Pitman & Sons. Reprinted, with a new introduction by Morgen Witzel, Bristol: Thoemmes, 2001.

——. 1927. *The Home-maker and Her Job*. New York and London: D. Appleton & Co.

Gilbreth, Lillian M. and Gilbreth, Frank Bunker. 1916. *Fatigue Study: The Elimination of Humanity's Greatest Unnecessary Waste, a First Step in Motion Study.* London: G. Routledge.
——. 1917–19. *Applied Motion Study: A Collection of Papers on the Efficient Method to Industrial Preparedness.* New York: Sturgis & Walton; London: Routledge.
Gildersleeve, Genieve. 1920. The Private Secretary – To Be or Not to Be? *Bulletin of the National Committee of the Bureau of Occupations* 1 (October): 3.
Gill, Miss. 1891. Is Type-writing a Successful Occupation for Educated Women? *Englishwoman's Review*, n.s. 210 (April): 82–8.
——. 1892. Type Writing: As It Is and as It Ought to Be. *Englishwoman's Review*, n.s. 214 (April 15): 87–90.
Gill, Minna P. 1921. Trade Investigations, as Conducted through Merchandising Departments of Newspapers. B.B.A. thesis, University of Texas.
——. 1927. *Freight Rates and Agriculture: A List of References.* Washington: U.S. Bureau of Agricultural Economics Library.
Gill, Minna and Lillian Crans, comp. 1928. *The Meat Industry in the United States: A Selected List of References on the Economic Aspects of the Industry, Including Meat Packing, Published since 1918.* Washington: U.S. Department of Agriculture, Bureau of Agricultural Economics.
Gillespie, Frances Elma. 1918. The Commerce of Ireland during the Thirteenth and Fourteenth Centures. A.M. thesis, University of Chicago (history).
——. 1923. The Political History of the English Working Classes, 1850–1867. Ph.D. thesis, University of Chicago (history).
——. 1927. *Labor and Politics in England, 1850–1867.* Durham, N.C.: Duke University Press.
——. 1931. Book Review of "The Church of England and Social Reform since 1854" by Donald O. Wagner. *Journal of Modern History* 3(4) (December): 661–.
——. 1931. Book Review of "A History of the English Corn Laws, 1660–1846" by Donald Grove Barnes. *Journal of Modern History* 3(2) (June): 311–.
——. 1934. Book Review of "The Condition of the Working Class in Britain" by Allen Hutt. *Journal of Political Economy* 42: 549–.
[Gilman,] Charlotte Perkins Stetson. 1893. *The Labor Movement.* Prize essay read before the trades and labor unions of Alameda County, September 5, 1892. Oakland, Calif.: Alameda County Federation of Trades. Reprinted in Larry Ceplair, ed., *Charlotte Perkins Gilman: A Nonfiction Reader.* New York: Columbia University Press, 1991.
——. 1895. Women's Discussion of the Labor Problem (Symposium). The Solution to the Labor Question. *Arena* 14(2) (October): 272–4.
——. 1898. *Women and Economics: A Study of the Economic Relation between Men and Women as a Factor in Social Evolution.* Boston: Small, Maynard & Co. Reprinted with an introduction by Carl N. Degler. New York: Harper & Row, 1962. Reprinted, with introduction by Michael Kimmel and Amy Aronson, Berkeley, Calif.: University of California Press, 1998.
——. 1898. Economic Basis of the Woman Question. *Woman's Journal 40* (1 October). Partially reprinted in Aileen Kraditor, ed., *Up from the Pedestal: Land-*

mark Writings in the American Woman's Struggle for Equality. Chicago: Quadrangle Books, 1968.

——. 1899. What Work Is. *Cosmopolitan* 27 (October): 678–82.

——. 1899. The Woman's Congress of 1899. *Arena* 22(3) (September): 342–50.

——. 1899. Woman's Economic Place. *Cosmopolitan* 27 (July): 309–13.

Gilman, Charlotte Perkins [Stetson]. 1900/1901. *Concerning Children.* Boston: Small, Maynard; London: Putnam. Reprinted Walnut Creek, Calif.: Rowman & Littlefield, 2003.

——. 1901. Too Wise. *Philistine* 12(6) (May): 188–.

——. 1903. *The Home: Its Work and Influence.* New York: McClure, Phillips. Reprinted New York: Source Book Press, 1970. Reprinted Urbana, Ill.: University of Illinois Press, 1972.

——. 1904. *Human Work.* New York: McClure Phillips.

——. 1904. The Growing Power of Woman: Impressions of the Congress in Berlin: With Illustrations. *Booklovers Magazine* 4(3) (September): 385–.

——. 1904. International Duties. *Armenia* 1(1) (October): 10–.

——. 1906. *Women and Economics.* With an introduction by Stanton Coit. London: Putnam's Sons.

——. 1907. Discussion of Professor Carver's Paper. *American Sociological Society, Papers and Proceedings* 2 (December): 28–.

——. 1907. Discussion of Professor Commons' Paper. *American Sociological Society, Papers and Proceedings* 2 (December): 163–.

——. 1907. Discussion of Professor Giddings' Paper. *American Sociological Society, Papers and Proceedings* 2 (December): 186–.

——. 1907. The Extent of Child Labor in the United States. Discussion on Child Labor in the United States. *American Economic Association, Publications* 3(8:1) (February): 260–.

——. 1907. Why Cooperative Housekeeping Fails, *Harper's Bazar* 41 (July).

——. 1908. The Basis of Social Conflict: Comment. *American Journal of Sociology* 13(5): 644.

——. 1908. Class Conflict in America: Comment. *American Journal of Sociology* 13(6): 781–.

——. 1908. Contradictions of Ideas and Beliefs: Comment. *American Journal of Sociology* 13(6) (May): 804–.

——. 1908. How Home Conditions React upon the Family. *American Sociological Society, Papers and Proceedings* 3 (December): 16–.

——. 1908. A Social Puzzle. *Public* 10(515) (February 15): 1,094–.

——. 1908. To the Wise – A Bargain. *Public* 10(516) (February 22): 1,116–.

——. 1908. Up and Down. *Public* 10(511) (January 18): 998–.

——. 1908. A Suggestion on the Negro Problem. *American Journal of Sociology* 14(1) (July): 78–85.

——. 1909. Why Walk Backward? *Appleton's Magazine* 13(6) (June): 666–.

——. 1909–17. *The Forerunner.* A periodical of works by Gilman, published in 7 vols. New York: Charlton Company. Reprinted New York: Greenwood

Reprint Corp., 1968. Reprinted New York: New York Source Book Press, 1970.

——. 1910. The "Anti" and the Fly. *American Suffragette* 2(2) (October): 12–.

——. 1910. Reasonable Resolutions. *The Forerunner* (January), vol. 1, no. 3. New York: Charlton Company.

——. 1910–11. *Our Androcentric Culture*. Serialized in *The Forerunner*, vol. 2. New York: Charlton Company. Reprinted as *The Man-Made World, or, Our Androcentric Culture*, New York: New York Source Book Press, 1970.

——. 1910–11. *What Diantha Did*. Serialized in *The Forerunner*, vol. 1. New York: Charlton Company.

——. 1911. Two Storks. *Public* 14(667) (January 13): 38–.

——. 1912. *Moving the Mountain*. Serialized in *The Forerunner*, vol. 4. New York: Charlton Company.

——. 1912. Education and Social Progress. *American Teacher* 1: 134–.

——. 1912. Housekeeping. *McCall's* (December).

——. 1912. Some Sins Are Worse Than Others. *Public* 15(764) (November 22): 1,121–.

——. 1913. The Arrested Development of Women. *New Statesman* 2, Supplement (November 1).

——. 1913. On a Branch. *Public* 16(812) (October) 24: 1,024–.

——. 1913. The Waste of Private Housekeeping. *American Academy of Political and Social Science, Annals* 48 (July): 91–.

——. 1913. The Women Selling Eggs. *The Forerunner*, vol. 4(2): 54.

——. 1914. Herland. Serialized in *The Forerunner*, vol. 6. New York: Charlton Company. Reprinted New York: Pantheon Press, 1979.

——. 1916. The Foolish Fifty. *Public* 19(942) (April 21): 375–.

——. 1916. Right Preparedness. *American Teacher* 5: 85–.

——. 1916. Wanted, a Railroad Cafeteria. *The Forerunner*, vol. 7, 1: 33. New York: Charlton Company.

——. 1916. With Her in Ourland: Sequel to Herland. *The Forerunner*, vol. 7. New York: Charlton Company. Reprinted Westport, Conn.: Greenwood Press, 1997.

——. 1916. Wouldn't You Think? *Public* 19(946) (May 19): 473–.

——. 1917. The Housekeeper and the Food Problem. *American Academy of Political and Social Science, Annals* 74 (November): 123–.

——. 1919. The Influence of Women on Public Life. *Public* 22(1104) (May 31): 571–.

——. 1919. The Socializing of Education. *Public* 22(1096) (April 5): 348–.

——. 1921. Making Towns Fit to Live in. *Century Illustrated Monthly Magazine* 102 (May/October): 361–.

——. 1921/2. Do Women Dress to Please Men? *Century Illustrated Monthly Magazine* 103 (November/April): 651–.

——. 1922. Vanguard, Rear-guard, and Mud-guard. *Century Illustrated Monthly Magazine* 104 (May/October): 348–.

——. 1922/3. Cross-Examining Santa Claus. *Century Illustrated Monthly Magazine* 105 (November/April): 169–.

——. 1922/3. His Religion and Hers: What Her Religion Will Do for the World. *Century Illustrated Monthly Magazine* 105 (November/April): 676–, 855–.

——. 1923. *His Religion and Hers: A Study of the Faith of Our Fathers and the Work of Our Mothers*. New York: Century Co. Reprinted Westport, Conn.: Hyperion Press, 1976; Walnut Creek, Calif.: AltaMira Press, 2003.

——. 1923. Is America Too Hospitable? *Forum* 70(4) (October).

——. 1923. The New Generation of Women. *Current History (New York)* 18(5) (August): 731–.

——. 1925. A Little Educational Fortune-telling. *Century Illustrated Monthly Magazine* 110 (May/October): 706.

——. 1925. The Nobler Male. *Forum* 74(1) (July): 19–.

——. 1925. Wash-tubs and Woman's Duty. *Century Illustrated Monthly Magazine* 110 (May/October): 152.

——. 1925. What Our Children Might Have. *Century Illustrated Monthly Magazine* 110 (May/October): 706.

——. 1925/6. Mind-stretching. *Century Monthly Magazine* 111 (November/April): 217–.

——. 1926. These Too, Too Solid Ghosts. *Forum* 75(2) (February): 238–.

——. 1927. Woman's Achievements since the Franchise. *Current History (New York)* 27(1) (October): 7–.

——. 1928. Thrills, Common and Uncommon. *Forum* 80(1) (July): 97–.

——. 1929. Feminism and Social Progress. In Baker Brownell, ed., *Man and His World*, Vol 7: *Problems of Civilization*. New York: D. Van Nostrand Company.

——. 1929. Sex and Race Progress. In V. F. Calverton and S. D. Schmalhausen, eds., *Sex in Civilization*. New York: MacCaulay.

——. 1935. The Right to Die – I. *Forum and Century* 94(5) (November): 297–.

——. 1940. For Us. *International Journal of Religious Education* 17(2) (October): 27–.

——. 1940. For Us. *International Journal of Religious Education* 17(4) (December): 29–.

Gilman, Charlotte Perkins and Aletta H. Jacobs. 1900. *De economische toestand der vrouw; een studie over de economische verhouding tusschen mannen en vrouwen als een factor in de sociale evolutie*. Haarlem: Tjeenk Willink.

Gilson, Mary Barnett. 1910/1919. *Work of the Employment and Service Department of the Clothcraft Shops*. Cleveland, Ohio: s.n.

——. 1916. The Relation of Home Conditions to Industrial Efficiency. *American Academy of Political and Social Science, Annals* 65 (May): 277–.

——. 1918. Taking Stock of Ideals – a War Measure. *Industrial Management* 55 (January/June): 235–.

——. 1921. Wages of Women in Industry. *Industrial Management* 62(1) (July 1): 37.

——. 1924. Scientific Management and Personnel Work: Why a Science Management Plant Offers the Proper Environment for the Highest Type of Personnel Work. *Bulletin of the Taylor Society* 9(1).

——. 1927/8. Book Review of "The Economic Basis of Fair Wages" by Jacob Dolson Cox. *Personnel Journal* 6 (June/April): 134–.
——. 1928. Existing Plans for Unemployment Insurance in the U.S. *American Federationist* 35(9) (September): 1,114–.
——. 1930. Great Britain's Experience with Unemployment Insurance. *American Labor Legislation Review* 20: 262–6.
——. 1931. *Unemployment Insurance in Great Britain: The National System and Additional Benefit Plans.* New York: Industrial Relations Counselors.
——. 1932/3. Book Review of "The Co-operation of the United States with the League of Nations and with the International Labour Organisation" by Ursula P. Hubbard. *American Journal of Sociology* 38(1/6): 804–.
——. 1932/3. Book Review of "Hours of Labor" by Lazare Teper. *American Journal of Sociology* 38(1/6): 803–.
——. 1932/3. Book Review of "Woman Labour in India" by Rajani Kanta Das. *American Journal of Sociology* 38(1/6): 341–.
——. 1933/1936. *Unemployment Insurance.* University of Chicago Public Policy Pamphlets, no. 3. Chicago, Ill.: University of Chicago Press.
——. 1934. Book Review of "Insecurity: A Challenge to America" by Abraham Epstein. *Journal of Political Economy* 42: 553–.
——. 1934. The New British Unemployment Insurance Act. *American Labor Legislation Review* 24: 111–14.
——. 1934/5. Book Review of "The Labor of Women in the Production of Cotton" by Ruth Allen. *American Journal of Sociology* 40(1/6): 559–.
——. 1934/5. Book Review of "Unemployment Insurance" by S. P. Lowes and St. V. F. Coules. *American Journal of Sociology* 40(1/6): 274–.
——. 1935/6. Book Review of "The Employment Exchange Service of Great Britain" by T. S. Chegwidden and G. Myrddin-Evans. *American Journal of Sociology* 41(1/6): 417–.
——. 1935/6. Book Review of "Standards of Unemployment Insurance" by Paul H. Douglas. *American Journal of Sociology* 41(1/6): 256–.
——. 1936/7. Book Review of "The International Protection of Labor: International Labor Organization, History and Law" by Boutelle Ellsworth Lowe. *American Journal of Sociology* 42(1/6): 296–.
——. 1937. They that Have Eyes to See. *American Federationist* 44(10) (October): 1,068–.
——. 1938/9. Book Review of "The Legal Protection of the Worker's Job" by James Rowland. *American Journal of Sociology* 44(1/6): 319–.
——. 1938/9. Book Review of "Profit Sharing for Wage Earners" by C. Canby Balderston. *American Journal of Sociology* 44(1/6): 318–.
——. 1939. Book Review of "Men without Work: A Report Made to the Pilgrim Trust" by Pilgrim Trust. *Journal of Political Economy* 47: 147–.
——. 1939. Our Business: The General Welfare. Through a Social Security Program We Seek to Alleviate the Hazards of Modern Life. *American Association of University Women, Journal* 33(1) (October): 17–.

——. 1940. *What's Past Is Prologue: Reflections on My Industrial Experience.* New York and London: Harper & Brothers.

——. 1940. Scientific Management and the "Cultural Lag." *Advanced Management* 5(4) (October/December): 180–.

——. 1940/1. Book Review of "Labor Policy under Democracy" by Clay Packer Malick. *American Journal of Sociology* 46(1/6): 762–.

—— 1940/1. Book Review of "Management and the Worker" by F. J. Roethlisberger and William Dickson. *American Journal of Sociology* 46(1/6): 98–.

Gilson, Mary Barnett and E. J. Riches. 1930. *Employers' Additional Unemployment Benefit Schemes in Great Britain.* Geneva: International Labour Office. Reprinted in *International Labour Review* 21(3) (March 1930): 348–.

Gilson, Mary Barnett. Papers (Archival Material, fourteen items), 1909–59. Papers of Mary Barnett Gilson, including three diary-memorandum books, 1909, 1926, and 1959, from trips to Europe, which contain narrative entries, as well as notes on accommodations, engagements, and persons she met; and letters, 1937–1938, from Herbert G. Williams, Neville Chamberlain, and Henry L. Stimson, concerning British and American policy toward Japan in 1932, Chamberlain's lack of popularity in the United States, and other matters. In the Southern Historical Collection, University of North Carolina at Chapel Hill (#3855).

Givens, Meredith Bruner. 1929. Measurability of Unemployment and Related Trends. *Journal of the American Statistical Association* 24, Supplement (March): 33–41.

——. 1931. Statistical Measures of Social Aspects of Unemployment. *Journal of the American Statistical Association* 26 (September): 303–18.

——. 1933/1986. *Employment during the Depression.* New York: National Bureau of Economic Research.

——. 1934. Measurement of Unemployment (Roundtable Discussion). *American Economic Review* 24 (March): 89–.

——. 1935. Statistical Implications of the Social Security Program. *Journal of the American Statistical Association* 30 (December): 651–61.

——. 1936. Industrial Instability and Unemployment Insurance. *Personnel Journal* 15(1) (May): 1–.

Givens, Meredith Bruner and Ernestine Wilke. 1933. A Guide to Statistical Series Relating to Wages in the United States. Part 4. In Stuart A. Rice, *Report to the President's Research Committee on Social Trends, on Social Statistics in the United States.* Ann Arbor, Mich.: Edwards Brothers.

[Glasier,] Katharine St. John Conway [Bruce] [Mrs. John Bruce Glasier]. 1894. *The Cry of the Children.* Manchester: Labour Press Society. [*novel*]

——. 1894. *Husband and Brother: A Few Chapters in a Woman's Life of To-day, and, From Key-Note to Dominant.* Bristol: Arrowsmith. [*novel*]

——. 1895. *The Road to Socialism.* Manchester. Labour Press Society.

——. 1896. *Aimee Furniss, Scholar.* London: Clarion. [*novel*]

——. 1900. *Socialism for Children.* City Branch Pamphlets, no. 6. London: City of London Branch of the Independent Labour Party.

——. 1909. *Socialism and the Home.* London: Independent Labour Party.

——. 1914. The Part Women Played in Founding the ILP [Independent Labour Party]. *Labour Leader* (9 April).

——. 1918. The Labour Women's Battle with Dirt. In M. Phillips, ed., *Women and the Labour Party*. London: Headley Brothers; New York: B. W. Huebsch.

——. 1929. *Socialism for Beginners*. London: Independent Labour Party Publication Department.

Glasier, Katharine Bruce and John Bruce Glasier. 1890. *The Religion of Socialism: Two Aspects*. Labour Press Pamphlet, no. 18. Manchester: Labour Press Society.

Glasser, Carrie. 1940. *Wage Differentials: The Case of the Unskilled*. New York: Columbia University Press.

——. 1941. Wage Differentials: The Case of the Unskilled. Ph.D. thesis, Columbia University.

Gleason, Caroline [Sister Miriam Teresa]. 1914. *Report of the Industrial Welfare Commission of the State of Oregon on the Power Laundries in Portland*. Salem, Oreg.: Oregon Industrial Welfare Commission.

——. 1924. Legislation for Women in Oregon. Ph.D. thesis, Catholic University of America (sociology, political science).

——. 1931. *Oregon Legislation for Women in Industry*. Washington: U.S. Women's Bureau.

Glover, Katherine. 1908/9. Working for an Education in a Southern School. *Craftsman* 15 (October/March): 707–.

——. 1931. White House Conference on Child Health and Protection. *Childhood Education* 7: 517–.

——. 1935. The TVA – a New World Begins. *Forum and Century* 93(1) (January): 42.

——. 1939. *America Begins Again, the Conquest of Waste in Our Natural Resources*. London: McGraw-Hill.

Glück, Elsie. 1925. Wage Theories – Yesterday and Today. *American Federationist* 32(7/12) (July/December): 1,163–.

——. 1927. The Significance of Labor's Wage Statement. *American Federationist* 34(1/6) (January/June): 214–.

——. 1929. *John Mitchell, Miner: Labor's Bargain with the Gilded Age*. New York: John Day Co.

——. 1929. John Mitchell, Miner: Labor's Bargain with the Gilded Age. Ph.D. thesis, University of Wisconsin–Madison (economics).

——. 1934. Book Review of "Beside Galilee" by Hector Bolitho. *American Academy of Political and Social Science, Annals* 172 (March): 178–.

——. 1935. *Introduction to American Trade Unionism*. New York: Affiliated Schools for Workers.

——, ed. 1937. *Does Norwegian Labor Seek the Middle Way?*, by Finn Moe. New York: League for Industrial Democracy.

——. 1937. *Introduction to American Trade Unionism with Supplement*. New York: Affiliated Schools for Workers.

——, comp. 1940. *Handbook of Federal Labor Legislation*, vol. I: *Labor Standards on Government Contract Work and Work Financed by the United States.* U.S. Department of Labor, Division of Labor Standards Bulletin, no. 39. Washington: U.S. Government Printing Office.

——. 1940. Book Review of "Sidney Hillman, Labor Stateman" by George Soule. *Jewish Social Studies* 2: 231–.

Gnauck-Kühne, Elisabeth. 1892. *Das Universitätsstudium der Frauen; ein Beitrag zur Frauenfrage.* Oldenburg: Schulz.

——. 1893. *Ursachen und Ziele der Frauenbewegung.* Berlin: Lesser.

——. 1895. *Die soziale Lage der Frau.* Lecture held at the 6th Evangelical Social Congress, Erfurt, 6 June 1895. Berlin: O. Liebmann.

——. 1896. Die Lage der Arbeiterinnen in der Berliner Papierwaren-Industrie. *Jahrbuch für Gesetzgebung, Verwaltung und Volkswirtschaft im deutschen Reich*, n.s. 20(2): 25–.

——. 1904. *Die deutsche Frau um die Jahrhundert-wende: statistische Studie zur Frauenfrage.* Berlin: Liebmann.

——. 1905. *Einführung in die Arbeiterinnenfrage.* Monchen-Gladbach, Germany: Zentralstelle des Volksvereins für das kath. Deutschland.

——. 1907. Die Arbeitszeit in Wasch- und Plättanstalten. *Jahrbuch für Gesetzgebung, Verwaltung und Volkswirtschaft im deutschen Reich* 31(4): 315–.

——. 1909/1912/1914/1920/1921/1928. *Das soziale Gemeinschaftsleben im deutschen Reich: Leitfaden der Wirtschafts und Bürgerkunde für höhere Schulen, Kurse und zum Selbstunterricht.* Monchen-Gladbach: Volksvereins-Verlag.

——. 1915. *Dienstpflicht und Dienstjahr des weiblichen Geschlechts.* Tübingen: J. C. B. Mohr (Paul Sieback).

——. 1916. Book Review of "Die Heimarbeit" by Käthe Gaebel. *Zeitschrift für Politik* 9: 603–.

——. 1917. Wohlfahrtspflege, Caritas und soziale Arbeit. *Jahrbücher für Nationalökonomie und Statistik* 109(1) (July): 77–.

Godfrey, Eleanor Elsabeth Smith. *See* Smith [Godfrey], Eleanor.

Goetz, Mary Rachel Marshall. 1927. The Scientific Background of the Industrial Revolution: The Steam Engine as a Type Case. M.A. thesis, University of Chicago (economics, history).

Goetz, Rachel Marshall and Ursula Batchelder Stone. 1937. *Chicago: World Trader.* Chicago: League of Nations Association, Midwest Office.

Going, Margaret Chase. *See* Woodhouse, Margaret Chase Going.

Goldman, Emma. 1908. *A Beautiful Idea.* The lecture which Emma Goldman was to have read before the Edelstadt Social, March 17, 1908, at Workingmens' Hall, 12th and Waller Streets, Chicago. Chicago: J. C. Hart & Co., printers.

——. 1908. *What I Believe.* New York: Mother Earth Publishing Association.

——. 1909. *The White Slave Traffic.* New York: Mother Earth Publishing Association.

——. 1910. *Anarchism and Other Essays.* New York: Mother Earth Publishing Association. Reprinted New York: Dover Publications, 1917.

——. 1911. *Anarchism: What It Really Stands For.* New York: Mother Earth Publishing Association.
——. 1911/1916. *Marriage and Love.* New York: Mother Earth Publishing Association.
——. 1913. *Syndicalism the Modern Menace to Capitalism.* New York: Mother Earth Publishing Association.
——. 1913. *The Tragedy of Woman's Emancipation.* New York: Mother Earth Publishing Association.
——. 1918. *The Truth about the Boylsheviki.* New York: Mother Earth Publishing Association.
——. 1919. *A Fragment of the Prison Experiences of Emma Goldman and Alexander Berkman in the State Prison at Jefferson City, Mo., and the U.S. Penitentiary at Atlanta, Ga., February, 1918–October, 1919.* New York: S. Comyn.
——. 1922. *The Crushing of the Russian Revolution.* London: Freedom Press.
——. 1923. *My Disillusionment in Russia.* Garden City, N.Y.: Doubleday, Page & Co.
——. 1924. *My Further Disillusionment in Russia.* Garden City, N.Y.: Doubleday, Page.
——. 1930/1939. *The Place of the Individual in Society.* Chicago: Free Society Forum.
——. 1934. Was My Life Worth Living? *Harper's Magazine* 170 (December): 52–8.
——. 1938. *Trotsky Protests Too Much.* Glasgow: Anarchist Communist Federation.
——. Publisher and proprietor, *Mother Earth*, monthly magazine devoted to social science and literature, 12 vols, 1906–17; editor, April 1915–August 1917.
Goldman, Fay. 1935. A Statistical Survey of the Distribution and Dispersion of Certain Retail Prices for February, 1933, June, 1933, and February, 1934. M.A. thesis, University of Chicago (economics).
Goldmark, Josephine Clara. 1903. Children Who Work at Night. *Charities; a Weekly Review of Local and General Philanthropy* 10: 569.
——. 1904. Child Labor, Street Labor and Juvenile Delinquency. *Political Science Quarterly* 19: 417.
——. 1904/5. Holiday Faces. *Charities; a Weekly Review of Local and General Philanthropy* 13: 184.
——. 1905. *The Necessary Sequel of Child-labor Laws.* New York?: National Consumers' League?. Reprinted from the *American Journal of Sociology* 11(3) (November 1905): 312–25.
——. 1906. Working Women and the Laws; a Record of Neglect. *Annals of the American Academy of Political and Social Science* 28: 261.
——. 1907/1990. *Labour Laws for Women in the United States.* London: Women's Industrial Council. Reprinted from the *Annals of the American Academy of Political and Social Science* (September 1906).
——. 1907 Child Labor Legislation. *American Academy of Political and Social Science, Annals* 29, supplement (January).
——. 1908. Child Labor Legislation. Handbook, 1908. *American Academy of Political and Social Science, Annals* 31 (January).

——. 1910. The Illinois Ten-hour Decision. In Helen Marot, ed., *The Economic Position of Women.* New York: U.S. Academy of Political Science. Also published in Henry Raymond Mussey, ed., *Proceedings of the Academy of Political Science in the City of New York.* New York: Columbia University.

——. 1912. *Fatigue and Efficiency, a Study in Industry.* New York: Charities Publication Committee.

——. 1912. *Handbook of Laws Regulating Women's Hours of Labor: A Standard Law Embodying the Best Provisions of the Most Effective Statutes Now in Force.* New York: National Consumers' League.

——. 1913. Labor Laws for Women. *Survey* (January 25).

——. 1914. Facts and Social Progress. *Standard* 1(4) (December): 109–.

——. 1916. *Tenement Home Work and the Courts.* New York: National Consumers' League.

——. 1917. *Fatigue and Efficiency: A Study in Industry.* New York: Russell Sage Foundation.

——. 1918. Some Considerations Affecting the Replacement of Men by Women Workers. *American Journal of Public Health* 8(4) (April): 270–.

——. 1918. Some Considerations Affecting the Replacement of Men by Women Workers. *United States Bureau of Labor Statistics, Monthly Review* 6 (January/June): 56–64.

——. 1923. *Nursing and Nursing Education in the United States.* New York: Macmillan Company.

Goldmark, Josephine and Mary Della Hopkins. 1920. *Comparison of an Eight-hour Plant and a Ten-hour Plant.* Washington: U.S. Government Printing Office.

Goldmark, Josephine Clara and Madeleine Wallin Sikes. 1905. *Child Labor Legislation: Schedules of Existing Statutes and the Standard Child Labor Law Embodying the Best Provisions of the Most Effective Measures Now in Force. Handbook 1905.* New York: National Consumers' League.

——. 1906. *Child Labor Legislation: Schedules of Existing Statutes and Standard Child Labor Law Embodying the Best Provisions of the Most Effective Measures Now in Force. Handbook 1906.* New York: National Consumers' League.

Goldmark, Josephine Clara. Coauth. *See* Goldmark, Pauline Dorothea; Sykes, Madeleine Wallin.

Goldmark, Pauline [Dorothea]. 1907. *Do Children Work in the Canneries?* New York: Consumers' League.

——. 1908. *Women and Children in the Canning Industry: An Investigation in New York State.* New York: Russell Sage Foundation.

——. 1910. *Child Labor in Canneries.* New York: U.S. National Child Labor Committee.

——. 1912. *Notes on an Industrial Survey of a Selected Area in New York City with Respect to Sanitary Conditions in the Factories.* Albany: J. B. Lyon Company, State Printers. Reprint of Appendix V to Preliminary Report of the New York State Factory Investigating Commission, submitted to the Legislature March 1, 1912.

——. 1912. The Relation of a Neighborhood Survey to Social Needs. *Academy of Political Science, Proceedings* 2(4) (July): 51–.

——. 1914. *West Side Studies*. New York: Survey Associates, Inc.

——. 1915. Report of the Committee on Field Secretary. *College Settlements Association Quarterly* 1(2) (December): 20–.

——. 1917. *Memorandum to the Public Service Commission of New York, First District, on the Proposed Plan to Provide for Fair and Reasonable Wages and Working Conditions and to Prevent Interruption of the Service on Street Railroads*. New York: National Consumers' League.

——. 1917. The Energies of Men in Wartime. *Independent* (April 28).

——. 1919. Women in the Railroad Service. *Academy of Political Science, Proceedings* 8(2) (February): 17–.

——. 1919. Women in the Railroad World. *Annals of the American Academy of Political and Social Science* 86 (November): 214–.

Goldmark, Pauline Dorothea, Josephine Clara Goldmark, Florence Kelley, and Minnie Bronson. 1912. The Truth about Wage-earning Women and the State: A Reply to Miss Minnie Bronson. In *Three Arguments against Woman Suffrage*. Concord, N.H.: Concord Equal Suffrage Association.

Goldsmith, Margaret L[eland]. 1920. Flexibility Clauses in Agreements in the Printing Industry. *American Economic Review* 10 (March): 104–5.

——. 1935. *Seven Women against the World*. London: Methuen. Reprinted 1976, Westport, Connecticut: Hyperion Press.

——. 1939. *The Trail of Opium, the Eleventh Plague*. London: R. Hale, Ltd.

——. 1939. Advertisements in German Newspapers. *Nineteenth Century and After* 126 (July/December): 761–.

Gooch [Iglehart], Fanny Chambers. 1887. *Face to Face with the Mexicans: The Domestic Life, Educational, Social and Business Ways, Statesmanship and Literature, Legendary and General History of the Mexican People, as Seen and Studied by an American Woman during Seven Years of Intercourse with Them*. New York: Fords, Howard, & Hulbert; London: Sampson Low, Marston, Searle & Rivington.

Goodale, Elaine. See Eastman, Elaine Goodale.

Goodale, Frances Abigail Rockwell, ed. 1893. *The Literature of Philanthropy*. New York: Harper & Brothers.

Goodman, Pearl and Elsa Ueland. 1910. The Shirtwaist Trade. *Journal of Political Economy* 18(10) (December): 816–28.

Goodrich-Freer, Miss A. 1899. Horticulture as a Profession for the Educated. *Nineteenth Century* 46 (November): 769–.

Goodwin, Christina. 1895. An Appeal to Housekeepers. *Forum* 19 (August): 753–60.

Goodwin, Maud Wilder. 1893. The Anti-slavery Legacy. In Frances A. Goodale, ed., *The Literature of Philanthropy*. New York: Harper Bros.

——. 1894. *The Colonial Cavalier; or, Southern Life before the Revolution*. New York: Lovell, Coryell. Reprinted New York: Arno Press, 1975.

Goold, Miss A. J. 1890. Irish Industrial Organisations. *Englishwoman's Review*, n.s. 205 (May): 198.

Gordon, Florence. 1894. Comments [on "The Economic Position of Women" by L. MacDonald]. *Australian Economist* IV(3) (April 23): 393–6.

——. 1894. The Conditions of Female Labour and the Rates of Women's Wages in Sydney. *Australian Economist* IV(7) (August 23): 423–9.

——. 1894. Reply to Comments. *Australian Economist* IV(10) (November 23): 454; IV(11) (December 31): 459–60.

Gordon, Mrs. J. E. H. [Alice Mary]. 1895. The After-careers of University-educated Women. *Nineteenth Century* 37 (June): 955–60.

——. 1940. Japan's Balance of International Payments, 1903–31. In Elizabeth B. Schumpeter, ed., *The Industrialization of Japan and Manchukuo*. New York: Macmillan.

Gordon, Margaret Maria. 1854. *Sunbeams in the Cottage, or, What Women May Do: A Narrative Chiefly Addressed to the Working Classes*. Edinburgh: Thomas Constable and Co.; London: Hamilton, Adams, and Co.

——. 1854. *Work, or, Plenty to Do and How to Do It*. New York: A. D. F. Randolph.

——. 1861. *Household Economy; A Manual Intended for Female Training Colleges and the Senior Classes of Girls' Schools*. Edinburgh: J. Gordon.

Gordon, Margaret S. 1937. Japanese Banks and War Loans. *Far Eastern Survey* 6(1/25): 223–.

——. 1940. Japan's Balance of International Payments, 1903–31. In Elizabeth B. Schumpeter, ed., *The Industrialization of Japan and Manchukuo*. New York: Macmillan.

Gordon, Maria Matilda Ogilvie. 1908. *A Handbook of Employments Specially Prepared for the Use of Boys and Girls on Entering the Trades, Industries, and Professions*. Aberdeen: Rosemount Press.

——. 1911. *Juvenile Employment Bureau*. Wellington: Mackay. Also published in *Journal of the Department of Labour* XIX(223) (September 1911).

——. 1912. Juvenile Employment Exchanges. *Women's Industrial Notes* (January).

Gordon, Mildred Larcom Jones. 1921. *State Laws Affecting Working Women*. Bulletin of the Women's Bureau, no. 16. Washington: U.S. Government Printing Office.

——. 1924. *State Laws Affecting Working Women: Hours, Minimum Wage, Home Work*. Bulletin of the Women's Bureau, no. 40. Washington: U.S. Government Printing Office.

——. 1927. *State Laws Affecting Working Women: Hours, Minimum Wage, Home Work*. Washington: U.S. Women's Bureau.

——. 1928. *The Development of Minimum-wage Laws in the United States, 1912 to 1927*. Bulletin of the Women's Bureau, no. 61. Washington: U.S. Government Printing Office.

——. Coauth. *See* Best, Ethel Lombard; Manning, Caroline; Peterson, Agnes Lydia.

Gordon-Cumming, Constance F[rederica]. 1881. *At Home in Fiji*. London: William Blackwood.

——. 1882. Wheat, Wine and Wool [California commerce]. *Contemporary Review* 42 (September): 343–60.

——. 1883. The Locust War in Cyprus. *Nineteenth Century* 14 (August): 300–16.

——. 1884. The World's Oil-supply in the Nineteenth Century. *Blackwood's* 136 (September): 336–62.
——. 1885. Locusts and Farmers of America. *Nineteenth Century* 17(95) (January): 133–53.
——. 1885. The Lowlands of Moray, in the Fourteenth and Nineteenth Centuries. *National Review* 4 (January): 642–57.
——. 1887. Our Oldest Colony [Bombay]. *Macmillan's* 55 (January): 218–23.
——. 1892. *Two Happy Years in Ceylon*. London: William Blackwood.
——. 1892. *Work for the Blind in China, Parts I & II*. London: Gilbert & Rivington.
Gore-Booth, Eva. 1900–10. *Women Workers and Parliamentary Representation*. Textile Tracts, no. 1. Manchester, UK: Lancashire and Cheshire Women Textile and other Workers' Representation Committee.
——. 1900–10. *Women's Right to Work*. Manchester, UK: Manchester and Salford Women's Trade and Labour Council.
Gorgas, Nellie. 1937. The Storage and Issuance of Hospital Supplies. M.A. thesis, University of Chicago (health sciences, health care management).
——. 1940. The Storage and Issuance of Hospital Supplies. *Journal of Business* 13(2) (April): 172–204.
——. 1940. The Storage and Issuance of Hospital Supplies (Continued). *Journal of Business* 13(3) (July): 275–315.
Gostling, Sarah S. 1885. Education in India: "Why It Takes More to Cure a European of Ignorance Than It Does a Native." London: s.n.
——. 1886. The Poverty of India and the Land Question: Thoughts Evolved Out of the Late Mahometan Riots at Delhi and Etawah. Paper read at a special meeting of the London Ayra Samaj. London: Ayra Samaj.
——. 1887. India's Position, Social and Economic. Paper read at a special meeting under the auspices of the Indian Society, March 8, 1887. London: C. Cordingley.
Gottheiner, Elisabeth. 1903. *Studien über die Wuppertaler Textilindustrie und ihre Arbeiter (Natur und Staat)*. Leipzig: Duncker & Humblot.
——. 1905. Book Review of "Eine soziologische Betrachtung" by Waldemar Mitscherlich and Entstehung der deutschen Frauenbewegung. *Jahrbücher für Nationalökonomie und Statistik* 3(30:4) (October): 552–.
——. 1905. Soziale Literatur über die Frauenfrage. *Archiv für Sozialwissenschaft und Sozialpolitik (Tübingen)*: 724–.
——. 1909/10. Die deutschen politischen Parteien und ihre Stellung zur Frauenfrage. *Zeitschrift für Politik* 3: 581–.
——. 1910/11. Book Review of "Die moderne Frauenbewegung" by Käthe Schirmacher. *Zeitschrift für Politik* 4: 417.
——. 1910/11. Book Review of "Politisches Handbuch für Frauen." *Zeitschrift für Politik* 4: 417.
Gould, Elenor Renwick. 1933. Merchandising Profits and the Business Cycle as Reflected by Chain Stores and Department Stores. M.A. thesis, University of Minnesota.

Gould, Elizabeth Porter. 1890/1. A Look at Labor and Charity. *Chautauquan* 12 (October/March): 369–.

Grady, Eleanor Hundson. 1931. Epigraphic Sources of the Delphic Amphictyony. Ph.D. thesis, Columbia University (history).

——. 1939. Teaching Labor Problems by the Case Method. *American Economic Review* 29 (June): 345–7.

Graffenried, Clare de. 1890. *The Needs of Self-supporting Women.* Studies in Historical and Political Science, 8th series, series ed. Herbert Baxter Adams. Baltimore: Johns Hopkins University.

——. 1890. Child-labor. In W. F. Willoughby and Clare de Graffenreid, *Two Essays on Child Labor. Publications of the American Economic Association*, 1st series, 5(2) (March): 72–149 [194–271].

——. 1891. The Georgia Cracker in the Cotton Mills. *Century Magazine* 41 (February): 483–98.

——. 1891. A Town Minus Poverty. *Chautauquan* 13 (April/September): 656.

——. 1891. Women in the London County Council. *Chautauquan* 13 (June): 357.

——. 1893. The Condition of Wage Earning Women. *Forum* 15 (March): 68–82.

——. 1893. London Parks for the People. *Chautauquan* 17 (April/September): 336–.

——. 1893. Trades-unions for Women. *Lend a Hand* 10(2) (February): 103.

——. 1895. Industrial Education. *American Federationist* 2(3) (May): 44–.

——. 1896. *Typical Alley Houses in Washington.* Bulletin No. 7. Washington: Woman's Anthropological Society.

——. 1896. Compulsory Education. *Lend a Hand* 16 (June): 415–23.

——. 1896. The Need of Better Homes for Wage-earners. *Forum* 21 (May): 301–12.

——. 1896. The New Woman and Her Debts. *Popular Science Monthly* 49 (September): 664–72.

——. 1896. Some Social Economic Problems. *American Journal of Sociology* 2(2) (September): 190–201.

Gragg, Mabel Taylor. 1930. Testing Advertising. *Harvard Business Review* 9 (October): 111–23.

Graham, Irene J[eanette]. 1915. Working Hours of Women in Chicago. *Journal of Political Economy* 23(8) (October): 822–31.

——. 1929. Family Support and Dependency among Chicago Negroes: A Study of Unpublished Census Data. *Social Service Review* 3(1/4) (March/December): 541–.

——. 1929. Negroes in Chicago, 1920: an Analysis of United States Census Data. (Chicago, Illinois). A.M. thesis, University of Chicago (sociology).

——. 1929/30. The Negro Family in a Northern City. *Opportunity: Journal of Negro Life* 8(2) (February 1930): 48–. A portion is also printed in *Social Service Review* (December 1929).

Graham, Mary. 1895. The Relations Between Education and Poverty. Ph.D. thesis, Yale University.

Grand, Sarah. 1894. The New Aspect of the Woman Question. *North American Review* 158 (March): 270–6. Reprinted in Andrea Broomfield and Sally Mitchell, eds., *Prose by Victorian Women: An Anthology*. New York: Garland Publishing, 1995.

——. 1898. *The Modern Man and Maid.* New York: T. Y. Crowell.

Grant, Anne MacVicar. 1813. *Sketches of Intellectual Education, and Hints on Domestic Economy Addressed to Mothers: with an Appendix, Containing an Essay on the Instruction of the Poor.* Baltimore: Edward J. Coale.

Grant, I[sabel]. F[rances]. 1920/1. An Old Scottish Handicraft Industry in the North of Scotland. *Scottish Historical Review* 18: 277–.

——. 1922. The Survival of the Small Unit in Industry. *Economic Journal* 32 (December): 489–505.

——. 1924. *Every-day Life of an old Highland Farm.* London: Longmans, Green & Co.

——. 1924. The Income of Tenants on a Scotch Openfield Farm in the Eighteenth Century. *Economic Journal* 34 (March): 83–9.

——. 1924. Three Official Reports upon the Agricultural Depression. *Economica* 4 (November): 336–52.

——. 1925. Highland Rural Industries. *Edinburgh Review* 241(491) (January): 167–.

——. 1926. The Social Effects of the Agricultural Reforms and Enclosure Movement in Aberdeenshire. *Economic History* 1 (January): 89–116.

——. 1928. Some Accounts of Individual Highland Sporting Estates. *Economic History* 1 (January): 405–11.

——. 1930. *The Social and Economic Development of Scotland before 1603.* Edinburgh and London: Oliver and Boyd.

——. 1934. *The Economic History of Scotland.* London: Longmans, Green and Co.

——. 1936. *The Lordship of the Isles.* Moray Press.

Grant, Margaret. 1937. *More Security for Old Age; a Report and a Program.* New York: Twentieth Century Fund.

——. 1939. *Old-age Security: Social and Financial Trends.* Washington: Committee on Social Security, Social Science Research Council.

——. 1940. Old-age Security: Social and Financial Trends. Ph.D. thesis, Columbia University (sociology).

Grant, Ruth Fulton. 1934. *The Canadian Atlantic Fishery.* Toronto: Ryerson Press.

Gras, E. C. 1936. *Descriptive Economics for Beginners.* New York: Holt.

Gray, Emma J. 1897. Family Co-operative Housekeeping. *Harper's Bazar* 30 (May 8): 390–1.

Gray, Greta. 1932. Changes in the Household Resulting from the Industrial Revolution, *Social Forces* 11(2) (December): 242–8.

Gray, Greta and Ruth Staples. 1928. Housing Needs of Children. *Social Forces* 7(2)(December): 250–2.

Gray, Greta and Violet Wolfe. 1933. Food Expenditures of Seven Industrial Families in Los Angeles. *Social Science* 8(1) (January): 34–.

Gray, Greta. Coauth. *See* Clark, Marjorie Ruth.

Greaves, Ida C. 1935. *Modern Production among Backward Peoples*. London: George Allen and Unwin, Ltd.

——. 1935/6. A Modern Colonial Fallacy. *Foreign Affairs; an American Quarterly Review* 14(1/4): 627–.

Greie, Johanna. 1888. [Is it necessary for women to organize themselves? Original in German.] *Der Sozialist* (January 14).

Green, Alice Stepford. 1894. *Town Life in the Fifteenth Century*. London: Macmillan.

Green, Constance McLaughlin. 1937. History of Holyoke, Massachusetts: A Case History of the Industrial Revolution in America. Ph.D. thesis, Yale University (history). (Received Yale's Eggleston prize in history.)

——. 1939. *Holyoke, Massachusetts: A Case History of the Industrial Revolution in America*. New Haven, Conn.: Yale University Press.

Green, E. M. 1899. Native Unrest in South Africa. *Nineteenth Century* 46 (November): 708–16.

Green, Elsa Goodwin. 1898. *Raiders and Rebels in South Africa*. London: G. Newnes.

Green, Gertrude. 1894. *The History of the Poor Law: With Other Lectures Delivered to Working Class Audiences, and a Few Collected Verses*. Manchester: Labour Press Society Ltd.

Green, Hetty. 1900. The Benefits of Business Training for Women. *Woman's Home Companion* (February): 8.

Green, Marjorie E. 1930. Family Allowances [letter to the editor]. *Nation and Athenaeum* 47(16) (July 19): 496–.

——. 1938. *Family Allowances*. London: Family Endowment Society.

Green, Dr. Mary E. 1897/8. Household Economics. *Chautauquan* 26 (October/March): 535–.

Greene, Catherine Dem. 1938. The Dynamic Balance Sheet: A German Theory of Accounting. Ph.D. thesis, University of California–Berkeley.

Greene, Mary A. 1890. Privileged Communications in Suits Between Husband and Wife. *American Law Review* 24(5) (September/October): 779.

——. 1891/2. Legal Domestic Relations. *Chautauquan* 14 (October/March): 592.

——. 1891/2. The Legal Relation of Parent and Child. *Chautauquan* 14 (October/March): 463.

——. 1891/2. A Woman Lawyer. *Chautauquan* 14 (October/March): 218.

——. 1892. Legal Business Transactions. *Chautauquan* 15 (April/September): 347.

——. 1892. Promissory Notes and Bank Checks. *Chautauquan* 15 (April/September): 81.

——. 1892. Woman's Position in Law. *Chautauquan* 15 (April/September): 634.

——. 1893. Married Women Property Acts in the U.S., and Needed Reforms Therein. *Albany Law Journal* 48: 206–.

——. 1894. Results of the Woman-suffrage Movement. *Forum* 17 (June): 413–24.

——. 1897. Evolution of the American Fee-simple. *American Law Review* 31: 227–.

Greenwell, Dora. 1862. Our Single Women. *North British Review* 36 (February): 62–87.

——. 1873. The East African Slave Trade, *Contemporary Review* 22 (June): 138–64.

Greenwood, Mrs. [Madeleine.] 1895. The Need for More Classification in Workhouses. *Englishwoman's Review*, n.s. 228 (October): 217.

——. 1897. Small Laundries. *Westminster Review* 147 (June): 698–701.

——. 1899. Freedom of Contract for the Unrepresented. *Westminster Review* 151 (May): 554–7.

Gregory, Mary Huston. 1911. *Checking the Waste: A Study in Conservation.* Indianapolis: Bobbs-Merrill.

Grenfell, Alice. 1895. Contemporary Socialists and Women. *Shafts* 3 (September).

Greville, Lady Beatrice Violet Graham. 1884. Social Reforms for the London Poor. *Fortnightly Review*, n.s. 35 [o.s. 41] (January): 21–30.

——. 1892. Man-servants in England. *National Review* 18 (February): 812–20.

Grey, Maria Georgina. 1875. *Old Maids: A Lecture.* London: W. Ridgway.

——. 1884. The Women's Education Movement. In Theodore Stanton, ed., *The Woman Question in Europe: A Series of Original Essays.* London: Sampson Low Marston, Searle; and New York: G. P. Putnam's Sons.

Grier, Lynda. 1925. The Meaning of Wages. *Economic Journal* 35 (December): 519–35.

——. 1926. Book Review of "The Economics of Private Enterprise" by J. H. Jones. *Economic Journal* 36: 610–.

——. 1929. Women's Work and Training. *Nash's Magazine 1927* 83(432) (May): 64–.

——. Coauth. *See* Ashley, Annie.

Grimes, Barbara. 1925. Constitutional Law: Police Power: Minimum Wage for Women. *The Supreme Court and Minimum Wage Legislation.* National Consumers' League. New York: New Republic.

Grinberg, Suzanne and Alice La Mazière. 1917. *Les Carrières féminines*, Paris: s.n.

Gripenberg, Baroness Alexandra. 1895. Women's Work in Finland. *Englishwoman's Review* XXVI, n.s. 225 (January): 3–9.

——. 1896. Women's Meetings in Finland. *Englishwoman's Review* XXVII, n.s. 232 (October): 219–.

——. 1898. The Woman Question in the Parliament of Finland. *Englishwoman's Review* XXIX, n.s. 238 (April): 125–.

——. 1899. Special Labour Legislation for Women. *Englishwoman's Review* XXX, n.s. 242 (April): 166–68.

Grobben, Margaret Maud. 1937. *The Cooperative Loan Agency; a Phase of Consumer Credit.* New York: Consumer Credit Institute of America, Inc.

——. 1938. *Report on the Small Loan Situation in the State of Georgia.* New York: Consumer Credit Institute of America.

——. 1938. Volume and Classification of Consumer Loans. *American Academy of Political and Social Science, Annals* 196 (March): 74–.

——. 1940. *Industrial Banking: A Phase of Consumer Credit.* New York: Consumer Credit Institute of America.

Grogan, Mrs. Mercy. 1880. *How Women May Earn a Living.* London, Paris and New York: Cassell, Petter, Galpin & Co.

Grünfeld, Judith. 1913. Die leitenden sozial- und wirtschaftsphilosophischen Ideen in der deutschen Nationalökonomie und die Überwindung des Smithianismus bis auf Mohl und Hermann. Doctoral thesis, University of Tübingen. Vienna: C. Konegen (E. Stülpnagel).

——. 1928. De Vakbeweging in Rusland. *Socialistische gids* 13(12) (December): 1,087–.

——. 1934. Rationalization and the Employment and Wages of Women in Germany. *International Labor Review* 29(5) (May): 605–32.

——. 1934. Vrouwenarbeid in het teeken van de mechanisatie. *Socialistische gids* 19(5) (May): 372–.

Gundselman, Myrtle Annice. 1926. Consumer Demand for Apples in Chicago (Illinois). M.A. thesis, University of Chicago (economics, agricultural).

Gunn, Grace. 1928. The Classification of Solutions of a Diophantine Equation. M.A. thesis, Northwestern University.

Gurney, Mary. 1872. *Are We to Have Education for Our Middle Class Girls?* London: William Ridgway.

Gwatkin, Idella. *See* Swisher, Idella Gwatkin [Mrs. Carl B. Swisher].

Gwin, Helen Clara. 1928. Depreciation of China, Glassware, and Silver in Institution Situations. M.A. thesis, University of Chicago (economics).

H

Haass, Charlotte Augusta Clara. 1908. Trades in the Inscriptions of Campania (France). M.A. thesis, University of Chicago (economics, history).

Hadcock, Editha. 1931. The Labor Problem in the Rhode Island Cotton Industry. A.M. thesis, Brown University.

Haddon, Charlotte. 1871. Nursing as a Profession for Ladies. *Saint Paul's Magazine* 8: 458–61.

Hagenauer, S. 1931. *Das "justum pretium" bei Thomas von Aquino. Ein Beitrag sur Geschichte der objektiven Werttheorie.* Stuttgart: Kohlhammer.

Hahn, Margaret. 1927. Voting Provisions in Public Utility Preferred Stock Issues of 1925. *Land Economics* 3 (February): 100–2.

Hainisch, Marianne. 1875. *Die Brotfrage der Frau.* Vienna: Gistel.

Haldane, Elizabeth S. 1897. Friendly Societies for Women. *National Review* 28: 559.

——. 1897. Jacob Böhme and His Relation to Hegel. *Philosophical Review* VI (March): 146–61.

——. 1908. Sick Nursing in the Territorial Army. *Contemporary Review* 94 (July/December): 356–.

——. 1918. Women and the Civil Service. *Fortnightly Review* (April): 593–.

——. 1922. Nursing as a Profession. *Nineteenth Century and After* 92 (July/December): 442–.

——. 1924. Adult Education in Rural Districts. *Nineteenth Century and After* 95 (January/June): 609–.

Hale, Mrs. H. G. 1915. Women in the Furnishing Trades in London. *Women's Industrial News* (October).

Hale, Mrs. Sarah Josepha. 1840. Domestic Economy. *Godey's Lady's Book, and Ladies' American Magazine* 20: 42, 86, 154.

Haley, Lucia. 1927. *Oregon: A Preliminary List of the Sources of Agricultural and Related Statistics of the State.* Washington: U.S. Bureau of Agricultural Economics.

——. 1935. General Education and Technical Training of Librarians of Land-grant Colleges. *Library Journal* 60(18) (October 15): 785–.

Hall, Bessie Louisa. 1929. Mothers' Assistance in Philadelphia. Actual and Potential Costs. Ph.D. thesis, Bryn Mawr College (sociology).

Hall, Mrs. Cecil. 1884. *A Lady's Life on a Farm in Manitoba.* London: W. H. Allen.

Hall, Frances Adkins. 1939. *Statistical Measurement in Group Work: A Manual on Statistical Records for Use by Staff Members*. Washington: U.S. Children's Bureau.

Hall, Helen. 1930. When Detroit's Out of Gear. *Survey Graphic* 17(1) (April): 9–14, 51–4.

——. 1931. *Shall We Stick to the American Dole?* New York: National Federation of Settlements.

——. 1933. English Dole and American Charity. *Atlantic Monthly* 151 (January/June): 538–.

——. 1933. Miners Must Eat. Atlantic Review 152 (July/December): 153–.

——. 1934. The American Dole in the Light of Mental Hygiene. *American Labor Legislation Review* 24: 11–21.

——. 1934. Current American Methods of Handling Unemployed in the Light of Present Mental Hygiene Knowledge. *American Sociological Society, Publication* 28(2) (June): 128.

——. 1934. A Dental Clinic on Wheels. *NEA Bulletin (Journal of the National Education Association)* 23(3) (March): 91–.

——. 1934. Insure the Worker! The Case for Social Security. *Forum and Century* 91(6) (June): 344–.

——. 1937. Creativeness in Settlement Work. *Standard* 23(4) (January): 85–.

Hall, Dr. Lucy M. 1885. Tenement Houses. *Journal of Social Science* 20 (June): 91–7.

——. 1888. Unsanitary Conditions in Country Homes. *Journal of Social Science* 25 (December): 59–74.

Hall, Margaret Winslow. *See* Cole, Margaret Winslow Hall.

Hall, Marguerite Franklyn. 1939. Medical Relief in Michigan. *Pi Lambda Theta Journal* 17(3) (March): 79–.

Hall, Wilhelmina L. 1887. *Boarding-out, as a Method of Pauper Education and a Check on Hereditary Pauperism*. Paper read at the Birmingham meeting of the British Association for the Advancement of Science, September 1886, with appendix. London: Hatchards.

Hallett, Caroline M. 1885. *How to Be Well: A Few Words to Working Women.* London: Walter Smith.

Hallowell, Anna. 1880. The Care and Saving of Neglected Children. *Journal of Social Science* 12 (December): 117–24.

Halsey, Olga S. 1915. Compulsory Unemployment Insurance in Great Britain. *American Labor Legislation Review* 5: 265.

——. 1916. Compulsory Health Insurance in Great Britain. *American Labor Legislation Review* 6: 127. Reprinted in John R. Commons (ed.) *Trade Unionism and Labor Problems*, second series. Boston: Ginn and Co.

——. 1916. The Reaction of the British Health Insurance upon Existing Charities. *Proceedings of N.Y. Conference on Hospital Social Service* III.

——. 1920. Recent Progress in Social Insurance Throughout the World. *American Labor Legislation Review* 10: 151.

——. 1921. The British National System of Unemployment Insurance – Its Operation and Effects. In John R. Commons (ed.), *Trade Unionism and Labor Problems*, 2nd series. Boston: Ginn and Co.

——. 1927. No "Demoralization" under British Unemployment Insurance; Adverse Charges Unfounded. *American Labor Legislation Review* 17: 244–.

——. 1929. A Superior Book on Unemployment Insurance. *American Labor Legislation Review* 19: 282–.

——. 1930. Manufacturers' Report is Biased and Superficial. *American Labor Legislation Review* 20: 259–60.

——. 1932. Wages and Unemployment Insurance in Great Britain. *American Federationist* 39(7) (June): 752–.

——. 1932/3. Book Review of "The British System of Social Insurance: History and Description" by Percey Cohen. *American Journal of Sociology* 38(1/6): 658–.

——. 1933/4. Book Review of "Unemployment Insurance and Various Forms of Relief for the Unemployed" by International Labour Conference. *American Journal of Sociology* 39(1/6): 556–.

——. 1935/6. Book Review of "The Development of Social Insurance and Minimum Wage Legislation in Great Britain: A Study of British Social Legislation in Relation to a Minimum Standard of Living" by Helen Fisher Hohman. *American Journal of Sociology* 41(1/6): 137–.

Hamburger, Estelle. 1939. *It's a Woman's Business.* New York: Vanguard.

Hamilton, Alice. 1911. Lead Poisoning in Illinois. *American Economic Review* 1(2) (April): 257–64.

——. 1911. Lead Poisoning in Illinois. *American Labor Legislation Review* 1: 17–.

——. 1911. White-lead Industry in the United States. *Bulletin of the Bureau of Labour* (July).

——. 1912. *Lead Poisoning in Potteries, Tile Works, and Porcelain Enameled Sanitary Ware Factories.* Bulletin of the United States Bureau of Labor, no. 104. Industrial Accidents and Hygiene Series, no. 1. Washington: U.S. Government Printing Office.

——. 1914. *Lead Poisoning in the Smelting and Refining of Lead.* Washington: Bureau of Labor Statistics.

——. 1914. Lead Poisoning in the United States. *American Journal of Public Health* 4(6) (June): 477–.

——. 1915. *Lead Poisoning in the Manufacture of Storage Batteries.* Bulletin of the United States Bureau of Labor Statistics, no. 165. Industrial Accidents and Hygiene Series, no. 6. Washington: U.S. Government Printing Office.

——. 1915. *Lead Poisoning in the Smelting and Refining of Lead.* Bulletin of the United States Bureau of Labor Statistics, no. 141. Industrial Accidents and Hygiene Series, no. 4. Washington: U.S. Government Printing Office.

——. 1915. Occupational Disease Clinic of New York City Health Department. *United States Bureau of Labor Statistics, Monthly Review* 1(5) (November): 7–19.

——. 1916. Industrial Anilin Poisoning in the United States. *United States Bureau of Labor Statistics, Monthly Review* 2 (January/June): 535–46.

——. 1916/17. Book Review of "Brief for the Defendant in Error" by Felix Frankfurter and Josephine Goldmark. *American Journal of Sociology* 22(1/6): 686.

——. 1916/17. Book Review of "The Case for the Shorter Work Day" by the Supreme Court of the United States. *American Journal of Sociology* 22(1/6): 686.
——. 1917. *Industrial Poisons Used or Produced in the Manufacture of Explosives*. U.S. Bureau of Labor Statistics, no. 219. Industrial Accidents and Hygiene Series, no. 14. Washington: U.S. Government Printing Office.
——. 1917. Dope Poisoning in the Manufacture of Airplane Wings. *United States Bureau of Labor Statistics, Monthly Review* 5 (July/December): 656–63.
——. 1917. Industrial Poisons Used in the Making of Explosives. *United States Bureau of Labor Statistics, Monthly Review* 4 (January/June): 177–98.
——. 1917. Toxic Jaundice in Munition Workers: A Review. *United States Bureau of Labor Statistics, Monthly Review* 5 (July/December): 263–74.
——. 1918. Causation and Prevention of Trinitrotoluene (TNT) Poisoning. *United States Bureau of Labor Statistics, Monthly Review* 6 (January/June): 1,285–98.
——. 1918. Dinitrophenol Poisoning in Munition Works in France. *Monthly Labor Review* 7 (July/December): 718–26.
——. 1918. Dope Poisoning in the Making of Airplanes. *United States Bureau of Labor Statistics, Monthly Review* 6 (January/June): 289–316.
——. 1918. Prophylaxis of Industrial Poisoning in the Munition Industries. *American Journal of Public Health* 8(2) (February): 125–.
——. 1918. Protection of Health of Munition Workers in Italy, Translated and Summarized. *United States Bureau of Labor Statistics, Monthly Review* 6 (January/June): 184–90.
——. 1919. *Do Women in Industry Need Special Health Legislation*. Pamphlet. The Consumers' League of Connecticut, no. 12. Harvard, Conn.: Consumers' League of Connecticut.
——. 1919. *Women in the Lead Industries*. Bulletin of the United States Bureau of Labor Statistics, Industrial Accidents and Hygiene Series, no. 253. Washington: U.S. Government Printing Office.
——. 1919. Industrial Poisoning in American Anilin Dye Manufacture. *Monthly Labor Review* 8(2) (February): 199–215.
——. 1919. New Scientific Standards for Protection of Workers. *Academy of Political Science, Proceedings* 8(2) (February): 23–.
——. 1919. Occupational Diseases in Pennsylvania. *Monthly Labor Review* 9(1) (July): 170–80.
——. 1919. Practical Points in the Prevention of TNT Poisoning. *Monthly Labor Review* 8(1) (January): 248–72.
——. 1921. *Industrial Poisoning in Making Coal-tar Dyes and Dye Intermediates, April, 1921*. Bulletin of the United States Bureau of Labor Statistics, Industrial Accidents and Hygiene Series, no. 280. Washington: U.S. Government Printing Office.
——. 1921/1927. *Poverty and Birth Control*. New York: American Birth Control League, Inc.
——. 1924. Protection for Women Workers. *Forum* (August): 152–.
——. 1925. *Industrial Poisons in the United States*. New York: Macmillan.

——. 1925. Book Review of "Industrial Poisons in the United States". *Industrial Management* 70 (July/December): 64–.
——. 1926. *Women Workers and Industrial Poisons.* Washington: U.S. Women's Bureau.
——. 1926. Prevalence of Industrial Lead Poisoning in the United States. In Joseph S. Aub, Laurence T. Fairhall, A. S. Minot, and Paul Reznikoff, *Lead Poisoning.* Baltimore: Wilkins & Wilkins Co.
——. 1929. Nineteen Years in the Poisonous Trades. *Harper's Monthly Magazine* 159(953) (October): 580–.
——. 1929. The Opposition to Health Insurance. *American Labor Legislation Review* 19: 404–.
——. 1930. State Pensions or Charity? *Atlantic Monthly* 145 (January/June): 683–.
——. 1931. What about the Lawyers? *Harper's Monthly Magazine* 163(977) (October): 542–.
——. 1931/2. Book Review of "Occupational Diseases in Relation to Compensation and Health Insurance" by Rosamond W. Goldberg. *American Journal of Sociology* 37(1/6): 1,009–.
——. 1932. American and Foreign Labor Legislation: A Comparison. *Social Forces* 11(1) (October): 113–19.
——. 1933. Forward with Hitler: A Communication. *Living Age* 344 (August): 484–.
——. 1933. Hitler Speaks. *Atlantic Monthly* 152 (July/December): 399–.
——. 1933. Industrial Hygiene. *American Journal of Public Health and the Nation's Health* 23(4) (April): 332–.
——. 1934. *Industrial Toxicology.* Harper's Medical Monographs, 2nd ed. New York: Harper.
——. 1934. The Plight of the German Intellectuals. *Harper's Monthly Magazine* 168(1004) (January): 159–.
——. 1936. *Recent Changes in the Painters' Trade.* U.S. Division of Labor Standards Bulletin no. 7. Washington: U.S. Government Printing Office.
——. 1936. The Development of the Synthetic Textile Fibre Industry in the United States and Some Associated Health Hazards. Paper read at the 23rd Annual Convention of the International Association of Industrial Accident Boards and Commissions, Topeka, Kansas, September 21–24, 1936 [typescript].
——. 1936. Industrial Poisons. *American Federationist* 43(7) (July): 707–.
——. 1938. Healthy, Wealthy – if Wise – Industry. *American Scholar* 7(1) (Winter): 12–.
——. 1940. *Occupational Poisoning in the Viscose Rayon Industry.* Washington: U.S. Government Printing Office.
——. Coauth. *See* Cohn, Adele.
——. Papers located in the Schlesinger Library, Radcliffe College.
Hamilton, Cicely. 1909. *Marriage as a Trade.* London: Chapman and Hall; New York: Moffat, Yard & Co.
Hamilton, Gail. Pseud. *See* Dodge, Mary A.

Hamilton, Lady Margaret. 1892. Household Clubs: How Will They Affect Small Households? *Nineteenth Century* 31 (January/June): 807–.

Hamilton, Mary E. 1924. *The Policewoman. Her Service and Ideals*. New York: Frederick A. Stokes Company.

Hammond, [Lucy] Barbara Bradby. 1904. Equal Pay for Equal Work. *Women's Industrial News* (September).

——. 1922. *William Lovett, 1800–1877*. London: Fabian Society.

——. 1928. Urban Death-rates in the Early Nineteenth Century. *Economic History* 1 (January): 419–28. Reprinted London: Macmillan, 1928.

——. 1931. Two Towns' Enclosures. *Economic History* 2 (January): 258–66.

[Hammond,] [Lucy] Barbara Bradby and Anne Black. 1899. Women Compositors and the Factory Acts. *Economic Journal* 9(34) (June): 261–6.

Hammond, [Lucy] Barbara Bradby and John Lawrence le Breton Hammond. 1911. *The Village Labourer, 1760–1832: A Study in the Government of England before the Reform Bill*. London: Longmans Green. Reprinted New York: A. M. Kelley, 1967; London and New York: Longman, 1978.

——. 1917. *The Town Labourer, 1760–1832: The New Civilisation*. London: Longmans Green.

——. 1919. *The Skilled Labourer, 1760–1832*. London: Longmans Green.

——. 1923. *Lord Shaftesbury*. London: Constable. 4th ed., London: Longmans Green, 1936.

——. 1925. *The Rise of Modern Industry*. London: Methuen & Co. Reprinted New York: Harcourt Brace, 1926.

——. 1930. *The Age of the Chartists, 1832–1854: A Study of Discontent*. London: Longmans Green.

——. 1934. *The Bleak Age*. London and New York: Longmans, Green. Reprinted London and New York: Penguin Books, 1947.

Hanks, Ethel E. Coauth. *See* Matthews, Ellen Nathalie; [Woodbury], Helen L[aura] Sumner.

Hann, Helen, Nebeker, Rhonda and Stiebeling, Hazel Katherine. 1938. *Food Consumption of Children at the National Child Research Center*. Circular, United States Department of Agriculture, no. 481. Washington: U.S. Department of Agriculture.

Hanna, Lavone Agnes. 1927. British Taxes Since the World War (Interwar Period). M.A. thesis, University of Chicago (economics, finance).

Hannay, Annie Murray Macgregor. 1927. *Control of Production of Agricultural Products by Governments*. Washington: s.n.

——. 1931. *The Influence of Weather on Crops, 1900–1930: A Selected and Annotated Bibliography*. Washington: U.S. Bureau of Agricultural Economics.

——. 1936. *A Chronicle of Industry on the Mill River*. Northampton, Mass.: Smith College Department of History.

——. 1940. *Price Fixing by Government in Foreign Countries, 1926–1939*. Washington: s.n.

Hannay, Annie Murray Macgregor, A. M. Murray [May] Coult, Lillian Crans, and Mary G. Lacy. 1933. *Measures Taken in Foreign Countries to Relieve Agricultural Indebtedness*. Washington: U.S. Bureau of Agricultural Economics Library.

Hannay, Annie Murray. Coauth. *See* Bercaw, Louise Oldham; Lacy, Mary Goodwin.

Hanson, Alice C. 1934. Book Review of "Apartment House Increases and Attitudes toward Home Ownership" by Coleman Woodbury. *Journal of Political Economy* 42: 844–6.

——. 1934. Book Review of "Cost of Living Studies, III. The Food of Twelve Families of the Professional Class" by Mary Gorringe Luck and Sybil Woodruff (Heller Committee for Research in Social Economics of the University of California). *Journal of Political Economy* 42: 844–6.

——. 1934. Book Review of "Cost of Living Studies, V: How Mexicans Earn and Live" by Constantine Panunzio. *Journal of Political Economy* 42: 844–6.

——. 1934. Book Review of "The Economic Basis for the Teacher's Wage" by Lester Dix. *Journal of Political Economy* 42: 286.

——. 1934. Book Review of "Women in the Twentieth Century: A Study of Their Political, Social and Economic Activities" by Sophonisba Breckinridge. *Journal of Political Economy* 42: 411.

——. 1939. Workers' Education on the March. *American Teacher* 23(7) (April): 15.

Hanson, Alice and Paul Douglas. 1930. The Wages of Domestic Labor in Chicago, 1890–1929. *Journal of the American Statistical Association* 25 (March): 47–50.

Harbert, Mrs. 1880. Social Economy in Illinois. *Journal of Social Science* 11 (May): 103–5.

Hardy, M. 1936. *The Influence of Organized Labor on the Foreign Policy of the United States*. Liège: Vaillant-Carmanne.

Hardy, Sara McLean. *See* McLean-Hardy, Sara.

Harkness, Margaret E. 1881. Women as Civil Servants. *Nineteenth Century* 10 (September): 369–81.

——. 1882. Railway Labour. *Nineteenth Century* 12 (November): 721–32.

——. 1883. The Municipality of London. *National Review* 1 (May): 395–407; 2 (September): 96–.

——. [as "John Law"] 1887. *A City Girl: A Realistic Story*. London: Vizetelly. Reprinted London and New York: Garland Publishing, 1984. [*novel*]

—— [as "John Law"]. 1888. *Out of Work*. London: Swan Sonnenschein. Reprinted London: Merlin Press, 1990. [*novel*]

—— [as "John Law"]. 1889. *Captain Lobe: A Story of the Salvation Army*. London: Hodder & Stoughton. [*novel*]

—— [as "John Law"]. 1889. *Toilers in London: or Inquiries Concerning Female Labour in the Metropolis*. London: Hodder and Stoughton.

—— [as "John Law"]. 1890. *A Manchester Shirtmaker: A Realistic Story of To-day*. London: Authors' Co-operative Publishing Co.

—— [as "John Law"]. 1891. A Year of My Life. *New Review* 5 (October): 375–84.

—— [as "John Law"]. 1893. The Children of the Unemployed. *New Review* 8 (February): 228–36.

—— [as "John Law"]. 1894. A Week on a Labour Settlement. *Fortnightly Review*, n.s. 56 (August): 206–13.

—— [as "John Law"]. 1905. *George Eastmont, Wanderer*. London: Burns & Oates. [*novel*]

Harland, Marion. Pseud. *See* Terhune, Mary Virginia Hawes.

Harley, Gertrude. 1925. Multi-family Housing Units and Urban Tenancy. *Land Economics* 1 (July): 371–2.

Harper, Elsie Dorothy. 1931. *Out of a Job: Proposals for Unemployment Insurance*. New York: Woman's Press.

——. 1934. *From Pay Day to Pay Day*. New York: Woman's Press.

——. 1935. *Primer of Economics: Certain ABC's of the Present Situation and What (May) Be Made out of Them*. New York: Woman's Press.

Harper, Elsie Dorothy and Ruth Steinmetz. 1934. *Unemployment's Humpty Dumpty: A Study Course in Three Lessons for the Busy Woman*. New York: Woman's Press.

Harper, Frances Ellen Watkins. 1866. We Are All Bound up Together. *Proceedings of the Eleventh National Woman's Rights Convention*. New York: Robert J. Johnston.

——. 1878. Colored Women of America. *Englishwoman's Review* ix, n.s. 57 (January 15): 10–14.

——. 1891. Duty to Dependent Races. Speech given at the 1891 annual meeting of the National Council of Women. In Rachel Foster Avery, ed., *Transactions of the National Council of Women of the United States*. Philadelphia: J. B. Lippincott.

——. 1894. Woman's Political Future. In May Wright Sewall, ed., *The World's Congress of Representative Women*. Chicago: Rand McNally.

Harrington, Virginia Draper. 1927. New York and The Embargo of 1807. *New York State Historical Association, Quarterly Journal* 8(2) (April): 143–.

——. 1932. The Place of the Merchant in New York Colonial Life. *New York History* 13(4) (October): 366–.

——. 1935. *The New York Merchant on the Eve of the Revolution*. New York: Columbia University Press.

——. 1935. The New York Merchant on the Eve of the Revolution. Ph.D. thesis, Columbia University (history).

Harris, Lilian. 1895. *Abolition of Overtime for Women*. Investigation Papers, no. 2. Manchester: Women's Co-operative Guild.

——. 1897. *The Prevention of Smoke*. Public Health Papers, no. 3. Manchester: Women's Co-operative Guild.

——. 1897. *The Treatment of Women Employees in the Co-operative Movement: Being a Report of an Enquiry into the Wages, Hours, and Conditions of Women Working in Co-operative Stores in 1895*. Manchester: Co-operative Newspaper Society.

——. 1908. The Propertied Vote for Women [letters to the editor]. *Nation* 4(10) (December 5): 380–.

——. 1912. Maternity Benefit and the Doctors [letter to the editor]. *Nation* 11(11) (June 15): 404–.

——. 1923. *The Position of Employees in the Co-operative Movement*. London: Fabian Society. Reprinted New York: Kraus Reprint, 1969.

Harris, Lilian, Emily Tomlinson, and Emily Ashton. 1908. A Woman's Charter [letter to the editor]. *Nation* 2(18) (February 1): 640–.

Harris, Lilian. Coauth. *See* Davies, Margaret Llewelyn.

Harris, Mary Dormer. 1921. *A Social and Industrial History of England before the Industrial Revolution.* London, Glasgow: Collins.

Harrison, Amy. 1901. The Inspection of Women's Workshops. *Economic Review* (January).

——. 1904. *Women's Industries in Liverpool: An Enquiry into the Economic Effects of Legislation Regulating the Labour of Women.* London: Williams & Norgate for the University Press of Liverpool.

Harrison, Mrs. Frederick. 1903. The "Woman Who Toils" in America. *Nineteenth Century* (December).

——. 1904. Social Life in England. *Cornhill Magazine* 89: 187.

Harrison, Lucia Caroline [Carolyn]. 1918–33. Two papers entitled "Some relations of the fur trade to the historical development of the Middle West", undated; and "Salt industry as a factor in the history of the Middle West", 1918, M.S. thesis Ogden Graduate School of Science, University of Chicago (geography).

——. 1919. *The Salt Industry as a Factor in the History of the Middle West.* M.S. thesis, University of Chicago (history).

——. 1935. *Daylight, Twilight, Darkness, and Time; Their Distribution over the Earth and Their Relationships to Human Affairs.* New York: Silver, Burdett and Company.

——. 1935. Dominica: A Wet Tropical Human Habitat. *Economic Geography* 11(1) (January): 62–76.

Harrison, Mary. 1893. Cookery as a Business. *Nineteenth Century* 34 (July/December): 110–20.

Hart, Alice Marion [Rowlands] [Mrs. Ernest Hart]. 1885. *Cottage Industries: And What They Can Do for Ireland.* London: Smith, Elder & Co.

Hart, Mary H. 1880. *The Children of the Street: Mary Carpenter's Work in Relation to our Own.* London: Sonnenschein and Allen.

——. 1882. *A Brief Sketch of the "Maison Leclaire"...and Its Founder.* London: Decorative Co-operators' Association.

——. 1885. *Poverty and Its Remedy: Papers on the Reconciliation of Capital and Labour.* London: Decorative Co-operators' Association.

——. 1885. *A Practical Method of Reconciling Capital and Labour: An Interview with Miss Mary H. Hart.* Reprinted from the *Pall Mall Gazette* (February 18, 1885).

——. 1885. Obstacles to Industrial Reform. Paper read at the Industrial Remuneration Conference, January. *Report of Proceedings and Papers of the Industrial Remuneration Conference, January 1885.* London: Cassell. Book reprinted 1968, New York: Augustus M. Kelley.

——. 1885. The Organisation of Labour. *Charity Organisation Review* 8 (August 15): 347.

Hartley, Olive Pierce. 1928. *The Trade in Iodine.* Washington: U.S. Bureau of Foreign and Domestic Commerce.

Hartman, Erika. *See* Schoenberg, Erika Hartman.

Hartsough, Mildred Lucile. 1924. The Development of the Twin Cities (Minneapolis and St. Paul) as a Metropolitan Market. Ph.D. thesis, University of Minnesota (economics).

——. 1925. *The Twin Cities as a Metropolitan Market: A Regional Study of the Economic Development of Minneapolis and St. Paul.* University of Minnesota Studies in the Social Sciences, no. 18. Minneapolis: University of Minnesota.

——. 1925/6. Book Review of "An Economic History of Russia" by Mavor. *Social Forces* 4(1/4): 841.

——. 1925/6. Book Review of "England on the Eve of the Industrial Revolution" by Moffitt. *Social Forces* 4(1/4): 848.

——. 1925/6. Book Review of "The History of the Standard Oil Company" by Tarbell. *Social Forces* 4(1/4): 842.

——. 1925/6. Book Review of "The Oil Industry and the Competitive System" by Stocking. *Social Forces* 4(1/4): 842.

——. 1925/6. Book Review of "Russia Today." *Social Forces* 4(1/4): 841.

——. 1926. *Transportation as a Factor in the Development of the Twin Cities.* Saint Paul, Minn.: s.n.

——. 1926. Transportation as a Factor in the Development of the Twin Cities. *Minnesota History* 7(3) (September): 218–.

——. 1926/7. Book Review of "Historical Foundations of Trade-mark Law" by Schechter. *Social Forces* 5(1/4): 176.

——. 1926/7. Book Review of "A History of Agriculture in Europe and America" by Gras. *Social Forces* 5(1/4): 175.

——. 1926/7. Book Review of "History of Economic Progress in the United States" by Jennings. *Social Forces* 5(1/4): 177.

——. 1929. The Concept of Regionalism as Applied to Western Germany. *American Sociological Society, Papers and Proceedings* 24 (December): 12–.

——. 1930. Business Leaders in Cologne in the Nineteenth Century. *Journal of Economic and Business History* 2 (February): 332–52.

——. 1931. Cologne, the Metropolis of Western Germany. *Journal of Economic and Business History* 3 (August): 574–601.

——. 1931. The Rise and Fall of the Stinnes Combine. *Journal of Economic and Business History* 3 (February): 272–95.

——. 1932. A New Treatise on Bookkeeping under the Fuggers. *Journal of Economic and Business History* 4 (May): 539–51.

Hartt, Irene W. 1895. *How to Make Money, Although a Woman.* New York: J. S. Ogilvie Publishing Co.

Harvey, Edith C., transl. 1905. *Socialism and Positive Science* by Enrico Ferri. 2nd ed. London: Independent Labour Party. 4th ed., 1906.

——, transl. 1909. *Evolutionary Socialism: A Criticism and Affirmation* [*Die Voraussetzungen des Sozialismus und die Aufgaben der Sozialdemokratie*] by Eduard Bernstein. London: Independent Labour Party.

——. 1909. *Labour Laws for Women and Children in the United Kingdom.* London: Women's Industrial Council.

Haskins, M. L. and E. T. Kelly. 1921. Foundation of Industrial Welfare. *Economica* (May) 1(2): 116–31.

Haslam, Anna. 1898. Irishwomen and the Local Government Act. *Englishwoman's Review*, n.s. 239 (October): 221–5.

Hasse, Adelaide Rosalia. 1901. How May Government Documents Be Made More Useful to the Public? *Public Libraries* 6(1) (January): 28–34.

——. 1907. *Index of Economic Material in Documents of the States of the United States: Maine, 1820–1904*. Washington: Carnegie Institution.

——. 1907. *Index of Economic Material in Documents of the States of the United States: New Hampshire*. Washington: Carnegie Institution.

——. 1907. *Index of Economic Material in Documents of the States of the United States: New York, 1789–1904*. Washington: Carnegie Institution.

——. 1907. *Index of Economic Material in Documents of the States of the United States: Vermont, 1789–1904*. Washington: Carnegie Institution.

——. 1907. Public Documents. *Bulletin of the American Library Association* 1(4) (July): 132–.

——. 1908. *Index of Economic Material in Documents of the States of the United States: California, 1849–1904*. Washington: Carnegie Institution.

——. 1908. *Index of Economic Material in Documents of the States of the United States: Massachusetts, 1789–1904*. Washington: Carnegie Institution.

——. 1908. *Index of Economic Material in Documents of the States of the United States: Rhode Island, 1789–1904*. Washington: Carnegie Institution.

——. 1908. *Materials for a Bibliography of the Public Archives of the Thirteenth Original States. Covering the Colonial Period and the State Period to 1789*. Washington: U.S. Government Printing Office.

——. 1909. *Index of Economic Material in Documents of the States of the United States: Illinois, 1809–1904*. Washington: Carnegie Institution.

——. 1910. *Index of Economic Material in Documents of the States of the United States: Delaware, 1789–1904*. Washington: Carnegie Institution.

——. 1910. *Index of Economic Material in Documents of the States of the United States: Kentucky, 1729–1904*. Washington: Carnegie Institution.

——. 1912. *Index of Economic Material in Documents of the States of the United States: Ohio, 1787–1904*. Carnegie Institution of Washington Publication, no. 85, vol. 11. Washington: Carnegie Institution.

——. 1914. *Index of Economic Material in Documents of the States of the United States: New Jersey, 1789–1904*. Washington: Carnegie Institution.

——. 1916. Library Preparedness in the Fields of Economics and Sociology. *American Library Association, Bulletin* 10 (4) (July): 202–.

——. 1916. Library Preparedness in the Fields of Economics and Sociology. *Library Journal* 41(8) (August): 557–.

——. 1917. Making a Market in Libraries. *Library Journal* 42(4) (April): 270–.

——. 1917. Public Libraries and Business Men. *Library Journal* 42(3) (March): 185–.

——. 1917. Women in Libraries. *Association of Collegiate Alumnae, Journal* 11(2) (October): 73–.

——. 1918. This Business of Ours. *Public Libraries* 23 (July): 303–5.

——. 1918. Do Libraries Impede Research? *Special Libraries* 9(7/8) (September/October): 155–.

——. 1919–22. *Index of Economic Material in Documents of the States of the United States: Pennsylvania, 1790–1904*. Washington: Carnegie Institution.

——. 1934. *Non-institutional Relief Measures of the States and Territories, California*. Washington: U.S. Federal Emergency Relief Administration.

——. 1935. *A Selected List of References on Old Age Security*. Washington: Federal Emergency Relief Administration.

——. 1935. *Selected References on Old Age Security: United States, Massachusetts*. Washington: Federal Emergency Relief Administration.

——. 1936–40. *Report on the Study and Investigation of the Work, Activities, Personnel and Functions of Protective and Reorganization Committees Pursuant to Section 211 of the Securities Exchange Act of 1934*. 8 vols. Washington: U.S. Government Printing Office for the Securities and Exchange Commission.

——. 1937. *Bibliography on Urban Real Estate Appraisals*. Washington: Joint Committee on Appraisal and Mortgage Analysis.

Hasse, Adelaide Rosalia and Elizabeth Ketcham. 1937. *Public Welfare Organization in the United States: A Synopsis of Opinion*. Washington: Works Projects Administration.

Hatcher, Orie Latham. 1927. *Occupations for Women*. Richmond, Va., and Atlanta, Ga.: Southern Woman's Educational Alliance.

——. 1930. *Rural Girls in the City for Work*. Richmond, Va.: Garrett & Massie, Inc.

Hatfield, Mary Lewis Nash. 1924. Indiana Housing. Ph.D. thesis, Indiana University (economics).

Hatfield, Myrtle Lohner. 1936. An Analysis of Some Grocery Store Practices from the Viewpoint of the Woman Buyer. M.A. thesis, University of Chicago (business administration, marketing).

——. 1937. Customer Attitude toward Chicago Grocery-store Practices. *Journal of Business of the University of Chicago* 10(3) (July): 233–50.

Hathaway, Ella S. 1927. The Fur Industry of the United States. A.M. thesis, University of Chicago (economics, commerce-business).

Hathway, Marion. 1927. *The Vocational Guidance Training and Placement of Crippled Children in Chicago*. A.M. thesis, University of Chicago, School of Social Service Administration (education, vocational).

——. 1928. *The Young Cripple and His Job*. Chicago: University of Chicago Press.

——. 1930. *The Cost and Volume of Social Work and Public Health in Seattle, 1929*. Seattle: Department of Sociology, University of Washington, in co-operation with the Seattle Community Fund.

——. 1930. The Migrant Family and Social Agencies in Washington: The Registration of Migrant Families by Family Welfare Agencies in Nine Cities in Washington. *Social Forces* 9(2) (December): 232–5.

——. 1933. The Migratory Worker and Family Life. Ph.D. thesis, University of Chicago (sociology).

——. 1934. *The Migratory Worker and Family Life: The Mode of Living and Public Provision for the Needs of the Family of the Migratory Worker in Selected Industries in the State of Washington.* Chicago: University of Chicago Press.

——. 1937. The Right to Training. *Social Work Today* 5(1) (October): 11–.

——. 1939. *Trade Union Organization for Professional Workers.* New York: Social Service Employees' Division of the United Office and Professional Workers of America, CIO. Reprinted from *Social Work Today* (June 1939).

——. 1939. Social Work and Labor. *Social Work Today* 6(9) (June): 32–.

Hautzinger, Amélie. 1894. *Die weibliche Berufswahl; Handbuch für Frauenbildung und Frauenerwerb. Mit einem Anhange: Studien- und Stipendienfonds, Unterstützungs- und Pensions anstalten.* Berlin: Steinitz.

Haward, Winifred Ida. 1926. Economic Aspects of the Wars of the Roses in East Anglia. *English Historical Review* XLI: 170–89.

——. 1929. Gilbert Debenham: A Medieval Rascal in Real Life. *History* XIII: 300–14.

——. 1933. The Relations between the Lancastrian Government and the Merchants of the Staple from 1449–1461. In Edna Eileen Power, ed., *Studies in English Trade in the Fifteenth Century.* London: Routledge.

Haweis, Mary Eliza. 1889. *The Art of Housekeeping: A Bridal Garland.* London: Sampson Low, Marston, Searle and Rivington.

——. 1899. Servants and Served. *Contemporary Review* 75: 505–14.

Hawes, Annie. 1912. *Methods of Sanitary Inspection in American Cities.* M.A. thesis, University of Nebraska (Lincoln Campus).

Hawkins, Hildred Moser and Caroline Manning. 1926. *Women in the Fruit-growing and Canning Industries in the State of Washington: A Study of Hours, Wages and Conditions.* Bulletin of the Women's Bureau, no. 47. Washington: U.S. Government Printing Office.

Hawkins, Hildred Moser and Ruth Irene Voris. 1926. *Women in Oklahoma Industries: A Study of Hours, Wages, and Working Conditions.* Washington: U.S. Women's Bureau.

Hawley, Edith. 1929. *Nutritive Value and Cost of Food Served to College Students.* Circular, United States Department of Agriculture, no. 89. Washington: U.S. Department of Agriculture.

——. 1932. *Economics of Food Consumption.* 1st ed. New York and London: McGraw-Hill Book Company, Inc.

Hayes, Alice. 1891. Can a Poor Girl Go to College? *North American Review* 152 (May): 624–31.

Hayes, Elinor [Guthrie]. 1922. The Employees' Publication. *University Journal of Business* 1(1) (October): 81–94.

——. 1922. A Survey of Employee's Publications. A.M. thesis, University of Chicago (commerce and administration).

——. 1932/3. Selecting Women for Shop Work. *Personnel Journal* 11 (June/April): 69–.

Hayes, Mary Holmes Stevens. 1915. In Memoriam: Eliza L. Clark. *Volta Review* 17(6) (June): 245.

——. 1923. The Use of Mental Tests in an Educational or Vocational Guidance Program in Fourteen Cities. Summary. *National Vocational Guidance Association Bulletin* 1(8) (March): 131–.

——. 1926/7. Edgerton: Vocational Guidance and Counseling. *Journal of Personnel Research* 5 (May/April): 533–.

——. 1928. The Work of the Vocational Service for Juniors in New York City. *Vocational Guidance Magazine* 7(1) (October): 9–.

——. 1931. Junior Placement in Unemployment. *American Federationist* 38(12) (December): 1,470–.

——. 1931/2. Training Counselors by Apprenticeship. *Personnel Journal* 10: 329–.

——. 1932/3. Book Review of "How Workers Find Jobs" by deSchweinitz. *Personnel Journal* 11 (June/April): 187–.

——. 1935. Plans for Disseminating Occupational Information. *Occupations: The Vocational Guidance Magazine* 14(3) (December): 240–.

——. 1936. Guidance for Minority Groups. *Occupations: The Vocational Guidance Magazine* 14(6) (March): 555–.

——. 1936. Junior Employment Counseling under the National Youth Administration. *Child* 1(3) (September): 15–.

——. 1937. Present-day Youth and the NYA. *Occupations: The Vocational Guidance Magazine* 15(4) (January): 301–.

——. 1938. NYA Youth Placement. *Occupations: The Vocational Guidance Magazine* 16(8) (May): 737–.

——. 1939. Government Agencies and Vocational Guidance. *Occupations: The Vocational Guidance Magazine* 17(6) (March): 507–.

——. 1940. Expediting the NYA Program. *Child* 5(3) (September): 81–.

——. 1940. Job Hunts for Youth. *Occupations: The Vocational Guidance Magazine* 19(3) (December): 177–.

Hayes, Mary Holmes Stevens. Coauth. *See* Matthews, Ellen Nathalie.

Haynes, Dorothy. 1915. A Comparative Study of the Occupations of Men and Women, with Special Reference to Their Mutual Displacement, from the Census Returns, 1861–1911, with Diagrams. *Women's Industrial News* (October).

Haynes, Elizabeth Ross. 1921. *Unsung Heroes; the Black Boy in America; Negroes in Domestic Service in the United States.* New York: DuBois and Dill.

——. 1922. Two Million Negro Women at Work. *Southern Workman* 51 (February): 64–72.

——. 1923. Negroes in Domestic Service in the United States. M.A. thesis, Columbia University (sociology). Also published in *Journal of Negro History* 8 (October 1923): 384–442.

——. 1925. Margaret Murray Washington. *Opportunity* 3(31) (July): 207–.

Hazard [Sprague], Blanche Evans. 1913. The Organization of the Boot and Shoe Industry in Massachusetts before 1875. *Quarterly Journal of Economics* 27 (February): 236–62.

——. 1915. *The Life of Primitive Woman.* Ithaca, N.Y.: New York State College of Agriculture at Cornell University.

——. 1921. *The Organization of the Boot and Shoe Industry in Massachusetts Before 1875*. Cambridge, Mass.: Harvard University Press.

——. 1935. Jacob Adams' Shoemaking Accounts. *Business History Review* 9 (December): 86–92.

Hearst, Helen Louise. 1929. *The Coffee Industry of Central America*. S.M. thesis, University of Chicago (geography).

——. 1932. Coffee Industry of South America. *Economic Geography* 8(1) (January): 53–66.

Heather-Bigg, Ada. 1886. Female Labour in the Nail Trade. *Fortnightly Review*, n.s. 39 (January/June): 829–38.

——. 1889. Pocket-money Wages. Paper read at the Denison Club, January 16. *Charity Organisation Review* 52 (April): 164–9.

——. 1891. Women and the Glove Trade. *Nineteenth Century* 30 (December): 939–50.

——. 1893. What is Fashion? *Nineteenth Century* 33(192) (February): 235–48.

——. 1894. The Cry against Home Work. *Nineteenth Century* 36(214) (December): 970–86.

——. 1894. The Wife's Contribution to Family Income. *Economic Journal* 4(13) (March): 51–8.

Heggie, Helen E. 1928. Developments in Municipal Ownership of Electric Plants in Minnesota. *Land Economics* 4 (August): 289–94.

Helm, Florence. 1934. Country Banking in Missouri, 1920–1932. Ph.D. thesis, Yale University (economics).

——. 1939. *Banking Developments in Missouri, 1920–1936*. Sedalia, Mo.: Missouri Bankers Association.

Henderson, Bertha. 1922. *Farm Lands Available for Settlement*. Farmers' Bulletin, United States Department of Agriculture, no. 1271. Washington: U.S. Department of Agriculture.

——. 1924. *Buying a Farm in an Undeveloped Region*. U.S. Department of Agriculture Farmers' Bulletin, no. 1,385. Washington: U.S. Department of Agriculture.

——. 1926. State Policies in Agricultural Settlement. *Land Economics* 2 (July): 284–96; A Correction. *Land Economics* 3 (February 1927): 102–3.

Hennefrund, Helen Emma. 1938. *The Soybean Industry*. Washington: U.S. Government Printing Office.

Hennefrund, Helen Emma and Mary G. Lacy. 1939. *Part-time Farming in the United States: A Selected List of References*. Washington: U.S. Government Printing Office.

——. 1939. *The Peanut Industry: A Selected List of References on the Economic Aspects of the Industry, 1920–1939*. Washington: U.S. Government Printing Office.

Hennefrund, Helen Emma. Coauth. *See* Bercaw, Louise Oldham; Olcott, Margaret Thompson.

Hennell, Mary. 1844. *An Outline of the Various Social Systems and Communities Which Have Been Founded on the Principle of Co-operation*. London: Longman, Brown, Green, and Longmans. Originally published as an Appendix in Charles Bray,

The Philosophy of Necessity, or, The Law of Consequences as Applicable to Mental, Moral, and Social Science. London: Longman, Orme, Brown, Green, and Longmans, 1841.

Henrotin, Ellen. 1897. Women in Finance. *National Magazine, an Illustrated American Monthly* 7: 51–.

——. 1899. *The Attitude of Women's Clubs and Associations towards Social Economics.* Bulletin of the U.S. Department of Labor no. 23. Washington: U.S. Government Printing Office.

Henry, Alice. 1903/4. The Special Moral Training of Girls. *International Journal of Ethics* 14: 1–15.

——. 1906. Industrial Democracy: The Australian Labour Movement. *Outlook* (November 3): 566–70.

——. 1908. Suffrage Notes from Australia. *Public* 11(530) (May 29): 207–.

——. 1909. Book Review of "An Australian Indictment of English Civilization." *Public* 12(596) (September 3): 861–.

——. 1910. The Campaign in Illinois for the Ten-hour Law. *American Federationist* 17(8) (August): 669–.

——. 1910. Sociological Meetings in St. Louis. *Public* 13(634) (May 27): 485–.

——. 1910. Women and the Trade-union Movement in the United States. In Helen Marot, ed., *The Economic Position of Women.* New York: Academy of Political Science. Also published in Henry Raymond Mussey, ed., *Proceedings of the Academy of Political Science in the City of New York.* New York: Columbia University.

——. 1910. The Women's Trade Union League. *Public* 13(644) (August 5): 738–.

——. 1915. *The Trade Union Woman.* New York: Appleton.

——. 1916/17. Book Review of "The Trade Union Woman" by Nathan Fine. *International Journal of Ethics* 27: 532–.

——. 1918. The Education Situation in England. *American Teacher* 7(5/6) (May/June): 113.

——. 1923. *Women and the Labor Movement.* New York: George H. Doran Co.; New York: Macmillan Co., 1927.

——. Edited Life and Labor, monthly publication of the U.S. Women's Trade Union League, 1911–1915.

——. Papers held at the National Library of Australia.

Herb, Mamie Idella. 1931. *Business and Banking Periodicals Reviewing the Business Situation.* Washington: U.S. Government Printing Office.

——. 1935. *Consumption of Fruits and Vegetables in the United States.* Washington: U.S. Government Printing Office.

Herb, Mamie Idella and Louise O. Bercaw. 1929. *Olives and Olive Oil; Selected References on the Culture of Olives and the Economic Aspects of the Industry.* Washington: U.S. Department of Agriculture.

Herb, Mamie Idella and Marion Etta Wheeler. 1939. *Agricultural Relief Measures Relating to the Raising of Farm Prices – 75th Congress, January 5, 1937 to June 16, 1938.* U.S. Bureau of Agricultural Economics Bibliography no. 76. Washington: U.S. Government Printing Office.

Herb, Mamie Idella, Louise Oldham Bercaw, Vajen Eilleen Hitz Fischer, and Marion Etta Wheeler. 1927. *Agricultural Relief Measures Relating to the Raising of Farm Prices*. Washington: U.S. Bureau of Agricultural Economics.

Herb, Mamie Idella. Coauth. *See* Bercaw, Louise Oldham.

Herbert, Lady Lea. 1875. The Workhouse Children. *Irish Monthly* 3: 119–.

Herbst, Alma. 1930. The Negro in the Slaughtering and Meat Packing Industry in Chicago. Ph.D. thesis, University of Chicago (economics).

——. 1932. *The Negro in the Slaughtering and Meat-packing Industry in Chicago*. Hart, Schaffner & Marx prize essays, 52. Boston: Houghton Mifflin.

Héricourt, Jenny d'. 1860. *La Femme affranchie: Réponse a Mm. Michelet, Proudhon, E. de Girardin, A. Comte et aux autres novateurs modernes*. 2 vols. Brussels: A. Lacroix. English ed., *A Woman's Philosophy of Woman: An Answer to Michelet, Proudhon, Girardin, Legouvé, Comte, and Other Modern Innovators*. New York: Carleton, 1864.

Hernaman, Irene. 1915. A Bibliography on Displacement. *Women's Industrial News* (October).

Herrick, Dr. Mary E. 1892. The Tenement House and the Children. *Journal of Social Science* 29 (August): 25–33.

Herring, Harriet L[aura]. 1923. Personnel Studies in Southern Industries – A Study of Labor Turnover. *Journal of Social Forces* 1(3) (March): 245.

——. 1925. Morituri te salutamus. *Journal of Social Forces* 3(3) (March): 511–12.

——. 1926. The Beginnings of Industrial Social Work. *Social Forces* 5(2) (December): 317–24.

——. 1926. Book Review of "Welfare Work in Industry" by Kelly. *Social Forces* 5(1/4): 193–.

——. 1927. The Beginnings of Industrial Social Work. *Social Forces* 5(3) (March): 502–7.

——. 1927/8. Book Review of "The Young Employed Girl" by Ormsbee. *Social Forces* 6(1/4): 498–.

——. 1928. Tracing the Development of Welfare Work in the North Carolina Textile Industry. *Social Forces* 6(4) (June): 591–8.

——. 1928. Working Mothers and Their Children. *Family* 9(7) (November): 234–.

——. 1929. *Welfare Work in Mill Villages: The Story of Extra-mill Activities in North Carolina*. Chapel Hill, N.C.: University of North Carolina Press.

——. 1929. Cycles of Cotton Mill Criticism. *South Atlantic Quarterly (SAMLA)* 28: 113–.

——. 1930. *Worker and Public in the Southern Textile Problem*. Greensboro, N.C.: Industrial Seminar for Ministers.

——. 1930. The Social Problem of Labor Organization Casualties. *Social Forces* 9(2) (December): 267–73.

——. 1930. Toward Preliminary Social Analysis: I. The Southern Mill System Faces a New Issue. *Social Forces* 8(3) (March): 350–9.

——. 1930/1. Book Review of "I Go South" by Shumway. *Social Forces* 9(1/4): 427.

——. 1930/1. Book Review of "The Industrial Revolution in the South" by Broadus Mitchell and George S. Mitchell. *Social Forces* 9(1/4): 427.

——. 1930/1. Book Review of "Industrial Village Churches" by Brunner. *Social Forces* 9(1/4): 427.

——. 1930/1. Book Review of "Leave Me with a Smile" by Springs. *Social Forces* 9(1/4): 427.

——. 1930/1. Book Review of "Soldiers of Progress and Industry" by Hornady. *Social Forces* 9(1/4): 427.

——. 1930/1. Book Review of "Strike!" by Vorse. *Social Forces* 9(1/4): 427.

——. 1931. Early Industrial Development in the South. *American Academy of Political and Social Science, Annals* 153 (January): 1–.

——. 1931. Social Development in the Mill Village: A Challenge to the Mill Welfare Worker. *Social Forces* 10(2) (December): 264–71.

——. 1933. Industrial relations in the South and the NIRA. *Social Forces* 12(1) (October): 124–31.

——. 1933. Book Review of "Beyond Desire" by Anderson. *Social Forces* 11(1/4): 295.

——. 1933. Book Review of "Call Home the Heart" by Burke. *Social Forces* 11(1/4): 295.

——. 1933. Book Review of "Sand in My Shoes" by Ripley. *Social Forces* 11(1/4): 295.

——. 1933. Book Review of "To Make My Bread" by Lumpkin. *Social Forces* 11(1/4): 295.

——. 1934/5. Some Costs of Economy in Schools. *Social Forces* 13(1) (October): 85–91.

——. 1936/7. Book Review of "A Footnote to Folly: Reminiscences of Mary Heaton Vorse." *Social Forces* 15(1/4): 136.

——. 1938. The Clement Attachment: An Episode of Reconstruction Industrial History. *Journal of Southern History* 4 (February/November): 185–.

——. 1938/9. Book Review of "Mingled Yarn" by Ethridge. *Social Forces* 17(1/4): 616.

——. 1939. The Outside Employer in the Southern Industrial Pattern. *Social Forces* 18(1) (October): 115–26.

——. 1939/40. Book Review of "Between the Devil" by Edmunds. *Social Forces* 18(1/4): 594.

——. 1939/40. Book Review of "Boss Man" by Cochran. *Social Forces* 18(1/4): 615.

——. 1939/40. Book Review of "Child Labor Legislation in the Southern Textile States" by Davidson. *Social Forces* 18(1/4): 601–.

——. 1939/40. Book Review of "Unions of Their Own Choosing" by Brooks. *Social Forces* 18(1/4): 612–.

——. 1940. *Southern Industry and Regional Development.* Chapel Hill, N.C.: University of North Carolina Press.

——. 1940/1. Book Review of "The City on the Hill" by Sims. *Social Forces* 19(1/4): 591–.

——. 1940/1. Book Review of "Industrial Opportunity in the Tennessee Valley of Northwestern Alabama" by Otte. *Social Forces* 19(1/4): 448–.

——. 1940/1. Book Review of "Holyoke, Massachusetts: A Case History of the Industrial Revolution in America" by Green. *Social Forces* 19(1/4): 138–.

——. 1940/1. Book Review of "The South in Progress" by Lumpkin. *Southern Economic Journal* 7(1/4): 429–.

Herring, Harriet L., Rutillius Harrison Allen, Leonard S. Cottrell, Willard W. Troxell, and A. D. Edwards. 1937. *Part-time Farming in the Southeast.* Washington: Works Progress Administration.

Herring, Harriet L., Rupert B. Yance, and Thomas J. Woofter. 1935. *A Survey of the Catawba Valley: a Study Made by the Institute for Research in Social Science for the Tennesse Valley Authority.* Chapel Hill, N.C.: University of North Carolina.

Herring, Harriet L. Papers held at the University of North Carolina, Chapel Hill.

Herrmann, Helen. 1938. *Ten Years of Work Experience of Philadelphia Machinists.* National Research Project on Reemployment Opportunities and Recent Changes in Industrial Techniques, Philadelphia Labor Market Studies [Report no. P–5]. Philadelphia: University of Pennsylvania, Wharton School of Finance and Commerce, Industrial Research Department.

Herron, Belva Mary. 1905. *The Progress of Labor Organization among Women: Together with Some Considerations Concerning Their Place in Industry.* Urbana, Ill.: University of Illinois Press.

——. 1907. Factory Inspection in the United States. *American Journal of Sociology* 12(4) (January): 487–99.

Hertzler, Joyce Oramel. 1920. The History of Utopian Thought. Ph.D. thesis, University of Wisconsin–Madison (sociology).

——. 1923. *The History of Utopian Thought.* New York: Macmillan Company.

——. 1924. Book Review of "Lindeman's Social Discovery." *Journal of Philosophy* 21(20) (September 25): 557–.

——. 1925/6. The Sociological Uses of History. *American Journal of Sociology* 31(1/6): 173–.

——. 1927. On the Board of Directors of the National Council for the Social Studies. *American Sociological Society, Papers and Proceedings* 22 (December): 310–.

——. 1927/8. Unsocial Trends. *Sociology and Social Research* 12: 512–.

——. 1928. *Social Progress: A Theoretical Survey and Analysis.* New York and London: Century Co.

——. 1929. *Social Institutions.* 1st ed. New York: McGraw-Hill Book Company, Inc.

——. 1930/1. Book Review of "Man's Social Destiny" by Charles A. Ellwood. *American Journal of Sociology* 36(1/6): 164–.

——. 1931/2. The Desirability and the Possibility of an Examination of the Social Thought of the Ancient Civilizations. *Social Forces* 10(1/4): 328–.

——. 1932/3. The Social Wisdom of the Primitives with Special Reference to Their Proverbs. *Social Forces* 11(1/4): 313–.

——. 1933. Book Review of "American Population Before the Federal Census of 1790" by Evarts B. Greene and Virginia D. Harrington. *American Academy of Political and Social Science, Annals* 167 (March): 246–.

——. 1933. Book Review of "Salaries and the Cost of Living in Twenty-seven State Universities and Colleges 1913–1932" by Viva Boothe. *American Academy of Political and Social Science, Annals* 167 (March): 236–.

——. 1933/4. On Golden Rules. *International Journal of Ethics* 44: 418–.

——. 1933/4. The Social Wisdom in the Ancient Egyptian Precepts. *Social Forces* 12(1/4): 174–.

——. 1934. Book Review of "Institutional Behavior" by Floyd Henry Allport. *American Academy of Political and Social Science, Annals* 171 (January): 296–.

——. 1934. Book Review of "Social Change and Social Problems" by James H. S. Bossard. *American Academy of Political and Social Science, Annals* 176 (November): 243–.

——. 1934. Race Relations and Certain Frontiers. Paper selected from the proceedings of the twenty-eighth annual meeting of the American sociological society. In Edward Byron Reuter, ed., *Race and Culture Contacts.* New York and London: McGraw-Hill Book Co.

——. 1935. Book Review of "Contemporary American Institutions" by F. Stuart Chapin. *American Academy of Political and Social Science, Annals* 182 (November): 221–.

——. 1936. *The Social Thought of the Ancient Civilizations.* 1st ed. New York and London: McGraw-Hill Book Company, Inc.

——. 1936. Book Review of "The Middle Classes Then and Now" by Franklin Charles Palm. *American Academy of Political and Social Science, Annals* 188 (November): 377–.

——. 1936. Book Review of "Preface to a Christian Sociology" by Cyril E. Hudson. *American Sociological Review* 1(1/6): 1,028–.

——. 1936. Book Review of "Die Religion der Ägypter" by Adolph Erman. *American Sociological Review* 1(1/6): 872–.

——. 1937. Book Review of "The Natural History of a Social Institution – the Y.W.C.A." by Mary S. Sims. *American Sociological Review* 2(1/6): 295.

——. 1937. Book Review of "Principles and Laws of Sociology" by Harold A. Phelps. *American Academy of Political and Social Science, Annals* 190 (March): 251–.

——. 1937. Book Review of "Social Institutions" by Lloyd Vernor Ballard. *American Sociological Review* 2(1/6): 295.

——. 1937/8. Book Review of "Culture and Conscience" by William Creighton Graham and Herbert Gordon May. *American Journal of Sociology* 43(1/6): 501–.

——. 1938. American Regionalism and the Regional Sociological Society. *American Sociological Review* 3(1/6): 738–.

——. 1938. Book Review of "Never to Die: The Egyptians in Their Own Words Selected and Arranged with Commentary" by Josephine Mayer and Tom Prideux. *American Sociological Review* 3(1/6): 913.

——. 1938. Book Review of "Sacrifices in Ancient Israel: Their Origins, Purposes and Development" by W. O. E. Oesterley. *American Sociological Review* 3(1/6): 913.

——. 1938/9. The Typical Life Cycle of Dictatorships. *Social Forces* 17(1/4): 303–.

——. 1939. Book Review of "Maximilien Robespierre: Nationalist Dictator" by James Michael Eagan. *American Sociological Review* 4(1/6): 123–.

——. 1939. Book Review of "Political Institutions: A Preface" by Edward McChesney Sait. *American Sociological Review* 4(1/6): 125–.

——. 1939/40. Book Review of "Society in Transition" by Harry Elmer Barnes. *American Journal of Sociology* 45(1/6): 941–.

——. 1939/40. The Causal and Contributory Factors of Dictatorship. *Sociology and Social Research* 24: 3–.

——. 1939/40. The Effects of Dictatorship. *Sociology and Social Research* 24: 111–.

——. 1939/40. Some Notes on the Social Psychology of Regionalism. *Social Forces* 18(1/4): 331–.

——. 1939/40. Some Sociological Aspects of American Regionalism. *Social Forces* 18(1/4): 17–.

——. 1940. Book Review of "The Incorrigible Idealist" by Elinor Pancoast and Anne E. Lincoln. *American Academy of Political and Social Science, Annals* 212 (November): 273–.

——. 1940. Crises and Dictatorships. Comment by Clifford Kirkpatrick. *American Sociological Review* 5(1/6): 157–.

——. 1940. On Golden Ages: Then and Now. *South Atlantic Quarterly (SAMLA)* 39: 318–.

——. 1940/1. Book Review of "The Social Mind: Foundations of Social Philosophy" by John Elof Boodin. *American Journal of Sociology* 46(1/6): 257–.

Herzfeld, Elsa G. 1905. Superstitions and Customs of Tenement-house. *Charities; a Weekly Review of Local and General Philanthropy* 14: 983.

——. 1905. The Tenement-house Family. *Independent* 59: 1,520.

——. 1906. *Family Monographs: The History of Twenty-four Families Living in the Middle West Side of New York City*. New York: Publisher of Charities.

Hess, Edith. 1922. State Regulation of Woman and Child Labor in Kansas. M.A. thesis, University of Kansas.

Hewart, Beatrice. 1898. The Wages of London Vestry Employees. *Economic Journal* 8(31) (September): 407–14.

——. 1900. The Cloth Trade in the North of England in the Sixteenth and Seventeenth Centuries. *Economic Journal* 10 (March): 20–31.

Hewes, Amy. 1899/1900. Seminar Notes: Social Institutions and the Riemann Surface. *American Journal of Sociology* 5(1/6): 392–.

——. 1903. The Part of Invention in the Social Process. Ph.D. thesis, University of Chicago (sociology).

——. 1915. *Industrial Home Work in Massachusetts*. Boston: Women's Educational and Industrial Union, Labor Bulletin No. 101.

——. 1915. Book Review of "The Middle West Side: A Historical Sketch." *American Economic Review* 5 (September): 629–30.

——. 1915. Book Review of "Mothers Who Must Earn." *American Economic Review* 5 (September): 629–30.

——. 1917. *Women as Munition Makers: A Study of Conditions in Bridgeport, Connecticut.* New York: Russell Sage Foundation.

——. 1918. *Work of the Women's Branch of the Industrial Service Section in the Chicago District from April 23, 1918 to December 13, 1918.* Chicago: United States Army Ordnance Department Industrial Service Section.

——. 1919. Dependents of College Teachers. *Journal of the American Statistical Association* 16 (December): 502–11.

——. 1919. The Training Course for Health Officers. *Intercollegiate Community Service Quarterly* 4(3) (April): 11–.

——. 1920. Book Review of "Working Life of Women in the Seventeenth Century." *American Economic Review* 10 (September): 577–81.

——. 1920. Labor Conditions in Soviet Russia. Note. *Journal of Political Economy* 28(9) (November): 774–83.

——. 1922. The Attitude of the Soviet Government toward Cooperation. *Journal of Political Economy* 30(3) (June): 412–16.

——. 1922. Guild Socialism: A Two Years' Test. *American Economic Review* 12(2) (June): 209–37.

——. 1922. Russian Wage Systems under Communism. *Journal of Political Economy* 30(2) (April): 274–8.

——. 1922. Standardization of Tapping Test. Mount Holyoke College, Hadley, Mass. *Journal of Applied Psychology* 6: 113–.

——. 1923. Trade Union Development in Soviet Russia. *American Economic Review* 13(4) (December): 618–37.

——. 1923. Russian Industry under Labor Union Rule. *Current History (New York)* 18(3) (June): 456–.

——. 1923/4. Note on the Racial and Educational Factors in the Declining Birth-rate. *American Journal of Sociology* 29(2) (September): 178–87.

——. 1924. Book Review of "The Cooperative Movement in Russia." *American Economic Review* 14(4) (December): 787.

——, ed. 1925. *Women Workers and Family Support: A Study Made by Students in Economics Courses at Bryn Mawr Summer School.* Washington: U.S. Government Printing Office.

——. 1925. The Changing Structure of the Bargaining Unit of Labor. *Quarterly Journal of Economics* 39(4) (August): 612–34.

——. 1925. A Study of Delinquent Girls at Sleighton Farm. Assisted by Misses Arnold, Buck, Merriam and Stockover. *Journal of the American Institute of Criminal Law and Criminology and Police Science* 15(4) (February): 598–.

——. 1926. *Changing Jobs: A Study Made by Students in the Economics Course under the Direction of Prof. Amy Hewes.* Bulletin of the Women's Bureau, no. 54. Washington: U.S. Government Printing Office.

——. 1926. Book Review of "Protective Labor Legislation with Special Reference to Women in the State of New York." *American Economic Review* 16(3) (September): 498–9.

——. 1926. The Task of the English Coal Commission. *Journal of Political Economy* 34(1) (February): 1–12.

——. 1927. Book Review of "The Woman Worker and the Trade Unions." *American Economic Review* 17(3) (September): 526–9.

——. 1927. Bryn Mawr Summer School. *American Federationist* 32(7/12) (July/December): 654–.

——. 1927. The Injured Workman under the New York Compensation Law. *Social Service Review* 1(1/4) (March/December): 606–.

——. 1927. The Savings of Women Workers. *American Federationist* 34(1/6) (January): 72–.

——. 1928. Functional Representation in the International Labor Organization. *American Political Science Review* 22(2) (May): 324–38.

——. 1929/30. Municipal Spending. *Social Forces* 8(1/4): 274–.

——. 1930. *The Contribution of Economics to Social Work.* New York: Columbia University Press.

——. 1930. Economic Myths. *Social Service Review* 4(1/4) (March/December): 23–.

——. 1930. France's Social Insurance Laws. *Current History (New York)* 32(6) (September): 1,150–.

——. 1930/1. Electrical Appliances in the Home. *Social Forces* 9(1/4): 235–.

——. 1932. Employment of Older Persons in Springfield (Mass.) Department Stores. U.S. Bureau of Labor Statistics, *Monthly Labor Review* 35(4) (October): 773–.

——. 1932. The Transformation of Soviet Trade Unions. *American Economic Review* 22(4) (December): 605–19.

——. 1933. *Women Workers in the Third Year of the Depression: A Study made by Students in the Economics Courses at the Bryn Mawr Summer School.* Washington: U.S. Government Printing Office.

——. 1933. The Conference at Work. *American Academy of Political and Social Science, Annals* 166 (March): 86–.

——. 1934. Britain's Care of the Jobless. *Current History (New York)* 41(3) (December): 284–.

——. 1935. Why Pupils Leave High School. *School Review* 43 : 287–94.

——. 1935. Women Wage Earners and the NRA. *American Federationist* 42(2) (February): 155–.

——. 1939. Review of Holyoke, Massachusetts: A Case History of the Industrial Revolution in America. *American Economic Review* 29(4) (December): 823–6.

——. 1940/1. Recent Municipal Spending. *Social Forces* 19(1/4): 547–.

Hewes, Amy, Raymond T. Bye, Broadus Mitchell, William W. Hewett, Paul M. O'Leary, and Maynard Krueger. 1940. Round Table on Problems in Teaching Economics. *American Economics Review Supplement* 30(1) (March): 106–11.

Heyman, Eleanor. 1933. The Value of the Service: Its Various Meanings and Uses. *Land Economics* 9 (August): 252–65.

[Heyrick,] Elizabeth Coltman. 1824. *Immediate, Not Gradual Abolition; or, An Inquiry into the Shortest, Safest, and Most Effectual Means of Getting Rid of West Indian Slavery*. London: J. Hatchard & Son; New York: J. V. Seaman, 1825.

——. 1828. *Apology for Ladies' Anti-slavery Associations*. London: J. Hatchard and Son.

——. 1828. *Appeal to the Hearts and Consciences of British Women*. Leicester: A. Cockshaw.

——. 1829. *No British Slavery, or, An Invitation to the People to Put a Speedy End to It*. Birmingham: B. Hudson; London: J. Hatchard.

Hicks, Amie. 1885. Women and Socialism. *Justice* (25 April).

Hicks, Frances. 1896. Dressmakers and Tailoresses. In Frank W. Galton, ed., *Workers on Their Industries*. London: Charles Scribner & Sons.

Hicks, Ursula K. 1934. Taxation and Production: The Wicksell Analysis. *Review of Economic Studies* 2(1) (October): 18–30.

——. 1935. Local Public Debt in England and Wales. *Economica* 2(6) (May): 204–19.

——. 1936. Some Effects of Financial Policy on the Distribution of Income in Great Britain Since the War. *International Labour Review* 34 (November): 594–617.

——. 1937. Book Review of "Co-ordination and Planning in the Local Authority" by H. R. Page. *Economic Journal* 47: 734.

——. 1937. Book Review of "An Introduction to Economic Analysis and Policy" by J. E. Meade. *Economic Journal* 47: 90.

——. 1937. Book Review of "The Making of Moscow" by E. D. Simon *et al*. *Economic Journal* 47: 734.

——. 1937. Book Review of "The Ratepayer's Money" by A. Collins. *Economic Journal* 47: 734.

——. 1937. Book Review of "Sweden: The Middle Way" by M. W. Childs. *Economic Journal* 47: 342.

——. 1938. *The Finance of British Government, 1920–1936*. London: Oxford University Press.

——. 1938. Book Review of "A Century of City Government" by Shena D. Simon. *Economic Journal* 48(191) (September): 537–40.

——. 1938. Book Review of "Miti e Paradossi della Giustizia Tributaria" by L. Einaudi. *Economic Journal* 48: 719.

——. 1938. Book Review of "Personal Income Taxation" by H. C. Simons. *Economic Journal* 48: 719.

——. 1938. Review of Central and Local Finance in Germany and England. *Economic Journal* 48(190): 287–9.

——. 1939/40. Book Review of "English Grants in Aid" by H. R. Bowen. *Economic History Review* 10: 183–.

——. 1940. Book Review of "La Politica Annonaria dell'Italia durante la Grande Guerra" by U. Ricci. *Economica* 7: 348–.

——. 1940. *The Taxation of Excess Profits in Wartime*. Manchester: Norbury, Lockwood.

Hidy, Muriel E. 1939. George Peabody, Merchant and Financier, 1829–1854. Ph.D. thesis, Radcliffe College (economics).

Higgs, Mary Kingsland. 1904. *How to Deal with the Unemployed*. London: S. C. Brown, Langham & Company, Ltd.

——. 1904. *The Tramp Ward*. Manchester and London: John Heywood. Also printed in the *Contemporary Review* 85 (May 1904): 649–.

——. 1904. Tramps and Wanderers. *Nineteenth Century and After, a Monthly Review* 56: 55.

——. 1905. The Geology of Society. *Contemporary Review* 87 (January/June): 552–.

——. 1905. *Three Nights in Women's Lodging Houses*. Pamphlet. Oldham: Printed for private circulation.

——. 1906. *Glimpses into the Abyss*. London: P. S. King and Son.

——. 1906. Mankind in the Making. *Contemporary Review* 89 (January/June): 830–.

——. 1912. *How to Start a Women's Lodging Home*. Pamphlet. London: P. S. King.

——. 1914. *My Brother the Tramp: Studies in the Problem of Vagrancy*. London: Student Christian Movement.

——. 1924. *Down and Out: Studies in the Problem of Vagrancy, Being a Revised Edition of My Brother the Tramp*. London: Student Christian Movement.

——. 1928. *Casuals and Their Casual Treatment*. Pamphlet. London: King.

——. 1931. *Where Shall He Live?* London: P. S. King.

Higgs, Mary and Edward E. Hayward. 1910. *Where Shall She Live? The Homelessness of the Woman Worker*. Written for the National Association for Women's Lodging-houses. London: P. S. King & Son.

Hilbourne, Charlotte S. 1863. *Effie and I, or Seven Years in a Cotton Mill: A Story of the Spindle City*. Cambridge, Mass.: Allen and Farnham.

Hilfer, Irma. 1938. Differential Effect in the Butter Market. *Econometrica* 6 (July): 270–84.

Hill, Alicia. 1853. American Slavery and "Uncle Tom's Cabin." *North British Review* 18 (January): 235–58.

——. 1853. Free and Slave Labour. *North British Review* 19 (August): 445–61.

Hill, Caroline Miles. 1898. On Choice. *American Journal of Psychology* 9: 587–90.

——. 1902. Book Review of "Democracy and Social Ethics" by Jane Addams. *American Academy of Political and Social Science, Annals* 20 (July/December): 424–.

——. 1904. The Economic Value of the Home [Book Review of "The Home, Its Work, and Its Influence" by Gilman]. *Journal of Political Economy* 12 (June): 408–19.

——. 1907. Voluntary Organizations, a Proposed Study in Social Psychology. *Psychological Bulletin* 4: 375–.

——. 1907/8. Book Review of "What is History?" by Karl Lamprecht. *American Journal of Sociology* 13(1/6): 278–.

Hill, Caroline R. Coauth. *See* Smith, Mrs. Corinna Haven Putnam.

Hill, Florence Davenport. 1868. *Children of the State: The Training of Juvenile Paupers*. London: Macmillan.

——. 1869. *The Boarding-out System Distinguished from Baby Farming and Parish Apprenticeship: A Paper Read before the National Association for the Promotion of Social Science, at Bristol, October 5th, 1869*. Bristol: Arrowsmith.

——. 1870. The Family System for Workhouse Children. *Contemporary Review* 15 (September): 240–73.

——. 1884. *The Boarding-out System – Discussion in the Plymouth Court of Guardians on the Boarding-out System Which Was followed by Its Unanimous Adoption*. London: Knight & Co.

——. 1893. The System of Boarding-out Pauper Children. *Economic Journal* 3(9) (March): 62–73.

Hill, Georgiana. 1896. *Women in English Life from Medieval to Modern Times*. 2 vols. London: Richard Bentley.

Hill, Joanna Margaret. 1868. How Can We Eradicate the Pauper Taint from Our Workhouse Children? Paper read at the Social Science Congress held at Birmingham, 1868. Birmingham: s.n.

——. 1873. Workhouse Girls: What They Are and How to Help Them. *Macmillan's* 28 (June): 132–9.

——. 1875. Homes for the Homeless. *Macmillan's* 32 (June): 133–40.

——. 1890. The Poor Law Act of 1889, as Affecting Deserted Children, with Special Reference to the Clause Concerning Compulsory Payment by Parents. Paper read at the West Midland Poor Law Conference, Malvern, May 1890. London: Knight.

——. 1896. The Pseudo and the Real "Cottage Homes" for Pauper Children. *Westminster Review* 146 (December): 660–75.

Hill, Miss Miranda. 1888. Life on Thirty Shillings a Week. *Nineteenth Century* 23 (January/June): 458–63.

Hill, Octavia. 1866. Cottage Property in London. *Fortnightly Review* 6 (November): 681.

——. 1869. The Importance of Aiding the Poor Without Almsgiving. Paper read at the National Association for the Promotion of Social Science.

——. 1869. Organized Work among the Poor: Suggestions Founded on Four Years' Management of a London Court. *Macmillan's Magazine* 20 (July): 219–26.

——. 1871. Blank Court; or, Landlords and Tenants. *Macmillan's Magazine* 24 (October): 456–65.

——. 1872. The Work of Volunteers in the Organization of Charity. *Macmillan's Magazine* 26 (October): 441–.

——. 1873–1907. *Letter to My Fellow-workers, to Which Are Added Accounts of Donations Received for Work among the Poor during 1894*. London: George Pulman (published annually).

——. 1874. The Homes of the London Poor. *Macmillan's Magazine* 30 (June): 131–8.

——. 1875. *Homes of the London Poor*. London: Macmillan & Co.

——. 1875. Space for the People. *Macmillan's Magazine* 32 (August): 328.

——. 1876. A More Excellent Way of Charity. *Macmillan's Magazine* 35 (December): 126–31.

——. 1876. Our Common Land. *Macmillan's Magazine* 33 (April): 536–9.

——. 1876. A Word on Good Citizenship. *Fortnightly Review*, n.s. 20 (September): 321–.

——. 1877. *Our Common Land (and Other Short Essays)*. London: Macmillan.

——. 1877. *District Visiting*. London: Longmans, Green and Co.

——. 1877. The Future of our Commons. *Fortnightly Review*, n.s. 22 (November): 631–41.

——. 1883. Common Sense and the Dwellings of the Poor. *Nineteenth Century* 14(82) (December): 925–33.

——. 1884. Colour, Space and Music for the People. *Nineteenth Century* 15 (May): 741–52.

——. 1886. Amateur Work. *Lend a Hand* 1(1) (January): 36–.

——. 1888. More Air for London. *Nineteenth Century* 23 (February): 181–8.

——. 1889. A Few Words to Fresh Workers. *Nineteenth Century* 26 (September): 452–61.

——. 1889. On the Charity Organisation Society. *Charity Organisation Review* 52 (April): 162–.

——. 1891. Our Dealings with the Poor. *Nineteenth Century* 30 (August): 161–70.

——. 1892. Influence on Character. In Charles Booth, ed., *Life and Labour of the People in London*, vol. 3. London: Macmillan.

——. 1893. Trained Workers for the Poor. *Nineteenth Century* 33 (January): 36–43.

——. 1894. Our Poor. *Lend a Hand* 12(1) (January): 54.

——. 1898. The Need of Thoroughness in Charitable Work. *Charity Organisation Review* 23 (November): 233–9.

——. 1899. The Open Spaces of the Future. *Nineteenth Century* 46 (July): 26–35.

——. 1901. The Relations between Rich and Poor. *Charity Organisation Review* 54 (June): 306–.

——. 1905. Natural Beauty as a National Asset. *Nineteenth Century and After* 58 (July/December): 935–.

——. 1909. *Memorandum on the Report of the Royal Commission on the Poor Laws and Relief of Distress....* London: P. S. King & Son.

——. 1921. *House Property & Its Management: Some Papers on the Methods of Management Introduced by Miss Octavia Hill and Adapted to Modern Conditions*. London: G. Allen & Unwin.

—— [unsigned]. 1934. *Housing Estate Management by Women (Being an Account of the Development of the Work Initiated by Octavia Hill)*. London: Society of Women Housing Estate Managers.

——. Coauth. *See* Chase, Ellen.

Hill, Polly. 1940. *The Unemployment Services, a Report Prepared for the Fabian Society*. London: G. Routledge & Sons.

Hillel, Felicia. 1885/6. Scientific Farming. *Chautauquan* 6 (October/July): 161–.

——. 1886/7. Pensions and Pensioners. *Chautauquan* 7 (October/July): 549–.

——. 1889/90. Working-girls. *Chautauquan* 10 (October/March): 328–.

Hillyer, Cecile May. 1937. Relief and Housing of Unattached Women in Chicago. M.A. thesis, University of Chicago (sociology, public and social welfare).

——. Coauth. *See* Byrne, Harriet Anne.

Hirschler, Diana. 1894. Union in Philadelphia. *Arena* 9(4) (March): 548–52.

Hirschmann, Ida. 1935. The Surplus of Women and the Declining Birth Rate. *Sociological Review* 27 (July): 344–58.

Hirst, Margaret E[sther]. 1909. *Life of Friedrich List and Selections from His Writings*. With an introduction by F. W. Hirst. London: Smith, Elder.

——. 1913. *The Story of Trusts*. London: Collins.

Hoar, Hannah Marceline [Dayle]. 1924. *Chicle and Chewing Gum: A Review of Chicle Production and Sources of Supply, and the Chewing Gum Industry and Trade*. Bureau of Foreign and Domestic Commerce (Department of Commerce) Trade Information Bulletin, no. 197. Washington: U.S. Government Printing Office.

——. 1924. *World Trade in Chromite*. Washington: U.S. Bureau of Foreign and Domestic Commerce.

——. 1926. *Potash: Significance of Foreign Control and Economic Needs of Domestic Development*. Washington: U.S. Bureau of Foreign and Domestic Commerce.

——. 1930. *The Coal Industry of the World with Special Reference to International Trade in Coal*. Washington: U.S. Bureau of Foreign and Domestic Commerce.

Hobart, Lady [Mary]. 1884. *Help for the Helpless: London's Bitter Cry Hushed in Canada*. East London Family Emigration Society. London: J.F. Shaw.

Hobart-Hampden [Donaldson], Lady Albinia. 1898. The Working Girl of To-day. *Nineteenth Century* 43 (May): 724–30.

Hobbs, Margaret A. 1918. War Time Employment of Women. *American Labor Legislation Review 8* (December): 332–8.

——. Coauth. *See* Andrews, Irene Osgood.

Hobhouse, Emily. 1900. Dust-women. *Economic Journal* 10(39) (September): 411–20.

——. 1900. Women Workers: How They Live, How They Wish to Live. *Nineteenth Century* (March): 471–.

——. 1901. Concentration Camps. *Contemporary Review* 80 (July/December): 528–.

——. 1909. The People's Suffrage Federation [letter to the editor]. *Nation* 6(3) (October 16): 121–.

——. 1914. A Song for Humanity [letter to the editor]. *Nation* 16(3) (October 17): 65.

——. 1915. A New Kind of Munition [letter to the editor]. *Nation* 17(13) (June 26): 421–.

——. 1915. Prisoners of War [letter to the editor]. *Nation* 16(18) (January 30): 558–.

——. 1916. A German Official's View of Peace [letter to the editor]. *Nation* 20(3) (October 21): 113–.

Hobson, Elizabeth Christophers Kimball and Charlotte Everett Wise Hopkins. 1896. *A Report Concerning the Colored Women of the South*. Baltimore: Trustees of the John F. Slater Fund. J. Murphy & Co., Printers.

Hobson, Florence. 1895. Sex Prejudice and Women's Progress. *Humanitarian* 6 (June): 442–.

Hodge, Margaret. 1898. Technical Education in Germany. *Australian Economist* VI(4): 25–9.

Hodgen, Margaret Trabue. 1920. *Factory Work for Girls*. New York: Woman's Press.

——. 1925. *Workers' Education in England and the United States*. London: K. Paul, Trench, Trubner & Co., Ltd.

——. 1925. Workers' Education in England and the United States. Ph.D. thesis, University of California–Berkeley (education).

Hodgson, Geraldine Emma. 1909. *The Parliamentary Vote and Wages*. London: National Union of Women's Suffrage Societies.

Hoerle, Helen Christine and Florence B. Saltzberg, 1919. *The Girl and the Job*. New York: Henry Holt.

Hoey, Jane M. 1936. *Aid to Dependent Children under the Social Security Act*. Washington: Bureau of Public Assistance, Social Security Board.

——. 1936. *Public Assistance under the Social Security Act for the Needy Aged, the Needy Blind, Dependent Children*. Washington: Bureau of Public Assistance, Social Security Board.

Hoffman, H. 1935. *Landwirtschaft und Industrie in Württemberg insbesondere im Industriegebiet der Schwäbischen Alb. Zum wirtschaftlichen Schicksal Europas, II*. Berlin: Junker and Dünnhaupt.

Hogarth [Courtney], Janet E. 1896. The German Insurance Laws. *Economic Journal* 6(22) (June): 283–94.

——. 1897. Book Review of "Der Arbeiterschutz" by Dr. Kuno Frankenstein. *Economic Journal* 7(26) (June): 252–3.

——. 1897. The Monstrous Regiment of Women. *Fortnightly Review* 62: 926–36.

Hogg, Edith F. 1887. The Fur-pullers of South London. *Nineteenth Century* 42 (November): 734–43.

——. 1887. School Children as Wage Earners. *Nineteenth Century* 42 (August): 235–44.

——. 1900. Wage-earning Children. *Economic Review*.

Hogg, Margaret Hope. 1921. Dependents on Women Wage Earners. *Economica* 1 (January): 69–86; (May): 111–12.

——. 1927. The Determination of the Mean Derivation for Graded Data. *Journal of the American Statistical Association* 22(160) (December): 501–4.

——. 1930. Sources of Incomparability and Error in Employment–Unemployment Surveys. *Journal of the American Statistical Association* 25(171) (September): 284–94.

——. 1930/1. Book Review of "Real Wages in the United States, 1890–1926" by Paul H. Douglas. *American Journal of Sociology* 36(1/6): 654–.

——. 1931. A Distortion in the Cost of Living Index [Notes]. *Journal of the American Statistical Association* 26(173) (March): 52–7.

——. 1932. *The Incidence of Work Shortage. Report of a Survey by Sample of Families Made in New Haven, Connecticut, in May–June, 1931.* New York: Russell Sage Foundation.

——. 1934. Revising the Wage Earners' Cost-of-living Index. *Journal of the American Statistical Association* 29(185), Supplement (March): 120–4.

Hoggan, Dr. Frances E[lizabeth] [Morgan]. 1882. Medical Women for India. *Contemporary Review* 42 (July/December): 267–75.

——. 1884. *The Position of the Mother in the Family in Its Legal and Scientific Aspects.* Read at the annual congress of the National Association for the Promotion of Social Science. Manchester: A. Ireland and Co.

Hohman, Helen Fisher. 1926. The Use of Cost-of-living Figures in Wage Adjustments. *Journal of Political Economy* 34 (August): 525–9.

——. 1928. The Trade Board Acts and the Social Insurance Acts in Relation to a Minimum Standard of Living in Great Britain – A Study of Attitudes Toward Poverty and Methods of Dealing with It – 1880–1926. Ph.D. thesis, University of Chicago (economics).

——. 1933. *The Development of Social Insurance and Minimum Wage Legislation in Great Britain: A Study of British Social Legislation in Relation to a Minimum Standard of Living.* Boston: Houghton Mifflin.

——. 1934. Book Review of "Labor Economics and Labor Problems" by Dale Yoder. *Journal of Political Economy* 42: 571–.

——. 1934. The Status of Unemployment Insurance in Great Britain. *Journal of Political Economy* 42 (December): 721–2.

——. 1940. *Old Age in Sweden.* Washington: Social Security Board.

——. 1940. Review of Public Assistance, vol. I: American Principles and Policies in Five Parts with Select Documents. *American Economic Review* 30(4) (December): 910–11.

——. 1940. Social Democracy in Sweden. *Social Security Bulletin* 3(2) (February): 3–.

Hollingsworth, Helen. Coauth. *See* Monroe, Day.

Holmes, Ann C. 1935. The Sources of Capital in American Expansion, 1815–1840. M.A. thesis, University of Chicago (economics, history).

Holmes, Lizzie M. 1898. Woman's Future Position in the World. *Arena* 20 (September): 333–43.

——. 1905. Women Workers of Chicago. *American Federationist* 12 (August): 507–10.

Holst, Elise and E[linor]. Pancoast. 1921. The Danish Technological Institute. *Journal of Political Economy* 29(6) (June): 514–16.

——. 1921. Scientific Method in Job Analysis. *Journal of Political Economy* 29(6) (June): 508–16.

Holtzmeyer, Genie. 1887. How an English Girl Sought to Make a Living. *Lippincott's* 40 (July/December): 422.

Holyoake, Emilie A. 1893. The Capacity of Women for Industrial Union. *Westminster Review* 139 (February): 164–8. Reprinted as pamphlet, London: Women's Trade Union League.

——. 1895. The Need of Organisation among Women. In Frank W. Galton, ed., *Workers on Their Industries*. London: Swan Sonnenschein.

Homan, Jeanette. 1933. Adjusting for the Changing Date of Easter in Economic Series. Note. *Journal of the American Statistical Association* 28 (September): 328–32.

Homan, Jeanette *et al.* 1935. Discussion: Security in Employment. *Academy of Political Science, Proceedings* 16(3) (June): 93–.

Hood, Robin. 1932. The Loray Mill Strike. M.A. thesis, University of North Carolina at Chapel Hill.

——. 1933/4. Book Review of "The Yellow Dog Contract" by Seidman. *Social Forces* 12(1/4): 154–.

——. 1934/5. A Bibliography on Southern Labor. *Social Forces* 13(1/4): 133–.

——. 1934/5. Book Review of "The American Federation of Labor" by Lorwin. *Social Forces* 13(1/4): 618–.

——. 1936. *Industrial Social Security in the South*. Chapel Hill, N.C.: University of North Carolina Press.

——. 1936. Some Basic Factors Affecting Southern Labor Standards. *Southern Economic Journal* 2(4) (April): 45–60.

Hoon, Beth E. [Elizabeth Evelynola]. 1938. *The Organization of the English Customs System, 1696–1786*. New York: Appleton-Century for the American Historical Association.

Hopkins, [Jane] Ellice. 1870. *Work among the Lost*. London: William Macintosh.

——. 1874. *The Visitation of Dens. An Appeal to the Women of England*. London: Hatchards.

——. 1875. *An English Woman's Work among Workingmen*. New Britain, Conn.: John A. Williams.

——. 1877. *Work in Brighton; or, Woman's Mission to Women*. London: Hatchards.

——. 1879. *Notes on Penitentiary Work*. London: Hatchard's.

——. 1881. *Preventive Work; or, The Care of our Girls*. London: Hatchards.

——. 1882. *The Legal Protection of the Young*. London: Strangeways.

——. 1882. The Industrial Training of Pauper and Neglected Girls. *Contemporary Review* 42 (July): 140–54.

——. 1883. *England's Law for Women and Children*. London: Hatchards.

——. 1883. Social Wreckage. *Chautauquan* 4 (October): 40–.

——. 1883. Social Wreckage. *Contemporary Review* 44 (July): 94–104.

——. 1884. *Drawn unto Death: A Plea for the Children Coming under the Industrial Schools Act Amendment 1880*. London: Hatchard's.

——. 1885. The Protection of Girls: The Apocalypse of Evil. *Contemporary Review* 48 (September): 332–42.

Hopkins, Mary Alden. 1916/17. This Matter of the Eight-hour Day. *Century Illustrated Monthly Magazine* 93 (November/April): 346–.

Hopkins, Mary Della. 1917. An Experiment in Hours. *New Republic* 11 (June): 157.

——. 1928. *The Employment of Women at Night*. Washington: U.S. Women's Bureau.

——. Coauth. *See* Goldmark, Josephine.

Hopkinson, Mrs. C. A. 1868. The Poor in Cities. *Atlantic Monthly* 22 (July): 52–6.

Horst, Sheila T. van der. *See* Van der Horst, Sheila T.

Hotchkiss, Irma H. 1919. *Prices of Fish and Oysters*. U.S. War Industries Board Price Bulletin, no. 22. Washington: U.S. Government Printing Office.

Hotelling, Susanne. 1939. Book Review of "Les Fluctuations économiques et l'interdépendance des marches" by B. Chait. *Journal of Political Economy* 47: 281–.

——. 1940. Les Fluctuations économiques et l'interdépendance des marchés: A Rejoinder. *Journal of Political Economy* 48 (October): 744–6.

Hough, Eleanor Margaret. 1928. Organization Trends in Cooperative Cotton Marketing Associations in the United States. M.A. thesis, George Washington University.

——. 1932. *The Co-operative Movement in India: Its Relation to a Sound National Economy*. London: P. S. King & Son.

——. 1932. The Co-operative Movement in India: Its Relation to a Sound National Economy. Ph.D. thesis, George Washington University (economics, history).

——. 1933. The Economic Aspects of Hindu Thought. *Aryan Path* 4(5) (May): 299–.

——. 1939. Proprietary Thoughts. *Aryan Path* 10(2) (February): 100–.

Houghteling, Leila. 1926. The Income and Standard of Living of Unskilled Laborers in Chicago. Ph.D. thesis, University of Chicago (sociology).

——. 1927. The Budget of the Unskilled Laborer. *Social Service Review* 1(1/4) (March/December): 1–.

——. 1927. Charity and Women's Wages. *Social Service Review* 1(1/4) (March/December): 390–.

Houghteling, Leila and Ethel Austin Martin. 1927. *The Income and Standard of Living of Unskilled Laborers in Chicago*. Social Science Studies, no. VIII. Chicago: University of Chicago Press.

Houghton, Louise S. 1888. Farming for Women. *Lend a Hand* 3(5) (May): 289–.

——. 1889. Women and War Policies. *North American Review* 148 (January/June): 652.

——. 1893. Children of the Dependent Poor: How Shall We Educate Them? *Century Illustrated* 46 (July): 478–9.

Houghton, Ruth. 1929. The Silk Industry in Northampton. Thesis, Smith College, Northampton, Mass.

Houghton, Ruth E. and D. W. Ellsworth. 1926. A New Weekly Index of Commodity Prices. *Journal of the American Statistical Association* 21(156) (December): 471–5.

Houghton, Ruth and Marjory P. Nield. 1937. Placement Trends for College Women. *Occupations: The Vocational Guidance Magazine* 15(9) (June): 877–.

Houk, Edna Catherine Jackson. 1893. *Women Wealth-winners or How Women Can Earn Money*. Cincinnati, Ohio: H. H. Bevis.

Hourwich, Andria Taylor and Gladys Louise Palmer. 1936. *I Am a Woman Worker: A Scrapbook of Autobiographies*. New York: Affiliated Schools for Workers, Inc.

Hourwich, Marie. 1911. The Early History of the Cigarmaker's Union 1851–1879. M.A. thesis, Johns Hopkins University.

Howard, Louise Ernestine Matthaei. 1920. *Germany in Revolution: The First Phase.* London: Swarthmore Press Ltd.; Harcourt, Bruce & Howe.

——. 1935. *Labour in Agriculture: An International Survey.* Oxford: Oxford University Press.

Howard, Louise Ernestine Matthaei and Beryl Hearnden, eds. 1939. *What Country Women Use.* London: G. Allen & Unwin Ltd.

Howard, Lady Mabel. 1898. Nursing the Poor in Their Homes. *Nineteenth Century* 44 (November): 835–.

Howe, Julia Ward. 1859. *A Trip to Cuba.* Originally serialized in *Atlantic Monthly*, 1859. Reprinted as a book, Boston: Ticknor and Fields, 1860; New York: Negro Universities Press, 1969.

——. 1874. *Sex and Education: A Reply to Dr. E. H. Clarke's "Sex in Education."* Cambridge, Mass.: Roberts Brothers. Reprinted New York: Arno Press, 1972.

——. 1881. Changes in American Society. *Journal of Social Science* 13 (March): 170–88.

——. 1882. The Industrial Value of Woman. *North American Review* 135 (November): 433–46.

——. 1886/7. Women in the Professions. *Chautauquan* 7 (October/July): 460–.

——. 1888. Men, Women, and Money. *Forum* 5 (June): 461–8.

——. 1891. Introduction. In Annie Nathan Meyer, ed., *Woman's Work in America.* New York: Henry Holt.

——. 1896. Shall the Frontier of Christendom be Maintained? *Forum* 22 (November): 321–6.

Howe, Julia Ward *et al.* 1890/1. Domestic Service, A Symposium. *Chautauquan* 12 (October/March): 636–.

Howes, Annie. 1885. *Health Statistics of Women College Graduates.* Report of a Special Committee of the Association of Collegiate Alumnae. Boston: Massachusetts Bureau of Statistics of Labor.

Howes, Ethel Puffer and Myra Reed Richardson. 1923. *How to Start a Cooperative Kitchen.* Booklet. Woman's Home Companion. New York: Crowell.

——. 1923. *How to Start a Cooperative Laundry.* Booklet. Woman's Home Companion.

——. 1923. *How to Start a Cooperative Nursery.* Booklet. Woman's Home Companion.

Howitt, Mary Botham. 1842. *Little Coin, Much Care, or, How Poor Men Live: A Tale for Youth.* London: Thomas Tegg; New York: D. Appleton.

——. 1842. *Work and Wages, or, Life in Service.* London: Thomas Tegg; New York: D. Appleton.

——. 1843. *Love and Money: An Every Day Tale.* London: Thomas Tegg. [*juvenile fiction*]

Howland, Katherine E[leanor]. 1922. A Statistical Study of Poor Relief in Massachusetts. *Journal of the American Statistical Association* 18 (December): 480–9.

——. 1923. Social Service in Relation to Those Patients in the Boston State Hospital Not over Twenty-five Years of Age at First Admission. *Mental Hygiene* 7 (January/October): 804–30.

Howland, Marie. 1873. The Patrons of Husbandry. *Lippincott's* 12 (September): 338–42.

Hoyt, Elizabeth Ellis. 1925. Foundations of Economic Value. Ph.D. diss., Radcliffe College (economics).

——. 1926. *Primitive Trade: Its Psychology and Economics*. London: Kegan Paul, Trench, Trubner. Economics Classics Reprint, New York: Augustus M. Kelley, 1968.

——. 1927. Determination of Rural Standards of Living. *Journal of Farm Economics* 9 (April): 216–22.

——. 1928. *The Consumption of Wealth*. New York: Macmillan.

——. 1932/3. Research in the Social Problems of Old Age. *Social Forces* 11(1/4): 398–.

——. 1934. Review of Women in the Twentieth Century: Their Political, Social and Economic Activities. *American Economic Review* 24(2) (June): 353–4.

——. 1938. *Consumption in Our Society*. New York: McGraw-Hill.

——. 1939. Book Review of "Income and Consumption" by Roland S. Vaile and Helen G. Canoyer. *Annals of the American Academy of Political and Social Science* 203 (May): 248–.

Hoyt, Elizabeth Ellis and V. C. Meints. 1932. Academic Incomes and Planes of Living. *American Economic Review* 22 (March): 78–81.

Hoyt, Elizabeth Ellis and Ethyl Cessna Morgan. 1931. *Value of Family Living on Iowa Farms*. Iowa Agricultural Experiment Station Bulletin, no. 281. Ames, Iowa: Agricultural Experiment Station, Iowa State College of Agriculture and Mechanical Arts.

Hubback, Eva M. 1928. The Case for Equal Franchise. *Fortnightly Review*, n.s. 123 (January/June): 526.

——. 1929. The Age of Marriage. *Nation and Athenaeum* 45(1) (April 6): 9.

——. 1929. Unjust Wills. *Fortnightly Review*, n.s. 125 (January/June): 541.

——. 1930. The Problem of Maternal Mortality. *Nation and Athenaeum* 47(20) (August 16): 611.

——. 1931. Disinherited Families. *Nation and Athenaeum* 48(21) (February 21): 656.

——. 1936. Children and Unemployment Assistance. *New Statesman and Nation*, n.s. 12(288) (August 29): 280.

——. 1937. Family Allowances in Relation to Population Problems. *Sociological Review* 29 (July): 272–.

Hubback, Eva M. and M. E. Green. 1933. Family Endowment, Part II: A Proposal for Constructive Eugenics in England. *Eugenics Review* 25 (April): 33–.

Hubback, Mrs. F. W. 1914. Women in Industry. *New Statesman* (February 21).

——. 1914. Women's Wages. *New Statesman* (February 21).

Hubbard, Louisa M., ed. 1875. *The Year-book of Women's Work*. London: Labour News Publishing Office. Later editions, titled the *Englishwoman's Year-book and Directory*, published annually, London: Adam & Charles Black, 1882–1916.

——. 1893. Statistics of Women's Work. In Angela Burdett-Coutts, ed., *Women's Mission*. London: Sampson, Low, Marston and Co.

Hudson, Harriet Dufresne. 1936. The Progressive Miners of America: A Study in Dual Unionism. MA thesis, University of Chicago (economics).

Huey, Katharine. 1916. *Problems Arising and Methods Used in Interviewing and Selecting Employees*. Philadelphia: American Academy of Political and Social Science. Reprinted from the *Annals of the American Academy of Political and Social Science*, Philadelphia (May 1916).

——. 1926. *Handling Employment in a Period of Declining Business*. New York: American Management Association.

Hughan, Jessie Wallace. 1911. *American Socialism of the Present Day*. New York: John Lane Company.

——. 1911. *The Present Status of Socialism in America*. New York and Cambridge, UK: Cambridge University Press.

——. 1911. The Present Status of Socialism in America. M.A. thesis, Columbia University.

——. 1913. *The Facts of Socialism*. New York and London: John Lane Co.

——. 1928. *What Is Socialism?* New York: Vanguard Press.

Hughes, Catharine. 1891. Woman's Work in America. *Chautauquan* 13 (April/September): 505–.

Hughes, Gwendolyn Salisbury. 1925. *Mothers in Industry: Wage-earning Mothers in Philadelphia*. New York: New Republic.

——. 1925. Mothers in Industry: Wage-earning by Mothers in Philadelphia. Ph.D. thesis, Bryn Mawr College (economics).

Hughes, Violet. 1934. *A Social Survey of the East Kent Coalfield*. Ph.D. thesis, London School of Economics.

Hume-Rothery, Mary. 1870. *A Letter Addressed to the Right Hon. W. E. Gladstone, M.P., and the Other Members of Her Majesty's Government and of Both Houses of Parliament, Touching the Contagious Diseases Acts of 1866 and 1869, and Their Proposed Extension to the Civil Population of This Kingdom*. Manchester: Abel Heywood and Son.

Humes, Elizabeth. 1928. *The Italian Chemical Industry*. Washington: U.S. Bureau of Foreign and Domestic Commerce.

——. 1930. *Italian Chemical Developments in 1928 and 1929*. Washington: U.S. Bureau of Foreign and Domestic Commerce.

Humphreys, Jennett. 1883. Some Sick Poor. *Cornhill Magazine*, n.s. 1 [o.s. 48] (July): 113–23.

Humphreys, Mary Gay. 1884. Norman Fisher-folk. *Harper's Magazine* 69 (November): 842–55.

——. 1891. Saleswomen and Domestic Service. *Chautauquan* 13 (April/September): 83–.

——. 1896. The New York Working Girl. *Scribner's Magazine* 20: 502.

——. 1901. Trade Unions in Japan. *Century Magazine* (April): 892.

——. 1901. The Men of New Japan. *Century Illustrated Monthly Magazine* 62 (May/October): 825–.

——. 1911/12. The Ways of Women Ranchers. *Century Illustrated Monthly Magazine* 83 (November/April): 525–.

Hungerford, Mary C. 1895. Domestic Service. *Lippincott's Monthly Magazine* 56 (July/December): 566.

Hunt, Caroline L. 1908. *Home Problems from a New Standpoint.* Boston: Whitcomb and Barrows.

——. 1909. Woman's Public Work for the Home: An Ethical Substitute for Cooperative Housekeeping. *Journal of Home Economics* 1 (June): 219–24.

Hunt, Elizabeth Pinney, ed. 1926. *Arthur Young on Industry and Economics; Being Excerpts from Arthur Young's Observations on the State of Manufactures and His Economic Opinions on Problems Related to Contemporary Industry in England.* Philadelphia: Bryn Mawr College.

Hunter, Frances L. 1922. Slave Society on the Southern Plantation. *Journal of Negro History* 7(1) (January): 1–10.

Hunter, Mary. 1918. Sectionalism in Connection with the Price, the Size of Tract, and the Distribution of the Proceeds of the Sales of the Public Lands. M.A. thesis, University of Chicago (economics, history).

Huntington, Emily Harriet. 1928. Cyclical Fluctuations in the Cotton Manufacturing Industry. Ph.D. thesis, Radcliffe College (economics).

——. 1935/6. Recent Legislation: The California Unemployment Insurance Law. *California Law Review* 24: 288–.

——. 1936. The Benefit Provisions of State Unemployment Insurance Law. *Law and Contemporary Problems* 3: 20–.

——. 1939. *Unemployment Relief and the Unemployed in the San Francisco Bay Region, 1929–1934.* Berkeley: University of California Press.

Huntington, Emily Harriet and Mary G. Luck. 1937. *Living on a Moderate Income: The Incomes and Expenditures of Street-car Men's and Clerks' Families in the San Francisco Bay Region.* Institute of Pacific Relations International Research Series. Berkeley: University of California.

——. 1938. *Living on a Moderate Income.* London: Oxford University Press.

Huntington, Emily. Coauth. *See* Okey, Ruth.

Huntley, Kate Eleanor. 1931. *Financial Trends of Agencies Engaged in Giving Outdoor Relief in New York City: a Section of the Study of Financial Trends of Organized Social Work in New York City.* New York: Welfare Council of New York City.

——. 1935. *Financial Trends in Organized Social Work in New York City.* New York: Welfare Council of New York City.

Huntley, Kate Eleanor and Wilford Isbell King. 1928. *Trends in Philanthropy: A Study in a Typical American City* [New Haven, Conn.]. New York: National Bureau of Economic Research, Inc.

Hurd, Mabel. 1899. Book Review of "Women and Economics" by Charlotte Perkins Stetson. *Political Science Quarterly* 14(4) (December): 712–13.

Hurst, Marion and Mildred Thompson. 1939. *Household Employees Handbook.* Oklahoma City: Dewing Publishing Company.

Hurtrel, Alice. 1887. *La Femme, sa condition sociale, depuis l'antiquité jusqu'à nos jours.* Paris: G. Hurtrel.

[Husband,] Mary S. Gilliland. 1894. Women in the Community and in the Family. *International Journal of Ethics* 5(1) (October): 28–43.

——. 1895. Book Review of "Practicable Socialism: Essays on Social Reform" by Samuel and Henrietta Barnett. *International Journal of Ethics* 5(4) (July): 530–1.

——. 1898. Book Review of "The Morality of Marriage, and Other Essays on the Status and Destiny of Woman" by Mona Caird. *International Journal of Ethics* 9 (October): 131–2.

Hussey, Miriam. Coauth. *See* Bezanson, Anne.

Hutchins, B[essie]. L[eigh]. [Elizabeth] 1899–1900. Notes Toward the History of London Wages. *Economic Journal* 9(36) (December): 599–605.

——. 1900. Notes Towards the History of London Wages. Part II. *Economic Journal* 10 (March): 103–4.

——. 1900. The Regulation of Wages by Guilds and Town Authorities. *Economic Journal* 10 (September): 404–11.

——. 1901. Historical Development of the Factory Acts. In Mrs. Sidney Webb, ed., *The Case for the Factory Acts*. London: Grant Richards.

——. 1904. The Employment of Women in Paper Mills. *Economic Journal* 14 (June): 235–48.

——. 1904. A Note on the Distribution of Women in Occupations. *Royal Statistical Society Journal*, series A, 67 (September): 479–90.

——. 1905. Book Review of "Infantile Mortality and Infants' Milk Depôts" by G. F. McCleary. *Economic Journal* 15: 211–.

——. 1905. Note on the Distribution of Women in Relation to the Birth-Rate [miscellanea section]. *Journal of the Statistical Society* (March): 95–103.

——. 1905. The Writings of Walther Lotz. *Economic Review* (January).

——. 1906. *Labour Laws for Women in Australia and New Zealand*. London: Women's Industrial Council.

——. 1906. *Women's Wages in England in the Nineteenth Century*. London: Women's Industrial Council.

——. 1906. Book Review of "The Factory Legislation of the State of New York" by F. R. Fairchild. *Economic Journal* 16: 407–.

——. 1906. An Enquiry into the Salaries and Hours of Work of Typists and Shorthand Writers. *Economic Journal* 16 (September): 445–9.

——. 1907. *Home Work and Sweating: The Causes and the Remedies*. London: Fabian Society.

——. 1907. *Labour Laws for Women in France*. London: Women's Industrial Council.

——. 1907. The Control of Sweating. *Economic Review* (October): 403–9.

——. 1908. *The Public Health Agitation, 1833–48*. London: A. C. Fifield.

——. 1908. Book Review of "British Freewomen: Their Historical Privilege" by C. C. Stopes. *Sociological Review* 1: 198–.

——. 1908. Book Review of "Factory and Shop Acts of the British Dominions" by Violet Markham. *Sociological Review* 1: 311–.

——. 1908. Book Review of "Woman in Transition" by Annette M. B. Meakin. *Sociological Review* 1: 93.

——. 1908. Gaps in Our Factory Legislation. *Economic Journal* 18 (June): 221–30.

——. 1909. *Working Women and the Poor Law*. London: Women's Industrial Council.

——. 1909. Book Review of "Makers of Our Clothes" by Mrs. Carl Meyer and Clementina Black. *Economic Journal* 19(75) (September): 422–4.

——. 1909. Book Review of "Report on the Employment of Children" by Constance Smith. *Sociological Review* 2: 93.

——. 1909. Book Review of "Women in Industry from Seven Points of View" by Constance Smith. *Sociological Review* 2: 309–.

——. 1909. Some Aspects of Women's Life and Work. *Women's Trade Union Review* (July).

——. 1909. Statistics of Women's Life and Employment. *Royal Statistical Society Journal*, series A, 72 (June): 205–37.

——. 1909. Woman's Industrial Career. *Sociological Review* (October): 338–48.

——. 1909/10. Book Review of "The Problem of Practical Eugenics" by Karl Pearson. *Eugenics Review* 1 (April/January): 209–.

——. 1910. Book Review of "Education of Women" by Marion Talbot. *Sociological Review* 3: 339–.

——. 1910. Book Review of "English Poor Law Policy" by S. Webb and B. Webb. *Sociological Review* 3: 337.

——. 1910. Book Review of "A Modern Humanist" by B. Kirkman Gray. *Sociological Review* 3: 330–.

——. 1910. Book Review of "Poor Law Reform" by Sir Wm. Chance. *Sociological Review* 3: 337.

——. 1910. Book Review of "Royal Commission on the Poor Laws" by A. D. Steel-Maitland and Rose E. Squire. *Sociological Review* 3: 86–.

——. 1910. Book Review of "Women in Industry" by Edith Abbott. *Sociological Review* 3: 340–.

——. 1910. Children's Care Committees [letter to the editor]. *Nation* 6(16) (January 15): 644–.

——. 1911. Book Review of "The Living Wage of Women Workers" by Louise M. Bosworth. *Sociological Review* 4: 361–.

——. 1911. Book Review of "The Position of Women, Active and Ideal." *Sociological Review* 4: 360–.

——. 1911. Book Review of "The State and the Doctor" by S. Webb and B. Webb. *Sociological Review* 4: 75–.

——. 1911. The Working Life of Women. Fabian Women's Groups Series. *Fabian Tract* 157: 3–14.

——. 1911/12. The "Corruption" of the Citizenship of the Working Man, I. *Hibbert Journal* 10 (October/July): 697–.

——. 1912. Book Review of "The Distribution of Income" by W. Smart. *Sociological Review* 5: 274.

——. 1912. Book Review of "Socialism and Character" by V. D. Scudder. *Sociological Review* 5: 274.

——. 1912. Charles Dickens and the Social Movement. *Sociological Review* 5: 115–.

——. 1913. *Conflicting Ideals, Two Sides of the Woman's Question*. London: T. Murby.

——. 1913. Book Review of "The Family" by C. F. Thwing and Carrie Thwing. *Sociological Review* 6: 277–.

——. 1913. Book Review of "Psychology and Industrial Efficiency" by H. Munsterberg. *Sociological Review* 6: 266–.

——. 1913. Book Review of "The Public Feeding of Elementary School-Children" by Phyllis D. Winder. *Sociological Review* 6: 179–.

——. 1913. Book Review of "The Real Democracy: First Essays of the Rota Club" by J. E. F. Mann, N. J. Sievers, and R. W. T. Cox. *Sociological Review* 6: 278–.

——. 1913. Book Review of "Sociology in Its Psychological Aspect" by C. A. Ellwood. *Sociological Review* 6: 183–.

——. 1913. Book Review of "Women and Social Progress" by S. Nearing and N. Nearing. *Sociological Review* 6: 8–.

——. 1913. The Capitalist Versus the Home. *New Statesman* 2, Supplement (November 1): xiii–.

——. 1913. Fatigue and Efficiency. *Sociological Review* (January): 30–.

——. 1913. Truck Fines and Deductions. *Women's Industrial News* (January).

——. 1914. Book Review of "English Industries in the Middle Ages" by L. F. Salzmann. *Sociological Review* 7: 82–.

——. 1914. Book Review of "Making Both Ends Meet" by S. A. Clark and E. Wyatt. *Sociological Review* 7: 286–.

——. 1914. Women in Trade Unionism. *New Statesman* (February 21): vi–ix.

——. 1915. *Women in Modern Industry*. London: G. Bell and Sons, Ltd. Reprinted West Yorkshire: E. P. Publishing Ltd, 1978.

——. 1915. Book Review of "Livelihood and Poverty" by A. L. Bowley and A. R. Burnett-Hunt. *Sociological Review* 8: 189.

——. 1915. Book Review of "The Measurement of Social Phenomena" by A. L. Bowley. *Sociological Review* 8: 189.

——. 1915. Book Review of "Social Work in London: a History of the Charity Organisation Society" by Helen Bosanquet. *Sociological Review* 8: 61–.

——. 1916. Book Review of "Domestic Service" by C. V. Butler. *Economic Journal* 26: 361–.

——. 1916. Book Review of "Report on Women and Child Wage Earners in the United States." *Economic Journal* 26: 525–.

——. 1916. The Position of the Woman Worker after the War. *Economic Journal* 26 (June): 183–91.

——. 1916/17. Book Review of "Distributive Justice" by J. A. Ryan. *Sociological Review* 9: 117–.

——. 1916/17. Book Review of "New Ideals in Business" by Ida M. Tarbell. *Sociological Review* 9: 186.

——. 1916/17. Book Review of "The Organisation of Labour" by W. O. Weyforth. *Sociological Review* 9: 186.

——. 1917. *Women in Industry after the War*. London: Athenaeum.

——. 1918. Book Review of "A New Way of Housekeeping" by Clementina Black. *Economic Journal* 28(111) (September): 331.

——. 1918. Book Review of "The Woman's Part: A Record of Munitions Work" by L. K. Yates. *Sociological Review* 10: 146.

——. 1918. Book Review of "Women in the Engineering Trades" by Barbara Drake. *Sociological Review* 10: 146.

——. 1919. The Demobilisation of Juvenile Workers. *Contemporary Review* (February): 196–.

——. 1920. Book Review of "Modern Industry and the Individual" by Robert B. Wolf. *Economic Journal* 30: 232.

——. 1920. Book Review of "Non-financial Incentives" by Robert B. Wolf. *Economic Journal* 30: 232.

——. 1920. Book Review of "Securing the Initiative of the Workman" by Robert B. Wolf. *Economic Journal* 30: 232.

——. 1921. Book Review of "International Labour Legislation" by H. J. W. Hethrington. *Sociological Review* 13: 255–.

——. 1921. Book Review of "The I.W.W." by F. P. Brissenden. *Sociological Review* 13: 258–.

——. 1921. The Creative Impulse in Industry. *Contemporary Review* (February): 207–14.

——. 1921. The Present Position of Industrial Women Workers. *Economic Journal* 31 (December): 462–71.

——. 1922. Book Review of "Labour in Transition" by W. Aylott Orton. *Sociological Review* 14: 69.

——. 1922. Book Review of "Labour Organisation" by George O'Bryan. *Sociological Review* 14: 69.

——. 1922. Some Psychological Characteristics of Pacifist Literature. *Sociological Review* 14: 233–.

——. 1926. Book Review of "Family Welfare Work in a Metropolitan Community" by Sophonisba P. Breckinridge. *Sociological Review* 18: 174.

——. 1926. Book Review of "My Apprenticeship" by Beatrice Webb. *Sociological Review* 18: 159–.

——. 1926. Book Review of "Wages and the Family" by Paul H. Douglas. *Sociological Review* 18: 174.

——. 1927. Book Review of "Labor Economics" by Solomom Blum. *Sociological Review* 19: 183–.

——. 1927. Book Review of "The Worker in Modern Economic Society" by Paul H. Douglas. *Sociological Review* 19: 261–.

——. 1928. Book Review of "Humanity and Labour in China" by Adelaide M. Anderson. *Sociological Review* 20: 262–.

Hutchins, Elizabeth Leigh and Amy Harrison Spencer. 1903/1907/1911/1926. *A History of Factory Legislation*. Westminster: P. S. King.

Hutchins, Elizabeth Leigh [B. L.]. Coauth. *See* MacDonald, Margaret Ethel Gladstone; Webb, Beatrice Potter.

——. Published in *The Englishwoman.*

Hutchins, Grace. 1922. For Group Discussion. *World Tomorrow* 5(2) (February): 59–.

——. 1923. Our Inferiority Complex. *World Tomorrow* 6(12) (December): 362–.

——. 1924. Prophets and the People. *World Tomorrow* 7(6) (June): 182–.

——. 1927. Gandhi in the Villages. *World Tomorrow* 10(5) (May): 202–.

——. 1929. *Labor and Silk.* New York: International Publishers.

——. 1933. *Children under Capitalism.* New York: International Publishers.

——. 1933/1934. *Women Who Work.* New York: International Publishers.

——. 1933. Mashenka Ivanova, Textile Worker. *Soviet Russia Today* 2(1) (March): 9–.

——. 1934. Soviet Textile Workers. *Soviet Russia Today* 3(8) (October): 12–.

——. 1935. *What Every Working Woman Wants.* New York: Workers Library Publishers.

Hutchinson, Emilie Josephine. 1914. The Socializing Influence of the Ballot upon Women. *American Academy of Political and Social Science, Annals* 56 (November): 105–.

——. 1914/15. Vocational Interests of College Women. *Columbia University Quarterly* 17: 227–.

——. 1918. Book Review of "Industrial Experience of Trade School Girls in Massachusetts." *Political Science Quarterly* 33: 607–.

——. 1918. Book Review of "The Trade Union Woman" by Alice Henry. *Political Science Quarterly* 33: 113–.

——. 1919. *Women's Wages: A Study of the Wages of Industrial Women and Measures Suggested to Increase Them.* Columbia University Studies in History, Economics, and Public Law, vol. 89, no. 1. New York: Longmans. Reprinted New York: AMS Press, 1968.

——. 1919. Women's Wages: A Study of the Wages of Industrial Women and Measures Suggested to Increase Them. Ph.D. thesis, Columbia University.

——. 1928. The Economics of Marriage. *World Tomorrow* 10(6) (June): 271–.

——. 1928. Women and the Ph.D. *American Association of University Women, Journal* 22(1) (October): 19–.

——. 1929. The Economic Problems of Women. *American Academy of Political and Social Science, Annals* 143 (May): 132–.

——. 1930. *Women and the Ph.D.: Facts from the Experiences of 1,025 Women Who Have Taken the Degree of Doctor of Philosophy Since 1877.* Institute of Women's Professional Relations Bulletin, no. 2. Greensboro, N.C.: North Carolina College for Women.

——. 1934. The Committee's Work. *American Association of University Women, Journal* 27(3) (April): 163–.

Hutchinson, Ruth Gillette. 1926. What's in a College Week. *School and Society* 24(625) (December 18): 768–.

——. 1931. *State-administered Locally-shared Taxes: Development in the State and Local Tax Systems of the United States.* New York: Columbia University Press. Reprinted in New York: AMS Press, 1968.

——. 1931. State-administered Locally-shared Taxes: Development in the State and Local Tax Systems of the United States. Ph.D. thesis, Columbia University (economics).

Hutchinson, Ruth Gillette and Mabel Newcomer. 1932. Taxation of Land Values in Canada. *Journal of Political Economy* 40 (June): 366–78.

Hutchinson, Ruth Gillette, A. R. Hutchinson, and Mabel Newcomer. 1938. A Study of Business Mortality; Length of Life of Business Enterprises in Poughkeepsie, New York, 1843–1936. *American Economic Review* 28 (September): 497–514.

Huxley, Mrs. Henriette. 1899. The Gold Diggings at Bathurst in 1851. *Nineteenth Century* 45 (June): 962–72.

Hyatt-Woolf, Annie C. 1897. "Women's Educational and Industrial Union" – Some Women Workers. *Englishwoman* 5 (June): 297.

Hyde, Elizabeth A. 1918. Social Betterment Work among Employees' Families. *United States Bureau of Labor Statistics, Monthly Review* 6 (January/June): 195–205.

Hyde, Elizabeth Adshead, and Ruth Irene Voris. 1924. *Women in New Jersey Industries: A Study of Wages and Hours.* Washington: U.S. Women's Bureau.

——. 1926. *Women in Mississippi Industries: A Study of Hours, Wages and Working Conditions.* United States Women's Bureau Bulletin, no. 55. Washington: U.S. Government Printing Office.

Hyde, Elisabeth Adshead. Coauth. *See* Best, Ethel Lombard; Manning, Caroline; Peterson, Agnes Lydia; Winslow, Mary Nelson.

Hyde, Mary A. 1863. *How to Win Our Workers. A Short Account of the Leeds Sewing School for Factory Girls. By Mrs. Hyde. Dedicated, by Permission, to the Earl of Carlisle.* London: Macmillan and Co.

Hysell, Helen. 1922. *The Science of Purchasing.* New York: D. Appleton.

——. 1922. Capacity for Detail as an Executive Asset. *Industrial Management* 64(3) (September): 138–.

——. 1924. *Handling Callers in the Business Office.* New York: Purchasing Agent Co., Inc.

——. 1926. Every Purchasing Agent is an Engineer. *Industrial Management* 71(2) (February): 104–.

I

Ichenhäuser, Eliza. 1894. *Der gegenwärtige Stand der Frauenfrage in allen Culturstaaten; eine vergleichende Studie.* Leipzig: Rossberg.

——. 1897. *Erwerbsmöglichkeiten für Frauen; praktischer Ratgeber für erwerbsuchende Frauen in allen Angelegenheiten der Vorbildung, der Anstellung und der sozialen Selbstandigkeit. Nebst Nachweis von Wohlfahrtseinrichtungen.* 2nd ed. Berlin: Ebhardt.

——. 1899. *Zur Frauenfrage.* 2nd ed. Berlin: C. Duncker.

——. 1900. *Die Dienstbotenfrage und ihre Reform.* Berlin: H. Walther.

——. 1905. *Die Journalistik als Frauenberuf.* Berlin: Frauen-Rundschau.

——. 1909. *Zur Ehereform.* Gautzsch bei Leipzig: F. Dietrich.

Ihrer, Emma. 1893. *Die Organisationen der Arbeiterinnen Deutschlands: ihre Entstehung und Entwickelung.* Berlin: self-published.

——. 1898. *Die Arbeiterinnen im Klassenkampf: Anfänge der Arbeiterinnen-Bewegung, ihr Gegensatz zur bürgerlichen Frauenbewegung und ihre nächsten Aufgaben.* Hamburg: Verlag der Generalkommission der Gewerkschaften Deutschlands.

Ilbert, Lettice. *See* [Fisher,] Lettice Ilbert.

Innis, Mary Quayle. 1922/3. In the Sugar Bush. *Canadian Forum* 3: 143–.

——. 1923/4. The Wood-Box. *Canadian Forum* 4: 144–.

——. 1927/8. The Trader. *Canadian Forum* 8: 752–.

——. 1932/3. Apology for Parents. *Canadian Forum* 13: 209–.

——. 1933/4. A Century of Progress. *Canadian Forum* 14: 72–.

——. 1933/4. The Gift. *Canadian Forum* 14: 349–.

——. 1935/1943/1945/1948/1954. *An Economic History of Canada.* Toronto: Ryerson Press.

——. 1936. The Record of an Epidemic. *Dalhousie Review* 16: 371–5.

——. 1937. The Industrial Development of Ontario: 1783–1820. *Ontario Historical Society Papers and Records* 32: 104–13. Reprinted in J. K. Johnson, *Historical Essays on Upper Canada.* Toronto: McClelland and Stewart, 1975.

——. 1937. Philip Henry Gosse in Canada. *Dalhousie Review* 17: 55–60.

——. 1940. A Galt Centenary. *Dalhousie Review* 19: 495–501.

Irby, Paulina. 1889. Bosnia and Its Land Tenure. *Contemporary Review* 56 (July): 28–40.

Irwin, Margaret Hardinge. 1893. *The Conditions of Women's Work in Laundries: Report of an Inquiry Conducted for the Council of the Women's Protective and Provident*

League of Glasgow. Glasgow: Women's Protective and Provident League of Glasgow.

——. 1894. *Women's Employment in Shops. Report of an Inquiry Conducted for the National Federated Council for Women's Trades*. London: National Federated Council for Women's Trades.

——. 1896. *Home Work amongst Women.* I[–II]: *Report of an Inquiry Conducted for the Glasgow Council for Women's Trades.* Glasgow: Council of the Women's Protective and Provident League.

——. 1896. *Women's Industries in Scotland.* Paper read before the Philosophical Society of Glasgow, March 18, and published in the *Proceedings of the Philosophical Society of Glasgow, 1895–96*. Glasgow: Philosophical Society of Glasgow.

——. 1897. The Problem of Home Work. *Westminster Review* 148 (November): 541–57.

——. 1899. The Shop Seats Bill Movement. *Fortnightly Review*, n.s. 66 (July): 123–31.

——. 1900?. *Women's Work in Tailoring and Dressmaking: Report of an Inquiry Conducted for the Scottish Council for Women's Trades*. Glasgow: Scottish Council for Women's Trades.

——. 1902. *The Problem of Home Work*. Glasgow: Scottish Co-operative Wholesale Society. Reprinted Glasgow: K. & R. Davidson, 1903.

——. 1903. Public Work for Women on Local Government Boards as Factory Inspectors. In J. Hogarth *et al.*, *Education and Professions*. London: Chapman & Hall.

——. 1909. *Home Work in Ireland: Report of an Enquiry by Margaret H. Irwin, Secretary, Scottish Council for Women's Trades*. Glasgow: Scottish Council for Women's Trades/Union for the Abolition of Sweating.

——. 1910. *The Housing of Potato Diggers*. Glasgow: Scottish Council for Women's Trades/Union for the Abolition of Sweating.

——. 1910. The Bitter Cry of the Irish Home Worker. *Nineteenth Century* 68 (October): 703–.

——. Coauth. *See* Kendal, Madge; Orme, Eliza.

Iselin, Helen. 1890/1. Tenement House Visiting. *Chautauquan* 12 (October/March): 517–.

Ives, Alice E. 1890. The Domestic Purse Strings. *Forum* 10 (September): 106–14.

J

Jackson, Helen Hunt. 1881. *A Century of Dishonor: A Sketch of the U.S. Government's Dealings with Some of the Indian Tribes*. New York: Harper; London: Chatto & Windus.

——. 1884. *Ramona: A Story*. Boston: Roberts, and London: Macmillan. [*novel*]

Jackson, Helen Hunt and Abbot Kinney. 1883. *Report on the Condition and Needs of the Mission Indians of California*. Washington: U.S. Government Printing Office.

Jackson, Kathleen C. 1926. The Financing of Highways in California, 1850–1925. M.A. thesis, Stanford University.

Jackson, Mary E. 1918. The Colored Woman in Industry. *Crisis* 17 (November): 12–17.

Jacobi, Mary Putnam. 1882. Shall Women Practice Medicine? *North American Review* 134 (January): 52.

Jacobs, Aletta H. 1899. *Vrouwenbelangen*. Amsterdam: L. J. Veen.

——. 1913. *Reisbrieven uit Afrika en Azië: benevens eenige brieven uit Zweden en Noorwegen*. Almelo, Netherlands: W. Hilarius.

Jacobs, Aletta H. and Carel Victor Gerritsen. 1906. *Brieven uit en over Amerika*. Amsterdam: F. van Rossen.

Jacobs, Aletta H., Carrel Victor Gerritsen, and H. J. Mehler. 1900. *La Femme et le féminisme*. Paris, V. Giard & E. Brière.

Jacobs, Harriet Ann and Lydia Maria Child. 1861. *Incidents in the Life of a Slave Girl*. Boston: Published for the author. Reprinted 1987, Cambridge: Harvard University Press.

Jacobs, Katharine. 1925. *Livestock Financing*. Washington: U.S. Government Printing Office.

——. 1933. *Farm Mortgages in the United States*. Washington: U.S. Government Printing Office.

——. 1935. *Livestock Financing in the United States*. Washington: U.S. Government Printing Office.

——. 1936. State Publications – The Cataloguers' Viewpoint. *Agricultural Library Notes* 11(5) (May): 287–.

Jacobs, Katharine and Mary G. Lacy. 1927. *A List of International Organizations Interested in Agriculture*. Washington: U.S. Government Printing Office.

Jacobs, Katharine. Coauth. *See* Day, Emily Louise.

Jacquelin, D. G. 1939. *Swiss–American Economic Relations*. Geneva: Geneva Research Centre.

Jaeger, Ruth Muller. 1922. Stabilization of the Foreign Exchanges. Ph.D. thesis, Columbia University (economics).

——. 1925. *The United States of Brazil, a Comparison with the United States of America*. New York: Paine, Webber.

Jaffe, Madeline. 1936. *Trends in Farm Population in the United States, 1909–1936*. Survey of Effects of Changing Agricultural Techniques on Employment in Agriculture, Report no. 1. Washington: National Research Project of the Works Progress Administration.

Jamara, Ann. 1929. Comparative Trends in Productivity in English and American Cotton Mills. Ph.D. thesis, University of Wisconsin.

James, Miss M. H. 1894. The Struggles of the Untrained Lady. *Monthly Packet* 8 (December): 715–.

James, Margaret. 1927. Social and Economic Policy and Projects during the Interregnum, 1640–60. Ph.D. thesis, University of London.

——. 1927. Summaries of Theses: Social and Economic Policy and Projects during the Interregnum. *Institute of Historical Research, Bulletin* 5(14) (November): 106–.

——. 1928. Tragedy in Homes of Injured Workers While Congress Neglects to Provide Accident Compensation. *American Labor Legislation Review* 18: 61–.

——. 1930. *Social Problems and Policy during the Puritan Revolution, 1640–1660*. London: Routledge.

——. 1937. The Effect of the Religious Changes of the Sixteenth and Seventeenth Centuries on Economic Theory and Development. In E. Eyre, ed., *European Civilization: Its Origin and Development*. Vol. V: *Economic History of Europe since the Reformation*. New York: Oxford University Press.

James, Margaret and Maureen Weinstock. 1935. *England during the Interregnum (1642–1660)*. London: Longmans.

Jameson, Mrs. Anna. 1843. The Condition of the Women and the Female Children. *Athenaeum* 16 (March 18): 257–9.

——. 1852. *Sketches in Canada: And Rambles among the Red Men*. London: Longman, Brown, Green, and Longmans.

——. 1855. *Sisters of Charity, Catholic and Protestant, Abroad and at Home*. 2nd ed., enlarged, and with a new preface. London: Longman, Brown, Green, & Longmans.

——. 1856. *The Communion of Labour: A Second Lecture on the Social Employments of Women*. London: Longman, Brown, Green, Longmans, & Roberts.

——. 1857. *Sisters of Charity; and, The Communion of Labour. Two Lectures on the Social Employments of Women*. Boston: Ticknor and Fields. New British ed., enlarged and improved with a prefatory letter to the Right Hon. Lord John Russell, president of the National Association for the Promotion of Social Science, on the present condition and requirements of the women of England. London: Longman, Brown, Green, 1859.

Jardon, Cornelia. 1892. *Die Frau und Bebel's Utopien*. Minden: in Commission bei T. C. C. Bruns' Verlag.

Jastrow, Henriette. 1897. Workers' Insurance Legislation in Germany. *Fortnightly Review*, n.s. 61 (o.s. 67) (March): 379–86.

——. 1899. Domestic Servants in Germany: Their Economic, Social and Legal Position. *Economic Journal* 9(36) (December): 625–33.

Jeans, Victorine. 1892. *Factory Act Legislation, Its Industrial and Commercial Effects, Actual and Prospective*. Cobden Prize Essay for 1891. London: T. Fisher and Unwin.

——. 1892. Effets de la legislation sur les fabriques en Angleterre. *Revue d'économie politique* 6: 55–.

Jebb, Louisa. *See* Wilkins, Louisa Jebb.

Jefferson, Olive Ruth. 1892/3. Southern Women at Home. *Chautauquan* 16 (October/March): 720–.

——. 1892/3. Women Down South. *Chautauquan* 16 (October/March): 592–.

——. 1893. The Negro Women of the South. *Chautauquan* 17 (April/September): 464–, 623–.

——. 1893. Southern Negro Women. *Chautauquan* 18 (October): 91–.

——. 1893. Southern Women in Education. *Chautauquan* 17 (April/September): 204–.

——. 1893. Southern Women at Work. *Chautauquan* 17 (April/September): 348–.

——. 1893/4. Southern Women in the North. *Chautauquan* 18 (October/March): 212–.

Jellicoe, Anne. 1862. *Women's Supervision of Women's Industry*. London: Emily Faithfull.

——. 1862. On the Conditions and Prospects of Young Women Employed in the Manufactories in Dublin. Paper read at the conference of the National Association for Promotion of Social Science, London, 1861. *English Woman's Journal* 8 (February): 107–11.

Jennings, Henrietta Cooper. 1927. The Political Theory of State-supported Elementary Education in England, 1750–1833. Ph.D. thesis, Bryn Mawr College (education).

——. 1928. *The Political Theory of State-supported Elementary Education in England, 1750–1833*. Lancaster, Pa.: Lancaster Press.

——. 1938. The Development of the Use Tax. *American Economic Review* 28(4) (December): 684–7.

——. 1939. *The Consumer in Commercial Banking*. New York: Consumer Credit Institute of America.

——. 1940. Review of Industrial Banking: A Phase of Consumer Credit. *American Economic Review* 30(3) (September): 640–1.

Jennings, Hilda. 1929. Relief in South Wales. *Charity Organisation Quarterly* 3(3) (July): 121–.

——. 1930. *The Private Citizen in Public Social Work*. London: G. Allen & Unwin Ltd.

——. 1930. Social Surveys: Brynmawr. *Sociological Review* 22: 146–.

——. 1932. Book Review of "Cecil Clare North: The Community and Social Welfare." *Sociological Review* 24: 325–.

——. 1934. *Brynmawr: A Study of a Distressed Area, Based on the Results of the Social Survey Carried out by the Brynmawr Community Study Council*. London: Allenson & Co., Ltd.

——. 1934. Brynmawr. *Charity Organisation Quarterly* 8(4) (October): 150–.

Jennings, Sister Marietta. 1939. *A Pioneer Merchant of St. Louis, 1810–1820: The Business Career of Christian Wilt*. New York: Columbia University Press.

——. 1940. Notes on Joseph Hertzog, an Early Philadelphia Merchant. *Business History Review* 14 (November): 65–76.

——. 1940. A Pioneer Merchant of St. Louis, 1810 to 1820: The Business Career of Christian Wilt. Ph.D. thesis, Columbia University (economics).

Jersey, Countess of [Child-Villiers, Margaret Elizabeth]. 1885. *The Speeches of the Countess of Jersey*. Revised. Bicester: T. W. Pankhurst.

——. 1887. *The Rise of English Liberty: An Address to the Middleton Conservative Association*. Oxford: Mid-Oxon Conservative Association.

——. 1888. The Romance of a Mine. *National Review* 11 (July): 701–10.

——. 1889. The Hindu at Home. *Nineteenth Century* 25 (January/June): 653–.

——. 1892. A French Colony [New Caledonia]. *Nineteenth Century* 32 (October): 524–35.

——. 1893. Three Weeks in Samoa. *Nineteenth Century* 33 (January/June) 249–.

——. 1893. The Transformation of Japan, I: Feudal Times. *Nineteenth Century* 34 (September): 369–83.

——. 1893. The Transformation of Japan, II: The Era of Meiji. *Nineteenth Century* 34 (October): 570–83.

——. 1898. White Slaves: A True Tale. *Nineteenth Century* 43 (March): 417–30.

Jeter, Helen Rankin. 1920. A Summary of Juvenile Court Legislation in the United States. A.M. thesis, University of Chicago (commerce and administration).

——. 1924. The Chicago Juvenile Court. Ph.D. thesis, University of Chicago (sociology).

——. 1927. *Trends of Population in the Region of Chicago*. Chicago: University of Chicago Press.

——. 1928. Statistical Terminology in the Family Welfare Field. *Social Service Review* 2(1/4) (March/December): 357–.

——. 1929. Book Review of "Trends of Population in the Region of Chicago". *Sociological Review* 21: 168–.

——. 1929. Some Statistics of Family Welfare and Relief in Chicago – 1928. *Social Service Review* 3(1/4) (March/December): 448–.

——. 1930. *Registration of Social Statistics for the Year 1928*. Chicago: Joint Committee of the Association of Community Chests and Councils and the Local Community Research Committee of the University of Chicago.

——. 1930. Receipts and Expenditures of Social Agencies during the Year 1928. *Social Service Review* 4(1/4) (March/December): 343–.

——. 1933. *The Administration of Funds for Unemployment Relief by the Los Angeles County Department of Charities Prior to November 24, 1933.* Los Angeles: Los Angeles (County) Emergency Relief Committee.

——. 1933. *Salaries, Education, Training and Experience of Social Workers in Family Welfare and Relief Agencies in Chicago, October 1, 1932.* Preliminary report prepared by Helen R. Jeter for the Committee on Research of the Chicago Council of Social Agencies and the Advisory Committee on Relief and Service of the Cook County Bureau of Public Welfare, February 6, 1933. Chicago: s.n.

——. 1933. Salaries and Professional Education of Social Workers in Family and Relief Agencies in Chicago. *Social Service Review* 7(1/4) (March/December): 225–.

——. 1934. *Hospital Facilities for the Care of the Sick Poor in Los Angeles.* Partial and Preliminary Report Presented to the Joint Committee of the Budget Committee of the Los Angeles Community Welfare Federation, the Health Committee of the Council of Social Agencies and the Hospital Council of Southern California, August 20. Los Angeles: s.n.

——. 1938. Counting the Recipients of Public Assistance and the Dollars They Receive. *Social Security Bulletin* 1(5) (May): 11–.

——. 1938. Interchange of Relief Information among Departments of Public Welfare of Large Cities. *Social Security Bulletin* 1(6) (June): 14–.

——. 1939. Future of the Private Field – II. *Social Work Today* 6(8) (May): 5–.

——. 1940. Hospital Morbidity Reporting. *American Journal of Public Health and the Nation's Health* 30(4) (April): 417–.

Jeter, Helen Rankin and A. W. McMillen. 1929. The Results of a First Year's Program for the Central Registration of Social Statistics. *Journal of the American Statistical Association* 24(165), Supplement. *Proceedings of the American Statistical Association* (March): 174–9.

Jeune, Lady [Susan] Mary [St. Helier], Baroness. 1885. Helping the Fallen. *Fortnightly Review*, n.s. 38. (November) 669–.

——. 1885. Saving the Innocents. *Fortnightly Review*, n.s. 38 (September): 345–.

——. 1888. The Creed of the Poor. *National Review* 11 (June): 553–66.

——. 1889. Technical Education for Women in England and Abroad. *National Review* 12 (February): 736–50.

——. 1889. Women of Today, Yesterday and Tomorrow. *National Review* 14 (December): 547–61.

——. 1890. Holidays for Poor Children. *New Review* 2 (May): 455–65.

——. 1890. The Homes of the Poor. *Fortnightly Review*, n.s. 47 (January): 67–80.

——. 1892. The Servant Question. *Fortnightly Review*, n.s. 52 (July): 65–73.

——. 1893. Amusements of the Poor. *National Review* 21 (May): 303–.

——. 1893. Introduction. In *Ladies at Work; Papers on Paid Employments for Ladies, by Experts in the Several Branches.* Reprinted, after revision, from the *Monthly Packet.* London: A. D. Innes & Co.

——. 1893. The Poor Children's Holiday. *Fortnightly Review*, n.s. 53 (June): 846–.

——. 1894. *Lesser Questions.* London and Sydney: Remington.

——. 1894. Our Domestic Servants. *New Review* 10 (May): 572–9.

——. 1894. The Revolt of the Daughters. *Fortnightly Review*, n.s. 55 (February): 267–.

——. 1895. The Ethics of Shopping. *Fortnightly Review*, n.s. 57 (January): 123–32.

Jeune, Lady [Susan] Mary [St. Helier], Baroness. Coauth. *See* Corelli, Marie.

Jevons, Harriet Winefrid. 1913. The Industrial Training and Placing of Juveniles in England. *Journal of Political Economy* 21 (March): 243–54.

——. 1934. William Stanley Jevons. *Econometrica* 2 (July): 225–31.

Jex-Blake, [Dr.] Sophia. 1869. Medicine as a Profession for Women. In Josephine Butler, ed., *Woman's Work and Woman's Culture, A Series of Essays*. London: Macmillan.

——. 1872. *Medical Women: Two Essays*. Edinburgh: William Oliphant.

——. 1875. The Practice of Medicine by Women. *Fortnightly Review*, n.s. 17 (March): 392–.

——. 1886. *Medical Women: A Thesis and a History*. London: Hamilton, Adams.

——. 1887. Medical Women. *Nineteenth Century* 22 (November): 692–707.

Johansen, Dorothy O. 1936. Simeon G. Reed, Pioneer. *Business History Review* 10 (June): 37–43.

——. 1940. Book Review of "Cavalcade of the Rails" by Morse. *Pacific Northwest Quarterly* 31(3) (July): 355–.

——. 1940. Organization and Finance of the Oregon Iron and Steel Company, 1880–1895. *Pacific Northwest Quarterly* 31(2) (April): 123–.

——. 1941. Capitalism on the Far Western Frontier: The Oregon Steam Navigation Company. Ph.D. thesis, University of Washington.

Johnsen, Julia Emily, compiler. 1922. *Cancellation of the Allied War Debt*. New York: H. W. Wilson.

——. 1922. *Kansas Court of Industrial Relations*. New York: H. W. Wilson.

——. 1922. *Selected Articles on Social Insurance*. New York: H. W. Wilson.

——. 1923. *Selected Articles on Government Ownership of Coal Mines*. New York: H. W. Wilson.

——. 1926. *Child Labor*. New York: H. W. Wilson.

——. 1926. *Government Regulation of the Coal Industry*. New York: H. W. Wilson.

——. 1927. *Agriculture and the Tariff*. New York: H. W. Wilson.

——. 1928. *Federal and State Control of Water Power*. New York: H. W. Wilson.

——. 1929. *Financing the State Highways*. New York: H. W. Wilson.

——. 1930. *Conscription of Wealth in Time of War*. New York: H. W. Wilson.

——. 1931. *Capitalism on Trial*. New York: H. W. Wilson.

——. 1931. *Stabilization of Employment*. New York: H. W. Wilson.

——. 1933. *Federal Aid to Education*. New York: H. W. Wilson.

——. 1935. *Collective Bargaining*. New York: H. W. Wilson.

——. 1935. *Old Age Pensions*. New York: H. W. Wilson.

——. 1935. *Socialization of Medicine*. New York: H. W. Wilson.

——. 1936. *Consumers' Cooperatives*. New York: H. W. Wilson.

——. 1936. *Government Ownership of Electric Utilities*. New York: H. W. Wilson.

——. 1940. *Interstate Trade Barriers*. New York: H. W. Wilson.
——. 1940. *The National Labor Relations Act*. New York: H. W. Wilson.
——. 1940. *Trade Unions and the Anti-trust Laws*. New York: H. W. Wilson.
Johnsen, Julia Emily and Edna Dean Bullock. 1917. *Selected Articles on Single Tax*. 2nd ed. New York: H. W. Wilson.
Johnson, Amanda. 1919. *The Michigan Fur Trade*. Lansing, Mich.: Michigan Historical Commission.
——. 1925. The Michigan Fur Trade. Ph.D. thesis, University of Chicago (history).
Johnson, Borghild Eleanor. 1931. Household Employment in Chicago. Ph.D. thesis, University of Chicago (home economics).
——. 1933. *Household Employment in Chicago*. Washington: U.S. Women's Bureau.
Johnson, E. M. 1939. *The Administration of Minimum Wage Laws in the United States*. Geneva and Washington: International Labour Office.
Johnson, Elizabeth Forrest. 1922. A Statistical Study of the Business Management of Twenty-four Private Schools. *School and Society* 16(395) (July 22): 99–.
Johnson, Elizabeth Sands. 1918–35. Child Labor Legislation. In John R. Commons *et al.*, *History of Labor in the United States*, vol. 3 (of 4). New York: Macmillan.
——. 1927. *Opportunities and Conditions of Work for Minors under 18 in the Glassware Industry*. Harrisburg, Pa.: Pennsylvania Bureau of Women and Children.
——. 1939. *Welfare of Families of Sugar-beet Laborers: A Study of Child Labor and Its Relation to Family Work, Income, and Living Conditions in 1935*. United States Children's Bureau Publication, no. 247. Washington: U.S. Government Printing Office.
——. 1940. Coal-mine Order Issued Under Hazardous-occupations Program. *Child* 5(3) (September): 83–.
Johnson, Elizabeth S., Evelyn Mead Hughes, Mary Henriette Letsche, Valda Constance Noll, and Sara Eleanor [Robin] Smith. 1933. *Women Workers after a Plant Shutdown*. Pennsylvania Department of Labor and Industry Special Bulletin, no. 36. Harrisburg, Pa.: Department of Labor and Industry.
Johnson, Elizabeth S. Coauth. *See* McConnell, Jessie Beatrice; Smaltz, Rebecca Glover.
Johnson, Helen Louise. 1914. The Meaning of the Label. *Pictorial Review* (August): 10, 54.
——. 1917. The Consumer's Responsibility. *Pictorial Review* (January): 18, 32.
Johnson, Mary A. 1889. One Reason for the Inefficiency of Women's Work. *Century Illustrated Monthly Magazine* 38 (July): 477–8.
Johnstone, Catherine Laura. 1898. *The British Colony in Russia*. London: Roxburghe Press.
Johnstone, Christian Isobel. 1832. The Irish Peasantry. *Tait's Edinburgh Magazine* 1 (May): 151–.
——. 1832. Miss Edgeworth's Works. *Tait's Edinburgh Magazine* 1 (June): 279–85.
——. 1832. Miss Martineau's "Illustrations of Political Economy." *Tait's Edinburgh Magazine* 1 (August): 612–18.

——. 1833. Miss Martineau's "Berkeley the Banker." *Tait's Edinburgh Magazine* 3 (April): 92–6.

——. 1833. The Slave Trade: Voyages to Western Africa. *Tait's Edinburgh Magazine* 1 (March): 789–99.

——, ed. 1836. *True Tales of the Irish Peasantry as Related by Themselves.* Excerpts from the report of the Poor-law Commissioners. Edinburgh: P. Brown.

——. 1836. The Final Report of the Irish Poor Law Commissioners. *Tait's Edinburgh Magazine,* n.s. 3 (o.s. 7) (May): 338–9.

——. 1836. The First Report of the Irish Poor Law Commission. *Tait's Edinburgh Magazine,* n.s. 3 (o.s. 7) (January): 10–16.

——. 1836. Pictures of Ireland from the Life: Report of the Irish Poor Law Commissioners. *Tait's Edinburgh Magazine,* n.s. 3 (o.s. 7) (March): 141–56.

——. 1837. The Condition of the Labouring Poor and the Management of Paupers in Scotland. *Tait's Edinburgh Magazine,* n.s. 7 (o.s. 11) (November): 681–96; (December): 749–60.

——. 1837. A Poor Law for Ireland. *Tait's Edinburgh Magazine,* n.s. 4 (o.s. 8) (March): 189–93.

——. 1838. Abolition of Negro Apprenticeships – Sturge and Harvey's Tour in the West Indies in 1837. *Tait's Edinburgh Magazine,* n.s. 8 (March): 135–48.

——. 1844. The Report of the Poor Law Commissioners for Scotland. *Tait's Edinburgh Magazine,* n.s. 11 (o.s. 15) (July): 409–13.

Jolley, Vivian Dake. 1939. Legal Regulation of Accounting. Ph.D. thesis, University of Chicago.

Jolliffe, Muriel Florence. 1935. *The United States as a Financial Centre, 1919–1933 with Reference to Imports and Exports of Capital.* Cardiff: University of Wales Press Board.

——. 1938. The Movement of Capital to and from the United States in 1935 and 1936. *Quarterly Journal of Economics* 53 (November): 150–9.

——. 1939. Fresh Light on John Francis Bray, Author of Labour's Wrongs and Labour's Remedy. *Economic History* (February): 240–4.

Jones, Alice Hanson. 1928. Economic Theories of Consumption as Applied to Labor. M.A. thesis, University of Washington.

——. Coauth. *See* Williams, Faith Moors.

Jones, Anna Maria. 1927. *Wales.* Oxford: Clarendon Press.

Jones, Carrie Maude. 1933. Apartment House Bonds: Some Plans for Reorganizing Defaulted Issues. Part I. *Land Economics* 9 (November): 358–67.

——. 1933. Some Plans for the Financial Reorganization of Apartment Buildings in Cook County with Particular Reference to the Treatment of Real Estate First Mortgage Bonds. M.A. thesis, Northwestern University.

——. 1934. Apartment House Bonds: Some Plans for Reorganizing Defaulted Issues. Part II. *Land Economics* 10 (February): 67–77.

——. 1934. Further Developments in Reorganization of Defaulted Real Estate Bond Issues. *Land Economics* 10 (November): 423–6.

——. 1936. Book Review of "How to Make a Real Property Survey." *Land Economics* 12 (May): 197–8.

——. 1936. Trustees under Real Estate Indentures. *Land Economics* 12 (August): 302–3.

——. 1940. Percentage Leases. Chicago: Brokers' Division, National Association of Real Estate Boards.

Jones, Mary H. 1925. *Autobiography of Mother Jones*, ed. Mary F. Parton. Chicago: C. H. Kerr. Reprinted New York: Arno Press, 1969.

Jones, Rosalie Gardner. 1922. *Influence on International Relations of the Different Standards of Living in Different Countries*. D.C.L.: American University, Political Science, International Law and Relations.

——. 1923. *The American Standard of Living and World Co-operation*. Boston and New York: Cornhill Publishing Company.

Jordan, Edna M. 1937. *Livestock, Meats, and Wool: Market Statistics and Related Data, 1936*. Washington: U.S. Bureau of Agricultural Economics.

Joseph, Margaret F. W. 1933. A Discontinuous Cost Curve and the Tendency to Increasing Returns. *Economic Journal* 43 (September): 390–8.

——. 1935/6. A Note on Index Numbers. *Review of Economic Studies* 3: 155–.

——. 1936. Further Notes on Index Numbers. II. Mr. Lerner's Supplementary Limits for Price Index Numbers. *Review of Economic Studies* 3 (February): 155–7.

——. 1939. The Excess Burden of Indirect Taxation. *Review of Economic Studies* 6 (June): 226–31.

Juillerat, Mme. Paul. 1911. L'Activité féminine en France. *Revue économique internationale* (August).

K

Kapriste, Countess Anna. 1895. The Position of Russian Women. *Humanitarian* 7 (October): 275–.

Kaufman, Edith R. 1934. Early Protectionist Theory in the United States. M.A. thesis, Clark University.

Keefer, Mary Wysor. 1933. State Care for the Sick Poor in Indiana with Special Reference to the Indiana University Hospitals. M.A. thesis, University of Chicago (sociology, public and social welfare).

——. Coauth. *See* Breckinridge, Sophonisba Preston; Shaffer, Alice.

Kehaya, Kalliope A. 1884. The Orient. in Theodore Stanton, ed., *The Woman Question in Europe*. London: Sampson Low, Marston, Searle.

Keith, Ethel Hannah. 1938. The Home and Social Background of the Women of Samuel Huston College for Negroes During 1937–38. M.S. thesis, Kansas State University.

Keith, Hannah L. 1900. *An Historical Sketch of Internal Improvements in Michigan, 1836–46*. Ann Arbor, Mich.: Michigan Political Science Association. Also published in *Publications of the Michigan Political Science Association* IV(1) (July 1900).

Keith, Theodora. 1907/8. Economic Condition of Scotland under the Commonwealth and the Protectorate. *Scottish Historical Review* 5: 273–.

——. 1908/9. Scottish Trade with the Plantations before 1707. *Scottish Historical Review* 6: 32–.

——. 1909. The Economic Causes for the Scottish Union. *English Historical Review* 24: 44–.

——. 1910. *Commercial Relations of England and Scotland, 1603–1707*. With a preface by W. Cunningham. Cambridge, UK: Cambridge University Press.

——. 1912/13. The Influence of the Convention of the Royal Burghs of Scotland on the Economic Development of Scotland before 1707. *Scottish Historical Review* 10: 250–.

——. 1912/13. The Origin of the Convention of the Royal Burghs of Scotland: with a Note on the Connection of the Chamberlain with the Burghs. *Scottish Historical Review* 10: 384–.

——. 1913. The Trading Privileges of the Royal Burghs of Scotland. *English Historical Review* 28: 454-, 678–.

——. 1915/16. Municipal Elections in the Royal Burghs of Scotland, from the Union to the Passing of the Scottish Burgh Reform Bill in 1833. *Scottish Historical Review* 13: 266–.

——. 1915/16. Municipal Elections in the Royal Burghs of Scotland prior to the Union. *Scottish Historical Review* 13: 111–.

Keithan, Elizabeth Frederica. 1935. The Cacao Industry of the Major Producing Regions of Latin America. M.S. thesis, University of Chicago (geography).

——. 1939. Cacao Industry of Brazil. *Economic Geography* 15(2) (April): 195–204.

——. 1940. Cacao in Costa Rica. *Economic Geography* 16(1) (January): 79–86.

Kelley[-Wischnewetsky], Florence [Josephine]. 1882. Need Our Working Women Despair? *International Review* 13 (November): 517–27.

——. 1882. On Some Changes in the Legal Status of the Child Since Blackstone. *International Review* 13 (August): 7–98.

——. 1886. Die Sozialdemokratie und die Frage der Frauenarbeit: Ein Beitrag zur Programmfrage [Social democracy and the question of women's work: a contribution to the platform question]. *Der Sozialdemokrat: Zentral-Organ der deutschen Sozialdemokratie* (Zurich) 33 (August 11); 34 (August 18); 35 (August 25).

——, transl. 1887. *The Condition of the Working Class in England in 1844*, by Friedrich Engels. New York: J. W. Lovell.

——, transl. 1887. *The Object of the Labor Movement*, by Johann Jakoby. New York: New York Labor News Company.

——. 1887. The Need of Theoretical Preparation for Philanthropic Work. In Helen Hiscock Backus, ed., *The Need and the Opportunity for College-trained Women in Philanthropic Work*. New York: New York Association of Collegiate Alumnae.

——. 1889. *Our Toiling Children*. Chicago: Woman's Temperance Publication Association.

——. 1889. The Labour Question: Is Slavery Yet Abolished?: A Social Democratic Address in Memory of Thomas Paine. Address delivered February 3, 1889, in Philadelphia. London: W. Reeves.

——. 1890. Child Labor. In *Fifth Annual Report of the Bureau of Labor Statistics of the State of Connecticut for the Year Ending November 30, 1889*. Hartford, Conn.: Case, Lockwood and Brainard.

——. 1890. Child Labor in the US. *Our Day* 6 (September): 192–7.

——. 1890. The Evil of Child Labor. *Frank Leslie's Illustrated Weekly* 70 (February): 84–.

——. 1890. White Child Slavery. In White Child Slavery: A Symposium. *Arena* 1 (December): 594–951.

——. 1891. A Decade of Retrogression. *Arena* 4 (August): 365–72.

——. 1893. The Sweating System in Chicago. Part 2 of Illinois Bureau of Labor Statistics, *Seventh Biennial Report, 1892*. Springfield, Ill.: H. K. Rokker, State Printer and Binder.

——. 1893. Working Women in Chicago. Part 1 of Illinois Bureau of Labor Statistics, *Seventh Biennial Report, 1892*. Springfield, Ill.: H. K. Rokker, State Printer and Binder.

——. 1894. Factory Legislation in Illinois. In *Proceedings of the Seventh Annual Convention of the International Association of Factory Inspectors of North America, Held at Chicago, Illinois, Sept. 19–22, 1893*. Cleveland, Ohio: Forest City Printing House.

——. 1895. Child Labor in Illinois. In *Proceedings of the Ninth Annual Convention of the International Association of Factory Inspectors of North America, Held at Providence, Rhode Island, Sept. 3–5, 1895*. Cleveland, Ohio: Forest City Printing House.

——. 1895. Die Fabrik-Gesetzgebung der Vereinigten Staaten [Factory legislation in the United States]. *Archiv fur Soziale Gesetzgebung und Statistik* 8: 192–209.

——. 1895. The Need of Uniformity in Labor Legislation. In *Proceedings of the Eighth Annual Convention of the International Association of Factory Inspectors of North America, Held at Philadelphia, Pennsylvania, Sept. 25–28, 1894*. Cleveland, Ohio: Forest City Printing House.

——. 1895. The Sweating System. In [Residents of Hull House,] *Hull House Maps and Papers*. New York: Thomas Y. Crowell. Reprinted New York: Arno Press, 1970.

——. 1896. *The Working Child*. Chicago: William C. Hollister & Brother.

——. 1896. The Working Child. In *Proceedings of the 23rd National Conference of Charities and Correction*: 161–5. Boston: G. Ellis.

——. 1896. The Working Boy. *American Journal of Sociology* 2(3) (November): 358–68.

——. 1897. Child Labor. *Charities Review* 6 (May): 221–9.

——. 1897. Evolution of the Illinois Child Labor Law. In *Proceedings of the Eleventh Annual Convention of the International Association of Factory Inspectors of North America, Held at Detroit, Michigan, Aug. 31 and Sept. 1–2, 1897*. Lansing, Mich.: Robert Smith Printing.

——. 1897. Little Girls in Factories. *Chautauquan* 26 (October): 88–.

——. 1897. The Sweating System. In *Proceedings of the Tenth Annual Convention of the International Association of Factory Inspectors of North America, Held at Toronto, Canada, Sept. 1–3, 1896*. Chicago: Harman, Geng.

——. 1897. Trade and Technical Education of Girls. *Chautauquan* 26 (December): 309–.

——. 1897. Die weibliche Fabrikinspektion in der Vereinigten Staaten [Women factory inspectors in the United States]. *Archiv fur Soziale Gesetzgebung und Statistik* 11: 128–42.

——. 1897. Women and Girls in Sweat-shops. *Chautauquan* 25 (September): 655.

——. 1898. Drei Entscheidungen oberster Gerichte über den gesetzlichen Arbeitstag in den Vereinigten Staaten [Three Supreme Court decisions on the legal limitation of the working day in the United States]. *Archiv für Soziale Gesetzgebung und Statistik* 12: 744–74.

——. 1898. The Hours of Work for Women and Children. *Chautauquan* 26 (January): 430–.

——. 1898. Die gesetzliche Regelung der Kinder Arbeit im Staate Illinois [The legal regulation of child labor in the state of Illinois]. *Archiv für Soziale Gesetzgebung und Statistik* 12: 530–50.

——. 1898. Hull House. *New England Magazine* 18 (July): 550–66.

——. 1898. The Illinois Child Labor Law. *American Journal of Sociology* 3(4) (January): 490–501.

——. 1898. Das Sweating-system in den Vereinigten Staaten [The sweating system in the United States]. *Archiv für Soziale Gesetzgebung und Statistik* 12: 208–32.

——. 1898. The United States Supreme Court and the Utah Eight-hours' Law. *American Journal of Sociology* 4(1) (July): 21–34.

___. (1898). Working Women's Need of the Ballot. In Susan B. Anthony and Ida Husted Harper, eds., History of Woman Suffrage, vol. 4. New York: Fowler and Wells, 1902.

——. 1899. Aims and Principles of the Consumers' League. *American Journal of Sociology* 5(3) (November): 289–304.

——. 1899. Die Italiener Chicagos. *Archiv für soziale Gesetzgebung und Statistik* 13: 291–.

——. 1899. Principles of the Consumers' League. *Journal of Social Science* 37 (December): 111–22.

——. 1900. Labor Legislation and Philanthropy in Illinois. *Charities Review* 10(7) (September): 285–.

——. 1901. Das Fabrikinspektorat von New York und seine Stellung zur Arbeiterschutzgesetzgebung. *Archiv für soziale Gesetzgebung und Statistik* 16: 414–.

——. 1902. Child Labor Legislation. *Annals of the American Academy of Political and Social Science* 20(1): 155–.

——. 1903/1904. *The Travesty of Christmas*. New York: National Consumers' League.

——. 1903. A Boy-Destroying Trade. *Charities* XI: 15–19.

——. 1903. An Effective Child-labor Law: A Program for the Current Decade. *American Academy of Political and Social Science, Annals* 21 (May): 438–.

——. 1904. *Institution-factories*. New York: National Consumers' League. Reprinted from *Charities* (March 5, 1904).

——. 1904. Child Labor in the United States. *Charities* (August 20).

——. 1904. Has Illinois the Best Laws in the Country for the Protection of Children? *American Journal of Sociology* 10(3) (November): 299–314.

——. 1904/5. Book Review of "Poverty" by Robert Hunter. *American Journal of Sociology* 10(1/6): 555–.

——. 1905. *Child Labor Legislation and Enforcement in New England and the Middle States*. Address delivered at First Annual Meeting of the National Child Labor Committee in New York. New York: National Child Labor Committee.

——. 1905/1910/1914. *Some Ethical Gains through Legislation*. New York: Macmillan Co. Reprinted New York: Arno Press, 1969.

——. 1905. Child Labor Legislation and Enforcement in New England and the Middle States. *American Academy of Political and Social Science, Annals* 25 (January/June): 480–.

——. 1905 or 1906. Women in Trade Unions. *Outlook* lxxxiv: 926–31.

——. 1906/1910/1919. *Woman Suffrage: Its Relation to Working Women and Children.* Political Equality Series. Warren, Ohio. New York: National Woman Suffrage Publishing Co., Inc., Publishers for the National American Woman Suffrage Association.

——. 1906. The Federal Government and the Working Children. *American Academy of Political and Social Science, Annals* 27 (January/June): 289–.

——. 1906/7. Unskilled Mothers. *Century Illustrated Monthly Magazine* 73 (November/April): 640–.

——. 1907. Obstacles to the Enforcement of Child Labor Legislation. *American Academy of Political and Social Science, Annals* 29 (January/June): 50–.

——. 1908. *Laws for the Children's Welfare: An Ideal Attainable in 1920.* Journal of Proceedings and Addresses. S.l.: National Education Association of the United States.

——. 1909. The Invasion of Family Life by Industry. *American Academy of Political and Social Science, Annals* 34 (July/December): 90–.

——. 1910. Industrial Work of Married Women. *Academy of Political Science, Proceedings* 1(1) (October): 90–.

——. 1910. Married Women in Industry. In Helen Marot, ed., *The Economic Position of Women.* In Henry Mussey, ed., *Proceedings of the Academy of Political Science in the City of New York* 1(1) (October). New York: Columbia University.

——. 1910. The Problem of Sweating in America. *Chautauquan* 60 (September/November): 414–.

——. 1910. The Sex Problems in Industrial Hygiene. *American Journal of Public Hygiene* 20(2) (May): 252–.

——. 1911. *The Abolition of Child Labor.* New York: National American Woman Suffrage Association.

——. 1911. Child Labor: The Standard Minimum Age for Beginning to Work for Wages. *Twentieth Century Magazine* 5(1) (November): 30–.

——. 1911. Child Labor: The Standard Minimum Age for Beginning to Work for Wages, Part II. *Twentieth Century Magazine* 5(2) (December): 104–.

——. 1911. Minimum-wage Boards. *American Journal of Sociology* 17(3) (November): 303–14.

——. 1911. Our Lack of Statistics. *American Academy of Political and Social Science, Annals* 38(1) (July): 94–.

——. 1912. *Minimum Wage Boards.* New York: National Consumers' League.

——. 1912. *Minimum-wage Laws.* New York: National Consumers' League.

——. 1912. *A Privileged Industry.* New York: National Consumers' League. Reprinted from *Twentieth Century Magazine.*

——. 1912. Labor of Women and Children in Tenements. *Academy of Political Science, Proceedings* 2(4) (July): 114–.

——. 1912. Minimum-wage Laws. *Journal of Political Economy* 20 (December): 998–1,010.

——. 1912. Standards of Life and Labor: Child Labor, a Privileged Industry (Fourth in the Series). *Twentieth Century Magazine* 6(3) (July): 32–.

——. 1912. Standards of Life and Labor: Child Labor, the Standard Minimum Age for Beginning to Work. *Twentieth Century Magazine* 5(4) (February): 370–.
——. 1912/13. Book Review of "A New Conscience and an Ancient Evil" by Jane Addams. *American Journal of Sociology* 18(1/6): 271–.
——. 1913. *The Present Status of Minimum Wage Legislation.* New York: National Consumers' League.
——. 1914. *Modern Industry in Relation to the Family, Health, Education, Morality.* London: Longmans.
——. 1914. The Latest Ethical Gains through Legislation. *Standard* 1(2) (October): 54–.
——. 1914. Women and Social Legislation in the United States. *American Academy of Political and Social Science, Annals* 56 (November): 62–.
——. 1915. *What Women Might Do with the Ballot: The Abolition of Child Labor.* New York: National American Woman Suffrage Association.
——. 1915. Children in the Cities. *National Municipal Review* 4(2) (April): 197–.
——. 1915. The La Follette Law from the Consumers' Point of View. *Academy of Political Science, Proceedings* 6(1) (October): 90–.
——. 1915. Twenty-five Years of the Consumers' League Movement. *Survey* (November 27).
——. 1916. *Women in Industry: The Eight Hours Day and Rest at Night Upheld by the United States Supreme Court.* New York: National Consumers' League.
——. 1919. *Wage-earning Women in War Time: The Textile Industry, with Special Reference in Pennsylvania and New Jersey to Woollen and Worsted Yarn, and in Rhode Island to the Work of Women at Night.* New York: National Consumers' League. Also published in the *Journal of Industrial Hygiene* (October 1919).
——. 1922. *Twenty Questions about the Federal Amendment Proposed by the National Woman's Party.* Pamphlets in American History, no. WO 186. New York: National Consumers' League.
——. 1922. The Denial of Education. *World Tomorrow* 5(3) (March): 78–.
——. 1922. Industrial Conditions as a Community Problem with Particular Reference to Child Labor. *American Academy of Political and Social Science, Annals* 103 (September): 60–.
——. 1923. *Progress of Labor Legislation for Women.* Reprinted from the National Conference of Social Work, Fiftieth Annual Session, Washington, D.C., May 16–23, 1923.
——. 1923. Laborers in Heat and in Heavy Industries. *American Academy of Political and Social Science, Annals* 109 (September): 175–.
——. 1923. The Sterling Discrimination Bill. *Crisis* 26 (October): 252–.
——. 1924. Leisure by Statute for Women. *The Woman Citizen* (May 17).
——. 1928. Leisure by Law for Women. *Social Service Review* 2(1/4) (March/December): 24–.
——. 1931. Why the Children's Bill Did Not Pass. *American Labor Legislation Review* 21(2) (June): 175–.

——. 1939. *The Development in the United States of Legislation Concerning Women's Remunerative Work in Gainful Occupations: A Study*. Columbus, Ohio: Central Ohio Alumnae Chapter, Pi Lambda Theta.

Kelley, Florence J. and Marguerite Marsh. 1929. Labor Legislation for Women and Its Effects on Earnings and Conditions of Labor. *Annals of the American Academy of Political and Social Science* 143 (May): 286–.

——. 1929. A Skeleton in Industry's Closet: Youth's Compensation for Industrial Injuries. *Diritto del lavoro* 3(1): 425–.

Kelley, Florence and Dorothy Myers. 1926/1927. *Children's Compensation for Industrial Accidents: How the States Love Their Children*. No. 1, A Preliminary Study. New York: National Consumers' League.

Kelley, Florence and Alzina Stevens. 1895. Wage Earning Children. In [Residents of Hull House,] *Hull House Maps and Papers*. New York: Thomas Y. Crowell.

Kelley, Florence Josephine and Lazare Wischnewetsky. 1887. *Die Arbeiterbewegung in Amerika*. New York: L. Weiss.

Kelley, Florence. Coauth. *See* Beard, Mary Ritter; Goldmark, Pauline Dorothea; Nicholes, Anna E.

——. Personal papers at the New York Public Library. New National Consumer League Papers are at the Library of Congress. She also has papers included in the Jane Addams papers at Swarthmore College, the Lillian Wald Papers at the New York Public Library and Columbia University, the Consumers' League of Massachusetts Papers at the Schlesinger Library, and the Henry Demarest Lloyd Papers at the State Historical Society of Wisconsin.

Kelley, M[ary]. E. J. 1888. Tariff Acts under the Confederation. *Quarterly Journal of Economics* 4 (July): 473–81.

——. 1893. The Value of a Pen-name. *Writer* 6(9) (September): 171–.

——. 1896. Woman in Business. *Lippincott's* 57 (June): 850–3.

——. 1897. Strikes as a Factor in Progress. *North American Review* 164 (January): 24–31.

——. 1897. The [Trade] Union Label. *North American Review* 165 (July): 26–36.

——. 1898. Women Factory Workers. *Outlook: A Family Paper* 58 (January 29): 269–70.

——. 1898. Women and the Labor Movement. *North American Review* 166(4) (April): 408–17.

——. 1899. Women and the Drink Problem. *Catholic World* 69 (August): 678–87.

Kellogg, Julia A. 1895. Women's Discussion of the Labor Problem: Land and Money. *Arena* 14 (October) 268–71.

Kellogg, Ruth Mary. 1927. Child Labor Legislation in New York State. M.A. thesis, University of Chicago.

——. 1933. *The United States Employment Service*. Chicago: University of Chicago Press.

——. 1933. Standards of Service for a Public Employment Office. *American Federationist* 40(2) (February): 145–.

——. 1933/4. Book Review of "Statistical Procedure of Public Employment Offices" by Annabel M. Stewart and Bryce M. Stewart. *American Journal of Sociology* 39(1/6): 416–.

——. 1934/5. Book Review of "An International Study of Placing Activities" by Employment Exchanges. *American Journal of Sociology* 40(1/6): 561–.

Kellor, Frances Alice. 1900. Criminal Sociology. *Arena* 23 (January and March): 301 and 516.

——. 1900. My Experiments with the Kymograph. *Harper's Bazar* 33 (November 10): 1,755–60.

——. 1900. Psychological and Environmental Study of Women Criminals I. *American Journal of Sociology* 5(4) (January); II 5(5) (March).

——. 1901. *Experimental Sociology*. New York: Macmillan.

——. 1901. Childhood Influences. *Arena* 26 (July/December): 304–.

——. 1901. The Criminal Negro. *Arena* 25 (January/June): 59, 190, 308, 419, 510.

——. 1901. Environmental Influences (The Criminal Negro). *Arena* 26 (July/December): 521–.

——. 1904/1915. *Out of Work: A Study of Employment Agencies, Their Treatment of the Unemployed, and Their Influence upon Home and Business*. New York and London: Putnam.

——. 1904. The Intelligence Office. *Atlantic Monthly* 94: 458–.

——. 1905. Associations for Protection of Colored Women. *Colored American Magazine* 9(6) (December): 695–.

——. 1905. Opportunities for Southern Negro Women in Northern Cities. *Voice of the Negro* 2(7) (July).

——. 1907. The Immigrant Woman. *Atlantic Monthly* 100: 401–.

——. 1908. Protection of Immigrant Women. *Atlantic* 101 (February): 246–.

——. 1910. *Notaries Public and Immigrants*. New York: s.n.

——. 1911. Needed – A Domestic Immigration Policy. *North American Review* 193 (April).

——. 1912. What Women Can Do for the Progressive Cause – Why They Should Do It. *Progressive Bulletin* 1–2.

——. 1914. *Immigrants in America: Program for a Domestic Policy*. New York: Committee for Immigrants in America.

——. 1914. *Who Is Responsible for the Immigrant?* S.l.: s.n.

——. 1914. The Crying Need for Connecting up the Man and the Job. *Survey* 31 (February 7).

——. 1914. The Education of the Immigrant. *Educational Review* 48 (June).

——. 1914. Is Unemployment a Municipal Problem? *National Municipal Review* 3(2) (April): 366–.

——. 1914. Justice for the Immigrant. *American Academy of Political and Social Science, Annals* 52 (March): 159–.

——. 1914. A New Spirit in Party Organization. *North American Review* 199 (June).

——. 1914. Organizing to Fight Unemployment Effectively. *Survey* 31 (February 14).
——. 1914. Three Bills to Distribute Labor and Reduce Unemployment. *Survey* 31 (March 7).
——. 1914. The Way Out of the Unemployment Situation. *Survey* 31 (February 21).
——. 1915. *Out of Work: A Study of Unemployment*. New York: Putnam.
——. 1915. Unemployment and Immigration. *Annals of the American Academy of Political and Social Science* 61 (September): 40–.
——. 1915. Unemployment in American Cities: The Record for 1914–15. *National Municipal Review* 4(3) (July): 420–.
——. 1915. Unemployment in Our Cities. *National Municipal Review* 4(3) (January): 69–.
——. 1915/16. *The Immigrants in America Review*. 2 vols. New York: Committee Immigrants in America.
——. 1916. *Straight America: A Call to National Service*. New York: Macmillan.
——. 1916. Americanization: A Conservation Policy for Industry. *American Academy of Political and Social Science, Annals* 65 (May): 240–.
——. 1916. Americanization, an Opportunity. *Association of Collegiate Alumnae, Journal* 10(1) (September): 7–.
——. 1916. How to Increase Night-school Attendance among the Foreign-born. *School and Society* 3(68) (April 15): 569–.
——. 1916. Lo, the Poor Immigrant. *Atlantic* 17 (January).
——. 1916/17. Women in the Campaign. *Yale Review* 6: 233–.
——. 1917. *The Americanization of Workmen around the Lime Plant*. S.l.: National Lime Manufacturers' Association.
——. 1917. Engineering Methods Must Replace Paternalism in the Handling of Labor. *Engineering News-Record* (April 12). Reprinted New York: Immigration Committee of the Chamber of Commerce of the United States of America, 1917.
——. 1917. Women in the Campaign. *Yale Review* 6 (January).
——. 1918. *The Americanization of Women: A Discussion of an Emergency Created by Granting the Vote to Women in New York State*. Lecture delivered in the course on citizenship of the New York State Woman's Suffrage Party in the City of New York, Murray Hill Hotel, January 17, 1918. New York: s.n.
——. 1918. *Industrial Americanization*. Americanization Pamphlets. New York: National Americanization Committee.
——. 1918. *Neighborhood Americanization: A Discussion of the Alien in a New Country and of the Native American in His Home Country*. Address delivered in the course of lectures on citizenship before the Colony Club in New York City, February 8, 1918. Pamphlets in American History, European War, EW 496. New York: National Americanization Committee.
——. 1918. *Welfare or Manpower Engineering*. New York: National Americanization Committee.

——. 1919. *What Is Americanization?* Americanization Pamphlets. New York: National Americanization Committee. Also printed in the *Yale review* (January 1919): 282–99.

——. 1919. Immigration in Reconstruction. *North American Review* 209 (February): 199–.

——. 1920. *Immigration and the Future.* New York: George H. Doran.

——. 1920. *The Inside of Bolshevism Addressed to Credit Men.* Address before the New York Credit Men's Association, Hotel Astor, New York, January 27, 1920. New York: s.n.

——. 1920. Conservation. *Personnel* 2(9) (September): 1–.

——. 1921. *Federal Administration and the Alien.* New York: George H. Doran.

——. 1921. Future Immigration. *North American Review* 214 (July): 13–.

——. 1921. Immigration and the Future. *Annals of the American Academy of Political and Social Science* 93 (January): 201–.

——. 1923. Women in British and American Politics. *Current History (New York)* 17(5) (February): 831–.

——. 1924. *Security Against War.* New York: Macmillan.

——, ed. 1931. *Report for 1926–1931.* Arbitration Association Administration of Commercial Arbitration under the Code of Arbitration. Practice and Procedure of the American Arbitration Tribunal, Supplement no. 1. New York: Commerce Clearing House, Inc., Loose Leaf Service Division of the Corporation Trust Company.

——. 1934. *Arbitration in the New Industrial Society.* New York: McGraw-Hill.

——. 1940. Arbitration as a Phase of the Procedure for the Settlement of Inter-American Controversies. *Proceedings of the Eighth American Scientific Congress* 10 (May).

Kellor, Frances Alice and J. Noble Braden. 1931. *Code of Arbitration.* New York: Commerce Clearing House, Inc.

Kellor, Frances Alice and Antonia Hatvany. 1925. *The United States Senate and the International Court.* New York: Thomas Seltzer.

Kelly, E. T. and M. L. Haskins. 1921. Foundations of Industrial Welfare. *Economica* 1/2(2) (May): 116–.

Kempe, Dorothy. 1912. Book Review of "Social Conditions in Oxford" by C. Violet Butler. *Economic Journal* 22(88) (December): 611–13.

Kelso, Tessa L. 1893. Some Economical Features of Public Libraries. *Arena* 7 (May): 709–13.

Kempin, Emilie. 1892. *Die Stellung der Frau; nach den zur Zeit in Deutschland gültigen Gesetzes-Bestimmungen sowie nach dem Entwurf eines bürgerlichen Gesetzbuches für das Deutsche Reich.* Leipzig: Allgemeiner Deutschen Frauenverein/Schäfer.

Kendal, Madge, Janet Elizabeth Hogarth Courtney, Beatrice Orange, Louise Jopling, Mary Frances Billington, Ethel F. Lamport, Margaret H. Irwin and Mabyn Armour. 1902. *Education and Professions.* London: Chapman & Hall.

Kendall, Edith. 1910. The Conquest of Poverty. How the Protestant Churches Are Awakening to the Problem. *Metropolitan Magazine* XXXIV: 105–12.

Kendall, Elizabeth Kimball. Coauth. *See* Coman, Katharine.

Kenealy, Arabella. 1890. Talent of Motherhood. *National Review* 16 (December): 446–59.

——. 1891. A New View of the Surplus of Women. *Westminster Review* 136 (November): 465–7.

Kennard, Mrs. Arthur. 1891. Ferdinand Lassalle. *Nineteenth Century* 30 (July/December): 361–.

Kennedy, Aileen Elizabeth. 1933. The Development and the Interpretation of the Ohio Poor Law. M.A. thesis, University of Chicago (law).

Kennedy, Aileen Elizabeth and Sophonisba Preston Breckinridge. 1934. *The Ohio Poor Law and Its Administration*. Service Monographs, no. 22. Chicago: University of Chicago Press.

Kennedy, Louise Venable. 1930. The Negro Peasant Turns Cityward: Effects of Recent Migrations to Northern Centers. Ph.D. thesis, Columbia University (history). Studies in History, Economics, and Public Law, no. 329. New York: Columbia University Press; P. S. King.

Kenyon, Nora. 1934. Labour Conditions in Essex in the Reign of Richard II. *Economic History Review* 4 (April): 429–51.

Kenyon, Ruth [E.]. 1908. The Problem of the Watering-place. *Economic Review* (January).

——. 1910/1919. *A History of Socialism*. Manuals for the Millions, no. 14. London: Mowbray.

——. 1910. Social Conditions and the Principles of 1834. *Economic Review*.

——. 1921/1964. *Unemployment*. Major Issue of the Day, no. 3. Guilford: Christian Social Council.

——. 1931. *The Catholic Faith and the Industrial Order*. London: P. Allan.

——. 1931. India and Her Problems. *International Journal of Religious Education* 8(3) (November): 22–.

——. 1932. Studies in the Social Outlook of the Tractarians (II). Keble and Pusey. *Theology* 25(145) (July): 24–.

——. 1932. Two Studies in the Social Outlook of the Tractarians (I). Newman. *Theology* 24(144) (June): 317–.

——. 1933. The "Lux Mundi" School as Continuators of the Tractarian Sociology. *Theology* 26(151) (January): 16–.

Kerchner, Anne Lenore. 1935. Going Value in Public Utility Rate Making. M.A. thesis, University of Chicago (economics, commerce-business).

[Kerr,] May Walden. 1900. *Women and Socialism*. Chicago: Charles H. Kerr.

——. 1901. *Socialism and the Home*. Chicago: Charles H. Kerr.

Keston-Conrad, Else. 1910. Zur Dienstbotenfrage. *Archiv für Sozialwissenschaft* (September).

Kettler, Frau. J. 1890. The Woman Question in Germany. *Chautauquan* 10 (March): 708–.

Key, Ellen Karolina Sofia. 1888. *Om eganderätt och myndighet för den gifta kvinnan: tvänne föredrag hållna i Helsingfors den 16: de och 17: de september, 1887*. Helsingfors: Finsk kvinnoförenings förlag.

——. 1896. *Missbrukad kvinnokraft, och Naturenliga arbetsområden för kvinnan.* Stockholm: A. Bonnier.

——. 1896. *Till Ellen Key. Kvinnoffrågans prima principia.* Helsingfors: Wentzel Hagelstam.

Kiehel, Constance Amelia. 1932. *Unemployment Insurance in Belgium: A National Development of the Ghent and Liège Systems.* New York: Industrial Relations Counselors.

——. 1933. Book Review of "The Coming Struggle for Power" by John Strachey. *American Academy of Political and Social Science, Annals* 170 (November): 173.

——. 1933. Book Review of "From Chaos to Control" by Norman Angell. *American Academy of Political and Social Science, Annals* 170 (November): 179.

——. 1933. Book Review of "Human Aspects of Unemployment and Relief" by James M. Williams. *American Academy of Political and Social Science, Annals* 167 (March): 235–.

——. 1933. Book Review of "Industry and Society" by Arthur James Todd. *American Academy of Political and Social Science, Annals* 170 (November): 179.

——. 1933. Book Review of "Statistical Procedure of Public Employment Offices" by Annabel M. Stewart and M. Bryce. *American Academy of Political and Social Science, Annals* 170 (November): 178.

——. 1937. Security of Job Tenure and Trade-union Out-of-work Benefits, 1926–1929 and 1930–1933. *American Economic Review* 27(3) (September): 452–67.

——. 1938. Unemployment Insurance in Belgium. Ph.D. thesis, University of Wisconsin–Madison (economics).

——. 1939. *The Maritime Industry and Unemployment Compensation.* Washington: Social Security Board, Divsions of Research and Statistics.

Kies, Marietta. 1891. The Ethical Principle in Industrial Relations. *Publications of the American Economic Association,* series I, VI(1/2) (January/March): 46–8.

——. 1891/2. Book Review of "The Land and the Laborers" by Charles William Stubbs. *Annals of the American Academy of Political and Social Science* 2 (July/June): 278.

——. 1894. *Institutional Ethics.* Boston: Allyn and Bacon.

Kilduff, Vera Rachel Reynolds. 1939. An Analysis of the Development of Canadian–American Trade. Ph.D. thesis, Brown University (economics).

Killough, Lucy Burton Winsor. 1920. Swindling in the Sale of Securities and the Blue Sky Law as a Remedy. M.A. thesis. Leland Stanford Junior University.

——. 1925. *The Tobacco Products Industry in New York and Its Environs: Present Trends and Probable Future Developments.* New York: Regional Plan of New York and Its Environs.

——. 1925. The Tobacco Products Industry in New York and Its Environs: Present Trends and Probable Future Developments. Ph.D. thesis, Columbia University (economics).

——. 1940. Tax Exempt Industries in Rhode Island. *National Tax Association, Bulletin* 26(2) (November): 34–.

King, Annie R. 1894. Woman in Charity Works. *Chautauquan* 19 (April/September): 754–.

King, Mrs. E. M. 1873. Co-operative Housekeeping. *Contemporary Review* 23 (December): 66–91.

Kingsbury, Elizabeth. 1883. *Work for Women*. London: Bickers and Son.

Kingsbury, Mary M. *See* [Simkhovitch,] Mary M. Kingsbury.

Kingsbury, Susan Myra. 1905. *An Introduction to the Records of the Virginia Company of London, with a Bibliographical List of the Extant Documents*. Washington: U.S. Government Printing Office.

——. 1905. An Introduction to the Records of the Virginia Company of London, with a Bibliographical List of the Extant Documents. Ph.D. thesis, Columbia University (history).

——. 1906/1933/1935. *The Records of the Virginia Company of London*. Washington: U.S. Government Printing Office.

——. 1906. Report of Sub-committee on Relation of Children to Industries. *Massachusetts Commission on Industrial and Technical Education Report*.

——. 1908. A Comparison of the Virginia Company with the Other English Trading Companies of the Sixteenth and Seventeenth Centuries. In *American Historical Association, Annual Report for the Year 1906*: 171–6.

——. 1908. Efficiency and Wage of Women in Gainful Occupations. *Association of Collegiate Alumnae, Publications* 3(18) (December): 19–.

——. 1910. Economic Efficiency of College Women. *Association of Collegiate Alumnae, Publications* 3(20) (February): 1–.

——. 1910. Opportunities for Women Trained in Research: Economic Research. In Agnes Perkins, ed., *Vocations for the Trained Woman: Opportunities Other than Teaching*. New York: Longmans Green & Co.

——. 1910. Standards of Living and the Self-dependent Woman. In Helen Marot, ed., *The Economic Position of Women*. In Henry Raymond Mussey, ed., *Proceedings of the Academy of Political Science in the City of New York* 1(1) (October). New York: Columbia University.

——. 1911/1971. Introduction. In Susan Myra Kingsbury, Charles Edward Person, and Edith Gertrude Solenberger, eds., *Labor Laws and Their Enforcement with Special Reference to Massachusetts*. New York: Longmans, Green. Reprinted, New York: Arno Press, 1971.

——. 1913. Book Review of "Seasonal Trades" by various writers. *American Economic Review* 3: 400–.

——. 1913. Book Review of "Women in the Bookbinding Trade" by Mary van Kleeck. *American Economic Review* 3: 667–.

——. 1915. Book Review of "Citizens in Industry" by Henderson. *Psychological Bulletin* 12: 477–.

——. 1915. Book Review of "Crippled Children" by Reeves. *American Economic Review* 5(1/2): 385–.

——. 1916. The Education of Women as Measured in Civic and Social Relations. *College Settlements Association Quarterly* 1(4) (June): 1–.

——. 1917. Book Review of “Survey of Wage-earning Girls below Sixteen Years of Age in Wilkes-Barre, Pennsylvania, 1915” by Atherton. *American Economic Review* 7(1/2): 165.

——. 1917. Book Review of “Wage Worth of School Training” by Hedges. *American Economic Review* 7(1/2): 166.

——. 1918. Book Review of “Industrial Conditions in Springfield, Illinois” by Odencrantz and Potter. *American Economic Review* 8(1/2): 375–.

——. 1918. The New Community Service at Home and Abroad. *Intercollegiate Community Service Quarterly* 3(2) (January): 1–.

——. 1919. The Problem of Educating a Democracy. Discussion. *American Sociological Society, Papers and Proceedings* 14 (December): 160–.

——. 1919. Training for Industrial Supervision and Employment Management and for Community Work. *Intercollegiate Community Service Quarterly* 4(3) (April): 5–.

——. 1920. Relation of Women to Industry. *American Sociological Society, Papers and Proceedings* 15 (December): 141–.

——. 1921. Relation of Women to Industry. *American Sociological Society Publications* (May).

——. 1932. Social Process in Russia. *American Sociological Society, Publication* 26(3) (December): 68–.

——. 1933. Measuring the Ethics of American Newspapers. *Journalism Quarterly* 10.

——. 1934. Measuring the Ethics of American Newspapers. *Journalism Quarterly* 11.

——. 1937. *Newspapers and the News, and Objective Measurement of Ethical and Unethical Behavior by Representative Newspapers.* New York: G. P. Putnam’s Sons.

——. 1939. *Economic Status of University Women in the U.S.A. Report of the Committee on Economic and Legal Status of Women, American Association of University Women in Cooperation with the Women’s Bureau, United States Department of Labor.* Bulletin of the U.S. Women’s Bureau, no 170. Washington: U.S. Government Printing Office.

——. 1939. A Study of the Economic Status of University Women. Summary and Conclusions. *American Association of University Women, Journal* 32(4) (June): 224–.

Kingsbury, Susan Myra and Mildred Fairchild. 1932. *Employment and Unemployment in Pre-war and Soviet Russia.* Schiedam, Holland: De Eendracht.

——. 1935. *Factory, Family, and Woman in the Soviet Union.* New York: G. P. Putnam’s Sons. Reprinted New York: AMS Press, 1974.

Kingsbury, Susan Myra and Mabelle Moses. 1915. *Licensed Workers in Industrial Home Work in Massachusetts, Analysis of Current Records under the Auspices of the Bureau of Research, Women’s Educational and Industrial Union.* Massachusetts State Board of Labor and Industries, Industrial Bulletin, no. 4. Boston: Wright & Potter, State Printers.

Kingsbury, Susan M., George E. Putnam, Mildred Fairchild, Calvin B. Hoover, Mabel Newcomer, William Adams Brown, Jr., and Paul Haensel. 1931.

Russian Economic Situation. *American Economic Review*, Supplement 21(1) (March): 37–53.

Kingsbury, Susan Myra. Coauth. *See* Allinson, May; Cohn, Adele; Francke, Marie; Martin, Eleanor.

Kingsford, Jane. 1896/7. Progressive Housekeeping. *Chautauquan* 24 (October/March): 211–, 331–, 472–.

Kingsley, Mary H[enrietta]. 1896. The Development of Dodos. *National Review* 27 (March): 66–79.

——. 1897. *Travels in West Africa, Congo Francais, Corisco and Cameroons*. London and New York: Macmillan.

——. 1897. African Religion and Law. *National Review* 29 (September): 122–39.

——. 1898. The Hut-tax in Africa. *Spectator* 84 (March 19): 407–8.

——. 1898. Liquor Traffic with West Africa. *Fortnightly Review* 69 (n.s. 63) (April): 537–60.

——. 1899. *The Story of West Africa*. London: H. Marshall & Son.

——. 1899/1901. *West African Studies*. London and New York: Macmillan. 2nd ed. with additional chapters, 1901.

Kirsten, Mary. 1938. Current Trends in Real Estate. *Land Economics* 14 (November): 454–8.

Kistler, Thelma Maddie. 1938. *The Rise of Railroads in the Connecticut River Valley*. Smith College Studies in History, vol. xxiii, no. 4 (July). Northampton, Mass.: Department of History of Smith College.

——. 1939. Rise of Railroads in the Connecticut River Valley. Ph.D. thesis, Cornell University (economics).

Kittredge, Dorothea Davis. 1923. The Influence of Certain Factors on the Increase in Cost of Living, 1913 to 1920, as Interpreted by Partial Correlations. M.A. thesis, George Washington University.

——. 1923. A Suggestion for Determining a Living Wage. *American Economic Review* 13 (June): 225–9.

Klärmann, Sophie. 1912/1990. *Die freien Gewerkschaften in Gesetzgebung und Politik*. Leipzig: Duncker & Humblot; Bad Feilnbach, Germany: Schmidt.

Kleeck, Mary van. *See* van Kleeck, Mary.

Klem, Margaret Coyne. 1933. The Costs of Medical Care to the Family. *Journal of the American Statistical Association* 28(181), Supplement (March): 98–103.

——. 1935. *Medical Care and Costs in California Families in Relation to Economic Status*. San Francisco: State Relief Administration of California.

——. 1938. *A Plan for a Case Census of Recipients of Public Assistance Research Social Security Board, Bureau of Research and Statistics*. Social Security Board Bureau of Research and Statistics Report, no. 2. Washington: U.S. Government Printing Office.

Klingenstein, Miss L. 1912. Seamen's Allotment Notes. *Women's Industrial Notes* (January).

Klopfer, Helen L. 1936. Statistics of Foreign Trade of Philadelphia, 1700–1860. Ph.D. thesis, University of Pennsylvania (economics).

——. Coauth. *See* Palmer, Gladys Louise.

Knapp, Adeline. 1895. The Dignity of Labor: A Sketch from Life. *Arena* 11 (January): 258–60.

Knatchbull-Hugessen, the Hon. Eva. 1889. Higher Education of Women. *National Review* 13 (March): 33–.

Kneeland, Hildegard. 1930. The Work of the Rural Household. Ph.D. thesis, Robert Brookings.

——. 1938. *Consumer Incomes in the United States: Their Distribution in 1935–1936*. Washington: National Resources Committee, Industrial Committee.

——. 1939. *Consumer Expenditures in the United States: Estimates for 1935–36*. Washington: U.S. National Resources Committee, Industrial Committee.

Knightley, Lady. 1893. New Employments for Educated Women. *New Review* 9 (December): 577–.

Knowles, Lilian. 1904. Book Review of "Industrial Organisation in the Sixteenth and Seventeenth Centuries" by George Unwin. *Economic Journal* 14: 579.

——. 1905. Book Review of "The English Craft Gilds and the Government" by Stella Kramer. *Economic Journal* 15(60) (December): 543–8.

——. 1906. Book Review of "The Growth of the Manor" by Paul Vinogradoff. *Economic Journal* 15: 394.

——. 1906. Book Review of "Die oekonomische Entwicklung Europas bis zum Beginn der Kapitalisschen Wirtschafttisform" by M. Kowalewsky. *Economic Journal* 16: 116.

——. 1907. Book Review of "The Economic Development of a Norfolk Manor, 1086–1565" by Frances Gardiner Davenport. *Economic Journal* 17(66) (June): 267–9.

——. 1908. Book Review of "A History of Commerce" by Clive Day. *Economic Journal* 18: 83.

——. 1908. Book Review of "The Stannaries: A Study of the English Tin Miner" by George Randall Lewis. *Economic Journal* 18: 445–.

——. 1909. Book Review of "The King's Customs. An Account of Maritime Revenue and Contraband Traffic in England, Scotland, and Ireland, from the Earliest Times to the Year 1800" by Henry Alton and Henry Hurst Holland. *Economic Journal* 19: 440.

——. 1911. Book Review of "The King's Customs, Vol. II: An Account of Maritime Revenue, Contraband Traffic, the Introduction of Free Trade, and the Abolition of the Navigation and Corn Laws from 1801 to 1855" by Henry Atton and Henry Hurst Holland. *Economic Journal* 21: 92.

——. 1911. Book Review of "Die oekonomische Entwicklung Europas bis zum Beginn der kapitalistischen Wirtschaftsform" by Maxime Kowalewsky. *Economic Journal* 21: 438.

——. 1911. Book Review of "A Short History of English Agriculture" by W. H. R. Curtler. *Economic Journal* 21: 420.

——. 1914. Book Review of "Economic Organisation of England" by W. J. Ashley. *Economic Journal* 24: 566.

——. 1915. Book Review of "Economic History of England" by M. Briggs. *Economic Journal* 25: 402.

——. 1915. Book Review of "Industrial History of Modern England" by G. H. Perris. *Economic Journal* 25: 402.

——. 1918. Book Review of "Economic Development of Modern Europe" by F. A. Ogg. *Economic Journal* 28: 87.

——. 1919. Book Review of "Chartism and the Churches: A Study in Democracy" by H. N. Faulkner. *Economic Journal* 29: 203.

——. 1919. Book Review of "The Chartist Movement in its Social and Economic Aspects" by F. E. Rosenblatt. *Economic Journal* 29: 202.

——. 1919. Book Review of "The Decline of the Chartist Movement" by P. W. Slosson. *Economic Journal* 29: 202.

——. 1919. Book Review of "Historical Review of Economic Conditions of British Empire, 1815–1919" by W. Page. *Economic Journal* 29: 460.

——. 1919. New Light on the Economic Causes of the French Revolution. *Economic Journal* 29 (March): 1–24.

——. 1921. *The Industrial and Commercial Revolutions in Great Britain During the Nineteenth Century*. London: Routledge & Co.

——. 1922. Book Review of "Modern Economic History, with Special Reference to Australia." *Economic Journal* 32: 88–.

——. 1922. Book Review of "A Social and Industrial History of England before the Industrial Revolution" by M. D. Harris. *Economic Journal* 32(125) (March): 86–9.

——. 1924. *The Economic Development of the British Overseas Empire*. London: Routledge & Sons.

——. 1932. *Economic Development in the Nineteenth Century. France, Germany, Russia, and the United States*. London: Routledge.

——. Papers can be found at the British Library of Political and Economic Science, London School of Economics. Information on Knowles' archives is available on the web at http://www.aim25.ac.uk/cgi-bin/search2?coll—id=5632&inst—id=1.

Knox, Kethleen S. 1894. A Visit to an Industrial School. *Irish Monthly* 22.

Knudsen, Lila. 1938. Serial or Coherent Correlation in Price Series. *Journal of Farm Economics* 28 (May): 484–8.

——. 1940. Interdependence in a Series. *Journal of the American Statistical Association* 35 (September): 507–14.

Kock, Karin. 1927. The Organisation of the Swedish Money Market. *Economica* 7(19) (March): 63–73.

——. 1928. Bankwetgeving in Zweden. *Economisch-statistische Berichten* 13(630) (January 25): 82–.

——. 1928. Het Herstel van de Scandinavische Muntunie. *Economisch-statistische Berichten* 13(670) (October 31): 956–.

——. 1929. *A Study of Interest Rates*. London: P. S. King.

——. 1929. Industriëele vrede in Zweden. *Economisch-statistische Berichten* 14(693) (April 10): 350–.

——. 1929. Zweden en de ontwikkeling op de buitenlandsche geldmarkten. *Economisch-statistische Berichten* 14(713) (August 28): 781–.

——. 1930/1932. *Svenskt Bankväsen i Våra Dagar*. Stockholm: Kooperativa Förbundets Bokförlag.

——. 1930. De landbouwerisis. *Economisch-statistische Berichten* 15(731) (January 1): 10–.

——. 1931. *Skånska Privatbanken, Minnesskrift. På Uppdrag av Skandinaviska Kreditaktiebolaget.* Stockholm: P. A. Norstedt & Söner; Göteborg, Sweden: Skandinaviska Kreditaktiebolaget.

——. 1931. Capital Formation in Sweden 1924–1929. In *Arbetlöshetsutredningens betäkande* I: 542–8.

——. 1931. G. H. Aulin och Skånska Privatbanken. *Statsvetenskaplig tidskrift för politik, statistik, ekonomi* 13: 178–.

——. 1931. How Sweden Was Forced to Leave the Gold Standard. In Myrdal G., ed., *Sveriges väg genom penningkrisen.* Stockholm: Natur och Kultur.

——. 1932. *Skånska cement aktiebolag 1871–1931 Minnesskrift.* Uppsala: Almqvist & Wiksell.

——. 1932. *Skånska privatbanken.* Stockholm: Norstedt.

——. 1932. *Svenskt bankväsen i våra dagar.* Stockholm.

——. 1932. Les Monnaies scandinaves et leur détachement de l'or. *Revue d'économie politique* 46: 382–.

——. 1933. *Economic Essays in Honour of Gustav Cassell.* London: George Allen & Unwin.

——. 1933. The Banking System in the United States. *Svensk Sparbankstidskrif* 17: 133–50.

——. 1933. The Budget and Savings. *Svensk Sparkankstidskrift* 17: 73–80.

——. 1933. Paper Currency and Monetary Policy in Sweden. In Karin Kock, ed., *Economic Essays in Honor of Gustav Cassel.* London: George Allen & Unwin.

——. 1934. *Roosevelts Program ur Konjunktursynpunkt.* Ekonomiska Debatten, 3. Stockholm: Kooperativa Förbundets Bokförlaget.

——. 1934. *Sveriges Handelsekonomiska Läga.* Stockholm: A. Bonnier.

——. 1935. Konjunkturppsvingets Förlopp och Orsaker 1932–1934 [The course and causes of the business cycle upswing 1932–34]. *SOU* [Statens Offentliga Utredningar; or Official (Public) Investigations of the State (Government)] 1935(16). Also published Stockholm: Nord. bokh. i distr.

——. 1936. Memo on Economic and Social Trend Investigations. *Riksdagens protokoll 1936*, Bihang Saml. 1, 215: 30–4.

——. 1936. Wirtschaftspolitik und Kunjunkturaufschwung in Schweden 1933–1936. *Jahrbücher für Nationalökonomie und Statistik* 144(6) (December): 708–29.

——. 1937. *Smålands bank 1837–1937.* Jönkoping: s.n.

——. 1938. *Betänkande angående gift kvinnas förvärsarbete m. m.* Stockholm: I. Marcus boktryckeri-aktiebolag.

——. 1938. Crisis, Depression and Recovery in Sweden, 1929–1937. In Carl Jakob Herman Hallendorff and Adolf Schuck, eds., *History of Sweden.* Stockholm: C. E. Fritze, Ltd.

——. 1938. The Importance of Forestry and Forest Industries for the Economy. In *Utredning rörande skogsnäringens ekonomiska läge med förslag till åtgärder för höjande av näringens bärkraft Förberedande undersökningar och uttalanden*: 69–103. S.l.: s.n.

——. 1938. Women's Labour in Sweden. In *Betänkande ang gift kvinnas förvärsarbete m m ave av Kvinnoarbetskommitén*. Stockholm: I. Marcus boktryckeri-aktiebolag.

——. 1939. *Memorandum (3) on International Capital Movements and Economic Policy, Submitted to the Conference by the Swedish Co-ordinating Committee for International Studies*. Paris: International Institute of Intellectual Co-operation, League of Nations.

——. 1939. Några problem rörande definitioner och terminologi i teorien för de internationella kapitalrörelserna. *Ekonomisk Tidskrift* 41(4) (December): 311–.

——. 1939. Some Problems of Definitions and Terminology in the Theory of International Capital Movements. *Ekonomisk Tidskrift* 41: 311–24.

——. 1940. Hur Skall Kriget Betalas? *Ekonomisk Tidskrift* 42(2) (June): 49–.

Kock, Karin, E. Lindahl, and E. Dahlgren. 1937. *National Income of Sweden, 1861–1930*. Stockholm Economic Studies, nos. 5A and 5B. London: P.S. King and Son, Ltd.

Koempel, Leslie Alice. 1937. Measurement of Changes in the Standard of Living during a Depression. Ph.D. thesis, Bryn Mawr College (economics).

Koester, Genevieve. 1938. Chicago Real Estate Bonds, 1919–1938. Part I. *Land Economics* 15 (February): 49–58.

——. 1938. Chicago Real Estate Bonds, 1919–1938. Part II. *Land Economics* 15 (May): 201–11.

Komarovsky, Mirra. 1940. *The Unemployed Man and His Family: The Effect of Unemployment upon the Status of the Man in Fifty-nine Families*. New York: Institute of Social Research.

Kopald [Selekman], Sylvia. 1923. *Workers' Education in the United States: Report of Proceedings, Second National Conference on Workers' Education in the United States, 1922*. New York: Workers' Education Bureau of America.

——. 1924. *Rebellion in Labor Unions*. New York: Boni and Liveright.

——. 1924. Rebellion in Labor Unions. Ph.D. thesis, Columbia University (economics)

——. 1924. Where Are the Female Geniuses? In Freda Kirchwey, ed., *Our Changing Morality: A Symposium*. New York: A. and C. Boni. Reprinted in Aileen Kraditor, ed., *Up from the Pedestal: Selected Writings in the History of American feminism*. Chicago: Quadrangle, 1968.

Krahelska, Halina. 1932. *Praca kobiet w przemysle wspolczesnym* [Le Travail des femmes dans l'industrie contemporaine]. Warsaw, Poland: Instytugospodarstwa spolcznego.

Kramer, Martha J. 1939. Financial Management by 427 New York Farm Families from Marriage until 1935. Ph.D. thesis, Cornell University.

Kramer, Stella. 1905. *English Craft Gilds and the Government: An Examination of the Accepted Theory Regarding the Decay of the Craft Gilds*. New York: Columbia University Press. Reprinted New York: AMS Press, 1968.

——. 1905. English Craft Gilds and the Government: An Examination of the Accepted Theory Regarding the Decay of the Craft Gilds. Ph.D. thesis, Columbia University (history, economics, and public law).

——. 1908. The Amalgamation of the English Mercantile Crafts. *English Historical Review* 23.

——. 1927. *The English Craft Gilds: Studies in Their Progress and Decline.* New York: Columbia University Press. Reprinted New York: AMS Press, 1976.

Kratz, Althea Hallowell. 1940. Prosecutions and Treatment of Women Offenders and the Economic Crisis: Philadelphia, 1925–1934. Ph.D. thesis, University of Pennsylvania (sociology).

Kraus, Hertha. 1931/2. The Edge of the Precipice. *Canadian Forum* 12: 167–.

——. 1932. *Community Chests and Councils: Versuche genossenschaftliche Planung und Finanzierung der freien Wohlfahrtspflege in den Vereinigten Staaten.* Berlin: Vahlen.

——. 1933. Familienfürsorge. *Family* 14(8) (December): 271–.

——. 1934. *Work Relief in Germany.* New York: Russell Sage Foundation.

——. 1934. Participation of Family Welfare Agencies in a Housing Program. *Family* 14(10) (February): 336–.

——. 1935. *Aiding the Unemployed: A Survey of Methods and Trends in 24 Foreign Countries Made for Advisory Committee on Planning of the Temporary Emergency Relief Administration.* Albany, N.Y.: New York State Temporary Emergency Relief Administration.

——. 1939. Starting Life Anew in a Strange Country. *American Academy of Political and Social Science, Annals* 203 (May): 99–.

——. Personal and professional correspondence and other items (1918–68) relating to Kraus's activities as director of public welfare, Cologne, Germany, 1923–3; her work for U.S. Social Security Administration and involvement with U.N. Relief and Rehabilitation Administration, 1941–6; and her activities in refugee placement programs of American Friends Service Committee; together with scholarly articles and course material notebooks.

Kropotkin, Princess. 1898. The Higher Education of Women in Russia. *Nineteenth Century* 43 (January/June): 117–34.

Krout, Mary H. 1898. New Zealand and Its Resources. *Chautauquan* 28 (October): 57–.

Kruijf, Miss J. H. 1882. *Vrouwenarbeid onder vrouwen: Toespraak en mededeelingen van elders aan de Vrouwenvereeniging te Rotterdam.* The Hague: W. A. Beschoor.

Kuliscioff, Anna. 1890. Il monopolio dell'uomo: conferenza tenuta il 27 Aprile 1890 nelle sale del circolo filologico milanese. [The monopoly of man: address at the Philological Society of Milan]. Milan: Libreria Editrice Galli.

Kusch, Monica Henrietta. 1934. The Commercial Utilization of the Elbe River (Czech Republic, Germany). M.S. thesis, University of Chicago (geography).

——. 1937. Structure of Elbe River Traffic. *Economic Geography* 13(1) (January): 53–66.

Kyrk, Hazel. 1920. The Consumer's Guidance of Economic Activity. Ph.D. thesis, University of Chicago (economics).

——. 1923. *A Theory of Consumption*. Boston and New York: Houghton Mifflin; London: Pitman.

——. 1925. *The American Baking Industry, 1849–1923: As Shown in the Census Reports*. Stanford: Stanford University Press.

——. 1926. *Cost of Living on Iowa Farms. Part II, Household Expenditures*. Iowa Agricultural Experiment Station, Bulletin 237. Ames, Iowa: Agricultural Experiment Station, Iowa State College of Agriculture and Mechanic Arts.

——. 1929/1933. *Economic Problems of the Family*. New York: Harper.

——. 1929. The Economics of Consumption: Discussion. *Journal of Farm Economics* 11(4) (October): 575–7.

——. 1930. Education and Rational Consumption. *Journal of Educational Sociology* 4(1) (September): 14–19.

——. 1931/2. Book Review of "Cost of Living Studies. IV. Spending Ways of a Semi-skilled Group." *American Journal of Sociology* 37(1/6): 678–.

——. 1932. The Household Worker. *American Federationist* 39(1) (January): 33–.

——. 1932/3. Book Review of "The Home and the Child. Report of the Subcommittee on Housing and Home Management of the White House Conference on Child Health and Protection." *American Journal of Sociology* 38(1/6): 489–.

——. 1932/3. Book Review of "An International Enquiry into Costs of Living." *American Journal of Sociology* 38(1/6): 166–.

——. 1933/4. Book Review of "The Cost of Living in the United States in 1931." *American Journal of Sociology* 39(1/6): 434–.

——. 1933/4. Book Review of "Enquête sur les conditions de vie de chômeurs assurés" by Guillaume Jacquemyns. *American Journal of Sociology* 39(1/6): 133–.

——. 1934. Wastes in the Consumer's Dollar. *American Academy of Political and Social Science, Annals* 173 (May): 18–.

——. 1934–9?. *The Consumer and the Marketing System...Radio Talks Given in the Spring Quarter, 1934*. Chicago: University of Chicago Press.

——. 1934/5. Book Review of "Economics of Household Production" by Margaret G. Reid. *American Journal of Sociology* 40(1/6): 700–.

——. 1935. Who Shall Educate the Consumer? *American Academy of Political and Social Science, Annals* 182 (November): 41–.

——. 1936/7. Book Review of "Economics of the Household: Its Administration and Finance" (rev. ed.) by B. R. Andrews. *American Journal of Sociology* 42(1/6): 147–8.

——. 1936/7. Book Review of "Food, Health, and Income" by John Boyd Orr. *American Journal of Sociology* 42(1/6): 948–.

——. 1937. Methods of Measuring Variations of Family Expenditures: Discussion. *Journal of the American Statistical Association* 32(197) (March): 47–9.

——. 1937/8. Book Review of "Research Memorandum on Social Aspects of Consumption in the Depression" by Roland S. Vaile. *American Journal of Sociology* 43(1/6): 1,013.

——. 1939. Book Review of "The Consumer and the Economic Order" by Warren C. Waite and Ralph Cassady, Jr. *American Academy of Political and Social Science, Annals* 205 (September): 191–.

——. 1939. Book Review of "Consumption in Our Society" by Elizabeth Ellis Hoyt. *Journal of Political Economy* 47: 597–.

——. 1939. Book Review of "Merchandise Testing as a Guide to Consumer Buying" by Mabel Taylor Gragg with Neil H. Borden. *Journal of Political Economy* 47: 598–.

——. 1939. The Development of the Field of Consumption. *Journal of Marketing* 4 (July): 16–19.

——. 1939/40. Book Review of "The Consumers' Cooperative as a Distributive Agency" by Orin E. Burley. *American Journal of Sociology* 45(1/6): 947.

——. 1939/40. Book Review of "Does Distribution Cost Too Much?" by Paul W. Stewart, J. Frederic Dewhurst, and Louise Field. *American Journal of Sociology* 45(1/6): 947.

——. 1939/40. Book Review of "Proceedings of a National Conference on Consumer Education Held at Stephens College, Columbia, Missouri, April 3, 4, and 5, 1939. Next Steps in Consumer Education." *American Journal of Sociology* 45(1/6): 947.

——. 1940. The Consumer and the Economic Order. Part II. In Elizabeth Hoyt, *Consumption in Our Society*. Also published in the *Journal of Marketing* 4(4) (April 1940): 111–17.

Kyrk, Hazel, Day Monroe, Maryland Y. Pennell, and Edith D. Rainboth. 1940/1941. *Family Housing and Facilities, Five Regions*. Consumer Purchases Study: Urban, Village, and Farm, U.S. Department of Agriculture, Miscellaneous Publications, no. 402. Washington: U.S. Government Printing Office.

Kyrk, Hazel, Day Monroe, Lenore Monroe Stratton, and Ursula Batchelder Stone. 1938/1940. *Food Buying in Our Markets*. New York: M. Barrows & Co.

Kyrk, Hazel. Coauth. *See* Monroe, Day; Reid, Margaret Gilpin.

L

La Flesche [Picotte], Susan. 1888. An Indian Teacher. *Southern Workman* 17 (January): 12–.

——. 1891. The Omahas and Citizenship. *Southern Workman* 20 (April): 177–.

——. 1892. My Work as Physician among My People. *Southern Workman and Hampton School Record* 21 (August): 133–.

La Flesche [Tibbles], Susette [as "Bright Eyes"]. 1880. The Indian Question. *Christian Union* (March 10).

——. 1881. The Position, Occupation and Culture of Indian Women. Paper presented before the Association for the Advancement of Women.

La Follette, Cecile Tipton. 1934. *A Study of the Problems of 652 Gainfully Employed Married Women Homemakers.* New York: Teachers College, Columbia University.

——. 1934. A Study of the Problems of 652 Gainfully Employed Married Women Homemakers. Ph.D. thesis, Columbia University.

La Follette, Suzanne. 1926. *Concerning Women.* New York: Albert and Charles Boni.

——. 1929. women in the Modern World. In A. Johnson *et al., Civilization and Enjoyment.* New York: Van Nostrand.

——. 1935. American Art: Its Economic Aspects. *American Magazine of Art* 28(6) (June): 337–.

——. Founded and wrote in publication entitled *The Freeman,* 1920–4 and *The New Freeman,* 1930. Also contributed frequently to *Nation, New Republic,* and *Scribner's Magazine.*

Lacy, Mary [Goodwin]. 1915. Seed Values of Maize Kernels: Butts, Middles and Tips. *American Society of Agronomy, Journal* 7(1/6) (January/December): 159–.

——. 1918. Sources of Agricultural Statistics. *Library Journal* 43(12) (December): 869–.

——. 1919. List of References on Agricultural Libraries in the United States: Including Their History, Administration And Problems in General. *Special Libraries* 10(2) March): 53–.

——. 1920. Agencies Working for Agriculture. *Library Journal* 45(20) (November 15): 922–.

——. 1921. Government Regulation of Prices Before 1800 A.D. *Special Libraries* 12(3) (March): 50–.

——. 1921. The Library of the U.S. Department of Agriculture. *Library Journal* 46(11) (June 1): 493–.

——. 1923. *An Early Agricultural Periodical.* American Historical Association Annual Report for 1919. Washington: American Historical Association.

——. 1923. Reading List on General Economics. *Special Libraries* 14(2) (February): 25–.

——. 1924. *A Beginning of a Bibliography of the Literature of Rural Life.* Agricultural Economics Bibliography, no. 3. Washington: Bureau of Agricultural Economics Library.

——. 1925/1927/1930/1936/1938. *Agricultural Economics, a Selected List of References.* Washington: Bureau of Agricultural Economics.

——. 1925. *Long-time Agricultural Programs in the United States: National, Regional, and State.* Washington: Bureau of Agricultural Economics Library.

——. 1928. Report of the Committee of the Agricultural Libraries Section on Cooperative Aid. *Agricultural Library Notes* 3(5/7) (May/July): 237–.

——. 1929. Foreign Files in the Library of the U.S. Bureau of Agricultural Economics. *Special Libraries* 20(4) (April): 114–.

——. 1933. *Food Control during Forty-six Centuries: A Contribution to the History of Price-fixing.* U.S. Department of Agriculture, Bureau of Agricultural Economics. Reprint of an address before the Agricultural History Society from March 1922. Washington: Bureau of Agricultural Economics.

——, comp. 1934. *The American Farm Problem: A Selected List of Books and Pamphlets on the Economic Status of the Farmer and Measures for His Relief Since 1920.* Washington. U.S. Department of Agriculture, Bureau of Agricultural Economics.

Lacy, Mary Goodwin, Annie Murray Hannay, and Emily Louise Day. 1926. *Price Fixing by Governments 424 B.C.–1926 A.D.: A Selected Bibliography, Including Some References on the Principles of Price Fixing, and on Price Fixing by Private Organizations.* Washington: U.S. Department of Agriculture, Bureau of Agricultural Economics.

Lacy, Mary G. Coauth. *See* Bercaw, Louise Oldham; Colvin, Esther Marie; Hannay, Annie Murray Macgregor; Hennefrund, Helen Emma; Jacobs, Katharine; Olcott, Margaret Thompson; Wright, Icelle Emma.

Lalor, Mrs. [Mary] Power. 1891. Industries in Ireland. *Englishwoman's Review*, n.s. 211 (July): 156–8.

Lambert, Agnes. 1886. *A School Bank Manual: For the Use of Managers, Masters and Mistresses, and Teachers of Public Elementary Schools.* London: Cassell & Co.

——. 1886. Thrift among the Children. *Nineteenth Century* 19 (January/June): 539–60.

——. 1887. Progress of "Thrift Among the Children." *Nineteenth Century* 22 (July/December): 206–18.

——. 1898. Neglecting Our Customers. *Nineteenth Century* 44 (December): 940–56.

——. 1899. Neglecting Our Customers: A Postscript. *Nineteenth Century* 45 (January/June): 336–40.

Lammers, Mathilde. 1877. *Die Frau: ihre Stellung und Aufgabe in Haus und Welt.* Leipzig: Veit.

LaMotte, Ellen Newbold. 1920. *The Opium Monopoly*. New York: Macmillan.

Lampen, Dorothy. 1929. Economic and Social Aspects of Federal Reclamation. Ph.D. thesis, Johns Hopkins University (economics, history).

——. 1930. *Economic and Social Aspects of Federal Reclamation.* Baltimore: Johns Hopkins Press.

Lampérière, Anna. 1898. *Le Rôle social de la femme; devoirs, droits, éducation.* Paris: F. Alcan.

Landau, Sara. Papers primarily from 1910–86 collected in the Special Collections and Archives at the University Libraries of the University of Louisville. See http://special.library.louisville.edu/display-collection.asp?ID=563 for biographical information.

Landauer, Bella C[lara]. 1933/4. My Collection of Lottery Items and Trade Cards. *New-York Historical Society Quarterly Bulletin* 17 (April/January): 102–.

——. 1933/4. Some Trade Cards with Particular Emphasis on the Currier & Ives Contributions. *New-York Historical Society Quarterly Bulletin* 17 (April/January): 79–93.

——. 1934/5. Jumbo's Influence on Advertising or Some "Jumbo" Trade-cards. *New-York Historical Society Quarterly Bulletin* 18 (April/January): 43–52.

——. 1935. Tradecards: An Overlooked Asset. *Business History Review* 9 (May): 33–8.

Lander, Beatrice. 1902. The Relief of the Poor in Jersey. *Economic Journal* 12 (June): 192–201.

Lane, Marie Dresden and Francis Steegmuller. 1938. *America on Relief.* New York: Harcourt, Brace, & Co.

Lane, Rachel Penn. 1934. *Cotton and Cottonseed: A List of the Publications of the United States Department of Agriculture on These Subjects, Including Early Reports of the United States Patent Office.* Washington: U.S. Government Printing Office.

——. Coauth. *See* Day, Emily Louise.

Lane-Claypon [Forber], [Lady] Janet [Elizabeth]. 1909. The Waste of Infant Life. *Nineteenth Century and After* 65 (January): 48–.

——. 1910. Poor Law Babies. *Nineteenth Century* 68 (September): 450–.

——. 1917. State Midwifery Service. *Nineteenth Century and After* 81 (January/June): 895–.

——. 1920. *The Child Welfare Movement.* London: G. Bell and Sons, Ltd.

Laney, Lucy. 1899. The Burden of the Educated Colored Woman. The *Southern Workman and Hampton School Record* 28 (September): 341–4.

Lange, Helene. 1914. *Die Frauenbewegung in ihren modernen Problemen.* Leipzig: s.n. Reprinted Münster: Tendau-Verlag, 1980.

Langhorne, Mrs. Orra. 1880. Colored Schools in Virginia. *Journal of Social Science* 11 (May): 36–45.

Lanier, Mary J. *See* Magruder, Mary Jean Lanier.

Lapham, Ella C. 1886. Woman's Duty to Woman. *Forum* 1 (July): 455–67.

Lapham, Ella Caroline. 1901. The Industrial Status of Women in Elizabethan England. *Journal of Political Economy* 9(4) (September): 562–99.

Larcom, Lucy. 1881. Among Lowell Mill Girls: A Reminiscence. *Atlantic Monthly* 48 (November): 593–612.

——. 1882. American Factory Life. *Journal of Social Science* 16 (December): 141–6.

Larson, Agnes M. 1938. Some Aspects of the History of the White Pine Industry in the Upper Mississippi Region, with Special Reference to Minnesota. Ph.D. thesis, Radcliffe College (history).

——. Coauth. *See* Arny, Clara Maude Brown.

Larson, Ethel C. Yohe. 1923. Protection of Workers under Mexican State Labor Laws. *Monthly Labor Review* 17 (July/December): 13–25.

——. 1924. Comparison of Workmen's Compensation Laws of the Mexican States. *Monthly Labor Review* 18 (January/June): 1–10.

——. 1924. Labor Law of Durango, Mexico. *Monthly Labor Review* 18 (January/June): 185–96.

——. 1925. Labor Laws and Court Decisions. *Monthly Labor Review* 20 (January/June): 186–94.

Larson, Henrietta [Melia]. 1926. *The Wheat Market and the Farmer in Minnesota, 1858–1900.* New York: Longmans, Green & Co.

——. 1926. The Wheat Market and the Farmer in Minnesota, 1858–1900. Ph.D. thesis, Columbia University (economics, agricultural).

——. 1930. A Medieval Swedish Mining Company. *Journal of Economic and Business History* 2 (May): 545–59.

——. 1931. S. & M. Allen: Lottery, Exchange, and Stock Brokerage. *Journal of Economic and Business History* 3 (May): 424–45.

——. 1932. Book Review of "Norwegian–American Studies and Records." *North Dakota Historical Quarterly* 7(1) (October): 60–.

——. 1932. E. W. Clark & Co., 1837–1857: The Beginning of an American Private Bank. *Journal of Economic and Business History* 4 (May): 429–60.

——. 1934. A China Trader Turns Investor: A Biographical Chapter in American Business History. *Harvard Business Review* 12 (April): 345–58.

——. 1935. Book Review of "From Canoe to Steel Barge on the Upper Mississippi" by Hartsough. *Minnesota History* 16: 78–.

——. 1935. Book Review of "The New York Merchant on the Eve of the Revolution." *American Economic Review* 25(4) (December): 738–9.

——. 1935. Jay Cooke's Early Work in Transportation. *Pennsylvania Magazine of History and Biography* 59: 362–.

——. 1936. *Jay Cooke, Private Banker.* Cambridge: Harvard University Press.

——. 1937. The Implications for Education of Research in Business History. *Harvard Educational Review* 7(4) (October): 502–.

——. 1937. The Records of a Flour Milling Firm of Rochester, New York. *Business Historical Society, Bulletin* 11 (December): 108–.

——. 1938. The "John B. Alley," A Pioneer Locomotive. *Minnesota History* 19: 193–.

——. 1940. The Armor Business in the Middle Ages. *Business History Review* 14 (October): 49–64.

Laselle, Mary A. and Katherine E. Wiley. 1913. *Vocations for Girls*. New York: Houghton Mifflin.

Latham, Lucy Clare. 1928. The Decay of the Manorial System, during the First Half of the Fifteenth Century, with Special Reference to Manorial Jurisdiction and to the Decline of Villeinage, as Exemplified in the Records of Twenty-six Manors, etc. Ph.D. thesis, London School of Economics.

——. 1931. *The Manor*. Historical Association Leaflets, no. 83. London: G. Bell and sons.

——. 1933. Collection of the Wages of the Knights of the Shire in the Fourteenth and Fifteenth Centuries. *English Historical Review* XLVIII: 455–64.

Lathrop, Julia Clifford. 1905. *Suggestions for Visitors to County Poorhouses and to Other Public Charitable Institutions*. Chicago?: Public Charities Committee of the Illinois Federation of Women's Clubs.

——. 1912. The Children's Bureau. *American Journal of Sociology* 18 (Novemeber): 318–30.

——. 1916. *To the Members and Friends of the National Child Labor Committee: [on] the Campaign for the Federal Child Labor Law*... New York: National Child Labor Committee.

——. 1917. Public Protection of Maternity. *American Labor Legislation Review* 7: 27–.

——. 1917. Shall This Country Economize for or against Its Children? *National Education Association of the US., Journal of Proceedings and Addresses*: 76–80.

——. 1918. The Children's Bureau and Child Labor. *American Federationist* 25 (August/December): 908–.

——. 1918. *Provision for the Care of the Families and Dependents of Soldiers and Sailors*. New York: Academy of Political Science. Reprinted from *Proceedings of the Academy of Political Science* vii(4).

——. 1919. Income and Infant Mortality. *American Journal of Public Health* 9(4) (April): 270–.

——. 1921. Standards of Child Welfare. *American Academy of Political and Social Science, Annals* 98 (November): 1–.

——. 1925. Federal Safeguards of Child Welfare. *American Academy of Political and Social Science, Annals* 121 (September): 96–.

——. 1926. International Child Welfare Problems. *Academy of Political Science, Proceedings* 12 (July): 418–.

Latimer, Dr. Caroline. 1892. Medicine as a Profession for Women. *Monthly Packet* 4 (November): 542–.

——. 1898. Scientific Instruction in Girls' Schools. *Popular Science Monthly* 53 (June): 246–54.

Latimer, Elizabeth Wormeley. *Europe in Africa in the Nineteenth Century*. Chicago: A. C. McClurg & Co. Reprinted New York: Negro Universities Press, 1969.

Laut, A[gnes]. C[hristina]. 1899. Canada, Claims before Anglo-American Joint High Commission. *Review of Reviews* 19: 445.

——. 1901/2. Beaver Hunting. *Outing; the Gentleman's Magazine of Sport, Travel and Outdoor Life* 39: 470.

——. 1902/3. The American Invasion of Canada's Wheat Belt. *Century Illustrated Monthly Magazine* 65 (November/April): 481–.

——. 1903/4. Louisiana Purchase, Fights of the Fur Companies. *Century Illustrated Monthly Magazine* 45: 797.

——. 1905. Outlaw Hunters of Russia. *Outing Magazine* 46: 653.

——. 1905/6. Hudson Bay Fur Company and the French Raiders. Gamesters of the Wilderness. *Harper's Monthly Magazine* 112: 768.

——. 1905/6. Russian–American Fur Company. Sea Voyagers of the Northern Ocean. *Harper's Monthly Magazine* 112: 291.

——. 1905/6. Russian Fur Trade in the Pacific. *American Illustrated Magazine* 61: 60.

——. 1906. Problem of the Unemployed in England. *Review of Reviews* 33: 40.

——. 1907. The Fur Trade of the World (Illustrated). *World's Work* 14(1) (May).

——. 1907. Openings for Women in Canada. Illustrated from Photographs. *Pall Mall Magazine* 40 (July/December): 588–.

——. 1907. The Twentieth Century is Canada's. *World's Work* 13(4) (February).

——. 1909. On the Frontier of the Fur Country. *World's Work* 17(5) (March).

——. 1909. Railroad Fight for the Canadian Northwest. *World's Work* 18(1) (May).

——. 1914/1920/1922/1935. *The "Adventurers of England" on Hudson Bay: A Chronicle of the Fur Trade in the North.* Toronto: Glasgow, Brook & Co. Reprinted Toronto: University of Toronto Press, 1964.

——. 1914/15. The New Spirit among Women Who Work. *Century Illustrated Monthly Magazine* 89 (November/April): 927–.

——. 1915. *The Canadian Commonwealth.* Indianapolis: Bobbs-Merrill Company.

——. 1915. The Cost of Congestion. *World's Work* 30(4) (August): 446–.

——. 1916. Merchant Marine and the Farmer. *Forum* 56 (July/December): 735–.

——. 1919. In the Hells of Tehuantepec. *Forum* 61 (January/June): 641–.

——. 1920. Oil, Should It Be Nationalized? *Forum* 63(3) (March): 325.

——. 1920. Why Mexico Needs Our Help. *Forum* 64 (June/December): 404–.

——. 1921. *Canada at the Cross Roads.* Toronto: Macmillan.

——. 1921. *The Fur Trade of America.* New York: Macmillan.

——. 1928/9. Rivers of Gold. *Century Monthly Magazine* 117 (November/April): 734–.

——. 1928/9. Wheat, the Romantic Story of Our Basic Industry. *Century Monthly Magazine* 117 (November/April): 734–.

Law, Alice. 1895. The English "Nouveaux-Riches" in the Fourteenth Century. *Royal Historical Society, Transactions*, n.s. 9: 49–.

——. 1897. Brief Survey of English Towns and Roads in the 13th Century. *Economic Review* 7 (July): 289–.

——. 1898. Notes on English Medieval Shipping. *Economic Review* 8 (July): 349–.

——. 1903. Some Notable "Kings" Merchants. *Economic Review* (October).

Law, John. Pseud. *See* Harkness, Margaret.

Lawrance, Hannah. 1843. *The History of Woman in England, and Her Influence on Society and Literature, from the Earliest Period*, Vol. I: To the Year 1200. London: Henry Colburn.

——. 1869. The Condition of Englishwomen in the Middle Ages. *British Quarterly Review* 50 (July): 30–68.

——. 1870. The Education and Employment of Women. *British Quarterly Review* 52 (July): 31–57.

Lawrence, A. Susan. 1919. The Prevention of Unemployment. In Gertrude M. Tuckwell, Marion G. Phillips, and Susan A. Lawrence, *Labour Women on International Legislation Proposals for International Legislation.* London: Labour Party.

——. Coauth. *See* Bondfield, Margaret.

Lawrence, Margaret Oliver Woods. 1868. Women and Work. *Putnam's*, n.s. 1 (May 1868): 601–11. Reprinted in *Dublin University Magazine* 80 (December 1872): 670–82.

Lawrence, Marjorie. 1924. Distribution of Wealth at Death in Cook County. A.M. thesis, University of Chicago (economics, finance).

Lawrence, Susan. 1935. The Civil Servant and the Elected Person. *Public Administration (London)* 13(2) (April): 111–.

——. 1940. The New Poor Law. *Fabian Quarterly* 26.

Le Mesurier, Alice M. C. 1934. The Orphans' Inventories at the London City Guildhall. *Economic History Review* 5(1) (October): 98–103.

Le Plastrier, Jane. 1863. A Season with the Dressmakers, or the Experience of a First Hand. *English Woman's Journal* 11 (August): 407–9; 12 (September): 7–24; (October): 104–12; (November): 181–7; (December): 267–76.

Lease, Mary E[lizabeth]. [Clyens]. 1891. Women in the Farmers' Alliance. In Rachel Foster Avery, ed., *Transactions of the National Council of Women of the United States, Assembled in Washington, D. C., February 22 to 25 1891*. Philadelphia: J. B. Lippincott.

——. 1895. *The Problem of Civilization Solved.* Chicago: Laird & Lee.

Lecky, Mrs. 1896. A Warning to Imperialists. *Nineteenth Century* 40 (July): 19–26.

Lee, Alice. 1903. On the Relation between Rates, Expenditure on Remunerative Works, and Rate of Increase of Population in Fifty-eight British Municipalities. *Economic Journal* 13 (September): 424–9.

——. 1908. On the Manner in Which the Percentage of Employed Workmen in This Country Is Related to the Import of Articles Wholly or Mainly Manufactured. *Economic Journal* 18 (March): 96–191.

Lee, Mabel Ping-Hua. 1921. *The Economic History of China, with Special Reference to Agriculture.* New York: Columbia University Press. Reprinted New York: AMS Press, 1969.

——. 1921. The Economic History of China, with Special Reference to Agriculture. Ph.D. thesis, Columbia University (economics, history).

Leete, Mary Mather. 1927. *The Children's Bureau of Cleveland: A Study of the Care of Dependent Children in Cleveland, Ohio.* Washington: U.S. Children's Bureau.

Legg, Caroline Ella and Ella Gardner. 1931. *Leisure-time Activities of Rural Children in Selected Areas of West Virginia.* Washington: U.S. Government Printing Office.

Legg, Caroline and Ella Arvilla Merritt. 1940. Child Labor in Vegetable Canneries in Maryland. *Child* 5(2) (August): 35–.

Lehmann, Andrée. 1924. *De la Réglementation légale du travail féminin (étude de législation comparée)*. Paris: H. d'Arthez,.

Leichter, Käthe. 1918. Die handelspolitischen Beziehungen Österreich-Ungarns zu Italien. Thesis, Heidelberg.

——. 1924. Erfahrungen des österreichischen Sozialisierungsversuchs. In Hermann Otto Jenssen and Karl Kautsky, eds., *Der lebendige Marxismus*. Jena: Thüringer Verlagsanstalt und Drückerei.

——. 1926. *Handbuch der Frauenarbeit in Österreich*. Vienna: Kammer für Arbeiter und Angestellte.

——. 1927. *Frauenarbeit und Arbeiterinnenschutz in Österreich*. Vienna: Kammer für Arbeiter und Angestellte and Verlag "Arbeit und Wirtschaft."

——. 1928. *Wie leben die Wiener Heimarbeiter? Eine Erhebung über die Arbeits- und Lebensverhältnisse von tausend Wiener Heimarbeitern*. Vienna: Verlag Arbeit und Wirtschaft.

——. 1932. *So leben wir – 1320 Industriearbeiterinnen berichten über ihr Leben. Eine Erhebung*. Vienna: Verlag Arbeit und Wirtschaft.

——. 1932. Sanierung und Krise. In Julius Deutsch, ed., *Geschichte der österreichischen Gewerkschaftsbewegung im Weltkrieg und in der Nachkriegszeit*, vol. 2. Vienna: Wiener Volksbuchhandlung.

——. 1932. Vom revolutionären Syndikalimus zur Verstaatlichung der Gewerkschaften. In *Festschrift für Carl Grünberg*. Leipzig: C. L. Hirschfeld.

——. 1936. Interviews mit Schweizer Sachverständigen. In *Studien über Autorität und Familie*. Paris: F. Alcan/Institut für Sozialforschung, Frankfurt am Main.

Leigh, Frances Butler. 1883. *Ten Years on a Georgia Plantation since the War*. London: R. Bentley & Sons.

Leininger, Grace Carr. 1935. A Bibliography on Utility Holding Companies. *Land Economics* 11 (November): 419–24.

Lemaire, Minnie Ethel. 1932. *Land Utilization of Boylston and West Boylston*. M.A. thesis, Clark University.

——. 1935. The Quasi-Piedmont Characteristics of Marlborough. Ph.D. thesis, Clark University (physical geography).

——. 1936. The Artificial Pearl Industry of Cape Cod. *Journal of Geography* 35 (January/December): 243–.

——. 1937. Wachusett Reservoir: A Metropolitan Water Supply. *Economic Geography* 13(2) (April): 181–6.

Lemlich, Clara. 1912. The Inside of a Shirtwaist Factory: An Appeal to Women Who Wear Choice and Beautiful Clothing. *Good Housekeeping* 54(3) (March): 367–9.

Lenroot, Katherine F. 1940. American Childhood Challenges American Democracy. *Child* 5(1) (July).

Lenroot, Katherine F. and Martha May Eliot. 1937. Security for Children. In Martha D. Ring and Merrill Garver Murray, eds., *Social Security in America; the*

Factual Background of the Social Security Act as Summarized from Staff Reports to the Committee on Economic Security. Washington: U.S. Government Printing Office.

Lenroot, Katherine F., Ruby Steward, and John Rogers Commons. 1911. *Proposed Minimum Wage Law for Wisconsin Bill, 317 S.* Wisconsin: Wisconsin Consumers' League.

Lenroot, Katharine F. Coauth. *See* Lundberg, Emma Octavia.

Leonard, E[llen]. M. 1898. Relief of the Poor by State Regulation of Wages, 1629–40. *English Historical Review* 13(49) (January): 91–3.

——. 1900. *The Early History of English Poor Relief.* Cambridge, UK: Cambridge University Press.

——. 1905. The Inclosure of Common Fields in the Seventeenth Century. *Royal Historical Society, Transactions* 19: 101–.

Leppington, [Miss] C. H. [E.] 1891. Side Lights of the Commission on the Sweating System. *Westminster and Foreign Quarterly Review* 136 (September): 273–; (November): 504–.

——. 1891. Theatre: Work and Wages behind the Scenes. *National Review* 17: 245–.

——. 1891/2. Object Lessons in Socialism in Switzerland. *National Review* 18: 267.

——. 1892. Irish Labour Colonies for Prisoners. *Charity Organisation Review* 89 (May): 183–5.

——. 1892. Work and Wages in Hotels and Restaurants. *Good Words* 33: 754.

——. 1892/3. Mental and Moral Character of Mobs. *National Review* 20: 578.

——. 1893. The Conditions of State Relief in Denmark. *Economic Journal* 3(10) (June): 325–33.

——. 1893. The Teachings of the Labour Commission. *Contemporary Review* 64 (September): 388–404.

——. 1893. Three Solutions of the Industrial Problem. *Charity Organisation Review* 99 (April): 121–5.

——. 1894. University Extension and Workmen. *Charity Organisation Review* 113 (June): 258–63.

——. 1895. Employers and Employed. *Charity Organisation Review* 125 (June): 224–5.

——. 1896. The Industrial Union of Employers and Employed. *Charity Organisation Review* 133 (February): 63–4.

——. 1897. The Charity Organization-system of To-day. *Economic Review* 7 (January): 25–.

——. 1899. The English Poor Law and English Charities and Corrections. *Chautauquan* 28 (February): 452–7.

——. 1907. The Evolution of an Industrial Town. *Economic Journal* 17(67) (September): 345–57.

Leslie, Emma. 1870. *Teddy's Dream; or A Little Sweep's Mission.* London: James Nisbet.

——. 1891. *The Seed She Sowed: A Tale of the Great Dock Strike.* London: Blackie. [*novel*]

Leslie, Marion. 1899. Private Teaching as an Employment for Women. *Woman at Home* 8 (November): 152.

Leubuscher, Charlotte. 1913. *Der Arbeitskampf der englischen Eisenbahner im Jahre 1911. Mit einem einleitenden Überblick über die allgemeinen Entwicklungstendenzen in der heutigen englischen Arbeiterbewegung.* Munich: Duncker & Humblot.

——. 1913. Der Arbeitskampf der englischen Eisenbahner im Jahre 1911. Mit einem einleitenden Überblick über die allgemeinen Entwicklungstendenzen in der heutigen englischen Arbeiterbewegung. Thesis, Berlin.

——. 1916/17. Die Nationalisierung des Kapitals. *Archiv für Sozialwissenschaft und Sozialpolitik* 42: 505–.

——. 1917. Die ausländische Kapitalbeteiligung an der deutschen Industrie. *Schmollers Jahrbuch für Gesetzgebung, Verwaltung und Volkswirtschaft im deutschen Reich* 41(3): 329 –.

——. 1917. Book Review of "The Export of Capital. (Studies in Economic and Political Science, Nr. 38)" by C. K. Hobson. *Schmollers Jahrbuch für Gesetzgebung, Verwaltung und Volkswirtschaft im deutschen Reich* 41(3): 491–.

——. 1917. Book Review of "Der Schweizerische Kapitalexport (*Zeitschrift für Schweizerische Statistik und Volkswirtschaft* IV)" by Julius Landmann. *Schmollers Jahrbuch für Gesetzgebung, Verwaltung und Volkswirtschaft im deutschen Reich* 41(3): 494–.

——. 1921. *Sozialismus und Sozialisierung in England: ein Überblick über die neuere Entwicklung der sozialistischen Theorien und über die Probleme der Industrieverfassung in England.* Jena: G. Fischer.

——. 1921. Die Bewegung der englischen Bergarbeiter seit Beendigung des Krieges. *Jahrbücher für Nationalökonomie und Statistik* 117(3) (September): 251–.

——. 1922. Die Agrarfrage im deutschen Sozialismus der Gegenwart. *Jahrbücher für Nationalökonomie und Statistik* 118(4) (April): 289–.

——. 1922. Book Review of "Gewinnbeteiligung der Arbeitnehmer" by Bernhard Goldschmidt. *Jahrbücher für Nationalökonomie und Statistik* 119(5) (November): 451–.

——. 1923. Book Review of "Die ausländische Kapitalbeteiligung in Deutschland (*Handbücher der Industrie- und Handels-Zeitung* II)" by Hans Jürgen Kleist. *Jahrbücher für Nationalökonomie und Statistik* 120(2) (February): 175–.

——. 1923. Book Review of "Bergarbeiterbewegung und Kohlenwirtschaft in Grossbritannien während der letzten Jahre" (Sonderabdruck aus *Glückauf, berg- und hüttenmännische Zeitschrift* 57(36–39)) by H. E. Böker. *Jahrbücher für Nationalökonomie und Statistik* 120(1) (January): 71–.

——. 1923. Book Review of "Die englische Wirtschaft (*Handbuch der Englisch-Amerikanischen Kultur*)" by Hermann Levy. *Jahrbücher für Nationalökonomie und Statistik* 121(5) (November): 494–.

——. 1923. Book Review of "Gewerkschaftslehre" by Siegfried Nestriepke. *Jahrbücher für Nationalökonomie und Statistik* 120(2) (February): 181–.

——. 1923. Book Review of "Ein konsumgenossenschaftlicher Blick in die Zukunft. Vergangenheit, Gegenwart und Zukunft des konsumgenossenschaftlichen Grosseinkaufs" by Heinrich Kaufmann. *Jahrbücher für Nationalökonomie und Statistik* 120(4) (April): 376–.

——. 1923. Book Review of "Wandlungen des liberalen England durch die Kriegswirtschaft (Archiv für Sozialwissenschaft und Sozialpolitik, Ergänzungsheft XVIII)" by Charlotte Mendelsohn. *Jahrbücher für Nationalökonomie und Statistik* 120(1) (January): 87–.

——. 1923. Book Review of "Wiedergutmachung und Wirtschaft" (transl. Otto Eccius) by J. A. Hobson. *Jahrbücher für Nationalökonomie und Statistik* 120(2) (February): 186–.

——. 1924. Book Review of "Die Arbeitsleistung im deutschen Kalibergbau unter besonderer Berücksichtigung des hannoverschen Kalibergbaues (Sozialwissenschaftliche Forschungen)" by Wilhelm Röpke. *Jahrbücher für Nationalökonomie und Statistik* 122(1) (January/February): 127–.

——. 1924. Die Nationalökonomie. *Die Frau* 32: 219–20.

——. 1925. Die Berufslage der deutschen Hochschuldozentinnen. *Die Frau* 33: 533–7.

——. 1925. Book Review of "Abriss der Sozialpolitik" by Ludwig Heyde. *Jahrbücher für Nationalökonomie und Statistik* 123(4) (July/August): 578–.

——. 1925. Book Review of "Der Radikalismus in der deutschen Arbeiterbewegung. Ein soziologischer Versuch" by Kurt Geyer. *Jahrbücher für Nationalökonomie und Statistik* 123(6) (November/December): 871–.

——. 1926. Der sozialwissenschaftliche Gehalt von Beatrice Webbs Jugenderinnerungen. *Archiv für Sozialwissenschaft und Sozialpolitik* 56: 770–.

——. 1927. *Liberalismus und Protektionismus in der englischen Wirtschaftspolitik seit dem Kriege*. Jena: G. Fischer.

——. 1927. Book Review of "Internationale Sozialpolitik. Ihre geschichtliche Entwicklung und ihr gegenwärtiger Stand" by Friedrich Ritzmann. *Jahrbücher für Nationalökonomie und Statistik* 126(5) (May): 674–.

——. 1927. Book Review of "Die Persönlichkeit im Sozialismus. Beiträge zur philosophischen Begründung des Sozialismus" by Albert Kranold. *Jahrbücher für Nationalökonomie und Statistik* 127(2) (August): 343–.

——. 1928. Book Review of "Die Arbeitslosenversicherung in Grossbritannien (Zürcher Volkswirtschaftliche Forschungen 12)" by Emil Gsell. *Jahrbücher für Nationalökonomie und Statistik* 129(6) (December): 935–.

——. 1928. Book Review of "Grundriss der Finanzwissenschaft" by Karl Theodor von Eheberg. *Jahrbücher für Nationalökonomie und Statistik* 128(1) (January): 138–.

——. 1928. Book Review of "Nichtfiskalische Zwecke der Besteuerung. Ein Beitrag zur Steuertheorie und Steuerpolitik" by Dora Schmidt. *Jahrbücher für Nationalökonomie und Statistik* 128(4) (April): 622–.

——. 1928. Book Review of "Der Zusammenbruch des Sozialismus" by Arthur Shadwell. *Jahrbücher für Nationalökonomie und Statistik* 129(4) (October): 614–.

——. 1928. Das wirtschaftliche Reformprogramm der britischen Liberalen. *Jahrbücher für Nationalökonomie und Statistik* 128(5) (May): 731–.

——. 1929. Book Review of "Die Besteuerung der Erbschaften in den Einzelstaaten der Nordamerikanischen Union (Finanzwissenschaftliche und volkswirtschaftliche Studien 9)" by Herbert Schnieber. *Jahrbücher für Nationalökonomie und Statistik* 30(6) (June): 935–.

——. 1929. Book Review of "Die britische Wirtschaftspolitik nach dem Kriege" by F. Heyer. *Jahrbücher für Nationalökonomie und Statistik* 131(2) (August): 296–.

——. 1929. Book Review of "Die Finanzreform des Grafen Wallis und der Staatsbankerott von 1811" by Johanna Kraft. *Jahrbücher für Nationalökonomie und Statistik* 130(4) (April): 616–.

——. 1929. Book Review of "Grundzüge der Finanzwissenschaft (Wissenschaft und Bildung 246)" by Paul Mombert. *Jahrbücher für Nationalökonomie und Statistik* 130(2) February: 292–.

——. 1929. Book Review of "Grundzüge der französischen Volkswirtschaft 1913–1927" by von Ungern-Sternberg. *Zeitschrift für Politik* 18: 430–.

——. 1929. Book Review of "A Survey of the Social Structure of England & Wales as Illustrated by Statistics" by A. M. Carr-Saunders and Caradog Jones. *Jahrbücher für Nationalökonomie und Statistik* 130(5) (May): 793–.

——. 1930. Book Review of "Die Belastung der deutschen Wirtschaft durch die Sozialversicherung" by Alois Egger. *Jahrbücher für Nationalökonomie und Statistik* 132(3) (March): 456–.

——. 1930. Book Review of "Die Hauptfragen der Sozialpolitik" by Karl von Balás. *Vierteljahrschrift für Sozial- und Wirtschaftsgeschichte* 22(3/4): 476–7.

——. 1931. *Der südafrikanische Eingeborene als Industriearbeiter und als Stadtbewohner. Mit einer einleitenden Übersicht über die afrikanische Eingeborenenfrage*. Jena: Verlag von Gustav Fischer.

——. 1931. Book Review of "Die Einkommensteuern der grossen britischen Dominions unter Einschluss Britisch-Indiens (Finanzwissenschaftliche und volkswirtschaftliche Studien 18)" by Karl Theill. *Jahrbücher für Nationalökonomie und Statistik* 134(6) (June): 1,050–.

——. 1931. Eine englische Sozialenquete. *Jahrbücher für Nationalökonomie und Statistik* 135(6) (December): 897–.

——. 1931/2. Heinrich Herkner zum Gedächtnis. *Die Frau* 39: 641–4.

——. 1932. Book Review of "Probleme der sozialen Betriebspolitik." *Vierteljahrschrift für Sozial- und Wirtschaftsgeschichte* 25(1): 91–.

——. 1933. Book Review of "Die Ertragsfähigkeit der Getränkesteuern. Vergleichende Übersicht über die Voraussetzungen der Alkoholbesteuerung im deutschen Reich, in Grossbritannien, Frankreich, der Schweiz, Dänemark und den Vereinigten Staaten. Ein Beitrag zur deutschen Finanzreform" by Günter Schmölders. *Schmollers Jahrbuch für Gesetzgebung, Verwaltung und Volkswirtschaft im deutschen Reich* 57(3) (June): 144–.

——. 1933. Book Review of "Die Gestaltung der Handelspolitik in den wichtigsten Ländern" by Ders. *Vierteljahrschrift für Sozial- und Wirtschaftsgeschichte* 26(2): 199–200.

——. 1933. Book Review of "Grundlagen der Handelspolitik" by Heinrich Sieveking. *Vierteljahrschrift für Sozial- und Wirtschaftsgeschichte* 26(2): 199–200.

——. 1933. Book Review of "Grundlagen der Volkswirtschaftspolitik" by Franz Josef Weiss. *Vierteljahrschrift für Sozial- und Wirtschaftsgeschichte* 26(2): 199–200.

——. 1933. Book Review of "Internationale Wirtschaftspolitik und internationale Sozialpolitik" by Karl Pribram. *Vierteljahrschrift für Sozial- und Wirtschaftsgeschichte* 26(2): 199–200.

——. 1933. Book Review of "Soziale und wirtschaftspolitische Anschauungen in Deutschland" by Paul Mombert. *Vierteljahrschrift für Sozial- und Wirtschaftsgeschichte* 26(2): 199–200.

——. 1933. Book Review of "Unternehmertum und Wirtschaftsführung" by Johannes Gerhardt. *Vierteljahrschrift für Sozial- und Wirtschaftsgeschichte* 25(3): 299–300.

——. 1933. Heinrich Herkner als Sozialpolitiker. *Schmollers Jahrbuch für Gesetzgebung, Verwaltung und Volkswirtschaft im deutschen Reich* 57(1) (February): 13–.

——. 1933. Der südafrikanische Eingeborene als Industriearbeiter und als Stadtbewohner. *Archiv für Sozialwissenschaft und Sozialpolitik* 69: 115–.

——. 1939. Marketing Schemes for Native-grown Produce in African Territories. *Africa* 12(2): 163–.

Leuck, Miriam Simons. 1926. *Fields of Work for Women.* New York and London: D. Appleton & Company.

——. 1929. Women in Odd and Unusual Fields of Work. *American Academy of Political and Social Science, Annals* 143 (May): 166–.

Levett, Ada Elizabeth. 1927. The Financial Organization of the Manor. *Economic History Review* 1 (January): 65–86.

——. 1929. *English Economic History*. London: E. Benn. Chinese ed., *Ying-kuo ching chi shih*, Shang-hai: Shang Wu Yin Shu Kuan, 1930.

——. 1930. The Consumer in History. In Sir P. Redfern, ed., *Self and Society: Second Twelve Essays: Social and Economic Problems from the Hitherto Neglected Point of View of the Consumer.* Manchester: Ernest Benn Ltd.

——. 1932. Note on the Statutes of Labourers. *Economic History Review* 4 (October): 77–80.

——. 1938. *Studies in Manorial History.* Oxford: Clarendon Press.

Levett, Ada Elizabeth and A. Ballard. 1916. *The Black Death on the Estates of the See of Winchester.* Oxford Studies in Social and Legal History, vol. V. Oxford: Clarendon Press.

Levetus, Amelia Sarah. 1897. Working Women in Vienna. *Economic Journal* 7(25) (March): 101–9.

Lewis, Mrs. 1893. A Reformation of Domestic Service. *Nineteenth Century* 33 (January/June): 127–38.

Lewis, Ada Haeseler. 1928. A Study of Elizabethan Ship Money, 1588–1603. Ph.D. thesis, University of Pennsylvania (economics, history).

Lewis, Alice. 1900. The Housing of the Poor in London. *Economic Review* (April).

Lewis, Burdette Gibson. 1906. Our Trade Relations with Latin America. *Journal of Political Economy* 14 (December): 602–13.

——. 1922. Job Analysis in Prisons and State Institutions. *Academy of Political Science, Proceedings* 9(4) (January): 162–.

——. 1922/3. Will Women Dispel Popular Ignorance of Government? *Social Forces* 1(1/5): 608–.

——. 1933. Regionalism. A Plan for Uniting the States More Effectively. *Forum and Century* 89(3) (March): 136–.

——. 1935. *Social Study of Pittsburgh and Allegheny County*. Report on Public Welfare Institutions and Directors of the Poor. Chicago: American Public Welfare Association.

——. 1938. *Report of Investigation of Public Relief in the District of Columbia*. Washington: Subcommittees of the Committees on Appropriations of the Senate and the House of Representatives.

Lewis, Cleona. 1921. *A Secondary School Presentation of the Work of Trade and Traders*. M.A. thesis, University of Chicago (commerce and administration).

——. 1927. *The International Accounts. A Constructive Criticism of Methods Used in Stating the Results of International Trade, Service, and Financial Operations*. New York: Macmillan Co.

——. 1933. The International Balances. *American Academy of Political and Social Science, Annals* 170 (November): 162–.

——. 1935. The Trend of Savings, 1900–1929. *Journal of Political Economy* 43(4) (August): 530–47.

——. 1937. Book Review of "Germany's Foreign Indebtedness" by C. R. S. Harris. *Political Science Quarterly* 52: 298–.

——. 1938. *America's Stake in International Investments*. Washington: Brookings Institution.

Lewis, Mary A. 1882. The Salvation Army. *Macmillan's* 46 (September): 403–16.

Lewis, Sarah [unsigned]. 1839. *Woman's Mission*. London: John W. Parker; New York: Wiley & Putnam.

——. 1848. On the Social Position of Governesses. *Fraser's* 37 (April): 411–14.

Leybourne, Grace. 1934. The Future Population of Great Britain. *Sociological Review* 26: 130–.

——. 1934. The Number of Families in England and Wales. *Sociological Review* 26 (October): 407–.

——. 1937/8. Urban Adjustments of Migrants from the Southern Appalachian Plateaus. *Social Forces* 16(1/4): 238–.

——. 1938. A Declining Birth-rate and the Cost of Education. *Eugenics Review* 30(1) (April): 33–.

——. 1938. The Growth of Education in England and Its Influence on the Size of the Family. *Eugenics Review* 30(3) (October): 175–.

Lidgett, Elizabeth S. 1893. *Women as Guardians or as Work-house Visitors*. Manchester: s.n. Reprinted from the *Guardian*, Manchester. Microform, Gerritsen Collection of Women's History, no. 1722.

——. 1894. The Official Work of Women in Local Government. Paper read at the Conference of Women Workers, Glasgow. S.l.: s.n. Microform, Gerritsen Collection of Women's History, no. 1721.

——. 1897. Poor Law Children and the Departmental Committee. *Contemporary Review* 71 (February): 205–20.

Lieser, Helene. 1920. Währungspolitische Literatur der österreichischen Bankozettelperiode. M.S. thesis, University of Vienna.

——. 1922. Adam H. Müller, Versuche einer neuen Theorie des Geldes, mit erklärenden Ammerkungen versehen von Dr. Helen Lieser. In Othmar Spahn, ed., *Die Herdflamme. Sammlung der gesellschaftswissenschaftlichen Grundwerke aller Zeiten und Völker.* Jena: G. Fischer.

Liggett, Hazel Mary. 1921. *The Relation of Wages to the Cost of Living in Los Angeles, 1915–1920.* Los Angeles: University of Southern California.

Lincoln, Alice N. 1884. Three Years' Experience in Managing a Tenement House. *Century* 28 (May): 145–7.

——. 1894. Places of Discipline and Training for Able-bodied Paupers. *Charities Review* 4(2) (December): 87–.

——. 1895. Improved Dwellings. *Charities Review* 4(8) (June): 425–.

——. 1895. Individualism in Charities. *Lend a Hand* 14(6) (June): 411–.

Lindsay, Mrs. 1892. Trade Unions for Working Women. In *Women Workers. Papers read at a conference convened by the Liverpool Ladies Union of Workers among Women and Girls in November 1891.* Liverpool: Silbert G. Walmsley.

Lindsay, Helen. 1890. *Letters to Workmen; or Short Chapters on Many Subjects.* London: Elliot Stock.

Lindsay, Mary Rodgers. 1938. *Youth Gets Its Chance: A Study of N.Y.A. Workers in New York City – Their Characteristics, Use of Income and Attitudes Towards Their Jobs.* New York: National Youth Administration for New York City.

Lindsay, Matilda. 1929. Southern Women in Industry. *American Federationist* 36 (August): 973–4.

Link, Irene. 1937. *Relief and Rehabilitation in the Drought Area.* Research Bulletin, Series 5, Works Progress Administration, Division of Social Research, no. 3. Washington: Works Progress Administration.

——. Coauth. *See* Farnham, Rebecca Tufts.

Linnett, Amy and Sidney Webb. 1892. Women Compositors. *Economic Review* (January).

Linton, E[liza]. Lynn. 1862. Domestic life. *Temple Bar* 4 (February): 402–15.

——. 1868. The Girl of the Period. *Saturday Review* 25 (March). Reprinted in Andrea Broomfield and Sally Mitchell, eds., *Prose by Victorian Women: An Anthology*. New York: Garland Publishing, 1995.

——. 1868. What is Women's Work? *Saturday Review* 25 (February).

——. 1870. The Modern Revolt [of Women]. *Macmillan's* 23 (December): 142–9.

——. 1883. *The Girl of the Period and Other Social Essays Reprinted from the Saturday Review.* 2 vols. London: R. Bentley.

——. 1885. The Stage as a Profession for Women. *National Review* 5 (March): 8–19.

——. 1886. The Higher Education of Woman. *Fortnightly Review*, n.s. 40 (October): 498–510.

——. 1889. Democracy in the Household. *Forum* 8 (October): 209–17.

——. 1890. *About Ireland: A Political Essay.* London: Methuen.

——. 1891. The Judicial Shock to Marriage. *Nineteenth Century* 29 (January/June): 691–700.

——. 1891. The Revolt against Matrimony. *Forum* 10 (January): 585–96.

——. 1891. The Wild Women: As Politicians. *Nineteenth Century* 30 (July): 79–88.

——. 1891. The Wild Women: As Social Insurgents. *Nineteenth Century* 30 (October): 596–605.

——. 1892. The Partisans of the Wild Women. *Nineteenth Century* 31 (January/June): 455–64.

——. 1894. Professor Henry Drummond's Discovery [the law of altruism]. *Fortnightly Review*, n.s. 56 [o.s. 62] (September): 448–57.

——. 1895. Class Sympathies. *National Review* 26 (November): 400–8.

Litchfield, Susan Sophia Burr. 1922. The Operation of the Federal Farm Loan Act in the Eleventh District. A.M. thesis, Leland Stanford Junior University.

——. 1925. Farm Mortgage Credit in Kansas. Ph.D. thesis, Leland Stanford Junior University.

Little, Eleanor Howell. 1926. *Women in Supervisory Positions*. New York: American Management Association.

——. 1927. *Some Considerations in Installing a Salary Administration Plan*. American Management Association Office Management Series, no. 27. New York: American Management Association.

——. 1930. *The United States Rubber Company's Use of a Dismissal Wage*. New York: American Management Association.

——. 1937. *Relief without Politics*. Hartford?, Conn.: Emergency Relief Commission.

——. Eleanor H. Little papers, 1915–1986. Correspondence, published reports, personal papers, newspaper clippings, and photos, relating to Little's activities and interests. Includes correspondence and reports created as part of her work as administrator for Connecticut Emergency Relief Commission and photos documenting Rocky Neck State Park (near East Lyme, Conn.), Keney Park (Hartford, Conn.), and other commission projects; and information pertaining to her participation in the Connecticut House of Representatives and volunteer work with Connecticut Department of Correction. Correspondents include New Deal figures such as Corrington Gill, Harry Hopkins, and other members of the Federal Emergency Relief Administration.

Little, Esther. 1914. Book Review of "A Theory of Interest" by Hoag. *American Academy of Political and Social Science, Annals* 55 (September): 288–.

Little, Esther Louise. 1914. Budgets of Families and Individuals of Kensington, Philadelphia. Ph.D. thesis, University of Pennsylvania (economics).

Little, Esther Rhoda. 1929. Wholesale Price Movements in California, 1861–1866. M.A. thesis, University of California.

Livermore, Mary. 1883. *What Shall We Do with Our Daughters? Superfluous Women, and Other Lectures*. Boston: Lee & Shepard.

——. 1886. Co-operative Housekeeping. *Chautauquan* 6 (April): 396.

——. 1886. Woman's Work in Moral Reforms. *Chautauquan* 7 (October): 69–.

——. 1886/7. Homes Builded by Women, *Chautauquan* 7 (October/July): 408–, 473–.

——. 1886/7. Superfluous Women. *Chautauquan* 7 (October/July): 216.

——. 1889. Co-operative Experiment. *Nationalist* 1 (October): 198–203.

——. 1890. Shall Our Daughters Have Dowries? *North American Review* 151(6) (December): 763–6.

——. 1891. Cooperative Womanhood in the State. *North American Review* 153 (September): 283–95.

——. 1891. Woman in the State. In Annie Nathan Meyer, ed., *Woman's Work in America*. New York: Henry Holt. Reprinted New York: Arno Press, 1972.

Lizars, Robina and Kathleen Macfarlane Lizars. 1896. *In the Days of the Canada Company: The Story of the Settlement of the Huron Tract and a View of the Social Life of the Period*. Toronto: W. Briggs; Montreal: C. W. Coates.

Lloyd, Julia Margaret Fuller. 1893. The Negro and Civilization. In Frances A. Goodale, ed., *The Literature of Philanthropy*. New York: Harper Bros.

Loane, Helen Jefferson. 1937. Trade and Industry of the City of Rome (50 B.C.–200 A.D.). Ph.D. thesis, Johns Hopkins University (language and literature).

——. 1938. *Industry and Commerce of the City of Rome (50 BC–200 AD)*. Baltimore: Johns Hopkins Press. Reprinted in Philadelphia: Porcupine Press, 1979.

——. 1938. Industry and Commerce of the City of Rome (50 B.C.–200 A.D.). *Johns Hopkins University Studies in Historical and Political Science* 56(2).

Loane, M[artha]. 1905. *The Queen's Poor: Life as They Find It in Town and Country.* London: E. Arnold. Reprinted, with introduction by Susan Cohen and Clive Fleay, London: Middlesex University Press, 1998.

Lockett, Jeannie. 1885. Female Labour in Australia. *Nineteenth Century* 18 (October): 651–6.

——. 1889. The Labour Question in Australia from an Australian Point of View. *Westminster Review* 132 (December): 617–23.

——. 1890. Divorce Considered from a Woman's Point of View. *Westminster Review* 133 (May): 479–88.

——. 1890. Divorce in Australia. *Westminster Review* 134 (October): 368–76.

——. 1891. The Labour Battle in Australia. *Westminster Review* 135 (February): 134–46.

Lockwood, Belva Ann. 1888. My Efforts to Become a Lawyer. *Lippincott's Monthly Magazine* 41 (February): 215–29.

——. 1899. *Peace and the Outlook: An American View*. Washington: T. W. Cadick, printer.

——. Lockwood, Florence Bayard. 1880. The Principle of Volunteer Service. *Journal of Social Science* 12 (December): 125–34.

——. 1891. Working Girls Clubs. *Century Magazine* 41 (March): 793–.

Lockwood, Mary S. 1892. Women in the Treasury Department in Washington. *Chautauquan* 15 (April/September): 628–.

Loewenherz, Johanna. 1895. *Prostitution oder Production, Eigentum oder Ehe? Studie zur Frauenbewegung.* Neuwied, Germany: published by the author.

Logan, Mrs. General John A. 1886/7. Women in the Departments at Washington. *Chautauquan* 7 (October/July): 327–.

Logan, Olive. 1877. English Domestics and Their Ways. *Lippincott's* 20 (July–December): 758–.

Lohner, Myrtle M. 1937. Customer Attitude toward Chicago Grocerystore Practices. *Journal of Business* 10 (July): 233–50.

Lombroso-Ferrero, G[ina]. 1914. The Results of an Official Investigation Made in England by Dr. Goring to Test the Lombroso Theory. *Journal of Criminal Law and Criminology* 5: 207.

——. 1931. *The Tragedies of Progress.* New York: Dutton.

——. 1932. *La tragedia del progreso.* Madrid: M. Aguilar.

Londonderry, Marchioness of [Theresa Vane-Tempest-Stewart]. 1897. The "Conservative" Compensation (Workmen's) Bill of 1897. *Nineteenth Century* 42 (September): 349–52.

Longfield, Ada K[athleen]. 1921/4. Anglo-Irish Trade in the Sixteenth Century as Illustrated by the English Custom Accounts and Port Books. *Royal Irish Academy, Proceedings; Archaeology, Linguistic, and Literature* 36: 318–.

——. 1929. *Anglo-Irish Trade in the Sixteenth Century.* London: Routledge.

——. 1937. History of the Irish Linen and Cotton Printing Industry in the 18th Century. *Journal of Royal Society of Antiquaries of Ireland* LXVII: 26–.

——. 1938. History of Tapestry-making in Ireland in the 17th and 18th Centuries. *Journal of Royal Society of Antiquaries of Ireland*, series 7, 8(1): 91–.

——. 1940. History of Carpet-making in Ireland in the 18th Century. *Royal Society of Antiquaries of Ireland, Journal* 7(10:2) (June 30): 63–.

Longman, Mary. 1918. Women and Internationalism. In Marion Phillips, ed., *Women and the Labour Party.* London: F. Matthews.

Lonigan, Edna. 1931. *Unemployment in New York City: An Estimate of the Number Unemployed in December, 1930, and the Sources of Information on the Extent of Unemployment in New York City.* New York: Welfare Council of New York City.

——. 1939. The Effect of Modern Technological Conditions upon the Employment of Labor. *American Economic Review* 29(2) (June): 246–59.

Lonigan, Mary Edna. 1925. *Course of Employment in Sugar Refineries in New York State, 1914–1925.* New York Department of Labor Special Bulletin, no. 137. Albany, N.Y.: J. B. Lyon Company, Printers.

——. 1926. *Employment and Earnings of Men and Women in New York State Factories, June 1923–June 1925.* Albany, N.Y.: J. B. Lyon Company, Printers.

Lonsdale, Sophia. 1891. Women's Work among the Poor. *Monthly Packet* 11 (July): 32–.

——. 1895. *The Evils of a Lax System of Out-door Relief.* Paper read at the third meeting of the Charity Organisation Conference held at Cheltenham, April 30, 1895. London: Charity Organisation Society.

——. 1896. Women as Poor Law Guardians. *Charity Organisation Review* 142 (November): 464–7.

——. 1897. *The English Poor Laws, Their History, Principles and Administration.* Three lectures given at the University Settlement for Women, Southwark. London: P. S. King & Son. 3rd ed., revised and enlarged, Westminster: P. S. King, 1902.

Lord, Eleanor Louisa. 1891. *Educated Women as Factors in Industrial Competition.* Paper presented to the Association of Collegiate Alumnae. New York: Association of Collegiate Alumnae.

——. 1892. International Arbitration. *Annals of the American Academy of Political and Social Science* 2(4) (January): 471–87.

——. 1898. *Industrial Experiments in the British Colonies of North America.* Johns Hopkins University Studies in Historical and Political Science. Baltimore: Johns Hopkins Press.

Loudon, Mrs. Margracia. 1832. *Fortune-hunting: A Novel.* London: H. Colburn.

——. 1835. *Philanthropic Economy or The Philosophy of Happiness, Practically Applied to the Social, Political, and Commercial Relations of Great Britain.* London: Edward Churton.

——. 1842. *Corn Laws, Selections from Mrs. Loudon's "Philanthropic Economy."* London: National Anti-Corn-Law League/E. Churton. Reprinted Manchester: J. Gadsby, 1845.

——. 1849. *The Fortunes of Woman: A Novel.* New York: Stringer and Townsend.

Lough, Susan Madeline. 1909. The Judicial Systems of Massachusetts and Connecticut, 1629–1687. Ph.D. thesis, University of Chicago (history).

——. 1916. Trade and Industry in Ireland in the Sixteenth Century. *Journal of Political Economy* 24(7) (July): 713–30.

——. 1919. The English Government of Ireland during the Reign of Queen Elizabeth. Ph.D. thesis, University of Chicago (history).

Loughran, Miriam Elizabeth. 1921. The Historical Development of Child-labor Legislation in the United States. Ph.D. thesis, Catholic University of America (economics, history).

Low, Frances H[elena]. 1897. How Poor Ladies Live. *Nineteenth Century* 41 (March): 405–17.

——. 1897. How Poor Ladies Live: A Rejoinder and a "Jubilee" Suggestion. *Nineteenth Century* 42 (July): 161–8.

——. 1898. Gymnastic Teaching as a Profitable Employment for Educated Women. *Woman at Home* 7 (November): 157.

——. 1898. Laundry Superintendentships – a Profitable Employment for Educated Women. *Woman at Home* 7 (December): 313.

——. 1898. A Remedy for Baby-farming. *Fortnightly Review*, n.s. 63 (February): 280–6.

——. 1898. Tea and Luncheon Rooms: A Profitable Employment for Educated Women. *Woman at Home* 7 (October): 64.

——. 1899. Dispensing as an Employment for Educated Women. *Woman at Home* 8 (June): 862.

——. 1899. Dressmaking as an Employment for Educated Women. *Woman at Home* 8 (April): 653.

——. 1899. Nursing Children as an Employment for Educated Women. *Woman at Home* 8 (May): 777.

——. 1899. A Woman's Criticism of the Women's Congress. *Nineteenth Century* 46 (August): 192–202.

Lowell, Mrs. Charles Russell, C. R. Henderson, Robert D. M'Gonnigle, Levi L. Barbour, F. B. Sanborn, and Isaac P. Wright. 1900. Public Outdoor Relief. *American Journal of Sociology* 6(1) (July): 90–104.

Lowell, Josephine Shaw. [Mrs. C. R. Lowell] 1879. One Means of Preventing Pauperism. In *Proceedings of the National Conference of Charities and Correction.* Paper read at the Chicago Conference of Charities, June. New York: National Conference of Charities and Correction.

——. 1880. *Public Charities of New York City.* An appended paper from the Thirteenth Annual Report of the Board of Charities of the State of New York, made to the legislature February 5, 1880. Albany, N.Y.: Weed, Parsons.

——. 1880. *Reformatories for Women.* An appended paper from the Thirteenth Annual Report of the Board of Charities of the State of New York, February 5, 1880. Albany, N.Y.: State Board of Charities/Weed, Parsons & Co.

——. 1881. *Some Facts Concerning the Jails, Penitentiaries and Poorhouses of the State of New York.* New York: Lowell.

——. 1881. *A Statement on Behalf of the Several Penitentiaries in the State, Submitted at a Joint Session of the Senate and Assembly Committee on State Prisons, held Feb. 17th, 1881, in Opposition to the Bill for the Repeal of the Laws Authorizing the Incarceration of Felons in Penitentiaries.* Albany, N.Y.: s.n.

——. 1881. Considerations upon a Better System of Public Charities and Corrections for Cities. In *Proceedings of the National Conference of Charities and Correction.* New York: National Conference of Charities and Correction.

——. 1882. Report on the Public Charities of New York City. In *Fifteenth Annual Report of the State Board of Charities.* Albany, N.Y.: State Board of Charities.

——. 1882. Report in Relation to Out-door Relief Societies in New York City. In *Fifteenth Annual Report of the State Board of Charities.* Albany, N.Y.: State Board of Charities.

——. 1884. *Public Relief and Private Charity.* New York: G. P. Putnam's Sons. Reprinted New York: Arno Press, 1971.

——. 1885. *On the Relation of Employers and Employed.* Philadelphia: Philadelphia Society for Organizing Charity.

——. 1885. The Bitter Cry of the Poor in New York: Some of Its Causes and Some of Its Remedies. *Christian Union* 31: 6–7.

——. 1886. Dependent Children Supported by New York City. *Lend a Hand, a Journal of Organized Philanthropy* 1: 161.

——. 1887. *Report on the Public Charities of New York City for the Year 1886.* From the 20th Annual Report of the State Board of Charities. Albany, N.Y.: New York Board of Social Welfare.

——. 1888. The Organization of Charity. *Chautauquan* 9 (October): 80.

——. 1890. The Economic and Moral Effects of Public Outdoor Relief. In *17th Annual Proceedings of the National Conference of Charities and Correction*. New York: National Conference of Charities and Correction.

——. 1890. Report upon the Care of Dependent Children in the City of New York and Elsewhere. In *Twenty-third Annual Report of the State Board of Charities*. Albany, N.Y.: State Board of Charities.

——. 1891. Labor Organisation in England, as Affected by Law. *Charities Review, a Journal of Practical Sociology* 1 (November): 6–11.

——. 1891. Voluntary Arbitration. *Journal of Social Science* 28 (October): 66–85.

——. 1891. Women in Philanthropy – Charity. In Annie Nathan Meyer, ed., *Woman's Work in America*. New York: Henry Holt. Reprinted New York: Arno Press, 1972.

——. 1892. Workingmen's Rights in Property Created by Them [letter to the editor]. *New York Tribune* (July 15). Reprinted in William Rhinelander Stewart, ed., *The Philanthropic Work of Josephine Shaw Lowell*. New York: Macmillan, 1911.

——, ed. 1893. *Industrial Arbitration and Conciliation, Some Chapters from the Industrial History of the Past Thirty Years*. New York: G. P. Putnam and Sons.

——. 1893. A Chapter of Industrial History. *Charities Review* 2(7) (May): 365–70.

——. 1893. " O Felix Qui Causam Rerum Cognavit". *Charities Review* 2(8) (June): 420–6.

——. 1893. Industrial Peace. *Charities Review* 2(3) (January): 153–9.

——. 1894. Five Months' Work for the Unemployed in New York City. *Charities Review, a Journal of Practical Sociology* 3: 323–42.

——. 1894. The Great Coal Strike of 1894. *Charities Review* 4(1) (November): 41–5.

——. 1894. Industrial Peace. *American Federationist* 1(6) (August): 115.

——. 1894. Methods of Relief for the Unemployed. *Forum* 16 (February): 655–62.

——. 1895. *Poverty and its Relief: The Methods Possible in the City of New York*. National Conference of Charities and Corrections. Boston: G. H. Ellis.

——. 1895. Charity in New York City. *Lend a Hand, a Journal of Organized Philanthropy* 15: 6–.

——. 1896. *The Reform of the Civil Service and the Spoils System*. Paper read before the Women's Auxiliary of the Civil Service Reform Association and the League for Political Education, December 30. New York: Civil Service Reform Association. Reprinted in William Rhinelander Stewart, ed., *The Philanthropic Work of Josephine Shaw Lowell*. New York: Macmillan, 1911.

——. 1896. Charity Problems. *Charities Review* 5(3) (January): 123–7.

——. 1896. The True Aim of Charity Organization Societies. *Forum* 21 (June): 494–500. Reprinted in William Rhinelander Stewart, ed., *The Philanthropic Work of Josephine Shaw Lowell*. New York: Macmillan, 1911.

——. 1897. *Consumers' Leagues*. Boston: Church Social Union. Reprinted in William Rhinelander Stewart, ed., *The Philanthropic Work of Josephine Shaw Lowell*. New York: Macmillan, 1911.

——. 1897. *Rights of Capital and Labor and Industrial Conciliation.* Boston: Church Social Union. Reprinted in William Rhinelander Stewart, ed., *The Philanthropic Work of Josephine Shaw Lowell.* New York: Macmillan, 1911.

——. 1898. The Evils of Investigation and Relief. In *Charities* 1: 8–10. Reprinted in William Rhinelander Stewart, ed., *The Philanthropic Work of Josephine Shaw Lowell.* New York: Macmillan, 1911.

——. 1898. The Living Wage. Paper delivered at Cooper Union, New York. Reprinted in William Rhinelander Stewart, ed., *The Philanthropic Work of Josephine Shaw Lowell.* New York: Macmillan, 1911.

Lowenthal, Esther. 1911. *The Ricardian Socialists.* Studies in History, Economics and Public Law, vol. XLVI, no. 1, whole no. 114. New York: Faculty of Political Science of Columbia University. Reprinted Clifton, N.J.: A.M. Kelley, 1972.

——. 1911. The Ricardian Socialists. Ph.D. thesis, Columbia University (economics).

——. 1927. The Labor Policy of the Oneida Community Ltd. *Journal of Political Economy* 35 (February): 114–26.

——. 1927. Labor Policy of the Oneida Community Ltd. *Law and Labor* 9(8) (August): 223–.

——. 1932. Book Review of "A Lecture on Human Happiness" by John Gray. *Economica* 12: 477–.

Lowrie, Josephine A[gnes]. 1927. *Merchandise Repossessions in the Installment of Furniture Trade.* Columbia: University Bureau of Business Research.

——. 1928. *Accounting Requirements of a Small Hatchery: Preliminary Bulletin.* Special Bulletin of the Bureau of Business Research, College of Commerce and Administration, the Ohio State University. Columbus, Ohio: Ohio State University Press.

——. 1928. *Analysis of Revenues and Expenses of Ohio Daily Newspapers, Year 1925.* Columbus, Ohio: Ohio State University Press.

——. 1929. *The Cost of Handling Merchandise Returns* (Based upon a Survey of a Three-month Period in an Ohio Department Store). Special bulletin of the Bureau of Business Research. Columbus, Ohio: Ohio State University Press.

——. 1929. *Operating Expenses in Ohio Accredited Hatcheries, Year 1927.* Columbus, Ohio: Bureau of Business Research, Ohio State University, co-operating with the Ohio Poultry Improvement Association.

——. 1930. *A Manual for Record Keeping in Commercial Hatcheries.* Ohio State University Bureau of Business Research Monographs. Columbus, Ohio: Bureau of Business Research, College of Commerce and Administration, Ohio State University.

——. 1931. *Operating Results of Thirty Installment Retail Furniture Stores – 1928.* Columbus, Ohio: Ohio State University Press.

——. 1933. A Better Evaluation of Current Department Operations. *Journal of Retailing* 9(2) (July): 35–.

Lowrie, Kathleen B. and Elisabeth Jennison Benham. 1927. *Industrial Accidents to Women in New Jersey, Ohio, and Wisconsin.* Bulletin of the Women's Bureau, no. 60. Washington: U.S. Government Printing Office.

Lowrie, Kathleen B. Jennison. Coauth. *See* Peterson, Agnes Lydia.

Lubbock, Gertrude. 1895. *Some Poor Relief Questions. With the Arguments on Both Sides, Together with the Summary of the Report of the Royal Commission on the Aged Poor, and Extracts from the Evidence Taken before that Commission. A Manual for Workers.* With a preface by the Right Hon. Sir John Lubbock. London: John Murray.

Luck, Mary Gorringe and Sybil Woodruff. 1931. *Cost of Living Studies. III. The Food of Twelve Families of the Professional Class.* University of California Publications in Economics, vol. 5, no. 4. Berkeley: University of California Press.

Luck, Mary Gorringe. Coauth. *See* Huntington, Emily Harriet; Okey, Ruth Eliza.

Lüders, Marie Elisabeth. 1912/1990. *Die Fortbildung und Ausbildung der im Gewerbe tätigen weiblichen Personen und deren rechtliche Grundlagen.* Bad Feilnbach, Germany: Schmidt.

——. 1920. Die Entwickllung der gewerblichen Frauenarbeit im Kriege. II. *Schmollers Jahrbuch für Gesetzgebung, Verwaltung und Volkswirtschaft im deutschen Reich* 44(2): 253–.

——. 1935/1936/1937. *Das unbekannte Heer; Frauen kämpfen für Deutschland, 1914–1918.* Berlin: E. S. Mittler & Sohn.

——. 1937. *Volkdienst der Frau.* Berlin-Tempelhof: H. Bott.

Lueb, Lydia. 1929. Die Freizeit der Textilarbeiterinnen. Eine Untersuchung über die Verwendung der Freizeit der Arbeiterinnen des christlichen Textilarbeiterverbandes Bezirk Westfalen. Ph.D. thesis, University of Münster.

Lumpkin, Katharine [Du Pre]. 1928. Factors in the Commitment of Correctional School Girls in Wisconsin. Ph.D. thesis, University of Wisconsin–Madison (sociology).

——. 1931. Factors in the Commitment of Correctional School Girls in Wisconsin. *American Journal of Sociology* 37(2) (September): 222–30.

——. 1932. Parental Conditions of Wisconsin Girl Delinquents. *American Journal of Sociology* 38(2) (September): 232–9.

——. 1937. Democratic Ways in The USSR. *Soviet Russia Today* 6(2) (April): 10–.

——. 1939. Book Review of "Child Labor in the Southern Textile States" by Elizabeth H. Davidson. *Science & Society* 3: 553–.

——. 1939. The Child Labor Provisions of the Fair Labor Standards Act. *Law and Contemporary Problems* 6: 391–.

——. 1940. *The South in Progress.* New York: International Publishers.

Lumpkin, Katharine Du Pre and Mable Van Able Combs. 1934. *Shutdowns in the Connecticut Valley: A Study of Worker Displacement in the Small Industrial Community.* Northampton, Mass.: Department of History, Smith College.

Lumpkin, Katharine Du Pre and Dorothy Wolff Douglas. 1933. The Effect of Unemployment and Short-time during 1931 in the Families of 200 Alabama Child Workers. *Social Forces* 11(4) (May): 548–58.

——. 1937. *Child Workers in America.* New York: R. M. McBride & Company.

Lumsden, Miss. 1885. The Higher Education of Woman in Great Britain and Ireland. *Journal of Social Science* 20 (June): 49–60.

Lundberg, Emma Octavia. 1908. Personal Inefficiency as Related to Family and Social Conditions. Master's thesis, University of Wisconsin–Madison.

——. 1915. *Mental Defectives in the District of Columbia: A Brief Description of Local Conditions and the Need for Custodial Care and Training*. Washington: U.S. Children's Bureau.

——. 1916. *Cost of Living of Wage Earning Women in Wisconsin*. Madison, Wisc.: Wisconsin Industrial Commission.

——. 1917. *A Study of Mental Defectives in New Castle County, Delaware*. Washington: U.S. Children's Bureau.

——. 1918. Social Study of Mental Defectives in New Castle County, Delaware. *Journal of Criminal Law and Criminology* 8: 766.

——. 1920. *State Commission for the Study and Revision of Child-welfare Laws*. Washington: U.S. Government Printing Office.

——. 1921. Aid to Mothers with Dependent Children. *American Academy of Political and Social Science, Annals* 98 (November): 97–.

——. 1922. *County Organization for Child Care and Protection*. Washington: U.S. Children's Bureau.

——. 1922. Methods of Field Research by the Federal Children's Bureau. *American Sociological Society, Papers and Proceedings* 17 (December): 151–.

——. 1923. *Unemployment and Child Welfare: A Study Made in a Middle-Western and an Eastern City During the Industrial Depression of 1921 and 1922*. Washington: U.S. Government Printing Office.

——. 1924. *State Commissions for the Study and Revision of Child-welfare Laws*. Washington: U.S. Children's Bureau.

——. 1925. *Public Aid to Mothers with Dependent Children, Extent and Fundamental Principles*. Washington: U.S. Government Printing Office.

——. 1926. *Children of Illegitimate Birth*. Washington: U.S. Children's Bureau.

——. 1926. *The County as a Unit of an Organized Program of Child Caring and Protective Work*. Washington: U.S. Children's Bureau.

——. 1926. *Dependent and Delinquent Children in Georgia: A Study of the Prevalence and Treatment of Child Dependency and Delinquency in Thirty Counties with Special Reference to Legal Protection Needed*. Washington: U.S. Children's Bureau.

——. 1926. *Dependent and Delinquent Children in North Dakota and South Dakota: A Study of Prevalence, Treatment, and Prevention of Child Dependency and Delinquency in Two Rural States*. Washington: U.S. Children's Bureau.

——. 1926/1928. *Public Aid to Mothers with Dependent Children, Extent and Fundamental Principles*. Washington: U.S. Children's Bureau.

——. 1928. Progress of Mothers' Aid Administration. *Social Service Review* 2(1/4) (March/December): 435–.

——. 1932. The New York State Relief Administration. *Social Service Review* 6(1/4) (March/December): 545–.

——. 1933. *Child Dependency in the United States: Methods of Statistical Reporting and Census of Dependent Children in Thirty-one States*. New York: Child Welfare League of America.

——. 1933. *Food Allowance Standards in the Up-state Welfare Districts*. Albany: New York State Temporary Emergency Relief Administration.

——. 1933. *Local Administration of Public Relief.* Albany: New York State Temporary Emergency Relief Administration.

——. 1933. *Relief Funds for Shelter: Policies and Practice.* Albany: New York State Temporary Emergency Relief Administration.

——. 1933. *Social Service in Local Public Relief Administration.* Albany: New York State Temporary Emergency Relief Administration.

——. 1933. *Unmarried Mothers in the Municipal Court of Philadelphia: A Report.* By the Bureau of Municipal Research of Philadelphia. Philadelphia: Thomas Skelton Harris Foundation.

——. 1933. A State-wide Program of Constructive Public Relief. *Social Service Review* 7(1/4) (March/December): 463–.

——. 1934. *Mothers' Pensions in Florida, 1933.* Tallahassee, Fla.: Florida State Board of Public Welfare.

——. 1934. County Welfare Boards and Emergency Relief. *Social Service Review* 8(1/4) (March/December): 238–.

——. 1934. A State Plans Social Welfare Reconstruction. *Family* 15(2) (April): 38–. Reprinted New York: Family Welfare Association of America, 1934.

——. 1934. Who Are the New York Emergency Relief Families? *Social Service Review* 8(1/4) (March/December): 616–.

——. 1935. *Social Welfare in Florida.* Tallahassee, Fla.: State Board of Public Welfare, Publication no. 4.

——. 1935. A Cross-section of the Relief Load in Upstate New York. *Social Service Review* 9(1/4) (March/December): 484–.

——. 1937. *The Public Child-welfare Program in the District of Columbia.* U.S. Children's Bureau Publication, no. 240. Washington: U.S. Government Printing Office. 2nd ed., rev. enlarged, 1938.

——. 1939. Case Recording in Public Child-welfare Agencies. *Child* 4(4) (October): 105–.

Lundberg, Emma Octavia and Ada Ethel Barger. 1927/1936. *Handbook for the Use of Boards of Directors, Superintendents, and Staffs of Institutions for Dependent Children.* Washington: U.S. Children's Bureau.

Lundberg, Emma Octavia and Laura Hood. 1924/1926. *Foster-home Care for Dependent Children.* Washington: U.S. Children's Bureau.

Lundberg, Emma Octavia and Katharine F. Lenroot. 1920. *Illegitimacy as a Child-welfare Problem, Part I.* Children's Bureau Publication, no. 66. Washington: U.S. Government Printing Office.

——. 1922. *Illegitimacy as a Child-welfare Problem, Part II.* Children's Bureau Publication, no. 75. Washington: U.S. Government Printing Office.

——. 1925. *Juvenile Courts at Work: A Study of the Organization and Methods of Ten Courts.* U.S. Children's Bureau Publication, no. 141. Washington: U.S. Government Printing Office.

Lundberg, Emma Octavia and Mary E. Milburn. 1924. *Child Dependency in the District of Columbia: An Interpretation of Data Concerning Dependent Children under the Care of Public and Private Agencies.* Washington: U.S. Children's Bureau.

——. 1924. *What Child Dependency Means in the District of Columbia and How It Can Be Prevented.* Washington: U.S. Government Printing Office.

Lundberg, Emma Octavia. Coauth. *See* Springer, Ethel Maria.

——. Papers at Butler Library, Columbia University.

Lux, Käthe. 1907. Arbeiterbewegung und Arbeiterpolitik in Australasien 1890–1905. *Archiv für Sozialwissenschaft und Sozialpolitik* 6(24).

——. 1910. *Studien über die Entwicklung der Warenhäuser in Deutschland.* Jena: Gustav Fischer.

Luxemburg, Rosa. 1897. Die industrielle Entwicklung Polens. Ph.D. thesis, University of Zurich.

——. 1898. *Die industrielle Entwicklung Polens.* Leipzig: Duncker & Humblot. Published as *The Industrial Development of Poland*, transl. Tessa DeCarlo, with an introduction by Lyndon H. LaRouche, Jr. New York: Campaigner Publications, 1977.

——. 1899/1900. *Sozialreform oder Revolution? Mit einem Anhang: Miliz under Militarismus.* Berlin: Dietsch. English translation, *Reform or Revolution.* New York: Pathfinder Press, 1970.

——. 1900/1984. *W Obronie Narodowosci.* Warsaw: Wydawnictwa Artystyczne i Filmowe.

——. 1906. *Massenstreik, Partei und Gewerkschaften.* Hamburg: E. Dubber.

——. 1913. *Die Akkumulation des Kapitals. Ein Beitrag zur ökonomischen Erklärung des Imperialismus.* Leipzig: Frankes Verlag; Berlin: Buchhandlung Vorwarts, Paul Singer. 2nd ed., rev. and enlarged, published as *Die Akkumulation des Kapitals oder was die Epigonen aus der marxschen Theorie gemacht haben. Eine Antikritik.* English ed., trans. Agnes Schwarzschild, *The Accumulation of Capital.* London: Routledge & Kegan Paul Ltd., 1951; reprinted 2003.

——. 1916. *Die Krise der Sozialdemokratie, Anhang: Leitsätze über die Aufgaben der internationalen Sozialdemokratie.* Zurich: Verlagsdrukerei Union.

——. 1918/1969. *The Crisis in the German Social-Democracy.* New York: H. Fertig.

——. 1918. Die russische Tragödie. *Spartakusbrief* 11 (September): 2–4.

——. 1919. My Idea of Bolshevism. *Living Age* 8(300) (January/March): 583–.

——. 1922. *Die russische Revolution. Eine kritische Würdigung.* Berlin: Verlag Gesellschaft und Erziehung. English translation in *The Russian Revolution, and Leninism or Marxism.* Ann Arbor: University of Michigan Press, 1970.

——. 1925. *Einführung in die Nationalökonomie.* Berlin: E. Laub. Chapter 1, transl. T. Edwards, published as *What Is Economics?* New York: Pioneer Publishers. Reprinted London: Merlin, 1968, 1970.

——. 1932. Letters From Prison. *Adelphi* 2(5:2) (November): 123–.

——. 1933. Notes on the Russian Revolution. *Adelphi* 2(7:3) (December): 157–.

——. 1938. Letters from Prison. *Partisan Review* 5(1) (June): 3–.

——. 1954. *What Is Economics?* Chapter 1 of *Einführung in die Nationalökonomie,* transl. T. Edwards. New York: Pioneer Publishers. Reprinted London: Merlin, 1968, 1970.

Lyford, Carrie Alberta. 1923. *A Study of Home-Economics Education in Teacher-Training Institutions for Negroes.* Bulletin no. 79, Home Economics Series, no. 7.

S.l.: U.S. Office of Education. Reprinted New York: Negro Universities Press, 1969.

Lynd, Helen M[errell]. 1931/2. What Becomes of Mothers? *Child Study; a Journal of Parent Education* 9: 157–.

——. 1932. Parent Education and the Colleges. *American Academy of Political and Social Science, Annals* 160 (March): 197–.

——. 1937. Community Studies – Their Uses and Misuses. *American Association of University Women, Journal* 31(1) (October): 3–.

——. 1940. *Two Views of the Work of Women Today*. New York: Society for Ethical Culture.

——. 1940. Education for Contemporary Women. *Standard* 26(7) (April): 178–.

Lynskey, Elizabeth Mary. 1919. *The Organization and Government of the Roman Catholic Church, with Special Reference to the United States*. M.A. thesis, University of Minnesota.

——. 1929. The Diplomatic Protection of American Missionaries in China; and Nationalism and Internationalism: Features in the Governmental Structure of the Catholic Church. Ph.D. thesis, Robert Brookings.

——. 1931. *The Making of Our Nation*. New York and Chicago: Charles E. Merrill Company.

——. 1931. *Porto Rico and the United States; Study Presented to the Catholic Association for International Peace*. Catholic Association for International Peace (U.S.) pamphlet, no. 7. Committee on U.S. Dependencies. New York: Paulist Press.

——. 1934. *Manchuria: The Problem in the Far East*. Catholic Association for International Peace (U.S.) pamphlet, no. 12. New York: Paulist Press.

——. 1939/40. Book Review of "The Corporate State in Action" by Schmidt. *Catholic Historical Review* 25: 371–.

Lynskey, Elizabeth M. and Gwendoline Clabault Sauer. 1931. *The Beginnings of our Nation*. New York and Chicago: Charles E. Merrill Company.

Lyons, Vyvyan Ashleigh. 1920. *Wages and Empire*. London: Longmans, Green & Co.

Lyttelton, Katharine Sarah. 1892. Englishwomen in India. *New Review* 6 (June): 682–94.

M

McAdoo, Laura Sterette. 1899. Woman's Economic Status in the South. *Arena* 21 (June): 741–56.

McAnear, Beverly. 1940. Mr. Robert R. Livingston's Reasons against a Land Tax. *Journal of Political Economy* 48 (February): 63–90.

——. 1940. The Place of the Freeman in Old New York. *New York History* 21(4) (October): 418–.

McArthur, Ellen A. 1894. "The Boke Longyng to a Justice of the Peace" and the Assessment of Wages. *English Historical Review* 9(34) (April): 305–14.

——. 1898. A Fifteenth-century Assessment of Wages. *English Historical Review* 13(50) (April): 299–302.

——. 1898. Prices at Woodstock in 1604. *English Historical Review* 13(52) (October): 711–16.

——. 1900/1. Book Review of "The Early History of English Poor Relief" by E. M. Leonard. *International Journal of Ethics* 11: 379–.

——. 1906. Book Review of "The Acts and Ordinances of the Eastland Company" by Maud Sellers. *Economic Journal* 16: 584–.

——. 1908. Book Review of "British Committees, Commissions, and Councils of Trade and Plantations, 1622–1675" by Prof. Charles M. Andrews. *Economic Journal* 18: 448–.

——. 1909. Book Review of "The Black Death of 1348 and 1349" by Abbott Gasquet. *Economic Journal* 19: 106–.

——. 1909. Book Review of "The Enforcement of the Statutes of Labourers during the First Decade after the Black Death" by Bertha Haven Putnam. *Economic Journal* 19(76) (December): 585–8.

——. 1909. Book Review of "The Guilds and Companies of London" by George Unwin. *Economic Journal* 19: 438–.

——. 1909. A Parallel to the Suffragettes [letter to the editor]. *Nation* 4(20) (February 13): 751–.

——. 1910. Book Review of "Social England in the Fifteenth Century" by A. Abram. *Economic Journal* 20(78) (June): 263.

——. 1928. Sir Edmund Berry Godfrey, Woodmonger. *English Historical Review* 43: 78–.

McArthur, Ellen A. and William Cunningham. 1895. *Outlines of English Industrial History*. London: Macmillan. 2nd ed., Cambridge, UK: Cambridge University Press, 1898; 4th ed., 1920.

MacArthur, Kathleen [Walker]. 1916. The Government and the Women Workers [letter to the editor]. *Nation* 19(21) (August 19): 629–.

——. 1936. The Economic Ethics of John Wesley. Ph.D. thesis, University of Chicago Divinity School (religion).

——. 1938. *The Economic Ethics of John Wesley*. New York: Abingdon Press.

——. 1938. Book Review of "John Wesley's Awakening" by J. R. Joy. *Church History* 7(1) March: 74–.

——. 1939. Book Review of "Die Autoritätslehre in den Werken John Wesleys" by Frost. *Journal of Religion* 19: 72–.

——. 1939. Book Review of "England: Before and after Wesley" by Bready. *Journal of Religion* 19: 59–.

MacArthur, Kathleen and Margaret Llewelyn Davies. 1909. The Government and Women's Suffrage [letter to the editor]. *Nation* 6(10) December 4: 400–.

Macarthur, Mary R. 1908. Trade Unionism. In Gertrude M. Tuckwell, ed., *Woman in Industry from Seven Points of View*. London: Duckworth and Co. Reprinted Washington: NCR Microcard Editions, 1970.

——. 1911. Women and State Insurance. *Women's Trade Review* (July).

——. 1918. The Women Trade Unionists' Point of View. In M. Phillips, ed., *Women and the Labour Party*. London: F. Matthews.

——. 1919. American Health Insurance Bill Better than British Act. *American Labor Legislation Review* 9: 204.

——. 1919. Women Workers of England. In Margaret Grace Bondfield, Eleanor Barton, and Mary R. Macarthur, *English Women in the Labor and Co-Operative Movements: Three Speeches Delivered before the Seventh Biennial Convention of the National Women's Trade Union League, Philadelphia, June 2–7, 1919*. Chicago: Women's Trade Union League of America.

Macaulay, Catharine Graham. 1763–83. *History of England from the Accession of James I*. 8 vols. London: J. Nourse, W. Johnston, and C. Dilly.

——. 1770. *A Reply to Burke's Pamphlet Entitled "Thoughts on the Cause of the Present Discontents."* London: Edward and Charles Dilly.

——. 1774. *A Modest Plea for the Property of Copyright*. London: Edward and Charles Dilly.

——. 1775. *An Address to the People of England, Scotland and Ireland on the Present Important Crisis of Affairs*. London: Edward and Charles Dilly.

——. 1790. *Letters on Education*. London: C. Dilly.

——. 1790. *Observations on the Reflections of the Right Hon. Edmund Burke on the Revolution in France*. London: Charles Dilly.

McCann, Helen. 1940. The Business Papers of Emerson Cole. *Business History Review* 14 (December): 81–6.

McCartney, Martha Ann. 1927. The Influence of the Dutch on the Economic Life of England from 1600–1650. M.A. thesis, University of Minnesota.

McClenaghan, Barbara. 1924. *The Springs of Lavenham and the Suffolk Cloth Trade in the Fifteenth and Sixteenth Centuries*. Ipswich, UK: W. E. Harrison.

McClenahan, Bessie Averne. 1916. *The Social Survey*. State University of Iowa Extension Division Bulletin, no. 26. Iowa City: State University of Iowa.

——. 1918. *The Iowa Plan for the Combination of Public and Private Relief*. Iowa City: University of Iowa.

——. 1929/30. Locus and Status. *Sociology and Social Research* 14: 410–.

——. 1931/2. The Communality. *Sociology and Social Research* 16: 434–.

——. 1933/4. Preparation for Leisure. *Sociology and Social Research* 18: 140–.

——. 1935. The Child of the Relief Agency. *Social Forces* 13(4) (May): 560–7.

——. 1936/7. Relief and Security. *Sociology and Social Research* 21: 234–.

——. 1937/8. Group Work and Community Organization. *Sociology and Social Research* 22: 403–.

——. 1939/40. Group Work and Group Education. *Sociology and Social Research* 24: 240–.

——. 1940/1. The Tools and Techniques of Social Group Work. *Sociology and Social Research* 25: 332–.

McClure, Virginia Clay. 1934. Settlement of the Kentucky Appalachian Highlands. Ph.D. thesis, University of Kentucky (history).

McConnell, Dorothy Frances. 1935. *Women, War, and Fascism*. New York: American League against War and Fascism.

McConnell, Jessie Beatrice. 1928. *Migratory Child Workers and School Attendance*. Harrisburg, Pa.: Pennsylvania Bureau of Women and Children.

McConnell, Jessie Beatrice, Rebecca G. Smaltz, and Elizabeth S. Johnson. 1930. *Hours and Earnings of Men and Women in the Hosiery Industry*. Special Bulletin, no. 31. Harrisburg, Pa.: Pennsylvania Department of Labor and Industry.

McConnell, Jessie Beatrice. Coauth. *See* Smaltz, Rebecca Glover.

McCord, Elizabeth. 1932. *The Emergency Worker in Unemployment Relief*. New York: Family Welfare Association of America.

——. 1937. The Part of the Worker in the Community's Acceptance of Social Work. *Family* 17(9) (January): 294–.

McCord, Elizabeth, Wilma Van Dusseldorp, and Sybil Pease. 1936. *Social Work Practice in Three Rural Counties*. S.l.: Social Service Division, Federal Emergency Relief Administration.

McCord, Louisa Susanna [Mrs. D. J. McCord], transl. 1848. *Sophisms of the Protective Policy*, by Frederic Bastiat, translated from the French by Mrs. D. J. McCord. New York: George Putnam.

——. 1849. Justice and Fraternity. *Southern Quarterly Review* 15 (July): 356–74. Reprinted in Richard Lounsbury, ed., *Louisa S. McCord: Political and Social Essays*. Charlottesville, Va.: University Press of Virginia, 1995.

——. 1849. The Right to Labor. *Southern Quarterly Review* 16 (October): 138–60. Reprinted in Richard Lounsbury, ed., *Louisa S. McCord: Political and Social Essays*. Charlottesville, Va.: University Press of Virginia, 1995.

——. 1851. Diversity of the Races; Its Bearing upon Negro Slavery. *Southern Quarterly Review* 20 (April): 392–409. Reprinted in Richard Lounsbury, ed., *Louisa S. McCord: Political and Social Essays.* Charlottesville, Va.: University Press of Virginia.

——. 1851. Negro and White Slavery – Wherein Do They Differ? *Southern Quarterly Review* 20 (July): 118–32. Reprinted in Richard Lounsbury, ed., *Louisa S. McCord: Political and Social Essays.* Charlottesville, Va.: University Press of Virginia, 1995.

——. 1852. Enfranchisement of Woman. *Southern Quarterly Review* 21 (April): 322–41. Reprinted in Richard Lounsbury, ed., *Louisa S. McCord: Political and Social Essays.* Charlottesville, Va.: University Press of Virginia.

——. 1852. Negro Mania. *De Bow's Review* 12 (May): 507–24. Reprinted in Richard Lounsbury, ed., *Louisa S. McCord: Political and Social Essays.* Charlottesville, Va.: University Press of Virginia, 1995.

——. 1852. Woman and Her Needs. *De Bow's Review* 13 (September): 267–91. Reprinted in Richard Lounsbury, ed., *Louisa S. McCord: Political and Social Essays.* Charlottesville, Va.: University Press of Virginia, 1995.

——. 1853. British Philanthropy and American Slavery. *De Bow's Review* 14 (March): 258–80. Reprinted in Richard Lounsbury, ed., *Louisa S. McCord: Political and Social Essays.* Charlottesville, Va.: University Press of Virginia.

——. 1853. Charity Which Does Not Begin at Home. *Southern Literary Messenger* 19 (April): 193–208. Reprinted in Richard Lounsbury, ed., *Louisa S. McCord: Political and Social Essays.* Charlottesville, Va.: University Press of Virginia.

——. 1854. Carey on the Slave Trade. *Southern Quarterly Review* 25 (January): 115–53. Reprinted in Richard Lounsbury, ed., *Louisa S. McCord: Political and Social Essays.* Charlottesville, Va.: University Press of Virginia, 1995.

——. 1856. Slavery and Political Economy. *De Bow's Review* 21 (October): 331–49; (November): 443–67. Reprinted in Richard C. Lounsbury, ed., *Louisa S. McCord: Political and Social Essays.* Charlottesville, Va.: University Press of Virginia, 1995.

McCormick, Mary Josephine. 1929. *The Measurement of Home Conditions.* Washington: National Catholic School of Social Service.

——. 1931. A Scale for Measuring Social Adequacy. Ph.D. thesis, Catholic University of America (sociology).

——. 1932/3. Economic Depression and the School Child. *Thought; Fordham University Quarterly* 7: 448–.

McCourbrey, Margaret. 1922. The Irish "Woman with the Basket." *Irish Economist* (May).

[McCulloch,] Catharine G. Waugh. 1888. *Woman's Wages.* Rockford, Ill.: Daily Gazette Book and Job Office.

——. 1899. *Mr Lex: Or the Legal Status of Mother and Child.* Chicago: Flemming H. Revell Company.

McCulloch, Rhoda Elizabeth. 1920. *The War and the Woman Point of View.* Committee on the War and the Religious Outlook. New York: Association Press.

——. 1924. *And Who Is My Neighbor: An Outline for the Study of Race Relations in America.* National Conference on the Christian Way of Life. New York: Association Press.

——. 1924. *The Question of the "Right to Strike."* National Conference on the Christian Way of Life. Commission on Industrial Relations. New York: Association Press.

MacDonald, Alice. Coauth. *See* Stevenson, Marietta.

MacDonald, Lois. 1928. *Southern Mill Hills. A Study of Social and Economic Forces in Certain Textile Mill Villages.* New York: Alex L. Hillman.

——. 1929. *The Worker and the Machine Age: Economics Outlines, Syllabi, etc.* Burnsville, N.C.: Southern Summer School for Women in Industry.

——. 1929. Southern Mill Hills, a Study of Social and Economic Forces in Certain Textile Mill Villages. Ph.D. thesis, New York University (sociology).

——. 1932. Has Education Failed the South? *American Association of University Women, Journal* 25(2) (January): 65–.

——. 1934. *Wages and the Worker.* New York: Affiliated Schools for Workers, Inc.

——. 1936. The National Labor Relations Act. *American Economic Review* 26(3) (September): 412–27.

——. 1938. *Labor Problems and the American Scene.* New York: Harper.

MacDonald, Lois, Gladys Louise Palmer, and Theresa Wolfson. 1934. *Labor and the N.R.A.* New York: Affiliated Schools for Workers.

MacDonald, Louisa. 1893. The Economic Position of Women. *Australian Economist* III(11) (December 30): 367–72.

——. 1894. Reply [to remarks on The Economic Position of Women]. *Australian Economist* IV(3) (April 23): 396–8.

MacDonald, Margaret Ethel. 1908. Sweated Industries and Wages Boards. *Economic Journal* 18 (March): 140–5.

MacDonald, Margaret Ethel [Gladstone] and Elizabeth Leigh Hutchins. 1908. *Home Industries of Women in London: Report of an Inquiry by the Investigation Committee of the Council with an Account of the Development and Present Condition of Home Work in Relation to the Legal Protection of the Workers and Some Account of Foreign Experiments in Legislation.* London: Women's Industrial Council.

McDougall, Ellen M. L. 1893. How to Help Workhouse Girls and Women. *Sunday Magazine* 22 (May): 346.

McDowell, Mary Eliza. 1907. The Need for a National Investigation into Women's Work. *Charities and the Commons* 17 (October): 634–6.

——. 1907. Red Letter Day: First Interstate Convention of National Women's Trade Union League. *American Federationist* 14(9) (September): 678–.

——. 1909. *An Appeal to the Union Women.* Chicago: Women's Trade Union League of America.

——. 1910. A Practical Plea to Chicago Christians. *Public* 13(664) (December 23): 1,217–.

——. 1922. The Negro in Industry. *World Tomorrow* 5(3) (March): 72–.

——. 1923. Dr. Alice G. Masaryk at Work. *Czechoslovak Review* 7(3) (March): 54–.

——. 1929. Hovels or Homes? *Opportunity* 7(3) (March): 74–.

——. Published articles in *Survey*, *Charities*, *Outlook*, and the *Independent*.

McEnery, Mrs. M. B. 1890. Factory Inspection. In *Fourth Annual Convention of the International Association of Inspectors of Factories and Workshops of North America*. Boston: Wright and Potter.

MacFadyen, Irene [M. Ashby]. 1901. The Fight against Child Labor in Alabama. *American Federationist* 8 (May): 150–1.

——. 1901. Labor of Children in Southern Cotton-mills. *World's Work* 2: 1,290.

——. 1902. Abolish Child Labor. *American Federationist* 9(1) (January): 19–.

——. 1902. Child Life vs. Dividend. *American Federationist* 9(5) (May): 215–.

——. 1907. The Birth Rate and the Mother. *Nineteenth Century* 61 (March): 429–35.

McGill, Nettie Pauline. 1921. *Infant-welfare Work in Europe: An Account of Recent Experiences in Great Britain, Austria, Belgium, France, Germany, and Italy*. U.S. Children's Bureau Publication, no. 76. Washington: U.S. Government Printing Office.

——. 1921. Trend of Child Labor in the United States, 1913 to 1920. *Monthly Labor Review* 12 (January): 1–14.

——. 1925. *Vocational Guidance and Junior Placement: Twelve Cities in the United States*. Washington: U.S. Government Printing Office.

——. 1928. *Child Workers on City Streets*. Washington: U.S. Government Printing Office.

——. 1928. *Children in Street Work*. Washington: U.S. Children's Bureau.

——. 1931. *Child Labor in New Jersey*, part 3: *The Working Children of Newark and Paterson*. U.S. Department of Labor, Children's Bureau Publications, no. 199. Washington: U.S. Government Printing Office.

McGill, Nettie Pauline and Ellen N. Matthews. 1940. *Youth of New York City*. New York: Macmillan.

McGill, Nettie Pauline and Ella Arvilla Merritt. 1929. *Children in Agriculture*. U.S. Children's Bureau Publication, no. 187. Washington: U.S. Government Printing Office.

McGill, Nettie P. and Mary Skinner. 1929. *Child Labor in New Jersey*, part 1: *Employment of School Children*. U.S. Department of Labor, Children's Bureau Publications, no. 185. Washington: U.S. Government Printing Office.

McGill, Nettie Pauline and Ethel Maria Springer. 1923. *The Welfare of Children in Bituminous Coal Mining Communities in West Virginia*. U.S. Children's Bureau Publication, no. 117. Washington: U.S. Government Printing Office.

McGill, Nettie Pauline and Mary Mills West. 1920. *Child-welfare Programs*. Washington: U.S. Government Printing Office.

McGill, Nettie Pauline. Coauth. *See* Matthews, Ellen Nathalie; Skinner, Mary Elizabeth.

McGowan, Ellen B. Coauth. *See* Woolman, Mary Raphael Schenk.

McIlquham, Harriet. 1891. *The Enfranchisement of Women, an Ancient Right, a Modern Need. A paper read by Mrs. McIlquham (Poor Law Guardian) to the Bedminster (Bristol) Champion Habitation of the Primrose League, on the 11th December, 1891*. London: Women's Emancipation Union.

——. 1892. *The Rights and Duties of Women in Local Government.* Paper read at the Birmingham Conference, October 25, 1892. Manchester, UK: Women's Emancipation Union.

——. 1893. *The Duties and Rights of Women in Local Administration.* Paper read at the Women's Emancipation Union Conference, March 15, 1893. With an appendix on voting in local elections by Elizabeth C. Wolstenholme Elmy. Congleton, UK: Women's Emancipation Union.

——. 1894. *Women and the Parish Councils Act; the Past, Present and Future of Parochial and Poor Law Government.* Lecture delivered to the West Bristol Women's Liberal Association, 4 October, 1894. Congleton, UK: Women's Emancipation Union.

——. 1896. *Local Government and Its Limitations for Women.* London: Women's Printing Society.

——. 1896. *Local Government in England and Wales.* Paper read at the London Conference, October 14. Congleton, UK: Women's Emancipation Union.

——. 1899. *Women and the Local Franchise in England.* Women's Emancipation Union, no. 7. London: Women's Emancipation Union.

McIntosh, Maria J. 1850. *Woman in America: Her Work and Her Reward.* New York: D. Appleton & Co.

Machar, Agnes Maule. 1897. Outdoor Relief in Canada. *Charities Review* 6(5/6) (July/August): 457–68.

Mack, Ruth Prince. 1936. *Controlling Retailers: A Study of Cooperation and Control in the Retail Trade, with Special Reference to the NRA.* Studies in History, Economics and Public Law, edited by the Faculty of Political Science of Columbia University, no. 423. New York: Columbia University.

——. 1937. Controlling Retailers: A Study of Cooperation and Control in the Retail Trade with Special Reference to the N.R.A. Ph.D. thesis, Columbia University (economics).

[McKelvey,] Jean [Carol] Trepp. 1928. The Liverpool Movement for the Abolition of the English Slave Trade. *Journal of Negro History* 13(1/4) (January/October): 265–.

——. 1933. *Trade-union Interest in Production.* Ph.D. thesis, Radcliffe College.

McKelvey, Jean Carol Trepp. 1933. Union-management Co-operation and the Southern Organizing Campaign. *Journal of Political Economy* 41(5): 602–24.

——. 1939. *The Use of Field Work in Teaching Economics.* Bronxville, N.Y.: Sarah Lawrence College.

MacKenzie, W. A. 1921. Changes in the Standard of Living in the United Kingdom, 1860–1914. *Economica* (October): 211–30.

McKerlie, Helen. 1899. The Position of Women in Sweden. *Humanitarian* 14 (January): 48–.

McKillop, Margaret. 1911. *Economics, Descriptive and Theoretical, Part I: Descriptive.* London: Allman.

——. 1925. *Food Values: What They Are and How to Calculate Them.* 3rd ed. London: George Routledge & Sons Ltd.

——. 1929. The Family Budget on a Weekly Wage. *Listener* 1(15) (April 24): 563–.

——. 1929. The Family Budget on a Weekly Wage – II. *Listener* 1(16) (May 1): 608–.

McKinney, Miss. 1895. Remarks [on Women and Womanhood Suffrage by E. Badham]. *Australian Economist* IV(16) (June 21): 499.

Mackintosh, Margaret. 1924. *Government Intervention in Labour Disputes in Canada.* Kingston, Ontario Queen's University, Bulletin of the Departments of History and Political Science, no. 47. Kingston: Jackson Press. Also published in *Queen's Quarterly* 31 (August/May): 298–. Reprinted Ottawa: F. A. Alcand, Printer, 1925.

——. 1935. *Trade Union Law in Canada, January, 1935.* Ottawa: J. O. Patenaude, Printer to the King.

——. 1936. Collective Labor Agreements. *Personnel Journal* 15(4) (October): 151–.

——. 1936. Legislation Concerning Collective Labour Agreements. *Canadian Bar Review*, 14, parts 2 and 3.

——. 1938. *Canada and the I.L.O., February 1, 1938.* Compiled from memoranda prepared by Miss Margaret Mackintosh, Department of Labour, Canada, and an address delivered by her at the Pan-Pacific Women's Conference, Honolulu, 1934. Ottawa: International Labour Organisation and League of Nations Society in Canada.

——. 1938/1942. *An Outline of Trade Union History in Great Britain, the United States and Canada with Special Emphasis on the Causes Leading to the Present Division in the Canadian Labour Movement.* Ottawa: Canadian Department of Labour.

——. 1939. Workmen's Compensation in Canada. *International Labour Review* 40(1/6) (July/December): 1–.

Mackirdy, Olive Christian Malvery. 1907. *Baby Toilers.* London: Hutchinson.

——. 1907. *The Soul Market, with Which Is Included "The Heart of Things."* London: Hutchinson & Co.

——. 1908. *Thirteen Nights.* London: Hodder and Stoughton.

——. 1912. *The White Slave Market.* 7th ed. London: St. Paul & Co.

——. 1912. *A Year and a Day.* London: Hutchinson.

McKnight, Edna. 1931. Jobs – For Men Only? *Outlook and Independent* 159 (September 2): 12.

McLaughlin, Frances. 1891. The Problem of Domestic Service. *National Review* 17 (April): 214–27.

MacLean, Annie Marion. 1897. Factory Legislation for Women in the United States. *American Journal of Sociology* 3(2) (September): 183–205.

——. 1899. Factory Legislation for Women in Canada. *American Journal of Sociology* 5(2) (September): 172–81.

——. 1899. Homes for Working Women in Large Cities. *Charities Review* 9(5) (July): 215–28.

——. 1899. Two Weeks in Department Stores. *American Journal of Sociology* 4(6) (May): 721–41.

——. 1900. The Acadian Element in the Population of Nova Scotia. Ph.D. thesis, University of Chicago (sociology).

——. 1903. The Sweat-shop in Summer. *American Journal of Sociology* 9(3): 289–309.

——. 1905. Significance of the Canadian Migration. *American Journal of Sociology* 10(6): 814–23.

——. 1908. Life in the Pennsylvania Coal Fields. *American Journal of Sociology* 14(3) (November): 329–51.

——. 1909. With Oregon Hop Pickers. *American Journal of Sociology* 15 (July): 83–95.

——. 1910. *Wage-earning Women*. New York: Macmillan.

——. 1910. The Chicago Garment Makers. *Public* 13(662) (December 9): 1,166–.

——. 1915. Trade Unionism Versus Welfare Work for Women. *Popular Science Monthly* 87(1) (July).

——. 1915. The Plight of the Rich Man in a Democracy. *American Journal of Sociology* 21(3) (November): 339–45.

——. 1916/1919. *Women Workers and Society*. Chicago: A. C. McClurg & Co.

——. 1920/1. Book Review of "Italian Women in Industry" by Louise C. Odencrantz. *American Journal of Sociology* 26(1/6): 657–.

——. 1921. *Some Problems of Reconstruction*. Chicago: A. C. McClurg.

——. 1922. *Our Neighbors*. New York: Macmillan Co.

——. 1923. Four Months in a Model Factory. *Century Illustrated Monthly Magazine* 106 (May/October): 436–.

——. 1923. On Picket Duty. *Forum* 70(6) (December).

——. 1923. This Way Lies Happiness. *Open Court* 37: 24–.

——. 1925. *Modern Immigration: A View of the Situation in Immigrant Receiving Countries*. Lippincott Sociological Series. London: Lippincott.

——. 1931/2. I Become American. *Sociology and Social Research* 16: 427–.

McLean, Mrs. C. F. 1898. Henry George: A Study from Life. *Arena* 20 (September): 296–311.

McLean-Hardy, Sara. 1895. The Quantity of Money and Prices, 1860–1891: An Inductive Study. *Journal of Political Economy* 3 (March): 145–68.

MacLear, Anne Bush. 1908. Early New England Towns: A Comparative Study of Their Development. Ph.D. thesis, Columbia University (Studies in history, economics and public law, vol. 29, no. 1).

MacLeod, Emily Sarah. 1885. Home Truths on the Crofter Agitation. *Blackwood's* 138 (July): 92–100.

McMahan, Anna B. 1886. Something More about Domestic Service. *Forum* 1 (June): 399–403.

[Macmahon,] Edna Cers. 1930. Legal Action in Labor Disputes; and Report on Naturalization Procedure. Ph.D. thesis, Robert Brookings.

——. 1934. *Municipal Electric Plant Managers, Their Selection, Training, Salaries and Tenure with a List of Municipally Owned Plants in the United States*. Public Administration Service, Publication no. 38. Chicago: Public Administration Service.

McMahon, Theresa Schmid. 1909. Women and Economic Evolution; or, The Effects of Industrial Changes upon the Status of Women. Ph.D. thesis, University of Wisconsin–Madison (sociology).

——. 1912. Women and Economic Evolution; or, The Effects of Industrial Changes upon the Status of Women. University of Wisconsin Bulletin, no. 496. Madison, Wisc.: University of Wisconsin.

——. 1915. Book Review of "Out of Work: A Study of Unemployment." *American Economic Review* 5 (September): 614–15.

——. 1915. Public Regulation of Wages: Discussion. *American Economic Review*, Supplement, 5 (March): 278–99.

——. 1925. *Social and Economic Standards of Living*. Boston: D. C. Heath.

McMillan, Margaret. 1891. The Woman's Labour Day. *Westminster Review* 136 (November): 517–26.

——. 1895. *Samson*. London: Clarion. [*novel*]

——. 1896. *Child Labour and the Half-time System*. London: Clarion Newspaper Co.

——. 1897. Means and Ends in Education. In Edward Carpenter, ed., *Forecasts of the Coming Century*. Manchester, UK: Labour Press Society.

——. 1903. *Co-operators and the Labour Platform*. London: City of London Branch of the Independent Labour Party.

——. 1907. *Labour and Childhood*. London: Sonnenschein.

——. 1911. *The Child and the State*. The Socialist Library Series, IX. Manchester: National Labour Press.

——. 1917. The Care of Child Life. In W. H. Dawson, ed., *After-War Problems, by the Earl of Cromer, Viscount Haldane, the Bishop of Exeter, Professor Alfred Marshall, and Others*. New York: Macmillan.

——. 1918. The Nursery of Tomorrow. In M. Phillips, ed., *Women and the Labour Party*. London: F. Matthews.

McNerney, Blanche. 1911. A Cooperative Kitchen. *Journal of Home Economics* 3 (December): 464–6.

Maddison, Isabel. 1896. *Handbook of Courses Open to Women in British, Continental, and Canadian Universities*. New York: Macmillan.

——. 1899. *Handbook of British, Continental and Canadian Universities with Special Mention of the Courses Open to Women*. New York: Macmillan.

Magee, Mabel Agnes. 1927. The Women's Clothing Industry of Chicago with Special Reference to Relations between the Manufacturers and the Union. Ph.D. thesis, University of Chicago (economics).

——. 1930. *Trends in Location of the Women's Clothing Industry*. Chicago: University of Chicago Press.

Magnus, Erna. 1934. The Social, Economic, and Legal Conditions of Domestic Servants: I. *International Labour Review* (Geneva) 30 (August): 190–207.

——. 1934. The Social, Economic, and Legal Conditions of Domestic Servants: II. *International Labour Review* (Geneva) 30 (September): 336–64.

——. 1934. The Working of Social Insurance in Denmark. *International Labour Review* 30 (August): 208–.

Magnus, Lady [Katie Emanuel]. 1888. Charity in Talmudic Times. *National Review* 10 (January): 701–.

——. 1889. The Higher Education of Women. *National Review* 12 (January): 663–8.

——. 1900. A Solution of the Domestic Problem. *Macmillan's* 82 (October): 448–57.

Magruder, Mary [Jean] Lanier. 1924. *Wages*. New York: Harper.

——. 1924. The Early Development of Boston as a Commercial Center. Ph.D. thesis, University of Chicago (geography).

Maher, Amy [Grace]. 1925. Employers' Agents at Work Against Minimum Wage Legislation. *American Labor Legislation Review* 15: 114–.

——. 1925. Women Trade Unionists in the United States. *International Labour Review* 11(1/6) (January/June): 366–.

——. 1928. *Wage Rates, Earnings and Fluctuations of Employment: Ohio 1914–1926*. Toledo, Ohio: Information Bureau on Women's Work.

——. 1929. *Ohio Wage Earners in the Manufacture of Textiles and Textile Products, 1914–1927*. Toledo, Ohio: Information Bureau on Women's Work.

——. 1929. Ohio's Women Workers. *American Academy of Political and Social Science, Annals* 143 (May): 94–.

——. 1930. Effect of Concentration of Industry on Seasonal Variation of Employment. *Journal of the American Statistical Association* 25(169) (March): 41–6.

——. 1930. *Ohio Wage Earners in the Manufacture of Rubber Products, 1914–1928*. Toledo, Ohio: Toledo Consumers' League/H. J. Chittenden Co.

——. 1931. *The Business Cycle in Ohio, 1920–1929*. Toledo, Ohio: Information Bureau on Women's Work.

——. 1931. The Employment of Women… *Social Service Review* V(I) (March): 28–.

——. 1932. *Bookkeepers, Stenographers and Office Clerks in Ohio, 1914 to 1929*. Washington: U.S. Government Printing Office.

——. 1934. *Ohio Wage Earners in Restaurants, 1914–1932*. Toledo, Ohio: Information Bureau on Women's Work.

Mahler, Emma and Eleanor F. Rathbone. 1911. *Payment of Seamen: The Present System*. Liverpool: C. Tinling.

Mahn, Anny Wothe. 1886. *Das Gift unserer Zeit: Lösung der Frauenfrage*. Cannstatt, Germany: G. Ad. Stehn.

Maimesbury, Countess of. 1894. Village Life in England. *North American Review* 158(3)(March): 304–11.

Makower, Helen. 1937. *The Theory of Value on the Capital Market*. Ph.D. thesis, London School of Economics.

——. 1938. Elasticity of Demand and Stabilisation. *Review of Economic Studies* 6(1) (October): 25–32.

Makower, Helen and Robinson, H. W. 1939. Labour Potential in War-time. *Economic Journal* 49: 656–.

Mallet, Mrs. Charles. 1893. *Dangerous Trades for Women*. The Humanitarian League Publications, no. 9. London: William Reeves. Reprinted in Marie

Mulvey Roberts and Tamae Mizuta, eds., *Sources in British Feminism*, vol 3: *The Exploited: Women and Work*. London: Routledge/Thoemmes, 1993.

Mallock, Miss [Mary Margaret]. 1893. Restaurants for the Labouring Classes. *National Review* 21 (March): 62–70.

Mallon, Isabel Allderdice Sloan [as "Ruth Ashmore"]. 1898. *The Business Girl in Every Phase of her Life*. Philadelphia: Curtis Publications Co.; New York: Doubleday & McClure.

Maltais, Marie Ludovic. 1925. Les Syndicats catholiques canadiens: étude socio-économique. Ph.D. thesis, Catholic University of America (economics).

Mann, Julia deLacy, ed. 1931. The Teaching of Economic History in Universities. Part I. *Economic History Review* 3 (October): 197–218.

——, ed. 1932. The Teaching of Economic History in Universities. Part II. *Economic History Review* 3 (April): 325–45.

Manners, Janetta Hughan [Lady John Manners, Duchess of Rutland]. 1881. Employment of Women in the Public Service. *Quarterly Review* 151 (January): 181–200. Reprinted Edinburgh and London: William Blackwood and Sons, 1882.

——. 1884. A Plea for the Partial Emancipation of Certain English Bondmen and Bondwomen. *National Review* 3 (August): 735–44.

——. 1884. A Sequel to Rich Men's Dwellings. *National Review* 3 (March): 9–.

——. 1886. *A Sequel to Rich Men's Dwellings and Other Occasional Papers*. Edinburgh and London: W. Blackwood and Sons.

——. 1888. Are Rich Landowners Idle? *National Review* 10 (February): 836–40.

——. 1892. Thrift for the Poor, Part IV. *New Review* 7 (December): 679–82.

Manning, Caroline. 1930. *The Employment of Women in the Pineapple Canneries of Hawaii*. Bulletin of the Women's Bureau, no. 82. Washington: U.S. Government Printing Office.

——. 1930. *The Immigrant Woman and Her Job*. U.S. Department of Labor, Bulletin of the Women's Bureau, no. 74. Washington: U.S. Government Printing Office. Reprinted New York: Arno Press, 1970.

——. 1930. Industrial Woman Looks at Economic Old Age. *American Labor Legislation Review* 20: 445–7.

——. 1931. *Fluctuation of Employment in the Radio Industry*. Bulletin of the Women's Bureau, no. 83. Washington: U.S. Government Printing Office.

——. 1934. *The Employment of Women in Puerto Rico*. Bulletin of the U.S. Women's Bureau, no. 118. Washington: U.S. Government Printing Office.

——. 1934. *Hours and Earnings in Tobacco Stemmeries*. U.S. Women's Bureau Bulletin, no. 127. Washington: U.S. Government Printing Office.

Manning, Caroline and Harriet Anne Byrne. 1932. *The Effects on Women of Changing Conditions in the Cigar and Cigarette Industries*. Bulletin of the U.S. Women's Bureau, no. 100. Washington: U.S. Government Printing Office.

Manning, Caroline and Arcadia Dowdell Near Phillips. 1932. *Wage-earning Women and the Industrial Conditions of 1930: A Survey of South Bend*. Bulletin of the U.S. Women's Bureau, no. 92. Washington: U.S. Government Printing Office.

Manning, Caroline, Elizabeth Hyde, and Mary Viola Robinson. 1922. *Women in the Candy Industry in Chicago and St. Louis: A Study of Hours, Wages, and Working Conditions*. Bulletin of the Women's Bureau, no. 25. Washington: U.S. Government Printing Office.

——. 1922. *Women in Maryland Industries: A Study of Hours, Wages, and Working Conditions*. Washington: U.S. Women's Bureau.

Manning, Caroline, Elizabeth Adshead Hyde, Mary Loretta Sullivan, and Ethel Erickson. 1927. *Women in Delaware Industries*. Washington: U.S. Women's Bureau.

Manning, Caroline, Elizabeth Adshead Hyde, and Ruth Irene Voris. 1924. *Women in Missouri Industries: A Study of Hours and Wages*. Bulletin of the Women's Bureau, no. 35. Washington: U.S. Government Printing Office.

Manning, Caroline, Mary Viola Robinson, Mildred J. Gordon, and Elizabeth Adshead Hyde. 1923. *Women in Kentucky: A Study of Hours, Wages and Working Conditions*. U.S. Women's Bureau Bulletin, no. 29. Washington: U.S. Government Printing Office.

Manning, Caroline. Coauth. *See* Byrne, Harriet Anne; Hawkins, Hildred Moser; Parton, Mabel; Pidgeon, Mary Elizabeth; Reeves, Edith.

Manning, Phyllis Amy. 1932. *The Post-war Relation of Skilled and Unskilled Labour in the Printing, Building and Engineering Trades*. Ph.D. thesis, London School of Economics.

Manson, Grace [Evelyn]. 1924/5. Book Review of "Women and Leisure" by Pruette. *Journal of Personnel Research* 3: 398–.

——. 1927/8. Book Review of "Fields of Work for Women" by Leuck. *Personnel Journal* 6 (June/April): 133–.

——. 1931. *Occupational Interests and Personality Requirements of Women in Business and the Professions*. Ann Arbor, Mich.: University of Michigan, School of Business Administration, Bureau of Business Research.

Manson, Grace and Helen E. Cook. 1926/7. Abilities Necessary in Effective Retail Selling and a Method of Evaluating Them. *Journal of Personnel Research* 5 (May/April): 74–.

Manson, Grace and Margaret Elliott. 1929. Some Factors Affecting Earnings of Business and Professional Women. *American Academy of Political and Social Science, Annals* 143 (May): 137–.

Manson, Grace. Coauth. *See* Elliott, Margaret.

Marburg, Anita. 1925/6. Book Review of "Labor Attitudes and Problems" by Lasswell and Atkins. *Journal of Personnel Research* 4: 451–.

——. 1928. The Great War in Anthracite. Ph.D. thesis, Robert Brookings.

Marcet, Jane Haldimand. 1816. *Conversations on Political Economy; in Which the Elements of That Science Are Familiarly Explained*. London: Longman, Hurst, Rees, Orme, and Brown.

——. 1831. *Essays*. Cardiff, Wales: Society for the Improvement of the Working Population in the County of Glamorgan.

——. 1833/1834. *John Hopkins' Notions of Political Economy*. London: Longman, Rees, Orme, Brown, Green, & Longman.

——. 1851. *Rich and Poor: Dialogues on a Few of the First Principles of Political Economy.* London: Longman, Brown, Green, and Longmans.
March-Phillipps, Evelyn. 1892. A Dock Lodging-house. *Fortnightly Review*, n.s. 51 (May): 668–77.
——. 1892. The Working Lady in London. *Fortnightly Review*, n.s. 52 [o.s. 58] (August): 193–203.
——. 1893. The Progress of Women's Trade Unions. *Fortnightly Review*, n.s. 54 [o.s. 60] (July): 92–104.
——. 1893. Small Farms: A Contribution. *Fortnightly Review*, n.s. 53 [o.s. 59] (January): 91–100.
——. 1894. The New Factory Bill: As It Affects Women. *Fortnightly Review*, n.s. 55 [o.s. 61] (June): 738–48.
——. 1894. Women's Newspapers. *Fortnightly Review*, n.s. 56 (November): 661–70.
——. 1895 or 1898. *The Evils of Home Work for Women.* Investigation Papers, no. 3. Manchester, UK: Women's Co-operative Guild.
——. 1895. Factory Legislation for Women. *Fortnightly Review*, n.s. 57 [o.s. 63] (May): 733–44.
——. 1895. The New Journalism. *New Review* 13 (August): 182–9.
——. 1896. Women's Industrial Life. *Monthly Packet* 11 (April): 423–; (May): 530–.
——. 1897. Peasants of Romagna. *Fortnightly Review*, n.s. 62 [o.s. 68] (September): 407–17.
——. 1897. The Story of the Factory Acts. *Monthly Packet* 13 (January): 21–.
——. 1897. The Truck Acts. *Monthly Packet* 13 (April): 382–.
——. 1898. Poor Law Children. *Monthly Packet* 15 (February): 144–.
——. 1898. The Question of Women's Suffrage. *Monthly Packet* 15 (May): 509–.
——. 1898. Women and Parish Councils. *Monthly Packet* 15 (April): 385–.
——. 1898. Women and the School Board. *Monthly Packet* 15 (April): 385–.
——. 1898. Women as Inspectors. *Monthly Packet* 15 (March): 266–.
——. 1898. Women as Poor Law Guardians. *Monthly Packet* 15 (January): 23–.
——. 1899. American Women. *Monthly Packet* 17 (January): 25–.
——. 1899. French Women. *Monthly Packet* 17 (February): 140–.
——. 1899. German Women. *Monthly Packet* 17 (March): 258–.
——. 1899. Italian Women. *Monthly Packet* 17 (April): 384–.
——. 1899. Spanish Women. *Monthly Packet* 17 (May): 508–.
——. 1899. Swedish Women. *Monthly Packet* 17 (June): 619–.
——. 1908. The Working of Wages Boards. *Economic Review* (January).
Marchef-Girard, Mlle. J. 1860. *Les Femmes, leur passé, leur présent, leur avenir.* Paris: Louis Chappe.
——. 1886. *Cours d'économie domestique à l'usage des écoles normales.* Paris: s.n.
Marcy, Mary. 1911. *Shop Talks on Economics.* Chicago: Charles H. Kerr Cooperative.
——. 1921. *Open the Factories.* Chicago: C. H. Kerr.

Maresch, Elisabeth. 1938. *Ehefrau in Haushalt und Beruf eine statistische Darstellung für Wien auf Grund der Volkszählung vom 22. März, 1934*. Vienna: F. Deuticke.

——. 1938. Ehefrau in Haushalt und Beruf eine statistische Darstellung für Wien auf Grund der Volkszählung vom 22. März, 1934. Thesis, Vienna.

Margold, Stella Kaplan. 1933. *A Report on Export Credit Insurance in Germany*. Washington: s.n.

——. 1934. *Export Credit Insurance in Europe Today: A Study of the Sixteen European Export Credit Insurance Systems for the Formulation of a Pattern for an Entirely Government Operated or Partially Government Controlled Plan*. Washington: U.S. Government Printing Office.

——. 1934. *A Report on the Spanish Export Credit Scheme*. Washington: s.n.

——. 1935. *A Reciprocal Trade Agreement with the Union of Soviet Republics*. Washington: American Peace Society.

——. 1936. *Some Essential Facts on Government-aided Housing in Western Europe*. Washington: U.S. Bureau of Foreign and Domestic Commerce.

——. 1937. *Some Essential Facts on Government-aided Housing in Various British Empire Countries, Prepared from Reports of Foreign Offices of the Bureau of Foreign and Domestic Commerce and Other Information*. Washington: U.S. Department of Commerce, Bureau of Foreign and Domestic Commerce.

Mario, Signora Vedova. 1892. Peasant Life in Sicily. *Chautauquan* 15 (April/September): 316–.

Markham, Violet Rosa. 1900. *South Africa, Past and Present. An Account of its History, Politics and Native Africans*. London: Smith, Elder.

——. 1904. *The New Era in South Africa with an Examination of the Chinese Labour Question*. London: Smith, Elder, & Co.

——. 1905. The True Foundations of Empire: The Home and the Workshop. *Nineteenth Century and After* 58 (October): 570–.

——. 1906. Chaise-Dien, France. *Cornhill Magazine* 94: 534.

——. 1906. Lord Durham and the Colonies. *Nineteenth Century and After, a Monthly Review* 59: 914.

——. 1907. *Labour and Childhood*. London: Sonnenschein.

——. 1910. A Proposed Women's Council. *National Review* 55 (March/August): 1,029–.

——. 1913. *The South African Scene*. London: Smith, Elder.

——. 1915. Women Trade Unionists and the War. *Women's Trade Union Review* (July).

——. 1919. In a Devastated Area. *Fortnightly Review* 105 (January/June): 937–.

——. 1922. Occupation or Reparation. *Fortnightly Review* 112 (July/December): 383.

——. 1924. Racial and Political Issues in South Africa. *Edinburgh Review* 240(490) (October): 243–.

——. 1925. Greece and the Refugees from Asia Minor. *Fortnightly Review* 117 (January/June): 176–.

Markham, Violet R. and Mrs. James Carruthers. 1922. A True Path of Progress. *Nineteenth Century and After* 92 (July/December): 1,004–.

Markham, Violet R. and Edith Lyttelton. 1908. Personal Service among the London Poor [letter to the editor]. *Nation* 4(9) (November 28): 342–.

Markham, Violet Rosa and Edith Abraham Tennant. 1907/1908. *The Factory and Shop Acts of the British Dominions.* With a preface by Mrs. H. J. Tennant. London: Eyre and Spottiswoode.

Marks, Mary A. M. 1900. The Treatment of Subject Races. *International Journal of Ethics* 10: 417–.

——. 1908. *The Corn Laws: A Popular History*. London: Fifield.

——. 1908. *Landholding in England Considered in Relation to Poverty*. London: Fifield.

Marot, Helen. 1899. *A Handbook of Labor Literature. Being a Classified and Annotated List of the More Important Books and Pamphlets in the English Language.* Philadelphia: T. S. Leach & Co.

——, ed. 1910. *The Economic Position of Women.* New York: Academy of Political Science.

——. 1910. A Woman's Strike – an Appreciation of the Shirtwaist Makers of New York. In Helen Marot, ed., *The Economic Position of Women.* Also published in Henry Raymond Mussey, ed., *Proceedings of the Academy of Political Science in the City of New York.* New York: Columbia University.

——. 1914. *American Labor Unions, by a Member.* New York: Henry Holt and Company.

——. 1915. Trade Unions and Minimum Wage Boards. *American Federationist* 22(11) (November): 966–.

——. 1918. *Creative Impulse in Industry: A Proposition for Educators.* New York: E. P. Dutton and Company.

——. 1918. The Creative and Efficiency Concepts of Education. *Dial* 64 (January 3/June 6): 341–.

——. 1918. Reconstruction at Work. *Dial* 65 (June 20/December 28): 303–.

——. 1918/19. Labor at the Crossways. *Dial* 66 (December 28/July 12): 165–.

——. 1918/19. Labor Control of Government Industries. *Dial* 66 (December 28/July 12): 411–.

——. 1918/19. Reform – Why It Is Futile. *Dial* 66 (December 28/July 12): 293–.

——. 1919. The Labor Crisis. *Dial* 67 (July 12/November 29): 393–.

——. 1919. Responsible Unionism. *Dial* 67 (July 12/November 29): 131–.

——. 1920. Production and the Preservation of Initiative. *Annals of the American Academy of Political and Social Science* 91 (September): 14–.

Marot, Helen and Caroline L. Pratt. 1903. *Report of an Investigation Made in Philadelphia.* Pamphlets in American History, Labor, L 1025. Philadelphia: Philadelphia Branch of the Consumers' League.

Marot, Helen. Contributor to *Masses*, 1916–17.

Marsh, Elsie Agnes Gillespie. 1937. *The Economic Library of Jacob H. Hollander.* Baltimore: J. H. Furst Co.

Marsh, Marguerite. 1930. *Youth in Danger: A Study of Young Workers Injured in Georgia Industries*. New York: National Consumers' League, in Cooperation with the Industrial Commission of Georgia.

——. Coauth. *See* Kelley, Florence J.

Marshall, Dorothy. 1926. *The English Poor in the Eighteenth Century: A Study in Social and Administrative History*. London: George Routledge & Sons.

——. 1929. The Domestic Servants of the Eighteenth Century. *Economica*, n.s. 9 (April): 15–40.

——. 1937. The Old Poor Laws, 1662–1795. *Economic History Review* 8 (November): 38–47.

——. 1938. Book Review of "The Economy of Britain: A History" by H. M. Croome and R. J. Hammond. *Economica* 5: 370–.

Marshall, Mary Paley. 1893. Book Review of "Ladies at Work," with an introduction by Lady Jeune. *Economic Journal* 3(12) (December): 679–80.

——. 1895. Book Review of "Viertehalb Monate Fabrikarbeiterin: Eine praktische Studie" by Minna Wettstein-Adelt. *Economic Journal* 5(19) (September): 401–4.

——. 1896. Conference of Women Workers. *Economic Journal* 6(21) (March): 107–9.

——. 1902. Book Review of "Educated Working Women" by Clara E. Collet. *Economic Journal* 12(46) (June): 252–7.

——. 1922. Letter to J. M. Keynes. 27 July 1922, Keynes Collection, King's College, Cambridge, JMK EJ/6.4.

——. 1940. Obituary of Mary Wright [Kennedy], 1871–1875. Newnham College Roll *Letter* (January).

Marshall, Mary Paley and Alfred Marshall. 1879. *The Economics of Industry*. 2nd ed., London: Macmillan, 1881.

Marshall, Mary Rachel. *See* Goetz, [Mary] Rachel Marshall.

Martin, Anna. 1910/11. The Married Working Woman: A Study. *Nineteenth Century and After* 68 (December): 1,102–18; 69 (January): 108–22. Reprinted London: National Union of Women's Suffrage Societies, 1911. Reprinted New York: Garland Publishing, 1980.

——. 1913. The Mother and Social Reform. *Nineteenth Century and After* 73 (May): 1,060–79; (June): 1,235–55. Reprinted London: National Union of Women's Suffrage Societies.

——. 1918/19. The Irresponsibility of the Father. *Nineteenth Century and After* 84 (December): 1,091–103; 85 (March): 548–62; (May): 956–70.

Martin, Eleanor, Margaret A. Post, and Susan Myra Kingsbury. 1914. *Vocations for the Trained Woman: Agriculture, Social Service, Secretarial Service, Business of Real Estate*. Women's Educational and Industrial Union (Boston, Mass.), Department of Research. Studies in Economic Relations of Women, vol. 1, pt. 2. New York: Longmans, Green, and Co.

Martin, Ellen A. 1887. Admission of Women to the Bar. *Chicago Law Times* 1: 76–.

Martin, Frances. 1864. Blind Workers and Blind Helpers. *Cornhill's Magazine* 9 (May): 603–17.

——. 1879. A College for Working Women. *Macmillan's* 40 (October): 483–8.

——. 1881. The Other Side of the Question [training girls to work for the poor]. *Macmillan's* 43 (April): 461–4.

——. 1884. Holidays for Working Women. *Macmillan's* 49: 363–.

Martin, Margaret Evelyn. 1938. Aspects of Proletarianism in the Works of James Stephens. M.A. thesis, University of Texas.

Martindale, Hilda. 1938. *Women Servants of the State, 1870–1938: A History of Women in the Civil Service*. London: Allen & Unwin.

Martineau, Harriet. 1827. *The Rioters, or a Tale of Bad Times*. Wellington, Salop, UK: Houlston & Son.

——. 1829. *The Turn Out, or Patience the Best Policy*. Wellington, Salop, UK: Houlston & Son.

——. 1832–4. *Illustrations of Political Economy*, 9 vols. London: Charles Fox; Boston: Leonard Bowles. Reprinted, with a new introduction by Caroline Franklin, London: Thoemmes, 2001.

——. 1833–4. *Poor Laws and Paupers, Illustrated*. 4 vols. bound in 2. London: Charles Fox; Boston: Leonard Bowles. Reprinted, with a new introduction by Caroline Franklin, London: Thoemmes, 2001.

——. 1834. *Illustrations of Taxation*. 5 vols. bound in 2. London: Charles Fox. Reprinted, with a new introduction by Caroline Franklin, London: Thoemmes, 2001.

——. 1834. *The Tendency of Strikes and Sticks to Produce Low Wages and of Union between Masters and Men to Ensure Good Wages*. Durham, UK: J. H. Veitch.

——. 1837. *Society in America*. 3 vols. London: Saunders & Otley. Reprinted in Susan Hoecker-Drysdale, ed., *Harriet Martineau: Studies of America 1837–1868*. London: Thoemmes, 2003.

——. 1837. *Views of Slavery & Emancipation from "Society in America."* New York: Piercy & Reed.

——. 1838. *The Guide to Service: The Housemaid, the Lady's Maid, the Maid of All Work*. London: Charles Knight.

——. 1838. *How to Observe: Morals and Manners*. London: Charles Knight; New York: Harper & Brothers. Reprinted, ed. Michael R. Hill, New Brunswick, N.J.: Transaction Books, 1989. Reprinted in Susan Hoecker-Drysdale, ed., *Harriet Martineau: Studies of America 1837–1868*. London: Thoemmes, 2003.

——. 1838. *Retrospect of Western Travel*. 3 vols. London: Saunders & Otley; New York: Harper Brothers. New ed., with introduction by Daniel Feller, Armonk, N.Y.: M. E. Sharpe, 2000. Reprinted in Susan Hoecker-Drysdale, ed., *Harriet Martineau: Studies of America 1837–1868*. London: Thoemmes, 2003.

——. 1838. *Slavery in America, Being a Brief Review of Miss Martineau on That Subject*. Richmond: Thomas W. White.

——. 1838. Domestic Service. *Westminster Review* 29 (August): 405–32.

——. 1838. The Martyr Age of the United States. *Westminster Review* 32 (December): 1–59. Reprinted as *The Martyr Age of the United States*. New York: S. W. Benedict, 1839; Newcastle-upon-Tyne: Finlay and Charlton, 1840.

——. 1845. *Dawn Island*. Manchester, UK: Gadsby.

——. 1845–6. *Forest and Game-law Tales.* 3 vols. London: E. Moxon, Bradbury and Evans.

——. 1848. *Eastern Life, Present and Past.* 3 vols. London: Edward Moxon; Philadelphia: Lea & Blanchard.

——. 1849. *The History of England during the Thirty Years' Peace*, 1816–46. 2 vols. London: Charles Knight.

——. 1849. *Household Education.* London: Edward Moxon; Philadelphia: Lea & Blanchard.

——. 1852. *Letters from Ireland*, London: John Chapman. Letters reprinted from the *Daily News.*

——. 1853. *The Positive Philosophy of Auguste Comte, Freely Translated and Condensed.* 2 vols. London: John Chapman. Reprinted, with a new introduction by Caroline Franklin, London: Thoemmes, 2001.

——. 1853. The Condition and Prospects of Ireland. *Westminster Review* 59 [n.s. 3] (January): 35–62.

——. 1854. England's Foreign Policy. *Westminster Review* 61 [n.s. 5] (January): 190–232.

——. 1854. Results of the Census of 1851. *Westminster Review*, n.s. 5 [o.s. 61] (April): 323–57.

——. 1855. *The Factory Controversy; a Warning against "Meddling Legislation."* Manchester, UK: National Association of Factory Occupiers; printed A. Ireland & Co.

——. 1856. *A History of the American Compromises.* London: John Chapman. Reprinted, with additions, from the *Daily News.*

——. 1857. *British Rule in India: A Historical Sketch.* London: Smith, Elder & Co. Reprinted as *The History of British Rule in India.* London: Smith, Elder & Co., 1859.

——. 1857. *Corporate Traditions and National Rights: Local Dues on Shipping.* London: G. Routledge.

——. 1857. Female Dress in 1857. *Westminster Review* 68 (October): 315–40.

——. 1857. The "Manifest Destiny" of the American Union. *Westminster Review*, n.s. 12 [o.s. 68] (July): 137–76. Reprinted as pamphlet, New York: American Anti-Slavery Society.

——. 1858. *Suggestions toward the Future Government of India.* London: Smith, Elder & Co.

——. 1858. China: Past and Present. *Westminster Review* 69 [n.s. 13] (April): 370–401.

——. 1858. The Last Days of Church-rates. *Westminster Review* 70 [n.s. 14] (July): 30–52.

——. 1858. The Religion of Positivity. *Westminster Review* 69 (April): 305–50.

——. 1858. The Slave Trade in 1858. *Edinburgh Review* 108 (October): 541–86.

——. 1859. *Endowed Schools of Ireland.* London: Smith, Elder. Reprinted from the *Daily News.*

——. 1859. *England and Her Soldiers.* London: Smith, Elder & Co.

——. 1859. Female Industry. *Edinburgh Review* 109 (April): 293–336.

——. 1859. Secret Organisation of Trades. *Edinburgh Review* 110 (October): 525–63.

——. 1861. *Health, Husbandry and Handicraft*. Articles selected from various publications. London: Bradbury & Evans. Republished in part as *Our Farm of Two Acres*. New York: Bunce and Huntingdon, 1865.

——. 1862. Brewing of the American Storm. *Macmillan's* 6 (June): 97–107.

——. 1862. The English in the Eastern Seas. *Edinburgh Review* 116 (October): 398–417.

——. 1862. Modern Domestic Service. *Edinburgh Review* 115 (April): 409–39.

——. 1863. The Convict System in England and Ireland. *Edinburgh Review* 117 (January): 241–68.

——. 1863. Death or Life in India. *Macmillan's* 8 (August): 332–40.

——. 1864. Cooperative Societies in 1864. *Edinburgh Review* 120 (October): 407–36.

——. 1864. Middle Class Education in England: Boys. *Cornhill Magazine* 10 (October): 409–26.

——. 1864. Middle Class Education in England: Girls. *Cornhill Magazine* 10 (November): 549–68.

——. 1864. The Negro Race in America. *Edinburgh Review* 119 (January): 203–42.

——. 1865. Life in the Criminal Class. *Edinburgh Review* 122 (October): 337–71.

——. 1865. Nurses Wanted. *Cornhill Magazine* 11 (April): 409–25.

——. 1868. Salem Witchcraft. *Edinburgh Review* 128 (July): 1–47.

Martinengo-Cesaresco, Countess [Evelyn Carrington]. 1887. The Agricultural Crisis in North Italy. *National Review* 9 (August): 824–.

——. 1888. The Peasant in North Italy. *Scottish Review* 11 (January): 103–17.

Martínez Sierra, María. 1931. *La mujer española ante la República*. Madrid: s.n.

Martyn, Elisabeth. 1889. In Donegal [a plea for the Irish tenantry]. *Westminster Review* 132 (July): 97–105.

——. 1889. In Donegal: A Rejoinder. *Westminster Review* 132 (December): 635–54.

Martyn, Mrs. H. [Edith How]. 1922. The Methods of Appointment of Administrative and Clerical Staffs in the Local Government Service of England and Wales. *Economica* 4 (January): 51–68.

Marvin, Gertrude L. 1910. College Girls in Department Stores. In Agnes F. Perkins, ed., *Vocations for the Trained Woman: Opportunities Other than Teaching*. Boston: Women's Educational and Industrial Union.

Mason, Carol Young. 1925. *The Geography of the Cranberry Industry in Southeastern Massachusetts*. M.S. thesis, Clark University.

——. 1926. The Cranberry Industry in Massachusetts. *Economic Geography* 2(1) (January): 59–69.

——. 1936. Problems of New England Municipal Water Supplies. Ph.D. thesis, Clark University (geography).

——. 1936. Land Economy of Amberson Valley, Pennsylvania. *Economic Geography* 13(4) (July): 265–72.

——. 1937. Municipal Water Supplies of New England. *Economic Geography* 13(4) (October): 347–64.

——. 1939. Water in the Laramie Region of Wyoming. *Economic Geography* 15(3) (July): 271–82.

——. 1940. *Geography and Pan-Americanisms*. Maryville, Mo.: Northwest Missouri State College.

Mason, Carol Y. and Adagrace Rowlands. 1938. Panama Canal Traffic. *Economic Geography* 14(4) (October): 325–37.

Mason, Elizabeth H. 1904. *Practical Ideas for Profitable Home Work*. New York: Women's Work Publishing Co.

Mason, M. H. 1884. *Classification of Girls and Boys in Workhouses, and the Legal Powers of Boards of Governors for Placing Them Beyond the Workhouse*. London: Hatchards.

Mason, Mary G[ertrude]. 1936. Aspects of the Trade Between China and America, 1840–1870. *Business History Review* 10 (February): 24–8.

——. 1939. Western Concepts of China and the Chinese, 1840–1876. Ph.D. thesis, Columbia University (history).

——. 1939. *Western Concepts of China and the Chinese, 1840–1876*. New York: Seeman Printery.

Matheson, Marie Cecile. 1930. *Indian Industry, Yesterday, To-day and To-morrow*. National Christian Council of India. London and Bombay: H. Milford/Oxford University Press.

Matheson, M. Cecile and Hugh Martin, eds. 1917. *Citizenship; an Introductory Handbook*. London: Student Christian Movement.

Matthews, Ada M. 1925. The Physical Volume of Production in the United States for 1924. *Review of Economics and Statistics* 7 (July): 208–16.

——. 1926. New York Bank Clearings and Stock Prices, 1866–1914. *Review of Economics and Statistics* 8 (October): 184–98.

Matthews, Ellen Nathalie. 1931. The Employment Certificate. *American Federationist* 38(5) (May): 588–.

——. 1932. *The Illegally Employed Minor and the Workmen's Compensation Law*. U.S. Children's Bureau Publication, no. 214. Washington: U.S. Government Printing Office.

——. 1934. Accidents to Telegraph Messengers. *Monthly Labor Review* 38(1) January: 14–.

——. 1939?. *Memorandum on the Use of Social Service Exchange by Group Work Agencies in New York City*. New York: Research Bureau, Welfare Council of New York City.

——. 1939. New York City Studies the Use of Its Social Service Exchange. *Family* 20(3) (May): 92–.

——. 1939. Pioneering in Federal Labor Legislation. *Child* 4(2) (August): 39–.

Matthews, Ellen Nathalie and Helen Marietta Dart. 1924. *The Welfare of Children in Cotton-growing Areas of Texas*. Children's Bureau Publication, no. 134. Washington: U.S. Government Printing Office.

Matthews, Ellen Nathalie and Gertrude Underhill Light. 1923. *Child Labor and the Work of Mothers in the Beet Fields of Colorado and Michigan*. Washington: U.S. Children's Bureau.

Matthews, Ellen Nathalie and Mary E. Skinner. 1924. *Work of Children on Truck and Small-fruit Farms in Southern New Jersey*. U.S. Children's Bureau Publication, no. 132. Washington: U.S. Government Printing Office.

Matthews, Ellen Nathalie and Ethel Maria Springer. 1924. *Child Labor and the Work of Mothers on Norfolk Truck Farms*. U.S. Children's Bureau Publication, no. 130. Washington: U.S. Government Printing Office.

Matthews, Ellen Nathalie, Mathilde Selig, Ethel Edna Hanks Van Buskirk, and Alice Channing. 1930. *Children in Fruit and Vegetable Canneries: A Survey in Seven States*. Washington: U.S. Government Printing Office.

Matthews, Ellen Nathalie, Mary Hayes Stewart, Mary Holmes Stevens, Jeanette Eaton, Virginia Cleaver Bacon, and Nettie Pauline McGill. 1925. *Vocational Guidance and Junior Placement: Twelve Cities in the United States*. Children's Bureau Publication, no. 149. Washington: U.S. Government Printing Office.

Matthews, Ellen Nathalie. Coauth. *See* Byrne, Harriet Anne; Burke, Dorothy May Williams; Channing, Alice; McGill, Nettie Pauline.

Matthews, Lillian Ruth. 1912. Women in Trade Unions in San Francisco. Ph.D. thesis, University of California–Berkeley (economics, history).

——. 1913. *Women in Trade Unions in San Francisco*. Berkeley: University of California Press.

Maule, Frances. 1908. *Woman Suffrage in Finland*. New York: National American Woman Suffrage Association.

——. 1912. *Why Women Want to Vote*. New York: National American Woman Suffrage Association.

——. 1934. *She Strives to Conquer; Business Behavior, Opportunities and Job Requirements for Women*. New York: Funk & Wagnalls.

——. 1937. *Men Wanted; the New Opportunities and What They Demand*. New York: Funk & Wagnalls.

——. 1938. *The Road to Anywhere; Opportunities in Secretarial Work*. New York and London: Funk & Wagnalls.

——. 1939. *Your Next Job; How to Get It and Hold It*. New York and London: Funk & Wagnalls.

——. 1940. *Selling – a Job That's Always Open*. New York and London: Funk & Wagnalls.

Maule, Frances and Annie Gertrude Webb Porritt. 1915. *Woman Suffrage; History, Arguments and Results; a Collection of Seven Popular Booklets Covering Practically the Entire Field of Suffrage Claims and Evidence. Designed Especially for the Convenience of Suffrage Speakers and Writers and for the Use of Debaters and Libraries*. New York: National Woman Suffrage Publishing Co.

May, Elizabeth Stoffregen. 1936. *Government, Business, and the Individual: A Guide for Studying Current Controversy in Economic, Political, and Social Questions*. Washington: American Association of University Women.

——. 1940. *Social Welfare: A Guide for Studying the Welfare Facilities of the Local Community*. Washington: American Association of University Women.

Maynard, Cora. 1893. The Woman's Part. *Arena* 7 (March): 47–57.

Maynard, Edith L. 1902. *The Making of Earthenware and China and Its Dangers*. London: Christian Social Union?.

Maynard, Margaret. 1891. Domestic Service: The Kitchen Girl's Side. *Chautauquan* 13 (April/September): 350–.

Mayo, Miss C. M. 1898. *Co-operative House-Building*. Women's Co-operative Guild. Manchester: Co-operative Newspaper Society.

Mayo, Isabell F. 1899. Employments of Women. *Chambers's Journal*, series 6, 77(3): 628–52.

Mead, Lucia True Ames. 1889. *Memoirs of a Millionaire*. Boston and New York: Houghton, Mifflin. [*novel*]

——. 1897. *A Popular Fallacy*... [on the cost of living]. Boston: Women's Educational and Industrial Union.

——. 1899. *To Whom Much is Given*. New York and Boston: T. Y. Crowell & Co.

——. 1912. *Swords and Ploughshares or the Supplanting of the System of War by the System of Law*. New York: G. P. Putnam's Sons.

——. 1914. *Economic Facts for Practical People*. Washington: American Peace Society.

Meade, Emily Fogg. 1901. The Place of Advertising in Modern Business. *Journal of Political Economy* 9 (March): 218–42.

——. 1902. Book Review of "Educated Working Women" by Clara E. Collet. *American Academy of Political and Social Science, Annals* 20 (July/December): 436–.

——. 1903. Book Review of "The Woman Who Toils" by Mrs. John and Marie Van Vorst. *American Academy of Political and Social Science, Annals* 22 (July/December): 238–.

——. 1904/5. Italian Immigrant on the Land. *Charities; a Weekly Review of Local and General Philanthropy* 13: 541.

——. 1905. Book Review of "The Italian in America" by Eliot Lord, J. D. Trenor, and S. J. Barrows. *American Academy of Political and Social Science, Annals* 26 (July/December): 609–.

——. 1905. Italian Immigration Into the South. *South Atlantic Quarterly (SAMLA)* 4: 217–.

——. 1907. *Italian on the Land: A Study in Immigration*. Bulletin of the Bureau of Labor, no. 70. Washington: U.S. Government Printing Office.

——. 1907. Book Review of "The Family" by Helen Bosanquet. *American Academy of Political and Social Science, Annals* 30 (July/December): 173–.

Meiklejohn, Helen Everett. *See* Everett, Helen.

Meints, Viola Catherine. 1931. Incomes and Expenditures of Iowa State College Faculty Families. M.S. thesis, Iowa State College.

——. Coauth. *See* Hoyt, Elizabeth Ellis.

Melegari, Dora. 1899. The Woman Question in Italy. *Contemporary Review* 76 (July/December): 819–31.

Mell, Mildred Rutherford. 1938. Poor Whites of the South. *Social Forces* 17(2) (December): 153–67.

——. 1939/40. Book Review of "The Southern Poor-white from Lubberland to Tobacco Road" by McIlwain. *Social Forces* 18(1/4): 448–.

Mercier, Hélène. 1887. *Over arbeiderswoningen, Met afbeeldingen*. Haarlem: H. D. Tjeenk Willink.

——. 1889. *Verbonden schakels*. Haarlem: Tjeenk Willink.

——. 1897. *Social schetsen*. Haarlem: H. D. Tjeenk Willink.

Meredith, Mrs. Charles [Louisa Anne]. 1865. *The Lacemakers: Sketches of Irish Character, with Some Account of the Effort to Establish Lacemaking in Ireland*. London: Jackson, Walford, and Hodder.

Merlin, Maria de la Mercedes. 1844. The Introduction of Tobacco into Europe. *Bentley's Miscelleny* 15 (April): 379–84.

[Merriam,] Ida Sonntag Craven [Mrs. Mylon Merriam]. 1928. The Conquest of the Railroads; and The United States Shoe Machinery Corporation. Ph.D. thesis, Robert Brookings.

——. 1936. *The Employer–Employee Relationship in the Marketing of Gasoline*. Bureau of Research and Statistics Bureau Memorandum. Washington: U.S. Social Security Board, Bureau of Research and Statistics.

——. 1938. *Seasonal Workers and Unemployment Compensation*. Washington: Social Security Board, Bureau of Research and Statistics.

——. 1939. *State Statistical Analyses Relating to Unemployment Compensation Simplification*. Washington: Social Security Board, Bureau of Research and Statistics.

——. 1940. Extension of the Scope of National Assistance Programs in Great Britain. *Social Security Bulletin* 3(6) (June): 24–.

Merriam, Ida Craven and Diane Bochner. 1940. The Roles of Unemployment Insurance and Unemployment Assistance in Great Britain. *Social Security Bulletin* 3(3) (March): 3–.

Merrifield, Mary P. 1870. The Need of Sanitary Knowledge to Women. *Dublin University Magazine* 76 (September): 343–8.

Merriman, Effie Woodward. 1898. *How Women May Earn Money*. New York: F. M. Lupton Pub. Co.

Merritt, Ella Arvilla. 1924. *Legal Regulation of the Employment of Minors 16 Years of Age and Over*. Washington: U.S. Government Printing Office.

——. 1928. Laws and Ordinances Regulating the Work of Children in Street Trades. In Nettie Pauline McGill and Ella Arvilla Merritt, *Child Workers on City Streets*. Washington: U.S. Children's Bureau.

——. 1929. *State Laws and Local Ordinances Regulating the Street Work of Children: A Tabular Summary of Regulations in Effect in the United States*. United States Department of Labor, Children's Bureau, Chart no. 15. Washington: U.S. Government Printing Office.

——. 1929. Legal Regulation of the Employment of Children in Agricultural Pursuits. In Nettie Pauline McGill and Ella Arvilla Merritt, *Children in Agriculture*. Washington: U.S. Childrens' Bureau.

——. 1932. Review of the White House Conference Report on Child Labor. *Monthly Labor Review* 34(6) (June): 1,278–.
——. 1935. Child Labor under the N.R.A., as Shown by Employment Certificates Issued in 1934. *Monthly Labor Review* 41(6) (December): 1,477–.
——. 1939. Age Certificates for Young Workers under the Sugar Act. *Child* 4(4) (October): 93–.
——. 1940. Regulation of Child Labor in Industrialized Agriculture. *Child* 4(10) (April): 275–.
Merritt, Ella Arvilla and Caroline E. Legg. 1940. Child Labor in Vegetable Canneries in Maryland. *Child* 5(2) (August): 35–.
Merritt, Ella Arvilla. Coauth. *See* Dart, Helen Marietta; Legg, Caroline; McGill, Nettie Pauline; Skinner, Mary Elizabeth; [Woodbury], Helen L[aura] Sumner.
Merryweather, Mary. 1862. *Experiences of Factory Life: Being a Record of Fourteen Years' Work at Mr. Courtauld's Silk Mill at Halstead, in Essex*. London: E. Faithfull. Reprinted from the *Waverley*, a working women's journal.
Mertsky, Grace. 1928. The Assessment of Real Estate in Chicago, 1927. *Land Economics* 4 (February): 71–4.
Merwin, Virginia C. 1881. *The Relation of Women to Work in the Southern States.* Paper read before the Association for the Advancement of Women, at the annual congress, Boston, October 1880. Boston: New England Publishing Co.
Mesurier, Alice M. C. Le. *See* Le Mesurier, Alice M. C.
Meteyard, Eliza. 1872. *The Nine Hours' Movement: Industrial and Household Tales, etc.* London: Longman's, Green & Co.
Mettert, Margaret Jane Thompson. 1934. *State Reporting of Occupational Disease, Including a Survey of Legislation Applying to Women.* Bulletin of the Women's Bureau, no. 114. Washington: U.S. Government Printing Office.
——. 1935. *Industrial Injuries to Women in 1930 and 1931 Compared with Injuries to Men.* U.S. Women's Bureau Bulletin, no. 129. Washington: U.S. Government Printing Office.
——. 1936. *Summary of State Reports of Occupational Diseases.* Washington: U.S. Government Printing Office.
——. 1937. *Injuries to Women in Personal Service Occupations in Ohio.* Bulletin of the U.S. Women's Bureau, no. 151. Washington: U.S. Government Printing Office.
——. 1938. *Industrial Injuries to Women and Men, 1932 to 1934.* Bulletin of the U.S. Women's Bureau, no. 160. Washington: U.S. Government Printing Office.
——. Coauth. *See* Pidgeon, Mary Elizabeth.
Meyer, Adele Levis [Mrs. Carl Meyer] and Clementina Black. 1909. *Makers of Our Clothes; a Case for Trade Boards, Being the Results of a Year's Investigation into the Work of Women in London in the Tailoring, Dressmaking, and Underclothing Trades.* London: Duckworth & Co.
Meyer, Annie Nathan, ed. 1891. *Woman's Work in America.* New York: Holt. Reprinted New York: Arno Press, 1972.
——. 1897. To Him that Hath. *Lippincott's* 59 (January/June): 854–.

Meyerstein, Constance. 1896. The Education of Children under the Poor-Law: A Historical Summary: III. *Charity Organisation Review* 140 (September): 382–8.

Meynieu, Mary. 1839. *Elements d'économie politique, exposés dans une suite de dialogues entre un instituteur et son élève, à l'usage des écoles normales primaires*. Paris: A. Cherbuliez.

——. 1841. *Du Pauperisme anglais*. Paris: A. Cherbuliez.

——. 1859. Observations sur l'économie politique, à propos du Manuel de M. Baudrillart. *Journal des économistes* 65 (May).

——. 1860. *Quelques Mots sur le travail des femmes, à l'occasion d'un article de M. Jules Simon*. Paris: Imprimerie du Corps legislatif, A. H. Noblet.

Michel, Louise. 1898. *La Commune*. Paris: P.-V. Stock.

Michener, Anna Marguerite. 1920. *The Budget System of Frankfort-on-the-Main*. White Plains, N.Y.: Westchester Printing Service.

——. 1920. The Budget System of Frankfort-on-the-Main. Ph.D. thesis, Columbia University (economics, history).

Milburn, Mary E. Coauth. *See* Lundberg, Emma Octavia.

Milchrist, Elizabeth Hayward and Sophonisba Preston Breckinridge. 1927. *State Administration of Child Welfare in Illinois*. Chicago: University of Chicago Press.

[Miles,] Sibella E. Hatfield. 1844. *An Essay on the Factory Question*. London: R. Hastings.

Milhaud, Caroline. 1907. *L'Ouvrière en France: Sa Condition présente, les réformes nécessaires*. Paris: Alcan.

[Mill,] Harriet Taylor [Mrs. John Stuart Mill]. 1851/1868. The Enfranchisement of Women. *Westminster Review* 55 (July): 289–311. Reprinted New York: Office of *The Revolution*, 1868. Reprinted in Alice S. Rossi, ed., *Essays on Sex Equality*. Chicago: University of Chicago Press, 1970; with a new introduction by Kate Soper, London: Virago Press, 1983; in Ann P. Robson and John Robson, eds., *Sexual Equality: Writings by John Stuart Mill, Harriet Taylor Mill and Helen Taylor*. Toronto: University of Toronto Press, 1994; and in Jo Ellen Jacobs, ed., *The Complete Works of Harriet Taylor Hill*. Bloomington: Indiana University Press, 1998. (Authorship is disputed; possibly coauthored with John Stuart Mill.)

Miller, Edith M. 1927. *Credit, Prices and Prosperity*. Proceedings of Management Week series, October 28, 1927. Columbus, Ohio: Bureau of Business Research, College of Commerce and Administration, Ohio State University.

Miller, Emily Huntington. 1891/2. The Homes of Poverty. *Chautauquan* 14 (October/March): 336–.

——. 1896. The Tea Supply of the U.S. *National Magazine, an Illustrated American Monthly* 4: 553–.

Miller, Florence Fenwick. 1883. *Readings in Social Economy*. London: Longmans, Green.

——. 1883. Elementary Education in Social Economy. *Modern Review* 4 (July): 575–85.

——. 1884. *Harriet Martineau*. London: W. H. Allen.

——. 1901. Women as Workers at Home. *Temple Magazine*, V (September): 273.

Miller, Frieda S[egelke]. 1932. Woman's Place – What Will Determine It? *American Federationist* 39(3) (March): 287–.

——. 1938. International Regulation of Hours of Road Transport Workers. *American Labor Legislation Review* 28: 177–80.

——. 1940. *Workers' Health Hazards – Today and Tomorrow: Detection and Control of Silicosis and Other Occupational Diseases. What New York State Has Done, and the Job Ahead. A Progress Report to the Legislature of the State of New York.* New York: New York State Industrial Commission/State of New York Department of Labor.

——. Frieda Miller Papers, including private letters, diaries, as well as published public papers and articles are at the Schlesinger Library, Radcliffe College.

Miller, Margaret S. 1921. Co-operation in Russia. *Economica* 1(3) (October): 291–301.

——. 1921/2. Financial Reform in Soviet Russia. *Slavonic and East European Review* 10: 328–.

——. 1921/2. Financial Reform in Soviet Russia II. *Slavonic and East European Review* 10: 547–.

——. 1922/3. The Trade Balance of Russia. *Slavonic Review* 1: 401–.

——. 1925/6. Taxation in Soviet Russia, I (from the essay of Paul Haensel). *Slavonic Review* 4.

——. 1926. *Economic Development of Russia 1905–1914*. London: P. S. King & Son.

——. 1926/7. Taxation in Soviet Russia. *Slavonic Review* 5: 494–.

——. 1930/1. The Financing of Industry in Soviet Russia. *Slavonic and East European Review* 9: 13–.

——. 1930/1. The Planning System in Soviet Russia. *Slavonic and East European Review* 9: 449–.

——. 1931. Prosperity to a Time Schedule. *Listener* 5(128) (June 24): 1,047–.

——. 1932. Soviet Public Finance. *New Statesman and Nation* 3(64) (May 14): 640–.

——. 1933. *Financial Democracy*. London: L. and Virginia Woolf at the Hogarth Press.

——. 1935. What Freedom Means in Soviet Russia. *Listener* 13(318) (February 13): 261–.

——. 1936. Book Review of "Soviet Russia Fights Crime" by Lenka von Koerber. *Pacific Affairs* 9(2) (June): 299–.

——. 1936. A Survey of Soviet Finance. *Public Administration (London, UK)* 14(4) (October): 404–.

——. 1937. Review of "The Second Five Year Plan." *New Statesman and Nation* 13(327) (May 29): 893–.

——. 1938. Book Review of "Premature Subdivision and Its Consequences" by P. H. Cornick. *Public Administration (London, UK)* 16(3) (July): 349.

——. 1938. Book Review of "Urban Blight and Slums" by M. L. Walker. *Public Administration (London, UK)* 16(3) (July): 349.

——. 1939. Book Review of "Housing in America – Housing Comes of Age" by Michael W. Strauss And Talbot Wegg. *Public Administration (London, UK)* 17(1) (January): 96–.

——. 1939. Book Review of "Managing Low-rent Housing" by C. Kent Wright. *Public Administration (London, UK)* 17(4) (October): 439–.

——. 1940. Book Review of "Soviet Housing Law" by John N. Hazard. *Public Administration (London, UK)* 18(2) (April): 153–.

Milnes, Nora. 1916/17. Some Aspects of the Infant Welfare Question. *Sociological Review* 9: 121–.

——. 1917. Mint Records in the Reign of Henry VIII. *English Historical Review* 32: 270.

——. 1921. *Child Welfare from the Social Point of View*. London: J. M. Dent & Sons, Ltd.

——. 1926. *The Economics of Wages and Labour*. London: P. S. King.

——. 1929. Difficulties in Recruiting and Training Workers in a Social Case Agency. *Charity Organisation Quarterly* 3(1) (January): 21–.

——. 1931. Public Health and the Family. *Charity Organisation Quarterly* 5(4) (October): 148–.

——. 1932. Social Aspects of British Health Insurance. *Social Service Review* 6(1/4) (March/December): 581–.

——. 1936. *A Study of Industrial Edinburgh, 1923–1934*. London: P. S. King & Son.

——. 1937. Edinburgh – An Industrial Study. *Charity Organisation Quarterly* 11(3) (July): 207–.

Miner, Maude E[mma]. 1910. Probation Work for Women. *American Academy of Political and Social Science, Annals* 36 (July/December): 27–.

——. 1912. *The Problem of Wayward Girls and Delinquent Women*. Academy of Political Science Publication, vol. 2, no 4. New York: Academy of Political Science.

——. 1912. The Problem of Wayward Girls and Women Delinquents. *Academy of Political Science, Proceedings* 2(4) (July): 130–.

——. 1916. *Slavery of Prostitution: A Plea for Emancipation*. New York: Macmillan.

——. 1917. Book Review of "Slavery of Prostitution – A Plea for Emancipation." *Journal of Criminal Law and Criminology and Police Science* 8(1) (May): 152–.

——. 1917. Slavery of Prostitution: A Plea for Emancipation. Ph.D. thesis, Columbia University (sociology).

Mirlin, Margarete Ada Beney. 1939. Differentials in Industrial Wages and Hours in the United States. Ph.D. thesis, Columbia University.

Mitchell, Agnes W. 1939. The Labor Relations of a Large Steel Company in the Pittsburgh District. Ph.D. thesis, University of Pittsburgh (economics).

Monchow, Helen Corbin. 1928. *The Use of Deed Restrictions in Subdivision Development*. Studies in Land Economics, Research Monograph, no. 1. Chicago: Institute for Research in Land Economics and Public Utilities.

——. 1928. The California Planning Act of 1927. *Land Economics* 4 (May): 209–12.

——. 1928. The Cambridge Zoning Decision. *Land Economics* 4 (August): 322–4.

——. 1929. Finding a Base-year for the Study of Urban Problems. *Land Economics* 5 (August): 311–21.

——. 1930. Torrens System Upheld by the United States Supreme Court. *Land Economics* 6 (August): 311–21.

——. 1933. Population and Subdividing Activity in the Region of Chicago: 1871–1930. *Land Economics* 9 (May): 192–206.

——. 1936. County Zoning Authorized in Illinois. *Land Economics* 12 (February): 89–90.

——. 1936. New Departures in Subdivision and Control. *Land Economics* 12 (November): 417–19.

——. 1937. The Farm Tenancy Act. *Land Economics* 13 (November): 417–18.

——. 1937. Real Estate Subdividing in the Region of Chicago, 1871–1930. Ph.D. thesis, Northwestern University (economics).

——. 1938. Subdivision Legislation in 1937. *Land Economics* 14 (February): 83–4.

——. 1939. *Seventy Years of Real Estate Subdividing in the Region of Chicago*. Evanston, Ill.: Northwestern University.

——. 1939. California's Subdivision Control Sustained. *Land Economics* 15 (February): 97–8.

——. 1939. A Yardstick of Residential Lot Needs. *Land Economics* 15 (November): 474–7.

Monroe, Day. 1930. Chicago Families: A Study of Unpublished Census Data. Ph.D. thesis, University of Chicago (home economics).

——. 1933. Book Review of "Standardization of Consumers' Goods" by Jessie V. Coles. *American Academy of Political and Social Science, Annals* 168 (July): 245–.

——. 1939. *Family Income and Expenditures, Pacific Region.* U.S. Department of Agriculture, Miscellaneous Publications, no. 339. Washington: U.S. Government Printing Office.

Monroe, Day and Hazel Kyrk. 1937. Analyzing Families by Composition Type with Respect to Consumption. *Journal of the American Statistical Association* (May) 32: 35–9 .

Monroe, Day and Maryland Young Pennell. 1939. *How Professional Women Spend Their Money: An Analysis of 55 Account Books for 1938.* Washington: U.S. Department of Agriculture.

Monroe, Day, Dorothy S. Brady, June F. Constantine, and K. L. Benson. 1940/1941. *Family Expenditures for Automobile and Other Transportation, Five Regions.* Consumer Purchases Study: Urban, Village, and Farm, U.S. Department of Agriculture, Miscellaneous Publications, 436. Washington: U.S. Government Printing Office.

Monroe, Day, Dorothy S. Brady, Maryland Y. Pennell, and Miriam H. Coffin. 1940/1941. *Family Expenditures for Education, Reading, Recreation, and Tobacco, Five Regions.* Consumer Purchases Study: Urban, Village, and Farm, U.S. Department of Agriculture, Miscellaneous Publications, 464. Washington: U.S. Government Printing Office.

Monroe, Day, Dorothy S. Brady, Edith D. Rainboth, and Ellen D. Riley. 1940/1941. *Family Expenditures for Personal Care, Gifts, Selected Taxes, and Miscellaneous Items, Five Regions.* Consumer Purchases Study: Urban, Village, and Farm, U.S.

Department of Agriculture, Miscellaneous Publications, 456. Washington: U.S. Government Printing Office.

Monroe, Day, Helen Hollingsworth, and Margaret Perry Maryland. 1940/1941. *Family Expenditures for Furnishings and Equipment, Five Regions.* Consumer Purchases Study: Urban, Village, and Farm, U.S. Department of Agriculture, Miscellaneous Publications. Washington: U.S. Government Printing Office.

Monroe, Day, Lenore Monroe Stratton, Hazel Kyrk, and Ursula Batchelder Stone. 1925/1940. *Food Buying and Our Markets.* New York: M. Barrows & Co, Inc.

Monroe, Day, Elizabeth Phelps, and Idella G. Swisher. 1940. *Family Income and Expenditures: Middle Atlantic and North Central Region and New England Region. Part I: Family Income.* U.S. Department of Agriculture, Miscellaneous Publication, no. 370. Washington: U.S. Government Printing Office.

Monroe, Day. Coauth. *See* Brady, Dorothy S.; Kyrk, Hazel; Weiss, Gertrude Schmidt.

Montagu, Lady Cicely Susan. 1892. Thrift for the Poor. *New Review* (December): 673–9.

Montagu, Lily. 1896. The Condition of the Individual in a Socialistic State. *Westminster Review* 146 (October): 439–45.

Montefiore, Dora B. 1908. *Some Words to Socialist Women.* London: Twentieth Century Press.

——. 1909. *The Position of Women in the Socialist Movement.* London: Twentieth Century Press.

Montgomery, Louise. 1913. *The American Girl in the Stockyards District.* Chicago: University of Chicago Press.

——. 1921. The Invisible Strike. *World Tomorrow* 4(3) (March): 78–.

Moodie, Susanna. 1852. *Roughing It in the Bush, or, Life in Canada.* London: Richard Bentley; New York: G. P. Putnam. Reprinted Toronto: McClelland and Stewart, 1970.

Moody, Miss S. 1894/5. Aspects of Social Life in the East End of London. *Chautauquan* 20 (October/March): 399–.

Morant, Amy C. 1895. *The Crisis at Cardiff: A Critical Review of the Present Aspect of Trades Unionism in this Country.* London: Independent Labour Party.

——. 1895. *Liberalism Unveiled, or a Creed Without a Programme.* London: Independent Labour Party.

More, Hannah. 1777. *Essays on Various Subjects: Principally Designed for Young Ladies.* London: J. Wilkie and T. Cadell.

——. 1788. *Slavery, a Poem.* London: Printed for T. Cadell.

—— [as "Will Chip, a country carpenter"]. 1792. *Village Politics, Addressed to All the Mechanics, Journeymen, and Labourers, in Great Britain.* London: F. and C. Rivington.

——. 1795. *Hints to All Ranks of People, on the Occasion of the Present Scarcity.* Cheap Repository Tracts. London: J. Marshall.

——. 1795. *The History of Tom White, the Post Boy.* Cheap Repository Tracts. London: J. Marshall.

——. 1795. *The Market Woman, a True Tale; or Honesty Is the Best Policy.* Cheap Repository Tracts. London: J. Marshall.

——. 1795. *Patient Joe, or, the Newcastle Collier.* Cheap Repository Tracts. Bath: J. Marshall and R. White and S. Hazard. [*ballad*]

——. 1795. *The Riot; or, Half a Loaf is Better than No Bread.* Cheap Repository Tracts. London: J. Marshall and R. White and S. Hazard. [*ballad*]

——. 1795. *The Shepherd of Salisbury Plain.* Cheap Repository Tracts. London: J. Marshall.

——. 1795. *The Sorrows of Yamba; or the Negro Woman's Lamentation.* Cheap Repository Tracts. London: J. Marshall. [*ballad*]

——. 1795. *The Two Shoemakers.* Cheap Repository Tracts. London: J. Marshall.

——. 1795. *The Two Wealthy Farmers, or, the History of Mr. Bragwell.* Cheap Repository Tracts. London: J. Marshall.

——. 1796. *The Apprentice Turned Master.* Cheap Repository Tracts. London: J. Marshall.

——. 1796. *Betty Brown, the St. Giles's Orange Girl with an Account of Mrs. Sponge, the Money Lender.* Cheap Repository Tracts. London: J. Marshall, J. E. Evans.

——. 1796. *Black Giles the Poacher: With Some Account of a Family Who Had Rather Live by Their Wits than Their Work: Part I–II.* London: J. Marshall and R. White.

——. 1796. *The Cottage Cook; or Mrs. Jones' Cheap Dishes; Shewing the Way to Do Much Good with Little Money.* Cheap Repository Tracts. London: J. Marshall.

——. 1796. *The History of Charles Jones the Footman.* Cheap Repository Tracts. London: J. Marshall.

——. 1796. *The History of Idle Jack Brown, Being the Third Part of The Two Shoemakers.* Cheap Repository Tracts. London: J. Marshall.

——. 1796. *A Hymn of Praise for the Abundant Harvest of 1796.* Cheap Repository Tracts. London: J. Marshall.

——. 1796. *The Shop-keeper Turned Sailor, or, The Folly of Going out of Our Element.* London: J. Marshall.

——. 1797. *The History of Mr Fantom, the New-fashioned Philosopher.* Cheap Repository Tracts. London: J. Marshall.

——. 1799. *Strictures on the Modern System of Female Education. With a View of the Principles and Conduct Prevalent among Women of Rank and Fortune.* London: T. Cadell and W. Davies. Reprinted Bristol: Thoemmes Classics, 1995.

——. 1818. *Stories for the Middle Ranks of Society and Tales for the Common People.* London: T. Cadell and W. Davies.

——. 1840. *The Works of Hannah More.* New York: Harper & Brothers.

More, Louise Bolard. 1907. *Wage Earners' Budgets: A Study of Standards and Cost of Living in New York City.* With a preface by Franklin H. Giddings. New York: Henry Holt & Co.; London: G. Bell & Sons.

——. 1913. The Cost of Living for a Wage-earner's Family in New York City. *American Academy of Political and Social Science, Annals* 48 (July): 104–.

Morehouse, Frances Milton Irene and Sybil Fleming Graham. 1923. *American Problems: A Textbook in Social Progress.* Boston: Ginn.

Morel, Lydie. 1937. *Le Droit au travail de la femme mariée*. Geneva: Labor.

Morgan, Charlotte E. 1930. *The Origin and History of the New York Employing Printers' Association. The Evolution of a Trade Association*. New York: Columbia University Press.

[Morgan, Elizabeth] Chicago Trade and Labor Assembly. 1891. *The New Slavery. Investigation into the Sweating System as Applied to the Manufacture of Wearing Apparel*. Chicago: Detwiler.

Morgan, Joy Elmer 1912. *Selected Articles on Free Trade and Protection*. Minneapolis: H. W. Wilson company.

——. 1925. Child Labor and Big Business. *School and Society* 22(557) (August 29): 274.

——. 1926. The Future of the Child Labor Amendment. *School and Society* 23(575) (January 2): 17–.

——. 1930. The Causes of American Prosperity [letter to the editor]. *Nation and Athenaeum* 46(17) (January 25): 570–4.

——. 1932. *Prohibition and the Future of America*. Westerville, Ohio: American Issue Press.

——. 1934. *The New American Plan for Radio*. Washington: National Committee on Education by Radio.

——. 1934/5. Readjustments Which Need Emphasis in Business Education. *Journal of Educational Sociology* 8: 555–.

——. 1937. Your Profession in the Making. *NEA Bulletin* 26(1) (January): 27–.

Morgan, Joy Elmer and Edna Dean Bullock 1911/1914. *Selected Articles on Municipal Ownership*. 2nd ed. Enlarged. New York and White Plains, N.Y.: H. W. Wilson company.

Morgan, Margaret Lee. 1939. *The History and Economic Aspect of the Wichita Valley Irrigation Project*. M.A. thesis, Southern Methodist University.

Morgan, May Isabelle. 1926. The Development of Exchange. A.M. thesis, Washington University.

Morgan, Winona L. 1937. Changes in Socio-economic Status and Family Relationships Occurring within a Highly Selected Group during the Period from 1927–1933. Ph.D. thesis, University of Minnesota (sociology).

——. 1939. *The Family Meets the Depression: A Study of a Group of Highly Selected Families*. Minneapolis: University of Minnesota Press.

Morgenstern, Lina. 1891. *Die Stellung der Frau im Leben*. Kiel: Lipsius & Tischer.

——. 1893. *Frauenarbeit in Deutschland*. Berlin: Verlag der Deutschen Hausfrauen-Zeitung.

Morison, Dorothea Cotter. *See* Braithwaite, Dorothea Cotter Morison.

Morley, Edith J. 1914. The Economic Position of Women. *Economic Review* (October).

——. 1914. *Women Workers in Seven Professions: A Survey of Their Economic Conditions and Prospects*. London: Routledge.

Morrison, Anne Hendry. 1932. Women and Their Careers: A Study of Three Hundred and Six Women in Business and the Professions. Ph.D. thesis, Bryn Mawr College (sociology).

——. 1934. *Women and Their Careers a Study of 306 Women in Business and the Professions.* New York: National Federation of Business and Professional Women's Clubs, Inc.

Morrison, Frances. 1838. *The Influence of the Present Marriage System upon the Character and Interests of Females, Contrasted with that Proposed by Robert Owen, Esq.: A Lecture Delivered in the Social Institution, Shudehill, Manchester, on Sunday Evening, Sept. 2nd., 1838, Addressed Particularly to Females.* Manchester: A. Heywood.

Morriss, Margaret Shove. 1914. *Colonial Trade of Maryland, 1689–1715.* Baltimore: Johns Hopkins Press. Reprinted in Philadelphia: Porcupine Press, 1976.

——. 1914. Colonial Trade of Maryland, 1689–1715. Ph.D. thesis, Bryn Mawr College (economics).

Morrissy, Elizabeth. 1922. Graft in the Building Trades. M.A. thesis. Johns Hopkins University.

——. 1930. Unemployment Insurance in American Trade Unions. Ph.D. thesis, Johns Hopkins University.

——. 1940. Security – A Safeguard to Democracy. *Christian Scholar* 23(3) (February): 184–.

Morse, Annie Hooker. 1905. Social Economics. *Association of Collegiate Alumnae, Publications*, series 3, 10 (January): 36–.

Morse, Ruth. 1891. The Higher Education of Woman in Europe. *Chautauquan* 13 (April/September): 227.

Moses, Mabelle. 1911/1971. The Regulation of Private Employment Agencies in the United States. In Susan Myra Kingsbury, Charles Edward Person, and Edith Gertrude Solenberger, eds., *Labor Laws and Their Enforcement with Special Reference to Massachusetts.* New York: Longmans, Green.

——. Coauth. *See* Kingsbury, Susan Myra.

Mossell, Gertrude. 1894. *The Work of the Afro-American Woman.* Philadelphia: G. S. Ferguson. Reprinted New York and London: Oxford University Press, 1988. Online at the Digital Schomburg, http://digital.nypl.org/schomburg/writers—aa19/.

Mossell, Sadie Tanner *see* [Alexander] Sadie.

Moszkowska, Natalie. 1917. *Arbeiterkassen an den privaten Berg- und Hüttenwerken im Königreich Polen: ein Beitrag zur Geschichte der Wohlfahrtseinrichtungen der Arbeitgeber.* Stuttgart: Dietz.

——. 1917. Arbeiterkassen an den privaten Berg- und Hüttenwerken im Königreich Polen: ein Beitrag zur Geschichte der Wohlfahrtseinrichtungen der Arbeitgeber. Thesis, Zurich.

——. 1929. *Das marxsche System: ein Beitrag zu dessen Aufbau.* Berlin: Verlag Hans Robert Engelmann.

——. 1935. *Zur Kritik moderner Krisentheorien.* Prague: Michael Kacha Verlag.

Mott, Alice J. 1896. The Economic Bearing of Charity. *Lend a Hand* 16 (January): 54–.

——. 1896. Our Duty to Nature's Step-children. *Charities Review* 5 (June): 391–.

Mott, Lucretia. 1850. *Discourse on Woman. Delivered at the Assembly Buildings Dec. 17, 1849.* Revised by the Author. Philadelphia: T. B. Peterson.

Moulder, Priscilla E. 1899. The Industrial Position of Women. *Westminster Review* 151 (March): 318–23.

Moulthrop, Alice Louise. 1928. Economic Grievances of the New York Frontier to 1776. MA thesis, University of Chicago (economics, history).

Moulton, Elma Saunders. 1931. *Cotton Production and Distribution in the Gulf Southwest.* Washington: U.S. Government Printing Office.

——. 1938. *Atlas of Wholesale Grocery Trading Areas.* Washington: U.S. Bureau of Foreign and Domestic Commerce.

——. 1939. *Marketing Research Activities of Manufacturers.* Washington: U.S. Bureau of Foreign and Domestic Commerce.

——. 1940. *Sources of Regional and Local Current Business Statistics.* Washington: U.S. Bureau of Foreign and Domestic Commerce.

Mozley, Anne. 1869. Mr Mill on the Subjection of Women. *Blackwood's Magazine* 106 (September): 309–21. Reprinted in Andrew Pyle, ed., *The Subjection of Women: Contemporary Responses to John Stuart Mill.* Bristol: Thoemmes Press, 1995.

Mozzoni, Anna Maria. 1866. *Un passo avanti nella cultura femminile tesi e progetto.* Milano: Tip. Internazionale.

Mulhall, Marion. 1896. Boarding-out Workhouse Children. *New Ireland Review* (November).

——. 1896. Girls' Technical Schools on the Continent. *Contemporary Review* 70 (July): 136–.

Mulholland [Gilbert], Rosa. 1890. Linen-weaving in Skibbereen. *Irish Monthly* 18.

Müller, F[rances]. Henrietta. 1884. The Future of Single Women. London: Ballantyne, Hanson & Co., printers. Reprinted, with additions, from the *Westminster Review.*

——. 1885. The Work of Women as Poor Law Guardians. *Westminster Review,* n.s. 67 [old 123] (April): 386–95.

Muller, Helen Marie. 1928. *Installment Buying.* New York: H. W. Wilson.

——. 1929. *Government Fund for Unemployment.* New York: H. W. Wilson.

——. 1930. *County Manager Government.* New York: H. W. Wilson.

——. 1931. *Lobbying in Congress.* New York: H. W. Wilson.

——. 1931. *The World Court.* New York: H. W. Wilson.

——. 1933. *Federal Regulation of Motor Transport.* New York: H. W. Wilson.

——. 1934. *Federal Aid for the Equalization of Educational Opportunity.* New York: H. W. Wilson.

——. 1935. *Democratic Collectivism.* New York: H. W. Wilson.

——. 1935. *Lotteries.* New York: H. W. Wilson.

——. 1936. *The Seventh International Conference of American States.* M.A. thesis, Oklahoma Agricultural and Mechanical College.

Mulliken, Jean H. 1937. Competitive Conditions in the Long-staple Cotton Trade, with Special Reference to the Tariff. Ph.D. thesis, Radcliffe College (economics).

Murray, Alice Effie 1903/1907. *A History of the Commercial and Financial Relations between England and Ireland from the Period of the Restoration.* London: P. S. King.

Murray, Helen. 1939. *Welfare Needs of Migratory Agricultural Labor in Southern California.* M.S. thesis, University of Southern California.

Murray, Helen G. 1933. *Out of Work: Hunger and Relief.* Boston and Chicago: Pilgrim Press.

Murray, Helen Grace. 1913. *Social Movement in the American Churches.* M.A. thesis, University of Chicago (sociology).

Murray, Janet [H.]. 1930. The Wheat Position and Policy in Switzerland since the War, 1919–1929. M.A. thesis, Leland Stanford Junior University.

——. 1939. A Study of Factors Affecting the Price of Dry Edible Beans in the United States. Ph.D. thesis, University of Chicago. Also printed in the *Canadian Historical Review* XIX(4) (December 1938).

——. Coauth. *See* Brady, Dorothy S.

Murray, Jean E[lizabeth]. 1933. Book Review of "The Fur Trade in New England" by Moloney. *Canadian Historical Review* 14(1/4) (March/December): 342–.

——. 1937. The Fur Trade in New France and New Netherlands Prior to 1645. Ph.D. thesis, University of Chicago (history).

——. 1938. The Fur Trade in New France and New Netherlands Prior to 1645. *Canadian Historical Review* XIX(4) (December): 365–.

Mutton, Alice Florence Adelaide. 1938. The Black Forest: Its Human Geography. *Economic Geography* 14(2) (April): 131–53.

Mutton, Alice Florence Adelaide and A. E. Adams. 1939. Land Forms, Settlement, and Land Utilization in the Southern Allgau. *Economic Geography* 15(2) (April): 185–8.

Muzzey, Annie L. 1896. A Social Settlement. *Arena* 16 (August): 432–8.

——. 1899. The Hour and the Woman [Review of Charlotte Perkins Gilman, *Woman and Economics*]. *Arena* 22(2) (August): 263–72.

Myers, Dorothy Woodin. 1939. *One Family in Five: A Study of Families Receiving Assistance in January, 1939.* Providence, R.I.: Providence Council of Social Agencies.

——. Coauth. *See* Kelley, Florence.

Myers, Margaret Good. 1922. Monthly Production of Pig Iron, 1884–1903. *Journal of the American Statistical Association* 18 (June): 247–9.

——. 1930/1. Book Review of "The Labor Banking Movement in the United States" by Princeton University, Industrial Relations Section. *Personnel Journal* 9: 191–.

——. 1930/1. Book Review of "Robots or Men? A French Workman's Experience in American Industry" by Dubreuil. *Personnel Journal* 9: 264–.

——. 1931. *The New York Money Market*, Vol. I: *Origins and Development.* New York: Columbia University Press. Reprinted New York: AMS Press, 1971.

——. 1931. The New York Money Market, Vol. I: Origins and Development. Ph.D. thesis, Columbia University (economics, finance).

——. 1931/2. Book Review of "Cost of Living Studies II. How Workers Spend a Living Wage" by Peixotto. *Personnel Journal* 10: 67.

——. 1931/2. Book Review of "The Movement of Money and Real Earnings in the United States, 1926–28" by Douglas and Jennison. *Personnel Journal* 10: 67.

——. 1931/2. Book Review of "The National Income and Its Purchasing Power" by King. *Personnel Journal* 10: 67.

——. 1932. Book Review of "Le Crédit par acceptation: Paris, centre financier" by Pierre-Benjamin Vigreux. *Political Science Quarterly* 47: 301–.

——. 1935. Book Review of "Le Crédit" by Louis Baudin. *Political Science Quarterly* 50: 150–.

——. 1936. *Paris as a Financial Centre.* London: P. S. King & Son.

——. 1938. Book Review of "La Monnaie et la formation des prix. Partie I: Les Éléments" by Louis Baudin. *Political Science Quarterly* 53: 310–.

——. 1940. *Monetary Proposals for Social Reform.* New York: Columbia University Press. Reprinted New York: AMS Press, 1970.

N

Napier, Catherine. 1840. *Woman's Rights and Duties Considered with Relation to Their Influence on Society and on Her Own Condition. By a Woman.* 2 vols. London: John W. Parker.

Nash, Rosalind Nightingale [Mrs. Vaughan Nash]. 1892?. *Co-operative Production and the Needs of Labour*. London: s.n.

——. 1892. *Reduction of Hours of Work for Women. Some Points in the Time Regulations of the Factory Act.* By Mrs. Vaughan Nash. Investigation Papers, no. 1. Manchester, UK: Women's Co-operative Guild.

——. 1897. *The Accidents Compensation Act 1897.* Leicester, UK: Co-operative Printing Society.

——. 1897. *The Law Relating to Health in Factories and Workshops*. Manchester, UK: Women's Co-operative Guild.

——. 1898. Life and Death in the Potteries. Manchester, UK: Women's Co-operative Guild/Labour Press.

——. 1902. *How the Poor Live: A Review of Poverty, A Study of Town Life by B. S. Rowntree*. Manchester, UK: Women's Cooperative Guild.

——. 1906. *Sweated Industries: What Can Be Done?* Manchester, UK: Women's Co-operative Guild.

Nassau, Mabel Louise. 1915. *Old Age Property in Greenwich Village*. Greenwich House Series, no. 61. New York: Fleming H. Revell Company.

Nathan, Mrs. Maud. 1896. The Consumers' League. *Lend a Hand* 17(4) (October): 276.

——. 1898. The Consumers' Label. *North American Review* 166 (February): 250–4.

——. 1906. Women Who Work and Women Who Spend. *Annals of the American Academy of Politics and Social Science* XXVII: 646–50.

——. 1908. *The Housekeeper and the Ballot.* Warren, Ohio: National American Woman Suffrage Association.

——. 1908. *The Wage Earner and the Ballot.* Warren, Ohio: National American Woman Suffrage Association.

——. 1926. *The Story of an Epoch-making Movement* [Consumers' League efforts on behalf of labor]. Garden City, N.Y.: Doubleday, Page & Co. Reprinted New York: Garland Publishing, 1986.

Neal, Rachel. 1911. *Women Co-operators: Their Place and Work in the Movement.* Manchester: Co-operative Union.

Needleman, Rae Leona. 1930. The Status of Thirty Trade Union Carpenters, Madison, 1928–1929. B.A. thesis, University of Wisconsin.

——. 1938. *Tips in Relation to Wages under the Social Security Program.* Washington: Social Security Board, Bureau of Research and Statistics.

——. 1939. Are Domestic Workers Coming of Age? *American Federationist* 46(10) (October): 1,070–.

——. 1939. Domestic Workers in Private Homes. *Social Security Bulletin* 2(3) (March): 10–.

——. 1939. Problems of Payments in Kind. *American Federationist* 46(3) (March): 269–.

Neff, Wanda Fraiken. 1929. *Victorian Working Women: An Historical and Literary Study of Women in British Industries and Professions, 1832–1850.* New York: Columbia University Press.

——. 1929. Victorian Working Women: An Historical and Literary Study of Women in British Industries and Professions, 1832–1850. Ph.D. thesis, Columbia University (economics).

Neilson, Nellie. 1896/7. Boon-services on the Estates of Ramsey Abbey. *American Historical Review* 2: 213–24.

——. 1898. Economic Conditions on Ramsey Manors. Ph.D. thesis, Bryn Mawr College (history).

——. 1899. *Economic Conditions on the Manors of Ramsey Abbey.* Philadelphia: Press of Sherman & Co.

——. 1910. *Customary Rents.* Oxford: Clarendon Press.

——. 1928/9. English Manorial Forms. *American Historical Review* 34: 725–.

——. 1936. *Medieval Agrarian Economy.* New York: H. Holt and Company.

Nelken, Margarita. 1922. *La condición social de la mujer en España. Su estado actual; su posible desarrollo.* Barcelona: Editorial Minerva.

Nelson, Eleanor. 1931. Industry's Dead and Injured: The Need of More Complete Reports on Industrial Accidents. *State Government* 4(7) (July): 14–.

Nelson, Eleanor Crosby and Rebecca Tufts Farnham. 1933/1939. *Women at Work: A Century of Industrial Change.* United States Women's Bureau Bulletin, no. 161. Washington: U.S. Government Printing Office.

Nelson, Esther Ethel. 1938. International Trade between Gold and Silver Standard Countries. Ph.D. thesis, Radcliffe College (economics).

Nelson, Evelyn Gibson. 1930. History of the English Frame Work Knitting Industry in England. Ph.D. dissertation, Radcliffe College (economics).

——. 1930. The Putting-out System in the English Frame-work-knitting Industry. *Journal of Economic and Business History* 2 (May): 467–94.

Nelson, Nell. 1888. *The White Slave Girls of Chicago: Nell Nelson's Startling Disclosures of the Cruelties and Iniquities Practiced in the Workshops and Factories of a Great City.* Chicago: Barkley Publishing Co.

Nesbitt, Florence. 1917/18. Book Review of "The Minimum Cost of Living" by Winifred Stuart Gibbs. *American Journal of Sociology* 23(1/6): 277–.

——. 1918. *Household Management.* New York: Russell Sage Foundation.

——. 1919/1920. *The Chicago Standard Budget for Dependent Families.* Chicago: Chicago Council of Social Agencies.

——. 1923. *Standards of Public Aid to Children in Their Own Homes.* Washington: U.S. Children's Bureau.

——. 1926. Cause of Some Failures in the Work of the United Charities of Chicago. *Social Forces* 5(2) (December): 258–68.

——. 1926. Success and Failure in the Promotion of Normal Family Life. *Family* 7(8) (December): 234–.

——. 1927. *Study of a Minimum Standard of Living for Dependent Families in Los Angeles.* Los Angeles: Community Welfare Education.

——. 1933. Effects of the Depression on Standards of Work in Family Welfare Agencies. *Family* 13(10) (February): 324–.

Nestor, Agnes. 1910. *The Working Girl's Need of Suffrage.* Microfilm reproduction for History of Women, reel 948 no. 9,011.

——. 1926. The Women's Industrial Conference. *American Federationist* 33 (January/June): 296.

——. 1929. The Experiences of a Pioneer Woman Unionist. *American Federationist* 36 (August): 926.

——. 1930. What Labor Is Doing. *American Labor Legislation Review* 20: 290–2.

Netter, Yvonne. 1923. *Le Travail de la femme mariée, son activité professionnelle.* Paris: Presses Universitaires de France.

Neumann, Anna. 1911. *Die Bewegung der Löhne der ländlichen "freien" Arbeiter im Zusammenhag mit der gesamtwirtschaftlichen Entwicklung in Königreich Preussen gegenwärtigen Umfangs vom Ausgang des 18 Jahrhunderts bis 1850.* Berlin: Paul Parey.

——. 1914. Lohngestaltung auf dem Lande im Zusammenhange mit agrarischen Entwicklungen. *Schmollers Jahrbuch für Gesetzgebung, Verwaltung und Volkswirtschaft im deutschen Reich* 38(1): 361–.

Neville, Edith. 1919. *Family Life, Considered in Connection with the Proposals for the National Endowment of Motherhood.* London: Charity Organisation Society.

Newbigin, Marion Isabel. 1914. *The British Empire beyond the Seas, an Introduction to World Geography.* London: G. Bell and Sons Ltd.

——. 1917. *Man and his Conquest of Nature.* London: A. & C. Black.

——. 1918. Some Aspects of the Industrial Revolution in Western Europe. *Scottish Geographical Magazine* 34(7) (July): 251–.

——. 1924. *Commercial Geography.* New York: H. Holt.

——. 1932. *Southern Europe: A Regional and Economic Geography of the Mediterranean Lands.* London: Methuen & Co.

Newbold, Ethel M. 1926. *A Contribution to the Study of the Human Factor in the Causation of Accidents.* Industrial Fatigue Research Board Reports, no. 34. London: H.M. Stationery Office.

——. 1927. Practical Applications of the Statistics of Repeated Events, Particularly to Industrial Accidents. *Royal Statistical Society Journal,* series A, 90: 487–535, pt. 3.

——. Coauth. *See* Broughton, Gladys Mary.

Newcomb, Elizabeth D. 1922. Industrial Welfare Work in Great Britain. *International Labor Review* 5 (April): 553–71.

Newcomb, Elizabeth and L. H. Green. 1933. Industrial Relations – IX. Should Wages Be Settled by Law? *Listener* 9(233) (June 28): 1,024–.

Newcomer, Mabel. 1917. *Separation of State and Local Revenues in the United States*. Columbia University Studies in History, Economics and Public Law, vol. LXXVI, no. 2, whole no. 180. New York: Columbia University. Reprinted New York: AMS Press, 1968.

——. 1917. Separation of State and Local Revenues in the United States. Ph.D. thesis, Columbia University (economics).

——. 1924. *The Chemical Industry in New York and Its Environs: Present Trends and Probable Future Developments*. New York: Plan of New York and Its Environs.

——. 1924. *Financial Statistics of Public Education in the United States 1910–1920: A Report Reviewed and Presented by the Education Finance Inquiry Commission under the Auspices of the American Council on Education, Washington, DC*. New York: Macmillan Co.

——. 1924. Taxation of Billboards. *National Municipal Review* (July): 349–51.

——. 1927. The Phi Beta Kappa Student. *School and Society* 25(627) (January 1): 24–.

——. 1928. Tendencies in State and Local Finance and Their Relation to State and Local Functions. *Political Science Quarterly* 43 (March): 1–.

——. 1929. State Taxation of Interstate Income of Manufacturing Corporations. *National Tax Association, Bulletin* 15(1) (October): 10–.

——. 1930. The General Property Tax and the Farmer. *Journal of Political Economy* 38(1) (1930): 62–72.

——. 1932. *Use of State Revenues for the Support of Local Functions in New York*. Albany, N.Y.: New York State Commission for the Revision of the Tax Laws.

——. 1932. Taxation of Land Values in Canada. *Journal of Political Economy* 40(3) (June): 366–78.

——. 1934. Coordination of State and Local Revenues in Germany. *Taxbits* 1(4) (February): 4–.

——. 1935. Financing a Recovery Program with Tax Reductions in National Socialist Germany. *National Tax Association, Bulletin* 20(6) (March): 162–.

——. 1935. Locally Shared State Revenues. *National Municipal Review* 24(12) (December): 678–.

——. 1936. Coordination of Federal, State and Local Tax Systems. *Annals of the American Academy of Political and Social Science* (January): 39–47.

——. 1936. English Local Government Finance under the Local Government Act of 1929. *Political Science Quarterly* 11(4) (December): 538–68.

——. 1936. Equalization of Local Government Resources in Germany and England. *American Economic Review* 26(1) (March): 182–7.

——. 1936. Federal Tax Policy. *Taxbits* 3(3) (January): 25–.

——. 1936. Fiscal Relations of Central and Local Governments in Germany under the Weimar Constitution. *Political Science Quarterly* (June): 185–214.

——. 1937. *Central and Local Finance in Germany and England*. New York: Columbia University Press.

——. 1937. Analysis of the Nature of American Public Debts, Federal, State, and Local. *American Economic Review* 27(1) (March): 49–57.

——. 1937. European Taxation of Business. In E. C. Alvord, ed., *How Shall Business Be Taxed?* New York: Tax Policy League.

——. 1939. *You Are a Taxpayer*. Poughkeepsie, N.Y.: Vassar College.

——. 1939. Book Review of "Federal Tax Practice" by Robert Hiester Montgomery and James Marvin Haynes. *Annals of the American Academy of Political and Social Science* 203 (May): 251–.

——. 1939. Book Review of "A Study in English Local Authority Finance" by Joseph Sykes. *Journal of Political Economy* 47: 898–.

——. 1939. State Tariff Walls. *Taxes* 17(9) (September): 509–.

——. 1939?/1940?. Paying for Public Education. *New York State Education* (May): 626–7, 667–8.

——. 1940. *Taxation and Fiscal Policy*. New York: Columbia University Press.

——. 1940. Book Review of "Financing Economic Security in the United States" by William Withers. *Political Science Quarterly* 55: 312–.

Newcomer, Mabel and Evelyn S. Gibson. 1924. Vital Statistics for Vassar College. *American Journal of Sociology* 29(1/6): 430–.

Newcomer, Mabel and Margaret Perkins. 1939. Price Variations Among Poughkeepsie Grocers. *Journal of Marketing* 4 (July): 39–44.

Newcomer, Mabel. Coauth. *See* Hutchinson, Ruth Gillette.

Nicholas, Frieda J. 1932. The Assize of Bread in London during the Sixteenth Century. *Economic History* 2 (January): 323–47.

Nicholes, Anna E., Florence Kelley, and Jane Addams. 1910/1919. *Chicago Working Women Need Woman Suffrage in the New Charter*. Chicago: Woman's Trade Union League.

Nicholl, Edith Mary. 1890. A Virginia Poorhouse. *Temple Bar* 88 (February): 202–14.

Nichols, Jeannette Paddock. 1923. Harnessing College Power to Promote Public Welfare in the South. *Journal of Social Forces* 2(1) (November): 45–7.

——. 1924. *Alaska: A History of Its Administration, Exploitation, and Industrial Development during Its First Half Century under the Rule of the United States*. Cleveland, Ohio: Arthur H. Clark Co.

——. 1924. Alaska: A History of Its Administration, Exploitation, and Industrial Development during Its First Half Century under the Rule of the United States. Ph.D. thesis, Columbia University (history).

——. 1924. The Southern Mill Village Complex. II: Does the Mill Village Foster any Social Types? *Journal of Social Forces* 2(3) (March): 350–7.

——. 1930. Colonial Industries of New Jersey – 1618–1815. *Americana* 24(3) (July): 299–.

——. 1933. Silver Diplomacy. *Political Science Quarterly* 48: 565–.

——. 1934. Silver Inflation and the Senate in 1933. *Social Studies* 25(1): 12.

——. 1934/5. John Sherman: A Study in Inflation. *Mississippi Valley Historical Review* 21: 181–.

——. 1935. Pennsylvania and the Agitation for Cheap Money. *Pennsylvania Magazine of History and Biography* 59: 245–.

——. 1936. A Painful Lesson in Silver Diplomacy. *South Atlantic Quarterly (SAMLA)* 35: 251–.

——. 1937. *John Sherman and the Silver Drive of 1877–78: The Origins of the Gigantic Subsidy*. Columbus, Ohio: Ohio State Archaeological and Historical Society.

——. 1939. Book Review of "Money and Trade" by Rene Leon. *Political Science Quarterly* 54: 145–.

Nicholson, Mrs. Asenath [Hatch]. 1847. *Ireland's Welcome to the Stranger: or, Excursions through Ireland, in 1844 & 1845, for the Purpose of Personally Investigating the Condition of the Poor*. New York: Baker and Scribner; London: Charles Gilpin.

——. 1850/1851. *Lights and Shades of Ireland: Annals of the Famine in Ireland, in 1847, 1848, and 1849*. New York: E. French.

Nickell, Paulena. 1932. Rural Housing: A Study of the Housing of 316 Master Farm Homemakers with Special Reference to Adequacy. Ph.D. thesis, University of Minnesota (economics, agricultural).

Nicolitch, Suzanne D. 1934. *Le Socialisme et les femmes*. Paris: Librairie Populaire du Parti Socialiste.

Nienburg, Bertha Marie. 1920. *Industrial Opportunities and Training for Women and Girls*. Washington: U.S. Government Printing Office.

——. 1920. *Women in the Government Service*. Bulletin of the U.S. Women's Bureau, no. 8. Washington: U.S. Government Printing Office.

——. 1923. *The Woman Home-maker in the City: A Study of Statistics Relating to Married Women in the City of Rochester, N.Y., at the Census of 1920*. Washington: U.S. Government Printing Office for the Department of Commerce, Bureau of the Census.

——. 1926. *The Status of Women in the Government Service in 1925*. Washington: U.S. Government Printing Office.

——. 1935. *Potential Earning Power of Southern Mountaineer Handicraft*. Bulletin of the U.S. Women's Bureau, no. 128. Washington: U.S. Government Printing Office.

——. 1936. *A Policy Insuring Value to the Woman Buyer and a Livelihood to Apparel Makers*. Washington: U.S. Women's Bureau, Department of Labor.

——. 1936. *Reemployment of New England Women in Private Industry*. Washington: U.S. Women's Bureau, Department of Labor.

——. 1936. Industrial Self-regulation. *Personnel Journal* 15(6) (December): 214–.

——. 1939. *Conditions in the Millinery Industry in the United States*. Bulletin of the U.S. Women's Bureau, no. 169. Washington: U.S. Government Printing Office.

——. 1939. Women in the Nation's Economy. *American Association of University Women, Journal* 32(3) (April): 131–.

Nienburg, Bertha Marie and Bertha Blair. 1936. *Factors Affecting Wages in Power Laundries*. Bulletin of the U.S. Women's Bureau, no. 143. Washington: U.S. Government Printing Office.

Nienburg, Bertha Marie. Coauth. *See* Obenauer, Marie Louise.

Nightingale, Florence. 1854. *Letters from Egypt: A Journey on the Nile 1849–50*. London: Printed for private circulation.

——. 1860. Cassandra. In *Suggestions for Thought to the Searchers after Truth among the Artizans of England*. London: George E. Eyre and William Spottiswoode. Reprinted in Mary Poovey, ed., *Cassandra and Other Selections from Suggestions for Thought*. New York: New York University Press, 1992.

——. 1861. *Notes on Nursing for the Labouring Classes*. London: Harrison.

——. 1863. *How People May Live and Not Die in India*. London: Emily Faithfull.

——. 1863. *Sanitary Statistics of Native Colonial Schools and Hospitals*. London: Eyre & Spottiswoode.

——. 1865. *Note on the Aboriginal Races of Australia*. Paper read at the annual meeting of the National Association for the Promotion of Social Science, held at York, September 1864. London: Emily Faithfull.

——. 1869. A Note on Pauperism. *Fraser's*, n.s. 79 (March): 281–90.

——. 1874. *Life or Death in India*. A paper read at the meeting of the National Association for the Promotion of Social Science, Norwich, 1873. With an appendix on life or death by irrigation. London: Spottiswoode.

——. 1878. The People of India. Part I. *Nineteenth Century* 4 (August): 193–221.

——. 1878. The United Empire and the Indian Peasant. *Journal of the National Indian Association: In Aid of Social Progress in India* 90 (June): 232–45.

——. 1883. The Bengal Tenancy Bill. *Contemporary Review* 44 (October): 587–602.

——. 1883. The Dumb Shall Speak, and the Deaf Shall Hear; or, the Ryot, the Zemindar, and the Government. *Journal of the East India Association* 15 (July): 163–238.

——. 1883. Our Indian Stewardship. *Nineteenth Century* 14 (August): 329–38.

——. 1894. *Village Sanitation in India*. London: Spottiswoode.

Nisot, Marie-Thérèse. 1922. La Nationalité de la femme mariée d'après la loi belge du 15 mai 1922. *Revue de droit international et de législation comparée*, series 3, 3(4): 365–.

——. 1926. *Quelques Mesures protectrices de la première enfance dans les Divers Pays*. Brussels: Hill.

——. 1926. L'Institut international pour l'unification du droit privé. *Revue de droit international et de législation comparée*, series 3, 7(5): 577–.

——. 1927. Workers' Education in Belgium. *International Labour Review* (Geneva) 24 (July): 55–74.

——. 1928. Législations récentes sur la nationalité de la femme mariée. *Université de Bruxelles, Revue* 35(1): 95–.

——. 1928. La Nationalité de la femme mariée et la loi française du 10 août 1927. *Revue de droit international et de législation comparée*, series 3, 9(4/5): 646–.

——. 1932. The Status of Professional Workers in the Chemical Industry. *International Labour Review* 26(1/6) (July/December): 513–.

——. 1933. L'Universalité des conventions internationales du travail. *Université de Bruxelles, Revue* 38(3): 377–.

——. 1940. The Protection of Professional Titles: I. *International Labour Review* (January): 30–.

——. 1940. The Protection of Professional Titles: II. *International Labour Review* (February): 115–.

Noble, Emily Harris. 1931. *Status and Professional Preparation of Recreation Center Executives and Workers in California, 1929. A Report Prepared under the Sigmund Stern Foundation.* University of California Publications in Education, vol. 6, no. 4. Berkeley, Calif.: University of California Press. Reprinted New York: Johnson Reprint Corp., 1966.

——. 1931. The Policies of National Governments for the Provision of Recreation of the Wage Worker. Ph.D. thesis, University of California–Berkeley (economics).

Noble, Margaret W. 1891/2. The Progress of Colored People in Washington DC. *Chautauquan* 14 (October/March): 183–.

——. 1891/2. What Women Owe to Inventions. *Chautauquan* 14 (October/March): 725–.

——. 1893/4. Women Keepers for Women Convicts. *Chautauquan* 18 (October/March): 467–.

Noel, Felicia. 1904. Why So Many Women Cannot Find Work. *Irish Monthly* 32 (July).

Noll, Valda Constance [Lyons]. Coauth. *See* Johnson, Elizabeth S.; Palmer, Gladys Louise.

Norris, Ruby Turner. 1930. Some Contributions to the Theory of Wages Found in Business Cycle Literature. A.M. thesis, Leland Stanford Junior University.

——. 1936. The Physical Volume of American Foreign Trade with Leading Countries, 1920–1932. *Review of Economics and Statistics* 18 (May): 89–96.

——. 1938. American Foreign Trade, 1920–1932. Ph.D. thesis, Stanford University (economics).

——. 1939. The Analysis of Demand. *Quarterly Journal of Economics* 54 (November): 131–42.

Northrop, Mildred Benedict. 1923. Mothers' Pensions in Missouri. M.A. thesis, University of Missouri–Columbia.

——. 1938. *Control Policies of the Reichsbank, 1924–1933.* New York: Columbia University Press; London: P. S. King & Son, Ltd. Reprinted New York: AMS Press, 1968.

——. 1938. Control Policies of the Reichsbank, 1924–33. Ph.D. thesis, Columbia University (economics).

Norton, Caroline [Elisabeth] S[heridan]. 1836/1847. *A Voice from the Factories: in Serious Verse.* London: John Murray. American edition Boston: Putnam, 1847. Reprinted Oxford: Woodstock Books, 1994. Online at Indiana University's LETRS.

——. 1838. *The Separation of Mother and Child by the Law of "Custody of Infants" Considered.* London: Roake and Varty. Reprinted in Maria Mulvey Roberts and Tamae Mizuta, eds., *Perspectives on the History of British Feminism*, Vol. 3: *The Mothers: Controversies of Motherhood.* London: Routledge/Thoemmes, 1994.

—— [as "Pearce Stevenson, Esq."]. 1839. *A Plain Letter to the Lord Chancellor on the Infant Custody Bill.* London: James Ridgway. Online at Indiana University's LETRS.

—— [as "Libertas"]. 1848. *Letters to the Mob.* Reprinted from the "Morning Chronicle." London: Thomas Bosworth. Online at Indiana University LETRS.

——. 1854. *English Laws for Women in the Nineteenth Century.* London: Printed for private circulation [J. Wertheimer]. Reprinted Chicago: Academy Chicago, 1982. Online at Indiana University's LETRS.

——. 1855. *A Letter to the Queen on Lord Chancellor Cranworth's Marriage and Divorce Bill.* London: Longman, Brown, Green & Longmans. Online at Indiana University's LETRS.

——. 1856. *The Oppressed Condition of the Dressmakers' and Milliners' Assistants.* The Early Closing Association. London: Kent & Co.

Novich, Berta. 1907. *Maternità e Lavoro.* Milan: Remo Sandron.

Novikoff, Olga Alexeena. 1881. Emperor Alexander's Reforms. *Fraser's*, n.s. 23 [o.s. 103] (January): 30–52.

——. 1882. The Crisis in Serbia. *Contemporary Review* 41 (February): 290–307.

Nute, Grace Lee. 1921. American Foreign Commerce, 1825–1850. Ph.D. thesis, Radcliffe College (history).

——. 1923/4. James Dickson: A Fillibuster in Minnesota in 1836. *Mississippi Valley Historical Review* 10: 127–.

——. 1926. The American Fur Company's Fishing Enterprises on Lake Superior. *Mississippi Valley Historical Review* 12(4) (March): 483–.

——. 1927. The Papers of the American Fur Company: A Brief Estimate of Their Significance. *The American Historical Review* XXXII(3) (April).

——. 1930. Posts in the Minnesota Fur-trading area, 1660–1855. *Minnesota History* 11(4) (December).

——. 1935. *The Three Rivers (Trois-Rivières) Yearbook, 1935. An Annual Survey of Industry, Finance, Trade, Purchasing Power, Municipal and Other Developments in the City of Three Rivers, Province of Quebec, with Special "Economic Survey" Compiled for the "1935 Yearbook."* Three Rivers, Quebec: St. Maurice Valley Chronicle.

——. 1936. Book Review of "Hudson's Bay Company: A Brief History." *Minnesota History* 17: 74–.

O

O'Brien, Charlotte G. 1880. The Irish "Poor Man." *Nineteenth Century* 8(46) (December): 876–87.

——. 1881. Eighty Years [in Ireland]. *Nineteenth Century* 9 (March): 397–414.

——. 1881. The Emigration and Waste-land Clauses. *Fortnightly Review*, n.s. 29 (June): 757–66.

——. 1881. The Horrors of the Emigrant Ship. *Pall Mall Gazette* (May 6).

O'Connell, Mary Anne Bianconi [Mrs. Morgan John O'Connell]. 1879. A Plea for the Poor Hearth. *Irish Monthly* 7: 158–.

——. 1884. The Emigrant in New York. *Nineteenth Century* 16 (October): 530–49.

——. 1880. Poor Law Administration as It Affects Women and Children in Workhouses. *Journal of the Statistical and Social Inquiry Society of Ireland* 8 (April).

——'. 1886. *Munster Land-owning*. London and Dublin: W. Ridgway.

O'Connor, Mrs. Charles. 1879. Our Young Work Girls. *Irish Monthly* 7.

O'Connor, Elizabeth Paschal. 1933. The Worker's Equity in His Job. Ph.D. thesis, University of Wisconsin (economics).

O'Day, Laura. 1930. *Buffalo as a Flour Milling Center*. S.M. thesis, University of Chicago (geography).

——. 1932. Buffalo as a Flour Milling Center. *Economic Geography* 8(1) (January): 81–93.

O'Hare, Kate Richards. 1911. *The Church and the Social Problem*. Saint Louis, Mo.: National Ripsaw Publishing Co.

——. 1911. *Common Sense and the Liquor Traffic*. Saint Louis, Mo.: National Ripsaw Publishing Co.

——. 1911. *Law and the White Slave*. Saint Louis, Mo.: National Ripsaw Publishing Co.

——. 1919. *Americanism and Bolshevism*. St. Louis, Mo.: F. P. O'Hare.

——. 1919. *Socialism and the World War*. St. Louis, Mo: F. P. O'Hare.

——. 1921. *Crime and Criminals*. Girard, Kans: Frank P. O'Hare.

——. 1924. *Gateway to Freedom. The Story of How Workers are Co-operating in the Ownership, Management, Labor and Distribution of Products Where They Own Collectively All Productive Property*. Leesville, La.: Llano Co-operative Colony.

——. 1925. *Prison Labor for Private Profit: Survey and Report on the Prison Labor Situation: Submitted to the Joint Committee on Prison Labor of the Union-made Garment Manufacturers' Association of America and the United Garment Workers of America.* New York: Joint Committee on Prison Labor.

O'Neill, Ellen. 1850. *Extraordinary Confessions of a Female Pickpocket, Seventeen Years of Age, Now in the Preston House of Correction under Sentence of Transportation; Her Serious Charge against the Factory Overlookers of Manchester; also Her Revelations Respecting the Conduct of the Female Factory Operatives of Manchester; Together with her Exploits in Preston.* Preston: J. Drummond.

O'Neill, H. C. and Edith A. Barnett. 1888. *Our Nurses and the Work They Have to Do.* London: Ward, Lock.

O'Neill, H. C. Coauth. *See* Barnett, Edith A.

O'Reilly, Leonora. 1915. *A Working Women's Plea.* New York: New York State Women Suffrage Association.

O'Reilly, Mary [A.]. 1892. Child Labor in Pennsylvania. In *Proceedings of the 6th Annual Convention of Factory Inspectors.* International Association of Factory Inspectors of North America. Boston?: Wright and Potter?

——. 1893. *Report and Statistics of Women Wage Earners of City and County of Philadelphia.* Philadelphia: Committee on Social and Economic Science of the Philadelphia Woman's Auxiliary Committee, Columbian World's Fair.

O'Sullivan, Mary K. 1912. The Labor War at Lawrence. *Survey* 28 (April): 72–4.

Oakeshott, Grace [M.]. 1900. Women in the Cigar Trade in London. *Economic Journal* 10 (December): 562–72.

——. 1903. Artificial Flower-making: An Account of the Trade, and a Plea for Municipal Training. *Economic Journal* (March) 13: 123–31.

——. 1908. *Women's Trades.* Report of the Education Committee of the London County Council, Submitting Report by the Chief Inspector Presenting Reports on Women's Trades. London: Southwood, Smith & Co., Ltd.

Obenauer, Marie Louise. 1913. *Employment of Women in Power Laundries in Milwaukee: A Study of Working Conditions and of the Physical Demands of the Various Laundry Occupations.* Washington: U.S. Government Printing Office.

——. 1913. *Hours, Earnings, and Duration of Employment of Wage-earning Women in Selected Industries in the District of Columbia.* Bulletin of the U.S. Bureau of Labor Statistics, no. 116. Washington: U.S. Government Printing Office.

——. 1913. *Working Hours of Women in the Pea Canneries of Wisconsin, May 5, 1913.* Washington: U.S. Bureau of Labor Statistics.

——. 1924. Living Conditions among Coal Mine Workers of the United States. *American Academy of Political and Social Science, Annals* 111 (January): 12–.

——. 1932. *The Woman Power of the Nation, a Problem of Adjustment: Facts and Factors in Movements of American Women to Meet Changing Conditions in the Economic, Social and Civic Life of the Nation.* New York: Woman's Department, National Civic Federation.

Obenauer, Marie Louise and Helen V. Bary. 1917. *The Regulation of the Fruit and Vegetable Canning Industry of California, May 1917.* Sacramento: California State Printing Office for the California Industrial Welfare Commission.

Obenauer, Marie Louise and Bertha Marie Nienburg. 1915. *Effect of Minimum-wage Determinations in Oregon, July 1915*. Bulletin of the U.S. Department of Labor Statistics, whole no. 176. Women in Industry Series, no. 6. Washington: U.S. Government Printing Office.

Obenauer, Marie Louise and France W. Valentine. 1914. *Hours, Earnings, and Conditions of Labor of Women in Indian Mercantile Establishments and Garment Factories*. Washington: U.S. Commission on Industrial Relations.

Oberholtzer, Sara L. 1892/3 and 1893/4. School Savings Banks. *Annals of the American Academy of Political and Social Science* 3: 14–; and 4: 972–.

Odencrantz, Louise Christine. 1916. *Industrial Conditions in Springfield, Illinois: A Survey by the Committee on Women's Work and the Department of Surveys and Exhibits, Russell Sage Foundation*. New York: Department of Surveys and Exhibits, Russell Sage Foundation.

——. 1919. *Italian Women in Industry: A Study of Conditions in New York City*. New York: Russell Sage Foundation.

——. 1922. International Industrial Welfare Conference. *Personnel Administration* 10(6) (October): 3–.

——. 1922. Personnel Work in America. *Personnel Administration* 10(4) (August): 5–.

——. 1928/9. Cambridge Congress of the International Industrial Relations Association. *Personnel Journal* 7: 226–.

——. 1929. *The Social Worker in Family, Medical and Psychiatric Social Work*. New York: Harper & Brothers.

——. 1940. Recent Developments in Employment Services. *Occupations: The Vocational Guidance Magazine* 18(4) (January): 249–.

Ogg, Elizabeth. 1939. *Longshoremen and Their Homes: The Story of a Housing "Case" Study Conducted under the Auspices of Greenwich House*. New York: Greenwich House.

——. Coauth. *See* Wood, Edith Elmer.

Ogle-Moore, Helen and Edith Hare. 1896. The Work of Women in the White Lead Trade. In Jessie Boucherett and Helen Blackburn, eds., *The Conditions of Women and the Factory Acts*. London: Elliot Stock.

Okey, Ruth Eliza. 1918. Approximate Analysis of the Alcoholic Extract of the Root of Rumex Crispus, and a Comparison of the Hydroxy-Methyl Anthraquinones Present with Those from Certain Other Drugs. Ph.D. thesis, University of Illinois at Urbana–Champaign (health sciences).

——. 1933. *The Foods Chosen by Dependent Families: An Analysis of the Food Purchased by 25 Families Dependent on the Berkeley Welfare Society in May 1932*. Berkeley: University of California.

Okey, Ruth [Eliza] and Emily [Harriett] Huntington. 1932. *Adequate Food at Low Cost*. San Francisco: University of California, Heller Committee for Research in Social Economics.

——. 1933. *Okey–Huntington Allowances for Adequate Food at Low Cost*. Sacramento: California State Printing Office.

Okey, Ruth Eliza and Mary Gorringe Luck. 1934. *Nutritive Value of Foods Purchased by Dependent Families: A Study of Grocery Orders of 233 Families on Relief in Alameda County, California*. Berkeley: University of California.

Okey, Ruth Eliza. Collection of sixty-one Pamphlets from 1917–1965 available at University of California–Berkeley Library.

Okey, Mrs. Thomas. 1908. *Labour Laws for Women in Italy*. London: Women's Industrial Council.

Olcott, Margaret Thompson. 1922. *List of Serials Currently Received in the Library of the U.S. Department of Agriculture, Exclusive of U.S. Government Publications and Publications of the State Agricultural Colleges and Experiment Stations. Arranged by Title, by Subject, and by Region. January 1, 1922*. Washington: U.S. Government Printing Office.

——. 1925. *World Food Supply: A Selected Bibliography*. Washington: U.S. Government Printing Office.

——. 1926. *Alabama*. Washington: U.S. Government Printing Office.

——. 1928. *Taxation and the Farmer: A Selected and Annotated Bibliography*. Agricultural Economics Bibliography, no. 25. Washington: U.S. Department of Agriculture, Bureau of Agricultural Economics.

——. 1939. *Rural Psychology: A Partial List of References*. Washington: U.S. Government Printing Office.

——. 1939. *The World Food Supply: A Partial List of References, 1925–1939*. Washington: U.S. Government Printing Office.

Olcott, Margaret Thompson and Louise Oldham Bercaw. 1926. *Farm Youth: A Selected List of References to Literature Issued since January, 1920*. Washington: U.S. Department of Agriculture, Bureau of Agricultural Economics.

——. 1934. *State Measures for the Relief of Agricultural Indebtedness in the United States 1933 and 1934*. Washington: U.S. Department of Agriculture, Bureau of Agricultural Economics.

Olcott, Margaret Thompson and Margaret G. Lacy. 1929. *Large Scale and Corporation Farming: A Selected List of References*. Washington: U.S. Government Printing Office.

——. 1938. *Income: Selected References on the Concept of Income and Methods of Obtaining Income Statistics*. Agricultural Economics Bibliography, no. 73. Washington: U.S. Department of Agriculture, Bureau of Agricultural Economics.

Olcott, Margaret Thompson, Helen Emma Hennefrund, and Mary G. Lacy, comp. 1935. *Valuation of Real Estate with Special Reference to Farm Real Estate*. Washington: U.S. Government Printing Office.

Olcott, Margaret Thompson. Coauth. *See* Bercaw, Louise Oldham; Colvin, Esther Marie; Day, Emily Louise.

Oldfield, Laura. 1873. Children of the Poor. *Macmillan's* 27 (February): 335–44.

Oldham, Alice. 1890–1. The History of Socialism, Parts I, II, III. *National Review* 16 (November 1890): 310–34; (December 1890): 460–85; (January 1891): 621–49.

Oliphant, Margaret. 1856. The Laws Concerning Women. *Blackwood's* 79 (April): 379–87.

——. 1858. The Condition of Women. *Blackwood's* 83 (February): 139–54.

——. 1861. Social Science. *Blackwood's* 88 (December): 698–715.

——. 1866. The Great Unrepresented [women]. *Blackwood's* 100 (September): 367–79.

——. 1869. Mill on the Subjection of Women. *Edinburgh Review* 130 (October): 572–602. Reprinted in Andrew Pyle, ed., *The Subjection of Women: Contemporary Responses to John Stuart Mill*. Bristol: Thoemmes Press, 1995.

——. 1874. The Indian Mutiny: Sir Hope Grant. *Blackwood's* 115 (January): 102–20.

——. 1877. Harriet Martineau. *Blackwood's* 121 (April): 472–96.

——. 1880. The Grievances of Women. *Fraser's*, n.s. 21 [o.s. 101] (May): 698–710.

——. 1896. The Anti-marriage League. *Blackwood's* 159 (January): 135–49.

Oliphant, Rosamond Dale Owen. 1881. *Woman's Work*. Cincinnati: C. T. Woodrow & Co.

——. 1924. *I. Robert Owen, Co-operation Versus Communism; a Play in Four Acts. II. Arcadia, the Bridal Mystery; Illustrated in One Act*. Worthing: Hollands & Son.

Olson, Helen and A. B. Wolfe. 1919. War-time Industrial Employment of Women in the United States. *Journal of Political Economy* 27(8) (October): 639–69.

Oppenheimer, Mary S. 1897. Employers' Liability. *Charities Review* 6(4) (June): 326–31.

Orchard, Dorothy Johnson. 1929. Agrarian Problems of Modern Japan, Part I. *Journal of Political Economy* 37 (April): 129–49.

——. 1929. Agrarian Problems of Modern Japan, Part II. *Journal of Political Economy* 37 (June): 285–311.

——. 1930. Book Review of "The Effect of the World War upon the Commerce and Industry of Japan" by Kakujiro Yamasaki and Gotaro Ogawa. *Political Science Quarterly* 45: 309–.

——. 1930. China's Use of the Boycott as a Political Weapon. *American Academy of Political and Social Science, Annals* 152 (November): 252–.

——. 1933. China Boycotts Japan. *Asia* 33(1) (January): 10–.

——. 1934. Book Review of "China Industrial Handbooks; No. I, Kiangsu. First Series of the Reports by the National Industrial Investigation. Shanghai" by Chung Kuo Shih Yeh Chi I and Chiang Su Sheng. *Pacific Affairs* 7(1) (March): 95–.

——. 1935. Book Review of "The Dutch East Indies: Its Government, Problems and Politics" by Amry Vandenbosch. *Political Science Quarterly* 50: 473–.

——. 1935/1936. Man-Power in China. *Political Science Quarterly* 50(4) (December 1935); 51(1) (March 1936): 561–.

——. 1936. Book Review of "Made in Japan" by Guenther Stein. *Political Science Quarterly* 51: 621.

——. 1936. Book Review of "Social Aspects of Industrial Development in Japan" by Fernand Maurette. *Political Science Quarterly* 51: 621.

——. 1939. Flight to Chungking. *Amerasia* 3(9) (November): 403–.

——. 1939. The Outlook in Japan. *Amerasia* 3(10) (December): 465–.

——. 1940. *India Enters the Machine Age*. Columbia University Council for Research in the Social Sciences, Project 10, vol. 8. New York: Columbia University. Also published in *Asia* 40(4) (April): 212–.

——. 1940. Manchuria – A Pattern of the "New Order in East Asia." *Asia* 40(1) (January): 36–.

Orme, Eliza. 1893. *A Barmaid's Life as It Really Is: Facts Given in the Parliamentary Reports of the Labour Commission of 1893*. London: Church of England Temperance Society.

——. 1897. How Poor Ladies Live: A Reply. *Nineteenth Century* 41(242) (April): 613–19.

——. 1898. Prison Reform: Our Female Criminals. *Fortnightly Review*, n.s. 63 (May): 790–6.

Orme, Eliza, Clara Elizabeth Collet, Margaret H. Irwin, and May E. Abraham [Tennant]. 1893. *The Employment of Women: Reports by the Lady Assistant Commissioners on the Conditions of Work in Various Industries in England, Wales, Scotland and Ireland*. Presented to Parliament in February 1893. Royal Commission on Labour. London: Printed for H.M. Stationery Office, by Eyre and Spottiswoode. Cmnd 6703-V, 6894-VIII, 7063, and 7421.

Ormsbee, Elizabeth Paschal. 1934. The Worker's Equity in His Job. Ph.D. thesis, University of Wisconsin–Madison.

Ormsbee, Hazel Grant. 1926. The Young Employed Girl. Ph.D. thesis, Bryn Mawr College (economics).

——. 1927. *The Young Employed Girl*. New York: Woman's Press.

Ormsby, Hilda Rodwell. 1924. *London on the Thames: A Study of the Natural Conditions That Influenced the Birth and Growth of a Great City*. London: Sifton, Praed & Co.

——. 1931. *France: A Regional and Economic Geography*. New York: E. P. Dutton and Company.

——. 1932. Book Review of "Economic Geography of Europe" by W. O. Blanchard and S. S. Vischer. *Economica* 12: 276.

——. 1933. Book Review of "The Geography of the Mediterranean Region" by Ellen C. Semple. *Economica* 13: 108.

——. 1933. Book Review of "South Europe, a Regional and Economic Geography of the Mediterranean Lands" by Marion I. Newbigin. *Economica* 13: 108.

Ormsby, Margaret Anchoretta. 1935. Fruit Marketing in the Okanagan Valley of British Columbia. *Agricultural History* 9 (April): 80–97.

——. 1937. The Relations between British Columbia and the Dominion of Canada, 1871–1885. Ph.D. thesis, Bryn Mawr College (history).

Orr, Harriet K. 1935. Cooperation in Principle and Practice: The Trend in Wyoming. Ph.D. thesis, University of California–Berkeley (economics).

Osborn, Christabel [as "C.O."]. 1893. Report of the Bureau of Labour Statistics, Connecticut. *Economic Journal* 3(10) (June): 358–60.

—— [as "C.O."]. 1894. Compulsory Insurance: Special Report on Compulsory Insurance in Germany. *Economic Journal* 4(14) (June): 355–61.

—— [as "C.O."]. 1894. Report on Agencies and Methods for Dealing with the Unemployed. *Economic Journal* 4(13) (March): 181–5.

——. 1895. The Slums of Great Cities. *Economic Journal* 5(19) (September): 474–6.

——. 1895. Trade Depression in Maine. *Economic Journal* 5(19) (September): 476–7.

——. 1896. Agricultural Depression in New York State, USA. *Economic Journal* 6(22): 317.

——. 1896. Bulletin of the United States Labour Department, no. 1. *Economic Journal* 6(21) (March): 154–6.

——. 1896. Bulletin of US Department of Labour No. 2, Jan. 1896. *Economic Journal* 6(22) (June): 314–16.

——. 1896. Bulletins of the United States Labour Department, No. 3, No. 4, No. 5. *Economic Journal* 6(24) (December): 653–60.

——. 1897. Bulletins of the United States Department of Labour, nos. 7 and 9. *Economic Journal* 7(26) (June): 295–7.

——?. 1897. Congress of Economists at Brussels. *Economic Journal* 7(26) (June): 293–5.

——. 1898. *Domestic Service in the United States* by Lucy Maynard Salmon. *Economic Journal* 8(29) (March): 95–7.

——. 1898. Economic Aspects of the Liquor Problem. Twelfth Annual Report of the Commissioner of Labour, U.S.A. *Economic Journal* 8(32) (December): 572–7.

——. 1898. Railway Brotherhoods in the United States. *Economic Journal* 8(32) (December): 577–9.

——. 1899. The United States Bulletin of Labour. *Economic Journal* 9(35) (September): 483–9.

——, ed. 1900. *Manuals of Employment for Educated Women*, 1: *Secondary Teaching*; 2: *Elementary Teaching*; 3: *Sick Nursing*; 4: *Medicine*. London: Walter Scott.

——. 1900. Book Review of "Slavery as an Industrial System" by H. J. Niebohr. *Economic Journal* 10: 527–.

——. 1900. Bulletin of the United States Department of Labour [Notes and Memoranda]. *Economic Journal* 10: 582–.

——. 1901. Book Review of "Commerce and Christianity." *Economic Journal* 11: 200–.

——. 1901. Book Review of "Massachusetts Labour Legislation. An Historical and Critical Study" by Sarah Scovill Whittelsey. *Economic Journal* 11: 207–.

——. 1901. The Dockers' Strike at Marseilles. *Economic Journal* 11 (December): 604–7.

——. 1901. Trusts and Trade Combinations in Europe [Notes and Memoranda]. *Economic Journal* 11: 271–.

——. 1903. Book Review of "Constructive and Preventive Philanthropy" by Joseph Lee. *Economic Journal* 13: 588.

——. 1903. Book Review of "The Employment of Women in the Clothing Trade" by Maud Hurt Willett. *Economic Journal* 13(51) (September): 415–18.

——. 1903. Book Review of "A History of Factory Legislation" by B. L. Hutchins and A. Harrison. *Economic Journal* 13: 585–.

——. 1903. Book Review of "Our Benevolent Feudalism" by W. J. Ghent. *Economic Journal* 13: 588.

——. 1903. The Work of Women in France. *Economic Journal* 13 (March): 131–3.

——. 1904. Book Review of "Les Systèmes socialistes et l'évolution économique" by Maurice Bourguin. *Economic Journal* 14: 589–.

——. 1911. Rowtown Houses for Women. *Contemporary Review* 99 (June): 707–.

Osgood, Ellen. 1921/1935. *A History of Industry*. Boston: Ginn & Co.

Otenasek, Mildred B. 1939. Alexander Hamilton's Financial Policies. Ph.D. thesis, Johns Hopkins University (economics).

Otey, Elizabeth Dabney Langhorne Lewis. 1910. *The Beginnings of Child Labor Legislation in Certain States*. Washington: U.S. Bureau of Labor.

——. 1913. *Employers' Welfare Work, May 15, 1913*. Washington: U.S. Bureau of Labor Statistics.

——. 1924. *The Cotton Mill Workers on Jones Falls, Baltimore*. Pamphlet, no. 1. Baltimore: Christian Social Justice Fund.

——. 1928. Is the New South Forgetting the Human Side of Industry? *American Labor Legislation Review* 18: 26–.

——. 1931. Women and Children in Southern Industry. *American Academy of Political and Social Science, Annals* 153 (January): 163–.

——. 1939. Cash Benefits under Voluntary Disability Insurance. *Social Security Bulletin* 2(2) (February): 27–.

Otto, Louise. *See* [Peters] Louise Otto.

Otto, Rose, 1910. *Über Fabrikarbeit verheirateter Frauen*. Stuttgart and Berlin: J. G. Cotta.

Outwater, Olive E. 1920. An American Accident Table. *Journal of the American Statistical Association* 17 (December): 492–5.

Ovington, Mary White. 1905. The Negro Home in New York. *Charities* XV: 25–30.

——. 1911. *Half a Man: The Status of the Negro in New York*. New York: Longmans, Green.

——. 1914. *How the National Association for the Advancement of Colored People Began*. New York: National Association for the Advancement of Colored People.

——. 1927. *Portraits in Color*. New York: Viking Press.

Owen, Catherine. 1889. Are Women to Blame? *North American Review* 148 (May): 633–7.

——. 1889. Is Housekeeping a Failure? *North American Review* 148 (February): 254–7.

Owen, Marianne E. 1866. Criminal Women. *Cornhill Magazine* 14 (August): 152–60.

Owens, Martha J. 1895. How Many Women Are Going into Business. *Chautauquan* 21 (June): 337–.

——. 1895/6. How to Get a Business Education. *Chautauquan* 22 (September/March): 213–.

Owenson, Sydney [Lady Morgan]. 1825. *Absenteeism*. London: H. Colburn.

——. 1840. *Woman and Her Master*. London: H. Colburn.

P

Packard, Esther. 1915. *A Study of Living Conditions of Self-supporting Women in New York City*. New York: YWCA.

Pacquet-Mille, Mme. A. 1891. *Nouveau Guide pratique des jeunes filles dans le choix d'une profession.* Paris: Lecène, Oudin.

Page, Anne B. 1913. Labor Laws for Women and Children at Home and Abroad. *Women's Industrial News* (October).

Page, Frances Mary. 1929. "Bidentes Hoylandie" a Medieval Sheep Farm. *Economic History* 1 (January): 603–13.

——. 1929/30. The Customary Poor Law of three Cambridgeshire Manors. *Cambridge Historical Journal* 3: 125–.

Page Bates, Helen. *See* Bates, Helen Frances Page.

Paget, Lady [Walburga]. 1886. The Present State of Peasant Proprietors in Germany. *National Review* 8(46) (December): 542–8.

Palliser, Mrs. Bury [Fanny]. 1865. *History of Lace.* London: Sampson Low, Son, & Marston.

Pallister, Minnie. 1924. *The Orange-box. Thoughts of a Socialist Propagandist.* London: Leonard Parsons.

——. 1925. *Socialism, Equality and Happiness.* London: Independent Labour Party.

——. 1925. *Socialism for Women.* London: Independent Labour Party.

Palmer, Alice Freeman. 1891. A Review of the Higher Education of Women. *Forum* 12 (September): 28–40.

——. 1893. Some Lasting Results of the World's Fair. *Forum* 16 (December): 517–23.

Palmer, Gladys Louise. 1925. *Labor Relations in the Lace and Lace-curtain Industries in the United States.* Washington: U.S. Government Printing Office.

——. 1925. The Honors Courses Conference at the State University of Iowa. *School and Society* 21(547) (June 20): 749–.

——. 1925. Labor Relations in the Lace and Lace-curtain Industries. Ph.D. thesis, University of Pennsylvania (economics).

——. 1927. The Community Chest in Virginia Cities. *Social Forces* 6(2) (December): 229–36.

——. 1928. Trade Custom in the Lancashire Cotton Industry. *Journal of Political Economy* 36(3) (June): 391–8.

——. 1930. Job-conscious Unionism in the Chicago Men's Clothing Industry. *American Economic Review* 20(1) (March): 28–36.

——. 1931. *The Industrial Experience of Women Workers at the Summer Schools, 1928 to 1930*. Washington: U.S. Government Printing Office.

——. 1932. *Union Tactics and Economic Change: A Case Study of Three Philadelphia Textile Unions*. Philadelphia: University of Pennsylvania Press. Reprinted New York: Arno Press, 1971.

——. 1932. History of the Philadelphia District Textile Council. *American Federationist* 39(10) (October): 1,133–.

——. 1933. *Thirty Thousand in Search of Work*. Philadelphia: Pennsylvania Department of Labor and Industry/Pennsylvania State Employment Commission.

——. 1934. *Depression Jobs: A Study of Job Openings in the Philadelphia Employment Office, 1932–1933*. Philadelphia: Industrial Research Department, Wharton School of Finance and Commerce, University of Pennsylvania.

——. 1934. An Analysis of Labor Surplus in Philadelphia. *Occupations: The Vocational Guidance Magazine* 12(6) (February): 48–.

——. 1935. Characteristics of the Jobless. *Personnel Journal* 14(6) (December): 222–.

——. 1936. *The Incidence and Duration of Unemployment among New Applicants [at the] Philadelphia State Employment Office, 1934*. Philadelphia Employment Market Studies, Special Report A–7. Philadelphia: University of Pennsylvania, Wharton School of Finance and Commerce, Industrial Research Department.

——. 1936. Book Review of "The Clothing Workers" by J. Hardy. *American Academy of Political and Social Science, Annals* 184 (March): 220–.

——. 1937. *Recent Trends in Employment and Unemployment in Philadelphia*. Philadelphia Labor Market Studies Series, report no. P–1. Philadelphia: Univerisity of Pennsylvania, Wharton School of Finance and Commerce, Industrial Research Department.

——. 1939. *The Search for Work in Philadelphia, 1932–36: An Analysis of Records of the Philadelphia State Employment Office*. Philadelphia Labor Market Studies, Report no. P–7. Philadelphia: University of Pennsylvania, Wharton School of Finance and Commerce, Industrial Research Department.

——. 1939. The Convertibility List of Occupations and the Problems of Developing It. *Journal of the American Statistical Association* 34 (December): 693–708.

——. 1940. Review of Hours and Wages in American Organized Labor. *American Economic Review* 30(1) (March): 178–9.

Palmer, Gladys Louise and Margaret W. Bell. 1938. *Employment and Unemployment in Philadelphia in 1936 and 1937*. Works Progress Administration, National Research Project in cooperation with Industrial Research Department, University of Pennsylvania. Philadelphia Labor Market Studies, Report no. P–3. Philadelphia: University of Pennsylvania, Wharton School of Finance and Commerce, Industrial Research Department.

Palmer, Gladys Louise and Janet H. Lewis. 1939. *The Long-term Unemployed in Philadelphia in 1936: A Study of the Chief Wage Earners of Families on Relief for the*

Works Program for Two Years Prior to August 1936. Works Progress Administration, National Research Project in cooperation with Industrial Research Department, University of Pennsylvania. Philadelphia Labor Market Studies, Report no. P–8. Philadelphia: University of Pennsylvania, Wharton School of Finance and Commerce, Industrial Research Department.

Palmer, Gladys Louise and Ada M. Stoflet. 1938. *The Labor Force of the Philadelphia Radio Industry in 1936.* Philadelphia Labor Market Studies, Report no. P–2. Philadelphia: University of Pennsylvania, Wharton School of Finance and Commerce, Industrial Research Department.

Palmer, Gladys Louise and Katherine Dorothy Klueter Wood. 1936/1937. *Urban Workers on Relief,* vol. 1: *The Occupational Characteristics of Workers on Relief in Urban Areas,* May, 1934; vol. 2: *The Occupational Characteristics of Workers on Relief in 79 Cities,* May, 1934. Washington: Works Progress Administration. Reprinted New York: Da Capo Press, 1971.

Palmer, Gladys Louise, Kate Edelman, M. Eileen Leach, and Helen L. Klopfer. 1939. *Ten Years of Work Experience of Philadelphia Weavers and Loom Fixers.* National Research Project on Reemployment Opportunities and Recent Changes in Industrial Techniques, Philadelphia Labor Market Studies, Report no. P–4. Works Progress Administration, National Research Project in cooperation with Industrial Research Department, University of Pennsylvania. Philadelphia: University of Pennsylvania, Wharton School of Finance and Commerce, Industrial Research Department.

Palmer, Gladys Louise, Constance Willard Williams, and Valda Constance Lyons Noll. 1939. *Reemployment of Philadelphia Hosiery Workers after Shutdowns in 1933–34.* Works Progress Administration, National Research Project in cooperation with Industrial Research Department, University of Pennsylvania. Philadelphia Labor Market Studies, Report no. P–6. Philadelphia: University of Pennsylvania, Wharton School of Finance and Commerce, Industrial Research Department.

Palmer, Gladys Louise. Coauth. *See* Hourwich, Andria Taylor.

Pancoast, Elinor [Evangeline]. 1921. *The Prohibition of Night Work for Women.* Study Leaflet Series, no. 7, Pamphlets in American History. Washington: National League of Women Voters, Committee on Women in Industry.

——. 1922. *A Study of the Programs of Industrial Relations Issued by Twelve American Organizations.* M.A. thesis, University of Chicago.

——. 1927. The Photoengravers' Union. Ph.D. thesis, University of Chicago (economics).

——. 1936. Summer School for Office Workers. *American Federationist* 43(10) (October): 1,052–.

——. 1938. Social Education in an Adult Summer School. *Social Education* 2(8) (November): 536–.

Pancoast, Elinor and Anne E. Lincoln. 1940. *The Incorrigible Idealist: Robert Dale Owen in America.* Bloomington: Principia Press.

Pancoast, Elinor. Coauth. *See* Holst, Elise.

Pankhurst, E. Sylvia. 1919. *La Grande Conspiration contre le socialisme russe et allemand.* Petrograd: s.n.

——. 1919. *Housing & the Workers' Revolution: Housing in Capitalist Britain and Bolshevik Russia.* London: Workers' Socialist Federation.

——. 1921. *Soviet Russia as I Saw It.* London: Workers' Dreadnought Publishers.

——. 1922. *The Truth about the Oil War.* London: Workers' Dreadnought Publishers.

——. 1924. *Education of the Masses.* London: Workers' Dreadnought Publishers.

——. 1926. *India and the Earthly Paradise.* Bombay: Sunshine Publishing House.

——. 1930. *Save the Mothers. A Plea for Measures to Prevent the Annual Loss of about 3000 Child-bearing Mothers and 20,000 Infant Lives in England and Wales, and a Similar Grievous Wastage in Other Countries.* London: Knopf.

Papa, Mrs. Dario [Fidella Dinsmore]. 1898. Hunger and Poverty in Italy. *North American Review* 167(1) (July): 126.

——. 1899. The Italian Revolt. *Arena* 21(5) (May): 646–66.

Papworth, Lucy Wyatt. 1907. Laundry Work and Legislation. *Month: A Catholic Magazine* 109(515) (May): 468–.

Papworth, Lucy Wyatt and Dorothy M. Zimmern. 1912. *Clothing and Textile Trades.* London: Women's Industrial Council.

——. 1914. *The Occupations of Women According to the Census of England and Wales, 1911.* London: Women's Industrial Council.

——. 1915. *Women in Industry: A Bibliography.* London: Women's Industrial Council.

Paradise, Viola. 1922. *Child Labor and the Work of Mothers in Oyster and Shrimp Canning Communities on the Gulf Coast.* Washington: U.S. Department of Labor, Children's Bureau.

——. 1939. With the Immigrants' Protective League. *Child* 4(2) (August): 35–.

Parce, Lida. 1900. *The Cost of Living and the Ballot.* New York: National American Woman Suffrage Association.

——. 1908. *Lesson Outlines in the Economic Interpretation of History.* Girard, Kans.: Humanist Publishing Co.

——. 1913. *Economic Determinism, or the Economic Interpretation of History.* Chicago: C. H. Kerr & Co.

Parker, Coralie. 1928. *The History of Taxation in North Carolina during the Colonial Period.* New York: Columbia University Press.

——. 1928. The History of Taxation in North Carolina during the Colonial Period. Ph. D thesis, Columbia University.

Parker, Cornelia S[tratton]. 1920. The Human Element in the Machine Process. *American Academy of Political and Social Science, Annals* 90 (July): 88–.

——. 1921. Days in a Laundry. *Harper's Monthly Magazine* 143 (June/November): 380–.

——. 1921. In a Brassworks. *Harper's Monthly Magazine* 143 (June/November): 164–.

——. 1921. In a Dress Factory. *Harper's Monthly Magazine* 143 (June/November): 651–.

——. 1921. Labeling Pillow Cases in a Bleachery. *Harper's Monthly Magazine* 143 (June/November): 772–.

——. 1921. No. 1075 Packs Chocolates. *Harper's Monthly Magazine* 143 (June): 64–.

——. 1921/2. Working with the Working Woman – VI: Pantry Girl in a New York Hotel. *Harper's Monthly Magazine* 144 (December/May): 109–.

——. 1922. *Working with the Working Woman.* New York, London: Harper & Brothers.

Parker, Eliza R. 1886. *Economical Housekeeping: Complete System of Household Management for Those Who Wish to Live Well at a Moderate Cost: All Branches of Cookery Are Carefully Treated, and Information Given on Canning Fruits, Curing Meats, Making Butter, Washing, Ironing, Dyeing, Renovating, the Toilet, Care of the Sick, Rearing of Children, Cultivating Flowers, Bee Culture, Silk Culture, the Poultry Yard, and Much Else that Is Valuable to Every Housekeeper.* Toronto: J.S. Robertson.

Parker, Florence E[velyn]. 1918. Effect of Railway Nationalization on Wages, Hours, and Transportation Rates. *United States Bureau of Labor Statistics, Monthly Review* 6 (January/June): 1,071–92.

——. 1920. Aims and Possibilities of the Consumers' Cooperative Movement. *Monthly Labor Review* 10(6) (June): 117–22.

——. 1920. Comparative Study of the Cooperative Movement in Various Countries. *Monthly Labor Review* 11 (July/December): 153–67.

——. 1920. Consumers' Cooperative Wholesale Societies in the United States. *Monthly Labor Review* 10(4) (April): 117–28.

——. 1920. The Cooperative Movement in the United States. *Monthly Labor Review* 10(3) (March): 138–45.

——. 1920. Elements of Success and Possibilities of Saving in Cooperative Stores. *Monthly Labor Review* 11 (July/December): 136–.

——. 1921. All-American Cooperative Congress. *Monthly Labor Review* 12 (January/June): 118–21.

——. 1922. The Consumers' Co-operative Movement in the United States. *International Labour Review* (December): 917–.

——. 1923. *Consumers' Cooperative Societies in the United States in 1920.* Bulletin of the United States Bureau of Labor Statistics, Miscellaneous Series no. 313. Washington: U.S. Government Printing Office.

——. 1924. Development and Operation of Pilots' Associations at Representative Ports. *Monthly Labor Review* 19 (July/December): 16–36.

——. 1925. The Cooperative movement: A Selected Bibliography. *Monthly Labor Review* 20 (January/June): 201–32.

——. 1927. *Cooperative Movement in the United States in 1925 (Other than Agricultural).* Bulletin of the United States Bureau of Labor Statistics, Miscellaneous Series, no. 437. Washington: U.S. Government Printing Office.

——. 1928. *Beneficial Activities of American Trade Unions.* Bulletin of the U.S. Bureau of Labor Statistics, Miscellaneous Series. Washington: U.S. Government Printing Office.

——. 1929. *Cooperation of Trade-unions with Employers.* U.S. Bureau of Labor Statistics Bulletin, no. 465. Washington: U.S. Government Printing Office.

——. 1931. *Consumers' Credit, and Productive Cooperative Societies, 1929.* U.S. Bureau of Labor Statistics Bulletin, Miscellaneous Series no. 531. Washington: U.S. Government Printing Office.

——. 1934. Experience under State Old-age Pension Acts in 1933. *Monthly Labor Review* 39(2) (August): 255–.

——. 1934. Operation of Local Consumers' Cooperative Societies in 1933. *Monthly Labor Review* 39(5) (November): 1,041–.

——. 1934. Operations of Cooperative Credit Societies in 1933. *Monthly Labor Review* 39(3) (September): 551–.

——. 1935. *Consumers' Credit and Productive Cooperation in 1933.* U.S. Bureau of Labor Statistics Bulletin, no. 612. Washington: U.S. Government Printing Office.

——. 1935. Experience under State Old-age Pension Acts in 1934. *Monthly Labor Review* 41(2) (August): 303–.

——. 1935. Self-help Activities among the Unemployed in Washington, D.C. *Monthly Labor Review* 40(3) (March): 604–.

——. 1937. Consumers' Coöperation in the United States. *American Academy of Political and Social Science, Annals* 191 (May): 91–.

——. 1939. *Activities of Credit Unions.* Washington: U.S. Government Printing Office.

——. 1940. *Activities of Credit Unions in 1943–45*[?]. Washington: U.S. Government Printing Office for the U.S. Bureau of Labor Statistics.

Parker, Florence Evelyn and Jean Atherton Flexner. 1937. *Consumer Cooperatives in the United States. 1937–40.* U.S. Bureau of Labor Statistics, Serial no. R 1941–. Washington: U.S. Government Printing Office.

Parker, Florence Evelyn, Estelle M. Stewart, and Mary Conyington. 1929. *Care of Aged Persons in the United States.* U.S. Bureau of Labor Statistics Bulletin, Miscellaneous Series no. 489. Washington: U.S. Government Printing Office.

Parker, Helen Cameron. 1893. Technical Schools for Women. *Canadian* 1: 634–.

Parker, Ida White. 1923. Women in the Insurance Fields. *Businesswoman* (January): 17–18.

Parker, Jane M. 1898. Profit Sharing and Domestic Service. *North American Review* 166(5) (May): 639–.

Parker, N. 1884. *A Year's Work amongst Factory Girls.* London: Hatchards.

Parkes, Bessie Rayner. *See* Belloc, Bessie Rayner Parkes.

Parkhurst, Eleanor. 1937. Poor Relief in a Massachusetts Village in the Eighteenth Century. *Social Service Review* 11 (September): 446–64. Reprinted in Frank R. Brent and Steven J. Diner, eds., *Compassion and Responsibility: Readings in the History of Social Welfare and Policy in the United States.* Chicago: University of Chicago Press, 1980.

Parloa, Maria. 1879. *First Principles of Household Management and Cookery: A Textbook for Schools and Families.* Boston: Houghton, Osgood.

——. 1889. Is Housekeeping a Failure? *North American Review* 148 (February): 257–60.

——. 1898. *Home Economics, a Guide to Household Management Including the Proper Treatment of the Materials Entering into the Construction and the Furnishing of the House….* New York: Century Co.

——. 1906. *Home Economics.* New York: The Century Company.

Parmele, Mary. 1891. Thoughts about Money. *Lend a Hand* 6(5) (May): 293.

Parris, Marion. 1908. Total Utility and the Economic Judgment. Ph.D. thesis, Bryn Mawr College (economics).

——. 1909. *Total Utility and the Economic Judgment Compared with Their Ethical Counterparts.* Philadelphia: J. C. Winston Co.

——. 1911. Book Review of "The Common Sense of Political Economy" by P. H. Wicksteed. *American Academy of Political and Social Science, Annals* 37 (January/June): 574–.

Parsons, Lucy E. 1884. To Tramps, the Unemployed, the Disinherited, and Miserable. *Alarm* (October 4). Reprinted as leaflet, Chicago: International Working People's Association.

——, ed. 1884. *Anarchism: Its Philosophy and Scientific Basis as Defined by Some of Its Apostles: Writings of Albert R. Parsons.* Chicago: A. R. Parsons.

——. 1890s. The Principles of Anarchism: A Lecture. Chicago: L. E. Parsons.

Parten, Mildred Bernice. 1929. An Analysis of Social Participation, Leadership, and Other Factors in Pre-school Play Groups. Ph.D. thesis, University of Minnesota (sociology).

——. 1932. A Statistical Analysis of the Modern Family. *American Academy of Political and Social Science, Annals* 160 (March): 29–.

——. 1935. Book Review of "Elementary Statistics" by James G. Smith. *American Academy of Political and Social Science, Annals* 177 (January): 285–.

——. 1937. Size and Composition of American Families. *American Sociological Review* 2(1/6): 638–.

Parten, Mildred and Erika H. Schoenberg. 1937. Methods and Problems of Sampling Presented by the Urban Study of Consumer Purchases. *Journal of the American Statistical Association* 32(198) (June): 311–22.

Parton, Mabel. 1905. *Women's Work in Rubber Factories, Its Effect on Health: Report of an Investigation of Certain Trades.* Boston: Joint Committee on Sanitary and Industrial Conditions of the Massachusetts State Federation of Women's Clubs and the Women's Educational and Industrial Union.

——. 1905. *The Work of Women and Children in Cordage and Twine Factories, Its Effect on Health: Report of an Investigation of Certain Trades.* Boston: Joint Committee on Sanitary and Industrial Conditions of the Massachusetts State Federation of Women's Clubs and the Women's Educational and Industrial Union.

Parton, Mabel and Caroline Manning. 1911. Unregulated Conditions in Women's Work. In Susan Myra Kingsbury, Charles Edward Person, and Edith Gertrude Solenberger, eds., *Labor Laws and Their Enforcement with Special Reference to Massachusetts.* New York: Longmans, Green.

Parton, Sara Willis [as "Fanny Fern"]. 1855. *Ruth Hall: A Domestic Tale of the Present Time.* London: Routledge; New York: Mason Brothers. Reprinted London and New York: Penguin, 1997. [*novel*]

Paterson, Emma. 1874. The Position of Working Women and How to Improve It. *Labour News* (April).

——. 1875. The Position of Women Engaged in Handicrafts and Other Industrial Pursuits. *Englishwoman's Review*, n.s. 21 (January): 1–12. Reprinted as pamphlet, London: Women's Protective and Provident League.

——. 1885. Continuity of Employment and Rates of Wages. In *Industrial Remuneration Conference, 1885: The Report of Proceedings and Papers.* London: Cassell. Reprinted New York: Augustus M. Kelley, 1968.

——. 1886. Preface. In Thomas Paterson, *A New Method of Mental Science with Applications to Political Economy*. London: Women's Printing Society.

Patrick, Mary Mills. 1896. Education of Women in Turkey. *Forum* 21 (June): 440–8.

Patterson, Florence Edith. 1936. *The Development of the American Policy of Non-recognition.* S.M. thesis, University of Chicago (international relations).

Pattison, Emilia Frances Strong. *See* Dilke, Lady Emilia.

Pattison, Mary [Mrs. Frank Pattison]. 1913. Scientific Management in Home-making. *Annals of the American Academy of Political and Social Science* 48 (July): 96–8.

——. 1915. *The Business of Home Management.* New York: Robert McBride.

——. 1915. *The Principles of Domestic Engineering, or The What, Why and How of a Home; an Attempt to Evolve a Solution to the Domestic "Labor and Capital" Problem.* New York: Women's Club of New Jersey.

Patton, Francine E. 1893. *Illinois Women's Work.* Springfield, Ill.: Illinois State Register Print.

Patton, Mary Brown. 1937. *Suggested Family Budget at Minimum Cost.* Rev. ed. Columbus, Ohio: Department of Public Welfare, Division of Public Assistance, Bureau of Aid to Dependent Children.

Paulet, Lady Charlotte Josephine Howard. 1896. Early Days in Rhodesia. *New Review* 14 (June): 696–702.

Peabody, Elizabeth R. 1870. Industrial Schools for Women. *Harper's* 40 (May): 885–91.

Peck, Annie S[mith]. 1922. *Industrial and Commercial South America.* London: Fisher Unwin.

Peirce, [Harriet] Melusina Fay [Mrs. Charles Sanders Peirce] [as "Mrs. C. F. Peirce"]. 1868–9. Co-operative Housekeeping. *Atlantic Monthly* 22 (November): 513–24; (December): 682–97; 23 (January): 29–39; (February): 161–71; (March): 286–99.

——. 1870. *Cooperative Housekeeping: Romance in Domestic Economy.* Edinburgh: John Ross & Co; London: Sampson, Low, and Son and Marston.

——. 1884. *Co-operative Housekeeping: How Not to Do It and How to Do It, a Study in Sociology.* Boston: James R. Osgood & Co.

Peixotto, Jessica Blanche. 1900. A Comparative Study of the Principles of the French Revolution and the Doctrines of Modern French Socialism, with the

Origin and Development of Each. Ph.D. thesis, University of California–Berkeley (political science).
——. 1901. *The French Revolution and Modern French Socialism: A Comparative Study of the Principles of the French Revolution and the Doctrines of Modern French Socialism.* New York: T. Y. Crowell.
——. 1904. Bourgain's Examination of Socialism. *Journal of Political Economy* 13: 98–108.
——. 1908. Women of California as Trade Unionists. *Association of Collegiate Alumnae, Publications* 3(18) (December): 40–.
——. 1913. Relief Work of the Associated Charities. Part V in *San Francisco Relief Survey: The Organization and Methods of Relief Used after the Earthquake and Fire of April 18, 1906.* New York: Survey Associates.
——. 1915. New Ideals for the Schools. *Child Labor Bulletin* 4: 118–22.
——. 1916. California's Children: Some Recent Steps in State Child-Welfare Work. *Survey* 36: 537–40.
——. 1918. The Children's Year and the Woman's Committee. *Annals of the American Academy of Political and Social Sciences* 79: 257–62.
——. 1919. Minimum Wages for Minors. In *Standards of Child Welfare.* U.S. Children's Bureau Bulletin, no. 60. Washington: U.S. Government Printing Office.
——. 1923. *The Control of Poverty: Economics 180.* Berkeley: University of California Press.
——. 1923. Book Review of "The American Standard of Living and World Cooperation." *American Economic Review* 13(3) (September): 525–6.
——. 1923. The Case for Coeducation. *Forum* LXX: 2,059–66.
——. 1924. The Business Man and the Consumer. *Commercia* V: 2–9.
——. 1927. *Getting and Spending at the Professional Standard of Living: A Study of the Costs of Living of Academic Life.* New York: Macmillan.
——. 1927. Family Budgets. *American Economic Review* 17(1): 132–40.
——. 1928. *The Dependent Aged of San Francisco.* Berkeley: University of California Press.
——. 1928. Family Budgets of University Faculty Members. *Science*, n.s. LXVIII: 497–501.
——. 1929. *Cost of Living Studies II: How Workers Spend a Living Wage, a Study of the Incomes and Expenditures of Eighty-two Typographers' Families in San Francisco.* Berkeley: University of California Press.
Peixotto, Jessica Blanche and O. A. Jeschien. 1917. *The Economizer: An Efficient Household Account Book that Does Not Require Tedious Bookkeeping.* Berkeley: University of California Press.
Peixotto, Jessica Blanche *et al.* 1923. *Cost of Living Survey: Report to the California Civil Service Commission Relative to Cost of Living in California for Selected Family Groups.* Sacramento: California State Printing Office.
Peixotto, Jessica B. *et al.* 1932. *Budget for Dependent Families or Children: For Use by Social Welfare Agencies.* Berkeley, Calif.: University of California–Berkeley, Heller Committee for Research in Social Economics.

Peixotto, Jessica B. Papers located at the Bancroft Library, University of California, Berkeley.

Pelletier, Madeleine. 1914. *L'Education féministe des filles.* Paris: s.n.

——. 1922. *Mon Voyage aventureux en Russie communiste.* Paris: s.n.

——. 1926. *Capitalisme et communisme.* Nice: s.n.

Pennell, Elizabeth Robins. 1884. *Life of Mary Wollstonecraft.* Boston: Roberts Brothers.

Pennell, Maryland Young. Coauth. *See* Kyrk, Hazel; Monroe, Day.

Penny, Virginia. 1862. *How Women Can Make Money: Married or Single: In All Branches of the Arts and Sciences, Professions, Trades, Agricultural and Mechanical Pursuits.* Philadelphia: John E. Potter & Co. Also published as *The Employments of Women: A Cyclopaedia of Woman's Work.* Boston: Walker, Wise & Co. 2nd ed., titled *500 Employments Adapted to Women, Married or Single: In All Branches of the Arts and Sciences, Trades, Professions, Agricultural and Mechanical Pursuits, etc., with the Average Rate of Pay in Each.* Philadelphia: J. E. Potter & Co., 1868. Reprinted, with introduction by Leon Stein and Philip Taft, New York: Arno Press, 1971.

——. 1869. *Think and Act. A Series of Articles Pertaining to Men and Women, Work and Wages.* Philadelphia: Claxton, Remsen & Haffelfinger. Reprinted New York: Arno Press, 1971.

Penrose, Edith Tilton. 1940. *Food Control in Great Britain.* Geneva: International Labour Office.

Penson, Lilian M. 1924. *The Colonial Agents of the British West Indies: A Study in Colonial Administration Mainly in the Eighteenth Century.* London: University Press.

Perham, Margery F. 1934. Some Problems of Indirect Rule in Africa. *Journal of the Royal Society of Arts* 82 (May): 689–710.

——. 1937. *Native Administration in Nigeria.* London and New York: Oxford University Press.

Perkins, Agnes F., ed. 1910. *Vocations for the Trained Woman: Opportunities other than Teaching.* Introductory Papers. Boston: Women's Educational and Industrial Union.

Perkins, Frances [U.S. Secretary of Labor, 1933–45]. 1910. A Study of Malnutrition in 107 Children from Public School 51. Master's thesis, Columbia University.

——. 1931. Unemployment and Senator Wagner's Bills. Address before the Democratic Women's Luncheon Club of Philadelphia, April 13, 1931. Unpublished.

——. 1934. *People at Work.* New York: John Day Co.

——. 1934. *Proceedings of the National Conference for Labor Legislation.* Held at Washington, D.C., February 14 and 15, 1934. U.S. Bureau of Labor Statistics Bulletin, no. 583. Washington: U.S. Bureau of Labor Statistics.

——. 1935. *Report to the President of the Committee on Economic Security.* Washington: U.S. Government Printing Office.

——. 1939. *The International Labor Organization as an Agency of Democracy.* Address delivered to the Democratic Women's Luncheon Club of Philadelphia, March 27. Philadelphia: International Labour Organisation.

——. 1940. *The Worker's Stake in Safety.* Washington: U.S. Department of Labor/U.S. Government Printing Office.

——. Coauth. *See* Smith, Florence Patteson.

Perry, Lorinda. 1913. The Millinery Trade in Boston and Philadelphia: A Study of Women in Industry. Ph.D. thesis, Bryn Mawr College (economics, history).

——. 1916. *Millinery as a Trade for Women.* Studies in Economic Relations of Women, vol. V. New York: Longmans, Green & Company.

Peters, Iva L[owther]. 1916. A Questionnaire Study of Some of the Effects of Social Restrictions on the American Girl. *Pedagogical Seminary* 23: 550–69.

——. 1918. The Institutionalized Sex Taboo. Ph.D. thesis, Clark University (sociology).

——. 1922/3. The Concept of Repression in Analysis of Problems of the Family. *Sociology and Social Research* 7: 310–.

——. 1922/3. The New Place of Women in Community Life. *Sociology and Social Research* 7: 51–.

——. 1923. A Two-year Experiment with Vocational Guidance in a Woman's College. *Pedagogical Seminary* 30: 225–40.

——. 1924. A College Vocational Guidance Program. *School and Society* 20(503) (August 16): 201–.

——. 1924. The Practice of Vocational Guidance at Goucher College. *Vocational Guidance Magazine* 2(6) (March): 151–.

——. 1924/5. Book Review of "Economics of the Household: Its Administration and Finance" by Andrews. *Social Forces* 3(1/4): 355–.

——. 1925/6. A Social Interpretation: Maryland. *Social Forces* 4(1/4): 510–.

——. 1926. *Social and Vocational Orientation for College Women.* Richmond, Va.: Southern Woman's Educational Alliance/Goucher College, Baltimore.

——. 1927. An Adequate Program of Educational and Vocational Guidance in a College. *Vocational Guidance Magazine* 5(6) (March): 247–.

——. 1935. *Occupational Discriminations against Women: An Inquiry into the Economic Security of American Business and Professional Women.* New York: Publications Department, National Federation of Business and Professional Women's Clubs.

——. 1936. *A Study of Employability of Women in Selected Sections of the United States: Interview Study of 212 Business and Professional Women.* New York: National Federation of Business and Professional Women's Clubs, Inc.

Peters, Iva Lowther, Helen W. Atwater, and Katharine Dexter McCormick. 1919. *Agencies for the Sale of Cooked Foods without Profit: A Survey of Their Development with Particular Reference to Their Social and Economic Effect.* Washington: United States Council of National Defense Committee on Women's Defense Work.

Peters, Iva Lowther. Coauth. *See* Pruette [Fryer], Lorine.

[Peters,] Louise Otto. 1866. *Das Recht der Frauen auf Erwerb: Blicke auf das Frauenleben der Gegenwart.* Hamburg: Hoffmann & Campe.

——. 1870. *Der Genius der Menschheit: Frauenwirken im Dienste der Humanität: eine Gabe für Mädchen und Frauen.* Pest: A. Hartleben.

——. 1876. *Frauenleben im Deutschen Reich: Erinnerungen aus der Vergangenheit mit Hinweis auf Gegenwart und Zukunft.* Leipzig: M. Schäfer. Reprinted Cologne: Verlag M. Hutterman, Paderborn, 1988.

Peterson, Agnes Lydia. 1922. *Iowa Woman in Industry.* Bulletin of the Women's Bureau, no. 19. Washington: U.S. Government Printing Office.

——. 1929. *What the Wage-earning Woman Contributes to Family Support.* Bulletin of the Women's Bureau, no. 75. Washington: U.S. Government Printing Office. Also published in the *Annals of the American Academy of Political and Social Science* 143 (May 1929): 74–.

——. 1931. *Activities of the Women's Bureau of the United States.* Bulletin of the U.S. Women's Bureau, no. 86. Washington: U.S. Government Printing Office.

——. 1935. *A Survey of the Shoe Industry in New Hampshire.* Bulletin of the U.S. Women's Bureau, no. 121. Washington: U.S. Government Printing Office.

Peterson, Agnes Lydia, Ethel Lombard Best, Helen Bryan, Agnes Horne Campbell, and Mary Nelson Winslow. 1920. *Hours and Conditions of Work for Women in Industry in Virginia.* Bulletin of the U.S. Women's Bureau, no. 10. Washington: U.S. Government Printing Office.

Peterson, Agnes Lydia, Ethel Lombard Best, Mildred Larcom Gordon, and Mary Nelson Winslow. 1920. *Home Work in Bridgeport, Connecticut. December 1919.* Bulletin of the United States Women's Bureau, no. 9. Washington: U.S. Government Printing Office.

Peterson, Agnes Lydia, Ethel L. Best, and Mary Nelson Winslow. 1921. *Women Streetcar Conductors and Ticket Agents.* Washington: U.S. Women's Bureau.

Peterson, Agnes Lydia, Elizabeth Adshead Hyde, and Kathleen B. Jennison Lowrie. 1924. *Women in Alabama Industries: A Study of Hours, Wages and Working Conditions.* Washington: U.S. Government Printing Office.

Peterson, Florence. 1934. CWA. *Atlantic Monthly* 153 (January/June): 587–.

——. 1935. What Facts Must Be Gathered to Be Reported to Governmental Agencies? *Personnel* 12(1) (August): 135–.

——. 1937. Methods Used in Strike Statistics. *Journal of the American Statistical Association* 32 (March): 90–6.

——. 1938. *Strikes in the United States, 1880–1936.* U.S. Bureau of Labor Statistics Bulletin, no. 651. Washington: U.S. Government Printing Office.

——. 1940. Collective Bargaining in the United States. *International Labour Review* 41(1/6) (January/June): 479–.

Peterson, Marie Wilheminna. 1927. Timber: The Cash Crop of Sweden. M.S. thesis, University of Chicago (economics, agricultural).

Pethick, Emmeline. 1898. Working Girls' Clubs. In Will Reason, ed., *The University and Social Settlements.* London: Methuen & Co.

Pettengill, Lillian. 1903. *Toilers of the Home. The Record of a College Woman's Experience as a Domestic Servant.* New York: Doubleday, Page & Co.

Pfeiffer, Mrs. Emily Jane [Davis]. 1878. The Tyranny of Fashion. *Cornhill Magazine* 38 (July): 83–94.
——. 1880. Woman's Claim. *Contemporary Review* 39 (February): 265–77.
——. 1885. The Suffrage for Women. *Contemporary Review* 47 (March): 418–35.
——. 1888. *Women and Work, an Essay Treating on the Relation to Health and Physical Development of the Higher Education of Girls and the Intellectual or More Systemised Effort of Women.* Boston: Tickner & Co.; London: Trubner & Co.
Phelps, Edith May. 1909/1911. *Selected Articles on the Income Tax, with Special Reference to Graduation and Exemption.* Minneapolis: H. W. Wilson. 3rd, ed., New York: H. W. Wilson, 1917.
——. 1911. *Selected Articles on Federal Control of Interstate Corporations.* Minneapolis: H. W. Wilson. 2nd ed., White Plains, N.Y., and New York: H. W. Wilson, 1915.
——, comp. 1912. *Selected Articles on Government Ownership of Railroads.* Minneapolis: H. W. Wilson. 2nd enlarged ed., New York: H. W. Wilson, 1914. 3rd rev. ed., 1916. A 2nd vol. was published in 1919.
——. 1912. *Selected Articles on Government Ownership of the Telegraph.* Minneapolis: H. W. Wilson.
——. 1913. *Selected Articles on Panama Canal Tolls.* Minneapolis: H. W. Wilson.
——. 1913. *Selected Articles on the Parcels Post.* 2nd ed. Minneapolis: H. W. Wilson.
——. 1930. *The Socialization of Medicine.* New York: H. W. Wilson.
Phelps, Elizabeth Stuart. 1871. *The Silent Partner.* Boston: Osgood. [*novel*]
——. Coauth. *See* Brady, Dorothy S.; Monroe, Day.
Phelps, Katherine. 1939. A Flexible Method of Hand Tabulation. *Journal of Marketing* 3 (January): 265–8.
Philipps, Leonora. 1898. *A Dictionary of Employments Open to Women: With Details of Wages, Hours of Work, and Other Information.* London: Women's Institute.
Phillimore, Mrs. A. 1897. *The Housing of the People.* Manchester: Women's Cooperative Guild.
Phillimore, Margaret. 1897. Agricultural Laborer, Past and Present. *Economic Review* 7: 13.
——. 1897. Agricultural Laborer – A Rejoinder. *Economic Review* 7: 468.
Phillipps, Evelyn March. *See* March-Phillipps, Evelyn.
Phillipps, Miss. L[ucy]. F. March [unsigned]. 1869. *My Life, and What Shall I Do with It? A Question for Young Gentlewomen. By an Old Maid.* London: Longmans.
——. 1869. *Strong and Free; or, First Steps Towards Social Science.* London: Longmans, Green.
——. 1873. *English Matrons and Their Profession, with Some Considerations as to Their Various Offices, Their National Importance, and the Education They Require.* London: S. Low, Marston, Low, & Searle.
Phillips, Arcadia Dowdell [Near]. Coauth. *See* Manning, Caroline; Pidgeon, Mary Elizabeth; Smaltz, Rebecca G.
Phillips, Marion. 1906. Book Review of "Colonial Administration" by Paul S. Reinsch. *Economic Journal* 16(61) (March): 123–5.

——. 1906. Book Review of "L'Espansione commerciale e coloniale degli stati moderni" by Marco Fanno. *Economic Journal* 16(63) (September): 418–22.

——. 1906. Book Review of "Il Regime e la concessione delle terre nelle colonie moderne" by Marco Fanno. *Economic Journal* 16(61) (March): 121–3.

——. 1914. The Health of the Child. *Nation* 15(6) (May 9): 227–.

——. 1915. The Revolt of the Socialist Women of Germany. *Nation* 17(2) (April 10): 47.

——. 1915. The Women's International. *Contemporary Review* 107 (January/June): 646–.

——, ed. 1918. *Women and the Labour Party*. New York: B. W. Heubsch; London: Headley Bros.

——. 1919. The Employment of Children. In Gertrude M. Tuckwell, Marion G. Phillips, and Susan A. Lawrence, *Labour Women on International Legislation: Proposals for International Legislation*. London: Labour Party.

——. 1922. *Les Femmes et les enfants dans l'industrie textile: durée du travail & âge d'admission, rapports international*. Amsterdam: Fédération syndicale internationale.

——. 1922. *Women and Children in the Textile Industry: An International Survey of Hours of Work and Age of Entry*. Amsterdam: International Federation of Trade Unions.

——. 1926. Miners' Wives and Children [letter to the editor]. *Nation and Athenaeum* 39(00) (June 12): 271–3.

——. 1926. Miners' Wives and Children [letter to the editor]. *Nation and Athenaeum* 39(20) (August 21): 580–2.

——. 1927. *Women and the Miners' Lockout: The Story of the Women's Committee for the Relief of the Miners' Wives and Children*. London: Labour Publishing Company.

——. 1927. Labor and Poor-law Reform in England. *Social Service Review* 1(1/4) (March/December): 581–.

——. 1928. Case Papers as a Cure for Unemployment: A Reply to Mr. J. C. Pringle. *Social Service Review* 2(1/4) (March/December): 618–.

——. 1931/1934. *Socialism and Women*. Girard, Kans.; Haldeman-Julius Publication.

Phipps, Helen. 1924. The Agrarian Phase of the Mexican Revolution 1911–1920. *Political Science Quarterly* (March): 1–.

——. 1925. *Some Aspects of the Agrarian Question in Mexico: A Historical Study*. University of Texas Bulletin, no. 2,515. Austin, Tex.: University of Texas.

——. 1925. Some Aspects of the Agrarian Question in Mexico: A Historical Study. Ph.D. thesis, Columbia University (economics).

Phoebus, Gladys Edith. 1924. *Canadian Iron and Steel Industry and Trade*. Washington: U.S. Bureau of Foreign and Domestic Commerce.

——. 1926. *World Markets for Cutlery*. Washington: U.S. Bureau of Foreign and Domestic Commerce.

Phoebus, Mildred Anna. 1923. *Economic Development in Argentina Since 1921*. Washington: U.S. Bureau of Foreign and Domestic Commerce.

——. 1926. *Argentine Markets for United States Goods*. Washington: U.S. Bureau of Foreign and Domestic Commerce.

——. 1927. *Commercial Readjustment in Brazil, 1927.* U.S. Foreign and Domestic Commerce Bureau, Trade Information Bulletin, no. 560. Washington: U.S. Government Printing Office.
——. 1929. *Reajustamento commercial do Brasil: resumo de uma publicação do Departamento do Commercio dos Estados Unidos da America, remettida pela Embaixada do Brasil em Washington.* Brazilian Ministry of Foreign Relations, Economic Department. Rio de Janeiro: Imprensa Nacional. Abridged translation of the author's *Commercial Readjustment in Brazil, 1927.*
Pidgeon, Mary E[lizabeth]. 1925. The Power and Practice of Virginia County Boards. *National Municipal Review* 14(4) (April): 240–.
——. 1926. The Southern Conference on the Social Sciences. *School and Society* 23(590) (April 17): 501–.
——. 1929. *Negro Women in Industry in 15 States.* Washington: U.S. Government Printing Office.
——. 1930. *Women in 5- and 10-Cent Stores and Limited-price Chain Department Stores.* Bulletin of the U.S. Women's Bureau, no. 76. Washington: U.S. Government Printing Office.
——. 1931. *Wages of Women in 13 States.* Bulletin of the U.S. Women's Bureau, no. 85. Washington: U.S. Government Printing Office.
——. 1931. *Women in Industry: A Series of Papers to Aid Study Groups.* Washington: U.S. Women's Bureau.
——. 1932/3. Recent Changes in Occupations of Women. *Personnel Journal* 11 (June/April): 289–.
——. 1933. *Employment Fluctuations and Unemployment of Women: Certain Indications from Various Sources, 1928–31.* Bulletin of the U.S. Women's Bureau, no. 113. Washington: U.S. Government Printing Office.
——. 1933. Recent Changes in Occupations for Women. *Women Lawyers' Journal* 20(2) (May).
——. 1935. *Employed Women under N.R.A. Codes.* U.S. Women's Bureau Bulletin, no. 130. Washington: U.S. Government Printing Office. Reprinted in *Women in the Economy of the United States of America: Employed Women under NRA Codes.* New York: Da Capo Press, 1975.
——. 1936. *The Employed Woman Homemaker in the United States: Her Responsibility for Family.* Bulletin of the U.S. Women's Bureau, no. 148. Washington: U.S. Department of Labor.
——. 1936. *Summary of State Hour Laws for Women and Minimum-wage Rates.* Bulletin of the U.S. Women's Bureau, no. 137. Washington: U.S. Government Printing Office.
——. 1937. *Women in the Economy of the United States of America.* Bulletin of the U.S. Women's Bureau, no. 155. Washington: U.S. Government Printing Office. Reprinted in *Women in the Economy of the United States of America: Employed Women under NRA Codes.* New York: Da Capo Press, 1975.
——. 1938. *Differences in the Earnings of Women and Men.* Bulletin of the U.S. Women's Bureau, no. 152. Washington: U.S. Government Printing Office.

——. 1938. *Trends in the Employment of Women, 1928–36.* Bulletin of the U.S. Women's Bureau, no. 159. Washington: U.S. Government Printing Office.

——. 1938. *Women in Industry: A Series of Papers to Aid Study Groups.* Bulletin of the Women's Bureau, no. 164. Washington: U.S. Government Printing Office.

Pidgeon, Mary Elizabeth and Caroline Manning. 1932. *The Employment of Women in Slaughtering and Meat Packing.* Bulletin of the U.S. Women's Bureau, no. 88. Washington: U.S. Government Printing Office.

Pidgeon, Mary Elizabeth and Margaret Jane Thompson Mettert. 1939. *Employed Women and Family Support.* Bulletin of the U.S. Women's Bureau, no 168. Washington: U.S. Government Printing Office.

Pidgeon, Mary Elizabeth and Arcadia Dowdell [Near] Phillips. 1935. *Variations in Wage Rates under Corresponding Conditions.* Bulletin of the U.S. Women's Bureau, no. 122. Washington: U.S. Government Printing Office.

Pidgeon, Mary Elizabeth. Coauth. *See* Best, Ethel Lombard.

Pike, Violet [Leonard]. 1912. *New World Lessons for Old World Peoples.* New York: Women's Trade Union League.

——. 1912. *Women Workers in Factories in New York State.* Albany: J. B. Lyon.

Pimenoff, Lydia L. 1893. Science and the Woman's Question. *North American Review* 156 (January/June): 248–51.

Pinchbeck, Ivy. 1930. *Women Workers and the Industrial Revolution, 1750–1850.* London: Routledge; New York: F. S. Crofts & Co. Reprinted New York: A. M. Kelley, 1969; London: Cass, 1969.

Pinoff, Minna. 1867. *Die Erziehung der Frau zur Arbeit; ein Beitrag zur Lösung der socialen Frage der Frauen.* Breslau: Maruschke & Berendt.

——. 1867. *Reform der weiblichen Erziehung als Grundbedingung zur Lösung der socialen Frage der Frauen.* Breslau: Maruschke & Berendt.

——. 1869. *Die Lösing der Existenzfrage der Frau als Grundbedingung für die sittliche und geistige Gleichberechtigung der Frau.* Berlin: C. Heymann.

Pissarjevsky, Lydié. 1910. *Socialisme et féminisme.* Paris: Imprimerie Cooperative Ouvriçre.

Pitney, Augusta Anne. 1855. *Cottage Economy, by a Cottager. In Three Lectures Addressed to the Girls of the Westbourne National School.* London: Joseph Masters.

Plant, Marjorie. 1939. *The English Book Trade: An Economic History of the Making and Sale of Books.* New York: R. R. Bowker; London: George Allen & Unwin.

Plunket, Isabella Katherine. 1877. *Words of Help for Working Women; or, Short Addresses for Mothers' Meetings.* By the Honble. Isabel Plunket. London and Edinburgh: Gall & Inglis.

Poggi, Edith Muriel. 1928. The Red Land of Gwent in Eastern Monmouthshire. *Economic Geography* 4(1) (January): 31–43.

——. 1930. The Forest of Dean in Gloucestershire. *Economic Geography* 6(3) (July): 309–20.

——. 1930. The German Sugar Beet Industry. *Economic Geography* 6(1) (January): 81–93.

——. 1931?/1934?. The Prairie Province of Illinois: A Study of Human Adjustment to the Natural Environment. Ph.D., University of Illinois at Urbana–Champaign (ecology).

——. 1934. *The Prairie Province of Illinois: A Study of Human Adjustment to the Natural Environment.* Illinois Studies in the Social Sciences, vol. XIX, no. 3. Urbana, Ill.: University of Illinois.

Pollak, Hansi [P.]. 1933. Women Workers in Witswatersrand Industries. *South African Journal of Economics* 1: 58–.

——. 1934. Book Review of "The American Experiment: A Study of Bourgeois Civilization" by M. J. Bonn. *South African Journal of Economics* 2(3) (September): 332–.

——. 1934. Book Review of "From Wants to Satisfactions" by H. A. Jones. *South African Journal of Economics* 2(4) (December): 484–.

——. 1936. European Population Growth since Union. An Analysis of the Birth, Fertility and Death Rates with Reference to the Future Increase of Population. *South African Journal of Economics* 4: 1–.

——. 1937. South Africa. *Charity Organisation Quarterly* 11(3) (July): 167–.

——. 1940. State and Private Provisions for Soldiers' Dependants. *South African Journal of Economics* 8: 446–.

Pollak, Marianne. 1925. *Kind und Sozialismus.* Prague: Zentralstelle für das Bildungswesen der Deutschen Sozialdemokratischen Arbeiterpartei in der Tschechoslowakischen Republik.

——. 1930. Beruf und Haushalt. *Handbuch der Frauenarbeit in Österreich.* Vienna: Kammer für Arbeiter und Angestellte in Wien.

——. 1933. *Eine Frau studiert den Sozialismus.* Deutschen Sozialdemokratischen Arbeiterpartei in der Tschechoslowakischen Republik. Teplitz: Druck- und Verlagsanstalt Teplitz.

Pope, Dr. Emily F. 1881. The Practice of Medicine by Women in the United States. *Journal of Social Science* 14 (November): 178–87.

Popp, Adelheid. 1895. *Die Arbeiterin im Kampf um's Dasein.* Vienna: Verlag der Wiener Volksbuchhandlung, I. Brand.

——. 1930. *Der Weg zur Höhe: die sozialdemokratische Frauenbewegung Österreichs; ihr Aufbau, ihre Entwicklung und ihr Aufstieg.* 2nd ed. Vienna: Frauenzentralkomitee der Sozialdemokratischen Arbeiterpartei Deutschösterreichs.

Porter, Sylvia Field. 1934. Weekly columns in *American Banker.*

——. 1935–77. Financial columns in the *New York Post.*

——. 1939. *How to Make Money in Government Bonds.* New York: Harper.

Posanski, Susan Elrick. Coauth. *See* Stevenson, Marietta.

Post, Alice Thacher. 1895. Women's Discussion of the Labor Problem (Symposium). The Great Neighbor. *Arena* 14(2) (October): 274–7.

Potter, Beatrice. *See* Webb, Beatrice Potter.

Potter, Clara Sidney. 1889. Factory Conditions in New York. *Christian Union* 39: 566–.

Potter, Dorothy Shena. *See* Simon, Dorothy Shena Potter.

Potwine [Potwin], Marjorie A[della]. 1923. The Carolina Cotton Mills. M.A. thesis, University of Chicago (economics, history).

——. 1927. *Cotton Mill People of the Piedmont: A Study in Social Change.* New York: Columbia University Press.

Powell, Eleanor G. Coauth. *See* Sewell, Margaret A.

Powell, Leona Margaret. 1924. A History of the United Typothetae of America, with Especial Reference to Labor Policy. Ph.D. thesis, University of Chicago (economics).

——. 1925. Origin and Background of the United Typothetae of America. *University Business Journal* 4(1) (December): 1–20.

——. 1925. Typothetae and the Eight-hour Day. *Journal of Political Economy* 33(6) (December): 660–83.

——. 1926. *History of the United Typothetae of America.* Chicago: University of Chicago Press.

——. 1926. The Typothetae Division Plan and the Amalgamation Movement. *University Business Journal* 4(2) (April): 123–50.

——. 1926. Typothetae Experiments with Price Maintenance and Cost Work. *Journal of Political Economy* 34(1) (February): 78–99.

——. 1926. Typothetae as a Trade Association. *University Business Journal* 4(3) (July): 207–29.

——. 1936. Benefit Associations and the Depression. *Personnel* 13(2) (November): 69–.

——. 1937. Significant Literature on Labor Relations. *Personnel* 14(2) (November): 84–.

——. 1938. Book Review of "Conference Leader's Manual." *Management Review* 27(5) (May): 178–.

——. 1938. Book Review of "Personality in Formation and Action." *Management Review* 27(4) (April): 139–.

——. 1938. Book Review of "The Waterfront Labor Problem." *Management Review* 27(11) (November): 391–.

——. 1938. Current Labor and Personnel Literature. *Personnel* 14(3) (February): 150–.

——. 1938. Current Labor and Personnel Literature. *Personnel* 14(4) (May): 195–.

——. 1940. Book Review of "Business and the Public Library." *Management Review* 29(5) (May): 193–.

Power, Eileen [Edna]. 1917. By-elections under P.R. [letter to the editor]. *Nation* 21(10) (June 9): 247–.

——. 1917. The Cult of the Virgin in the Middle Ages. *Cambridge Magazine* (May 12): 594–6; (June 9): 710–12.

——. 1918. Medieval Ideas about Women. *Cambridge Magazine* (November 2).

——. 1919/20. English Craft Gilds in the Middle Ages. *History* 4: 211–.

——. 1922. *Medieval English Nunneries, c.1275–1535.* Cambridge, UK: Cambridge University Press.

——. 1922. Book Review of "A Plea for the Middle Ages." *Economica* 5 (June): 173–80.
——. 1923/4. Book Review of "The Cambridge History of British Foreign Policy. Vol. II" by Sir A. W. Ward and G. P. Gooch. *Economica* 3(4:11): 243–.
——. 1924/1925/1926/1929/1935/1939. *Medieval People.* London: Methuen & Co.; Garden City, N.Y.: Doubleday; Boston: Houghton Mifflin; New York: Barnes & Noble.
——. 1926. The Position of Women. In C. G. Crump and E. F. Jacob, eds., *The Legacy of the Middle Ages.* Oxford: Clarendon Press.
——. 1926/7. The English Wool Trade in the Reign of Edward IV. *Cambridge Historical Journal* 2: 17–.
——. 1927. *The Industrial Revolution, 1750–1850: A Select Bibliography.* Economic History Society Bibliographies, no. 1. London: Economic History Society.
——, transl. 1927. *Life and Work in Medieval Europe (Fifth to Fifteenth Centuries)*, by Prosper Boissonnade. London: K. Paul Trench, Trubner & Co.
——, transl. 1928. *The Goodman of Paris (Le Ménagier de Paris): A Treatise on Moral and Domestic Economy by a Citizen of Paris (c.1393).* London: G. Routledge.
——. 1929/30. Book Review of "The East India Company Trading to China, 1635–1834" by H. B. Morse. *Economic History Review* 2: 157–.
——. 1931. The Boxer Indemnity. *Nation and Athenaeum* 48(16) (January 17): 499–.
——. 1931. The Chinese Problem (Reviews). *New Statesman and Nation* 2(40) (November 28): 677–.
——. 1932. Our Debt to the Past – XI: Political Life and Thought in the Middle Ages. *Listener* 8(205) (December 14): 845–.
——. 1932. Our Debt to the Past – XII: Economic Ideas of the Middle Ages. *Listener* 8(206) (December 21): 904–.
——. 1933. *The Wool Trade in the Fifteenth Century.* London: G. Routledge.
——. 1933. The Foundations of the Chinese Problem. *New Statesman and Nation* 5(102) (February 4): 133–.
——. 1933. Traders of the Saharan Desert. *New Statesman and Nation* 6(134) (September 16): 330–.
——. 1934. Book Review of "Empire in the East" by Joseph Barnes, ed. *Pacific Affairs* 7(4) (December): 447–.
——. 1934. On Medieval History as a Social Study. *Economica* 1 (February): 13–29.
——. 1934/5. Book Review of "Close Rolls of the Reign of Henry III, 1259–61." *Economic History Review* 5: 134.
——. 1936. Book Review of "Parliamentary Taxes on Personal Property" by J. F. Willard. *Economica* 3: 338–.
——. 1936. Book Review of "A Source Book for Medieval Economic History" by R. C. Cave and H. H. Coulson. *Economica* 3: 351–.
——. 1936/7. Book Review of "Five Centuries of Religion, vol. III: Getting and Spending" by G. G. Coulton. *Economic History Review* 7: 87.

——. 1936/7. Book Review of "The Ordinance Book of the Merchants of the Staple" by E. E. Rich, ed. *Economic History Review* 7: 235.

——. 1936/7. Book Review of "Le Temporel et la situation financiere des établissements de l'Ordre de Cluny du XIIe au XIVe siecle, particulierement dans les provinces françaises" by Guy de Valous. *Economic History Review* 7: 87.

——. 1937/8. Book Review of "Economic and Social History of Medieval Europe" by H. Pirenne. *Economic History Review* 8: 82.

——. 1937/8. Book Review of "An Economic History of the British Isles" by Arthur Birnie. *Economic History Review* 8: 82.

——. 1937/8. Book Review of "Economic History of Europe" by Herbert Heaton. *Economic History Review* 8: 82.

——. 1938. Class; An Enquiry into Social Distinctions. *Listener* 20(510) (October 20): 817–.

——. 1938/9. Book Review of "Un Grand Commerce d'exportation au moyen âge" by Henri Laurent. *Economic History Review* 9: 195.

——. 1938/9. Book Review of "Les Villes de foires de Champagne des origines au début du XIVe siecle" by Elizabeth Chapin. *Economic History Review* 9: 195.

——. 1939/40. Book Review of "Calendar of Fine Rolls, vols. XVIII and XIX, 1445–52 and 1452–61." *Economic History Review* 10: 180–.

——. 1939/40. Book Review of "Close Rolls of the Reign of Henry III, 1268–72." *Economic History Review* 10: 155.

——. 1939/40. Book Review of "Curia Regis Rolls, vols. VII and VIII, 1213–15 and 1219–20." *Economic History Review* 10: 155.

——. 1939/40. Book Review of "Henri Mohammad and Charlemagne" by Pirenne. *Economic History Review* 10: 60–.

——. 1939/40. Book Review of "Histoire économique de la France, I: le moyen âge et l'ancien régime" by Henri Sée. *Economic History Review* 10: 69–.

——. 1939/40. Book Review of "The Worshipful Company of Poulters of the City of London" by P. E. Jones. *Economic History Review* 10: 72–.

——. 1940. The Fens. *New Statesman and Nation* 19(478) (April 20): 538–.

——. 1940. Topical History (Reviews). *New Statesman and Nation* 20(495) (August 17): 168–.

Power, Eileen Edna and M. M. Postan, eds. 1933. *Studies in English Trade in the Fifteenth Century*. London: G. Routledge.

Power, Eileen and F. W. Tickner 1926. Economic History [letter to the editor]. *Nation and Athenaeum* 39(21) (August 28): 608–10.

Praed, Mrs. Campbell. 1885. *Australian Life, Black and White*. London: Chapman and Hall.

Praga, Mrs. Alfred. 1899. *Appearances: How to Keep Them up on a Limited Income*. London: J. Lang.

Preston, Evelyn. 1923. The Pit Committee in the Illinois Coal Fields. M.A. thesis, University of Wisconsin, 1923.

Price, Enid M. 1919. *Changes in the Industrial Occupations of Women in the Environment of Montréal during the Period of the War, 1914–1918.* Montreal: Canadian Reconstruction Association.

Priestley, Mrs. [Eliza.] 1892. Housekeeping Schools. *Nineteenth Century* 32 (October): 652–9.

Pruette [Fryer], Lorine. 1923. Book Review of "How to Choose and Get a Better Job" by E. J. Kilduff. *Mental Hygiene* 7 (January/October): 198–200.

——. 1923/4. Book Review of "Woman, a Vindication" by Ludovici. *Social Forces* 2(1/5): 622.

——. 1923/4. Book Review of "Women and the Labor Movement" by Henry. *Social Forces* 2(1/5): 601.

——. 1923/4. Book Review of "Women in the Factory, an Administrative Adventure, 1893 to 1921" by Anderson. *Social Forces* 2(1/5): 601.

——. 1924. *Women and Leisure: A Study of Social Waste.* New York: E. P. Dutton & Co. Reprinted New York: Arno Press, 1972.

——. 1924. Women and Leisure: A Study of Social Waste. Ph.D. thesis, Columbia University (sociology).

——. 1924/5. Fads and Fancies in the Social Sciences. *Social Forces* 3(1/4): 442–.

——. 1925. Business Professions by Leading Specialists of New York City. In Douglas Fryer, *Vocational Self-guidance: Planning Your Work.* Philadelphia: J. B. Lippincott.

——. 1925. The Business Professions for Women. In Douglas Fryer, *Vocational Self-guidance: Planning Your Work.* Philadelphia: J. B. Lippincott.

——. 1925. Psychology – What Mental Tests Can Do for Industry. *Industrial Management* 70 (July/December): 270–.

——. 1925. Vocational Orientation for the College Student. *Educational Review* 69 (January/May): 83–.

——. 1925/6. Book Review of "Woman's Share in Social Culture" by Spencer. *Social Forces* 4(1/4): 243–.

——. 1926. Harriet Beecher Stowe and the Universal Backdrop. *Bookman* 64(1) (September): 18.

——. 1928. The Instinct(?) of Race Prejudice. *World Tomorrow* 11(7) (July): 304–.

——. 1929. The Married Woman and the Part-time Job. *American Academy of Political and Social Science, Annals* 143 (May): 301–.

——. 1936. Women Workers Have Come through. *American Scholar* 5(3) (Summer): 328–.

——. 1940. *Working with Words: A Survey of Vocational Opportunities for Young Writers.* New York: Funk & Wagnalls Co.

Pruette, Lorine and Iva Lowther Peters. 1934. *Women Workers through the Depression: A Study of White Collar Employment Made by the American Woman's Association.* New York: Macmillan.

Pryor, Margaret [Mrs. Harry Glicksman]. 1918. Changes in the Economic Position of Women in England and the United States Since August, 1914. M.A. thesis, University of Texas.

——. 1928. The Place of Consumption in Economic Theory. Ph.D. thesis, University of Wisconsin–Madison (economics).

Puffer, Evelyn H. 1939. A California Pioneer in Insurance. *Business History Review* 13 (June): 33–43.

Pugh, Mary Anderson. 1926. *Resources and Trade of the Philippine Islands.* Washington: U.S. Government Printing Office.

——. 1927. *Markets of the Netherlands East Indies.* Washington: U.S. Bureau of Foreign and Domestic Commerce.

——. 1929. *Economic Development of Siam.* Washington: U.S. Bureau of Foreign and Domestic Commerce.

Pulling, Hazel Adele. 1931. History of the Range Cattle Industry of Dakota. M.A. thesis, University of Chicago (economics, history).

Putnam, Bertha Haven. 1906. The Justices of Labourers in the 14th Century. *English Historical Review* 21: 517.

——. 1908. *The Enforcement of the Statutes of Laborers During the First Decade after the Black Death.* Studies in History, Economics and Public Law, vol. 32. New York: Columbia University.

——. 1908. The Enforcement of the Statutes of Laborers During the First Decade after the Black Death. Ph.D. thesis, Columbia University.

——. 1915/16. Maximum Wage-laws for Priests after the Black Death, 1348–1381. *American Historical Review* 21: 12–.

——. 1927. Northamptonshire Wage Assessments of 1560 and 1667. *Economic History Review* 1 (January): 124–34.

Putnam, Elizabeth C[abot]. 1887. *Real and Fancied Hardships of Working-girls.* Paper read before the associate members of the Girls Friendly Society at their annual meeting in Boston, May 3, 1887. Boston: s.n.

——, ed. 1893. *Massachusetts' Care of Dependent and Delinquent Children.* Boston: Massachusetts Board of Managers, World's Fair.

Q

Quinton, Amelia Stone [Mrs. Richard Stone]. 1890. Seven Ways to Help Indians: Annual Address of the President, November 1890. Philadelphia: Women's National Indian Association.

——. 1891. Care of the Indian. In Annie Nathan Meyer, ed., *Woman's Work in America*. New York: H. Holt & Co.

——. 1893. The Indian. In Frances A. Goodale, ed., *The Literature of Philanthropy*. New York: Harper Bros.

——. 1893. Women's Work for Indians. In Lydia H. Farmer, ed., *The National Exposition Souvenir: What America Owes to Women*. Buffalo: C.W. Houlton.

——. 1894. The Woman's National Indian Association. In Mary Kavanaugh Oldham, ed., *The Congress of Women Held in the Woman's Building, World's Columbia Exposition, Chicago, USA, 1893*. Cincinnati: E. R. Curtis & Co. Reprinted New York: Arno Press, 1974.

Quittner-Bertolasi, E. 1933. *Das Verhältnis von Trend und Konjunktursyklen als mathematisch-ökonomisches Problem*. Leipzig: Hans Buske.

R

Rae, Priscilla M. 1937. *The £ s. d. of National Defence.* London: William Hodge.

Ragen, Katherine M. 1937. Alexander Hamilton's Economic Policy. Ph.D. thesis, University of Wisconsin–Madison (economics).

Rainboth, Edith D. Coauth. *See* Brady, Dorothy S.; Kyrk, Hazel; Monroe, Day.

Ramabai Sarasvati, Pandita. 1888. *The High-caste Hindu Woman.* London: G. Bell.

Ramsay, E. 1875. Co-operative Housekeeping. *Englishwoman's Review*, n.s. 30 (October): 436.

Ramsey, Mary Louise. 1931. Aesthetic Considerations and Billboard Zoning. *Land Economics* 7 (May): 208–10.

——. 1931. Judicial Supervision of Commission Regulation: A Study of Court and Commission Relations in Massachusetts. Part I. *Land Economics* 7 (August): 225–36.

——. 1931. Judicial Supervision of Commission Regulation: A Study of Court and Commission Relations in Massachusetts. Part II. *Land Economics* 7 (November): 343–54.

——. 1932. The Interstate Commerce Commission on Depreciation Accounting. *Land Economics* 8 (August): 327–30.

——. 1934. Recent Developments in Low-cost Housing and Slum Clearance Programs. *Land Economics* 10 (February): 99–101.

——. 1937. Mortgage Foreclosures and Income Taxes. *Tax Magazine* 15(10) (October): 579–.

——. 1937. A New Theory of Corporate Domicile for Tax Purposes. *American Bar Association Journal* 23: 543–.

——. 1938. States' Rights and the Wagner Act Decisions. *Missouri Law Review* 3: 26–.

——. 1939. *An Analysis of 1935 Arkansas Bank Data.* Arkansas University, College of Business Administration Seminar Theses, no. 60. Fayetteville, Ark.: University of Arkansas.

——. 1940. Railroad Assessments in Illinois. *Taxes* 18(12) (December): 744–.

Ranck, Katherine Howland. Coauth. *See* Cavan, Ruth Shonle.

Rankin, Mary Theresa. 1916. *Arbitration and Conciliation in Australasia: The Legal Wage in Victoria and New Zealand.* London: George Allen & Unwin.

——. 1929. Book Review of "Evolution of Industrial Organisation" by B. F. Shields. *Economic Journal* 39: 267–.

——. 1930. Book Review of "Labour Organisation" by J. Cunnison. *Economic Journal* 40: 486–.

——. 1931. *Arbitration Principles and the Industrial Court.* London: P. S. King.

——. 1935. *Monetary Opinions and Policy, 1924–34.* London: P. S. King.

Rathbone, Eleanor [Florence]. 1898. Book Review of "Forecasts of the Coming Century" by A. P. Wallace *et al. International Journal of Ethics* 8(2) (January): 257–8.

——. 1899. Book Review of "A Study of Mary Wollstonecraft and the Rights of Woman" by Emma R. Clough. *International Journal of Ethics* 9(3) (April): 407–8.

——. 1904. *Report of an Inquiry into the Conditions of Dock Labour at the Liverpool Docks.* Liverpool: Northern Publishing Company.

——. 1909. *How the Casual Labourer Lives: Report of the Liverpool Joint Research Committee on the Domestic Condition and Expenditure of Certain Liverpool Labourers.* Liverpool: Liverpool Women's Industrial Council.

——. 1912. The Problem of Women's Wages: An Enquiry into the Causes of the Inferiority of Women's Wages to Men's. *Transactions of Liverpool Economic Society.*

——. 1914. *Report on the Condition of Widows under the Poor Law in Liverpool.* Liverpool: Liverpool Women's Industrial Council/Lee and Nightingale.

——. 1915. Naval and Military Pensions Bill [letter to the editor]. *Nation* 17(21) (August 21): 678–.

——. 1917. The Immediate Prospects of Women's Suffrage. *Athenaeum* 4615 (March): 137–.

——. 1917. The Remuneration of Women's Services. *Economic Journal* 27(105) (March): 55–68.

——. 1918. The Endowment of Motherhood. *Athenaeum* 4634 (October): 427–.

——. 1920. The New South Wales Scheme for the Grading of Wages According to Family Needs. *Economic Journal* 30(120) (December): 550–3.

——. 1920. Wages According to Family Needs. *Hibbert Journal* 19 (October/July): 712–.

——. 1924. *The Disinherited Family: A Plea for the Endowment of the Family.* London: Edward Arnold & Co.

——. 1924/5. Book Review of "The Disinherited Family." *International Journal of Ethics* 35: 94–.

——. 1925. Family Endowment in Its Bearing on the Question of Population. *Eugenics Review* 16(4) (January): 270–.

——. 1926. State Aid for Children's Allowance in the Mining Industry [letter to the editor]. *Nation and the Athenaeum* 39(7) (May 22): 171–3.

——. 1927. *The Disinherited Family: A Plea for Direct Provision for the Costs of Child Maintenance through Family Allowances.* London: G. Allen & Unwin.

——. 1927. *The Ethics and Economics of Family Endowment: The Social Service Lecture.* London: Epworth Press/J. Alfred Sharp.

——. 1927. The Government's Pledge on Equal Franchise [letter to the editor]. *Nation and Athenaeum* 41(4) (April 30): 107–10.

——. 1928. Women and the Guardians. *Nation and Athenaeum* 44(8) (November 24): 284–.

——. 1928/9. Has Katherine Mayo Slandered "Mother India"? *Hibbert Journal* 27 (October/July): 193–.

——. 1930. Towards Utopia – II: Family Endowment. *Listener* 3(61) (March 12): 462–.

——. 1930/1. Child Marriage in India. *Hibbert Journal* 29 (October/July): 609–.

——. 1931. The Case for University Representation. *Nation and Athenaeum* 48(14) (January 3): 452–.

——. 1931. Unemployment and the Family. *New Statesman and Nation* 2(20) (July 11): 38–.

——. 1931. University Representation [letter to the editor]. *Nation and Athenaeum* 48(21) (February 21): 660–2.

——. 1933. The Political Status of Indian Women. *Asiatic Review* 29(98) (April): 303–.

——. 1934. *Memorandum on the Scale of Needs Suitable for Adoption by the Unemployment Assistance Board in Assessing Assistance to Applicants under Part II of the Unemployment Act.* London: Children's Minimum Campaign Committee.

——. 1934. The Campaign for a Children's Minimum. *New Statesman and Nation* 7(172) (June 9): 873–.

——. 1934. Foreword. In E. Reiss, *Rights and Duties of Englishwomen.* Manchester: Sherratt and Hughes.

——. 1935. Brown Autocrats and White Bureaucrats. *New Statesman and Nation* 9(210) (March 2): 273–.

——. 1938. *War Can Be Averted: The Achievability of Collective Security.* London: V. Gollancz.

——. 1939. The Economics of the Family. *Fortnightly Review* 146 (July/December): 552–.

——. 1939. A Personal View of the Refugee Problem. *New Statesman and Nation* 17(425) (April 15): 568–.

——. 1940. *The Case for Family Allowances.* London: Penguin Books.

——. 1940. The Waste of Woman-power. *New Statesman and Nation* 19(486) (June 15): 743–.

——. 1940. Women in Dangerous Services. *New Statesman and Nation* 20(489) (July 6): 8–.

Rathbone, Eleanor F. and D. H. MacGregor. 1929. Should Wages Be Supplemented by Family Allowances? *Listener* 1(7) (February 27): 237–.

Rathbone, Eleanor. Coauth. *See* Strachey, Ray [Rachel Conn Costelloe Strachey].

Ratliff, Beulah Amidon. 1939. *Who Can Afford Health?* United States Public Health Service; United States Interdepartmental Committee to Coordinate Health and Welfare Activities, Public Affairs Pamphlets, no. 27. New York: Public Affairs Committee, Inc.

——. 1940. *This Business of Relief.* New York: s.n.

Ravenhill, Alice. 1897. *The Health of the Community: How to Promote It.* Public Health Papers, no. 1. Manchester: Women's Co-operative Guild.

——. 1898. *Elements of Sanitary Law.* London: Sanitary Publishing Co.

——. 1898. *How the Law Helps to Healthy Homes.* Women's Co-operative Guild series The Housing of the People, no. 1; Manchester, UK: Co-operative Newspaper Society.

——. 1905. *The Teaching of "Domestic Science" in the United States of America.* London: Wyman and Sons.

——. 1912. *Labor-saving Devices in the Household.* Logan, Utah: Utah Agricultural College.

Ravenhill, Alice and Catherine J. Schiff, eds. 1910. *Household Administration, Its Place in the Higher Education of Women.* London: G. Richards.

Rawlings, Gertrude Burford. 1898. *The Story of British Coinage, with One Hundred and Eight Illustrations.* London: George Newnes, Ltd.

Raymaker, Constance Louise. 1928. Unionism in the Bituminous Coal Industry. M.A. thesis, Northwestern University.

——. 1933. Machine Competition and Union Policies in the Printing Industry. Ph.D. thesis, Northwestern University (economics).

Raymond, Mme. W. 1929. *Le Travail des jeunes filles.* Montreal: L'École sociale populaire, Secrétariat de l'É.S.P. , L'Action paroissiale.

Rayne, Mrs. Martha Louise. 1883. *What Can a Woman Do; or, Her Position in the Business and Literary World.* Detroit: F. B. Dickerson & Co.

Reading, Anna W. 1891. Working Women "Versus" Workingmen. *Chautauquan* 14 (October): 79–.

Reaney, Isabel [Edis] [Mrs. G. S. Reaney]. 1889. Slave-driving by Public Companies. *Contemporary Review* 56 (November): 649–58.

——. 1890. *Temperance Sketches from Life, Inspiring and Helpful Stories for Practical Workers.* New York: American Tract Society.

Reddick, Olive I[rene]. 1924. Book Review of "The Acquisitive Society" by R. H. Tawney. *Indian Journal of Economics* 5 (October): 192–.

——. 1932. Labor Relations in Los Angeles. Ph.D. thesis, Radcliffe College (economics).

Reddish, Sarah. 1890. *Women's Guilds, with Special Reference to Their Claims on the Attention and Support of Educational Committees.* Bolton: Co-operation Educational Committees' Association.

——. 1890s. *Machinery Accidents.* Women's Co-operative Guild. Manchester: Co-operative Newspaper Society.

Redheffer, Ruth Alexander Tracy. 1932. The Economic Principles of Bolshevism. Ph.D. thesis, Northwestern University (economics).

Reed, Anna Y. 1917. *Newsboy Service.* Yonkers-on-Hudson, N.Y.: World Book Co.

——. 1922/3. Book Review of "Education and Industry" by Henry C. Link. *Elementary School Journal* 23(1/10): 793–4.

——. 1922/3. Child-labor Legislation – A Point of View. *Elementary School Journal* 23(1/10): 276–82.

——. 1927. *Human Waste in Education.* New York: Century.

——. 1929/30. Book Review of "A Personnel Study of Women Deans in Colleges and Universities" by Jane Louise Jones. *Elementary School Journal* 30(1/10): 67–9.

Reed, Helen Leah. 1897. Manual Training for Girls. *Harper's Bazar* 30 (April 10): 308–9.

Reed, Ruth. 1921. The Negro Women of Gainesville, Georgia. M.A. thesis, University of Georgia.

——. 1926. Negro Illegitimacy in New York City. Ph.D. thesis, Columbia (sociology).

——. 1934. *The Illegitimate Family in New York City: Its Treatment by Social and Health Agencies.* Studies of the Research Bureau of the Welfare Council, no. 11. New York: Columbia University Press for the Welfare Council of New York City.

Reeves, Edith. 1911. Labor Laws of Massachusetts, 1902–1910. In Susan Myra Kingsbury, Charles Edward Person, and Edith Gertrude Solenberger, eds., *Labor Laws and Their Enforcement with Special Reference to Massachusetts.* New York: Longmans, Green.

——. 1914. *Care and Education of Crippled Children in the United States.* New York: Survey Associates.

Reeves, Edith and Caroline Manning. 1911. Administration of Labor Legislation in the United States, with Special Reference to Massachusetts. In Susan Myra Kingsbury, Charles Edward Person, and Edith Gertrude Solenberger, eds., *Labor Laws and Their Enforcement with Special Reference to Massachusetts.* New York: Longmans, Green.

Reeves, Magdalen Stuart Robinson. 1913/1914. *Round about a Pound a Week.* London: G. Bell and Sons.

Reeves, Margaret. 1929. *Training Schools for Delinquent Girls.* New York: Russell Sage Foundation.

Reichardt, Mrs. [Annie]. 1891. Mohammedan Women. *Nineteenth Century* 29 (June): 941–52.

Reid, Helen. 1937. Michigan and the Policy of Free Homesteads, 1845–1862. M.A. thesis, Wayne State University.

Reid, Helen Dwight. 1932. *International Servitudes in Law and Practice.* Chicago: University of Chicago Press.

Reid, Helen R. Y. 1890s. *The Problem of the Unemployed.* Paper read before the Montreal local council. Montreal: National Council of Women.

Reid, Margaret Gilpin. 1930. Planning a County Nursing Program. *Public Health Nurse* (April).

——. 1931. Household Production: A Study of Its Economic Characteristics. Ph.D. thesis, University of Chicago (home economics).

——. 1934. *Economics of Household Production.* New York: John Wiley.

——. 1935. *Status of Farm Housing in Iowa.* Research Bulletin, no. 174. Ames, Iowa: Agricultural Experiment Station, Iowa State College of Agriculture and Mechanic Arts.

——. 1935. *Status of Town and Village Housing in Iowa.* Research Bulletin, no. 186. Ames, Iowa: Agricultural Experiment Station, Iowa State College of Agriculture and Mechanic Arts.

——. 1936. *Some Factors Affecting Improvement in Iowa Farm Family Housing.* Research Bulletin, no. 349. Ames, Iowa: Agricultural Experiment Station, Iowa State College of Agriculture and Mechanical Arts.

——. 1938. *Consumers and the Market.* New York: F. S. Crofts & Co.

——. 1939. *Consumers and the Market. Supplement.* New York: F. S. Crofts & Co.

——. 1939. Book Review of "Economics for Consumers" by Leland J. Gordon. *American Academy of Political and Social Science, Annals* 206 (November): 189–.

——. 1939. The United States Housing Act of 1937. *Journal of Home Economics* 29: 687–736.

——. 1940. Economics of Marriage and the Family. In Moses Jung, ed., *Modern Marriage.* New York: F. S. Crofts and Co.

——. 1940. Marketing Rewritten from the Consumer's Point of View. *Journal of Marketing,* part 2: 134–7.

Reid, Margaret Gilpin and Hazel Kyrk. 1929. An Estimate of the Number of Women Engaged in Homemaking. *Journal of Home Economics* 21: 424–6.

Reid, Margaret Gilpin and E. Schickele. 1936. Variations in Retail Prices of Certain Branded Foods. *Journal of Home Economics* 28: 691–5.

Reid, Marion Kirkland. 1843. *A Plea for Woman, Being a Vindication of the Importance and Extent of Her Natural Sphere of Action: With Remarks on Recent Works on the Subject.* Edinburgh: W. Tait.

Reid, Rachel R. 1921. *The King's Council of the North.* London: Longmans, Green & Co.

Reimers, Charlotte Engel. 1908. Book Review of "Das Dienstbotenproblem in den nordamerikanischen Staaten, und was es uns lehrt" by Else Conrad. *Jahrbuch für Gesetzgebung, Verwaltung und Volkswirtschaft im deutschen Reich* 32(3): 325–.

——. 1911. *Die deutschen Bühnen und ihre Angehörigen: Eine Untersuchung über ihre wirtschaftliche Lage.* Leipzig: Duncker & Humblot.

——. 1932. Der Methodenstreit in der Soziologie. *Schmollers Jahrbuch für Gesetzgebung, Verwaltung und Volkswirtschaft im deutschen Reich* 56(1) (February): 87–.

Reiss, Miss R. L. 1914. *The Report of the Land Enquiry Committee: A Reply to the Criticisms Contained in the "Grey Pamphlet."* London: Central Land and Housing Council.

——. 1914. Maintenance Grants under Separation Orders. *Women's Industrial News* (October).

Remick, Marie C. 1896. The Relation of Industrialism to Morality. *Arena* 17 (December): 32–41.

Remond, Sarah P[arker]. 1859. Speech Delivered at the Athenaeum, Manchester, England, 14 September 1859. *Manchester Weekly Times* (September 17) Reprinted in C. Peter Ripley, ed., *The Black Abolitionist Papers,* vol. 1. Chapel Hill, N.C.: University of North Carolina Press, 1985.

——. 1864. *The Negroes & Anglo-Africans as Freedmen and Soldiers.* Ladies' London Emancipation Society. London: Emily Faithfull.

——. 1868. Letter to the Editor. *Daily News* (London) (November 22). Reprinted in C. Peter Ripley, ed., *The Black Abolitionist Papers*, vol. 1. Chapel Hill, N.C.: University of North Carolina Press, 1985.

Reticker, Ruth. 1932. The Cost of Crime and Criminal Justice. *American Bar Association Journal* 18: 163–.

——. 1936. Labor Standards in NRA Codes. *American Academy of Political and Social Science, Annals* 184 (March): 72–.

——. 1940. Social Insurance Payments in the United States. *Social Security Bulletin* 3(3) (March): 27–.

——. Coauth. *See* Wiese, Mildred Janovsky.

Reynard, Hélène. 1913. *Business Methods and Secretarial Work for Girls and Women.* London: Sir I. Pitman & Sons, Ltd.

——. 1919. The Industrial Situation. *Economic Journal* 29 (September): 290–301.

——. 1920. Book Review of "Working Life of Women in the Seventeenth Century." *Economic Journal* 30(118) (June): 242–4.

——. 1920. The Guild Socialists. *Economic Journal* 30 (September): 321–30.

——. 1924. Book Review of "Economics for Helen" by H. Belloc. *Economic Journal* 34: 620–.

——. 1924. Book Review of "The Standard of Living" by N. H. Comish. *Economic Journal* 34: 452–.

——. 1928. Book Review of "Capitalist Combines" by G. M. Colman. *Economic Journal* 38 (151) (September): 445–7.

——. 1928. Book Review of "Co-operation, Its Problems and Possibilities" by A. H. Enfield. *Economic Journal* 38(151) (September): 445–7.

——. 1928. Book Review of "The Economic System." *Economic Journal* 38 (151) (September): 445–7.

——. 1929. Book Review of "Women and the Labor Movement." *Economic Journal* 39(155) (September): 435–7.

——. 1934. *Institutional Management & Accounts.* London and New York: Longmans, Green.

——. 1935. *What Is a Balance Sheet?* London: Faber & Faber Limited.

Reynolds, Bertha Capen. 1934. *Between Client and Community: A Study in Responsibility in Social Case Work.* Northampton, Mass.: Smith College School for Social Work.

Rhine, Alice Hyneman. 1891. Woman in Industry. In Annie N. Meyer, ed., *Woman's Work in America.* New York: Holt. Reprinted New York: Arno Press, 1972.

——. 1891. The Work of Women's Clubs. *Forum* 12 (December): 519–28.

[Rhys-Davids,] C[aroline]. A. Foley. 1893. Book Review of "Handbuch des Socialismus Lieferung I" by Dr. jur. Carl Stegmann and Dr. Phil. C. Hugo. *Economic Journal* 3(12) (December): 675–6.

——. 1893. Book Review of "Public Assistance of the Poor in France" by Emily Greene Balch, A.B., and of "Paris qui mendie, mal et remède" by Louis Paulian. *Economic Journal* 3(12) (December): 676–8.

——. 1893. Fashion. *Economic Journal* 3(11) (September): 458–74.

——. 1894. Book Review of "Primitive Civilisation; or, Outlines of the History of Ownership in Archaic Communities" by Edith J. Simcox. *Economic Journal* 4(16) (December): 701–4.

——. 1894. Book Review of "The Rights of Women, A Comparative Study in History and Legislation" by M. Ostrogorski and of "Woman, Her Position in the Past, Present and Future [Die Frau und der Sozialismus]" by August Bebel. *Economic Journal* 4(13) (March): 90–3.

——. 1894. Book Review of "The Royal Commission on Labour – The Employment of Women, Reports by Miss Orme, Miss Collet, Miss Abraham and Miss Irwin (Lady Assistant Commissioners) on the Conditions of Work in Various Industries." *Economic Journal* 4(13) (March): 185–91.

——. 1897. Book Review of "Rich and Poor" by Mrs. Bernard Bosanquet. *Economic Journal* 7(25) (March): 83–5.

——. 1901. Economic Conditions in Ancient India. *Economic Journal* 11 (September): 305–20.

——. 1901. Notes on Early Economic Conditions in Northern India. *Journal of the Royal Asiatic Society of Great Britain and Ireland*: 859–8. Article available online at http://pears2.lib.ohio-state.edu/FULLTEXT/JR-ENG/car.htm.

——. 1922. *Economic Conditions According to Early Buddhist Literature.* Cambridge History of India, vol. 1. Cambridge, UK: Cambridge University Press.

Rice, Mary L. 1897. *Abstract of New York State Laws Affecting the Rights and Property of Women.* Buffalo, N.Y.: Women's Educational and Industrial Union.

Rich, Margaret Elden. 1931. *The Administration of Relief in Unemployment Emergencies.* New York: Family Welfare Association of America.

——. 1938. Dealing with People in Need. In R. H. Kurtz, ed., *The Public Assistance Worker: His Responsibility to the Applicant, the Community, and Himself.* New York: Russell Sage Foundation.

——. Coauth. *See* Anderson, Harriet E.

Richards, Audrey Isabel, Ph.D. 1932. *Hunger and Work in a Savage Tribe: A Functional Study of Nutrition among the Southern Bantu.* London: G. Routledge.

——. 1932. An Anthropologist in Rhodesia. *Listener* 7(177) (June 1): 783–.

——. 1935. Tribal Government in Transition: The Babemba of North-Eastern Rhodesia. *Royal African Society, Journal* 34(137) (October): 1–26.

——. 1935. The Village Census in the Study of Culture Contact. *Africa* 8(1): 20–.

——. 1939. *Land, Labour and Diet in Northern Rhodesia: an Economic Study of the Bemba Tribe.* London: Humphrey Milford.

——. 1940. *Bemba Marriage and Modern Economic Conditions.* Livingstone, Northern Rhodesia: Rhodes–Livingstone Institute.

Richards, Ellen Henrietta [Swallow] [Mrs. R. H. Richards]. 1882. *The Chemistry of Cooking and Cleaning: A Manual for Housekeepers.* Boston: Estes & Lauriat.

——. 1889. *Domestic Economy as a Factor in Public Education.* New York: College for the Training of Teachers.

——. 1890. *The Relation of College Women to Progress in Domestic Science.* Paper presented to the Association of Collegiate Alumnae. New York?: Association of Collegiate Alumnae.

——. 1893. Scientific Cooking – Studies in the New England Kitchen. *Forum* 15 (May): 355–61.

——. 1897. *Municipal Responsibility for Healthy School-houses.* Concord, N.H.: Republican Press. Reprinted from *Transactions of the American Public Health Association.*

——. 1897. Domestic Science: What It Is and How to Study It at Home. *Outlook* 55 (April 24): 1,078–80.

——. 1898. *Food Materials and Their Adulterations.* New and corrected ed. Boston: Home Science Publishing Co.

——. 1899/1905. *The Cost of Living as Modified by Sanitary Science.* New York: J. Wiley & Sons.

——. 1899. *Plain Words about Food.* Boston: Rockwell & Churchill Press.

——. 1899. Waste of Energy in Organization. *Outlook. A Family Paper* 63: 928.

——. 1900. *University Laboratories in Relation to the Investigation of Public Health Problems and to Commercial Work.* Columbus, Ohio: Berlin Printing Co.

——. 1901/1913/1917. *The Cost of Food: A Study in Dietaries.* New York: John Wiley & Sons. 3rd ed. revised under the direction of John F. Norton.

——. 1905. *The Cost of Shelter.* 2nd ed. New York: J. Wiley & Sons.

——. 1905. Practical Suggestions for Applied Economics and Sociology in the College Curriculum. *Association of Collegiate Alumnae, Publications* 3(10) (January): 30–.

——. 1906. Wanted, a Test for "Man Power." Address delivered at the Seventh Annual Commencement, June 15, 1906, of the Thomas S. Clarkson Memorial School of Technology. *Clarkson Bulletin* III(3).

——. 1908/1911. *The Cost of Cleanness.* New York: J. Wiley & Sons.

——. 1908. *Home Economics in Elementary and Secondary Education.* S.l.: National Education Association of the United States.

——. 1908. Desirable Tendencies in Education for Women. *Association of Collegiate Alumnae, Publications* 3(17) (February): 25–.

——. 1910. *Euthenics: The Science of Controllable Environment.* Boston: Whitcomb & Barrow.

——. 1911. The Social Significance of the Home Economics Movement. *Journal of Home Economics* (April): 117–25.

Richards, Ellen H. and Marion Talbot, eds. 1887. *Home Sanitation: A Manual for Housekeepers.* Boston: Ticknor and Co.

Richards, Kirsten Daisy. 1940. The Export Trade of Chicago, 1890–1915. A.M. thesis, University of Chicago (economics, commerce-business).

Richardson, Anna Steese Sausser. 1909. *The Girl Who Earns Her Own Living.* New York: B. W. Dodge & Co.

——. 1916. *Adventures in Thrift.* Indianapolis: Bobbs-Merrill Co.

Richardson, Anne B. 1893. The Massachusetts System of Caring for State Minor Wards. In Elizabeth Cabot Putnam, ed., *Massachusetts' Care of Dependent and Delinquent Children.* Boston: Massachusetts Board of Managers, World's Fair.

Richardson [Lucas], Bertha J. 1904. *The Woman Who Spends: A Study of Her Economic Function.* Boston: Whitcomb and Barrows.

Richardson, Dorothy. 1903. *Report of Committee on the Economic Effect of Legislation Regulating Women's Labour.* British Association for the Advancement of Science.

——. 1905. *The Long Day; the Story of a New York Working Girl, as Told by Herself.* New York: Century Co.

——. 1906. The Difficulties and Dangers Confronting the Working Woman. *Annals of the American Academy of Political and Social Science* 27: 624–6.

Richardson, Eveline Mabel. *See* Burns, Eveline Mabel.

Riches, Naomi. 1932. A Study of Eighteenth Century Agriculture in the County of Norfolk, England. Ph.D. thesis, University of Chicago (history).

——. 1937. *The Agricultural Revolution in Norfolk.* Chapel Hill, N.C.: University of North Carolina Press.

Richmond, Mary E[llen]. 1896. Criticism and Reform in Charity. *Charities Review, a Journal of Practical Sociology* 5(4) (February): 169–81.

——. 1896. Married Vagabonds. *Lend a Hand, a Journal of Organized Philanthropy* 16: 103.

——. 1897. Home Making and Charity. *Charities Review* 6(2) (April): 118–26.

——. 1897. Training of Charity Workers. *Charities Review* 6(4) (June): 308–21.

——. 1897. Convention of Working Women's Clubs at Philadelphia. *Charities Review* 6(4) (June): 351–2.

——. 1899/1910. *Friendly Visiting among the Poor: A Handbook for Charity Workers.* New York: Macmillan.

——. 1900. What Is Charity Organization? *Charities Review* 9 (January): 490–500.

——. 1901. *Charitable Co-operation.* Boston: George H. Ellis. Reprinted from the *Proceedings of the Twenty-eighth National Conference of Charities and Correction*, 1901.

——. 1901. Some Methods of Cooperation in Charity. *Charities: A Weekly Review of Local and General Philanthropy* 7: 108, 196.

——. 1905. Public Subsidies to Private Institutions in Pennsylvania. *Charities; a Weekly Review of Local and General Philanthropy* 14: 843.

——. 1905/6. First Principles in the Relief of Distress. *Union Seminary Magazine* 17: 185–.

——. 1905/6. Retail Method in Reform and Reformers. *International Journal of Ethics Devoted to the Advancement of Ethical Knowledge and Practice* 16: 171.

——. 1907/1911. *The Good Neighbor in the Modern City.* Philadelphia: J. B. Lippincott.

——. 1911. *The Inter-relation of Social Movements.* Social Service Series, Bulletin no. 17. Boston: American Unitarian Association Department of Social and Public Service.

——. 1912. *How Social Workers Can Aid Housing Reform.* National Housing Association Publications, no. 15. New York: National Housing Association.

——. 1917. *Social Diagnosis.* New York: Russell Sage Foundation.

——. 1922. *What Is Social Case Work? An Introductory Description*. New York: Russell Sage Foundation.

——. 1922. Some Relations of Family Case Work to Social Progress. *Family* 3(5) (July): 99–.

——. 1933. Social Diagnosis (Marie Baum). *Archiv für Sozialwissenschaft und Sozialpolitik* 69: 93–.

Richmond, Mary Ellen, Joanna Carver Colcord, and Ruth Z. S. Mann, eds. 1930. *The Long View; Papers and Addresses by Mary E. Richmond*. New York: Russell Sage Foundation.

Riggs, Margaret Joanna. 1935. The Exploration and Pastoral Occupancy of Australia. S.M. thesis, University of Chicago (geography).

——. 1936. The Influence of the Pastoral Industry on Australian Exploration. *Economic Geography* 12(3) (July): 279–86.

——. 1938/9. Book Review of "Our Economic World" by D. O. Kinsman. *Southwestern Social Sciences Quarterly* 19: 338–.

Ring, Sister Mary Ignatius. 1931. Villeneuve-Bargemont, Catholic Social Protagonist: The First Important Precursor of Leo XIII. Ph.D. thesis, St. Louis University (economics, history).

——. 1935. *Villeneuve-Bargemont: Precursor of Modern Social Catholicism, 1784–1850*. Milwaukee, Wisc.: Bruce Publishing Company.

Risch, Erna. 1931. Encouragement and Aid to Immigrants, 1607–1830. Ph.D. thesis, University of Chicago (history).

——. 1936. Immigrant Aid Societies before 1820. *Pennsylvania Magazine of History and Biography* 60: 15–.

——. 1937. Encouragement of Immigration as Revealed in Colonial Legislation. *Virginia Magazine of History and Biography*, vol. 45. Richmond, Va.: Virginia Historical Society.

——. 1939. Joseph Crellius, Immigrant Broker. *New England Quarterly* 12(1/4): 241–.

[Ritchie,] [Lady] Anne Isabella Thackeray. 1861. Toilers and Spinsters. *Cornhill Magazine* 3: 318–31.

——. 1864. The End of a Long Day's Work [Nassau Senior]. *Cornhill Magazine* 10 (August): 253–6.

——. 1874. *Toilers and Spinsters and Other Essays*. London: Smith, Elder.

——. 1882. Miss [Maria] Edgeworth. *Cornhill Magazine* 46 (October): 404–26; (November): 526–45.

Ritchie, Ellen S. H. 1895. A National Waste: The Labour of Married Women. *Westminster Review* 144 (November): 545–.

Ritts, Elizabeth. Coauth. *See* Crook, Evelyn Buchan.

Robbins, Helen. 1928. A Comparison of the Effects of the Black Death on the Economic Organization of France and England. *Journal of Political Economy* 36 (August): 447–79.

Robbins, Jane E. 1894. Charity that Helps, and Other Charity. *Forum* 18 (December): 502–7.

Roberson, Nellie. 1922. The Organized Work of Women in One State. *Journal of Social Forces* 1(1) (November): 50–5.

——. 1923. The Organized Work of Women in One State. *Journal of Social Forces* 1(2) (January): 173–7.

——. 1923. The Organized Work of Women in One State. *Journal of Social Forces* 1(5) (September): 613–15.

Roberts, Hazel Van Dyke. 1935. *Boisguilbert, Economist of the Reign of Louis XIV.* New York: Columbia University Press.

——. 1935. Boisguilbert, Economist of the Reign of Louis XIV. Ph.D. thesis, Columbia University (economics).

Roberts, Mary Catherine. 1932. The Land Utilization of the Town of Lowville, Lewis County, N.Y. M.A. thesis, Clark University.

——. 1933. Rumania To-day. *Economic Geography* 9(3) (July): 230–55.

——. 1938. Cultural Adjustments in the Central Massachusetts Uplands. Ph.D. thesis, Clark University (geography).

Roberts-Austin, Mrs. 1894. The Proposed Imperial Exhibition of Women's Work. *Englishwoman's Review* XXV, n.s. 224 (October): 217.

Robertson, Anne Isabella. 1872. *Women's Need of Parliamentary Representation. A Lecture upon the Necessity of Giving Women the Parliamentary Franchise.* Irish National Society for Women's Suffrage. Dublin: R. D. Webb.

Robertson, Ina Cullom. 1924. The Relation of Geographic Factors to Land Utilization in the Ozark Region of Southern Illinois. M.A. thesis, Clark University.

——. 1928. The Ozark Orchard Center of Southern Illinois. *Economic Geography* 4(3) (July): 253–66.

——. 1929. *Syllabus for Economic Geography: Tentative.* Bismarck, N. Dak.: Department of Public Instruction, Knight Printing Co.

Robins, Margaret Dreier [Mrs. Raymond Robins]. 1907. *The Lot of the Woman Telegrapher: An Open Letter.* Chicago: Women's Trade Union League of Illinois.

——. 1910–19?. *The Progress of Industry: Standards Raised through Legislation.* Chicago: Educational Committee of the National Women's Trade Union League.

——. 1913. *Need of a National Training School for Women Organizers; the Minimum Wage, Industrial Education. Presidential Address to the Fourth Biennial Convention, National Women's Trade Union League, St. Louis, June 2, 1913.* Chicago: National Women's Trade Union League.

——. 1914. *Educational Plans of the National Women's Trade Union League.* Chicago: National Women's Trade Union League of America.

——. 1917. *Address of the President, Mrs. Raymond Robins at the Sixth Biennial Convention of the National Women's Trade Union League, Kansas City, Mo., June 3–9, 1917.* Chicago: National Women's Trade Union League.

——. 1919. *Address of Mrs. Raymond Robins, President of the National Women's Trade Union League of America: to the Seventh Biennial Convention, Philadelphia, June 2, 1919.* Chicago: National Women's Trade Union League.

——. 1919. *Self-government in the Workshop: The Demand of the Women's Trade Union League*. Chicago: National Women's Trade Union League of America. Reprinted from *Life and Labor* (April 1912).

——. 1921. *International Congress of Working Women, Meeting in Geneva, Switzerland, October 17, 1921: Address to the Delegates*. Chicago: National Women's Trade Union League of America.

Robinson, A[gnes]. Mary F[rances]. [Mme. James Darmesteter]. 1890. Rural Life in France in the Fourteenth Century. *Fortnightly Review*, n.s. 48 (November): 738–52; (December): 865–77.

——. 1890. The Workmen of Paris in 1390 and in 1890. *Fortnightly Review*, n.s. 48 [o.s. 54] (July): 82–106.

——. 1891. Private Life in France in the Fourteenth Century. *Fortnightly Review*, n.s. 50 (August): 244–58.

——. 1891. Private Life in France in the Fourteenth Century: The Middle Class. *Fortnightly Review*, n.s. 49. (May): 751–61.

——. 1892. France in the Fourteenth Century – V: The Jews. *Fortnightly Review*, n.s. 51. (March): 369–89.

Robinson, F[rances]. Mabel. 1887. Our Working Women and Their Earnings. *Fortnightly Review*, n.s. 42 (July): 50–63.

——. 1888. Pawnbroking in England and Abroad. *Fortnightly Review*, n.s. 44 (July): 69–88.

Robinson, Harriet [Jane] H[anson]. 1881. *Massachusetts in the Woman Suffrage Movement: A General, Political, Legal and Legislative History from 1774 to 1881*. Boston: Roberts Brothers.

——. 1882. Early Factory Life in New England. *Journal of Social Science* 16 (December): 127–40.

——. 1883. Early Factory Labor in New England. In *Fourteenth Annual Report of the Massachusetts Bureau of Statistics of Labor*. Reprinted Boston: Wright & Potter Printing Co., 1889.

——. 1898. *Loom and Spindle, or Life Among the Early Mill Girls, With a sketch of "The Lowell Offering" and Some of Its Contributors*. New York: T. Y. Crowell. Reprinted New York: T. Y. Crowell, 1983.

Robinson, Joan. 1932. Imperfect Competition and Falling Supply Price. *Economic Journal* 42(168) (December): 544–4.

——. 1933. *The Economics of Imperfect Competition*. London: Macmillan.

——. 1933. Book Review of "The Co-ordination of the Laws of Distribution" by P. H. Wicksteed. *Economic Journal* 43: 301–.

——. 1933. Book Review of "Theory of Economic Equilibrium" by Attilio Da Empoli. *Economic Journal* 43: 666–.

——. 1933. Decreasing Costs: A Reply to Mr. Harrod. *Economic Journal* 43(117) (September): 531–2.

——. 1933. The Imperfection of the Market: A Further Note. *Economic Journal* 43(169) (March): 113–25.

——. 1933. A Parable on Savings and Investment. *Economica* 13 (February): 75–84.

——. 1933. Shakespeare and Mr. Looney. *Cambridge Review* 54(1334) (May 12): 389–.

——. 1933. The Theory of Money and the Analysis of Output. *Review of Economic Studies* 1(1) (October): 22–6.

——. 1934. Book Review of "Increasing Return" by G. T. Jones and Colin Clark, ed. *Journal of Political Economy* 42: 694–.

——. 1934. Book Review of "The Rate of Interest in a Progressive State" by J. E. Meade. *Economic Journal* 44: 282–.

——. 1934. Euler's Theorem and the Problem of Distribution. *Economic Journal* 44(175) (September): 398–414.

——. 1934. Mr. Fraser on Taxation and Returns. *Review of Economic Studies* 1(2) (February): 137–40.

——. 1934. What Is Perfect Competition? *Quarterly Journal of Economics* 49(1) (November): 104–20.

——. 1935. Book Review of "German Monetary Theory, 1905–1933" by H. S. Ellis. *Economic Journal* 45: 729–.

——. 1935. A Fundamental Objection to Laissez-faire. *Economic Journal* 45(179) (September): 80–2.

——. 1935/6. A Note on Elasticity of Substitution. *Review of Economic Studies* 3: 148–.

——. 1936. Banking Policy and the Exchanges. *Review of Economic Studies* 3(3) (June): 226–9.

——. 1936. Book Review of "Bankers, Statesmen and Economists" by P. Einzig. *Economic Journal* 46: 122–.

——. 1936. Book Review of "Britain without Capitalists." *Economic Journal* 46: 704.

——. 1936. Book Review of "The Nature of the Capitalist Crisis" by J. Strachey. *Economic Journal* 46, 298–.

——. 1936. Book Review of "Patterns of Economic Activity" by A. Radford. *Economic Journal* 46: 706–.

——. 1936. Book Review of "The Trade Cycle" by R. F. Harrod. *Economic Journal* 46: 691–.

——. 1936. Disguised Unemployment. *Economic Journal* 46(182) (June): 225–37.

——. 1936. Disguised Unemployment. A Rejoinder. *Economic Journal* 46(184) (December): 759–60.

——. 1936. Dr. Machlup's Commonsense of the Elasticity of Substitution. *Review of Economic Studies* 3(2) (February): 148–50.

——. 1936. The Long-period History of Employment. *Zeitschrift für Nationalökonomie* 7 (March): 74–93.

——. 1936. The Long-period Theory of Employment. *Zeitschrift für Nationalökonomie* 7(1) (March 2): 74–.

——. 1937. *Essays in the Theory of Employment.* Oxford: B. Blackwell.

——. 1937/1938. *Introduction to the Theory of Employment.* London: Macmillan.

——. 1937. Book Review of "Abolish Slumps. A Diagnosis of the Trade Cycle" by A. W. Knight. *Economic Journal* 47: 339–.

——. 1937. Book Review of "Exchange Depreciation" by S. E. Harris. *Economic Journal* 47: 699–.

——. 1937. The Economic System in a Socialist State. *Cambridge Review* 58(1425) (February 26): 289–.

——. 1938. Book Review of "The Economics of Inflation" by C. Bresciani-Turroni. *Economic Journal* 48: 507–.

——. 1938. The Classification of Inventions. *Review of Economic Studies* 5(2) (February): 139–42.

——. 1938. The Concept of Hoarding. *Economic Journal* 48(190) (June): 231–6.

——. 1938. Essays in the Theory of Employment. *Annales sociologiques; Série D: Sociologie économique* 3: 70–.

——. 1939. Book Review of "Monetary Equilibrium" by G. Myrdal. *Economic Journal* 49: 493–.

——. 1940. Book Review of "Monetary Experiments" by R. A. Lester. *Economic Journal* 50: 280.

——. 1940. Book Review of "A Programme for Progress" by Strachey. *Political Quarterly (1930-)* 11: 280–.

——. 1940. Book Review of "The Real Cost of the War" by J. K. Horsefield. *Economic Journal* 50: 505.

——. 1940. Book Review of "Ways and Means of War" by G. Crowther. *Economic Journal* 50: 505.

Robinson, Lelia Josephine. 1890. *The Law of Husband and Wife Compiled for Popular Use*. Boston: Lee and Shepard; New York: C. T. Dillingham.

Robinson, Lona I. 1895. Representative Women on Social Problems: Is the Single Tax Enough? (Symposium) *Arena* 13 (August): 411–13.

Robinson, M[arjorie]. E. 1922. *Public Finance*. London: Nisbet & Co.; New York: Harcourt, Brace and Co. Reprinted London, Nisbet & Co., 1928.

Robinson, Margaret. 1898. Book Review of "The Cotton Industry: An Essay in American Economic History" by M. B. Hammond. *Economic Journal* 8(31) (September): 368–73.

——. 1900. Book Review of "Die Gewerkschastsbewegung: Darstellung der gewerkschaftlichen Organisation der Arbeiter und der Arbeitgeber aller Lander" by Von W. Kulemann. *Economic Journal* 10(38) (June): 218–21.

Robinson, Margaret Fothergill. 1911. *The Poor Law Enigma*. London: J. Murray.

——. 1913. *The Spirit of Association, Being Some Account of the Gilds, Friendly Societies, Co-operative Movement, and Trade Unions of Great Britain*. London: J. Murray.

Robinson, Mary Alice. 1931. Trade Between Britain and India. M.S. thesis, University of Chicago (political science, international law and relations).

Robinson, Mary V[iola]. 1940. Working Women. *Pi Lambda Theta Journal* 18(4) (May): 120–.

——. Coauth. *See* Best, Ethel Lombard; Manning, Caroline; Winslow, Mary Nelson.

Robinson, Mrs. T. 1855. The Private Life and Household of Charlemagne [Book review essay]. *North American Review* 81 (July): 112–59.

——. 1856. Slavery in Russia [Book review essay]. *North American Review* 82 (April): 293–318.

Robison, Sophia Moses. 1935. *An Inquiry into the Present Functioning of the Women's Court in Relation to the Problem of Prostitution in New York City*. New York: Welfare Council of New York City, Research Bureau.

——. 1937. Can Delinquency Be Measured? Ph.D. thesis, Columbia University (sociology).

Roche, Josephine A[spinwall]. 1918. *Wage Earning Women and Girls in Baltimore: A Study of the Cost of Living in 1918*. New York: National Consumers' League.

——. 1929. Seeking a New Era in the Industrial Relations of Colorado. *American Federationist* 36(11) (November): 1,320–.

——. 1937. Economic Health and Public Health Objectives. *American Journal of Public Health and the Nation's Health* 25(11) (November): 1,181–.

——. 1937. Health of the Nation's Workers. *Personnel Journal* 16(5) (November): 159–.

——. 1937. Medical Care as a Public Health Function. *American Journal of Public Health and the Nation's Health* 27(12) (December): 1,221–.

——. 1938. *Proceedings of the National Health Conference: July 18, 19, 20, 1938, Washington, D.C.* Harvard Medicine Preservation Microfilm Project, Part 2, 03895. Washington: U.S. Government Printing Office for the Interdepartmental Committee to Coordinate Health and Welfare Activities.

——. 1938. The Worker's Stake in a National Health Program. *American Labor Legislation Review* 28: 125–30.

——. 1939. *Broadcast on the Consumers' Stake in Labor Problems*. New York: National Consumers' League.

——. 1939. National Action for Health. *American Teacher* 23(8) (May): 9–.

——. 1939. National Action for Health. *Social Service Review* 13(1/4) (March/December): 579–.

Rochebillard, Marie Louise. 1904. *Les Syndicats d'ouvrières lyonnaises*. Lillie.

Rochester, Anna. 1914. *Children at Work on Men's Clothing*. New York: National Child Labor Committee, Inc.

——. 1918. *Child Labor in Warring Countries*. New York: National Labor Committee.

——. 1921. Immigration and Internationalism. *World Tomorrow* 4(11) (November): 336.

——. 1921. Immigration and Internationalism: II. *World Tomorrow* 4(12) (December): 375–.

——. 1922. What Eleven Families Spend. *World Tomorrow* 5(6) (June): 169–.

——. 1922. What Property Does to the Individual. *World Tomorrow* 5(4) (April): 105–.

——. 1923. The Future in the Present. *World Tomorrow* 6(7) (July): 203–.

——. 1924. The Pacifist's "Preparedness." *World Tomorrow* 7(7) (July): 213–.

——. 1925. Need We Fear Class-consciousness? *World Tomorrow* 8(1) (January): 5–.

——. 1925. Sowing the Wind. *World Tomorrow* 8(11) (November): 330–.

——. 1927. Glimpses of the New China. *World Tomorrow* 10(2) (February): 79–.

——. 1927. Notes from the Philippines. *World Tomorrow* 10(3) (March): 132–.

——. 1930. Communism: A World Movement. *World Tomorrow* 13(1) (January): 16–.

——. 1931. *Labor and Coal.* New York: International Publishers.

——. 1932. *Wall Street.* New York: International Pamphlets.

——. 1933. *Profits and Wages: The Effect of the Crisis on Employers' Incomes and Workers' Earnings.* 2nd ed. New York: International Pamphlets.

——. 1933. *Your Dollar under Roosevelt.* New York: Workers' Library.

——. 1934. Mining in the Soviet Union. *Soviet Russia Today* 3(10) (December): 12–.

——. 1936. *Rulers of America: A Study of Finance Capital.* New York: International Publishers; London: Lawrence & Wishart.

——. 1936/7. Book Review of "Rural Trends in Depression Years. A Survey of Village-centered Agricultural Communities, 1930–1936" by Edmund de Brunner and Irving Lorge. *Science & Society* 1: 570.

——. 1939. Book Review of "Changing Aspects of Rural Relief" by A. R. Mangus. *Science & Society* 3: 556.

——. 1939. Book Review of "Farming Hazards in the Drought Area" by R. S. Kifer and H. L. Stewart. *Science & Society* 3: 556.

——. 1939. Book Review of "Five Reports by W.P.A." *Science & Society* 3: 556.

——. 1939. Book Review of "Five Years of Rural Relief" by Waller Wynne, Jr. *Science & Society* 3: 556.

——. 1939. Book Review of "Forty Acres and Steel Mules" by Herman Clarence Nixon. *Science & Society* 3: 128.

——. 1939. Book Review of "Research Memorandum on Rural Life in the Depression" by Dwight Sanderson. *Science & Society* 3: 128.

——. 1939. Book Review of "Rural Families on Relief" by Carle C. Zimmerman and Nathan L. Whittan. *Science & Society* 3: 556.

——. 1939. Book Review of "Rural Youth, Their Situation and Prospects" by Bruce L. Melvin and Elna N. Smith. *Science & Society* 3: 556.

——. 1939. Book Review of "Seven Lean Years" by Ellen Winston. *Science & Society* 3: 556.

——. 1939. Book Review of "Social Problems in Agriculture. Record of the Permanent Agricultural Committee of the I.L.O." *Science & Society* 3: 556.

——. 1940. *Why Farmers Are Poor: The Agricultural Crisis in the United States.* New York: International Publishers.

——. 1940. On the Nature of Rent. *Science & Society* 4(1): 57–69.

Rollins, Alice W[ellington]. 1887/8. The New Uncle Tom's Cabin. *Forum* 4 (September/February): 220–7.

——. 1888. *Uncle Tom's Tenement: A Novel.* Boston: W. E. Smythe.

——. 1888. The Tenement-house Problem. *Forum* 5 (March/August): 207–15.

——. 1890. Shall Our Daughters Have Dowries? *North American Review* 151(6) (December): 766–9.

Rollins, Mabel Alice. 1940. Some Store Practices in the Sale of Washing Machines on Installment Credit. Ph.D. thesis, Cornell University (economics).

——. Coauth. *See* Canon, Helen.

Rolph, Inez Katherine. 1924. *Cooperative Retail Advertising.* Washington: U.S. Bureau of Foreign and Direct Commerce.

——. 1926. *Vehicular Traffic Congestion and Retail Business.* Washington: U.S. Bureau of Foreign and Domestic Commerce.

——. 1932. The Population Pattern in Relation to Retail Buying: As Exemplified in Baltimore. *American Journal of Sociology* 38(3) (November): 368–76.

——. 1933. *The Location Structure of Retail Trade Based on a Study of Baltimore.* Washington: U.S. Bureau of Foreign and Domestic Commerce.

——. 1936. *Retail Parcel Delivery Companies: Scope and Character of Service.* Washington: U.S. Bureau of Foreign and Domestic Commerce.

Roosevelt, Eleanor R. [Mrs. Franklin D.] 1933. *It's up to the Women.* New York: Frederick A. Stokes.

——. 1933. The Married Woman in Business. *Woman's Home Companion* 60 (November).

——. 1934. The National Conference on the Education of Negroes. *Journal of Negro Education* 3(4) (October): 573.

——. 1934. Subsistence Farmsteads. *Forum and Century* 91(4) (April): 199.

——. 1936. The Negro and Social Change – An Address. *Opportunity* 14(1) (January): 22.

——. 1940. Defense and the Minority Groups. *Opportunity* 18(12) (December): 356.

Rorer, Sarah T. 1895. Cooperation in Housekeeping. *Ladies' Home Journal* 12 (January).

Rose, Ernestine. 1917. *Bridging the Gulf; Work with the Russian Jews and Other Newcomers.* New York: Immigrant Publication Society.

Rose, Ernestine L. 1851. *An Address on Woman's Rights, Delivered before the People's Sunday Meeting, in Cochituate Hall Oct. 19, 1851.* Boston: J. P. Mendum.

Ross, Adelaide Sandars. 1882. Emigration for Women. *Macmillan's* 45 (February): 312–17.

Ross, Eva J[eany]. 1935/6. Belgian Catholics and the Land. *Catholic World* 142(847/852) (October/March): 140–.

——. 1937. Belgian Agricultural Cooperation: A Study in Social Adjustment. Ph.D. thesis, Yale University (sociology).

——. 1939. *What Is Economics? A Brief Survey of Our Economic Life.* Milwaukee, Wisc.: Bruce Publishing Company.

Ross, Janet Anne. 1893. Land Tenure in Tuscany. *Macmillan's* 71 (January): 195–8.

Ross, Lisa. 1912. *Weibliche Dienstboten und Dienstbotenhaltung in England.* Tübingen: J. C. B. Mohr. Reprinted Bad Feilnbach, Germany: Schmidt Periodicals, 1993.

——. 1912. Die weibliche Diensboten in England. Thesis, Heidelberg.

Ross, Mary. 1931. What Ten Million Women Want. *Parents* 6 (August): 15–16.

Rossiter, Elisabeth. 1882. Unnatural Children [ill health in slums]. *Fortnightly Review*, n.s. 31 [o.s. 37] (May): 612–19.

Roumania, Queen of [Carmen Sylva]. 1889. Peasant Life in Roumania. *Forum* 7 (June): 452–65.

Routledge, Florence. 1891. Trades Unionism among Women. *Fortnightly Review*, n.s. 49 [o.s. 55] (May): 746–50.

Routzahn, Mary Swain. 1920. *Travelling Publicity Campaigns: Educational Tours of Railroad Trains and Motor Vehicles*. New York: Russell Sage Foundation.

——. 1929. Why Have a Plan? *American Journal of Public Health and the Nation's Health* 19(5) (May): 513–.

——. 1937. Publicizing Human Needs. *Public Opinion Quarterly* 1(4) (October): 126–.

Rouzade, Léonie. 1880. *Développement du programme de la société l'Union des femmes: discours*. Paris: L'Union des femmes.

——. 1895. *Petit Catéchisme de morale laïque et socialiste*. Meudon: chez l'auteur.

——. 1896. *La Femme et le peuple. Organisation sociale de demain*. Meudon: En vente chez l'auteur.

Royden, A. Maude. 1912. *Votes and Wages: How Women's Suffrage Will Improve the Economic Position of Women*. London: National Union of Women's Suffrage Societies.

——. 1917. *Women and the Sovereign State*. London: Headley Bros.

——. 1919. *National Endowment of Motherhood*. London: Women's International League.

Royer, Clémence Auguste. 1862. *Théeorie de l'impôt, ou la Dîme sociale*. 2 vols. Paris: Guillaumin.

——. 1876. Les Phases sociales des nations. *Journal des économistes* (July).

——. 1877. Du Groupement des peuples et de l'hégémonie universelle. *Journal des économistes* (May).

Ruffin, Josephine St. Pierre. 1894. Women in Business. *Woman's Era* (March).

——. 1894. Women in Politics. *Woman's Era* (November).

——. 1896. Separate Car Law. *Woman's Era* (February).

Ruggles, Catherine G. 1937. The Financial History of Cambridge, 1846–1929. Ph.D. thesis, Radcliffe College (economics).

——. 1939. The Relation of Corporate Surpluses to Income and Employment. *American Economic Review* 29 (December): 724–33.

——. 1940. Book Review of "Illinois Tax Problems." *American Economic Review* 30: 901.

——. 1940. Book Review of "Property Taxes." *American Economic Review* 30: 902.

——. 1940/1. State Aid and Shared Taxes in Illinois. *Illinois Law Review* 35: 754–.

Rulo, Zallie. 1885. The Indian Woman. *Southern Workman* 14 (June): 62–.

Ruml, Frances. 1928. The Formative Period of Higher Commercial Education in American Universities. *Journal of Business of the University of Chicago* 1(2) (April): 238–63.

Rush, Caroline E. 1852. *The North and the South, or Slavery and Its Contrasts: A Tale of Real Life.* Philadelphia: Crissy & Markley. Reprinted New York: Negro Universities Press, 1968; Freeport, N.Y.: Books for Libraries Press, 1971.

Russell, the Hon. Mrs. Bertrand [Alys]. 1896. The Woman Movement in Germany. *Nineteenth Century* 40 (July/December): 97–104.

——. 1903. Four Days in a Factory. *Contemporary Review* 84 (July): 52–.

Russell, Frances E. 1895. Representative Women on Social Problems: Is the Single Tax Enough? (Symposium) *Arena* 13(3) (August): 418–24.

——. 1896. Is the Single Tax Enough? (Symposium): Foundation and Fellowship. *Arena* 15 (May): 960–4.

——. 1896. Is the Single Tax Enough? (Symposium): Notes in Reply. *Arena* 15 (January): 206–11.

Rutland, Duchess of [Lady John Manners]. See Manners, Janetta Hughan.

Ruutz-Rees, Janet E[mily]. 1882/3. Women's Wages. *Century Illustrated Monthly Magazine* 25 (November/April): 475–.

——. 1890. Wage Values in America: The Experience of a Bread-winner. *Westminster Review* 134 (July): 76–81.

Rye, Maria S. 1856. The Property of Married Women. *Englishwoman's Domestic Magazine* 8(5) (November): 234–8.

——. 1859. The Rise and Progress of Telegraphs. *English Woman's Journal* 4(22) (November): 256–63. Reprinted in Candida Ann Lacey, ed., *Barbara Leigh Smith Bodichon and the Langham Place Group*. London and New York: Routledge, 1987.

——. 1860. On Assisted Emigration. *English Woman's Journal* 5 (June): 235–40. Reprinted in Candida Ann Lacey, ed., *Barbara Leigh Smith Bodichon and the Langham Place Group*. London and New York: Routledge, 1987.

——. 1860–1. The Englishwoman in London. Serialized in *Englishwoman's Domestic Magazine.*

——. 1861. Emigration of Educated Women. Paper read at the National Association for Promotion of Social Science Congress in Dublin, 1861. *English Woman's Journal* 7 (March). Published as pamphlet, London: Emily Faithfull/Victoria Press.

——. 1861–3. The Domestic History of England. *Englishwoman's Domestic Magazine* (May 1861–April 1863). Serialized in 23 parts.

——. 1866. On Female Emigration. *Social Science Journal*: 445–56.

Rylah, Margaret. 1937. Book Review of "Crises and Cycles" by W. Ropke. *Economic Record* 13(25) (December): 305–.

——. 1938. National Income and Company Profits in Australia. *Economic Review* 14 (June): 98–104.

S

Sadlier, Mary Anne [Madden]. 1850. *Willy Burke; or, The Irish Orphan in America.* Boston: Donahoe. [*novel*]

——. 1861. *Bessy Conway; or, The Irish Girl in America.* New York: D. & J. Sadlier & Co. [*novel*]

Sainsbury, Ethel Bruce. 1908. *A Calendar of the Court Minutes, etc., of the East India Company, 1635–1639.* With an introduction and notes by William Foster. Oxford: Clarendon Press.

——. 1909. *A Calendar of the Court Minutes etc. of the East India Company, 1640–1643.* Oxford: Clarendon Press.

——. 1912. *A Calendar of the Court Minutes, etc. of the East India Company, 1644–1649.* Oxford: Clarendon Press.

——. 1913. *A Calendar of the Court Minutes, etc. of the East India Company, 1650–1654.* Oxford: Clarendon Press.

——. 1916. *A Calendar of the Court Minutes, etc., of the East India Company, 1655–1659.* Oxford: Clarendon Press.

——. 1922. *A Calendar of the Court Minutes, etc., of the East India Company, 1660–1663.* Oxford: Clarendon Press.

——. 1925. *A Calendar of the Court Minutes, etc., of the East India Company, 1664–1667.* Oxford: Clarendon Press.

——. 1929. *A Calendar of the Court Minutes, etc., of the East India Company, 1668–1670.* Oxford: Clarendon Press.

——. 1932. *A Calendar of the Court Minutes etc., of the East India Company, 1671–1673.* Oxford: Clarendon Press.

——. 1935. *A Calendar of the Court Minutes, etc., of the East India Company, 1674–1676.* Oxford: Clarendon Press.

——. 1939. *A Calendar of the Court Minutes, etc., of the East India Company, 1677–1679.* Oxford: Clarendon Press.

St. Leger, Mary and Kingsley Harrison. 1903. *The Wages of Sin.* New York: R. F. Fenno & Company.

Sainte-Croix, Avril de [Mme. Ghénia]. 1901. *La Serve: Iniquité sociale.* Paris: P. Dupont.

——. 1907. *Le Feminisme.* Paris: V. Giard and E. Brière.

——. 1919. *Le Travail des femmes et le demi-temps.* Paris: Le musée sociale.

Sakmann, Marianne. 1937. *Social Insurance for Salaried Employees in Austria*. Bureau Memorandum, no. 16. Washington: U.S. Social Security Board Bureau of Research and Statistics.

——. 1938. *Unemployment and Health Insurance in Great Britain, 1911–1937*. Washington: Social Security Board, Bureau of Research and Statistics.

——. 1938. Unemployment and Health Insurance in Great Britain, 1911–37. *Social Security Bulletin* 1(8) (August): 23–.

Salès, Mme. Maria J. [Saxton]. 1888. *The Master-key of Social Reform; or, the Gradual Abolition of Hereditary Property*. London: William Reeves.

Salmon, Lucy Maynard. 1892. Earnings of Women in Michigan. *Publications of the American Statistical Association* III(20) (December): 235–8.

——. 1892. A Statistical Inquiry Concerning Domestic Service. *Publications of the American Statistical Association*, n.s. III(18–19) (June/September): 89–118.

——. 1892. The Woman's Exchange – Charity or Business? *Forum* 13 (May): 394–406.

——. 1893. Book Review of "Women's Wages" by William Smart. *Journal of Political Economy* 1(4) (September): 608–10.

——. 1893. Domestic Service from the Standpoint of the Employee. *Cosmopolitan* (July).

——. 1893. Some Historical Aspects of Domestic Service. *New England Magazine* 8 (April): 175–84. Reprinted Boston: J. T. & E. Buckingham.

——. 1894. The Union of Utrecht. *American Historical Association Annual Report for the Year 1893*. Washington: U.S. Government Printing Office.

——. 1896. Book review of "William the Silent, Prince of Orange" by Ruth Putnam. *American Historical Review* 1 (January): 329–31.

——. 1897. *Domestic Service*. New York: Macmillan. 2nd ed., 1901. Reprinted New York: Arno Press, 1972.

——. 1898. Domestic Service I, II. *Chautauquan* 27 (April/September): 191-, 308–.

——. 1905. Recent Progress in the Study of Domestic Service. *Atlantic Monthly* 96: 628.

——. 1906. *Progress in the Household*. Boston and New York: Houghton, Mifflin & Co.

——. 1908. The Economics of Spending. *Association of Collegiate Alumnae, Publications* 3(18) (December): 85–.

——. 1909/10. Book Review of "Women in Industry – A Study in American Economic History" by Edith Abbott. *American Journal of Sociology* 15(1/6): 698–.

——. 1911. On the College Professor. *Library Journal* 36(2) (February): 51–.

——. 1912. Democracy in the Household. *American Journal of Sociology* 17(4) (January): 437–57.

——. 1912. The Evolution of the Teacher. *History Teacher's Magazine* 3(2) (February): 23–.

——. 1915. *The Dutch West India Company on the Hudson*. Poughkeepsie, N.Y.: Lansing & Broas.

——. 1917/18. Book Review of "Why Men Fight" by Bertrand Russell. *American Journal of Sociology* 23(1/6): 847–.

——. 1926/7. The Newspaper and Research. *American Journal of Sociology* 32(2) (September): 217–.

——. 1927. Place-names and Personal Names as Records of History. *American Speech* 2(1/12): 228–.

Salomon, Alice. 1902. *Soziale Frauenpflichten: Vorträge gehalten in deutschen Frauenvereinen*. Gerritsen Women's History, no. 2488. Berlin: O. Liebmann.

——. 1906. *Die Ursachen der ungleichen Entlohnung von Männer und Frauenarbeit*. Leipzig: Duncker & Humblot. Reprinted in Bad Feilnbach, Germany: Schmidt, 1990.

——. 1906. Book Review of "Heimarbeitsliteratur." *Jahrbücher für Nationalökonomie und Statistik*, series 3, 31(6) (June): 828–.

——. 1906. Book Review of "Die Weber in der Gegenwart. Sozialpolitische Wanderungen durch die Hausweberei und die Webfabrik" by Robert Wilbrandt. *Jahrbücher für Nationalökonomie und Statistik* series. 3, 32(1) (July): 136–.

——. 1907. *Labour Laws for Women in Germany*. History of Women, reel 938, no. 8,156. London: Women's Industrial Council.

——. 1907. Book Review of "Drei Klassen von Lohnarbeiterinnen in Industrie und Handel der Stadt Karlsruhe. Bericht, erstattet an das Grossherzoglilche Ministerium des Innern und herausgegeben von der Grossherzoglich Badischen Fabrikinspektion" by Marie Baum. *Jahrbücher für Nationalökonomie und Statistik*, series 3, 34(2) (August): 266–.

——. 1907. Book Review of "Die Heimarbeit in Berlin. Bericht der Handelskammer zu Berlin." *Jahrbücher für Nationalökonomie und Statistik*, series 3, 34(3) (September): 420–.

——. 1908. *Soziale Frauenbildung*. Leipzig and Berlin: B. G. Teubner.

——. 1908. Literatur zur Frauenfrage. Die Entwicklung der Theorie der Frauenbewegung. *Archiv für Sozialwissenschaft und Sozialpolitik* 26: 451–.

——. 1909/1926/1928. *Einführung in die Volkswirtslehre. Ein Lehrbuch für Frauenschulen*. Leipzig: B. G. Teubner.

——. 1909. Wirtschaftliche Probleme der Frauenbewegung. *Archiv für Rechts- und Wirtschaftsphilosophie* 2(3) (March): 359–.

——. 1910. Book Review of "Die Frauenfrage im Mittelalter. Zweiter Auflage" by Max Hafemann. *Jahrbuch für Gesetzgebung, Verwaltung und Volkswirtschaft im deutschen Reich* 34(3): 456–.

——. 1910. Book Review of "Die Schulspeisung (Heft 89 der Schriften des Deutschen Vereins für Armenpflege und Wohltätigkeit)" by Helene Simon. *Jahrbuch für Gesetzgebung, Verwaltung und Volkswirtschaft im deutschen Reich* 34(2): 392.

——. 1913. *Zwanzig Jahre soziale Hilfsarbeit. Anlässlich des zwanzig-jährigen Bestehens der "Mädchen- und Frauengruppen für soziale Hilfsarbeit" in Berlin im Auftrage des Vorstands Verfasst*. Karlsruhe I.B.: G. Braun.

——. 1915. Book Review of "Die Frau in Volkswirtschaft und Staatsleben der Gegenwart" by Gertrud Bäumer. *Zeitschrift für Politik* 8: 599–.

——. 1921. *Leitfaden der Wohlfahrtspflege.* Leipzig and Berlin: B. G. Teubner.

——. 1922. What Young Germany Is Thinking [letter to the editor]. *Nation and the Athenaeum* 32(4) (October 28): 153–.

——. 1922. Women in German Trade Unions. *Forum (New York)* 67(2) (February): 116–.

——. 1926. *Die deutsche Volksgemeinschaft; Wirtschaft, Staat, Soziales Leben, eine Einführung.* Leipzig: B. G. Teubner.

——. 1926. *Soziale Diagnose.* Die Wohlfahrtspflege in Einzeldarstellungen, 3. Berlin: C. Heymann.

——. 1931. *Die deutsche Volksgemeinschaft; Wirtschaft, Staat, Soziales Leben; eine Einführung,* 3rd. ed. Leipzig: B. G. Teubner.

——. 1931. Changes in Social Work in Germany. *Family* 11(10) (February): 325–.

——. 1932. *Soziale Führer: Ihr Leben, ihre Lehren, ihre Werke.* Wissenschaft und Bildung, 279. Leipzig: Quelle & Meyer.

——. Coauth. *See* Schmidt, Anna.

Salvanius, Sophie. 1890/1. Woman's Sphere from a German Standpoint. *Chautauquan* 12 (October/March): 783.

Samuels, Mrs. A. [Emma Margaret.] 1898. State Adoption of Street Arabs. *Fortnightly Review,* n.s. 63 (January): 111–18.

Samuelson, Marion Crawford. 1939. The Australian Case for Protection Reexamined. *Quarterly Journal of Economics* 54(1) (November): 143–51.

San Carlos de Pédroso, Marquise de. 1893. Middle Class Life in France. *North American Review* 156 (January/June): 478.

——. 1893. The French Peasantry. *North American Review* 157 (August): 209–14.

Sanborn, Kate. 1890. Reclaiming an Abandoned Farm. *Chautauquan* 12 (October): 74–.

Sanders, Elizabeth Elkins. 1828. *Conversations Principally on the Aborigines of North America.* Salem, Mass.: W. and S. B. Ives.

Sanders, Sue. 1940. *The Real Causes of Our Migrant Problem.* Los Angeles: Sue Sanders.

Sanger, Sophy. 1908. *Report on the Administration of Labour Laws in the United Kingdom.* London: Twentieth Century Press, Limited.

——. 1911. Book Review of "A History of California Labor Legislation" (with an Introductory Sketch of the San Francisco Labor Movement) by Lucile Eaves. *Economic Journal* 21(81) (March): 109–11.

——. 1911. Book Review of "Le Petit Commerce contre les grands magasins et les coopératives de consommation" by Henry Vouters. *Economic Journal* 21: 94–.

——. 1911. Book Review of "Social Insurance" by Henry Rogers Seager. *Economic Journal* 21: 107–.

——. 1911. Industrial Laws and International Agreement. *Clare Market Review* (January).

——. 1912. Book Review of "The Closed Shop in American Trade Unions" by F. T. Stockton. *Economic Journal* 22: 483–.

——. 1915. Book Review of "Labour Laws in Certain European Countries" by G. M. Price. *Economic Journal* 25: 234–.

——. 1915. Labour Legislation Affecting Young Persons and Children. *Women's International Quarterly* 4(1) (October): 12–.

——. 1916. Hours of Work. *Contemporary Review* 110 (July/December): 502–.

——. 1918. Hours of Work in Relation to Efficiency and Output. *Living Age* 8(292) (January/March): 33–.

——. 1918. Labour Questions in the Peace Settlement. *Contemporary Review* 114 (July/December): 436–.

——. 1921. *The Permanent Court of International Justice and "Labour Cases."* London: Roworth.

Sangster, Margaret Elizabeth Munson. 1895. Editorship as a Profession for Women. *Forum* 20 (December): 445–55.

Savage, Gertrude. 1894. The Scissors-grinder. *Arena* 9 (January): 253–60.

Savage, Sarah. 1814. *The Factory Girl.* Boston: Munroe, Francis and Parker. [*novel*]

——. 1823. *Advice to a Young Woman at Service; in a Letter from a Friend.* New York: New York Book Society.

Sawtelle, Lelia Robinson. 1890/1. How Marriage Affects a Woman's Property. *Chautauquan* 12 (October/March): 773–.

——. 1890/1. Points of Law which Women Should Understand. *Chautauquan* 12 (October/March): 221–.

——. 1890/1. What Constitutes a Legal Marriage? *Chautauquan* 12 (October/March): 651–.

——. 1891. How Marriage Affects a Woman's Wages or Business. *Chautauquan* 13 (April/September): 87–.

——. 1891. How a Married Woman May Make a Will. *Chautauquan* 13 (April/September): 224–.

——. 1891. What Contracts a Married Woman May Make. *Chautauquan* 13 (April/September): 365–.

——. 1891. What Support a Wife May Claim from her Husband. *Chautauquan* 13 (April/September): 517–.

Sawyer, Edith Orpha. 1931. Income and Expenditures of the Chicago YWCA from 1900 to 1928 (Illinois). M.A. thesis, University of Chicago (economics, commerce-business).

Sayles, Mary B. 1902. Tenement-house Conditions in Boston, in Jersey City. *Annals of the American Academy of Political and Social Science* 20 (July): 139.

——. 1903. Book Review of "Crime and Social Progress" by A. C. Hall. *American Academy of Political and Social Science, Annals* 21 (January/June): 465–.

——. 1903. Housing Conditions in Jersey City. *Annals of the American Academy of Political and Social Science* 21, supplement (January).

——. 1903. Work of a Woman Tenement-house Inspector. *Outlook. A Family Paper* 75: 116.

——. 1904. Settlement Workers and Their Work. *Outlook. A Family Paper* 78: 304.

——. 1904/5. Housing and Social Conditions in a Slavic Neighborhood. *Charities; a Weekly Review of Local and General Philanthropy* 13: 257.

——. 1905. Visiting Nurses and the Nurses' Settlement. *Outlook. A Family Paper* 81: 419.

Schaffner, Margaret Anna. 1902. The Territorial Tax Legislation of Michigan. *Publications of the Michigan Political Science Association* 5(1) (September).

——. 1903. The Labor Contract with Special Reference to Collective Bargaining in the United States. Ph.D. thesis, University of Wisconsin–Madison (economics).

——. 1905. *Railway Coemployment.* Wisconsin Free Library Commission, Legislative Reference Department, Comparative Legislation Bulletin, no. 1. Madison, Wisc.: Wisconsin Free Library Commission, Legislative Reference Department.

——. 1906. *Exemption of Wages.* Wisconsin Free Library Commission, Legislative Reference Department, Comparative Legislation Bulletin, no. 4. Madison, Wisc.: Wisconsin Free Library Commission, Legislative Reference Department.

——. 1906. *Taxation of Trust Companies.* Wisconsin Free Library Commission, Legislative Reference Department, Comparative Legislation Bulletin, no. 7. Madison, Wisc.: Wisconsin Free Library Commission, Legislative Reference Department.

——. 1906. *Trust Company Reserves.* Wisconsin Free Library Commission, Legislative Reference Department, Comparative Legislation Bulletin, no. 6. Madison, Wisc.: Wisconsin Free Library Commission.

——. 1906/7. Notes on Current Legislation. *American Political Science Review* 1(1/4): 438, 608.

——. 1907. *The Labor Contract from Individual to Collective Bargaining.* Madison, Wisc.: Bulletin of the University of Wisconsin.

——. 1907/8. The Initiative, the Referendum, and the Recall. *American Political Science Review* 2(1): 32–42.

——. 1907/8. Notes on Current Legislation. *American Political Science Review* 2(2): 255, 270, 273; 2(3): 411, 425, 440; 2(4): 562, 575, 600.

——. 1908. Industrial Disputes. Canadian Law of 1907. *American Political Science Review* 2(2) (February): 260-5.

——. 1909. Campaign Expenses a Public Charge. *American Political Science Review* 3: 382.

——. 1909. Notes on Current Legislation. *American Political Science Review* 3(1/4): 49, 205.

——. 1910. Effect of the Recent Boycott Decisions. *American Academy of Political and Social Science, Annals* 36 (July/December): 277–.

Schéfer, Mme. G. and Mme. Sophie Amis. 1889. *Travaux manuels et économie domestique à l'usage des jeunes filles.* Paris: C. Delagrave.

Scheftel, Yetta. 1907. Persistence of Poverty. M.A. thesis, University of Chicago (sociology).

——. 1916. *The Taxation of Land Value: A Study of Certain Discriminatory Taxes on Land.* Boston: Houghton Mifflin Company. Hart, Schaffner & Marx prize essays 22.

Schepeler-Lette, Anna and Jenny Hirsch. 1884. Germany. In Theodore Stanton, ed., *The Woman Question in Europe: A Series of Original Essays.* London: Sampson Low, Marston, Searle; New York: G. P. Putnam's Sons. Reprinted New York: Source Book Press, 1970.

Schiffman, Ruth Frances Yeomans. Coauth. *See* Boehmer, Florence Elsie; Woodhouse, Margaret Chase Going.

Schirmacher, Käthe. 1897. *Sociales Leben, zur Frauenfrage.* Paris and Leipzig: H. Welter.

——. 1898. *Le Féminisme aux États-Unis, en France, dans la Grande-Bretagne, en Suède, et en Russie.* Paris: A. Colin.

——. 1899. Salaires de femmes. *Revue de morale sociale* (December).

——. 1902. *Le Travail des femmes en France.* Paris: A. Rousseau.

——. 1902. Frauenarbeit in Frankreich. *Jahrbuch für Gesetzgebung, Verwaltung und Volkswirtschaft im Deutschen Reich,* n.s. 26(3): 337.

——. 1905/1909. *Die moderne Frauenbewegung: ein geschichtlicher Überblick.* Leipzig: B.G. Teubner.

——. 1905. Die Danziger Holzarbeiter. *Jahrbücher für Nationalökonomie und Statistik,* series 3, 29(6) (June): 815.

——. 1908. Die Ausländer und der pariser Arbeitsmarkt. *Archiv für Sozialwissenschaft und Sozialpolitik* 27: 234-, 447–.

Schlaugh, Margaret. 1940. The Revolt of 1381 in England. *Science & Society* 4(4): 414–32.

Schlesinger, Therese. 1919. *Die geistige Arbeiterin und der Sozialismus.* Vienna: Heller.

——. 1921. *Wie will und wie soll das Proletariat seine kinder erziehen?* Vienna: s.n.

——. 1928. *Die Frau im sozialdemokratischen Parteiprogramm.* Vienna: Verlag der Organisation Wien der Sozialdemokratischen Partei.

Schlumberger, Marguerite de Witt. 1911. *Aux Jeunes Ouvrières.* Paris: Fischbacher.

——. n.d. *Les Idées de Mrs. Olive Schreiner sur la femme et le travail.* Paris: s.n.

Schmahl, Mme. Henri [Jeanne]. 1892. The Present Position of Women in France. *Englishwoman's Review,* n.s. 216 (October): 220–30.

——. 1893. The Intellectual Inferiority of Women. *Englishwoman's Review,* n.s. 220 (October): 217.

——. 1894. Maria Deraismes and the Woman's Movement in France. *Englishwoman's Review,* n.s. 222 (April): 73.

——. 1896. Progress of the Women's Rights Movement in France. *Forum* 22 (September): 79–92.

——. 1905. *Raisons biologiques et économiques de l'inégalité de la femme dans le travail.* Paris: Impr. Lahure.

——. 1907. *Économie domestique.* Paris: chez l'auteur.

Schmidt, Anna, Gertrud Dyhrenfurth, and Alice Salomon. 1909. *Heimarbeit und Lohnfrage.* Jena: G. Fischer.

Schmidt, Gertrude. 1931. Zur Thrombosen- und Emboliefrage an Hand der Fälle der Breslauer Universitäts-Frauenklinik in den Jahren 1920 bis 1930. Ph.D. thesis, Breslau.

——. 1933. History of Labor Legislation in Wisconsin. Ph.D. thesis, University of Wisconsin–Madison (economics).

Schmidt, Gertrude and Faith M. Williams. 1935. New Study of Money Disbursements of Wage Earners and Lower-salaried Workers. *Monthly Labor Review* 40(4) (April): 861–.

Schmidt, Gertrude, Faith M. Williams, and Frances Rice. 1934. Changes in Cost of Living of Federal Employees 1928–33. *Monthly Labor Review* 39(1) (July): 213–.

Schmidt, Gertrude. Coauth. *See* Williams, Faith Moors.

Schneider, Florence Hemley. 1939. The Bryn Mawr Summer School for Women Workers in Industry: A Resident School in the Workers' Education Movement. Ph.D. thesis, Bryn Mawr College (sociology).

——. 1941. *Patterns of Workers' Education: The Story of the Bryn Mawr Summer School.* Washington: American Council on Public Affairs.

Schneider, Margaret Grant. 1937. *More Security for Old Age: A Factual Report.* New York: Twentieth Century Fund.

Schneider, Margaret Grant, Rufus S. Tucker, Alfred L. Bernheim, and Gardiner C. Means. 1938. Big Business: Its Growth and Its Place. *Journal of the American Statistical Association* 33(202) (June): 406–11.

[Schoenberg,] Erika Hartman. 1932. The Demand Curve for Cigarettes. M.A. thesis, University of Chicago (commerce and administration).

——. 1933. The Demand Curve for Cigarettes. *Journal of Business of the University of Chicago* 6(1) (January): 15–35.

——. Coauth. *See* Parten, Mildred.

Schreiner, Olive [as "Ralph Iron"]. 1883. *The Story of an African Farm: A Novel.* 2 vols. London: Chapman & Hall; Boston: Little, Brown. Online at Indiana University's LETRS.

—— [as "A Returned South African"]. 1891–6. Stray Thoughts on South Africa. *Fortnightly Review*, n.s. 50 (July 1891): 53–74; n.s. 59 (April 1896): 510–40; n.s. 60 (July): 1–35; n.s. 60 (August): 225–56.

——. 1896. The Boer. *Fortnightly Review*, n.s. 59 (April): 510–40.

——. 1897. *Trooper Peter Halket of Mashonaland.* London: T. Fisher Unwin; Boston: Roberts. Online at Indiana University's LETRS. [*novel*]

——. 1899. *The South African Question, by a British South African.* Cape Town: South Africa Newspaper Co.; Chicago: Charles H. Sergel Co. Reprinted from the *South African News.* British ed., *An English-South African's View of the Situation: Words in Season.* London: Hodder & Stoughton.

——. 1899. The Woman Question. *Cosmopolitan* (November): 45–54; (December): 182–92. Reprinted in Carol Barash, ed., *An Olive Schreiner Reader: Writings on Women and South Africa.* London: Pandora-Routledge, 1987.

——. 1900. The African Boer. *Cosmopolitan* 29 (September): 451–68; (October): 593–602.

——. 1909. *Closer Union: A Letter on the South African Union and the Principles of Government.* London: Fifield.

——. 1911. *Woman and Labour.* London: T. F. Unwin; Leipzig: B. Tauchnitz; Toronto: H. Frowde. Reprinted Johannesburg: Cosmos Publications, Commemorative Edition, 1975; London: Virago, 1985.

——. 1923. *Thoughts on South Africa.* London: Unwin.

Schreiner, Olive and Samuel C. Cronwright-Schreiner. 1896. *The Political Situation* [in Cape Colony]. London: T. Fisher Unwin. Online at Indiana University's LETRS.

Schumpeter, Elizabeth Boody. 1924. Cyclical Fluctuations in the Volume of Mining, 1913–23. *Review of Economics and Statistics* 6 (April): 77–92.

——. 1938. English Prices and Public Finance, 1660–1822. *Review of Economics and Statistics* 20 (February): 21–37.

——. 1938. How Strong Is Japan? Address to the Institute of Public Affairs, University of Virginia, Charlottesville, Va., July 12.

——. 1938. Japanese Economic Policy and the Standard of Living. *Far Eastern Survey* 7(1/25): 13–.

——. 1939. Is There an Open Door to China? Address given at the School of Politics, Foreign Affairs, Cambridge, Mass., and conducted by the Massachusetts League of Women Voters, Cambridge, Mass., January 19.

——. 1939. The Problem of Sanctions in the Far East. *Pacific Affairs* 12(3) (September): 245–.

——. 1940. *The Industrialization of Japan and Manchuko, 1930–1940: Population, Raw Materials, and Industry.* New York: Macmillan.

——. 1940. *The Problem of Sanctions in the Far East.* New York: Japan Institute.

——. 1940. The Policy of the United States in the Far East. *American Academy of Political and Social Science, Annals* 210 (July): 98–.

Schutrumpf, Emma Dorothea. 1931. *Broadcast Advertising in Latin America.* Washington: U.S. Government Printing Office.

——. 1932. *Broadcast Advertising in Asia, Africa, Australia, and Oceania.* Washington: U.S. Government Printing Office.

——. 1932. *Broadcast Advertising in Europe.* Washington: U.S. Government Printing Office.

——. 1939. *World Trade in Toys.* Washington: U.S. Bureau of Foreign and Domestic Commerce.

Scott, Jean Thomson. 1891/1892. The Conditions of Female Labour in Ontario, *Toronto University Studies in Political Science*, First Series, no. 3. Toronto: Warwick & Sons. Online at www.canadiana.org.

Scott, Rose. 1894. Remarks [on "The Economic Position of Women" by L. MacDonald]. *Australian Economist* IV(2) (March 27): 390.

——. 1894. Remarks on Presidential Address. *Australian Economist* IV(6) (July 26): 421–2.

——. 1895. Remarks [on "Women and Womanhood Suffrage" by E. Badham]. *Australian Economist* IV(15) (May 31): 492–4; IV(16) (June 21): 495–7.

Scouloudi, Irene. 1936. Alien Immigration and Alien Communities in London, 1558–1640. Ph.D. thesis, London School of Economics.

——. 1937/1941. Alien Immigration into and Alien Communities in London, 1558–1640. *Proceedings of the Huguenot Society of London* 16: 27–.

——. 1937/1941. Sir Theodore Turquet De Mayerne, Royal Physician and Writer, 1573–1655. *Huguenot Society of London, Proceedings* 16: 301–.

Scudder, Vita [Dutton]. 1890. *The Relation of College Women to Social Need.* Association of Collegiate Alumnae Publications, series 2, no. 30 (October): 1–16.

——. 1891. Socialism and Spiritual Progress, a Speculation: An Address Delivered before the Society of Christian Socialists, Boston. *Andover Review* 16 (July/December): 49–.

——. 1910. Religion and Socialism. *Harvard Theological Review* 3 (April): 230–47.

——. 1912. *Socialism and Character.* Boston and New York: Houghton Mifflin Co.

——. 1915. *Socialism and Sacrifice.* New York: Scholastic Literature.

——. 1917. *The Church and the Hour, Reflections of a Socialist Churchwoman.* New York: E. P. Dutton.

——. 1934. *The Christian Attitude toward Private Property.* Milwaukee, Wisc.: Morehouse Publishing Co.

——. 1934. *Church and Social Justice.* New York: National Council, Department of Christian Social Service.

Seaman, Elizabeth Cochrane [as "Nellie Bly"]. 1887. *Ten Days in a Madhouse.* New York: Munro.

—— [as "Nellie Bly"]. 1888. *Six Months in Mexico.* New York: Munro.

Seaman, Ethel Lillian. 1930. Some Economic Aspects of the Conflict between the Governor and the House of Representatives in Provincial Massachusetts, 1715–1727. M.A. thesis, University of Chicago (economics, history).

Searle, Joan Carol. 1935. An Inquiry into the Nature, Extent and Implications of the Socialism of the French Revolution during the Period of the Revolutionary Government (January 1793 to Thermidor 1794) with Special Attention to the Factors of Ideas and Popular Force. Ph.D. thesis, London School of Economics.

Sears, Amelia. 1913. *The Charity Visitor, A Handbook for Beginners.* Chicago: Department of Social Investigation, School of Civics and Philanthropy.

Sedgwick, Catherine Maria. 1853. Slavery in New England. *Bentley's Miscellany* 34 (October): 417–24.

Seebohm, M. E. 1927. *The Evolution of the English Farm.* Cambridge, Mass.: Harvard University Press.

Seeley, Bessie M. 1928. Opportunities for Women in Trust Work. *Bulletin of the American Institute of Banking* (October): 422.

Seipp, Emma. 1935. *A Study of One Hundred Clients of the Adjustment Service.* New York: American Association for Adult Education.

Selden, Catherine. 1893. The Tyranny of the Kitchen. *North American Review* 157 (October): 431–40.

Selekman, Sylvia Kopald. *See* Kopald, Sylvia.

Sellers, Edith. 1886. Old Age Pensions in Denmark. *Review of Reviews* 14 (December): 731.

——. 1891. Herr von Bodelschwingh and His Labour Colony. *Newbery House Magazine* IV (February): 226.

——. 1892. The Story of a Colony for Epileptics. *Contemporary Review* 62 (November): 683–91.

——. 1893. A Humane Poor Law. *Macmillan's* 67 (February): 277–83.

——. 1894. Anarchists' Utopia [on Kropotkin]. *Temple Bar* 103 (December): 521–8.

——. 1894. The Dockers' Restaurants. *Good Words* 35 (May): 327–.

——. 1894. Our Most Distinguished Refugee [Prince Kropotkin]. *Contemporary Review* 66 (October): 537–49.

——. 1894. The People's Kitchens in Vienna. *Nineteenth Century* 36 (November): 744–53.

——. 1894. The Vienna Poor Law System. *Charities Review* 3 (February): 168–.

——. 1895. Artels: Co-operation in Russia. *Chambers's Journal of Popular Literature, Science, and Arts* 12 (November): 705–.

——. 1895. A Colony for Lunatics. *Cornhill Magazine*, n.s. 24 [o.s. 71] (June): 577–83.

——. 1895. An Experiment in the Administration of the Poor Law. *Good Words* 36 (January): 30–.

——. 1895. How to Organise a People's Kitchen in London. *Nineteenth Century* 37 (March): 409–20.

——. 1895. Old Age Homes in Austria. *Nineteenth Century* 38 (August): 338–47.

——. 1896. Depauperised [the Scattered Cottage Homes system]. *New Review* 14 (April): 429–35.

——. 1896. The Ways of Beggars in Russia. *Good Words* 37: 195.

——. 1896. Wilhelm Liebknecht, Leader of the German Socialists. *Fortnightly Review*, n.s. 59 (June): 997–1,008.

——. 1896. The Working of the Old Age Relief Law in Copenhagen. *National Review* 28 (November): 390–9.

——. 1897. Story of a Philanthropic Pawnshop. *Eclectic Magazine* 128 (May): 706–12.

——. 1897. Story of a Philanthropic Pawnshop. *Living Age* 213 (May): 397–404.

——. 1897. Story of a Philanthropic Pawnshop. *National Review* 29 (April): 243–52.

——. 1897. Workhouse, An Old Folks' Retreat. *New Review* 17 (July): 95–104.

——. 1898. How the Poor Old Folk Fare in Other Lands. *Review of Reviews* 18 (July): 97–8.

——. 1898. How the Poor Old Folk Fare in Other Lands. *Temple Bar* 113 (April): 610–20.

——. 1898. Most Miserable Peasantry in Europe. *Living Age* 217 (April 16): 162–6.

——. 1899. In Vienna, in the Mad Year '48. *Living Age* 221 (June 17): 757–69.

——. 1899. In Vienna, in the Mad Year '48. *Temple Bar* 116 (April): 491–507.

——. 1899. An Open-air Reformatory. *National Review* 33 (August): 980.
——. 1900/1908/1983. *Foreign Solutions of Poor Law Problems.* London: H. Marshall.
——. 1900. Old Age Pensions in Denmark. *Contemporary Review* (September): 430–.
——. 1901. Pauper Children When George I. Was King. *Sunday Magazine* XXX (April): 229.
——. 1902. In Danish and Russian Old-age Homes. *Nineteenth Century and After* 52 (July/December): 643–.
——. 1902. In the Day-room of a London Workhouse. *Nineteenth Century and After* (September).
——. 1902. The Russian Temperance Committees. *Contemporary Review* 82 (July/December): 866–.
——. 1903. The Little Sister of the Poor. *Macmillan's Magazine* 88 (May/October): 28–.
——. 1903. Shifting Scenes in Rural Workhouses. *Nineteenth Century and After* 54 (July/December): 1,000–.
——. 1904. *The Danish Poor Relief System: An Example for England.* London: P. S. King and Co.
——. 1905. Official Poor Relief in Russia. *Nineteenth Century* 57 (June): 1020.
——. 1905. Poor-law Guardians; How They Spend Their Money. *Nineteenth Century and After, a Monthly Review* 58: 403.
——. 1905. Poor Relief in Berlin. *Contemporary Review* 88 (December): 857.
——. 1906. A Loafers' Reformatory. *Fortnightly Review* 85: 321.
——. 1906. Poor Relief in Vienna. *Contemporary Review* 90 (July/December): 837–.
——. 1907. Foreign Remedies for English Poor Law Defects. *Nineteeth Century* 62 (November): 770.
——. 1907. A Freedom Poor-law Experiment. *Nation* 1(26) (August 24): 927–.
——. 1907. Poor Relief in the Balkans. *Contemporary Review* 92 (August): 213.
——. 1907. The State Children of Hungary. *Contemporary Review* 91 (January/June): 329–.
——. 1908. *Foreign Solutions of Poor Law Problems.* London: H. Marshall & Son.
——. 1908. How Switzerland Deals with Her Unemployed. *Nineteenth Century and After* 64 (July/December): 763–.
——. 1908. Old-age Pensions and the Belongingless Poor. *Contemporary Review* 93 (February): 147.
——. 1908. Poor Relief in Switzerland. *Contemporary Review* 94 (October): 459.
——. 1908. The Power behind the Austrian Throne. *Fortnightly Review* 84 (July/December): 925–.
——. 1909. A High School of Danish Peasants. *Cornhill Magazine* 3(26): 356–.
——. 1909. Insurance against Unemployment Scheme. *Nineteenth Century* 65 (February): 272.
——. 1909. Poor Relief in Days to Come. *Nineteenth Century* 65 (May): 875.
——. 1909. Poor Relief in Switzerland II. *Contemporary Review* 95 (March): 349–.

——. 1910. Compulsory Insurance against Unemployment: A Swiss Scheme. *Nineteenth Century and After* 67 (January/June): 882–.
——. 1910. A Paupers' Restaurant and Home. *Cornhill Magazine* 3(28): 125–.
——. 1910. In Search of Homes for Old Age Pensioners. *Cornhill Magazine* 3(28): 511–.
——. 1910. A Self-supporting Penal Labour Colony. *Nineteenth Century* 67 (January): 108.
——. 1910. The Unemployable and the Unemployed. *Cornhill Magazine* 3(29): 611–.
——. 1911. Cassandra on Votes for Women. *Nineteenth Century and After* 69 (January/June): 487–.
——. 1911. Experiments in Cheap Catering. *Nineteenth Century and After* 76 (July/December): 1,123–.
——. 1911. Patriotism Here and Elsewhere. *Nineteenth Century and After* 70 (July/December): 969–.
——. 1912. Two Model States in What Concerns Children. *Contemporary Review* 102 (July/December): 534–.
——. 1912. Where Women Sit in Parliament. *Nineteenth Century and After* 72 (July/December): 167–.
——. 1913. For the Sake of Ratepayers and Old Age Pensioners. *Contemporary Review* 104 (July/December): 528–.
——. 1913. Sober by Act of Parliament. *Nineteenth Century and After* 73 (January/June): 1,294–.
——. 1914. A Shop-girls' Restaurant. *Cornhill Magazine* 3(37): 656–.
——. 1915. On the Entertaining of Refugees. *Nineteenth Century and After* 77 (January/June): 1,362–.
——. 1915. On the Providing of Work for Refugees. *Nineteenth Century and After* 78 (July/December): 837–.
——. 1916. An Antediluvian on the Education of Working-class Girls. *Living Age* 8(291) (October/December): 24–.
——. 1916. An Antediluvian on Education of Working-class Girls. *Nineteenth Century and After* 80 (July/December): 337–.
——. 1916. Montenegro: Patriotism without Compulsion. *Cornhill Magazine* 3(40): 99–.
——. 1916. A War Saving Worth Making. *Cornhill Magazine* 3(41): 89–.
——. 1916. Wilful Waste, Woeful Want. *Living Age* 8(289) (April/June): 202–.
——. 1916. Wilful Waste, Woeful Want. *Nineteenth Century and After* 79 (January/June): 670–.
——. 1917. Education in Copenhagen. *Nineteenth Century and After* 82 (July/December): 379–.
——. 1917. French Solution of Bread Problem. *Nineteenth Century and After* 81 (January/June): 1,028–.
——. 1917. A Mission of Manners. *Living Age* 8(298) (July/September): 409–.
——. 1917. On Manufacturing Grievances. *Nineteenth Century and After* 81 (January/June): 550–.

——. 1917. On Retail Dealing in Coal. *Cornhill Magazine* 3(43): 359–.
——. 1917. On Retail Dealing in Coal: An Amateur's Experiment. *Living Age* 8(295) (October/December): 426–.
——. 1917. Quarts Versus Noggins. *Fortnightly Review* 101 (January/June): 114–.
——. 1918. Boy and Girl War-products. *Nineteenth Century and After* 84 (July/December): 702–.
——. 1918. Elementary School Child's Mother. *Nineteenth Century and After* 83 (January/June): 553–.
——. 1918. On Fighting against Lying Rumors. *Living Age* 8(298) (July/September): 281.
——. 1918. On Fighting Lying Rumours. *Nineteenth Century and After* 83 (January/June): 1,284–.
——. 1919. Among Strikers' Womenfolk. *Nineteenth Century and After* 85 (January/June): 971–.
——. 1919. A Plea for Old-age Homes. *Cornhill Magazine* 3(47): 479–.
——. 1919. The Remaking of Village Life. *Living Age* 8(302) (July/September): 165–.
——. 1919/20. Grievance in the Village. *National Review* 74 (September/February): 846–.
——. 1920. Amateur Spreaders of Bolshevism. *Cornhill Magazine* 3(49): 413–.
——. 1920. Bolsheviki, Amateur. *Living Age* 8(307) (October/December): 479–.
——. 1920. From the Old-age Pensioners' Standpoint. *Nineteenth Century and After* 87 (January/June): 33–.
——. 1920. Sidelights on Employment Exchange Ways. *Cornhill Magazine* 3(48): 627–.
——. 1921. Norwegian Thrift in Poor Law Administration. *Cornhill Magazine* 3(51): 25–.
——. 1921. Temperance Made Easy. *Cornhill Magazine* 3(50): 455–.
——. 1921/2. The Manufacture of Girl-loafers. *National Review* 78 (September/February): 123–.
——. 1922. For Economy's Sake and Humanity's. *Cornhill Magazine* 3(52): 98–.
——. 1922. France's Fight against Her Falling Birth-rate. *Contemporary Review* 122 (December): 760.
——. 1922. An Unknown Quantity; the Woman as Voter. *Nineteenth Century and After* 91 (January/June): 504–.
——. 1922. Women Electors and their Ways. *Cornhill Magazine* 3(53): 433–.
——. 1922/3. Women Electors and Foreign Affairs. *National Review* 80 (September/February): 46–.
——. 1923. In Search of a Four-roomed Dwelling. *National Review* 80 (September/February): 736–.
——. 1923. The Swiss Solution of the Great Domestic Problem. *Cornhill Magazine* 3(54): 274–.
——. 1923. The Tragedy of the Middle Class in England and France. *Atlantic Monthly* 132 (July/December): 556–.
——. 1924. Self-supporting Village Clubs. *Cornhill Magazine* 3(56): 151–.

——. 1924. The Sifting and Sorting of the Poor: A Much-needed and Long-delayed Reform. *Contemporary Review* 125 (January/June): 451–.

——. 1924. The Voteless Women of France. *National Review* 83 (March/August): 878–.

——. 1924. Wilful Waste on Poor Relief. *Cornhill Magazine* 3(57): 318–.

——. 1924/5. The Old Age Pensioners' Grievances, Fictitious and Real. *National Review* 84 (September/February): 919–.

——. 1925. The Danish Solution of the Poor Relief Problem. *Nineteenth Century and After* 97 (January/June): 485–.

——. 1925. English Poor Relief Methods through Foreign Eyes. *Nineteeth Century* 98 (November): 679.

——. 1925. An Experiment for the Prevention of Baby-killing. *Cornhill Magazine* 3(58): 247–.

——. 1925. For the Sake of the New Poor. *Contemporary Review* 127 (January/June): 193–.

——. 1925. What the Old People Think of Their New Pension Law. *Cornhill Magazine* 3(59): 534–.

——. 1926. Among Fascismo's Friends and Foes. *Contemporary Review* 130 (July/December): 596–.

——. 1926. Where Loafers are Turned into Workers. *Cornhill Magazine* 3(61): 338–.

——. 1927. For England's Sake and the Children's. *Cornhill Magazine* 3(62): 220–.

——. 1927. Women Bolsheviks, and How They Are Manufactured. *Nineteenth Century and After* 102 (July/December): 822–.

——. 1928. Cobbett on Choosing a Wife. *Contemporary Review* 133 (January/June): 745–.

——. 1928. Men not Measures. *Cornhill Magazine* 3(64): 533–.

——. 1928. Women Bolsheviki Are Manufactured. *Living Age* 334 (January/August): 233–.

——. 1929. France and the Women's Vote. *Cornhill Magazine* 3(66): 158–.

Sellers, Maud. 1894. The City of York in the 16th Century. *English Historical Review* 9: 275.

——. 1897. York in the 16th and 17th Centuries. *English Historical Review* 12 (July): 437.

——. 1897. York in the Sixteenth and Seventeenth Centuries. *Review of Reviews* 16 (August): 146.

——. 1903. Girls' Secondary Education in Queensland. *Journal of Education* 25: 177–.

——, ed. 1906. *The Acts and Ordinances of the Eastland Company; Edited for the Royal Historical Society, from the Original Muniments of the Gild of Merchant Adventurers of York.* Royal Historical Society Publications, Camden Series. 3rd series, vol. XI. London: Royal Historical Society.

——. 1912–15. *The York Memorandum Book*, part I: *1376–1419*; part II: *1388–1493*. Publications of the Surtees Society, vols. 120 and 125. Durham, UK: Andrews & Co. for the Surtees Society.

——. 1918. *The York Mercers and Merchant Adventurers, 1356–1917*. Publications of the Surtees Society, vol. 129. Durham, UK: Andrews & Co. for the Surtees Society.

——. 1921. *A Short Account of the Mystery of Merchants and Company*: York: Merchant Adventurers of England.

Sells, Dorothy [, Ph.D.]. 1923. *The British Trade Boards System: An Inquiry into Its Operation*. London: P. S. King & Son, Ltd.

——. 1923. The Economic Effects of the British Trade Boards System. *International Labour Review* (August): 191–.

——. 1924. The Development of State Wage Regulation in Australia and New Zealand. *International Labour Review* 10: 607–29, 779–99, 962–1,004.

——. 1926. Apprenticeship – Its Status and Its Possibilities. *Industrial Management* 72 (July/December): 21–.

——. 1926. Apprenticeship – Its Status and Its Possibilities, I: Is the Apprenticeship System Reviving in American Industry? *Industrial Management* 71(5) (May): 278–.

——. 1926. Apprenticeship – Its Status and Its Possibilities, II. *Industrial Management* 71(6) (June): 351–.

——. 1926. Selected Bibliography on Apprentice Training. *Industrial Management* 72 (July/December): 28–.

——. 1927/8. Book Review of "How to Do Research Work" by Schluter. *Personnel Journal* 6 (June/April): 129–.

——. 1938. Collective Bargaining in Great Britain. *American Federationist* 45(3) (March): 258–.

——. 1938. The Settlement of Industrial Disputes in Great Britain. *Law and Contemporary Problems* 5: 321–.

——. 1939. *British Wages Boards: A Study in Industrial Democracy*. Washington: Brookings Institution.

Sells, Dorothy McDaniel. 1917. The Canadian Industrial Disputes Investigation Act of 1907. A.M thesis, University of Chicago (history).

Sewall, Hannah Robie. 1898. The Theory of Value Before Adam Smith. Ph.D. thesis, University of Minnesota.

——. 1901. *The Theory of Value Before Adam Smith*. New York: Macmillan for American Economic Association. Reprinted New York: A. M. Kelley, 1968, 1971.

——. 1904. *Child Labor in the U.S.* U.S. Bureau of Labor Bulletin, no. 52. Washington: U.S. Government Printing Office.

Sewall, May Wright. 1885. *A Report on the Position of Women in Industry and Education in the State of Indiana*. Indianapolis, Ind.: Carlon & Hollenbeck, printers.

——. 1894. *The World's Congress of Representative Women; a Historical Résumé for Popular Circulation of the World's Congress of Representative Women, Convened in Chicago on May 15, and Adjourned on May 22, 1893, under the Auspices of the Woman's Branch of the World's Congress Auxiliary*. 2 vols. Chicago: Rand McNally.

——. 1897. Coeducation in Secondary Schools and Colleges. *Arena* 17 (April): 767–75.

——. 1899. The International Council of Women. *Fortnightly Review*, n.s. 66 (July): 156–9.

Sewell, Margaret A. 1893. The Conditions of Effectual Work amongst the Poor: Paper read at the Bristol Conference of Women Workers, November 1892, by Margaret Sewell, Warden of the Women's University Settlement, Southwark. *Charity Organisation Review* 106 (November): 412–18.

——. 1898. Some Aspects of Charity Organisation. *Charity Organisation Review* n.s. 22 (January): 8–24.

Sewell, Margaret A. and Eleanor G. Powell. 1898. Women's Settlements in England. In Will Reason, ed., *The University and Social Settlements*. London: Methuen & Co.

Seymour, Flora Warren. 1916. The Indian Service – An Opportunity. *American Indian Magazine* 4(4) (October/December): 315–.

——. 1917. The Woman Lawyer and the War. *Women Lawyers' Journal* 7(3) (December): 17–.

——. 1924. Burlesquing the American Indian. *Women Lawyers' Journal* 13(2) (April 1): 3–.

——. 1924. The Delusion of the Sentimentalists. *Forum (New York, 1886)* 71(3) (March).

——. 1924. Land Titles in the Pueblo Indian Country. *American Bar Association Journal* 10: 36–.

——. 1926. Our Indian Land Policy. *Land Economics* 2 (January): 93–108.

——. 1931. Red Man and White. *Religious Education* 26 (January/December): 104–.

Seymour, Helen. 1937. The Organized Unemployed. M.A., University of Chicago (sociology, public and social welfare).

——. 1937. *When Clients Organize*. Chicago: American Public Welfare Association.

Shadd [Cary], Mary A. 1852. *A Plea for Emigration, or, Notes of Canada West in its Moral, Social, and Political Aspect: With Suggestions Respecting Mexico, West Indies, and Vancouver's Island, for the Information of Colored Emigrants*. Detroit: George W. Pattison.

Shaffer, Alice. 1935. The Indiana Poor Law and Its Administration. M.A. thesis, University of Chicago (political science, public administration).

Shaffer, Alice, Mary Wysor Keefer and Sophonisba Preston Breckinridge. 1936. *The Indiana Poor Law; Its Development and Administration with Special Reference to the Provision of State Care for the Sick Poor*. Social Service Monographs, no. 28. Chicago: University of Chicago Press.

Shallcross, Ruth Enalda. 1938. Some Problems in the Control of Industrial Homework: An Analysis of Homework Legislation and Administration in New York State. Ph.D. thesis, Bryn Mawr College (economics).

——. 1939. *Industrial Homework; An Analysis of Homework Regulations, Here and Abroad*. New York: Industrial Affairs Publishing Co.

——. 1940. *Position of Married Women in the Economic World*. New York: National Federation of Business and Professional Women's Clubs, Inc.

——. 1940. *Should Married Women Work?* Public Affairs Pamphlets, no. 49. New York: Public Affairs Committee, Inc.

Sharp, Amy. 1884. *The Legal Protection of Young Girls*. London: Hatchards.

——. 1895?. *What has a Woman to Do with Co-operation?* Manchester, UK: Women's Co-operative Union.

Sharp, Evelyn. 1908. Working Wives in Council (Communications). *Nation* 3(13) (June 27): 453–.

——. 1921. A Child's Guide to Unemployment. *Living Age* 8(308) (January/March): 398–.

——. 1921. Labor and Foreign Affairs in England. *World Tomorrow* 4(7) (July): 208–.

——. 1922. British Labour's Recent Work for Peace. *World Tomorrow* 5(1) (January): 402.

——. 1928. *Daily Bread*. London: Ernest Benn Ltd.

——. 1931. *The Problem That Is Germany*. London: Friends Service Council. Also published in the *Friend* (April 24, 1931).

——. 1933. *Buyers & Builders: A Jubilee Sketch of the Women's Co-operative Guild, 1883–1933*. Women's Co-operative Guild.

Shaughnessy, Margaret. 1935. A Pre-war Cycle in British Trade, 1885–1896. Ph.D. thesis, Radcliffe College (economics).

Shaw, Edith M. 1897. How Poor Ladies Might Live: An Answer from the Workhouse. *Nineteenth Century* 41: 242 (April): 620–7.

——. 1899. The Workhouse from the Inside. *Contemporary Review* 76 (October): 564–72.

Shaw, F. G. 1895/6. The Chartered Company and Matabililand. *National Review* 26 (September/February): 786.

Shaw, Fayette B. 1936. The Economic Development of Joliet, Illinois, 1830–1870. Ph.D. thesis, Harvard University (economics).

——. 1937. Transportation in the Development of Joliet and Will County. *Illinois State Historical Society, Journal* 30(1) (April): 85–.

Shaw, Flora L[ouise]. [Lady Lugard.] 1878. *Castle Blair: A Story of Youthful Days*. London: C. Kegan Paul. [*children's novel*]

——. 1887. The Story of Zebehr Pasha. *Contemporary Review* 52 (July–December): 333-, 564-, and 658–.

——. 1889. The British South Africa Company. *Fortnightly Review*, n.s. 46 (November): 662–8.

——. 1889. Dry-nursing the Colonies. *Fortnightly Review*, n.s. 46 (September): 367–79.

——. 1893. *Letters from Queensland, by the "Times" Special Correspondent*. London and New York: Macmillan. Reprinted from the (London) *Times* (December 1892, January and February 1893).

——. 1893. *Letters from South Africa*. London and New York: Macmillan. Reprinted from the (London) *Times* (July, August, September and October 1892).

——. 1893/4. The Australian Outlook. *Proceedings of the Royal Colonial Institute* 25: 138–.

——. 1894. Australia. *Scottish Geographical Magazine* 10(4) (April): 169–.

——. 1894/5. Colonial Expansion. *Proceedings of the Royal Colonial Institute* 26: 3–.

——. 1898. *The Story of Australia.* Story of the Empire Series. London: H. Marshall & Son.

——. 1899. Klondike. Paper read before the Royal Colonial Institute, January 31, 1899. *Proceedings of the Royal Colonial Institute* 30: 109–35.

——. 1903/4. Nigeria. *Society of Arts, Journal* 52 (November 20/November 11): 370–. [*note: she invented the name Nigeria*]

——. 1903/4. West African Negroland. *Royal Colonial Institute, Proceedings* 35: 300.

——. 1905. *A Tropical Dependency: An Outline of the Ancient History of the Western Soudan, with an Account of the Settlement of Northern Nigeria.* London: James Nisbet.

——. 1905. Book Review of "West African Research." *Outlook* 15(368) (February): 232.

——. 1905. The Tropics of the Empire. In Charles Sydney Goldman, ed., *The Empire and the Century: A Series of Essays on Imperial Problems and Possibilities by Various Writers.* London: John Murray. Reprinted, edited by Ewen Green, London: Routledge/Thoemmes, 1998.

Sheavyn, Phoebe [Anne Beale]. 1911. Professional Women. *The Position of Women – Actual and Ideal.* London: James Nisbet.

——. 1922. *Higher Education for Women in Great Britain.* London: International Federation of University Women.

Shedd, Helen Frances. 1892. Development of Our Industries through Patents. *Chautauquan* 15 (April): 37–.

——. 1892. The United States Patent Office. *Chautauquan* 15 (April/September): 170-, 281–.

Sheldon, Mary French. *See* French-Sheldon, Mary.

Sheppard, Mrs. G. W. [Emma]. 1857. *Experiences of a Workhouse Visitor.* London: James Nisbet & Co.

——. 1860. *An Out-stretched Hand to the Fallen.* London: James Nisbet & Co.

Sheppard, Kate. 1892. Economics. *Canterbury Times* (December 15): 6. Reprinted in M. Lovell-Smith, ed., *The Woman Question – Writings by the Women Who Won the Vote.* Auckland, New Zealand: New Women's Press, 1992.

——. 1899. Economic Independence of Married Women. Reprinted, with an introduction by Tessa Malcolm, in *Women's Studies Journal* 5(1) (1989): 3–24.

——. 1903. Editorial. *White Ribbon* (February): 6–7.

Sherman, Caroline B[aldwin]. 1917. Handling and Marketing Agricultural Food Products. *Journal of the Association of Collegiate Alumnae* 11(3) (November): 143–.

——. 1922. Penalties of Progress. *Journal of the American Association of University Women* 15(2) (January): 52–.

——. 1925. Rural Improvement through Encouragement. *South Atlantic Quarterly (SAMLA)* 24: 264–.

——. 1927. Long Time Programs for Agriculture. *South Atlantic Quarterly (SAMLA)* 26: 109–.

——. 1929. Rural Standards of Living. *South Atlantic Quarterly (SAMLA)* 28: 346–.

——. 1930/1932/1939. *Roadside Markets.* Washington: U.S. Bureau of Agricultural Economics/U.S. Department of Agriculture.

——. 1931/1940. *Is the Public Market a Good Civic Investment?* Washington: U.S. Government Printing Office.

——. 1931. Living Standards Reflected in Rural Fiction. *Rural America* 9(1) (January): 8–.

——. 1934. Rural Factories Play Their Part. *Rural America* 12(5) (May): 6–.

——. 1934. Small Factories in Rural Communities. The Small Industry and Standards of Living. *Journal of the American Association of University Women* 28(1) (October): 23–.

——. 1937/1939/1940. *The Farmer's Share of the Consumer's Food Dollar.* Washington: U.S. Government Printing Office.

——. 1937. The Legal Basis of the Marketing Work of the United States Department of Agriculture. *Agricultural History* 11 (October): 289–301.

——. 1937. Rural Fiction as Interpreter of Rural Life. *Rural Sociology* 2(1) (March): 36–.

——. 1938. Book Review of "Final Report of League of Nations Committee on the Relation of Nutrition to Health." *Rural Sociology* 3(1/4): 477–.

——. 1939. Book Review of "Readjustments of Agricultural Tenure in Ireland" by Elizabeth R. Hooker. *Journal of Farm Economics* 21(2) (May): 544–.

——. 1939. Land Plays New Role in Rural Fiction. *Agricultural Library Notes* 14(10) (October): 597–.

Sherwood, Mrs. Emily L. 1891/2. Opportunities for Women in Washington, D.C. *Chautauquan* 14 (October/March): 595.

Sherwood, Kate Brownlee. 1896. The March of Labor. *American Federationist* 3: 255.

Sherwood, Mrs. N. E. W. 1891. The Lack of Good Servants. *North American Review* 153 (November): 546–58.

——. 1891. Why Women Marry. *North American Review* 152 (March): 292–8.

Shields [Penn], Emma L. 1922. *Negro Women in Industry.* Washington: U.S. Women's Bureau.

——. 1932. Vocational Adjustment Problems of Negro Women in New York City. M.A. thesis, New York University.

Shine, Mary Lambert. 1922. Ideas of the Founders of the American Nation on Landed Property. Ph.D. thesis, University of Wisconsin–Madison (history).

——. 1925. The Public Leasehold System in the United States. *Land Economics* 1 (July): 322–35.

Shipley, Marie A. [Mrs. John B.] 1890. Bebel's Bricks or Bellamy's? *Liberty* 7(4) (June 21).

Shirreff, Emily. 1858. *Intellectual Education and Its Influence on the Character and Happiness of Women.* London: John W. Parker.

——. 1864. *The Chivalry of the South.* London: Emily Faithfull for the Ladies' London Emancipation Society.

——. 1864. *A Few More Words on the Chivalry of the South.* London: printed and published for the Ladies' London Emancipation Society by Emily Faithfull.

——. 1870. College Education for Women. *Contemporary Review* 15 (August): 55–66.

Shlakman, Vera. 1934/5. *Economic History of a Factory Town: A Study of Chicopee, Massachusetts.* Smith College Studies in History series, vol. 20. Northampton, Mass.: Smith College, Department of History. Reprinted New York: Octagon Books, 1969.

——. 1938. Economic History of a Factory Town: A Study of Chicopee, Massachusetts. Ph.D. thesis, Columbia University (economics).

——. 1939/40. Book Review of "Holyoke, Massachusetts: A Case History of the Industrial Revolution in America" by Green. *Southern Economic Journal* 6(1/4): 534–.

Shore, Louisa Catherine. 1874. The Emancipation of Women. *Westminster Review*, n.s. 46 [o.s. 102] (July): 137–74. Reprinted as *The Citizenship of Women Socially Considered.* London: Savill, Edwards and Co., 1874.

Sidgwick, Eleanor [Mildred Balfour]. 1890. *Health Statistics of Women Students of Cambridge and Oxford and of their Sisters.* Cambridge: Cambridge University Press.

——. 1897. *The Place of University Education in the Life of Women.* Address delivered at the Women's Institute on 23 November 1897. London: Transactions of the Women's Institute, no. 1.

——. 1897. *University Education of Women.* Lecture delivered at University College, Liverpool, in May 1896. Cambridge, UK: Macmillan & Bowes.

——. 1913. *The Progress of the Women's Suffrage Movement.* Address to the annual meeting of the Cambridge branch of the Conservative and Unionist Women's Franchise Association, May 23. Cambridge, UK: Bowes & Bowes.

——. 1913. *University Education for Women: Presidential Address Delivered to the Education Society, Manchester University on 21st November, 1912.* Manchester: Manchester University Press.

Simcox, Edith J[emima] (as "H. Lawrenny") 1872. Custom and Sex. *Fortnightly Review*, n.s. 11 (March): 310–23.

——. 1873. On the Influence of John Stuart Mill's Writings. *Contemporary Review* 22 (July): 297–317.

——. 1877. *Natural Law. An Essay in Ethics.* London: Trubner & Co.; Boston: James Osgood.

——. 1878. Organization of Unremunerative Industry. *Fraser's Magazine* 18 (November): 609–21.

——. 1879. Industrial Employment of Women. *Fraser's Magazine* 19 (February): 246–55.

——. 1880. Educational Progress in England. *Journal of Social Science* 12 (December): 29–43.

——. 1880. Ideals of Feminine Usefulness. *Fortnightly Review*, n.s. 27 (May): 656–71.

——. 1882. A Turning Point in the History of Co-operation. *Fraser's*, n.s. 26 (August): 222–35.

——. 1883. Book Review of "Groundwork of Economics" by Charles Devas. *Academy* (October 27): 275–6.

——. 1884. Eight Years of Co-operative Shirtmaking. *Nineteenth Century* 15(87) (June): 1,037–54.

——. 1885. Loss or Gain of the Working Classes during the Nineteenth Century. In *Industrial Remuneration Conference 1885: Report of Proceedings and Papers*. London: Cassell. Reprinted New York: Augustus M. Kelley, 1968.

——. 1887. The Capacity of Women. *Nineteenth Century* 22 (September): 391–402. Reprinted in Andrea Broomfield and Sally Mitchell, eds., *Prose by Victorian Women: An Anthology*. New York: Garland Publishing, 1995.

——. 1887. Women's Work and Women's Wages. *Longman's Magazine* 10 (July): 252–67. Reprinted in Andrea Broomfield and Sally Mitchell, eds., *Prose by Victorian Women: An Anthology*. New York: Garland Publishing, 1995.

——. 1894. *Primitive Civilisation; or Outlines of the History of Ownership in Archaic Communities*. 2 vols. London: Swan Sonnenschein; New York: Macmillan.

——. 1899. The Native Australian Family. *Nineteenth Century* 46 (July): 51–64.

Simey, Miss E. 1900. Economic Theory among the Greeks and Romans. *Economic Review, Published Quarterly for the Oxford University Branch of the Christian Social Union* 10: 462.

——. 1902. Luxury Ancient and Modern. *Economic Review* (April).

[Simkhovitch,] Mary Kingsbury. 1898. The Relation of the Settlement to Women and Children. *Charities* 1 (June): 5–7.

——. 1898. Socialism as an Educative and Social Force on the East Side. *Christian Social Union. Publications* 49 (May 15).

——. 1898. Women in Settlement Work in New York. *Municipal Affairs* 2: 458–.

——. 1902. Friendship and Politics and Religion. *Political Science Quarterly, a Review Devoted to the Historical, Statistical and Comparative Study of Politics, Economics and Public Law* 17: 189.

——. 1905/6. Public Library Assembly Halls in New York City. *Charities and the Commons* 15: 885.

——. 1906/7. Handicrafts in the City: What Their Commercial Significance Is under Metropolitan Conditions. *Craftsman* 11 (October/March): 363–.

——. 1907. The Settlement's Relation to Religion. *Annals of the American Academy of Political and Social Science* 30 (July/December): 490–.

——. 1910. A New Social Adjustment. In Helen Marot, ed., *The Economic Position of Women*. New York: Academy of Political Science. Also published in Henry Raymond Mussey, ed., *Proceedings of the Academy of Political Science in the City of New York*. New York: Columbia University, 1910.

——. 1917. *The City Worker's World in America*. New York: Macmillan.

——. 1917. The City's Care of the Needy. *National Municipal Review* 6: 182-, 255–.

Simkins, Ethel. 1926. *The Agricultural Geography of the Deccan Plateau of India*. The Geographical Teacher, Supplement, no. 2. London: G. Philip & Son, Limited.

——. 1933. The Coast Plains of South India, Part I. *Economic Geography* 9(1) (January): 19–50.

——. 1933. The Coast Plains of South India, Part II. *Economic Geography* 9(2) (April): 136–59.

Simmons, Nelly Booth. 1892. Battle Hymn of Labor. *Arena* 5 (March): 401–4. [*poem*]

Simon, Helene. 1897. Die Fabrik- und Sanitätsinsptektorinnen in England. *Jahrbuch für Gesetzgebung, Verwaltung und Volkswirtschaft im deutschen Reich* 21(3): 133–.

——. 1898. Die englische Fabrikgesetzgebung. *Jahrbuch für Gesetzgebung, Verwaltung und Volkswirtschaft im deutschen Reich* 22(2): 287–.

——. 1899. Entwicklung und gegenwärtige Organisation der englischen Fabrikinspektion. *Jahrbuch für Gesetzgebung, Verwaltung und Volkswirtschaft im deutschen Reich* 23(2): 209–.

——. 1902. Book Review of "Die Arbeiterschutzgesetzgebung in den europäischen Ländern" by J. H. Van Zanten. *Jahrbücher für Nationalökonomie und Statistik*, series 3, 24 (1) (July): 148–.

——. 1905/1925. *Robert Owen: sein Leben und seine Bedeutung für die Gegenwart*. Jena: G. Fischer.

——. 1905. Book Review of "A History of Factory Legislation. With a preface by Sidney Webb" by B. L. Hutchins and A. Harrison. *Jahrbuch für Gesetzgebung, Verwaltung und Volkswirtschaft im deutschen Reich* 29(1): 368–.

——. 1909. *William Godwin and Mary Wollstonecraft: eine biographisch-soziologische Studie*. Munich: O. Beck.

——. 1909. Das englische Kindergesetz. Ein Beitrag zur sozialen Theorie der Kinderrechte. *Jahrbuch für Gesetzgebung, Verwaltung und Volkswirtschaft im deutschen Reich* 33(3): 319–.

——. 1910. *Der Anteil der Frau an der deutschen Industrie. Schriften des ständigen Ausschusses zur Förderung der Arbeiterinnen-Interessen*, Heft 2. Jena: G. Fischer.

——. 1910. Book Review of "Die Aufgabe des Jugendgerichts" by Ben. B. Lindsey. *Jahrbuch für Gesetzgebung, Verwaltung und Volkswirtschaft im deutschen Reich* 34(1): 415–.

——. 1912. Book Review of "Arbeiterbildungswesen in Wien und Berlin (Freiburger volkswirtschaftliche Abhandlungen)" by Hertha Siemering. *Jahrbuch für Gesetzgebung, Verwaltung und Volkswirtschaft im deutschen Reich* 36(4): 423–.

——. 1914. Beruf, Familienstand und Altersaufbau. *Archiv für Frauenkunde und Eugenetik* 1: 183–.

——. 1915. Das Jugendrecht. Ein soziologischer Versuch. *Schmollers Jahrbuch für Gesetzgebung, Verwaltung und Volkswirtschaft im deutschen Reich* 39(1): 227–.

——. 1916. Das Bevölkerungsproblem. *Archiv für Frauenkunde und Eugenetik* 2: 67–.

——. 1917. Book Review of "Ein deutsches Jugendgesetz" by Felisch. *Schmollers Jahrbuch für Gesetzgebung, Verwaltung und Volkswirtschaft im deutschen Reich* 41(3): 500–.

——. 1919. *Robert Owen und der Sozialismus*. Berlin: P. Cassirer.

——. 1919. Book Review of "Behörden-Handbuch zum Gesetze über die Versorgung der Personen der Unterklassen des Reichsheeres, der Kaiserlichen

Marine und der Kaiserlichen Schutztruppen (Mannschaftsversorgungsgesetz) vom 31. Mai 1906" by Neier-Demming. *Schmollers Jahrbuch für Gesetzgebung, Verwaltung und Volkswirtschaft im deutschen Reich* 43(1): 393.

——. 1919. Book Review of "Behörden-Handbuch zum Mannschaftsversorgungsgesetz. Nachtrag mit vollständigem Sachverzeichnis nach Zeit- und Buchstabenfolge" by Meier-Demming. *Schmollers Jahrbuch für Gesetzgebung, Verwaltung und Volkswirtschaft im deutschen Reich* 43(1): 393.

——. 1922. *Aufgaben und Ziele der neuzeitlichen Wohlfahrtspflege.* Stuttgart: Dietz; Berlin: Buchhandlung Vorwärts.

——. 1925. *Landwirtschaftliche Kinderarbeit.* Berlin: F. A. Herbig Verlagsbuchhandlung, G.m.b.H.

——. 1928. *Elisabeth Gnauck-Kühne: Eine Pilgerfahrt.* Monchen-Gladbach: Volksverein.

Simon, S. Fanny. Coauth. *See* Clark, Marjorie Ruth.

[Simon,] Shena Dorothy Potter. 1910. The Movement for International Labour Legislation. *Economic Journal* 20 (September): 347–57.

——. 1932. Municipal Finance: Should the Manchester City Council Spend or Save? *Manchester School of Economics and Social Studies* 3(1): 15–20.

——. 1938. *A Century of City Government.* London: Allen & Unwin.

Simons, May Wood [Wood-Simons], transl. 1897. *Socialism, What It Is and What It Seeks to Accomplish*, by Wilhelm Liebknecht. Chicago: C. H. Kerr.

——, transl. 1899. *Frederick Engels: His Life, His Work and His Writings*, by Karl Kautsky. Chicago: C. H. Kerr & Co.

——. 1899. *Woman and the Social Problem.* Pocket Library of Socialism, no. 1 (March 15) Chicago: C. H. Kerr. Also published as *Woman and the Social Question.* Chicago: C. H. Kerr.

——. 1902. *Socialism and the Organized Labor Movement.* Pocket Library of Socialism, no. 39. Chicago: C. H. Kerr & Co.

——. 1904/5. Education in the South. *American Journal of Sociology* 10(1/6): 382–.

——. 1910. *History of Economic Thought in Relation to Industrial Conditions, 1814–1837.* Economics, Finance, and Administration Contributions, no. 24. Evanston, Ill.: Northwestern University. Available at http://staffweb.library.northwestern.edu/cm/NU%20MA%20Theses%20H.html.

——. 1910. Industrial Education in Chicago. *Pedagogical Seminary* 17: 398–418.

——. 1913. *Why the Professional Woman Should be a Socialist.* Pamphlet in American History, Socialism S 332. Chicago: Woman's National Committee of the Socialist Party.

——. 1930. Economic Theory in Relation to Industrial Conditions in the United States from 1783 to 1837. Ph.D. thesis, Northwestern University (economics, history).

——. 1931. The Changing American Home. *Current History (New York)* 33(5) (February): 697–.

Singleton, Evelyn Ellen. 1933. Workmen's Compensation in Maryland. Ph.D. thesis, Johns Hopkins University.

——. 1935. *Workmen's Compensation in Maryland.* Baltimore: Johns Hopkins University Studies in Historical and Political Science.

Sinnett, Jane Fry. 1849. Colonisation and Emigration. *Dublin Review* 26 (June): 316–37.

Sissman, Louise. 1936. Development of the Postal Savings System. *Journal of the American Statistical Association* 31(196) (December): 708–18.

——. 1938. The Postal Savings System and the Banks. *Southern Economic Journal* 4 (January): 339–51.

Sisson, Dorothy and R. H. Whitbeck. 1933. Irrigation in South America. *Economic Geography* 9(2) (April): 198–210.

Skene, Felicia. 1865. *Penitentiaries and Reformatories.* Edinburgh: Edmonston & Douglas.

——. 1889. *Scenes from a Silent World, or, Prisons and Their Inmates.* Edinburgh: W. Blackwood & Sons.

Skinner, Mary E[lizabeth]. 1928. *Child Labor in New Jersey*, part 2: *Children Engaged in Industrial Home Work.* U.S. Department of Labor, Children's Bureau Publications, no. 192.Washington: U.S. Government Printing Office.

——. 1933. Organizing for Children's Work. *International Journal of Religious Education* 9(11) (July): 18–.

——. 1938. *Prohibition of Industrial Home Work in Selected Industries under the National Recovery Administration.* U.S. Children's Bureau Publication, no. 244. Washington: U.S. Government Printing Office.

Skinner, Mary Elizabeth and Cawthon A. Bowen. 1932. *Children's Work in the Church, for the Church without Separate Departments.* Nashville, Tenn.: Cokesbury Press.

Skinner, Mary E. and Nettie Pauline McGill. 1928/1931. *Child Labor in New Jersey.* U.S. Children's Bureau. Washington: U.S. Government Printing Office.

Skinner, Mary Elizabeth and Ella Arvilla Merritt. 1936. *Industrial Home Work under the National Recovery Administration.* U.S. Children's Bureau Publication, no. 234. Washington: U.S. Government Printing Office.

Skinner, Mary Elizabeth. Coauth. *See* Beyer, Clara Mortenson; Burke, Dorothy May Williams; Channing, Alice; McGill, Nettie Pauline; Matthews, Ellen Nathalie.

Slaughter, Frances Elisabeth. 1893. The Subaltern in India a Hundred Years Ago. *Cornhill Magazine*, n.s. 21 [o.s. 68] (November): 474–82.

Smaltz, Rebecca G. and Arcadia N. Phillips. 1934. *Hours and Earnings in the Leather-glove Industry.* U.S. Women's Bureau Bulletin, no. 119. Washington: U.S. Government Printing Office.

Smaltz, Rebecca Glover, Jessie Beatrice McConnell, and Elizabeth S. Johnson. 1929. *Hours and Earnings of Men and Women in the Silk Industry.* Harrisburg, Pa.: Pennsylvania Bureau of Women and Children.

——. 1930. *Hours and Earnings of Men and Women in the Hosiery Industry.* Harrisburg, Pa.: Pennsylvania Bureau of Women and Children.

Smedes, Henrietta R. 1923. *Agricultural Graphics.* Chapel Hill, N.C.: University of North Caroline Press.

——. 1923 *North Carolina and the United States 1866–1922*. Chapel Hill, N.C.: University of North Carolina Press.

Smedley, Agnes. 1929. *Daughter of Earth*. New York: Coward-McCann. Reprinted Old Westbury, N.Y.: Feminist Press, 1973. [*novel*]

——. 1933. *Chinese Destinies: Sketches of Present-day China*. New York: Vanguard Press.

——. 1934. *China's Red Army Marches*. New York: International Publishers.

——. 1938. *China Fights Back: An American Woman with the Eighth Route Army*. New York: Vanguard Press; London: V. Gollancz.

Smedley, Constance and Ethel Snowden. 1910s. *Woman; Her Position To-day*. London: New Age Press.

Smedley, Menella B. 1870. The English Girl's Education. *Contemporary Review* 14 (April/July): 29–.

——. 1874. Workhouse Schools for Girls. *Macmillan's* 31 (November): 27–36.

——, ed. 1875. *Boarding-out and Pauper Schools Especially for Girls; Being a Reprint of the Principal Reports on Pauper Education in the Blue Book for 1873–4*. London: King.

——. 1880. Comparison between Boarding-out and Pauper Schools. *Journal of the Statistical and Social Inquiry Society of Ireland* 8 (April).

Smith, Addie Viola. 1931. *Motor Roads in China*. Washington: U.S. Bureau of Foreign and Domestic Commerce.

Smith, Mrs. Andrew H. 1890. Trained Nurses for the Sick Poor. *Chautauquan* 12 (October): 80–.

Smith, Constance [Isabella Stuart]. 1903. Dangerous Trades. *Economic Review* (October).

——. 1908. *The Case for Wages Boards*. London: National Anti-Sweating League.

——. 1908. *Child Labour*. London: A. R. Mowbray.

——. 1908. *Report on the Employment of Children in the United Kingdom*. London: International Association for Labor Legislation, British Section.

——. 1908. The Minimum Wage. In Gertrude M. Tuckwell, Constance Isabella Stuart Smith, Mary R. MacArthur, May Tennant, Nettie Adler, Adelaide Mary Anderson, and Clementina Black, *Woman in Industry from Seven Points of View*. London: Duckworth & Co.

——. 1909. *The Present Facts with Regard to Lead-poisoning*. Christian Social Union Leaflet, no. 12. 3rd ed. London: A. R. Mowbray.

——. 1914. The Workings of the Trade Boards Act in Great Britain and Ireland. *Journal of Political Economy* 22(7) (July): 605–29.

——. 1919. The Washington Labour Conference. *Nineteenth Century and After* 86 (July/December): 772–.

——. 1921. *Ten Hours*. New York: Harcourt, Brace & Co.

——. 1922/3. Constructive Welfare Work in Modern Industry. *Journal of the Royal Sanitary Institute* 43: 188–.

——. 1925. The Stockholm Conference on Life and Work. *Contemporary Review* 128 (July/December): 636.

——. 1927. *Factory Conditions in China*. London: League of Nations.

Smith, Constance and D. Shena Potter. 1912. The Insurance of Women Workers [letter to the editor]. *Nation* 10(23) (March 9): 949–.

Smith, Mrs. Corinna Haven Putnam and Caroline R. Hill. 1920. *Rising above the Ruins in France; an Account of the Progress Made since the Armistice in the Devastated Regions in Reestablishing Industrial Activities and the Normal Life of the People.* New York and London, G. P. Putnam's Sons.

Smith [Godfrey], Eleanor [Elsabeth]. 1933. Socio-economic Adjustments to the Unemployment Situation Made by a Group of Factory Women Inspectors Laid Off in 1930–32. M.A. thesis, Northwestern University.

——. 1936. The History of the Gold and Silver Thread Patent, 1611–1621. A.M thesis, University of Chicago (history).

Smith, Elizabeth Oakes Prince. 1838. *Riches without Wings; or, The Cleveland Family*, Boston: G. W. Light. [*novel*]

——. 1851. *Woman and Her Needs.* New York: Fowler & Wells. Reprinted in *Liberating the Home.* New York: Arno Press, 1974.

——. 1854. *The Newsboy.* Boston: Phillips Sampson. [*novel*]

——. 1889/1890. The Negro Question [correspondence]. *Open Court* 3: 2,110.

Smith, Ellen. 1915. *Wage-earning Women and Their Dependents.* Executive Committee, Fabian Women's Group. London: Fabian Society.

Smith, Ellen Ada. 1898. The Type-writing Clerk. *Longman's* 31 (March): 431–46.

Smith, Florence Patteson. 1932. *Chronological Development of Labor Legislation for Women in the United States.* Bulletin of the U.S. Women's Bureau, no. 66–II. Washington: U.S. Government Printing Office.

——. 1932. *Labor Laws for Women in the States and Territories: Hours, Home Work, Prohibited or Regulated Occupations, Seats, Minimum Wage.* U.S. Women's Bureau Bulletin, no. 98. Washington: U.S. Government Printing Office.

——. 1933. *Summary of Labor Legislation for Women, January to June 1933.* U.S. Women's Bureau Bulletin, no. 98, supplement. Washington: U.S. Government Printing Office.

——. 1937/1938. *State Labor Laws for Women: Part 1 – Summary.* U.S. Women's Bureau Bulletin, no. 156. Washington: U.S. Government Printing Office.

——. 1938. *State Labor Laws for Women: Part II – Analysis of Hour Laws for Women Workers.* Women's Bureau Bulletin, no. 156–II. Washington: U.S. Government Printing Office.

Smith, Florence Patteson, Frances Perkins, and Mary Anderson. 1940. *State Minimum-wage Laws and Orders, 1939.* U.S. Women's Bureau Bulletin, no. 167, supplement. Washington: U.S. Government Printing Office.

Smith, Florence Patteson. Coauth. *See* Beyer, Clara Mortenson.

Smith, Helen Evertson. 1896. Charities of the Poor. *Independent* 48 (May 28): 712.

——. 1896. Contract Housekeeping. *Independent* 48 (June 25): 882.

——. 1896. Dentistry as a Profession for Women. *Independent* 48 (December 31): 1,814.

——. 1896. Village Improvement Societies and Good Roads. *Independent* 48 (February 6): 175.

——. 1896. Women as Photographers. *Independent* 48 (November 5): 1,506.

——. 1897. Miles of Money. *Journal of Education* 46 (July 22): 55.

——. 1897. Women as Gardeners. *Independent* 49 (March 25): 394–5.

——. 1897. Women as Merchants and Shopkeepers. *Independent* 49 (June 17): 798.

——. 1898. Women as Architects. *Independent* 50 (April 21): 530.

——. 1898. Women as Cabinet-makers. *Independent* 50 (June 30): 870.

——. 1898. Women in the Business of Real Estate. *Independent* 50 (January 27): 134.

Smith, Hilda Caroline Miall. 1888. *The British Hive and its Working Bees*. London: W. Isbister.

Smith, Ilse M. 1932. The Status of the Retired Teacher. *Journal of the American Statistical Association* 27(177) (Supplement, Proceedings of the American Statistical Association) (March): 109–112.

Smith, Miss Laura A. 1888. Workers' Songs. *Nineteenth Century* 24 (August): 238–50.

Smith, Lucy Toulmin. 1869. *Lench's Trust: Copies of the Original Deeds upon Which It Rests and of Those upon Which It Is Now Administered with Translations, Together with Lists of the Feoffees since 1525, and a Calendar of Other Deeds Belonging to the Trust.* Birmingham: Printed for private circulation.

——. 1878. *Gleanings from an Old Account Book: Being Notes on the Accounts of the Feoffees of the Common Lands of Rotherham, A.D. 1549 to 1646.* Paper read before the Rotherham Literary & Scientific Society, November 19, 1877. Rotherham, UK: printed for the Society by A. Gilling.

——. 1879. *Old English Gilds, a Paper.* Paper read at the Rotherham Literary & Scientific Society, Highgate, London, February 1878. Rotherham, UK: Printed for the Society by A. Gilling.

——. 1890. Early Village Life. *Antiquary* 21(127) (June): 258–.

——. 1899. On Openings for Women in Library Work. *Library Association Record* 1(11) (November): 719.

——. 1907. The English Manor. *Quarterly Review* (July).

Smith, Lucy Wilmot. 1887. The Future Colored Girl. *Minutes and Addresses of the American National Baptist Convention, St. Louis, MO, Aug. 25–29, 1886.* Jackson, Miss.: Spelman College. Reprinted in Shirley Wilson Logan, ed., *We Are Coming: The Persuasive Discourse of Nineteenth-Century Black Women.* Carbondale, Ill.: Southern Illinois University Press, 1999.

Smith, Mary Phlegar. 1928. *Special Legal Relations of Married Women in North Carolina as to Property, Contracts, and Guardianship.* Chapel Hill, N.C.: University of North Carolina.

——. 1929. Legal and Administrative Restrictions Affecting the Rights of Married Women to Work. *Annals of the American Academy of Political and Social Science* 143 (May): 255–.

——. 1929/30. Book Review of "The City of Tomorrow, and Its Planning" by Corbusier. *Social Forces* 8(1/4): 458.

——. 1929/30. Book Review of "Our Cities To-day and To-morrow: A Survey of Planning and Zoning Progress in the United States" by Hubbard and Hubbard. *Social Forces* 8(1/4): 458.

——. 1930/1. Book Review of "American City Government and Administration" by Macdonald. *Social Forces* 9(1/4): 454–.

——. 1932. Trends in Municipal Administration of Public Welfare: 1900–1930. *Social Forces* 10(3) (March): 371–7.

——. 1933. Municipal Expenditures for Family Relief. *Social Forces* 11(3) (March): 370–3.

——. 1934/5. Book Review of "Methods of Statistical Analysis in the Social Sciences" by Davies and Crowder. *Social Forces* 13(1/4): 315–.

Smith, Mary Roberts. *See* Coolidge, Mary Elizabeth Burroughs Roberts.

Smith, Mildred Wretts. *See* Wretts-Smith, Mildred.

Smith, Rose. 1932. *Working Women and The Capitalist Crisis.* London: Communist Party of Great Britian.

——. 1933. *Women Into the Ranks!* London: Communist Party of Great Britian.

——. 1937. *Why We Pay More.* London: Communist Party of Great Britain.

Smith, Rose E. 1934. My Town – What Can I Do to Boost Its Credit? *National Municipal Review* 23(1) (January): 16–.

Smith, Vera Constance. 1935. *Free Banking; or A Reconsideration of the Historical and Analytical Basis of Central Banking.* Ph.D. thesis, London School of Economics.

——. 1936. *The Rationale of Central Banking.* London: P. S. King and Son. Reprinted Indianapolis: Liberty Press, 1990 (as *The Rationale of Central Banking: And the Free Banking Alternative*); Greenwich, Conn.: Committee for Monetary Research and Education, 1981.

——, ed. 1936. *Crisis and Cycles*, by Wilhelm Röpke. London: W. Hodge

——, transl. 1937. *The Limits of Economics*, by Oskar Morganstern. London: W. Hodge.

——, transl. 1940. *The Stock Market, Credit, and Capital Formation*, by Fritz Machlup. London: W. Hodge.

Smith, Zilpha Drew. 1888. Country Help for City Charities. *Lend a Hand* 3(11) (November): 640–.

——. 1890. Causes of Poverty. *Lend a Hand* 5(1) (January): 23.

——. 1892. The Education of the Friendly Visitor. *Charities Review* 2(1) (November): 48–.

Smyth, Eleanor C. 1907. *Sir Rowland Hill: The Story of a Great Reform.* London: Unwin.

——. 1918. *The Passing of the Penny Post.* Letchworth, UK: Letchworth Printers.

Snodgrass, Katharine. 1919. *Prices of Wool and Wool Products.* U.S. War Industries Board Price Bulletin, no. 24. Washington: U.S. Government Printing Office.

——. 1920. International Price Indexes. *Quarterly Publications of the American Statistical Association* 17(131) (September): 326–32.

——. 1920. Price Fluctuations in the Woolen Industry. *Annals of the American Academy of Political and Social Science* 89 (May): 55–.

——. 1921. Short Term Borrowing in British Finance, 1914–1920. *Journal of the American Statistical Association* 17 (June): 776–7.

——. 1922. The Federal Reserve Board's Price Index for Great Britain. *Journal of the American Statistical Association* 18 (June): 241–7.

——. 1928. *Copra and Coconut Oil.* Stanford: Stanford University Press.

——. 1930. *Margarine as a Butter Substitute.* Stanford: Food Research Institute, Stanford University.

Snowden, Ethel [Annakin] [Mrs. Philip Snowden]. 1907. *Labour Ideal Series. The Woman Socialist.* London: George Allen.

——. 1907. *Woman: A Few Shrieks! Setting Forth the Necessity of Shrieking Till the Shrieks Be Heard.* Letchworth, UK: Garden City Press, Ltd.

——. 1907. *The Woman Socialist.* London: G. Allen.

——. 1913. *The Feminist Movement.* London: Collins Clear-Type Press.

——. 1913. The Women's Pilgrimage. *Nation* 13(18) (August 2): 677–.

——. 1920. *Through Bolshevik Russia.* London and New York: Cassell.

——. 1921. *A Political Pilgrim in Europe.* New York: George Doran.

——. 1922. *What We Want and Why.* London: W. Collins Sons & Co. Ltd.

——. Coauth. *See* Smedley, Constance.

Sohr, Amélie. 1882. *Frauenarbeit in der Armen- und Krankenpflege, daheim und im Auslande; geschichtliches und kritisches.* Berlin: Julius Springer.

Solenberger, Alice Willard. 1911. *One Thousand Homeless Men: A Study of Original Records.* New York: Charities Publication Committee. Reprinted New York: Survey Associates, Inc., 1914.

Somerville, Mrs. Anne. 1851. Free Trade. *New Monthly Magazine* 92 (May): 62–6.

Sommer, Louise. 1914. Book Review of "De la Femme et de son rôle dans la société d'après les écrits Saint-Simoniens" by Patureau-Mirand. *Archiv für die Geschichte des Sozialismus und der Arbeiterbewegung* 4: 492–.

——. 1920/1925. *Die österreichischen Kameralisten in dogmengeschichtlicher Darstellung.* Studien zur Social-, Wirtschafts- und Verwaltungsgeschichte XII Heft. 1st ed. 2nd ed. Vienna: G. Konegen.

——. 1922. Book Review of "Zielenzieger, die alten deutschen Kamalisten." *Archiv für die Geschichte des Sozialismus und der Arbeiterbewegung* 10: 449–.

——. 1926. *Freihandel und Schutzzoll in ihrem Zusammenhang mit Geldtheorie und Währungspolitik.* Jena: G. Fischer.

——. 1926. *Mercantilisme et théoré de la valeur.* Paris: Librairie des sciences économiques et sociales, Marcel Rivière.

——. 1926. Marxismus und Religionsphilosophie. *Archiv für Sozialwissenschaft und Sozialpolitik* 56: 799–.

——. 1927. Mercantilisme et théorie de la valeur. *Revue d'histoire économique et sociale* 15: 5–.

——. 1928. Book Review of "Adam Smith und die gegenwärtige Volkswirtschaft" by N. Reichesberg. *Schmollers Jahrbuch für Gesetzgebung, Verwaltung und Volkswirtschaft im deutschen Reich* 52(3) (June): 153.

——. 1928. Book Review of "The Collected Papers of Studies in Economic History. Edited with an introductory memoir by K. H: Tawney. Published for the Royal Economic Society" by Georg Unwin. *Schmollers Jahrbuch für Gesetzgebung, Verwaltung und Volkswirtschaft im deutschen Reich* 52(5) (October): 178–.

——. 1928. Book Review of "Cours d'économie politique" by Henry Truchy. *Schmollers Jahrbuch für Gesetzgebung, Verwaltung und Volkswirtschaft im deutschen Reich* 52(3) (June): 153.

——. 1928. Book Review of "Die Freihandelslehre in Deutschland. Ein Beitrag zur Gesellschaftslehre des wirtschaftlichen Liberalismus" by Georg Mayer. *Schmollers Jahrbuch für Gesetzgebung, Verwaltung und Volkswirtschaft im deutschen Reich* 52(2) (April): 172–.

——. 1928. Book Review of "La Monnaie, ses systèmes et ses phénomènes, en Europe centrale" by Elemér Hantos. *Zeitschrift für schweizerische Statistik und Volkswirtschaft/Journal de statistique et revue économique suisse* 64(3): 443–.

——. 1928. Book Review of "Währungsideen und Währungsgestaltungen in der Gegenwart" by Prof. Fr. Gutmann. *Zeitschrift für schweizerische Statistik und Volkswirtschaft/Journal de statistique et revue économique suisse* 64(2): 297–.

——. 1928. Politique commerciale et politique monétaire. *Zeitschrift für schweizerische Statistik und Volkswirtschaft/Journal de statistique et revue économique suisse* 64(1): 1–.

——. 1928. Zur Methode der exakten und historischen Nationalökonomie. *Schmollers Jahrbuch für Gesetzgebung, Verwaltung und Volkswirtschaft im deutschen Reich* 52(4) (August): 31–.

——. 1929. Book Review of "Die Entwicklung zum Idealtypus. Eine methodologische Untersuchung über das Verhältnis von Theorie und Geschichte bei Menger, Schmoller und Max Weber" by Bernhard Pfister. *Schmollers Jahrbuch für Gesetzgebung, Verwaltung und Volkswirtschaft im deutschen Reich* 53(5) (October): 142–.

——. 1929. Book Review of "Geschichte der Volkswirtschaftslehre. Enzyklopädie der Rechts- und Staatswissenschaft, Abteilung Staatswissenschaft" by Edgar Salin. *Zeitschrift für schweizerische Statistik und Volkswirtschaft/Journal de statistique et revue économique suisse* 65(3): 441–.

——. 1929. Book Review of "Die internationale Konferenz für Wirtschaftsstatistik." *Zeitschrift für schweizerische Statistik und Volkswirtschaft/Journal de statistique et revue économique suisse* 65(1): 17–.

——. 1929. Book Review of "Theorie und Praxis staatlicher Kreditpolitik der Gegenwart. Recht und Staat in Geschichte und Gegenwart" by Edgar Salin. *Zeitschrift für schweizerische Statistik und Volkswirtschaft/Journal de statistique et revue économique suisse* 65(3): 443–.

——. 1930. Book Review of "Irrationales in der Nationalisierung, Mensch und Machine" by Gerhard Menz. *Schmollers Jahrbuch für Gesetzgebung, Verwaltung und Volkswirtschaft im deutschen Reich* 54(6) (December): 163–.

——. 1930. Book Review of "Méthode d'un rapprochement économique entre les différents pays" by Genéve. *Zeitschrift für schweizerische Statistik und Volkswirtschaft/Journal de statistique et revue économique suisse* 66(2): 254–.

——. 1930. Book Review of "The Morris Plan of Industrial Banking" by Peter W. Herzog. *Jahrbücher für Nationalökonomie und Statistik* 133(6) (December): 935–.

——. 1930. Book Review of "Principles of Economics" by Frederic B. Garver and Alvin Harvey Hansen. *Jahrbücher für Nationalökonomie und Statistik* 132(6) (June): 923–.

——. 1930. Französische Inflation in amerikanischer Beleuchtung. *Jahrbücher für Nationalökonomie und Statistik* 133(1) (July): 64–.

——. 1931. Book Review of "Beiträge zur Geschichte der Staatslehre" by Adolf Menzel. *Schmollers Jahrbuch für Gesetzgebung, Verwaltung und Volkswirtschaft im deutschen Reich* 55(5) (October): 171–.

——. 1931. Book Review of "Die Grundlagen des aufgeklärten Absolutismus. (List-Studien. Untersuchungen zur Geschichte der Staatswissenschaften)" by Peter Klassen. *Schmollers Jahrbuch für Gesetzgebung, Verwaltung und Volkswirtschaft im deutschen Reich* 55(3) (June): 178–.

——. 1931. Book Review of "Scambi internazionali e politica bancaria. In regime di moneta sana ed avariata. (Biblioteca di scienze moderne. Nr. 105)" by Attilio Cabiati. *Jahrbücher für Nationalökonomie und Statistik* 135(3) (September): 451–.

——. 1931. Book Review of "Strukturwandlungen der österreichischen Volkswirtschaft nach dem Kriege" by Hans Bayer. *Schmollers Jahrbuch für Gesetzgebung, Verwaltung und Volkswirtschaft im deutschen Reich* 55(2) (April): 169–.

——. 1931. Book Review of "Wallenstein als Volkswirt im Herzogtum Friedland (Prager Studien aus dem Gebiete der Geschichtswissenschaft, 19. Heft)" by Anton Ernstberger. *Jahrbücher für Nationalökonomie und Statistik* 135(4) (October): 612–.

——. 1931. Momberts Bevölkerungslehre. *Vierteljahrschrift für Sozial- und Wirtschaftsgeschichte* 24(2): 169–78.

——. 1932. Book Review of "Herrschaft und Wirtschaft. Grundlagen und Aussichten der Industriegesellschaft" by Sigmund Rubinstein. *Schmollers Jahrbuch für Gesetzgebung, Verwaltung und Volkswirtschaft im deutschen Reich* 56(4) (August): 137–.

——. 1932. Book Review of "Die öffentliche Unternehmung der Gegenwart" by Manuel Saitzew. *Zeitschrift für schweizerische Statistik und Volkswirtschaft/Journal de statistique et revue économique suisse* 68(1): 154–.

——. 1932. Book Review of "Die sozialwissenschaftliche Erkenntnis. Ein Beitrag zur Methodik der Gesellschaftslehre" by Ernst Seidler. *Schmollers Jahrbuch für Gesetzgebung, Verwaltung und Volkswirtschaft im deutschen Reich* 56(5) (October): 150–.

——. 1933. Book Review of "Guiccardinis finanzpolitische Anschauungen" by Gustav Fremerey. *Finanzarchiv* 1: 558–.

——. 1933. Book Review of "Technik und Wirtschaft in den geistigen Entscheidungen der Gegenwart" by Eugen Böhler. *Schmollers Jahrbuch für Gesetzgebung, Verwaltung und Volkswirtschaft im deutschen Reich* 57(3) (June): 140–.

——. 1933. Mitteleuropäische Kombinationen. *Jahrbücher für Nationalökonomie und Statistik* 138(4) (April): 541–.

——. 1933. Sozialwissenschaftliche Bausteine. *Schmollers Jahrbuch für Gesetzgebung, Verwaltung und Volkswirtschaft im deutschen Reich* 57(1) (February): 107–.

——. 1935. *Neugestaltung der Handelspolitik: Wege zu einem intereuropäischen Präferenzsystem.* Berlin: Carl Heymann.

——. 1936. Book Review of "Die staatsideologischen Voraussetzungen des Kampfes gegen die Meistbegünstigungsklausel." *Zeitschrift für öffentliches Recht* 16(2) (April 11): 265–.

——. 1936. Book Review of "Die wirtschaftsstrukturellen Voraussetzungen des Kampfes gegen die Meistbegünstigungsklausel." *Zeitschrift für schweizerische Statistik und Volkswirtschaft/Journal de statistique et revue économique suisse* 72(1): 29–.

——. 1937. Book Review of "Preussens Steuern vor und nach den Befreiungskriegen" by Rolf Grabower. *Finanzarchiv* 4: 513–.

——. 1939. Book Review of "Introduction à la sociologie envisagée comme connaissance de faits sociaux par les causes" by André deMaday. *Zeitschrift für schweizerische Statistik und Volkswirtschaft/Journal de statistique et revue économique suisse* 75(2): 274–.

——. 1940. Book Review of "Der Welthandel 1930 bis 1934" by J. E. Fischer. *Zeitschrift für schweizerische Statistik und Volkswirtschaft/Journal de statistique et revue économique suisse* 76(1): 117–.

Sorabji, Cornelia. 1891. Stray Thoughts of an Indian Girl. *Nineteenth Century* 30 (October): 638–42.

——. 1898. The Legal Status of Women in India. *Nineteenth Century* 44 (November): 854–66.

——. 1899. An Indian Plague Story. *Nineteenth Century* 46 (September): 410–31.

——. 1900. Behind the Purdah. *Macmillan's Magazine* 82 (July): 193–200.

Southworth, Shirley Donald. 1922. Some Recent Problems in Public Utility Valuation and Regulation. *American Economic Review* 12 (December): 606–13.

——. 1926. Branch Banking in the United States. Ph.D. thesis, Princeton University (economics, history).

——. 1928. *Branch Banking in the United States.* New York: McGraw-Hill Book Co.

——. 1932. Branch Banks for America. *American Federationist* 39(5) (May): 514.

Spaak, Marie. 1923. La Femme et la politique. *Avant l'Action féminine*, Brussels: s.n.

Spahr, Margaret. 1925. *The Supreme Court on the Incidence and Effects of Taxation: An Analysis of Economic Theory Embedded in the Constitutional Law Derived from the Explicit Tax Clause.* Smith College Studies in History Series, vol. 10, nos. 2–4. Northampton, Mass.: Smith College.

——. 1926. The Supreme Court on the Incidence and Effects of Taxation: An Analysis of Economic Theory Embedded in the Constitutional Law Derived from the Explicit Tax Clauses. Ph.D. thesis, Columbia University (economics).

——. 1930. Natural Law, Due Process, and Economic Pressure. *American Political Science Review (1927–)* 24(2) (May): 332–.

——. 1935. *Readings in Recent Political Philosophy.* New York: Macmillan.

Speek, Frances Valiant. 1934. *Housing College Students.* Washington: American Association of University Women.

——. 1935. Book Review of "College Women and the Social Sciences" by Herbert Elmer Mills and his former students. *Journal of Higher Education* 6: 113–.

——. 1936. What the Branches Are Doing. *Journal of the American Association of University Women* 29(3) (April): 182–.

Speek, Frances Valiant and Kathryn McHale. 1935. Book Review of "Housing College Students." *Journal of Higher Education* 6: 285–6–.

Speek, Frances Valiant. Contributor to Campus and Classroom. *Journal of the American Association of University Women*, 1934–6; Contributor to News of the Colleges. *Journal of the American Association of University Women*, 1937–8.

Spencer, Amy Harrison. Coauth. *See* Hutchins, Elizabeth Leigh.

Spencer, Anna Garlin. 1931. Should Married Women Work Outside the Home? *Eugenics* 4: 25–.

Spilman, Leona. 1940. A Comparison of Veblen's and Commons' Institutionalism. Ph.D. thesis, University of Wisconsin–Madison (economics).

Spofford, Mrs. Harriet Prescott. 1881. *The Servant Girl Question.* Boston: Houghton Mifflin and Co.

——. 1890. Shall Our Daughters Have Dowries? *North American Review* 151(6) (December): 752–5.

Sprague, Blanche Hazard. *See* Hazard [Sprague], Blanche Evans.

Spratt, Dora E. W. 1897. Earning a Living in China. *Lippincott's* 59 (January/June): 670–.

——. 1898. How They Live on Nothing a Year. *Lippincott's* 61 (January/June): 250–.

Spring-Rice, Margery. 1939. *Working Class Wives, Their Health and Conditions.* Harmondsworth, UK: Penguin.

Springall, Lillie Marion. 1936. *Labouring Life in Norfolk Villages, 1834–1914.* London: G. Allen & Unwin.

——. 1936. Labouring Life in Norfolk Villages, 1834–1914. Ph.D. thesis, London School of Economics.

Springer, Ethel Maria. 1923. *Canal-boat Children.* Washington: U.S. Government Printing Office for the U.S. Children's Bureau. Also published in *Monthly Labor Review* 16 (January/June 1923): 1–21.

Springer, Ethel Maria and Emma Octavia Lundberg. 1921. *Children Deprived of Parental Care: A Study of Children Taken under Care by Delaware Agencies and Institutions.* Washington: U.S. Children's Bureau.

Springer, Ethel Maria, Harriet Anne Byrne, and Helen Marietta Dart. 1923. *Child Labor in North Dakota.* U.S. Children's Bureau Publication, no. 129. Washington: U.S. Government Printing Office.

Springer, Ethel Maria. Coauth. *See* McGill, Nettie Pauline; Matthews, Ellen Nathalie.

Springer, Mary E. 1894. Cuban Women. *North American Review* 158(2) (February): 255–.

Spruill, Julia Cherry. 1935. Virginia and Carolina Homes before the Revolution. *North Carolina Historical Review* 12(4) (October): 320–.

——. 1936. Southern Housewives before the Revolution. *North Carolina Historical Review* 13(1) (January): 25–.

——. 1936. Women in the Founding of the Southern Colonies. *North Carolina Historical Review* 13(3) (July): 202–.

——. 1938. *Women's Life and Work in the Southern Colonies*. Chapel Hill, N.C.: University of North Carolina Press. Reprinted New York: Russell & Russell, 1969; New York: W. W. Norton, 1972.

——. 1940. Book Review of "The History of the Woman's Peace Party" by Degen. *Social Forces* 19(1/4): 593–.

Spry, Irene M. *See* Biss [Spry], Irene M.

Stacpoole, Florence. 1898. *Handbook of Housekeeping for Small Incomes*. London: Walter Scott.

Stacy, Enid. 1895. *Education: Its Meaning: A Socialist Point of View*. Manchester: Labour Press Society Ltd.

——. 1896. *Is Socialism Desirable? A Debate* [with Rev. A. Stacy]. Nottingham: Co-operative Printing Works.

——. 1897. A Century of Women's Rights. In Edward Carpenter, ed., *Forecasts of the Coming Century*. Manchester: Labour Press.

Staley, Helen. 1936. The Theory of Planned Public Works. A.M thesis, University of Chicago (economics).

Staniforth, Edith A. 1894. Women's Work in Sheffield Factories. *Sylvia's Journal* 2 (September): 565–.

Stanley, Mrs. Arthur. 1891. Cooperation in Housekeeping. *Good Housekeeping* 12 (March).

Stanley, [the Hon.] Maude A. 1878. *Work about the Five Dials*. London: Macmillan.

——. 1881. West-End Improvements. *Nineteenth Century* 9 (January/June): 849–55.

——. 1889. Clubs for Working Girls. *Nineteenth Century* 25 (January/June): 73–83.

——. 1890. *Clubs for Working Girls*. London: Macmillan.

Stanton, Elizabeth Cady. 1882. The Health of American Women. *North American Review* 135 (July/December): 510–.

——. 1884. The Need of Liberal Divorce Laws. *North American Review* 139(3) (September): 234–45.

——. 1891. Patriotism and Chastity. *Westminster Review* 135 (January): 1–5.

——. 1891. Where Must Lasting Progress Begin? *Arena* 4: 293–8.

——. 1892. Sunday at the World's Fair. *North American Review* 154(2) (February): 254–.

Starr, Ellen Gates. 1896. *Settlements and the Church's Duty*. Boston: Church Social Union.

Starrett, Helen E[kin]. 1885. *The Future of Educated Women*. With *Men, Women, and Money*, by Frances Ekin Allison. Chicago: Jansen, McClurg, and Co.

——. 1889. The Housekeeping of the Future. *Forum* 8 (September): 108–15.

——. 1890. The Future of Our Daughters. *Forum* 10 (October): 185–96.

——. 1896. *After College, What? For Girls*. New York: Thomas Y. Crowell.

Stearns, Bertha Monica. 1930. Early Factory Magazines in New England: The *Lowell Offering* and Its Contemporaries. *Journal of Economic and Business History* 2 (August): 685–705.

——. 1934. Miss Sedgwick Observes Harriet Martineau. *New England Quarterly* 7(1/4): 533–.

Stearns, Maude Ethel. 1929. Correlation between Lodgings of Homeless Men and Employment in New York City. *Journal of the American Statistical Association* 24(165) (Supplement, Proceedings of the American Statistical Association) (March): 182–90.

Stebbins, Sarah Bridges. 1876. A Woman in Business. *Demorest's Monthly Magazine*: 454–6.

Stecker, Margaret Loomis. 1916. The National Founders' Association. *Quarterly Journal of Economics* 30 (February): 352–86. Reprinted in John R. Commons (ed.) *Trade Unionism and Labor Problems*, second series. Boston: Ginn and Co.

——. 1918. The Founders, the Molders, and the Molding Machine. *Quarterly Journal of Economics* 32 (February): 278–308. Reprinted in John R. Commons (ed.) *Trade Unionism and Labor Problems*, second series. Boston: Ginn and Co.

——. 1921. Family Budgets and Wages. *American Economic Review* 11 (September): 447–65.

——. 1925. The New York Agreement 1899–1904: An Unsuccessful Experiment in Collective Bargaining. Ph.D. thesis, Cornell University (sociology, industrial and labor relations).

——. 1933. *Industrial Pension Systems*. New York: American Management Association.

——. 1936. *Inter-city Differences in the Cost of Living*. Research Bulletin, series I, no. 20. Washington: Works Progress Administration, Division of Social Research.

——. 1936. *Quantity Budgets of Goods and Services Necessary for a Basic Maintenance Standard of Living and for Operation under Emergency Conditions: Prepared as Weights for Retail Prices Used in Ascertaining the Cost of Living of Industrial, Service and Other Manual Workers of Small Means*. Research Bulletin, series 1, no. 21. Washington: Works Progress Administration.

——. 1937/1971. *Intercity Differences in Costs of Living in March, 1935–59 Cities*. New York: Da Capo Press.

Steel, Flora A[nnie]. 1899. East Indian Women. *North American Review* 169 (July/December): 846–.

——. Coauth. *See* Corelli, Marie.

Steevens, Christina. 1896. A Product of the Poor Law. *Blackwoods* 160 (October): 533–9.

Stein, Rose M[arian]. 1934. Socialist Action in Pennsylvania. *World Tomorrow* 17(3) (February 1): 56–.

——. 1938. The National Labor Relations Board in U.S.A. *Economic Journal* 48 (December): 685–94.

——. 1938. Cross-country. *Partisan Review* 4(3) (February): 44–.

——. 1940. Workers' Education: Today's Challenge. *Harvard Business Review* 18(2): 207–14.

Steinmetz, Ruth. Coauth. *See* Harper, Elsie Dorothy.

Stephen, Caroline E. 1871. *The Service of the Poor; Being an Inquiry into the Reasons for and against the Establishment of Religious Sisterhoods for Charitable Purposes.* London and New York: Macmillan.

——. 1879. Mistress and Servants. *Nineteenth Century* 6 (December): 1,051–63.

Stephens, Amy [as "Veva Karsland"]. 1891. *Women and their Work.* London: Samson Low, Marston.

Stephens, Kate. 1889. Advanced Education for Women. *Forum* 7 (March): 41–51.

——. 1896. Woman's Wages. *North American Review* 162(3) (March): 377–9.

Stephens, Laura. 1900. An Irish Workhouse. *New Ireland Review* 13 (May).

Stetson, Charlotte P. *See* Gilman, Charlotte Perkins.

Stevens, Alzina Parsons. 1893. The Evils of Child Labor. In *Proceedings of the 7th Annual Convention of Factory Inspectors.* Cleveland, Ohio: International Association of Factory Inspectors.

——. 1894. Child Slavery in America (Symposium): The Child, the Factory and the State. *Arena* 10(1) (June): 117–35.

——. 1894. The Tenement House Curse (Symposium): Some Chicago Tenement Houses. *Arena* 9(5) (April): 662–8.

——. 1896. The Working Child and the Inspector. In *Proceedings of the 10th Annual Convention of Factory Inspectors.* Cleveland, Ohio: International Association of Factory Inspectors.

——. 1898. Die Gewerkvereine der Vereinigten Staaten. *Archiv für soziale Gesetzgebung und Statistik* 12: 695–.

——. 1899. Life in a Social Settlement – Hull House, Chicago. *Self Culture* (March).

——. Coauth. *See* Kelley, Florence J.

Stevens, Leah [Ida]. 1934. *The Port of Vancouver.* S.M. thesis, University of Chicago (geography).

——. 1936. The Grain Trade of the Port of Vancouver, British Columbia. *Economic Geography* 12(2) (April): 185–96.

——. 1936. Rise of the Port of Vancouver, British Columbia. *Economic Geography* 12(1) (January): 61–70.

Stevenson, Hilda. 1893. Book Review of "The Inquisition of 1517. Inclosures and Evictions. Edited from the Lansdown Ms. I. 152" by I. S. Leadam. *Economic Journal* 3(10) (June): 280.

——. 1893. Book Review of "The Mark in Europe and America" by Enoch A. Bryan. *Economic Journal* 3(12) (December): 680–1.

——. 1893. Book Review of "The Old English Manor" by Charles M. Andrews. *Economic Journal* 3(11) (September): 494–5.

——. 1893. Book Review of "Two Thousand Years of Gild Life" by Rev. J. Malet Lambert. *Economic Journal* 3(9) (March): 106.

Stevenson, Marietta. 1932. How to Maintain Welfare Standards in a Depression. *Public Management* 14(12) (December): 377–.

——. 1932. An Interpretation of the Federal Relief Act. *Public Management* 14(8) (August): 249–.

——. 1932. The Out-of-work: The Story of What Several Legislatures Have Done toward the Relief of Jobless Citizens. *State Government* 5(2) (February): 3–.

——. 1933. The New Federal Relief Program. *Public Management* 15(5) (May): 133.

——. 1933. Rules for Spending Federal Relief Funds. *Public Management* 15(8) (August): 230–.

——. 1934. Standards of Public Aid. *Annals of the American Academy of Political and Social Science* 176 (November): 57–.

——. 1935. What Social Workers Are Thinking. *Public Management* 17(7) (July): 195–.

——. 1936. Old-age Assistance. *Law and Contemporary Problems* 3: 236–.

——. 1936. Old-age Assistance. *National Municipal Review* 25(4) (April): 205–.

——. 1937. Public Welfare Reorganization. *Social Service Review* 11(1/4) (March/December): 349–.

——. 1938. *Public Welfare Administration*. New York: Macmillan.

——. 1939. Recent Trends in Public Welfare Legislation. *Social Service Review* 13(1/4) (March/December): 440–.

Stevenson, Marietta and Lucy Williams Brown. 1933. *Federal and State Welfare for Unemployment Relief and National Recovery, 1933*. Chicago: Public Administration Service.

——. 1933. *Old Age Security and Unemployment Insurance*. Chicago: American Public Welfare Association.

Stevenson, Marietta and Alice MacDonald. 1939. *Digest of Public Welfare Legislation, 1939*. Chicago: American Public Welfare Association.

——. 1939. *State and Local Public Welfare Agencies*. Chicago: American Public Welfare Association.

Stevenson, Marietta and Susan Elrick Posanski. 1935. *Digest of Social Welfare Legislation, 1935*. Chicago: American Public Welfare Association.

——. 1935. *Federal and State Welfare*. Chicago: Public Administration Service.

Stewart, Estelle May. 1925. *The Cost of American Almshouses*. U.S. Bureau of Labor Statistics Bulletin, no. 386, Miscellaneous Series. Washington: U.S. Government Printing Office.

——. 1928. *Apprenticeship in Building Construction, April, 1928*. Washington: U.S. Government Printing Office for the U.S. Bureau of Labor Statistics.

——. 1934. British Health-insurance System. *Monthly Labor Review* 39(4) (October): 823–.

——. 1936. Origin and Significance of Labor Day. *Monthly Labor Review* 43(2) (August): 279–.

Stewart, Estelle May and Maude A. K. Wetmore. 1927. *Study of a Group of Almshouses in Connecticut, New Jersey, New York, and Pennsylvania*. New York: National Civic Federation, Woman's Department.

Stewart, Estelle M. Coauth. *See* Parker, Florence Evelyn.

Stewart, Margaret. 1936. Review of Soviet Trade from the Pacific to the Levant. *Economic Journal* 46(182) (June): 340–2.

Stewart, Margaret Winfield. 1915. Some Buried "Labor Laws." *American Federationist* 22(6) (June): 425–.

——. 1933/4. The Consumer and the N.R.A. *Social Forces* 12(1/4): 585–.

Stewart, Maria W. 1835. *Productions of Mrs. Maria W. Stewart.* Presented to the First African Baptist Church & Society of the City of Boston. Boston: Friends of Freedom and Virtue.

Stewart, Countess Mary Arabella Cecil. 1886. Women and Politics. *Nineteenth Century* 19 (June): 896–901.

Stewart, Stella. 1937. *Changes in Retail Prices of Gas, 1923–36.* Washington: U.S. Bureau of Labor Statistics.

Stewart, Stella and Ruth J. Powers. 1939. *Changes in Retail Prices of Electricity, 1923–38.* Washington: U.S. Bureau of Labor Statistics.

Stewart, Stella and Faith M. Williams. 1938. *Retail Prices of Food, 1923–36.* Washington: U.S. Bureau of Labor Statistics.

Stewart, Stella. Coauth. *See* Weiss, Gertrude Schmidt.

Stiebeling, Hazel Katherine. 1929. Studies of the Relation of Vitamin D to the Deposition of Calcium in the Bones of Experimental Animals, with Special Reference to the Quantitative Determination of Vitamin D. Ph.D. thesis, Columbia University (biochemistry).

——. 1931. *The Family's Food at Low Cost.* Revised. Washington: U.S. Government Printing Office.

——. 1932. The Foods We Need. *American Federationist* 39(8) (August): 891–.

——. 1933. *Food Budgets for Nutrition and Production Programs.* U.S. Department of Agriculture Miscellaneous Publication, no. 183. Washington: U.S. Department of Agriculture.

——. 1934. How to Conserve Nutritive Value of Diet Adjusted to Family Purse. *United States News* 2(4) (January 29): 58–.

——. 1936. Nutritive Value of Diets of Families of Wage Earners and Clerical Workers in North Atlantic Cities, 1934–35. *Monthly Labor Review* 43(1) (July): 14–.

——. 1939. *Nutrition in Relation to Farm Income, Home-production, and Land Use.* Presented March 3, 1939, at the Regional Extension Conference for Northeastern States, New York. Washington: U.S. Department of Agriculture, Extension Service.

——. 1940. Programs for Using Agricultural Surpluses to Reduce Malnutrition and to Benefit Farmers – Discussion. *Journal of Farm Economics* 22(1) (February): 337–.

Stiebeling, Hazel Katherine and Miriam Birdseye. 1931. *Adequate Diets for Families with Limited Incomes.* U.S. Department of Agriculture Miscellaneous Publication, no. 113. Washington: U.S. Department of Agriculture.

Stiebeling, Hazel Katherine and Rowena Schmidt Carpenter. 1936. *Diets to Fit the Family Income.* Washington: U.S. Government Printing Office.

Stiebeling, Hazel Katherine and Hazel Edith Munsell. 1932. *Food Supply and Pellagra Incidence in 73 South Carolina Farm Families.* Washington: U.S. Department of Agriculture.

Stiebeling, Hazel Katherine and Ester Hawley Funnell Phipard. 1939. *Diets of Families of Employed Wage Earners and Clerical Workers in Cities*. Circular no. 157. Washington: U.S. Department of Agriculture.

Stiebeling, Hazel Katherine. Coauth. *See* Hann, Helen Nebeker.

Stieda, Wilh. 1893. Child Laborers and their Protection in Germany. *Chautauquan* 18 (October): 88–.

Stillman, Bella H. 1890. Life in Modern Italy, the Peasant. *Chautauquan* 11 (April/September): 6–.

——. 1890. Life in Modern Italy, the Upper Classes. *Chautauquan* 11 (April/September): 267–.

Stites, Sara Henry. 1904. The Economics of the Iroquois. Ph.D. thesis, Bryn Mawr College (economics).

Stitt, Louise. 1925. A Study of Woman's Party Position on Special Labor Laws for Women. M.A. thesis, Ohio State University.

——. 1936. The Present Status of Minimum Wage Legislation in the United States. *Social Service Review* 10(1/4) (March/December): 109–.

——. 1939. State Fair Labor Standards Legislation. *Law and Contemporary Problems* 6: 454–.

Stitt, Louise and E. L. Bowers. 1932. Workmen's Compensation – What Next? *American Federationist* 39(7) (June): 798–.

Stitt, Louise. Coauth. *See* Weiss, Gertrude Schmidt.

Stocks, Mary [Danvers Brinton]. 1915. The Attempt to Fix Maximum Corn Prices in Germany, November, 1914. *Economic Journal* 25 (June): 274–80.

——. 1916. German Potato Policy. *Economic Journal* 26 (March): 57–61.

——. 1916. The Meat Problem in Germany. *Economic Journal* 26 (June): 168–73.

——. 1918. The Future of the Woman War Worker. *Athenaeum* 4625 (January): 21–.

——. 1918. The Future of the Woman War Worker. *Living Age* 8(296) (January/March): 809–.

——. 1920/1921. *The Industrial State: A Social and Economic History of England*. London: Collins' Clear-Type Press.

——. 1921. *The Meaning of Family Endowment*. London: Labour Publishing Co./G. Allen & Unwin, Ltd.

——. 1927. *The Case for Family Endowment*. London: Labour Publishing Co.

——. 1932/3. Eight Years' Industrial Conscription: A Suggestion from America. *Hibbert Journal* 31 (October/July): 252–.

——. 1937. Gambling: What Do We Pay and What Do We Get? *Listener* 17(419) (January 20): 102–.

——. 1937. London Government. *Political Quarterly (1930-)* 10: 365–.

Stoddart, Jane T. 1909. *The New Socialism: An Impartial Inquiry*. London: Hodder and Stoughton.

Stoffregen, Elizabeth C. *See* May, Elizabeth Stoffregen.

Stokes, Rose Harriet Pastor. 1906. The Condition of Working Women, from the Working Woman's Viewpoint. *Annals of the American Academy of Political and Social Science* 27: 165–75.

——. 1916. *The Woman Who Wouldn't.* New York: G. P. Putnam's Sons. [*play*]

Stone, Mrs. C. H. 1892. *The Problem of Domestic Service.* St. Louis, Mo.: Nelson Printing Co.

Stone, Natalia S. 1940. The College Girl and the Depression. *Journal of Educational Sociology* 13(6) (February): 336–51.

Stone, Sarah. 1937. *An Analysis of Vital Statistics in Duluth, Minnesota, for the Period 1900–1937.* Official Project, no. 465–71–3151. Duluth, Minn.: Duluth (Minn.) Health Department Works Progress Administration.

Stone, Ursula Batchelder. *See* Batchelder Stone, Ursula Chase.

Stopes, C[harlotte]. C[armichael]. 1894. *British Freewomen: Their Historical Privilege.* London: Swan Sonnenschein.

——. 1894. With All My Worldly Goods I Thee Endow. *Englishwoman's Review,* n.s. 223 (July): 157–64.

——. 1896. Unequal Justice to Women. Paper read at the London Conference of the Women's Emancipation Union, October 15, 1896. *Humanitarian* 9 (December 15): 441–. Reprinted as *The Women's Protest,* London: Women's Printing Society, 1896.

——. 1898. Some Women's Trades in Olden Times. *Englishwoman's Review* 29, n.s. 240 (October): 247–.

——. 1907. *The Sphere of "Man" in Relation to That of Woman in the Constitution.* London: T. F. Unwin.

——. 1908. The Constitutional Basis of Women's Suffrage. *Fortnightly Review* n.s. 84 (September). Reprinted Edinburgh: Darien Press, 1983.

——. 1909. Suffragette History [letter to the editor]. *Nation* 4(20) (February 13): 752–.

——. 1916. Shakespeare's Industry [letter to the editor]. *Nation* 19(2) (April 8): 46.

Stow, Mrs. J. W. [Marietta], ed. 1876. *Probate Confiscation; Unjust Laws Which Govern Woman.* San Francisco: Bacon & Co. Reprinted Boston: published and sold by the author, 1878. Reprinted New York: Arno Press, 1974. Fourth ed. (1879) reprinted Clark, N.J.: The Lawbook Exchange, Ltd., 2003.

——. 1879. *An Equal-rights Marriage Property Act and Comparative Law.* Washington?: s.n.

Stowe, Harriet Beecher. 1852. *Uncle Tom's Cabin; or, Life among the Lowly.* 2 vols. Boston: Jewett. British ed., *Uncle Tom's Cabin, or, Negro Life in the Slave States of America.* London: Simms and McIntyre.

——. 1853. *The Key to Uncle Tom's Cabin: Presenting the Original Facts and Documents upon Which the Story Is Founded, Together with Corroborative Statements Verifying the Truth of the Work.* Boston: Jewett; London: Sampson Low.

——. 1853. *Mrs. Stowe's Letter to the Women of England.* Edinburgh: Edinburgh Ladies' Emancipation Society.

——. 1863. A Reply to the Address of the Women of England [on slavery]. *Atlantic Monthly* 11 (January): 120–34.

——. 1863. Sojourner Truth, the Libyan Sibyl. *Atlantic Monthly* 11 (April): 473–81.

——. 1879. The Education of Freedmen. *North American Review* 128 (June): 605–15; 129 (July): 81–95.

——. 1879. Ireland's Daughters in Their New Homes. *Donahoe's Magazine* (January).

——. 1885. Mistress and Maid. *Donahoe's Magazine* (May).

——. Coauth. *See* Beecher, Catharine E.

Strachan, Grace Charlotte. 1910. *Equal Pay for Equal Work: The Story of the Struggle for Justice Being Made by the Women Teachers of the City of New York*. New York: B. F. Buck & Company.

Strachey, Ray [Rachel Conn Costelloe Strachey]. 1913. *Frances Willard, Her Life and Work*. Fleming H. Revell Company.

——. 1914. *A Quaker Grandmother, Hannah Whitall Smith*. New York and Chicago: Fleming H. Revell Company.

——. 1923. *Marching On*. New York: Harcourt, Brace and Co.

——. 1927. *Women's Suffrage and Women's Service: The History of the London and National Society for Women's Service*. London: Westminster, London and National Society for Women's Service.

——. 1928. *Shaken by the wind; a Story of Fanaticism*. New York: Macmillan.

——. 1928. Books about Women. *Nation and Athenaeum* 43(7) (May 19): 228–.

——. 1928. The Centenary of Josephine Butler: An Interview with Dame Millicent Garrett Fawcett. *Social Service Review* 2(1/4) (March/December): 1–.

——. 1928. Facing Facts. *Nation and Athenaeum* 43(8) (May 26): 250–.

——. 1929. Dame Millicent Fawcett. *Nation and Athenaeum* 45(19) (August 10): 616–.

——. 1929. Prudery and Nakedness. *Nation and Athenaeum* 45(24) (September 14): 763–.

——. 1931. *Millicent Garrett Fawcett*. London: J. Murray.

——. 1935. *Careers and Openings for Women: A Survey of Women's Employment and a Guide for Those Seeking Work*. London: Faber and Faber.

——. 1936. Women in Parliament. *Fortnightly* 140 (July/December): 336–.

——. 1937. The Insurance of Black Coated Workers. *Political Quarterly (1930-)* 8: 430–.

——. 1937. Marriage and Divorce. *Political Quarterly (1930–)* 8: 90–.

——. 1938. How to Build Your Own House. *Listener* 19(470) (January 12): 83–.

Strachey, Ray, Florence Nightingale, and Carrie Chapman Catt. 1928. *"The Cause"; a Short History of the Women's Movement in Great Britain*. London: G. Bell and Sons, Ltd.

Strachey, Ray [Rachel], Eleanor Rathbone, and Carrie Catt, eds. 1936. *Our Freedom and Its Results, by Five Women*. London: Leonard and Virginia Woolf at the Hogarth Press.

Stratton, Lenore Monroe. Coauth. *See* Kyrk, Hazel; Monroe, Day.

Strickland, Martha. 1883. The Right of Women to Office. *American Law Review* 17: 670.

Strong, Anna Louise. 1908. A Consideration of Prayer from the Standpoint of Social Psychology. Ph.D. thesis, University Of Chicago (philosophy).

——. 1908. Some Religious Aspects of Pragmatism. *American Journal of Theology* 12 (January/October): 231–40.
——. 1912. Child Welfare Exhibits. *National Municipal Review* 1(2) (April): 248–.
——. 1920. Centralia: An Unfinished Story. *Nation* 110 (April 17): 508–10.
——. 1923. Three Kinds of Transport (Verse). *Forum (New York, 1886)* 69 (January/June): 1,279–.
——. 1924. *The First Time in History: Two Years of Russia's New Life (August 1921 to December 1923)*. New York: Boni and Liveright.
——. 1924. Get Rich Quick in Poland. *Nation* 119 (August 13): 171–2.
——. 1924. Triumph of Lenin. *Nation* 118 (February 13): 159–60.
——. 1925. *Children of Revolution: Story of the John Reed Children's Colony of the Volga.* Seattle: Piggott Printing.
——. 1926. Chang and Feng and Wu. *Asia* 26(7) (July): 596–.
——. 1926. Jews of Russia Move Back to the Soil. *Current History (New York)* 25(1) (October): 82–.
——. 1926. New Women of Old Canton. *Asia* 26(6) (June): 493–.
——. 1926. A Night on the Transsiberian. *Century Monthly Magazine* 112 (May/October): 136–.
——. 1926. Three Men of Japan. *Asia* 26(3) (March): 228–.
——. 1927. *How Business Is Carried on in Soviet Russia.* Girard: Haldeman-Julius Publications.
——. 1927. *How the Communists Rule Russia.* Girard: Haldeman-Julius Publications.
——. 1927. *Peasant Life in Soviet Russia.* Girard: Haldeman-Julius Publications.
——. 1927. *Workers' Life in Soviet Russia.* Girard: Haldeman-Julius Publications.
——. 1927. The Germans Trade on the Yangtse. *World Tomorrow* 10(10) (October): 416–.
——. 1927. Head-High-in-the-Wind. *Harper's Monthly Magazine* 155(930) (November): 744–.
——. 1928. *New Lives for Old in Today's Russia; What Has Happened to the Common Folk of the Soviet Republic.* Girard: Haldeman-Julius Publications.
——. 1928. The Awakened Peasantry of China. *Asia* 28(1) (January): 32–.
——. 1928. Motoring out from China. *Asia* 28(9) (September): 708–.
——. 1928. Mrs. Sun Yat-sen Flees from Victory. *China Weekly Review* 46(9) (October 27): 287–.
——. 1928. Old and New Gods in Mongolia. *Asia* 28(7) (July): 564–.
——. 1928. Peasants and Soldiers in Hunan. *World Tomorrow* 11(6) (June): 269–.
——. 1928. Woman Citizens of the Soviet Union. *Asia* 28(4) (April): 294–.
——. 1928. Young China Tackles the Floods. *China Weekly Review* 45(9) (July 28): 291–.
——. 1929. Making Bolshevists of Central Asians. *Asia* 29(11) (November): 870–.
——. 1929. Samarkand Returns to Power. *Atlantic Monthly* 144 (July/December): 255–.
——. 1929. Small Town Politics. *Asia* 29(8) (August): 631–.

——. 1929. The Soviet Outpost in Asia. *Asia* 29(6) (June): 460–.
——. 1930. *Modern Farming – Soviet Style*. New York: International Pamphlets.
——. 1930. The Economic Paradox in Uzbekistan. *Contemporary Review* 138 (July/December): 218–.
——. 1930. Grasshoppers, Soliers, and Silk Weavers. *Atlantic Monthly* 146 (July/December): 673–.
——. 1930. Modern Farming – Soviet Style. *Atlantic Monthly* 146 (July/December): 112–.
——. 1930. The Soviet of the High Pastures. *Atlantic Monthly* 146 (July/December): 817–.
——. 1930. The Village of Wide Bounty. *Atlantic Monthly* 145 (January/June): 697.
——. 1931. *The Soviets Conquer Wheat: The Drama of Collective Farming*. New York: H. Holt.
——. 1931. At the Edge of Civilisation. *Contemporary Review* 140 (July/December): 504–.
——. 1931. Book Review of "Red Star in Samarkand." *Moslem World* 21: 215–.
——. 1932. *From Stalingrad to Kuzbas, Sketches of the Socialist Construction in the USSR*. New York: International Pamphlets.
——. 1934. *Dictatorship and Democracy in the Soviet Union*. International Pamphlets, no. 40. New York: International Pamphlets.
——. 1934. The Soviet President's Wife. *Asia* 34(2) (February): 97–.
——. 1934. Soviets Fight Bureaucracy. *American Mercury* 33 (September): 86–9.
——. 1934. The Soviets Pay Their Bills. *Forum and Century* 91(1) (January): 24–.
——. 1934. Stalin in Action. *Asia* 34(1) (January): 19–.
——. 1934. We Soviet Wives. *American Mercury* 32 (August): 415–23.
——. 1934. What Soviet Elections Are Like. *Soviet Russia Today* 3(10) (December): 5–.
——. 1935. *China's Millions; the Revolutionary Struggles from 1927 to 1935*. New York: Knight Publishing Co.
——. 1935. *Remaking an American*. Moscow: Co-operative Publishing Society of Foreign Workers in the U.S.S.R. Reprinted as *I Change Worlds; the Remaking of an American*, New York: H. Holt and Co., 1935; Garden City, N.Y.: Garden City Publishing Co., 1935, 1937.
——. 1935. *What about Russia? An Honest Reply to Honest Questions*. Political Pamphlets at the State University of New York at Albany, no. 552. New York: American Friends of the Soviet Union. Reprinted from *New Republic*.
——. 1935. Bread Rationing Ends in the USSR. *Soviet Russia Today* 3(11) (January): 11–.
——. 1935. Building Democracy. *Soviet Russia Today* 4(10) (December): 7–.
——. 1935. From Vladivostok to Moscow. *Soviet Russia Today* 4(4) (June): 6–.
——. 1935. Karelia Revisited after 13 Years. *Soviet Russia Today* 4(7) (September): 12–.
——. 1935. The Last Word in the Far East. *Asia* 35(10) (October): 594–.
——. 1935. May Day around the World. *Soviet Russia Today* 4(3) (May): 11–.

——. 1935. The Power of the Press in the USSR. *Soviet Russia Today* 4(1) (March): 10–.
——. 1935. Searching Out the Soviets. *New Republic* 83 (August 7): 354–9.
——. 1935. Two Economic Systems. *Soviet Russia Today* 4(9) (November): 32–.
——. 1935. The Voice of the Soviet Village. *Current History (New York)* 41(6) (March): 692–.
——. 1935. Were You Ever a Dictator? *Soviet Russia Today* 4(2) (April): 10–.
——. 1936. The Arctic Sea Route Is Open. *Asia* 36(2) (February): 94–.
——. 1936. Birobidjan. *Asia* 36(1) (January): 41–.
——. 1936. Free Women. *Asia* 36(5) (May): 327–.
——. 1936. A New Charter of Freedom. *Soviet Russia Today* 5(6) (August): 8–.
——. 1936. Soviet Democracy. *Soviet Russia Today* 4(12) (February): 13–.
——. 1936. Spain and the USSR. *Soviet Russia Today* 5(10) (December): 8–.
——. 1936. Stakhanovism Sweeps the USSR. *Soviet Russia Today* 4(11) (January): 10–.
——. 1936. The Terrorists' Trial. *Soviet Russia Today* 5(8) (October): 9–.
——. 1936. The Workers Find a Way. *Soviet Russia Today* 5(9) (November): 26–.
——. 1937. *The New Soviet Constitution, a Study in Socialist Democracy*. New York: H. Holt.
——. 1937. 100 Million Voters. *Soviet Russia Today* 6(10) (December): 7–.
——. 1937. An Author Visits Spain. *Communist Review* 4(6) (June): 24–.
——. 1937. Heroic Artists of U.S.S.R. *Communist Review* 4(7) (July): 25–.
——. 1937. I Watched the Soviets Grow. *Soviet Russia Today* 6(9) (November): 14–.
——. 1937. The People Make a Constitution. *Soviet Russia Today* 5(11) (January): 16–.
——. 1937. The Revolution Betrayed – by Whom? A Review. *Soviet Russia Today* 6(3) (May): 36–.
——. 1938. *One-fifth of Mankind*. New York: Modern Age Books.
——. 1938. China Moves Inland. *Asia* 38(6) (June): 369–.
——. 1938. The Chinese Spirit Goes Up. *Asia* 38(7) (July): 425–.
——. 1938. The Communists and China's Future – I: How Red Is China Now? *Asia* 38(8) (August): 457–.
——. 1938. Political Work of a Chinese Army. *Amerasia* 2(6) (August): 304–.
——. 1938. Security for Farmers. *Soviet Russia Today* 7(8) (November): 28–.
——. 1939. *Is the Soviet Union Turning from World Brotherhood to Imperialism?* Address delivered to the Community Church of Boston, Symphony Hall, Sunday, November 19, 1939. Boston: Community Church of Boston.
——. 1939. How I Saw Minsk. *Soviet Russia Today* 7(11) (February): 8–.
——. 1939. Human Values behind the War. *Soviet Russia Today* 8(7) (November): 22–.
——. 1939. Moscow: Out of the World? *Asia* 39(5) (May): 272–.
——. 1939. The Red Army Marches for Peace. *Soviet Russia Today* 8(6) (October): 13–.
——. 1939. Salaries for Mothers. *Soviet Russia Today* 7(12) (March): 17–.

——. 1939. Stalin: Some Notes on His Method. *Soviet Russia Today* 8(8) (December): 9–.

——. 1939. What Does Moscow Want? *Asia* 39(11) (November): 647–.

——. 1940. *My Native Land*. New York: Viking Press.

——. 1940. The Lithuanian Workers Take Command. *Soviet Russia Today* 9(8) (December): 7–.

——. 1940. The Myth of the German–Soviet Alliance. *Communist Review* 7(2) (February): 93–.

——. 1940. The Red Army in Lithuania. *Soviet Russia Today* 9(6) (October): 13–.

Strong, Helen Mabel. 1921. The Geography of Cleveland. Ph.D. thesis, University of Chicago (geography).

——. 1924. *Distribution of Agricultural Exports from the United States*. Washington: U.S. Bureau of Foreign and Domestic Commerce.

——. 1924. *Relation between Value and Volume of Agricultural Products*. Washington: U.S. Bureau of Foreign and Domestic Commerce.

——. 1925. Changes in Entrepot Markets for Tropical and Other Exotic Products. *Annals of the Association of American Geographers* 15: 180–.

——. 1925. Cleveland: A City of Contacts. *Economic Geography* 1(2) (July): 198–205.

——. 1927. Maps and Business. *Annals of the Association of American Geographers* 17: 15–.

——. 1932. Book Review of "Commercial Survey of the Pacific Northwest" by Edwin Bates. *Geographical Review* 22(3) (July): 505–.

——. 1932. Export Wheat Producing Regions. *Economic Geography* 8(4) (April): 161–90.

——. 1936. Regionalism: Its Cultural Significance. *Economic Geography* 12(4) (October): 392–410.

——. 1937. Regions of Manufacturing Intensity in the United States. *Annals of the Association of American Geographers* 27: 23–.

——. 1938. A Land Use Record in the Blackland Prairies of Texas. *Annals of the Association of American Geographers* 28: 128–.

Strong, Margaret Kirkpatrick. 1928. Public Welfare Administration in Canada. Ph.D. thesis, University of Chicago (sociology).

Stuart, Miss. 1888. Openings for Women in the Colonies. *Englishwoman's Review*, n.s. 177 (January): 6–.

Stuart-Wortley, Mrs. Jane. 1887. The East End as Represented by Mr. Besant. *Nineteenth Century* 22 (September): 361–77.

Stuckenberg, Mrs. J. H. W. 1896. Labor and Temperance. *American Federationist* 2(11) (January).

Sullivan, Mary Loretta. 1936. *Employment Conditions in Department Stores in 1932–33: A Study in Selected Cities of Five States*. U.S. Women's Bureau Bulletin, no. 125. Washington: U.S. Government Printing Office.

Sullivan, Mary Loretta and Bertha Blair. 1936. *Women in Texas Industries: Hours, Wages, Working Conditions, and Home Work*. U.S. Women's Bureau Bulletin, no. 126. Washington: U.S. Government Printing Office.

Sullivan, Mary Loretta and Ethel Erickson. 1927. *Women's Employment in Vegetable Canneries in Delaware.* U.S. Women's Bureau Bulletin, no. 62. Washington: U.S. Government Printing Office.

Sullivan, Mary Loretta. Coauth. *See* Manning, Caroline.

Sumner, Helen L. *See* [Woodbury,] Helen L[aura]. Sumner.

Sumner, Marion Richter. 1927. Public Utility Financing during the First and Second Quarter of 1927. *Land Economics* 3 (August): 331–3.

——. 1927. Public Utility Financing during the First and Second Quarter of 1927. *Land Economics* 3 (November): 430–2.

——. 1927. Public Utility Financing during the Year 1926. *Land Economics* 3 (May): 217–19.

——. 1931. Cost of Railway Capital through June, 1930. *Land Economics* 7 (February): 94–7.

——. 1931. Recent Developments in the Electric Light and Power Industry as Disclosed by the 1927 Census. *Land Economics* 7 (May): 200–3.

Sumner Boyd, Mary Brown. 1912. *A Strike Brought about by a Bundle of Dirty Linen.* New York: Allied Printing.

Surrey, Nancy Maria Miller. 1916. The Commerce of Louisiana During the French Regime, 1699–1763. Ph.D. thesis, Columbia University (economics).

Sutcliffe, Constance. 1897. Turkish Guilds. *Fortnightly Review*, n.s. 60 (December): 820–9.

Sutherland, Lucy Stuart. 1932. The Accounts of an Eighteenth-century Merchant. *Economic History Review* 3 (April): 367–87.

——. 1934. The Law Merchant in England in the Seventeenth and Eighteenth Centuries. *Transactions of the Royal Historical Society*, 4th series, 17: 149–76.

——. 1935. The Use of Business Records in the Study of History. *Bulletin of the Institute of Historical Research* 13(38) (November): 69–.

——. 1936. Sir George Colebrooke's World Corner in Alum, 1771–73. *Economic History* 3 (February): 237–58.

Sutherland, Stella Helen. 1931. The Distribution of Population in the American Colonies in the Revolutionary Period. Ph.D. thesis, University of Illinois (history, sociology).

——. 1936. *Population Distribution in Colonial America.* New York: Columbia University Press.

Sutter, Miss J. 1901. *Cities and Citizens.* London: Marshall.

Swainson, Beatrice M. 1935. Rural Settlement in North West Devon, England. *Economic Geography* 11(1) (January): 77–90.

Swallow, Mary Alma. 1932. History of the Development of the Means of Communication in the Country of Monmouth. Ph.D. thesis, London School of Economics (economics).

Swanwick, Helena M. 1913. *The Future of the Women's Movement.* London: G. Bell.

——. 1914. *Some Points of English Law Affecting Working Women as Wives and Mothers: Being Notes of Two Lectures of a Guides' Course Given to Members of the Women's Co-operative Guild.* Women's Co-operative Guild.

——. 1915. *Women and War.* Union of Democratic Control Pamphlet, no. 11. London: Union of Democratic Control. Reprinted, with a new introduction by Blanche Wiesen Cook, New York: Garland Publishers, 1972.

——. 1916. *The War in Its Effect Upon Women.* London: Women's International League for Peace and Freedom. Reprinted, with a new introduction by Blanche Wiesen Cook, New York: Garland Publishers, 1972.

——. 1921. *Women in the Socialist State.* Social studies series, Vol. 5. Manchester: National Labour Press.

——. 1929. *Labour's Foreign Policy: What Has Been and What Might Be.* Fabian Tract, no. 227. London: The Fabian Society.

Sweezy, Maxine Yaple. *See* Woolston, Maxine Bernard Yaple Sweezy.

Swett, Maud and John Rogers Commons. 1909. *Summary of Labor Laws in Force 1909; Woman's Work.* Madison, Wisc.: Parsons Printery.

Swift, Anna Hazel. 1929. *The American Chemical Industry.* U.S. Bureau of Foreign and Domestic Commerce Trade Promotion Series, no. 78. Washington: U.S. Government Printing Office.

——. 1929. *Chemical Industry and Trade of Switzerland.* Washington: U.S. Bureau of Foreign and Domestic Commerce.

——. 1931. *Chemical Industry and Trade of Portugal.* Washington: U.S. Bureau of Foreign and Domestic Commerce.

Swiney, Frances. 1899. *The Awakening of Women; or, Woman's Part in Evolution.* London: G. Redway.

[Swisher], Idella Gwatkin [Mrs. Carl B. Swisher]. 1930. *A History of the Tariff in the United States.* Pamphlets in American History, Tariffs, T 1466. Washington: Committee on Living Costs, National League of Women Voters.

——. 1930. The Reorganization of Medical Education in the United States. Ph.D. thesis, Robert Brookings.

——. 1931. *An Introduction to a Study of the Tariff.* Washington: Committee on Living Costs, National League of Women Voters.

——. Coauth. *See* Monroe, Day.

Sykes, Madeleine Wallin and Josephine C. Goldmark. 1904. *Child Labor Legislation Handbook, 1904.* New York: National Consumers' League.

Synnot, Henrietta. 1874. Little Paupers. *Contemporary Review* 25 (November): 954–72.

——. 1875. Institutions and Their Inmates. *Contemporary Review* 26 (August): 487–504.

T

Taeuber, Irene Barnes. 1931. *Changes in the Content and Presentation of Reading Material in Minnesota Weekly Newspapers, 1860–1929.* Ph.D. thesis, University of Minnesota.

——. 1933. Weekly Newspaper in Pioneer Minnesota. *Minnesota History* 14(4) (December).

——. 1936. Book Review of "Population Problems" by Thompson. *Rural Sociology* 1(3) (September): 384–.

——. 1938. Book Review of "Population Problems, 2nd ed." by Reuter. *Rural Sociology* 3(1/4): 114–.

——. 1939. Book Review of "Cityward Migration – Swedish Data" by Jane Moore. *Annals of the American Academy of Political and Social Science* 204 (July): 224–.

Tait, [D.] Christie. 1930. The International Organisation of Migration. *International Labour Review (Geneva)* 21 (February): 202–16.

——. 1935. Unemployment of Young People in Great Britain. *International Labour Review (Geneva)* 31 (February): 166–89.

——. 1936. Migration and Settlement in Australia, New Zealand. *International Labour Review* (July).

Talbert, Mary Burnett. 1902. Did the American Negro Make in the Nineteenth Century, Achievements Along the Lines of Wealth, Morality, Education, etc., Commensurate with His Opportunities? If So, What Achievements Did He Make? In Daniel Wallace Culp, ed., *Twentieth Century Negro Literature: or, A Cyclopedia of Thought on the Vital Topics Relating to the American Negro, by One Hundred of America's Greatest Negroes.* Naperville, Ill., and Toronto, Canada: J. L. Nichols & Co. Reprinted New York: Arno Press, 1969.

Talbot, Mrs. Emily. 1886. Methodical Education in the Social Sciences. *Journal of Social Science* 21 (September): 13–20.

——. 1886. Synopsis of Social Science Instruction in Colleges, 1886. *Journal of Social Science* 21 (September): xxxiv–xlix.

——. 1887. Social Science Instruction in Colleges. *Journal of Social Science* 22 (June): 7–27.

Talbot, Marion. 1896. Sanitation and Sociology. *American Journal of Sociology* 2 (July): 74–81.

——. 1897. Book Review of "Domestic Service" by Lucy M. Salmon. *Journal of Political Economy* 5(3) (June): 397–9.

——. Coauth. *See* Breckinridge, Sophonisba Preston; Richards, Ellen H.

Talbot, Mary [S]. 1895. Settlements on Houses for Women. *Economic Review* 5: 489–.

——. 1896. Miss Irwin's Report on Women's Employment in Shops in Glasgow. *Economic Review* 6 (October): 535–.

Tandy, Elizabeth Carpenter. 1926. Time Changes in Biologically Classified Mortality Rates. Sc.D.Hyg. thesis, Johns Hopkins University (general health sciences).

——. 1929. Trends in Juvenile Delinquency and Child Labor. *Journal of the American Statistical Association* 24(165) (Supplement, Proceedings of the American Statistical Association) (March): 180–81.

——. 1935. *Comparability of Maternal Mortality Rates in the United States and Certain Foreign Countries*. U.S. Children's Bureau Publication, no. 229. Washington: U.S. Government Printing Office.

——. 1937. *Infant and Maternal Mortality among Negroes*. U.S. Department of Labor, Children's Bureau Publication, no. 243. Washington: U.S. Government Printing Office.

——. 1940. *The Health Situation of Negro Mothers and Babies in the United States*. Washington: U.S. Department of Labor, Children's Bureau.

Tanino, Setsu. 1933. Welfare Facilities in the Mining Industry in Japan. *Industrial Welfare* (October).

——. 1934. Examples of Retirement Grant in the Mining Industry in Japan. *Industrial Welfare* (May).

——. 1935. The Examination of the Contribution of Employers to the Cost of Welfare Facilities in Mines. *Industrial Welfare* (March).

——. 1935. The Protection of Women Workers in Japan's Industries. *Labor Legislation* 2(2/3) and 3(2).

——. *c.*1935. Problems Relating to the Protection of Women Workers. Unpublished.

——. 1936. The Participation of Women in the Labour Force during the Past Five Years. *Industrial Welfare* (September).

——. *c.*1936. A Note of a Woman Probationary Factory Supervisor. Unpublished.

——. 1937. The Lives of the Women Who Retired from Spinning Work. *Industrial Welfare* (November).

——. 1937. The Record of Inspection in the Factory at the Headquarter of Gunze Spinning Corporation. *Industrial Welfare* (May).

——. 1937. The Working Clothes from Women. *Industrial Welfare* (January).

——. *c.*1938. On the Recruiting of Women and Minors. *Industrial Welfare*.

——. 1939. Women Works and Music. *Industrial Welfare* (February).

——. 1939. Women's Advance into Machine Shops and Their Adaptability. *Industrial Welfare* (September).

——. 1939. Women's Working Conditions in Factories and Their Protection during the Sino-Japanese Incident. *Social Works* (October).

——. 1939. Working Women and Welfare Facilities. *Welfare Japan* (November).

——. 1940. *Joshi Rodo ni Kansuru Hokoku*. Tokyo: Showa Kenkyukai Jimukyoku.

——. 1940. The Current Situation of Working Women. Published, but journal unknown.

——. 1940. The Report on Working Women. Paper presented at a meeting of Showa Kenkyukai, November.

——. 1940. Women's Labors and Vocational Guidance. *Scientific Industry* (April).

Tanino, Setsu and Suzuki Ryuji. 1931. On the Effect of the Prohibition of Night Work. *Industrial Welfare* (June).

Tanino, Setsu. Additional information on Setsu Tanino can be found in Robert W. Dimand, Mary Ann Dimand, and Evelyn L. Forget, eds., *A Biographical Dictionary of Women Economists*. Cheltenham, UK: Edward Elgar.

Tanner, Amy E. 1907. Salaries of Women Teachers in Institutions of Collegiate Rank. *Association of Collegiate Alumnae, Publications*, series 3, 15 (November): 20–.

Tanqueray, Mrs. Bertram. 1902. Agricultural Gangs. *Contemporary Review* (June).

Tapley, Elizabeth. 1895. Small Savings and How to Collect Them. *Charities Review* 5(2) (December): 99.

Tarbell, Ida M[inerva]. 1886. The Arts and Industries of Cincinnati. *Chautauquan* 7 (December): 160.

——. 1887. Women as Inventors. *Chautauquan* 7: 355–.

——. 1887. Women in Journalism. *Chautauquan* 7: 393.

——. 1887/8. The Agricultural Department at Washington. *Chautauquan* 8 (October/July): 614–.

——. 1893. Identification of Criminals by Bertillon System. *McClure's Magazine* 2: 355.

——. 1895. Napoleon I, Relations with the United States. *McClure's Magazine* 5: 24.

——. 1904. *The History of the Standard Oil Company*. New York: McClure, Phillips & Co. Reprinted London: Heinemann, 1905. New York: Macmillan, 1925.

——. 1905. J. D. Rockefeller. *McClure's Magazine* 25: 227, 386.

——. 1905. Standard Oil Co. and Kansas. *McClure's Magazine* 25: 469, 608.

——. 1905/6. Commercial Machiavellianism. *McClure's Magazine* 26: 453.

——. 1910. The Shirt-waist Strikers. *American Federationist* 17(3) (March): 209–.

——. 1911/1926. *The Tariff in Our Times*. New York: Macmillan.

——. 1912/1928. *The Business of Being a Woman*. New York: Macmillan.

——. 1913. The Cost of Living and Household Management. *Annals of the American Academy of Political and Social Science* 48 (July): 127–.

——. 1914. Effects of Safety on the Community. *NSC Proceedings* 3: 119–25.

——. 1916/1917. *New Ideals in Business: An Account of Their Practice and Their Effects upon Men and Profits*. New York: Macmillan.

——. 1916. What the Day's Work Means to Me. *Bookman* 43(1) (March): 59–.

——. 1917. Mobilizing the Women. *Harper's Monthly Magazine* 135(810) (November): 841–.

——. 1918. The College Woman's Call to Duty. *Journal of the Association of Collegiate Alumnae* 11(9) (May): 597–.

——. 1920. The New Place of Women in Industry. *Industrial Management* 60(4) (October): 265–.

——. 1920. The New Place of Women in Industry II. *Industrial Management* 60(5) (November): 329–.

——. 1920. The New Place of Women in Industry III. *Industrial Management* 60(6): 399–.

——. 1920. Shorter Hours Mean Increased Service. *American Labor Legislation Review* 10: 270–.

——. 1921. The New Place of Women in Industry IV. *Industrial Management* 61(1) (January 1): 51–.

——. 1921. The New Place of Women in Industry V. *Industrial Management* 61(3) (February 1): 135–.

——. 1921. The New Place of Women in Industry VI. *Industrial Management* 2(2) (August 1): 106–.

——. 1925. *The Life of Elbert H. Gary: The Story of Steel.* New York: Appleton.

——. 1930. Personal Responsibility for Accidents. *American Labor Legislation Review* 20: 420–.

——. 1931. The College Graduate in Her Community. *Journal of the American Association of University Women* 24(2) (January): 57–.

——. 1932. *Owen D. Young: A New Type of Industrial Leader.* New York: Macmillan Co.

——. 1934. New Dealers of the Seventies. Henry George and Edward Bellamy. *Forum and Century* 92(3) (September): 133–.

——. 1936. *The Nationalizing of Business, 1878–1898.* New York: Macmillan.

——. 1938/9. Would Miss Tarbell See Mr. Rogers? *Harper's Monthly Magazine* 178 (December/May): 138–.

Tarbell, Ida Minerva. A series of twelve papers may be found in *Industrial Management* covering the problem of women in industry. Tarbell's papers available at Allegheny College, Columbia University, the Drake Memorial Museum (Titusville, Pa.), Indiana University, the Library of Congress and Smith College.

Tawney, Jeannette. 1911. Women and Unemployment. *Economic Journal* 21 (March): 131–9.

——. 1925. *Chapters from Richard Baxter's Christian Directory (1673).* With a preface by the Right Rev. Charles Gore. London: Bell.

Taylor, Emily Constance. 1889. A Real Working Man. *Macmillan's* 60 (September): 356–62.

——. 1890. Work among the Country Poor. *Macmillan's* 61 (April): 423–32.

Taylor, Etta. 1893. *How: A Practical Business Guide for American Women of All Conditions and Ages, Who Want to Make Money but Do Not Know How.* Minneapolis: Taylor.

Taylor, Fanny Isabel. 1909. *A Bibliography of Unemployment and the Unemployed.* London: P. S. King.

Taylor, Frances [Fanny] M[argaret]. [Mother Magdalen Taylor]. 1857. Works of Charity. *Dublin Review* 42 (March): 123–42.

——. 1867. *Irish Homes and Irish Hearts*. Boston: P. Donahoe.

Taylor, Helen. 1865. Personal Representation [on T. Hare's "Election of Representatives"]. *Westminster Review*, n.s. 28 [o.s. 84] (October): 305–20.

——. 1866. Women and Criticism. *Macmillan's Magazine* 14 (September): 335–40. Reprinted in Ann P. Robson and John M. Robson, eds., *Sexual Equality: Writings by John Stuart Mill, Harriet Taylor Mill, and Helen Taylor.* Toronto: University of Toronto Press, 1994. Reprinted in Andrea Broomfield and Sally Mitchell, eds., *Prose by Victorian Women: An Anthology*. New York: Garland Publishing, 1995.

——. 1867. *The Claim of Englishwomen to the Suffrage Constitutionally Considered.* London, Trübner and Co. Originally published as '*The Ladies Petition*' in *Westminster Review* n.s. 31 (January): 63–79. Reprinted in Ann P. Robson and John M. Robson, eds., *Sexual Equality: Writings by John Stuart Mill, Harriet Taylor Mill, and Helen Taylor*. Toronto: University of Toronto Press, 1994. Reprinted in Andrea Broomfield and Sally Mitchell, eds., *Prose by Victorian Women: An Anthology*. New York: Garland Publishing, 1995. Online in Indiana University's LETRS.

——, ed. 1873. *The Autobiography of John Stuart Mill*. London: Longmans, Green, Reader, and Dyer.

——, ed. 1874. *Nature, the Utility of Religion and Theism: Three Essays on Religion*, by John Stuart Mill. London: Longmans, Green, Reader, and Dyer.

——. 1874. Industrial Education for Ladies. *Englishwoman's Review of Social and Industrial Questions*, n.s. 17 (January): 1–6.

——. 1877. The Influence of Women on Temperance. *Englishwoman's Review*, n.s. 46 (February): 53–7.

——. 1881. Women's Rights as Preached by Women. *Westminster Review*, n.s. 60 [o.s. 116] (October): 469–78. Reprinted in Robson and Robson eds., *Sexual Equality* (1994).

——. 1890. *The Restoration of Their Homes to the People: An Appeal to Women.* London: English Land Restoration League.

——. 1892. *Nationalisation of the Land.* London: Land Nationalisation Society. Reprinted from the *Liberal & Radical Year Book.*

Taylor, Mary. 1870. *The First Duty of Women. A Series of Articles Reprinted from the Victoria Magazine, 1865 to 1870*. London: Emily Faithfull.

Teleki von Srek, Jane F. H. Bickersteth. 1859. England's Political Position in Europe. *Westminster Review*, n.s. 15 [o.s. 71] (April): 535–61.

——. 1860. Austria and the Government of Hungary. *Westminster Review*, n.s. 17 [o.s. 73] (April): 457–85.

——. 1860. The Organisation of Italy. *Westminster Review*, n.s. 18 [o.s. 74] (October): 386–410.

——. 1861. The Sicilian Revolution. *Westminster Review*, n.s. 19 [o.s. 75] (April): 337–63.

Teller, Charlotte. 1901. A German View of "Woman's Sphere." *Journal of Political Economy* 10(1) (December): 110–12.

——. 1906. Women in Unions (Cloth Hat and Cap Makers). *American Federationist* 13(4) (April): 222–.

——. 1908. The National Socialist Convention. *Arena* 40 (July/December): 26–.

[Tennant,] May Edith Abraham [Mrs. H. Tennant]. 1896/1897/1901/1902/1905/1908. *The Law Relating to Factories and Workshops, Including Laundries and Docks.* Part I: *Practical Guide to the Law and Its Administration.* London: Eyre & Spottiswoode.

——. 1898. The Women's Factory Department. *Fortnightly Review*, n.s. 64 [o.s. 70] (July): 148–56.

——. 1908/1970. Infant Mortality. In *Woman in Industry from Seven Points of View.* Washington: NCR Microcard Editions.

——. Coauth. *See* Orme, Eliza; Markham, Violet Rosa.

Terhune, Mary Virginia [as "Marion Harland"]. 1871. *Common Sense in the Household, a Manual of Practical Housewifery.* New York: Scribner.

—— [as "Marion Harland"]. 1889. Are Women to Blame? *North American Review* 148 (May): 630–3.

—— [as "Marion Harland"]. 1889. The Incapacity of Business Women. *North American Review* 149 (December): 707–12.

—— [as "Marion Harland"]. 1889. Is Housekeeping a Failure? *North American Review* 148 (February): 250–4.

—— [as "Marion Harland"]. 1897/1899. *Colonial Homesteads and Their Stories.* New York: Putnam.

—— [as "Marion Harland"]. 1899. *Household Management.* New York: Home Topics Publishing.

Terrell, Mary [E.] Church. 1898. *The Progress of Colored Women.* Address delivered before the National American Women's Suffrage Association at the Columbia Theater, Washington, D.C., February 18, 1898, on the occasion of its fiftieth anniversary. Washington: Smith Brothers, Printers.

——. 1904. Lynching from a Negro's Point of View. *North American Review* 178 (June): 853–68.

——. 1904. The Progress of Colored Women. *Voice of the Negro* 1 (July): 292.

——. 1906. A Plea for the White South by a Colored Woman. *Nineteenth Century* 60 (July): 70–84.

——. 1907. Peonage in the United States: The Convict Lease System and the Chain Gangs. *Nineteenth Century* 62 (August): 306–22.

——. 1915. Woman Suffrage and the Fifteenth Amendment. *Crisis* 10 (August): 191.

Thibert, Marguerite. 1921. *Féminisme et socialisme d'après Flora Tristan.* Paris: M. Rivière.

——. 1923. Saint-simoniennes et pacifistes [Eugénie Niboyet and Pauline Roland]. *La Paix par le droit* 23(6) (June).

——. 1925. *Le Rôle social de l'art d'après Saint-Simon.* Paris: M. Rivière.

——. 1925. Le Rôle social de l'art d'après Saint-Simon. *Revue d'histoire économique et sociale* 13: 181–.

——. 1926. *Le Féminisme dans le socialisme français, de 1830 à 1850.* Paris: M. Giard.

——. 1926. *Le Rôle social de l'art d'après les saint-simoniens*. Paris: Librairie des Sciences Économiques et Sociales.

——. 1926. Le Féminisme dans le socialisme français, de 1830 à 1850. Ph.D. thesis, faculté des letters, l'Université de Paris.

——. 1930. *L'Émigration (immigration et migrations)*. Paris: Sirey.

——. 1933. Crise économique et travail féminin. *Revue internationale du travail* 27(4/5) (April/May).

——. 1933. The Economic Depression and the Employment of Women: I. *International Labour Review* 27(1/6) (January/June): 443–.

——. 1933. The Economic Depression and the Employment of Women: II. *International Labour Review* 27(1/6) (January/June): 620–.

Thomas, Bertha. 1873. A Vision of Communism. *Cornhill Magazine* 28 (September): 300–10.

——. 1874. Latest Intelligence from the Planet Venus [on women's suffrage]. *Fraser's*, n.s. 10 [o.s. 90] (December): 763. Reprinted in Harriet Devine Jump, ed., *Women's Writing of the Victorian Period 1837–1901, An Anthology*. New York and London: Palgrave-Macmillan, 1999.

——. 1879. Technical Training for Girls. *Fraser's*, n.s. 19 [o.s. 99] (March): 343–51.

Thomas, Dorothy Swaine. 1924. Changes in Marriage Seasons. *Economica* 10 (February): 97–106.

——. 1925/1927. *Social Aspects of the Business Cycle*. London: Routledge. Reprinted New York: Alfred A. Knopf, Inc., 1927; New York: Gordon and Breach, 1968.

——. 1925. Social Aspects of the Business Cycle. Ph.D. thesis, London School of Economics.

——. 1926. An Index of British Business Cycles. *Journal of the American Statistical Association* 21 (March): 60–3.

——. 1929. *Some New Techniques for Studying Social Behavior*. New York: Teachers College, Columbia University.

——. 1929. Statistics in Social Research. *American Journal of Sociology* 35(1) (July): 1–17.

——. 1931. The Observability of Social Phenomena with Respect to Statistical Analysis. *American Sociological Society, Publication* 25(2) (May): 193–.

——. 1931/2. Some Aspects of Socio-legal Research at Yale. *American Journal of Sociology* 37(1/6): 213–.

——. 1932. An Attempt to Develop Precise Measurements in the Social Behavior Field. *Sociologus* 8(4) (December).

——. 1935. Economic and Social Aspects of Internal Migrations: An Exploratory Study of Selected Swedish Communities. In Asher Achinstein, ed., *Economic Essays in Honor of Wesley Clair Mitchell*. New York: Columbia University Press.

——. 1936/7. Internal Migrations in Sweden: A Note on Their Extensiveness as Compared with Net Migration Gain or Loss. *American Journal of Sociology* 42(1/6): 345–.

——. 1937. The Analysis of Internal Migration in the Swedish Census of 1930. *Journal of the American Statistical Association* 32(197) (March): 124–30.

——. 1937. Social Aspects of the Business Cycle. *Annales sociologiques; Série D: Sociologie économique* 2: 91–.

——. 1937. Streams of Internal Migration: A Further Exploration with Swedish Data. *Rural Sociology* 2(2) (June): 148–.

——. 1938. *Research Memorandum on Migration Differentials.* New York: Social Science Research Council.

——. 1938. Determining Population in Intercensal and Postcensal Years by Means of Continuous Population Registers. *American Journal of Public Health and the Nation's Health* 28(1) (January): 28–.

——. 1938. Utilization of Social Security Data for Sociological Research. *American Sociological Review* 3(1/6) (October): 718–23.

——. 1939. Migration, Marriage, and Divorce. *Rural Sociology* 4(1/4): 155–.

Thomas, Dorothy Swaine, Alice M. Loomis, and Ruth E. Arrington. 1933. *Observational Studies of Social Behavior.* New Haven, Conn.: Institute of Human Relations, Yale University.

Thompson, Allison J. 1933/1934. *The Relation of Wealth to Economics.* Cleveland, Ohio: s.n.

Thompson, Clara Mildred. 1915. *Reconstruction in Georgia, Economic, Social, Political, 1865–1872.* New York: Columbia University Press.

——. 1915. Reconstruction in Georgia, Economic, Social, Political, 1865–1872. Ph.D. thesis, Columbia University (history).

Thompson, Donna. 1912. *A Study of One Hundred Fifteen Mothers Observed by the Social Service Department of Indiana University.* Bloomington: Indiana University Social Service Department.

——. 1914. The Associations of Dependence in Seven Hundred Families. M.A. thesis, Indiana University.

Thompson, Donna Fay. 1927. *Professional Solidarity among the Teachers of England.* Studies in History, Economics and Public Law, ed. by the Faculty of Political Science of Columbia University, 288. New York: Columbia University Press; London: P. S. King & Son.

——. 1927. Professional Solidarity among the Teachers of England. Ph.D. thesis, Columbia University (education).

Thompson, Flora McDonald. 1900. Retrogression of American Woman. *North American Review* 171: 748.

——. 1900. The Servant Question. *Cosmopolitan* XXVIII (March): 521–8.

——. 1902. The Work of Wives. *Arena* 27 (January/June): 68.

——. 1904. The Truth about Women in Industry. *North American Review* 178: 751.

——. 1904/5. How to Live within Your Income and Family Protection. *Cosmopolitan, a Monthly Illustrated Magazine* 38: 105.

——. 1913. *Letter from Flora McDonald Thompson: Petitioning the Secretary of Labor for the Establishment of a Bureau of Woman Labor in the Department of Labor.* Bureau of Woman Labor, 63rd congress, 1st session, Senate, doc. no. 38. Washington: Bureau of Woman Labor.

——. 1937. An Oxfordshire Hamlet in the "Eighties." *National Review* 109 (July/December): 222–.

——. 1938. May Day in the "Eighties." *National Review* 110 (January/June): 648–.

Thompson, Laura Amelia. 1914. *Laws Relating to "Mothers' Pensions" in the United States, Denmark, and New Zealand*. Washington: U.S. Children's Bureau.

——. 1919. *Recent Literature on Collective Bargaining*. Washington: U.S. Department of Labor Library.

——. 1920. *Hours of Work in Relation to Output: An Annotated List of References*. Washington: U.S. Department of Labor Library.

——. 1920. The Kansas Court of Industrial Relations: A List of References. *Library Journal* 45(19) (November 1): 887–.

——. 1921. *Recent Literature on Unemployment, with Particular Reference to Causes and Remedies*. Washington: U.S. Department of Labor Library.

——, comp. 1922. Workers' Education: A List of References (in English). *Monthly Labor Review* 14 (January/June): 181–98.

——. 1924. Labor Banks in the United States – a Selected List of References. *Library Journal* 49(6) (March 15): 281–.

——. 1924. Recent References on Adult Workers' Education. *Monthly Labor Review* 19 (July/December): 190–203.

——. 1925. *References on Child Labor and Minors in Industry, 1916–1924*. Washington: U.S. Children's Bureau.

——. 1925. Children in Street Trades in the United States: A List of References. *Monthly Labor Review* 21 (July/December): 81–92.

——. 1925. Federal Control of Child Labor: A List of References. *Monthly Labor Review* 20 (January/June): 71–101.

——. 1926. The Library of the United States Department of Labor. *Monthly Labor Review* 22(3) (March): 3–8.

——. 1927. Employee Stock Ownership in the United States: A Selected Bibliography. *Monthly Labor Review* 24(6) (June): 214–23.

——. 1927. The Five-day Week in Industry; a List of References. *Monthly Labor Review* 24(1) (January): 237–41.

——. 1927. Union–management Cooperation: A List of References. *Monthly Labor Review* 25(4) (October): 220–7.

——. 1927. Workers' Leisure – A Selected List of References. *Monthly Labor Review* 24(3) (March): 167–77.

——. 1928. Injunctions in Labor Disputes: Select List of Recent References. *Monthly Labor Review* 27(3) (September): 201–20.

——. 1929. Public Old-age Pensions in Canada. *Monthly Labor Review* 28(2) (February): 212–17.

——, comp. 1929. Public Old-age Pensions in Australia and New Zealand: A List of References. *Monthly Labor Review* 28(3) (March): 260–5.

——. 1929. A National Library Service for Labor. *American Federationist* 36(8) (August): 947–.

——. 1929. The Older Worker in Industry. List of References. *Monthly Labor Review* 29(1) (July): 237–42.

——. 1931. Five-day Week, and Other Recent Proposals for a Shorter Work Week – A List of References. *Monthly Labor Review* 32(2) (February): 247–.

——. 1931. National Economic Councils: A List of References. *Monthly Labor Review* 32(5) (May): 217–.

——. 1935. *Unemployment Insurance and Reserves in the United States, A Selected List of Recent References.* Washington: U.S. Department of Labor Library.

——. Coauth. *See* Fine, Ruth.

Thompson, Marie L. 1885. The Story of an Italian Workwoman's Life. *Lippincott's* 36 (July/December): 301–.

Thompson, Pauline Evelyn. 1934. *Uncle Sam and Unemployment.* New York: Bureau of Publications, Columbia University.

Thomson, Claudia. 1938. *World Acreage and Production of Tobacco by Countries.* Washington: United States Department of Agriculture, Bureau of Agricultural Economics.

——. 1938. Norway's Industrialization. *Economic Geography* 14(4) (October): 372–80.

Thomson, Edith Parker. 1897. What Women Have Done for the Public Health. *Forum* 24 (September): 46–55.

Thomson, Mary Horner. 1912. *Environment and Efficiency: A Study in the Records of Industrial Schools and Orphanages.* W. J. Ashleh, ed., with a preface by J. Rendel Harris. London: Longmans, Greene.

Thomson, Mrs. R. W. 1871. *The Rights of Labour and the Nine Hours' Movement. Addressed to the men of Newcastle.* Edinburgh: Edmonston & Douglas.

Thorne, Alison Comish. 1936. Capacity to Consume. *American Economic Review* 26 (June): 292–5.

——. 1939. Evaluations of Consumption in Modern Thought. Ph.D. thesis, Iowa State University (economics).

——. 1940/1. Evaluations of Consumption in Scale-of-living Studies. *Social Forces* 19(1/4): 510–.

Thornton, Gladys A. 1928. *A History of Clare, Suffolk.* Cambridge, UK: W. Heffer & Sons, Ltd.

——. 1928. A Study in the History of Clare, Suffolk; with Special Reference to Its Development as a Borough. Alexander Prize Essay, 1928. *Transactions of the Royal Historical Society* 4(11): 83–.

——. 1928. Summaries of Theses: A History of Clare, Suffolk, with Special Reference to Its Development as a Borough during the Middle Ages, and Its Importance as a Centre of the Woollen Industry in the Fifteenth–Seventeenth Centuries. *Bulletin of the Institute of Historical Research* 6(16) (June): 29–.

Thrupp, Sylvia [Lettice]. 1932. Summaries of Theses: A Study of the Merchant Class of London in the Fifteenth Century, with Special Reference to the Company of Grocers. *Bulletin of the Institute of Historical Research* 9(27) (February): 193.

——. 1933. The Grocers of London: A Study of Distributive Trade. In Edna Eileen Power, ed., *Studies in English Trade in the Fifteenth Century.* London: Routledge.

——. 1933. *A Short History of the Worshipful Company of Bakers of London*. Croydon, UK: Galleon Press.

Till, Irene. 1934. *The Price of Gasoline*. 2 parts in 1 vol. Consumers' Division Price Policy Report, no. 3–4. Washington: Consumers' Division, National Recovery Administration.

——. 1935/6. *Milk; a Study of the Ways of an Industry*. 2 vols. Washington: Consumers' Division, National Recovery Administration.

——. 1935/6. Book Review of "The Dairy Industry and the AAA" by Black. *Yale Law Journal* 45: 1,540–.

——. 1936. *The Price of Waste Paper*. Washington: Consumers' Project, under supervision of the U.S. Department of Labor.

——. 1937. The Fiction of the Quoted Price. *Law and Contemporary Problems* 4: 363–.

——. 1938. *Milk: The Politics of an Industry*. New York and London: McGraw-Hill.

——. 1938. Milk: The Politics of an Industry. Ph.D. thesis, Columbia University (political science).

Tilley, Miss. 1894. Remarks [on "Conditions of Female Labour" by F. Gordon]. *Australian Economist* IV(8) (September 24): 437–8.

——. 1895. Remarks [on "Women and Womanhood Suffrage" by E. Badham]. *Australian Economist* IV(16) (June 21): 499–501.

Tilley, Nannie May. 1931. Studies in the History of Colonial Granville County. M.A. thesis, Duke University.

——. 1934. The Settlement of Granville County. *North Carolina Historical Review* 11(1) (January): 1–.

——. 1936. Industries of Colonial Granville County. *North Carolina Historical Review* 13(4) (October): 273–.

——. 1938/9. England and the Confederacy. *American Historical Review* 44: 56–.

——. 1939. The Bright-tobacco Industry, 1860–1929. Ph.D. thesis, Duke University (history).

Tisch, Cläre. 1932. *Wirtschaftsrechnung und Verteilung im zentralistisch organisierten sozialistischen Gemeinwesen*. Wuppertal-Elberfeld: Scheschinski.

——. 1932?. Wirtschaftsrechnung und Verteilung im zentralistisch organisierten sozialistischen Gemeinwesen. Thesis, Bonn.

——. 1934. *Organisationsformen der deutschen Mittelindustrie*. Frankfurt: Vittorio Klostermann.

——. 1934. *Der wirtschaftliche Sinn der bisherigen Rechtsprechung des deutschen Kartellgerichts*. Frankfurt: Vittorio Klostermann.

Tod, Isabella M. S. 1867. Advanced Education for Girls of the Upper and Middle Classes. Paper read before the National Association for the Promotion of Social Science. *Transactions of the National Association for the Promotion of Social Science*. London: Victoria Press.

——. 1874. *On the Education of Girls of the Middle Classes*. Issued by the National Union for Improving the Education of Women. London: William Ridgway. Reprinted from the *Leisure Hour*.

——. 1875. On the Principles on Which Plans for the Curative Treatment of Habitual Drunkards Should Be Based. *Journal of the Statistical and Social Inquiry Society of Ireland* 6(7) (May).

——. 1878. Boarding-out of Pauper Children. *Journal of the Statistical and Social Inquiry Society of Ireland* 7(5) (August).

——. 1881. The Place of Women in Administration of the Irish Poor Law. *Englishwoman's Review*, n.s. 103 (November): 481–9.

——. 1884. Women's Suffrage: A Liberal View of the Situation. *Englishwoman's Review*, n.s. 136 (August): 347–57. Reprinted London: J. Bale & Sons.

——. 1887. Municipal Franchise for Women in Ireland. *Englishwoman's Review* 170 (July): 291–3.

Todd, Marion Marsh. 1886. *Protective Tariff Delusion.* Battle Creek, Mich.: Gage. Reprinted Chicago: F. J. Schulte & Co., 1892.

——. 1890. *Prof. Goldwin Smith and his Satellites in Congress.* Battle Creek, Mich.: W. C. Cage.

——. 1893. *Railways of Europe and America; or, Government Ownership. With Notes from Official Sources.* Boston: Arena Publishing Company. Reprinted Lansing, Mich.: W. Emery, 1897.

——. 1894. *Honest (?) John Sherman, or A Foul Record.* Lansing, Mich.: H. D. Reprogle & Co.

——. 1895. *Rachel's Pitiful History*. Springport, Mich.: s.n. [*fiction*]

Todes, Charlotte. 1931. *Labor and Lumber*. New York: International Publishers. Reprinted New York: Arno Press, 1975.

——. 1932. *The Injunction Menace*. New York: International Pamphlets.

[Tonna,] Charlotte Elizabeth. 1827. *The System: A Tale of the West Indies*. London: Frederick Westley and A. H. Davis. [*novel*]

——. 1832. *Combination: A Tale, Founded on Facts.* Dublin: Religious Tract and Book Society of Ireland, W. Curry. [*novel*]

——. 1838. *Letters from Ireland.* London: Seeley and Burnside.

——. 1841. *Helen Fleetwood: A Tale of the Factories*. London: Seeley and Burnside. [*novel*]

—— [unsigned]. 1843. *The Perils of the Nation: An Appeal to the Legislature, the Clergy, and the Higher and Middle Classes.* London: Seeley, Burnside and Seeley.

——. 1843. *The Wrongs of Woman.* 4 vols. London: W. H. Dalton. Reprinted New York : M. W. Dodd, 1844.

Tooker, Elva. 1934. A Kentucky Merchant's Problems in the Early Nineteenth Century. *Business History Review* 8 (October): 81–8.

Tough, Rosalind. 1925. Growth of Urban Populations in the United States. *Land Economics* 1 (April): 226–36.

——. 1932. Building Costs and Total Costs at Sunnyside Gardens, Long Island. *Land Economics* 8 (May): 164–74.

——. 1932. Production Costs, Building Costs, and Total Costs at Sunnyside Gardens, L.I. *Journal of Land & Public Utility Economics* (February): 43–54.

——. 1933. Sunnyside Gardens in Queens, New York: A Valuation of a Limited Dividend Housing Project. Ph.D. thesis, Northwestern University (economics).

Townsend, Emily. 1911/1988. The Case against the Charity Organization Society. Fabian Pamphlet No. 158. Reprinted in S. Alexander, ed., *Women's Fabian Tracts*. London and New York: Routledge.

Townsend, Genevieve. 1932. *Consumer Loans in Wisconsin*. With a Preface by John R. Commons. Madison, Wisc.: s.n.

——. 1932. A Credit Union for College Teachers. *American Teacher* 16(7) (April): 14–.

Townsend, Mary Elizabeth. 1883. *Friendly Letters to Young Women in Business*. London: Hatchards. Reprinted by request from *Friendly Work*.

Townsend, Mary Evelyn. 1921. *Origins of Modern German Colonialism, 1871–1885*. New York: Longmans, Green & Co.

——. 1921. Origins of Modern German Colonialism, 1871–1885. Ph.D. thesis, Columbia University (history).

——. 1928. The Contemporary Colonial Movement in Germany. *Political Science Quarterly* 43: 64–.

——. 1930. *The Rise and Fall of Germany's Colonial Empire, 1884–1918*. New York: Macmillan Company.

——. 1930. German and Polish Conflicting Interests. *Current History (New York)* 32(2) (May): 333–.

——. 1938. The German Colonies and the Third Reich. *Political Science Quarterly* 53: 186–.

Toynbee, Mrs. 1900. Poverty and the Poor Law. *Economic Review*.

Toynbee, Gertrude. 1885. Sanitary Aid Committees. *Charity Organisation Review* 1 (January 15): 5–7.

——. 1911. *Reminiscences and Letters of Joseph and Arnold Toynbee*. London: Glaisher.

Traill, Catherine Parr Strickland. 1836. *The Backwoods of Canada: Being Letters from the Wife of an Emigrant Officer, Illustrative of the Domestic Economy of British America*. London: C. Knight & Co. Reprinted Toronto: McClelland & Stewart, 1989.

Trask, Katrina. 1895. Motherhood and Citizenship: Woman's Wisest Policy. *Forum* 18 (January): 609–15.

——. 1895. The Obligation of the Inactive. *Forum* 20 (December): 489–91.

Travers, Rosalind. 1909. Citizen Rights and Citizen Duties [letter to the editor]. *Nation* 6(1) (October 2): 15–.

——. 1910. Russia and Finland [letter to the editor]. *Nation* 7(4) (April 23): 123–.

——. 1911. Conditions of Women's Work in Finland. *Clare Market Review* (January).

——. 1911. The Dismemberment of Finland [letter to the editor]. *Nation* 9(24) (September 9): 843–.

——. 1912. As Others See Us [letter to the editor]. *Nation* 11(22) (August 31): 799–.

——. 1913. Concerning the Library Censor [letter to the editor]. *Nation* 13(26) (September 27): 952–.

——. 1913. The Extension of Russian Jurisdiction in Finland [letter to the editor]. *Nation* 13(14) (July 5): 531–.

Travers, Rosalind and H. M. Swanwick, 1910. The Next Step in Women's Suffrage [letters to the editor]. *Nation* 6(21) (February 19): 810–.

Trench, Maria. 1876. Sick-nurses. *Macmillan's* 34 (September): 422–9.

——. 1883. At the Docks. *Longman's* 2 (August): 416–.

——. 1883. Girl-children of the State. *Nineteenth Century* 13 (January): 76–87.

——. 1886. The "Donna." *Longman's* 7 (January): 327–.

——. 1887. The "Donna" in 1886. *Longman's* 9 (January): 299–.

——. 1888. The Unemployed and the "Donna" in 1887. *Longman's* 11 (January): 301–8.

——. 1889. The Unemployed and the "Donna" in 1888. *Longman's* 13 (January): 290–300.

——. 1890. The "Donna" in 1889. *Longman's* 15 (January): 288–.

——. 1891. The "Donna" in 1890. *Longman's* 17 (January): 323–.

——. 1895. The "Donna" in 1894. *Longman's* 25 (January): 304–.

——. 1896. The "Donna" in 1895. *Longman's* 27 (January): 270–.

——. 1897. The "Donna" in 1896. Longman's 29 (January): 274–.

——. 1898. The Story of the "Donna." *Longman's* 31 (January): 259–72.

Trepp, Jean Carol. *See* McKelvey, Jean Carol Trepp.

Trevor, Daphne. 1935. Some Sources of the Constitutional Theory of the Abbé Sieyès I. *Politica* 1(3) (February): 325–.

——. 1935. Some Sources of the Constitutional Theory of the Abbé Sieyès II. *Politica* 1(4) (August): 443–.

——. 1936. Public Opinion and the Acquisition of Bechuanaland and Rhodesia. Ph.D. thesis, London School of Economics.

——. 1936. South African Native Taxation. *Review of Economic Studies* 3(3) (June): 217–25.

——. 1937. Native Provident Societies in French West Africa. *South African Journal of Economics* 5 (September): 243–53.

Trimmer, Mrs. Sarah. 1787. *The Œconomy of Charity; or, an Address to Ladies Concerning Sunday Schools; The Establishment of Schools of Industry under Female Inspection; and the Distribution of Voluntary Benefactions.* London: Bensley. Also published as *The Œconomy of Charity; or, An Address to Ladies; Adapted to the Present State of Charitable Institutions in England: with a Particular View to the Cultivation of Religious Principles, among the Lower Orders of People.* 2 vols. London: J. Johnson and F. and C. Rivington, 1801.

——. 1792. *Reflections upon the Education of Charity Schools: With the Outlines of a Plan of Appropriate Instruction for the Children of the Poor.* London: T. Longman.

Tristan. Flora. 1838. *Pérégrinations d'une paria.* Paris: Arthus-Bertrand. New English ed., *Peregrinations of a Pariah*, transl. Charles de Salis, with introduction by Joanna Richardson. London: Folio Society. 1986. English ed., transl. and ed. Jean Hawkes. London: Virago Press, 1986.

——. 1840. *Promenades dans Londres.* Paris: H.-L. Delloye; London: W. Jeffs. New English edition. *The London Journal of Flora Tristan, 1842* or, *The Aristocracy and the Working Class of England.* Transl. by Jean Hawkes. London: Virago, 1982.

——. 1843. *Union ouvrière.* Paris: Prévot. English ed., *The Workers' Union,* transl. with an introduction by Beverly Livingston. Urbana and London: University of Illinois Press, 1983.

Trollope, Frances. 1840. *The Life and Adventures of Michael Armstrong, the Factory Boy.* London: Henry Colburn; New York: Harper & Bros. [*novel*]

True, Ruth Smiley. 1914. *The Neglected Girl.* West Side Studies Series, vol. 1, part 2. New York: Survey Associates for the Russell Sage Foundation.

——. 1914. *West Side Studies: Boyhood and Lawlessness.* West Side Studies Series, vol. 1, part 1. New York: Survey Association.

True, Ruth Smiley, Elizabeth Wagnet, and Elizabeth Brandeis. 1919. *Report on the General Policy of Certain Federal Departments Toward the Open or Preferential Shop, Toward Discrimination and Toward the Right of Workers to Organize in Trade Unions.* Addressed to the Department of Labor, U.S. War Labor Policies Board. S.l.: s.n.

Tuckwell, Gertrude M[ary]. 1894. *The State and Its Children.* London: Methuen; New York: Scribner's.

——. 1895. *Women's Work and Factory Legislation: The Amending Act of 1895.* Paper read before the Fabian Society. London: Fabian Society.

——. 1898. Commercial Manslaughter [lead poisoning]. *Nineteenth Century* 44 (August): 253–8.

——. 1899. A Seventeen Hours' Working Day. *Fortnightly Review*, n.s. 65 [o.s. 71] (May): 783–8.

——. 1900. The Government Factory Bill of 1900. *Fortnightly Review* (June): 972–.

——. 1901. The More Obvious Defects in Our Factory Code. In Mrs. Sidney Webb, ed., *The Case for the Factory Acts.* London: Grant Richards.

——. 1903. *Industrial Work and Industrial Laws.* Westminster, London: Industrial Law Committee.

——. 1904. The Industrial Position of Women. *Independent Review* (August).

——. 1906. Women's Opportunity: An Opportunity Plea for Reforms in Conditions of Female Labour. *Fortnightly Review* (March).

——. 1908. T*he Factory Laws Relating to Women.* London: A. R. Mowbray.

——. 1908. The Regulation of Woman's Work. In Gertrude M. Tuckwell, Constance Isabella Stuart Smith, Mary R. MacArthur, May Tennant, Nettie Adler, Adelaide Mary Anderson, and Clementina Black, *Women in Industry from Seven Points of View.* London: Duckworth & Co. Reprinted Washington: NCR Microcard Editions, 1970.

——. 1910. The Lock-out at Cradley Heath [letter to the editor]. *Nation* 7(23) (September 3): 803–.

——. 1910. Sweating [letter to the editor]. *Nation* 1(9) (April 27): 350–.

——. 1919. Equal Pay for Equal Work. *Fortnightly Review* 1 (January): 63–76.

——. 1919. The Human Interest in Industry. *Fortnightly Review* 106 (July/December): 91–.

——. 1919. Women's Employment. In Gertrude M. Tuckwell, Marion G. Phillips, and Susan A. Lawrence, *Labour Women on International Legislation Proposals for International Legislation*. London: Labour Party.

——. 1920. Women in Industry. *Nineteenth Century* 87 (February): 331–.

——. 1921. The Story of the Trade Board Acts. *Contemporary Review* 120 (November): 600–.

——. 1923. A Popular Whip. *Contemporary Review* 124 (July/December): 773–.

——. 1926. National Health and the Royal Commission. *Contemporary Review* 129 (January/June): 750–.

——. 1930. Looking Backwards – VI. Fifty Years of Social Reform. *Listener* 3(58) (February 19): 323–.

——. 1930/1. Address on the Share of the Health Visitor in the Maternity Services of Local Authorities. *Journal of the Royal Sanitary Institute* 51: 466.

Tuckwell, Gertrude and Constance Smith. 1908/1910. *The Worker's Handbook*. London: Duckworth.

Tuckwell, Gertrude M., Madeline J. Symons, Margaret G. Bondfield, and A. Susan Lawrence. 1926. Mary Macarthur [letter to the editor]. *Nation and the Athenaeum* 38(24) (March 13): 804.

Tuckwell, Gertrude M. Coauth. *See* Bondfield, Margaret.

Turner, Alice Lee. 1925. Communistic Colonies in California. M.A. thesis, University of California Berkeley.

Turner, Alice Willard. 1939. Friends in Canadian Bond, Stock, and Commodity Markets 1928 to 1938. *Journal of the American Statistical Association* 34 (June): 291–8.

Turner, Jennie Willing McMullin, comp. 1916. *Workmen's Compensation in Wisconsin, 1905–1913: Planks in Party Platform and History of Bills, with Votes*. Pamphlets in American History. Madison, Wisc.: s.n.

——. 1922. Thinking and Planning. Health and Happiness. Profit-sharing That Failed. From Scientific Management to Unionism. Joint Control. Ph.D. thesis, University of Wisconsin (business administration).

——. 1923. *Apprentice Education: A Survey of Part-time Education and Other Forms of Extension Training in Their Relation to Apprenticeship in the United States*. United States Federal Board for Vocational Education, Agricultural Series, no. 25. Washington: U.S. Government Printing Office.

——. 1923. Women's Rights by Blanket Legislation. *Wisconsin Law Review* 2(2) (January): 103–.

——. 1935. Old Age Pensions: Direct, National, Equal, Universal. *American Federationist* 42(1) (January): 16–.

Turner, Lillian A. 1915. Votes for Housewives. *Crisis* (August). New York: Crisis Publishing Co.

Turner, Mrs. Loretta E. 1902. *How Women Earn a Competence*. Oberlin, Ohio: News Printing Company.

Turner, Victoria B[riggs]. 1921. *Mutual Relief Associations among Government Employees in Washington, D.C.* Washington: U.S. Bureau of Labor Statistics.

——. 1921. Australia and South Africa. Labor Unrest. *Monthly Labor Review* 13 (July/December): 7–37.

——. 1921. Egypt – Labor Unrest. *Monthly Labor Review* 13 (July/December): 30–49.

——. 1921. India – Labor Unrest. *Monthly Labor Review* 13 (July/December): 32–53.

——. 1921. Labor Unrest in Great Britain. *Monthly Labor Review* 12 (January/June): 193–212.

——. 1921. New Zealand – Labor Conditions and Legislation. *Monthly Labor Review* 13 (July/December): 17–31.

——. 1922. Agricultural Wage Earners in the United States. *Monthly Labor Review* 15 (July/December): 22–40.

——. 1923. Agricultural Wage Earners in France. *Monthly Labor Review* 17 (July/December): 34–46.

——. 1923. Great Britain – Industrial Unrest. *Monthly Labor Review* 16 (January/June): 37–51.

[Twining, Louisa (unsigned).] 1857. *Metropolitan Workhouses and Their Inmates.* London: Longman, Brown, Green, Longmans, & Roberts.

Twining, Louisa. 1858. *Workhouses and Women's Work. Also, a Paper on the Condition of Workhouses, Read in the Social Economy Department of the National Association for the Promotion of Social Science, at Birmingham, October, 1857.* London: Longman, Brown, Green, Longmans, & Roberts.

——. 1862. *A Few Words on Social Science to Working People.* London: Emily Faithfull/Victoria Press.

——. 1862. *Our Poor Laws and our Workhouses.* London: Emily Faithfull/Victoria Press.

——. 1866. *A Letter to the President of the Poor Law Board, on Workhouse Infirmaries.* London: William Hunt.

——. 1880. *Recollections of Workhouse Visiting and Management during Twenty-five Years.* London: C. Kegan Paul. Reprinted, with additions, from *New Quarterly* (October 1879): pp 283–306.

——. 1882. *State Organisation and Voluntary Aid.* London: Family Welfare Association. Reprinted from the *Charity Organisation Reporter* 428–31 (May–June).

——. 1886. Workhouse Cruelties. *Nineteenth Century* 20 (November): 709–14.

——. 1887. *A Letter on Some Matters of Poor Law Administration.* London: W. Ridgway.

——. 1887. Suggestions for Women Guardians. *Englishwoman's Review*, n.s. 173 (September 15): 385.

——. 1887. Women's Work: Official and Unofficial. *National Review* 9 (July): 659–67.

——. 1888. Some Facts in the Working of the Poor Law. *National Review* 11 (June): 523–31.

——. 1889. *Poor Relief in Foreign Countries, and Out-door Relief in England.* London and New York: Cassell & Co.

——. 1889. Poor Law Infirmaries and Their Needs. *National Review* 13 (July): 630–42.

——. 1890. The Duty of Workhouse Visiting. *Monthly Packet* (March). Reprinted London: Family Welfare Association.

——. 1890. Women as Public Servants. *Nineteenth Century* 28 (December): 950–8.

——. 1891. Nursing in Workhouses. Paper read before the Ladies' Conference, Liverpool. Liverpool: Gilbert G. Walmsely, printer.

—— (unsigned). 1892. *Out-relief and Charity: Notes by a Lady Guardian*. London: F. Kirby, printer.

——. 1893. *Suggestions for Women Guardians.* London: Society for Promoting the Return of Women as Poor Law Guardians.

——. 1894. Private, Unofficial Visitation of Public Institutions. *Charities Review* 3 (February): 183–.

——. 1894. Women as Official Inspectors. *Nineteenth Century* 35(205) (March): 489–94.

——. 1898. *Workhouses and Pauperism and Women's Work in the Administration of the Poor Law.* London: Methuen.

——. 1898. Women as Poor Law Inspectors. *Englishwoman's Review*, n.s. 239 (July): 153.

——. 1899. The Official Work of Women. *Englishwoman's Review*, n.s. 242 (April): 81.

——. 1903. *Thoughts on Some Social Questions Past and Present with Additions and Letters on Charitable Institutions, etc., in Paris, Russia, Spain, and Holland from 1855 to 1881.* London: E. Stock. Reprinted from the *Churchman* (1901, 1902, 1903).

——. 1901. Poor Law and Poverty. *Economic Review* (July).

——. 1901. Women on Boards and Committees of Management in Hospitals. *Englishwoman's Review* 250 (April): 101–.

U

Ueland, Elsa. Coauth. *See* Goodman, Pearl.

Ullian, Frieda Silbert. 1938. Some Economic Aspects of the Social Security Act as an Instrument of Social Control. Ph.D. thesis, Radcliffe College (economics).

Unwin, Mrs. Cobden. 1913. *The Land Hunger – Life under Monopoly*. London: Fisher Unwin.

Upton, Harriet Taylor. 1922. Machine and the Woman. *Ladies' Home Journal* 39 (October): 13.

——. 1925. What Halts the Child Labor Amendment? *Woman Citizen*, n.s. 9 (February 21): 9.

Usborne, Mrs. H. M., ed. 1917. *Women's Work in War Time: A Handbook of Employments*. London: T. W. Laurie, Ltd.

Utley, F. 1937. *Japan's Feet of Clay*. New York: Norton.

V

Vaile, Gertrude. 1923. An Organization Problem of Public Welfare Departments. *Annals of the American Academy of Political and Social Science* 105 (January): 144–.

——. 1923. Our Interpretation of the True Place of Family Life. *Family* 4(6) (October): 153–.

——. 1931. Services of Local Mothers' Aid Workers in a Small Community. *Family* 12(8) (December): 235–.

——. 1938. Tying in with the Community. In R. H. Kurtz, ed., *The Public Assistance Worker: His Responsibility to the Applicant, the Community, and Himself.* New York: Russell Sage Foundation.

——. 1940. Family Case Work and Public Assistance. *Family* 21(8) (December): 247–.

Valesh, Eva McDonald. 1892. The Strength and Weakness of the People's Movement. *Arena* 5 (May): 726–31.

——. 1893. The Tenement House Problem in New York. *Arena* 7 (April): 580–6.

——. 1894. Settled by Arbitration. *American Federationist* 1(5) (July): 97–.

——. 1896. Conditions of Labor in Europe. *American Federationist* 3: 23, 41, 64, 83, 111, 155.

——. 1896. Woman and Labor. *American Federationist* 2(11) (January): 221–.

——. 1901. Review of Current Economics. *American Federationist* 8(8) (August): 301–.

——. 1901. A Score of American Federation of Labor Conventions. *American Federationist* 8(12) (December): 517.

——. 1901. Three Notable Lines of Labor Work. *American Federationist* 8(11) (November): 457.

——. 1902. A Historical Conference. *American Federationist* 9(11) (November): 793.

——. 1906. Wage-working Women. *American Federationist* 13(12) (December): 963–7.

——. 1907. Child Labor. *American Federationist* 14(3) (March): 157.

——. 1907. An Instructive Exhibit. *American Federationist* 14(9) (September): 681.

——. 1908. Women in Welfare Work. *American Federationist* 15 (April): 282–4.

——. 1909. "Au Revoir" to Samuel Gompers. *American Federationist* 16(7) (July): 606–.

——. 1909. Child Labor Legislation. *American Federationist* 16(8) (August): 668.

——. 1909. Problems to be Solved. *American Federationist* 16(10) (October): 864–.

——. 1909. The Right to Quit. *American Federationist* 16(9) (September): 764–.

Valette, Aline. 1893. *Cahier des doléances féminines, 1er mai 1893….* Fédération française des sociétés féministes. Paris: L'Harmonie Sociale.

——. 1895. *Socialisme et sexualisme.* Paris: A. M. Beaudelot.

——. 1898. *La Journée de la petite menagere.* Travaux manuels pour les filles. Paris: G. Delarue.

Van der Horst, Sheila T. 1934. Poor Law Legislation. *South African Journal of Economics* 2 (September): 298–305.

——. 1935. Some Effects of Industrial Legislation on the Market for Native Labour in South Africa. *South African Journal of Economics* 3 (December): 481–501.

——. 1939. Report of the Native Farm Labour Committee, 1937–39. *South African Journal of Economics* 7 (December): 462–71.

Van der Veen, Margrieta. 1898. Book Review of "The Standard of Life and Other Studies" by Mrs. Bernard Bosanquet. *Economic Journal* 8(32) (December): 517–20.

——. 1898. The Conference on Women's Work at the Hague. *Economic Journal* 8 (September): 404–7.

——. 1898. Home Work in Berlin. *Economic Journal* 8 (March): 143–6.

Van Deraa, Patricia Macasalyn. 1936. REA Allotments and Loans. *Land Economics* 12 (November): 427–9.

van Dorp, E[lisabeth]. C[aroline]. 1915. Book Review of "The Theory of Money and Dutch Currency" by H. Fryda. *Economic Journal* 25: 411–.

——. 1919. The Deviation of Exchanges. *Economic Journal* 29 (December): 497–503.

——. 1919/20. Die Bestimmungsgründe der intervalutarische Kurse. *Weltwirtschaftliches Archiv* 15: 29–39.

——. 1920. Abnormal Deviations in International Exchanges. *Economic Journal* 30 (September): 411–14.

——. 1920/1. Zur neueren geldtheoretischen Literatur II. *Archiv für Sozialwissenschaft und Sozialpolitik* 47: 889–.

——. 1921. Book Review of "Introduction to the Doctrine of the Stability in Value of Currency" by G. M. V. Stuart. *Economic Journal* 31: 240–.

——. 1931. Agio oder Lohnfonds? *Archiv für Sozialwissenschaft und Sozialpolitik* 66: 284–319.

——. 1933. Löhne und Kapitalzins. *Zeitschrift fü [ED1]r Nationalökonomie* 4: 254–66.

——. 1937. *Noch Communisme, Noch Dictatuur; een Staatkundig Voorstel.* Haarlem: De Erven F. Bohn n.v.

——. 1937. *A Simple Theory of Capital, Wages, and Profit or Loss.* London: P. S. King.

van Etten, Ida M. 1887. Working Women. *North American Review* 144(3) (March): 312–15.

——. 1888. Industrial Training in the Public Schools: In the New York Catholic Protectory. *Century Illustrated Monthly Magazine* 35 (January): 486–7.

——. 1891. *The Condition of Women Workers under the Present Industrial System.* Address delivered at the National Convention of the American Federation of Labor, Detroit, Michigan, December 8, 1890. Washington: American Federation of Labor; New York: Concord Cooperative Print.

——. 1892. The Socialist Labor Party in New York: A Criticism. New York: s.n.

——. 1893. Russian Jews as Desirable Immigrants. *Forum* 15 (April): 172–82.

van Hoesen, Antoinette. 1891. Woman's Department in the Columbian Exposition. *Chautauquan* 13 (April/September): 518–.

van Kleeck, Mary. 1906. Working Hours of Women in Factories. *Charities and the Commons* (6 October). Reprinted New York: Charity Organization Society.

——. 1908. Child Labor in New York City Tenements. *Charites and the Commons* (January 18).

——. 1910. Changes in Women's Work in Binderies. In Helen Marot, ed., *The Economic Position of Women.* New York: Academy of Political Science. Also published in Henry Raymond Mussey, ed., *Proceedings of the Academy of Political Science in the City of New York.* New York: Columbia University, 1910.

——. 1910. The Shirtwaist Strike and Its Significance. Unpublished lecture, Mary van Kleeck Papers, Box 29, Sophia Smith Collection, Smith College, Northampton, Mass.

——. 1913. *Artificial Flower Makers.* New York: Survey Associates, Inc.

——. 1913. *Women in the Bookbinding Trade.* New York: Survey Associates.

——. 1914. *Wages in the Millinery Trade.* Albany: printed by Lyon for New York (State) Factory Investigating Commission.

——. 1914. *Working Girls in Evening Schools: A Statistical Study.* New York: Survey Associates.

——. 1915. *Facts About Wage-earners in the United States Census, a Series of Diagrams Used in the Course on Industrial Conditions in the New York School of Philanthropy.* New York: New York School of Philanthropy.

——. 1915/1916. *Industrial Investigations of the Russell Sage Foundation with Bibliography of Publications of the Foundation Concerning Industry.* New York: Committee on Women's Work.

——. 1915. The Effect of Unemployment on the Wage Scale. *Annals of the American Academy of Political and Social Science* 61 (September): 90–.

——. 1916. *Positions in Social Work: A Study of the Number, Salaries, Experience, and Qualifications of Professional Workers in Unofficial Social Agencies in New York City.* New York: New York School of Philanthropy.

——. 1917. *Employment of Women in the Storage and Warehousing Depots of the United States Army.* U.S. War Industries Board, Storage Bulletin no. 9. Washington: U.S. Government Printing Office.

——. 1917. *A Seasonal Industry: A Study of the Millinery Trade in New York.* New York: Russell Sage Foundation.

——. 1918. *Industrial Standards in War Time.* Toledo: Toledo Consumers' League.

——. 1918. Case Work and Social Reform. *Annals of the American Academy of Political and Social Science* 77 (May): 9–.

——. 1918. A Census of College Women: (A Report of an Investigation for the A.C.A. in Cooperation with Eight Colleges and One Co-educational University). *Journal of the Association of Collegiate Alumnae* 11(9) (May): 557–.

——. 1919. *Suffragists and Industrial Democracy*. New York: National Woman's Suffrage Publishing Co., Inc.

——. 1919. Federal Policies for Women in Industry. *Annals of the American Academy of Political and Social Science* 81 (January): 87–.

——. 1919. The Task of Working Women in the International Congress. Address at the First International Congress of Working Women, Washington, D.C., October 28, 1919.

——. 1919. Women's Invasion of Industry and Changes in Protective Standards. *Proceedings of the Academy of Political Science* 8(2): 7–.

——. 1919. Women-workers during Reconstruction. *American Labor Legislation Review* 9: 62.

——. 1919/20. Book Review of "Women's Wages" by Emilie J. Hutchinson. *American Journal of Sociology* 25(1/6): 497–.

——. 1921. Women and Machines. *Atlantic Monthly* 127 (February): 250–.

——. 1922. The Professional Organization of Social Work. *Annals of the American Academy of Political and Social Science* 101 (May): 158–.

——. 1923. *What Industry Means to Women Workers*. U.S. Women's Bureau Bulletin, no. 31. Washington: U.S. Government Printing Office.

——. 1923. [Chapter in] Committee on Unemployment and Business Cycles, ed., *Business Cycles and Unemployment*. Washington: U.S. Government Printing Office; New York: McGraw-Hill.

——. 1924. Association's Relation to Social and Economic Position of Women. *Journal of the American Association of University Women* 18(1) (October): 18–.

——. 1925. *Employees' Representation in Steel and Coal: A Study of the Rockefeller Plan*. New York: Russell Sage Foundation.

——. 1925. *Outline of a Paper on Procedure Followed in Studying the Industrial Representation Plan of the Colorado Fuel and Iron Company*. New York: Personnel Research Foundation, Inc.

——. 1925. [?] Cannot Be Won by Constitutional Amendment. *Journal of the American Association of University Women* 18(3) (March): 21–.

——. 1925. Sharing Management with the Workers. *Journal of Social Forces* 3(3) (March): 506–10.

——. 1925/6. Procedure Followed in Studying the Industrial Representation Plan of the Colorado Fuel and Iron Company. *Journal of Personnel Research* 4: 133–.

——. 1926. The Interview as a Method of Research: Its Importance as an Essential Element of the Total Procedure of an Investigation Involving Human Relations. *Bulletin of the Taylor Society* (December): 268–74.

——. 1926. Modern Industry and Society. *American Federationist* (June): 698–.

——. 1927. Employment Statistics and Trade Unions. *American Federationist* 34(1/6) (January/June): 419–.

——. 1927. How the United States Can Aid the International Labor Organization through Research. *American Labor Legislation Review* 17: 168.
——. 1927. Measuring Employment in a Municipality. *National Municipal Review* 16(5) (May): 317–.
——. 1927. What Will You Do Next? *American Federationist* 34(7/12) (July/December): 1,090–.
——. 1928. Recent Gains in Industrial Relations. *World Tomorrow* 11(5) (May): 208–.
——. 1929. *How to Organize: A Problem.* Resumé of Findings, One Day Institute on Trade Union Organization. Chicago: Women's Trade Union League of America.
——. 1929. Human Relations in a Scientific Organization of Industry. *Factory and Industrial Management* 78(4) (October): 817–.
——. 1931. Planning and the World Paradox. *Survey Graphic* 1 (November).
——. 1931/2. The Personnel Manager in the World Workshop. *Personnel Journal* 10: 265–.
——. 1933. Dictatorships and Democracy. *Soviet Russia Today* 2(9) (November): 7–.
——. 1933. Nira Versus Piatiletka: Can Capitalism Plan? *Soviet Russia Today* 2(7) (September): 3–.
——. 1933. Scientific Management in the Second Five-year Plan. *Soviet Russia Today* (November) 2(4): 4–.
——. 1934. *Miners and Management: A Study of the Collective Agreement between the United Mine Workers of America and the Rocky Mountain Fuel Company, and an Analysis of the Problem of Coal in the United States.* New York: Russell Sage Foundation.
——. 1934. Book Review of "Master Craftsmen." *Yale Review* 23(4) (June): 831–.
——. 1934. Common Goals of Labor and Social Work. *Social Work Today* 2(1) (October): 4–.
——. 1934. An Open Letter from Mary van Kleeck. *Social Work Today* 1(1) (March/April): 12–.
——. 1934. Racial Conflict and Economic Competition. *Crisis* 41 (February): 45–.
——. 1934/5. The Workers' Bill for Unemployment. *New Republic* LXXXI: 121–4.
——. 1935. A Planned Economy. *Soviet Russia Today* 4(9) (November): 58–.
——. 1935. Sources of Power for the Social Work Program. *Social Work Today* 3(3) (December): 8–.
——. 1936. *Creative America: Its Resources for Social Security.* New York: Covici, Friede.
——. 1936. Book Review of "Unemployment: An International Problem. A Report by a Study Group of Members of the Royal Institute of International Affairs." *Pacific Affairs* 9(3) (September): 485–.
——. 1936. The Social Challenge to University Women. *Journal of the American Association of University Women* 29(2) (January): 67–.

——. 1937. Book Review of "The Soviets." *Soviet Russia Today* 6(4) (June): 24–.
——. 1937. Soviet Planning. *Soviet Russia Today* 6(9) (November): 17–.
——. 1938. The Moscow Trials. *Pacific Affairs* 11(2) (June): 233–.
——. 1938. Trade Unions and Soviet Security. *Soviet Russia Today* 7(8) (November): 18–.
——. 1938. Book Review of "Unemployment: An International Problem." *Pacific Affairs* 9(3) (September): 485–.
——. 1939. Labor and World Democracy. *Social Work Today* 6(4) (January): 18–.
——. 1940. Industrial Productivity and Labor Legislation. *American Labor Legislation Review* 30: 76–80.
——. 1940. Social Work and Changing Technology. *Social Work Today* 7(9) (June): 21–.
——. 1940. Social Work in the World Crisis. *Social Work Today* 7(6) (March): 5–.
——. 1940. World Democracy Needs the Soviet Union. *Soviet Russia Today* 9(6) (October): 15–.
van Kleeck, Mary and Mary L. Fleddérus, eds. 1935. *On Economic Planning: Papers Delivered at the Regional Study Conference of the International Industrial Relations Institute, New York, November 23–27, 1934*. New York: Covici, Friede.
van Kleeck, Mary. Papers in the Sophia Smith Collection, Smith College, and at the Walter Reuther Library at Wayne State University.
van Rensselaer, M[ariana]. G. [Mrs. Schuyler van Rensselaer]. 1892. The Development of American Homes. *Forum* 13 (January): 667–76.
——. 1892. The Waste of Women's Intellectual Force. *Forum* 13 (July): 616–28.
——. 1899. Our Public Schools. *North American Review* 169 (July): 77–.
Van Vorst, Mrs. J. [Bessie] 1904/5. Poor Children of Paris. *Harper's Monthly Magazine* 110: 248.
—— 1908. *The Cry of the Children*. New York: Moffat Yard & Co.
Van Vorst, Mrs. J. and Marie Van Vorst. 1903. *The Woman Who Toils; Being the Experiences of Two Ladies as Factory Girls*. New York: Doubleday, Page & Co.
Van Vorst, M[arie]. 1902. Life of Women in Factories. *Everybody's Magazine* 7: 361, 413, 540.
——. 1904. Lady and the Property. *Lippincott's Magazine* 73: 80.
——. 1904. When in Disgrace with Fortune; a Story. *Harper's Monthly Magazine* 109: 516.
——. 1905. *Amanda of the Mill*. New York: Dodd, Mead & Co.
——. 1905. The Sheathing of the Blade. *Harper's Monthly Magazine* 111: 117.
Van Vorst, Marie Louise and Bessie McGinnis Van Vorst. 1902. *Philip Longstreth, a Novel*. New York: Harper and Brothers.
Venter, Jewell. 1928. Possibilities of Rubber Production in Caribbean America. *Economic Geography* 4(4) (October): 381–4.
Verkade-Cartier van Dissel, Eline Francoise. 1937. *De Mogelijkheid van Landbouw-Kolonisatie voor Blanken in Suriname* Amsterdam: H.J. Paris.
Verney, Lady [Frances Parthenope Nightingale]. 1869. Female Education in France. *Fraser's Magazine* 80 (September): 366–79.

——. 1870. The Powers of Women, and How to Use Them. *Contemporary Review* 14 (July): 523–41.

——. 1871. Class Morality. *St Paul's Magazine* 8 (June): 259–68.

——. 1882. Autumn Jottings in France. (Peasant Proprietorship – II). *Contemporary Review* 41 (April): 560–82.

——. 1882. Peasant Properties in Auvergne. *Contemporary Review* 42 (December): 954–72.

——. 1882. Peasant Proprietors in France I, Jottings in France in September and October. *Contemporary Review* 41 (January): 1–26.

——. 1885. *Cottier Owners, Little Takes and Peasant Properties.* A Reprint, with additions, of *Jottings in France, Germany, and Switzerland.* London: Longmans, Green.

——. 1885. *Peasant Properties and Other Selected Essays.* 2 vols. London: Longmans, Green & Co. Essays collected from the *Contemporary Review* and *Fraser's Magazine.*

——. 1885. Foreign Opinions on Peasant Properties. *Nineteenth Century* 18 (November): 794–803.

——. 1885. "Little Takes" in England, vs. Peasant Properties in France and Germany. *Contemporary Review* 47 (May): 675–82.

——. 1886. Allotments. *Nineteenth Century* 19 (June): 902–13.

——. 1886. Rural Italy and Peasant Properties. *Nineteenth Century* 19 (February): 226–37.

——. 1887. Peasant Properties in France, 1787–1887. *National Review* 10 (December): 549–64.

——. 1887. Rural Life in Russia. *Nineteenth Century* 21 (January): 133–47.

——. 1888. *How the Peasant Owner Lives in Parts of France, Germany, Italy, Russia.* London and New York: Macmillan and Co.

——. 1889. Six Generations of Czars. *Nineteenth Century* 25 (June): 827–37.

——. 1891. *Essays and Tales.* London: Simpkin, Marshall.

——. 1896. Some Seventeenth-century Matrons and Their Housekeeping. *Longman's* 27(160) (February): 353–62.

Viau, Sister Joseph Marie. 1938. The Problem of Hours and Wages in American Organized Labor. Ph.D. thesis, Columbia University.

——. 1939. *Hours and Wages in American Organized Labor*. New York: Putnam's.

——. 1939. Book Review of "De la France d'avant guerre à la France d'aujourd'hui" by Rist and Pirou. *American Economic Review* 29: 827–.

Vlasto, Olga. 1926. Family Allowances and the Skilled Worker. *Economic Journal* 36 (December): 577–85.

[Vogts,] Miriam Beard. 1938. *A History of the Business-man*. New York: Macmillan.

——. 1962. *A History of Business*, vol. 1: *From Babylon to the Monopolists*; vol. 2: *From the Monopolists to the Organization Man*. Ann Arbor, Mich.: University of Michigan Press. First published as *A History of the Business-Man*, 1938.

von Franken, Constanze. 1898. *Katechismus der weiblichen Erwerbs- und Berufsarten.* Leipzig: M. Hesse.

von Gayette-Georgens, Jeanne Marie. 1872. *Die Frauen in Erwerb und Beruf; zwölf Vorträge*. Berlin: Deutsches Verlags-Institut.

von Koribout-Daschkewitsch, Nina. 1890/1. The Russian Peasant Woman. *Chautauquan* 12 (October/March): 654–.

von Lovasy, Gertrude. 1937. Zur Entwicklung des wirtschaftlichen Kapitalverkehrs in den letzten zehn Jahren. *Zeitschrift für Bankwesen* 2: 206–18.

von Reifenstein, Ida Kortzfleisch. 1895. *Der freiwillige Dienst in der wirtschaftlichen Frauen-Hochschule.* Hannover: C. Meyer.

von Troll-Borostyani, Irma. 1878. *Die Mission unseres Jahrhunderts; eine Studie über die Frauenfrage.* Pressburg, Austria: Gustar Heckenast.

——. 1888. *Die Gleichstellung der Geschlechter und die Reform der Jugend-Erziehung.* Zurich: Verlags-Magazin.

——. 1894. *Das Recht der Frau. Eine sociale Studie.* Berlin: S. Fischer.

von Wächter, Anna. 1861. *Der weibliche Beruf; Gedanken einer Frau.* Stuttgart: A. Krabbe.

Voris, Ruth Irene. 1925. *Standard and Scheduled Hours of Work for Women in Industry: A Study Based on Hour Data from 13 States.* Washington: U.S. Women's Bureau.

Voris, Ruth Irene and Ethel Lombard Best. 1926. *Women in Illinois Industries: A Study of Hours and Working Conditions.* Bulletin of the U.S. Women's Bureau, no. 51. Washington: U.S. Department of Labor, Women's Division.

Voris, Ruth Irene. Coauth. *See* Best, Ethel Lombard; Hawkins, Hildred Moser; Hyde, Elizabeth Adshead; Manning, Caroline.

Vorse, Mary Marvin Heaton. 1920. *Men and Steel.* New York: Boni and Liveright.

——. 1926. The War in Passaic. *Nation* 122 (March): 280–1.

——. 1927. *The Passaic Textile Strike, 1926–1927.* Passaic, N.J.: General Relief Committee of Textile Strikers.

——. 1929. Gastonia. *Harper's Monthly Magazine* 159 (November 19): 701–5.

——. 1930. *Strike!* New York: H. Liveright.

——. 1935. From Flathead to Blackfeet. *Indians at Work* 3(3) (September 15): 31–6.

——. 1938. *Labor's New Millions.* New York: Modern Age Books.

Vrooman, Grace. 1895. Manual Training for Women and the Problem of Domestic Service. *Arena* 14: 308–16.

W

Waggaman, Mary T[heresa]. 1919. Efforts to Standardize the Working Day for Domestic Service. *Monthly Labor Review* 9(2) (August): 206–13.

——. 1919. First International Congress of Working Women, Washington, D.C. *Monthly Labor Review* 9(6) (December): 280–90.

——. 1919. Growth of Trade-unionism among British Women during the War. *Monthly Labor Review* 8(6) (June): 298–303.

——. 1920. Labor Colonies for the Feeble-minded. *Monthly Labor Review* 11 (July/December): 12–19.

——. 1921. Canada – Labor Unrest. *Monthly Labor Review* 13 (July/December): 21–32.

——. 1921. Collection of Wage Claims by State Labor Offices. *Monthly Labor Review* 12 (January/June): 72–81.

——. 1921. Some Developments in the Movement for "Family Wages." *Monthly Labor Review* 13 (July/December): 9–19.

——. 1922. Efforts to Regularize Employment in Seasonal Trades. *Monthly Labor Review* 14 (January/June): 157–68.

——. 1923. Extension of the "Family-wage" System in France and Belgium. *Monthly Labor Review* 17 (July/December): 1–17.

——. 1923. Immigrant Aid: Legislative Safeguards, and Activities of Bureau of Immigration. *Monthly Labor Review* 16 (January/June): 22–35.

——. 1923. Immigrant Aid: State Activities. *Monthly Labor Review* 17 (July/December): 240–62.

——. 1924. Immigrant Aid: National, Nongovernmental Activities. *Monthly Labor Review* 18 (January/June): 187–99.

——. 1926. *Family Allowances in Foreign Countries.* U.S. Bulletin of the Bureau of Labor Statistics, Miscellaneous Series, no. 401. Washington: U.S. Government Printing Office.

——. 1935. Progress of Social Insurance in Japan. *Monthly Labor Review* 40(3) (March): 656–.

Wagner, Augusta Bertha. 1938/1987. *Labor Legislation in China.* Westport, Conn.: Hyperion Press.

——. 1939. The International Labor Organization and the Regulation of Labor Conditions in China. *Yenching Journal of Social Studies* II(1) (July): 1–.

——. 1940. Book Review of "An Outline of International Price Theories" by Wu Ch'i-Yuen. *Yenching Journal of Social Studies* 2(2) (February): 321–.

——. 1940. Labor Legislation in China. Ph.D. thesis, Columbia University (economics).

Wagner, Gertrud. 1938. Market Research: A Critical Study. *Review of Economic Studies* 5(2) (February): 132–8.

Waite, Marie. 1939. A History of the Nutrition and Clothing Service of the Illinois Emergency Commission, February, 1932 through June, 1936. A.M. thesis, University of Chicago (sociology).

——. Coauth. *See* Weiss, Gertrude Schmidt.

Wakefield, Priscilla [Bell]. 1798. *Reflections on the Present Condition of the Female Sex, with Suggestions for Its Improvement.* London: J. Johnson and Darton and Harvey. 2nd ed., London: Darton, Harvey and Darton, 1817.

——. 1801. *The Juvenile Travellers; Containing the Remarks of a Family during a Tour through the Principal States and Kingdoms of Europe, etc.* With a map. London: Darton & Harvey.

——. 1804. *A Family Tour through the British Empire Containing Some Account of Its Manufactures, Natural and Artificial Curiosities, History and Antiquities: Interspersed with Biographical Anecdotes: Particularly Adapted to the Amusement and Instruction of Youth.* London: Darton and Harvey.

——. 1806. *Excursions in North America, Described in Letters from a Gentleman and his Young Companion, to Their Friends in England.* London: Darton and Harvey.

——. 1814. *The Traveller in Africa: Containing Some Account of the Antiquities, Natural Curiosities, and Inhabitants, of Such Parts of that Continent and Its Islands, as Have Been Most Explored by Europeans. The Route Traced on a Map, for the Entertainment and Instruction of Young Persons.* London: Darton, Harvey, and Darton.

——. 1817. *The Traveller in Asia: or, a Visit to the Most Celebrated Parts of the East Indies and China. With an Account of the Manners of the Inhabitants, Natural Productions, and Curiosities. For the Instruction and Entertainment of Young Persons.* London: Darton, Harvey, and Darton.

Wakefield, Roberta P. 1923/1926. *Shipment of Samples and Advertising Matter to Europe.* Washington: U.S. Bureau of Foreign and Domestic Commerce.

——. 1924. *Shipment of Samples and Advertising Matter to Latin America and the West Indies.* Washington: U.S. Bureau of Foreign and Domestic Commerce.

——. 1928. *Shipment of Samples and Advertising Matter to the British Empire.* Washington: U.S. Bureau of Foreign and Domestic Commerce.

——. 1934. *Preparing Shipments to British Countries: Documentary Requirements and Customs Regulations.* Washington: U.S. Bureau of Foreign and Domestic Commerce.

——. 1937. *Tariff Handbook on Canned Foods in the Western Hemisphere.* Trade Promotion Series, no. 85. Washington: U.S. Bureau of Foreign and Domestic Commerce.

——. 1937. Some Factors in Cuba's Foreign Trade. *Economic Geography* 13(2) (April): 109–31.

——. 1939. *Foreign Marks of Original Regulations.* Department of Commerce, Bureau of Foreign and Domestic Commerce, Division of Foreign Tariffs. Washington: U.S. Government Printing Office.

——. 1939. *Preparing Shipments to British Countries (Except Canada): Documentary Requirements and Customs Regulations.* Washington: U.S. Bureau of Foreign and Domestic Commerce.

——. 1940. *Foreign Import Duties and Regulations on Fresh Fruits and Vegetables.* Washington: U.S. Bureau of Foreign and Domestic Commerce.

Wakefield, Roberta P. and Florence Isabelle Kehr Ioannou. 1927. *Export Duties of the World.* Washington: U.S. Government Printing Office.

Wakeman, Antoinette van H. 1892. Women as Stock Farmers. *Chautauquan* 15 (September): 736–.

——. 1895. Women Fruit Farmers in California. *Chautauquan* 20 (February): 596–.

Wald, Lillian D. 1902. Nurses' Settlement. *American Journal of Nursing* 2 (May): 567–75.

——. 1906. Child Labor. *American Journal of Nursing* 6 (March): 366–9.

——. 1906. Henry Street Settlement, New York. *Charities and the Commons* 16 (April 7): 35–41.

——. 1906. Organization amongst Working Women. *Annals of the American Academy of Political and Social Science* 27 (May): 638–45.

——. 1907. *Boarded-out Babies.* New York: Association of Neighborhood Workers of the City of New York.

——. 1907. Child Labor. *American Journal of Nursing* 7 (June): 471–93.

——. 1909. Need for a Federal Children's Bureau. *Annals of the American Academy of Political and Social Science* 33, Supplement (March): 23–8.

——. 1912. Doctor and the Nurse in Industrial Establishments. *American Journal of Nursing* 12 (February): 403–8.

——. 1912. Doctor and the Nurse in Industrial Establishments. *Proceedings of the Academy of Political Science* 2 (January): 93–8.

——. 1913. Sanitary Control of an Industry by the Industry Itself. *Public Health Nurse Quarterly* 5 (April): 13–21.

——. 1915. *House on Henry Street.* New York: H. Holt & Co. Reprinted New Brunswick, N.J.: Transaction Publishers, 1991.

——. 1915. House on Henry Street. *Atlantic* (March): 289–300; (April): 464–73; (May): 649–62; (June): 806–17; (July): 69–83; (August): 240–50.

——. 1916. Vocational Scholarships. *Child Labor Bulletin* 5 (May): 7–8.

——. 1923. Fifty Years of Child Welfare. *Survey* 50 (May 1): 181–3.

——. 1924. Public Health in Soviet Russia. *Survey* 53 (December 1): 270–4.

——. 1930. Helping the Workers. *Outlook and Independent* 156 (September 24): 158.

——. 1932. Twentieth Anniversary of the Federal Children's Bureau. *National Conference of Social Work*: 33–40.

——. 1933. Forty Years of Service to the Sick and Poor. *American Journal of Nursing* 33 (April): 326.

——. 1933. Forty Years on Henry Street. *Survey* 69 (May): 192.

——. 1933. Lean Years. *Atlantic* (December): 650–9.

——. 1933. Russia, from Henry Street. *Survey Graphic* 22 (November): 555–7.

——. 1934. *Windows on Henry Street.* Boston: Little, Brown & Co.

Wald, Lillian D. and Frances Alice Kellor. 1910. Construction Camps of the People. *Survey* 23 (January 1): 449–65.

Wald, Lillian D. and Henry Moscowitz. 1912. Taking Stock in New York's Factories. *Survey* 27 (March 16): 1,928–9.

Walden, Sarah S. W. 1916. Review of Industrial Home Work in Massachusetts. *American Economic Review* 6 (June): 400–3.

——. 1917. Book Review of "The Boot and Shoe Industry in Massachusetts as a Vocation for Women." *American Economic Review* 7 (March): 147–50.

——. 1917. Book Review of "Millinery as a Trade for Women." *American Economic Review* 7 (March): 147–50.

[Wales, Abigail Frothingham.] 1844. *Reminiscences of the Boston Female Asylum.* Boston: Eastburn's Press.

Walker, Helen M. 1933. Some Data Regarding 162 Families Affected by Unemployment Known to the Cleveland Associated Charities. *The Family*, Supplement, 14(4) (June). New York: Family Welfare Association of America.

Walker, Helen Mary. 1929. *Studies in the History of Statistical Method, with Reference to Certain Educational Problems.* Baltimore: Williams & Wilkins Co. Reprinted New York: Arno Press, 1975.

——. 1929. Studies in the History of Statistical Method with Special Reference to Certain Educational Problems. Ph.D. thesis, Columbia University (statistics).

Walker, Helen W. 1928/9. Mexican Immigrants and American Citizenship. *Sociology and Social Research* 13: 465–.

——. 1928/9. Mexican Immigrants as Laborers. *Sociology and Social Research* 13: 55–.

Walker, Mabel Louise 1930. *Municipal Expenditures.* Johns Hopkins University Studies in Historical and Political Science, Extra Volumes, new series, no. 13. Baltimore: Johns Hopkins Press; New York: AMS Press, 1983.

——. 1930. Budget-making in Seven Cities. *National Municipal Review* 19(5) (May): 302–.

——. 1930. Municipal Expenditures. Ph.D. thesis, Johns Hopkins University (economics, finance).

——. 1930. Unemployment Survey. *American Labor Legislation Review* 20: 375–409.

——. 1931. The Dole in New York City. *American Labor Legislation Review* 21(1) (March): 48–.

——. 1931. Running Away with a Word. *American Labor Legislation Review* 21(2) (June): 221–.

——. 1931. Spiritual Responses. *American Labor Legislation Review* 21(3) (September): 339–.

——. 1931. The Urge to Organize. *American Labor Legislation Review* 21(2) (June): 228–.

——. 1933. *The General Sales Tax: Unwise, Unscientific, Unjust.* New York: General Welfare Tax League.

——. 1933. *Why the Sales Tax Is Bad.* New York: General Welfare Tax League.

——. 1934. *Where the Sales Tax Falls.* New York: Tax Policy League.

——. 1934. Getting Acquainted with Taxes. *Independent Woman* (February).

——. 1934. Overhauling State Revenue Systems. *National Municipal Review* 23(8) (August): 424–.

——. 1934. The States' Search for Money. *National Municipal Review* 23(7) (July): 366–.

——. 1935. *The Home Owner and the Sales Tax.* New York: Tax Policy League.

——. 1935. The Sales Tax on Trial. *National Municipal Review* 24(5) (May): 258–.

——. 1936. Notes on Books and Materials in Public Finance. *Annals of the American Academy of Political and Social Science* 183 (January): 233–.

——. 1937. The Challenge of the Trailer. *National Municipal Review* 26(5) (May): 230–.

——. 1938. *Urban Blight and Slums: Economic and Legal Factors in Their Origin, Reclamation, and Prevention.* Cambridge, Mass.: Harvard University Press.

——. 1940. State and Local Protectionism. *Taxes* 18(7) (July): 407–.

Walker, Mary L. and Mona Wilson. 1905. *Report on Housing and Industrial Conditions and Medical Inspection of School Children.* Dundee: J. Lenge & Co., Ltd.

Walker, Sophia A. 1929. Carpet-baggers. *Journal of Negro History* 14(1) (January): 44–59.

Walter, Henriette Rose, comp. 1916. *Investigations of Industries in New York City, 1905–1915: A List of Published Reports.* New York: Russell Sage Foundation.

——. 1917. *Munition Workers in England and France; a Summary of Reports Issued by the British Ministry.* New York: Russell Sage Foundation.

Wandle, Mrs. Jaennie Taylor, comp. 1896. *Employments and Professions for Women.* London and New York: Butterick Publishing Co.

Ward, Barbara. 1938. *The International Share-out.* London: Nelson.

——. 1939. Planned Economy in Catholic Social Thought. *Dublin Review*, series 4, 204(408) (January/March): 85–.

Ward, Gertrude. 1935. The Education of Factory Child Workers, 1833–1850: A Study of the Effects of the Education Clauses in the Factory Act of 1833. *Economic History* 3 (February): 110–24.

Ward, Grace F. 1911/1971. Weakness of the Massachusetts Child Labor Laws. In Susan Myra Kingsbury, Charles Edward Person, and Edith Gertrude Solenberger, eds., *Labor Laws and Their Enforcement with Special Reference to Massachusetts.* New York: Longmans, Green.

Ward, Grace Faulkner. 1918. The Early History of the Merchant Staplers. *English Historical Review* 33: 297–.

Ward, Mrs. Humphry [Mary Augusta Arnold]. 1894. *Marcella.* London: Smith, Elder; New York: Macmillan. Online at Indiana University's LETRS [*social reform novel*]

——. 1896. *Sir George Tressaday*. London: Smith, Elder; New York: Macmillan. Originally serialized in *Century Magazine* (November 1895–October 1896). [*novel*]

Ward, Mrs. Humphry *et al.* 1889. An Appeal Against Female Suffrage. *Nineteenth Century* 25 (June): 781–8.

Ward, Margaret Henshaw. 1929. The Sacred Trust of Civilization. Ph.D. thesis, Robert Brookings.

Ward, Susan Hayes. 1886/7. In-door Employments for Women. *Chautauquan* 7 (October/July) 259–.

——. 1888. More Work for Women. *Chautauquan* 8(7) (April): 426–8.

Ware, Caroline Farrar. 1925. The Industrial Revolution in the New England Cotton Industry. Ph.D. thesis, Radcliffe College (history).

——. 1926. The Effect of the American Embargo, 1807–1809, on the New England Cotton Industry. *Quarterly Journal of Economics* 40 (August): 673–88.

——. 1931. *The Early New England Cotton Manufacture: A Study in Industrial Beginnings*. Boston: Houghton Mifflin. Reprinted New York: Russell and Russell, 1966; New York: Johnson Reprint Corp., 1966; Boston: Houghton Mifflin, 1973.

——. 1932. Book Review of "The New Survey of London Life and Labour. Volume I: Forty Years of Change." *Political Science Quarterly* 47: 141–3.

——. 1932. Methods of Conducting a Sociological Study of a Highly Disorganized Urban Area. *American Sociological Society, Publication* 26(3) (December): 200–.

——. 1932. Methods of Studying a Highly Disorganized Urban Area. *Social Forces* 10(3) (March): 378–82.

——. 1934. *The Worker Goes to Market*. New York: American Labor Education Service, Inc.

——. 1935. *Greenwich Village, 1920–1930: A Comment on American Civilization in the Post-war Years*. Boston: Houghton Mifflin; New York: Octagon Books. Reprinted New York: Harper & Row, 1965; New York: Octagon Books, 1977; Berkeley: University of California Press, 1994.

——. 1935. What Hope for the Consumer? The Need for a New Voice in Industrial Policy. *Journal of the American Association of University Women* 28(3) (April): 145–.

——. 1936. Book Review of "Social Settlements in New York City: Their Activities, Policies, and Administration" by Albert J. Kennedy, Kathryn Farra, and Neva Ruth Deardorff, eds. *American Journal of Sociology* 41(4): 522–.

——. 1937. The Strategic Role of the Consumer. Dollars-and-cents Economies Are Not the Whole of the Consumer's Problem. *Journal of the American Association of University Women* 31(1) (October): 14–.

——. 1938. The Need for a Federal Consumer Agency. The Consumer Looks to the National Government for Essential Services. *Journal of the American Association of University Women* 31(2) (January): 79–.

——. 1940. *The Cultural Approach to History*. New York: Columbia University Press.

——. 1940. Book Review of "A Social Study of Pittsburgh" by Philip Klein *et al.* *American Journal of Sociology* 45(4): 614–15.

——. Papers located at the Franklin D. Roosevelt Library and in the National Consumers League at the Library of Congress.

Ware, Edith E. 1932. *Business and Politics in the Far East.* New Haven: Yale University Press for the Carnegie Endowment for International Peace.

Warren, Mrs. Eliza. 1865. *How I Managed My House on Two Hundred Pounds a Year.* London: Houlston and Wright.

——. 1866. *Comfort for Small Incomes.* London: Published at the office of the Ladies' Treasury.

Warriner, Doreen, Ph.D. 1931. *Combines and Rationalisation in Germany, 1924–1928.* London: P. S. King & Son, Ltd.

——. 1931. Agricultural Survivals in Central Europe. *Slavonic (and East European) Review* 10: 357–62.

——. 1931. The Margarine Monopoly and the Consumer. *Review of International Co-operation* 24(6) (June): 201–.

——. 1931. Schumpeter and the Conception of Static Equilibrium. *Economic Journal* 41 (March): 38–50.

——. 1931. Wheat and the Consumer. *Review of International Co-operation* 24(10) (October): 368–.

——. 1931. Wheat and the Consumer. II. The Possibilities of International Control. *Review of International Co-operation* 24(11) (November): 420–.

——. 1932. Preferences and Imperialism. Report of the Special Committee of the British Union on State Purchase and Imperial Trade. *Review of International Co-operation* 25(7) (July): 267–.

——. 1932. Present Day Economic Problems. The Elimination of Profits. *Review of International Co-operation* 25(4) (April): 134–.

——. 1932. Present Day Economic Problems. Progress and the Price Level. *Review of International Co-operation* 25(5) (May): 179–.

——. 1932. Present Day Economic Problems. What Is Co-operative Economics? *Review of International Co-operation* 25(3) (March): 81–.

——. 1932. The Tariff and the Standard of Living. *Review of International Co-operation* 25(2) (February): 58–.

——. 1932/3. Czechoslovakia and Central European Tariffs, I. *Slavonic and East European Review* 11: 314–.

——. 1932/3. Czechoslovakia and Central European Tariffs, II. *Slavonic and East European Review* 11: 543–.

——. 1933. Rationalisation and the Consumer. *Review of International Co-operation* 26(1) (January): 27–.

——. 1933. The World Economic Conference. A Retrospect, 1927–1933. *Review of International Co-operation* 26(5) (May): 161–.

——. 1933/4. Czechoslovakia and Central European Tariffs, III. *Slavonic and East European Review* 12: 107–.

——. 1937/8. The Population Question in Eastern Europe. *Slavonic and East European Review* 16: 629–.

——. 1939. *Economics of Peasant Farming*. New York: Oxford University Press.

——. 1940. *Eastern Europe after Hitler*. London: Fabian Society.

——. 1940. Book Review of "Modern Turkey" by Parker and Smith. *Political Quarterly (1930-)* 11: 422.

——. 1940. Book Review of "Turkey at the Straits" by Shotell and Deak. *Political Quarterly (1930-)* 11: 422.

Warriner, Doreen and E. Shenkman. 1933. Book Review of "Results of State Trading." *Annals of Collective Economy* 9: 382–.

Warwick, Frances Evelyn Maynard Greville, Countess of, ed. 1898. *Progress in Women's Education in the British Empire, Being the Report of the Education Section, Victorian Era Exhibition, 1897*. London, New York, and Bombay: Longmans, Green and Co.

Washington, Margaret J. Murray [Mrs. Booker T. Washington]. 1894. *Work for the Colored Women of the South*. Tuskegee, Ala.: Normal School Press.

——. 1895. Club Work among Negro Women. In H. F. Kletzing and W. H. Crogman, eds., *Progress of a Race, or, The remarkable advancement of the Afro-American Negro from the Bondage of Slavery, Ignorance and Poverty, to the Freedom of Citizenship, Intelligence, Affluence, Honor and Trust*. Naperville, Ill.: J. L. Nichols and Co.

——. 1905. The Advancement of Colored Women. *Colored American Magazine* 8(4) (April): 183.

Waterman, Elizabeth Lane. *See* Gilboy, Elizabeth [Lane] Waterman.

Waters, Charlotte Mary. 1920. *A School Economic History of England*. Oxford: Clarendon Press.

——. 1925. *An Economic History of England, 1066–1874*. London: Oxford University Press.

——. 1926. *A Short Survey of the Economic Development of England and the Colonies, 1874–1914*. London: N. Douglas.

Watson, Amey [Brown] E[aton] [Ph.D.]. 1918. The Illegitimate Family. *Annals of the American Academy of Political and Social Science* 77 (May): 103–.

——. 1923. *Illegitimacy: Philadelphia's Problem and the Development of Standards of Care*. Washington: U.S. Children's Bureau.

——. 1929. Employer–Employee Relationships in the Home. *Annals of the American Academy of Political and Social Science* 143 (May): 49–.

——. 1932. *Household Employment in Philadelphia*. Washington: U.S. Women's Bureau.

——. 1932. The Reorganization of Household Work. *Annals of the American Academy of Political and Social Science* 160 (March): 165–.

——. 1937. Domestic Service. *Encyclopaedia of the Social Sciences* 5: 198–206.

Watson, Annah Robinson. 1895. The Attitude of Southern Women on the Suffrage Question. *Arena* 11 (February): 363–9.

Waugh, Catharine. *See* McCulloch, Catharine Waugh.

Wead, Margaret. 1932. Drifts in Unemployment Relief. *Family* 13(7) (November): 223–.

——. 1932. Unemployment relief in the family welfare field. *Social Forces* 11(2) (December): 214–18.

——. 1933. The Roof over Their Heads. *Family* 14(5), Supplement (July): 177–.

——. 1935. Local Membership Plans in Family Welfare Agencies. *Family* 16(4) (June): 102–.

[Webb,] Beatrice Potter. 1886. A Lady's View of the Unemployed at the East. *Pall Mall Gazette* (February 18).

——. 1887. The Dock Life of East London. *Nineteenth Century* 22 (October): 483–99. Included in Charles Booth, ed., *Life and Labour of the People in London.* London and Edinburgh: Williams & Norgate, 1889.

——. 1888. East London Labour. *Nineteenth Century* 24(138) (August): 161–83.

——. 1888. Pages from a Work-girl's Diary. *Nineteenth Century* 24 (September): 301–14.

——. 1888. The Sweating System II. *Charity Organisation Review* 37 (January): 12–17.

——. 1889. The Docks. In Charles Booth, ed., *Life and Labour of the People in London.* London and Edinburgh: Williams & Norgate, 1889.

——. 1889. The Jewish Community. In Charles Booth, ed., *Life and Labour of the People in London.* London and Edinburgh: Williams & Norgate, 1889.

——. 1889. The Tailoring Trades. In Charles Booth, ed., *Life and Labour of the People in London.* London and Edinburgh: Williams & Norgate, 1889.

——. 1890. The Lords and the Sweating System. *Nineteenth Century* 27(160) (June): 885–905.

——. 1891/1893/1895/1899. *The Co-operative Movement in Great Britain.* London: S. Sonnenschein & Co.; New York: C. Scribner's Sons. Reprinted London: G. Allen, 1914; London: G. Allen and Unwin, 1920, 1930; Aldershot, UK: Gower, 1987.

——. 1892. *How Best to Do Away with the Sweating System.* Paper read at the 24th Annual Conference of the Co-operative Societies, Rochdale, June 1892. Manchester: Co-operative Union, Ltd.

——. 1892. *The Relationship between Co-operation and Trade Unionism.* Paper read at a conference of trade union officials and co-operators, Tynemouth, August 15, 1892. Manchester: Co-operative Union, Ltd.

——. 1892. Co-operation among Women. In *Women Workers: Papers Read at a Conference Convened by the Liverpool Ladies Union of Workers among Women and Girls in Nov. 1891.* Liverpool: Silbert G. Walmsley.

——. 1893. Comment en finir avec le Sweating system? *Revue d'économie politique* 7: 963–.

——. 1894. The Failure of the Labour Commission. *Nineteenth Century* 34(209) (July): 2–22.

——. 1896. *Women and the Factory Acts.* Fabian Tract, no. 67. London: Fabian Society. Reprinted in Sally Alexander, ed., *Women's Fabian Tracts.* London and New York: Routledge, 1988; and in M. Mulvey Roberts and T. Mizuta, eds., *Controversies in the History of British Feminism*, Vol. 2: *The Workers, Women and Labour.* London: Routledge/Thoemmes, 1995.

——, ed. 1901. *The Case for the Factory Acts.* With a preface by Mrs. H. Ward. London: Grant Richards.

——. 1901. The Economics of Factory Legislation. In Mrs. Sidney Webb, ed., *The Case for the Factory Acts.* London: Grant Richards.
——. 1909. *The Charter of the Poor.* London: Christian Commonwealth Co.
——. 1909. *A Crusade against Destitution.* London: National Committee for the Prevention of Destitution.
——. 1909. *The Minority Report of the Poor Law Commission*, part 1: *The Break-up of the Poor Law*; part 2: *The Public Organisation of the Labour Market.* London: Fabian Society.
——. 1909. The Break-up of the Poor Law [letter to the editor]. *Nation* 5(16) (July 17): 570–.
——. 1910. *The Minority Report in Its Relation to Public Health and the Medical Profession.* London: National Committee to Promote the Break-up of the Poor law.
——. 1910. *The New Crusade against Destitution: Being an Exposition of the Minority Report of the Poor Law Commission.* Manchester: National Labour Press.
——. 1910. The Midwives Bill [letter to the editor]. *Nation* 7(22) (August 27): 769–.
——. 1912. *Complete National Provision for Sickness: How to Amend the Insurance Act.* London: Standing Joint Committee of the Independent Labour Party and the Fabian Society.
——. 1913. "Preface" to *The Case for the National Minimum.* London: National Committee for the Prevention of Destitution.
——. 1913. The Soul of Japan. *New Statesman* 1, Supplement (April 12): xiii–.
——, ed. 1913. Special Supplement on the Awakening of Women. *New Statesman* 2 (November).
——. 1913. What Is Socialism? *New Statesman* 1 (April 12/October 4).
——. 1914. The Falling Birth-rate. *New Statesman* 3 (April 11/October 3): 428–.
——. 1914. The Individual, Other Individuals, and the Community. *New Statesman* 3 (April 11/October 3): 395–.
——. 1914. Maternity under Free Conditions. *New Statesman* 3 (April 11/October 3): 461–.
——. 1914. Motherhood and Citizenship. *New Statesman* 3(58): 10–11.
——. 1914. Personal Rights and the Woman's Movement: Equal Remuneration for Men and Women. *New Statesman* 3 (August): 525–7.
——, ed. 1914. Personal Rights and the Woman's Movement: The Right of Women to Free Entry into All Occupations. *New Statesman* 3 (July): 493–4.
——. 1914. Personal Rights and the Women's Movement v. Equal Remuneration for Men and Women. *New Statesman* 1 (August): 525–7.
——, ed. 1914. Special Supplement on Women in Industry. *New Statesman* 2 (February).
——. 1914. Voteless Women and Social Revolution. *New Statesman* (February): 584–.
——. 1915. Special Supplement on English Teachers and Their Professional Organisation. *New Statesman* 5 129 (September).
——. 1916. *A Woman's Appeal: Personal Expenditure in Wartime.* S.l.: s.n.

——. 1917. *The Health of Working Girls: A Handbook for Welfare Supervisors and Others.* London: Blackie and Son.

——. 1918. *The Abolition of the Poor law.* Fabian Tract, no 185. London: Fabian Society.

——. 1918. The End of the Poor Law. In M. Phillips, ed., *Women and the Labour Party.* London: F. Matthews. Reprinted London: Headley Bros. Ltd, 1919.

——. 1918. Preface. In A. E. Metcalf, ed. *Woman: A Citizen.* London: Allen & Unwin.

——. 1919. *The Wages of Men and Women: Should They Be Equal?* London: Fabian Society.

——. 1919. Minority Report. In Sir James Richard Atkin, ed. *War Cabinet Committee on Women in Industry.* London: H.M. Stationery Office.

——. 1921. The Co-operative Movement of Great Britain and Its Recent Developments. *International Labour Review* (November).

——. 1926. *My Apprenticeship.* London: Longmans.

——. 1928. *The Discovery of the Consumer.* Self and Society Booklets, no. 3. London: Ernest Benn Ltd.

——. 1928. *The English Poor Law, Will It Endure?* Sidney Ball lecture, November 21, 1927. London: Milford, Oxford University Press.

——. 1931. *A New Reform Bill.* Fabian Tract, no. 236. London: Fabian Society.

——. 1933. Vladimir Ilyich. *New Statesman and Nation* 6(133) (September 9): 301–.

——. 1935. Soviet Communism. *New Statesman and Nation* 9(211) (March 9): 322–.

——. 1938. Individual Liberty in the USSR. *Soviet Russia Today* 7(7) (October): 8–.

——. 1938. A New Civilization. *Soviet Russia Today* 7(2) (April): 11–.

——. 1940. A Vital Discovery in the Social Sciences. *Soviet Russia Today* 9(2) (June): 8–.

Webb, Beatrice Potter and Sidney [James] Webb. 1894/1896/1902/1911/1920/1926/1935. *The History of Trade Unionism.* London and New York: Longmans, Green & Co. Reprinted London: printed by the authors for the Amalgamated Society of Engineers, 1898; London: Chiswick Press, 1912; Basingstoke: Palgrave Macmillan, 2003.

——. 1896. Arbitration in Labour Disputes. *Nineteenth Century* 40 (November): 743–58.

——. 1896. The Method of Collective Bargaining. *Economic Journal* 6(21) (March): 1–29.

——. 1896. Der Normalarbeitstag und die englischen Gewerkschaften. *Archiv für soziale Gesetzgebung und Statistik* 9: 440–.

——. 1896. Primitive Democracy in British Trade Unionism. *Political Science Quarterly* 11(3) (September): 397–432.

——. 1896. Representative Institutions in British Trade Unionism. *Political Science Quarterly* 11(4) (December): 640–71.

——. 1896. The Standard Rate. *Economic Journal* 6(23) (September): 356–88.

——. 1897/1902/1914/1920/1926. *Industrial Democracy*. 2 vols. London and New York: Longmans, Green & Co. Reprinted 2003, Basingstoke: Palgrave Macmillan.

——. 1897. Die englischen Gewerkvereine nach ihrem wirtschaftlichen Wert. *Archiv für soziale Gesetzgebung und Statistik* 11: 323–.

——. 1897. Die Stellung der britischen Gewerkvereine gegenüber der Einführung neuer Arbeitsmethoden. *Archiv für soziale Gesetzgebung und Statistik* 10: 83–.

——. 1897. Die theoretische Basis der britischen Gewerkvereine. *Archiv für soziale Gesetzgebung und Statistik* 11: 1–.

——. 1898/1902/1906/1920. *Problems of Modern Industry.* London and New York: Longmans, Green & Co. Reprinted 2003, Basingstoke: Palgrave Macmillan.

——. 1903. *The History of Liquor Licensing in England, Principally from 1700 to 1830.* London and New York: Longmans, Green & Co.

——. 1904. The Assize of Bread. *Economic Journal* 14(2): 196–218.

——. 1906–29. *English Local Government from the Revolution to the Municipal Corporations Act.* 9 vols. London and New York: Longmans, Green. Reprinted, with additional essays by B. Keith-Lucas, G. J. Ponsonby, L. Radzinowicz, and W. A. Robson, London: Frank Cass, 1963.

——. 1909. *The Break-up of the Poor Law. Part One of the Minority Report of the Poor Law Commission.* London and New York: Longmans, Green & Co.

——. 1909. *The Public Organisation of the Labour Market: Being Part Two of the Minority Report of the Poor Law Commission.* London and New York: Longmans, Green & Co.

——. 1910. *English Poor Law Policy.* London and New York: Longmans, Green, & Co.

——. 1910. *The State and the Doctor.* London and New York: Longmans, Green & Co.

——. 1911. *The Prevention of Destitution.* London and New York: Longmans, Green & Co.

——. 1911. *The Sphere of Voluntary Agencies in the Prevention of Destitution.* London: National Committee for the Prevention of Destitution.

——. 1920. *A Constitution for the Socialist Commonwealth of Great Britain.* London and New York: Longmans, Green & Co.

——. 1921. *The Consumers' Co-operative Movement.* London and New York: Longmans, Green & Co. Reprinted by the authors for cooperative students, Edinburgh: R. & R. Clark, 1930.

——. 1922. Book Review of "Consumers' Co-operative Movement." *International Co-operative Bulletin* 15: 22–.

——. 1923. *Decay of Capitalist Civilisation.* Westminster, London: Fabian Society and G. Allen and Unwin. Reprinted 1970, Freeport, N.Y.: Books for Libraries Press.

——. 1930. English Local Government: English Poor Law History. *Diritto del lavoro* 4(1): 223–.

——. 1932. *Methods of Social Study*. London and New York: Longmans, Green. Reprinted 1975, Cambridge: Cambridge University Press.

——. 1935. *Soviet Communism: A New Civilisation?*, vol. 1: *The Constitution*; vol. 2: *Social Trends in Soviet Communism*. London and New York: Longmans, Green & Co. Reprinted New York: Scribner's Sons, 1937. 2nd ed., London: V. Gollancz, 1937; New York: Scribner, 1938.

——. 1936. *Is Soviet Communism a New Civilisation?* London: Left Review.

——. 1936. *Soviet Communism: Dictatorship or Democracy?* London: Left Review.

Webb, [Beatrice Potter] Mrs. Sidney, B. L. Hutchins, and the Fabian Society. 1909. *Socialism and National Minimums*. Fabian Socialist Series, no. 6. London: A. C. Fifield.

Webb, Catherine. 1891. Can Women Raise Their Husbands' Wages? *Trade Unionist* (October 3, October 10). Reprinted Manchester, UK: Co-operative Printing Society.

——. 1892. *The Women's Guild and Store Life*. London: Women's Co-operative Guild.

——. 1894. *Should Co-operative Employees Understand the Principles of the Movement, and If So, How Are They to Be Taught?* Manchester, UK: Women's Co-operative Guild.

——. 1896. *The Machinery of the Cooperative Movement*. Manchester, UK: Co-operative Union.

——. 1897. *High Dividends and What They Mean*. Women's Co-operative Guild. Manchester, UK: Co-operative Printing Society.

——. 1903. An Unpopular Industry. *Nineteenth Century* (June).

——, ed. 1904. *Industrial Co-operation: The Story of a Peaceful Revolution. Being an Account of the History, Theory, and Practice of the Co-operative Movement in Great Britain and Ireland*. Manchester: Co-operative Union Ltd. Tenth edition, 1926.

——. 1927. *The Woman with the Basket; the History of the Women's Co-operative Guild, 1883–1927*. Manchester: Co-operative Wholesale Society's Printing Works.

Webb, Elizabeth Yates [Mrs. Roy Veatch]. 1929. The Development of the Textile Industry in North Carolina. Ph.D. thesis, Robert Brookings.

——. 1932. Cotton Manufacturing and State Regulation in North Carolina, 1861–65. *North Carolina Historical Review* 9(2) (April): 117–37.

——. 1939. A Lincoln Penny – and Our Thoughts. *Crisis* 46 (May): 142–.

Webb, Ursula. *See* Hicks, Ursula K.

Weber, Marianne [Schnitzer]. 1906. *Beruf und Ehe: Die Beteiligung der Frau an der Wissenschaft. Zwei Vorträge*. Gerritsen Women's History, no. 3046. Berlin-Schöneberg: Buchverlag der "Hilfe."

——. 1907. *Ehefrau und Mutter in der Rechtsentwicklung*. Tübingen: Mohr.

——. 1912. Autorität und Autonomie in der Ehe. *Logos* 3: 103–.

——. 1913. Die Frau und die objektive Kultur. *Logos* 4: 328–.

——. 1919. *Frauenfragen und Frauengedanken: Gesammelte Aufsatze*. Tübingen: J. C. B. Mohr.

——. 1925. *Fichte's Sozialismus und sein Verhältnis zur marx'schen Doktrin. Volkswirtschaftliche Abhandlungen der badischen Hochschulen*, 4. Band, 3. Heft. Tübingen: J. C. B. Mohr (Paul Siebeck).

Weber, Mathilde Walz. 1884. *Die Mission der Hausfrau.* Herzberg: C. F. Simon.

——. 1888. Ein Besuch in Zürich bei den weiblichen Studierenden der Medizin; ein Beitrag zur Klärung der Frage des Frauenstudiums. In *Die Frau in gemeinnützigen Leben.* Stuttgart: W. Rohlhammer.

——. 1893. *Ärztinnen für Frauenkrankheiten eine ethische und sanitäre Notwendigkeit.* Berlin, L. Oehmigke.

——. 1894. *Warum fehlt es an Diakonissinnen und Pflegerinnen?* Berlin: L. Oehmigke.

——. 1895. *Unsere Hausbeamtinnen; Stüssen Hausdamen, Gesellschafterinnen, Kinderfräulein. Mitteilungen über Zwecke und Ziele des neuen Vereins für Hausbeamtinnen.* Berlin: L. Oehmigke.

Webster, Cynthia. 1896. Indian Girls as Teachers. *Red Man* 13 (March): 2–.

Wedgwood, Julia. 1869. Female Suffrage, Considered Chiefly with Regard to Its Indirect Results. In Josephine Butler, ed., *Woman's Work and Woman's Culture, a Series of Essays.* London: Macmillan.

——. 1872. Female Suffrage in Its Influence on Married Life. *Contemporary Review* 20 (August): 360–70.

——. 1873. *The Political Claims of Women.* London National Society for Women's Suffrage. London: W. Wilfred Head.

Weiss, Gertrude Schmidt. 1933. History of Labor Legislation in Wisconsin. Ph.D. thesis, University of Wisconsin–Madison (economics).

Weiss, Gertrude Schmidt, Marie Waite, Louise Stitt, and Stella Stewart. 1938. *Factors to Be Considered in Preparing Minimum-wage Budgets for Women.* Miscellaneous Publication, U.S. Department of Agriculture. Washington: U.S. Department of Agriculture.

Weiss, Gertrude Schmidt, Kathryn Elizabeth Cronister, and Day Monroe. 1939. *Family Income and Expenditures: Plains and Mountain Region. Part 1: Family Income.* United States Department of Agriculture, Miscellaneous Publication, no. 345. Washington: U.S. Government Printing Office.

Weiss, Gertrude S. Coauth. *See* Brady, Dorothy S.

Welch, Mrs. Margaret. 1894. Newspaper Work for Women. *Journal of Social Science* 32 (November): 110–16.

Wells, Emilie Louise. 1911. Book Review of "The Economic Position of Women." *American Economic Review* 2 (June): 363–5.

——. 1912. Woman and Child Wage-earners in the United States. *American Economic Review* 2 (June): 436–42.

——. 1915. Book Review of "Report of the Bureau of Labor on the Conditions of Wage-earning Women and Girls." *American Economic Review* 5 (September): 615–17.

Wells[-Barnett], Ida B. 1892. *Southern Horrors. Lynch Law in All Its Phases.* New York: New York Age Print. Reprinted in Trudier Harris, ed., *Selected Works of Ida B. Wells-Barnett.* New York and Oxford: Oxford University Press, 1991; and in Jacqueline Jones Royster, ed., *Southern Horrors and Other Writings: The*

Anti-Lynching Campaign of Ida B. Wells, 1892–1900. Boston: Bedford Books, 1997.

——. 1895. *A Red Record. Tabulated Statistics and Alleged Causes of Lynchings in the U.S., 1892–1893–1894*. Chicago: Donohue & Henneberry. Reprinted in Trudier Harris, ed., *Selected Works of Ida B. Wells-Barnett*. New York and Oxford: Oxford University Press, 1991; and in Jacqueline Jones Royster, ed., *Southern Horrors and Other Writings: The Anti-Lynching Campaign of Ida B. Wells, 1892–1900*. Boston: Bedford Books, 1997.

——. 1920. *The Arkansas Race Riot*. Chicago: [Hume Job Print].

Wells[-Barnett], Ida B. and Ferdinand Barnett. 1893. *The Reason Why the Colored American Is Not in the World's Columbian Exposition*. Chicago: published by the author. Reprinted, ed. Robert W. Rydell, Urbana: University of Illinois Press, 1999.

Wells, Kate Gannett. 1880. The Transitional American Woman. *Atlantic Monthly* 46 (December): 817–23.

——. 1880. Women in Organizations. *Atlantic Monthly* 46 (September): 360–8.

——. 1881. Caste in American Society. *Atlantic Monthly* 48 (December): 823–31.

——. 1890. Some Facts Concerning State Aid to Higher Education in New England. *New England Magazine* 8(4) (June): 469–75.

——. 1891. Why More Girls Do Not Marry. *North American Review* 152 (February): 175–82.

——. 1893. The Servant Girl of the Future. *North American Review* 157 (December): 716–21.

Wendt, Laura. 1931. *On Certain Frequency Functions Involving the Absolute Values of Deviations*. M.A. thesis, University of Texas at Austin.

——. 1938. Census Classifications and Social Security Categories. *Social Security Bulletin* 1(4) (April): 3–.

——. 1940. *State Difference in Income Distribution: Figures Based on the Study of Consumer Purchases*. Washington: U.S. Social Security Board.

Wentworth, Edna C. 1939. Book Review of "Levels of Living in the Ilocos Region" by Horacio Lava. *Pacific Affairs* 12(2) (June): 233–.

Wentworth, Edna Louise Clark. 1922. History of the Controversy between Labor and Capital in the Slaughtering and Meat Packing Industries in Chicago. M.A. thesis, University of Chicago (sociology).

——. 1928. *The Changing Uses of Textile Fibers in Clothing and Household Articles*. U.S. Department of Agriculture, Miscellaneous Publication, no. 31. Washington: U.S. Department of Agriculture.

Wergeland, Agnes [Mathilde]. 1900. Slavery in Germanic Society during the Middle Ages. Part I. *Journal of Political Economy* 9(1) (December): 98–120.

——. 1901. Graham on English Political Philosophy. *Dial, a Monthly Review and Index of Current Literature* 30: 336.

——. 1901. Slavery in Germanic Society during the Middle Ages. Part II. *Journal of Political Economy* 9(3) (June): 398–422.

——. 1902. Slavery in Germanic Society during the Middle Ages. Part III. *Journal of Political Economy* 10(2) (March): 230–54.

——. 1903. History of the Working Classes in France: Mediaeval Period. *Journal of Political Economy* 11(4) (September): 568–93.

——. 1904. History of the Working Classes in France: Renaissance and Modern Period. *Journal of Political Economy* 12(2) (March): 225–53.

——. 1905. History of the Working Classes in France: 1789–1870. *Journal of Political Economy* 13(3) (June): 419–48.

——. 1912. *Amerika, og andre digte.* Decorah, Iowa: B. Anundsen Publishing Co.

——. 1914. *Efterladte digte.* Minneapolis, Minn.: Free Church Book Concern.

——. 1916. *History of the Working Classes in France: A Review of Levasseur's Histoire des classes ouvrières et de l'industrie en France avant 1789.* Chicago: University of Chicago Press. Reprinted from the *Journal of Political Economy* 13(3) (June 1905).

——. 1916. *Slavery in Germanic Society during the Middle Ages.* Chicago: University of Chicago Press.

Werner, [Dr.] Alice. 1898. Locusts [in Africa]. *Longman's* 32 (August): 309–17.

——. 1906. *The Natives of British Central Africa.* Series: Native Races of the British Empire. London: A. Constable & Co.

——. 1917. The So-called Black Peril in South Africa. *Crisis* 14 (September): 249–.

——. 1928. The Voice of Africa. *Africa* 1(2): 249.

——. 1932. African Economics and African Administration. *Journal of the African Society* 31(124) (July): 245–.

——. 1934. The Best of a Bad Job. *African Observer* 1(5) (September): 67–.

——. Coauth. *See* Colenso, Harriette E.

Wertheimer, Mildred Salz. 1924. The Pan-German League, 1890–1914. Ph.D. thesis, Columbia University (history).

——. 1932. Appendix: Balance of Germany's Commodity Trade. *Foreign Policy Reports* 7(26) (March 2): 475.

——. 1932. Appendix: Foreign Investments in Germany (end of July 1931). *Foreign Policy Reports* 7(26) (March 2): 475.

——. 1932. Appendix: Germany's Balance of International Payments. *Foreign Policy Reports* 7(26) (March 2): 475.

——. 1932. Appendix: Inter-allied Payments Due to the United States during the Fiscal Year 1932. *Foreign Policy Reports* 7(26) (March 2): 474.

——. 1932. Appendix: Receipts and Expenditures of German Public Administration, 1926–1931. *Foreign Policy Reports* 7(26) (March 2): 475.

——. 1932. Attempts at Reparation Settlement. *Foreign Policy Reports* 7(26) (March 2): 456.

——. 1932. Attempts to Curtail Borrowing Unsuccessful. *Foreign Policy Reports* 7(26) (March 2): 460.

——. 1932. Budgetary Deficit and Public Debt Increase. *Foreign Policy Reports* 7(26) (March 2): 462.

——. 1932. The Crisis in Germany. *Foreign Policy Reports* 7(26) (March 2): 465.

——. 1932. The Effects of the Depression on Germany. *Foreign Policy Reports* 7(26) (March 2): 461.

——. 1932. Efforts Made to Balance the Budget. *Foreign Policy Reports* 7(26) (March 2): 462.
——. 1932. Foreign Exchange Transactions Centralized. *Foreign Policy Reports* 7(26) (March 2): 468.
——. 1932. France. *Foreign Policy Reports* 7(26) (March 2): 473.
——. 1932. German Borrowing Abroad. *Foreign Policy Reports* 7(26) (March 2): 457.
——. 1932. German Expenditures on Public and Private Works. *Foreign Policy Reports* 7(26) (March 2): 459.
——. 1932. Germany. *Foreign Policy Reports* 7(26) (March 2): 472.
——. 1932. Germany's Balance of International Payments. *Foreign Policy Reports* 7(26) (March 2): 461.
——. 1932. Great Britain. *Foreign Policy Reports* 7(26) (March 2): 473.
——. 1932. High Interest Rates Attract Foreign Capital. *Foreign Policy Reports* 7(26) (March 2): 458.
——. 1932. The Hoover Moratorium. *Foreign Policy Reports* 7(26) (March 2): 464.
——. 1932. International Attempts to Assist Germany. *Foreign Policy Reports* 7(26) (March 2): 466.
——. 1932. Introduction. *Foreign Policy Reports* 7(26) (March 2): 455.
——. 1932. Italy. *Foreign Policy Reports* 7(26) (March 2): 473.
——. 1932. Lausanne Conference Summoned for June 1932. *Foreign Policy Reports* 7(26) (March 2): 473.
——. 1932. Laval and Hoover Discuss Inter-governmental Obligations. *Foreign Policy Reports* 7(26) (March 2): 470.
——. 1932. Provisional "Standstill Agreement." *Foreign Policy Reports* 7(26) (March 2): 467.
——. 1932. Rationalization of Industry. *Foreign Policy Reports* 7(26) (March 2): 460.
——. 1932. Reich Takes Measures Toward "Self-Help." *Foreign Policy Reports* 7(26) (March 2): 466.
——. 1932. Report of the Young Plan Advisory Committee. *Foreign Policy Reports* 7(26) (March 2): 471.
——. 1932. The Second "Standstill Agreement." *Foreign Policy Reports* 7(26) (March 2): 469.
——. 1932. United States. *Foreign Policy Reports* 7(26) (March 2): 471.
——. 1932. Vulnerable Position of the Reichsbank. *Foreign Policy Reports* 7(26) (March 2): 463.
——. 1934. Economic Structure of the Third Reich. *Foreign Policy Reports* X(15) (September 26).
Wescott, Dorothy. 1931. Production. *American Journal of Sociology* 36(6) (May): 900–.
——. 1933. The Volume of Industrial Production in the United States for 1932. *Review of Economics and Statistics* 15 (February): 36–44.
——. 1934. Indexes of Industrial Production for Various Countries. *Review of Economics and Statistics* 16 (December): 256–60.

——. 1939. Review of the First Quarter of 1939. *Review of Economic Statistics* 21(2) (May): 9–96.

——. 1939. Review of the Second Quarter of 1939. *Review of Economic Statistics* (August): 131–40.

Wescott, Dorothy and W. L. Crum. 1938. Review of the Second Quarter of 1938. *Review of Economic Statistics* 20(3) (August): 142–8.

——. 1938. Review of the Third Quarter of 1938. *Review of Economic Statistics* 20(4) (November): 193–200.

——. 1939. Review of the Year 1938. *Review of Economic Statistics* 21(1) (February): 40–8.

Wescott, Dorothy and R. A. Gordon. 1937. Review of the First Quarter of 1937. *Review of Economic Statistics* 19(2) (May): 100–8.

Wescott, Dorothy, W. L. Crum, and R. A. Gordon. 1937. Review of the Third Quarter of 1937. *Review of Economic Statistics* 19(4) (November): 203–12.

——. 1938. Review of the First Quarter of 1938. *Review of Economic Statistics* 20(2) (May): 89–96.

——. 1938. Review of the Year 1937. *Review of Economic Statistics* 20(1) (February): 43–52.

West, Mary Allen. 1891. Protective Agency for Women and Children. *Chautauquan* 13 (April/September): 511–.

West, Miriam E[sther]. 1929. *Employment Indexes in the United States and Canada.* New York: American Statistical Association Committee on Governmental Labor Statistics.

——. 1930. An Historical Study of the Theories and Policies of Stabilization of the Value of Money. Ph.D. thesis, University of Wisconsin–Madison (economics).

——. 1939. *Productivity and Employment in Selected Industries.* W.P.A., National Research Project. National Bureau of Economic Research Report, no. N–2. Philadelphia: W.P.A. National Research Project.

West, Miriam E. and Katharine Frances Ball. 1920. *Household Arithmetic.* Philadelphia and London: Lippincott.

West, Rebecca. 1918. Women as Brainworkers. In M. Phillips, ed., *Women and the Labour Party.* London: F. Matthews.

Weston, Janet Louise. 1927. Relations between Variations in Income Tax Rates and in Reported Individual Incomes. Ph.D. thesis, Leland Stanford Junior University.

——. 1934. Farm Real Estate Taxes Since 1913. *Bulletin of the National Tax Association* 20(3) (December): 78–.

Wetherell, Jane J. 1890/1. Railroad Passenger Fares in Hungary. *Annals of the American Academy of Political and Social Science* 1 (July/June): 103–.

——. 1890/1. Railroad Passenger Tariffs in Austria. *Annals of the American Academy of Political and Social Science* 1 (July/June): 462–.

Wettstein-Adelt, Minna. 1893. *3 ½ Monate Fabrik-Arbeiterin.* Berlin: J. Laiser.

Wheeler, A. Emily F. 1886. Business Education for Girls. *Chautauquan* 7 (October): 3–.

Wheeler, Anna Doyle. 1830. The Rights of Women. *The British Co-operator* (April).

——. 1833. Letter by "Vlasta" to *The Crisis* (May 13). Reprinted in Maria Mulvey Roberts and Tamae Mizuta, eds., *Controversies in the History of British Feminism,* Vol. 4: *The Rebels, Irish Feminists.* London: Routledge/Thoemmes, 1995.

——. 1833. Letter to the Editor of *The Crisis* (August 31). Reprinted in Maria Mulvey Roberts and Tamae Mizuta, eds., *Controversies in the History of British Feminism,* Vol. 4: *The Rebels, Irish Feminists.* London: Routledge/Thoemmes, 1995.

Wheeler, Marion Etta. Coauth. *See* Bercaw, Louise Oldham; Herb, Mamie Idella.

Wheeler, Miriam. 1895. Labor Chant. *American Federationist* 1(12) (February): 281.

Wheelock, Jemima. 1890. A Woman's Work in the World. *Red Man* 10 (May): 7–.

Whitbeck, Florence. 1927. A Geographical Interpretation of Porto Rico. Ph.D. thesis, University of Wisconsin–Madison (geography).

——. 1928. New York Barge Canal – Expectations and Realizations. *Economic Geography* 4(2) (April): 196–206.

Whitcomb, Carrie Niles. 1896. Training-schools for Domestic Servants. *Century* 52 (May/October): 795.

Whitcomb, Emeline S. 1931. *Homemaking Education, Biennial Survey of Education in the United States, 1928–1930,* vol. 1. Bulletin no. 20. Washington: U.S. Government Printing Office.

White, Amber Blanco. 1934. *The Nationalisation of Banking.* London: Allen & Unwin and the Fabian Society.

White, Frances Emily. 1875. Woman's Place in Nature. *Popular Science Monthly* 6 (January).

White, Sallie Elizabeth Joy. 1899. *Business Openings for Girls.* New York and Akron, Ohio: Werner Co.

Whitehead, Celia Baldwin. 1896. Representative Women on Social Problems: Is the Single Tax Enough? (Symposium): Henry George and Nehemiah. *Arena* 15 (January): 196–201.

Whiteman, Mary P. 1890s. Saleswomen in the Great Stores. *Cosmopolitan*: [79]–85.

Whiting, Eleanor. 1898. Women's Work and Wages. *Lippincott's Magazine* 61 (May): 670–7.

Whitley, Margaret. Coauth. *See* Bulley, A. Amy.

Whitney, Anice L[add]. 1917. Clubs, Gymnasium, and Recreation Grounds for Employees. *United States Bureau of Labor Statistics, Monthly Review* 5 (July/December): 1,035–46.

——. 1917. Lunch Rooms for Employees. *United States Bureau of Labor Statistics, Monthly Review* 5 (July/December): 1,279–87.

——. 1917. Medical, Hospital, and Surgical Treatment for Employees. *United States Bureau of Labor Statistics, Monthly Review* 5 (July/December): 471–9.

——. 1917. Rest and Recreation Rooms and Rest Periods for Employees. *United States Bureau of Labor Statistics, Monthly Review* 5 (July/December): 789–94.
——. 1918. Administration and Costs of Industrial Betterment for Employees. *United States Bureau of Labor Statistics, Monthly Review* 6 (January/June): 691–7.
——. 1918. Communal Kitchens in European Countries. *United States Bureau of Labor Statistics, Monthly Review* 6 (January/June): 1,420–5.
——. 1918. Establishment Disability Funds, Pension Funds, and Group Insurance for Employees. *United States Bureau of Labor Statistics, Monthly Review* 6 (January/June): 444–56.
——. 1918. Social and Educational Advantages for Employees. *United States Bureau of Labor Statistics, Monthly Review* 6 (January/June): 206–12.
——. 1919. Development of Shop Committee Systems. *Monthly Labor Review* 9(5) (November): 225–33.
——. 1921. Japan – Labor Unrest. *Monthly Labor Review* 13 (July/December): 53–63.
——. 1921. Labor Unrest in Belgium. *Monthly Labor Review* 12 (January/June): 147–54.
——. 1921. Labor Unrest in France. *Monthly Labor Review* 12 (January/June): 188–200.
——. 1921. Scandinavian Countries and Finland – Labor Unrest. *Monthly Labor Review* 13 (July/December): 20–36.
——. 1923. Health and Welfare Activities in the Government Printing Office. *Monthly Labor Review* 16 (January/June): 1–13.
——, transl. 1925. Belgian Law on Insurance of Workers against Old Age and Premature Death. *Monthly Labor Review* 20 (January/June): 155–7.
——. 1928. *Health and Recreation Activities in Industrial Establishments, 1926*. Washington: U.S. Bureau of Labor Statistics.
——. 1934. *Operation of Unemployment Insurance Systems in the United States and Foreign Countries*. Washington: U.S. Government Printing Office, Bureau of Labor Statistics, U.S. Department of Labor.
——. 1934. Operation of Unemployment-benefit Plans in the United States up to 1934, Part 2: Trade-union Plans. *Monthly Labor Review* 39(1) (July): 1–.
Whitney, Caroline. 1929. Mr. Shafer on the Equation of Exchange and the Business Cycle. *American Economic Review* 19(1) (March): 76–7.
——. 1932. Book Review of "Brokers' Loans" by Lewis H. Haney, Lyman S. Logan, and Henry S. Gavens. *Political Science Quarterly* 47: 444–.
——. 1932. The Equation of Exchange and the Price Stabilization Problem. *American Economic Review* 22(2) (June): 231–40.
——. 1934. *Experiments in Credit Control: The Federal Reserve System*. New York: Columbia University Press; London: P. S. King & Son.
——. 1934. Experiments in Credit Control: The Federal Reserve System. Ph.D. thesis, Columbia University (economics).
——. 1939. *What Price Milk?* New York: Caroline Whitney Memorial Fund.
Whitney, Jessamine Sophia. 1934. *Death Rates by Occupation*. New York: National Tuberculosis Association.

Whittelsey, Sarah Scovill, Ph.D.. 1900. *Massachusetts Labour Legislation. An Historical and Critical Study*. Philadelphia: American Academy of Political and Social Science.

——. 1901. Massachusetts Labor Legislation. *Annals of the American Academy of Political and Social Science* 17, supplement (January).

——. 1902. Tendencies of Factory Legislation and Inspection in the United States. *Annals of the American Academy of Political and Social Science* 20: 235.

——. 1902/3. Women and the Study of Social Sciences in Collegiate Training. *Education; a Monthly Magazine Devoted to the Science, Art, Philosophy and Literature of Education* 23: 98.

Whitton, Charlotte E[lizabeth]. 1922. *Some Aspects of the Immigration Problem*. Toronto: College Press, Ltd. for the Social Service Council of Canada, Committee on Industrial Life and Immigration.

——. 1923/4. The Immigration Problem for Canada. *Queen's Quarterly* 31 (August/May): 388–.

——. 1924. *The Immigration Problem for Canada*. Kingston: Jackson Press.

——. 1936. *Social Work at the League of Nations*. Canadian Welfare Council Publication, no. 81. Ottawa: Canadian Welfare Council.

——. 1939. Controlling the Public Welfare Bill. In H. M. Cassidy and Charlotte Whitton, *Facing up to Public Welfare Costs and Services*. Ottawa: Canadian Welfare Council.

Whitton, Charlotte and Elizabeth King. 1928. *Report of the Royal Commission Appointed by Order-in-council Number 747–28 to Inquire into the Administration of the Child Welfare Division of the Department of Health and Public Welfare, 1928*. Ottawa: Royal Commission to Inquire into the Administration of the Child Welfare Division.

Whitwell, Catherine Vale. 1819. *An Address to Mothers in the British Empire in Which a Scheme of Simplicity and Economy Is Illustrated, and the Establishment of a Free School for the Daughters of Professional Men Who Have Lost Their Property Recommended*. London: G. Wilson.

Widtsoe, Rose Homer. 1922. Studies in the Family Budget. M.A. thesis, University of California.

——. 1931. An Inquiry into Food Legislation: Federal and State of California. Ph.D. thesis, University of California (economics).

Wiener, Miriam. 1931. *Jobs, Jobs, Jobs: A Simple Method of Correcting Our Economic System, Creating Prosperity, Eliminating Unemployment and Poverty, and Reducing Crime, Disease, and Radical Activities*. New York: Golden Era Publishing Co.

Wiese, Mildred Janovsky and Ruth Reticker. 1930. *The Modern Worker*. New York: Macmillan.

Wigder, Clara F. 1925. Farm-mortgage Interest Rates. *Land Economics* 1 (January): 102–17.

Wigley, Mrs., S. S. 1880. *Workers at Home. A Companion to "Our Home Work."* London: James Nisbet & Co.

Wilcox, Ella Wheeler. 1890. Competition between Men and Women in Business. *Chautauquan* 12 (November): 233–.

Wilhelmi, Hedwig Henrich. 1890. *Frauenrecht ist Menschenrecht.* Cologne: Franz Greven.

——. 1893. *Das Recht der Frauen zum Studium und ihre Befähigung für alle Berufsarten.* Munich: Majer & Finckh.

Wilke, Ernestine. 1938. Conference on Employment and Payroll Statistics. *Journal of the American Statistical Association* 33(203) (September): 575–9.

——. Coauth. *See* Givens, Meredith Bruner.

Wilkie, Harriet Cushman. 1894. Russian Cottage Industries. *Chautauquan* 19 (April): 76–.

Wilkins, Louisa Jebb [Mrs. R.]. 1906. *How Landlords Can Create Small Holdings: Some Examples.* London: Murray.

——. 1906. *The Working of the Small Holdings Act, with Suggestions for Its Amendment.* London: Murray.

——. 1907. *The Small Holdings of England: A Survey of Various Existing Systems.* London: Murray.

——. 1907. The English Aspect of the Small Holding Question. *Economic Journal* 17 (June): 171–9.

——. 1910. *The Small Holdings Controversy: Tenancy v. Ownership.* London: King.

——. 1911. Book Review of "La Crise et l'évolution de l'agriculture en Angleterre de 1875 à nos jours" by Pierre Besse. *Economic Journal* 21: 86–.

——. 1915. *The Work of Educated Women in Horticulture and Agriculture.* London: J. Truscott and Son, Ltd. Reprinted as *The Training and Employment of Educated Women on Horticulture and Agriculture.* Westminster, London: Women's Farm and Garden Union, 1916.

——. 1920. *Report of Sub-committee Appointed to Consider the Employment of Women in Agriculture in England and Wales.* Board of Agriculture and Fisheries. London: H.M. Stationery Office.

Wilkinson, Ellen Cicely. 1929. *Clash, a Novel.* London: G. G. Harrap & Co. Ltd.

——. 1930. Towards Utopia – IV. Can Men and Women Be Really Equal? *Listener* 3(64) (April 2): 587–.

——. 1939. *The Town That Was Murdered – The Life-story of Jarrow.* London: Gollancz.

Wilkinson, Ellen, W. J. Mabon Evans, W. M. V. Thomas, and G. H. Jones. 1936. Marriage on the Dole. *Listener* 15(366) (January 15): 102–.

Wilkinson, Jeannette G. 1885. The Inspection of Workshops in London. By a Working Woman. *Charity Organisation Review* 9 (September 15): 380–.

Wilkinson, Lily Gair. 1905?. *Revolutionary Socialism and the Woman's Movement.* Edinburgh: Socialist Labour Party.

——. 1914. *Woman's Freedom.* London: Freedom Press.

Willard, Frances E[lizabeth]. 1885/6. Women in Journalism. *Chautauquan* 6 (October/July): 576.

——. 1889. An Interview with Edward Bellamy. *Our Day* 4(22) (October 10).

——. 1892. The Coming Brotherhood. *Arena* 6 (August): 317–24.

Willard, Frances Elizabeth, ed., with Helen M. Winslow and Sallie E. J. White. 1897. *Occupations for Women: A Book of Practical Suggestions for the Material*

Advancement, the Mental and Physical Development, and the Moral and Spiritual Uplift of Women. Cooper Union, N.Y.: Success Co.

Willeford, Mary Bristow. 1932. Income and Health in Remote Rural Areas: A Study of 400 Families in Leslie County, Kentucky. Ph.D. thesis, Columbia University (health sciences).

Willett, Mabel Hurd. 1902. *Employment of Women in the Clothing Trade.* New York: Columbia University Press. Reprinted New York: AMS Press, 1968.

——. 1902. Employment of Women in the Clothing Trade. Ph.D. thesis, Columbia University (economics, commerce-business).

Williams, Caroline E. 1877. *Protective and Provident Union among Women. A Paper Read at the Social Science Congress at Liverpool, October 1876.* London: Women's Protective and Provident League.

Williams, Constance. 1939. Industrious Idleness. *Aryan Path* 10(8) (August): 378–.

Williams, Constance Willard. Coauth. *See* Palmer, Gladys Louise.

Williams, Faith Moors. 1922. *The Economic Situation in Europe.* New York: Institute of International Education.

——. 1924. *The Food Manufacturing Industries in New York and Its Environs: Present Trends and Probable Future Developments.* New York: Regional Plan of New York and Its Environs.

——. 1924. The Food Manufacturing Industries in New York and Its Environs: Present Trends and Probable Future Developments. Ph.D. thesis, Columbia University (economics, agriculture).

——. 1929. The Measurement of the Demand for Food. *Journal of the American Statistical Association* 24 (September): 288–95.

——. 1934. Measuring Changes in Cost of Living of Federal Employees Living in Washington. *Monthly Labor Review* 38(3) (March): 511–.

——. 1935. *Studies of Family Living in the United States and Other Countries: An Analysis of Material and Method.* Washington: U.S. Department of Agriculture.

——. 1936. Food Consumption at Different Economic Levels. *Monthly Labor Review* 42(4) (April): 889–.

——. 1936. Money Disbursements of Wage Earners and Clerical Workers in 11 New Hampshire Communities. *Monthly Labor Review* 42(3) (March): 554–.

——. 1936. Money Disbursements of Wage Earners and Clerical Workers in Richmond Birmingham and New Orleans. *Monthly Labor Review* 42(5) (May): 1457–.

——. 1937. *Family Living in Knott County, Kentucky.* U.S. Department of Agriculture Technical Bulletin, no. 576. Washington: U.S. Department of Agriculture.

——. 1937. Methods of Measuring Variations in Family Expenditures. *Journal of the American Statistical Association* 32(197) (March): 40–6.

——. 1940. Factors to Be Considered in Measuring Intercity and Interregional Differences in Living Costs. *Journal of the American Statistical Association* 35 (September): 471–82.

Williams, Faith Moors and Helen Connolly. 1930. *Bibliography on Studies of Costs and Standards of Living in the United States.* Washington: U.S. Department of Agriculture, Bureau of Home Economics.

Williams, Faith Moors and Alice Hanson Jones. 1939. *Money Disbursements of Wage Earners and Clerical Workers in Five Cities in the Pacific Region, 1934–36*. U.S. Bureau of Labor Statistics Bulletin, no. 639. Washington: U.S. Government Printing Office.

——. 1939. *Money Disbursements of Wage Earners and Clerical Workers in Five Cities in the West North Central-Mountain Region, 1934–36*. U.S. Bureau of Labor Statistics Bulletin, no. 641. Washington: U.S. Government Printing Office.

——. 1939. *Money Disbursements of Wage Earners and Clerical Workers in the North Atlantic Region, 1934–36*. U.S. Bureau of Labor Statistics Bulletin, no. 637. Washington: U.S. Government Printing Office.

Williams, Faith Moors and Julia Etta Lockwood. 1930. *Economic Study of Food Consumed by Farm and Village Families in Central New York*. Ithaca, N.Y.: Cornell University Bulletin.

Williams, Faith M. and Gertrude Schmidt. 1935. New Study of Money Disbursements of Wage Earners and Lower-salaried Workers. *Monthly Labor Review* 40(4) (April): 861–.

Williams, Faith M., Gertrude Schmidt, and Frances Rice. 1934. Changes in Cost of Living of Federal Employees in the District of Columbia from 1928 to 1933. *Monthly Labor Review* 39(1) (July): 213–.

Williams, Faith Moors, Alice Hanson Jones, and Genevieve Beckwith Wimsatt. 1940. *Money Disbursement of Wage Earners and Clerical Workers in Eight Cities in the East North Central Region, 1934–36*. Washington: U.S. Government Printing Office.

Williams, Faith Moors. Coauth. *See* Schmidt, Gertrude; Stewart, Stella; Woodhouse, Margaret Chase Going.

Williams, Fannie Barrier. 1894. The Present Status and Intellectual Progress of Colored Women. Address delivered before the Congress of Representative Women, World's Columbian Exposition, 1893. In May Wright Sewall, ed., *The World's Congress of Representative Women*. Chicago: Rand, McNally & Co. Reprinted in Mary Jo Deegan, ed., *The New Woman of Color: The Collected Writings of Fannie Barrier Williams, 1893–1918*. DeKalb, Ill.: Northern Illinois University Press, 2002. Address sometimes is titled "The Intellectual Progress of the Colored Women of the U.S. since the Emancipation Proclamation."

——. 1900. The Colored Woman and her Part in Race Regeneration. In Booker T. Washington *et al.*, *A New Negro for a New Century: An Accurate and Up-to-date Record of the Upward Struggles of the Negro Race*. Chicago: American Publishing Co.

——. 1904. Industrial Education: Will It Solve the Negro Problem? *Colored American Magazine* 7(7) (July): 491–

——. 1904. The Smaller Economies. *Voice of the Negro* 1(5) (May).

——. 1904.The Club Movement Among Colored Women. *Voice of the Negro* 1(3) (March).

——. 1906. A New Method of Dealing With the Race Problem. *Voice of the Negro* 3(7) (July).

Williams, [Lady] Gertrude [Rosenblum]. 1923. *Social Aspects of Industrial Problems.* London: P. S. King.

——. 1923/4. Book Review of "Social Aspects of Industrial Problems" by C. D. Burns. *International Journal of Ethics* 34: 397–.

——. 1927. *A Synopsis of Economics.* London: Methuen.

——. 1936. *The State and the Standard of Living.* London: P. S. King.

——. 1938. Book Review of "Toward Industrial Peace in Australia" by O. De R. Foenander. *Economic Journal* 48(189) (March): 118–19.

——. 1938. A Study in the Industrial Career of Secondary School Boys. *Sociological Review* 30: 400–.

——. 1940. Book Review of "Unemployment and the Unemployed" by H. W. Singer. *Economic Journal* 50(198/199) (June/September): 290–2.

——. 1940. Book Review of "The Unemployment Services" by Polly Hill. *Economic Journal* 50(198/199) (June/September): 289–90.

——. 1940. Book Review of "The Voluntary Citizen" by Constance Braithwaite. *Economic Journal* 50(198/199) (June/September): 287–9.

Williams, Mrs. Harold. 1921. The Bolshevist Food System. *Nineteenth Century* (September).

Williams, Judith Blow. 1916. A Guide to Some Aspects of English Social History, 1750–1850. Ph.D. thesis, Columbia University (library science).

——. 1926. *A Guide to the Printed Materials for English Social and Economic History, 1750–1850.* New York: Columbia University Press.

——. 1930. Book Review of "The Coal Industry of the Eighteenth Century" by Thomas Southcliffe Ashton and Joseph Sykes. *Political Science Quarterly* 45: 464–.

——. 1931. Book Review of "England's Crisis" by Andre Siegfried. *Political Science Quarterly* 46: 603–.

——. 1932. Book Review of "The Cotton Trade and Industrial Lancashire, 1600–1780" by Alfred P. Wadsworth and Julia De Lacy Mann. *Political Science Quarterly* 47: 127–.

——. 1933. Book Review of "Economic Development in the Nineteenth Century" by L. C. A. Knowles. *Political Science Quarterly* 48: 315–.

——. 1935. Book Review of "British Regulation of the Colonial Iron Industry" by Arthur Cecil Bining. *Political Science Quarterly* 50: 156–.

——. 1935. The Development of British Trade with West Africa, 1750 to 1850. *Political Science Quarterly* 50: 194–.

——. 1935. The Establishment of British Commerce with Argentina. *Hispanic American Historical Review* 15: 43–.

——. 1937. Book Review of "Economic History of Europe" by Herbert Heaton. *Political Science Quarterly* 52: 465–.

——. 1938. Unemployment in the Learned Professions. *Cambridge Review* 59(1443) (January 14): 173–.

Williamson, Martha Burton. 1898/9. Some American Women in Science. *Chautauquan* 28 (October/March): 161–8, 361–8, and 465–73.

Wilson, Charlotte. 1886. *Social Democracy and Anarchism, [and] The Principles and Aims of Anarchists*. London: s.n. Reprinted (respectively) from *The Practical Socialist* (January) and *The Present Day* (July).

——. 1886. *Three Essays on Anarchism*. Reprinted Sanday, Orkney, UK: Over the Water and Cienfuegos Press, 1979.

——. 1886. *What Is Socialism?* Fabian Tract no. 4. London: Fabian Society.

——. Wrote articles for *Justice, The Practical Socialist*, and *The Present Day*.

Wilson, Eleanor Mary Carus. *See* Carus-Wilson, Eleanor Mary.

Wilson, Elizabeth Campbell. 1934. Unemployment Insurance and the Stability of Wages in Great Britain. *International Labour Review, Geneva* 30 (December): 767–96.

Wilson, Elizabeth Webb. 1934. The Distribution of Disability Costs. Ph.D. thesis, Radcliffe College (economics).

Wilson, Harriet E. 1859. *Our Nig: or, Sketches from the Life of a Free Black, in a Two Story White House, North, Showing that Slavery's Shadows Fall Even There. By "Our Nig."* Boston: George C. Rand and Avery. Reprinted, edited by Henry Louis Gates, Jr., New York: Random House, 1983.

Wilson, Margery Evelyn. 1919. The Growth of Child Labor Legislation in the United States. M.A. thesis, George Washington University.

Wilson, Martha Elizabeth. 1925. The Ocean Port of Chicago. Ph.D. thesis, London School of Economics.

Wilson, Mona. 1897. Parliamentary Papers. *Economic Journal* 7(28) (December): 638–9.

——. 1898. The Conference of Women Workers. *Economic Journal* 8(29) (March): 133–5.

——. 1898. Employers' Liability and Workmen's Compensation. *Westminster Review* 149 (February): 194–203.

——. 1899. *Our Industrial Laws; Working Women in Factories, Workshops, Shops and Laundries, and How to Help Them*. Ed. and with a preface by Mrs H. J. [May] Tennant. London: Duckworth.

——. 1901. Annual Report of the Chief Inspector of Factories and Workshops for the year 1900. [Notes and Memoranda] *Economic Journal* 11: 451–.

——. 1901. Contracting-out from the Workmen's Compensation Act. *Economic Journal* 11 (March): 23–30.

——. 1901. The Factory and the Workshops Acts Amendment Bill. *Economic Journal* 11 (June): 268–71.

——. 1901. Report from the Select Committee of the House of Lords on Early Closing of Shops [Notes and Memoranda] *Economic Journal* 11: 449–.

——. 1901/2. Book Review of "The Case for the Factory Acts" by Mrs. Sidney Webb. *International Journal of Ethics* 12: 522–.

——. 1902. Book Review of "Dangerous Trades" by Thomas Oliver. *Economic Journal* 12: 398–.

——. 1902. Book Review of "Labour Legislation, Labour Movements, Labour Leaders" by George Howell. *Economic Journal* 12: 393–.

——. 1938/9. Book Review of "Women Servants of the State" by Hilda Martindale C.B.E. *English* 2: 391–.

Wilson, Mona and Edward Goldie Howarth, eds. 1907. *West Ham: A Study in Social and Industrial Problems; Being the Report of the Outer London Inquiry Committee.* London: J. M. Dent & Co.

Wilson, Mona and Mary L. Walker. 1905. *Report on Housing and Industrial Conditions in Dundee.* Dundee, Scotland: John Long.

Wilson, Mona. Coauth. *See* Walker, Mary L.

Winder, Phyllis D. 1913. *The Public Feeding of Elementary School Children: A Review of the General Situation, and an Inquiry into Birmingham Experience.* W. J. Ashley, ed., with a preface by Norman Chamberlain. London: Longmans, Green.

Windett, Nancy. 1933. *Australia as Producer and Trader, 1920–1932.* New York: Oxford University Press.

——. 1935. Book Review of "Wheat and the AAA" by Joseph Stancliffe Davis. *Annals of the American Academy of Political and Social Science* 182 (November): 196–.

Winnemucca, Sarah. 1883. *Life among the Piutes: Their Wrongs and Claims.* Ed. Mrs Horace Mann. Boston: Privately printed. Reprinted Reno: University of Nevada Press, 1994.

Winslow, Emma Annie. 1918. *My Money Won't Reach: The Experience of 377 Self-supporting Families in New York City in Endeavoring to Make Their Incomes Provide the Essentials for Healthful Living.* New York: Committee on Home Economics, Charity Organization Society of the City of New York.

——. 1919. *Budget Planning in Social Case Work.* Bulletin no. 3. New York: Committee on Home Economics, Charity Organization Society of the City of New York.

——. 1920. The New Visiting Housekeeper: Her Training and Her Work. *Family* 1(3) (May): 11–.

——. 1922. Changes in Food Consumption among Working-class Families. *Economica* 2(6) (October): 256–71.

——. 1923. Budget Studies and the Measurement of Living Costs and Standards. Ph.D. thesis, London School of Economics.

——. 1933. Trends, Problems, and Policies in Relief Statistics. *Social Service Review* 7(1/4) (March/December): 11–.

——. 1937. *Trends in Different Types of Public and Private Relief in Urban Areas, 1929–1935.* U.S. Children's Bureau Publication, no. 237. Washington: U.S. Government Printing Office.

Winslow, Helen M. 1896. Some Newspaper Women. *Arena* 17 (December): 127–42.

Winslow, Mary Nelson. 1920. *Hours and Conditions of Work for Women in Industry in Virginia. March, 1920.* Bulletin of the Women's Bureau, no. 10. Washington: U.S. Government Printing Office.

——. 1921. *Health Problems of Women in Industry.* Washington: U.S. Women's Bureau.

——. 1921. *Some Effects of Legislation Limiting Hours of Work for Women.* Bulletin of the Women's Bureau, no. 15. Washington: U.S. Government Printing Office.

——. 1922. Medians of Women's Earnings in Four States. *Journal of the American Statistical Association* 18 (March): 106–8.

——. 1924. *Married Women in Industry*. Washington: U.S. Women's Bureau.

——. 1927/8. The Effect of Labor Laws for Women. *Personnel Journal* 6 (June/April): 242–.

——. 1928. *The Effects of Labor Legislation on the Employment Opportunities of Women.* U.S. Women's Bureau Bulletin, no. 65. Washington: U.S. Government Printing Office.

——. 1929. The Effects of Labor Legislation on Women's Work. *Annals of the American Academy of Political and Social Science* 143 (May): 280–.

Winslow, Mary Nelson and Elizabeth Adshead Hyde. 1923. *The Share of Wage-earning Women in Family Support.* Bulletin of the Women's Bureau, no. 30. Washington: U.S. Government Printing Office.

Winslow, Mary Nelson and Mary Viola Robinson. 1924. *Radio Talks on Women in Industry*. Washington: U.S. Women's Bureau.

Winslow, Mary Nelson. Coauth. *See* Peterson, Agnes Lydia.

Winsor, Lucy Burton. *See* Killough, Lucy Burton Winsor.

Wischnewetsky, Florence Kelley. *See* Kelley, Florence.

Wishard, Margaret N. 1891/2. How Women Figure in the Eleventh Census. *Chautauquan* 14 (October/March): 466–.

Withington, Anne. 1919. The Telephone Strike. *Survey* 42 (April): 146.

Witmer, Helen Elizabeth. 1928. Relations between the United States and Mexico during the Harding–Coolidge Administrations. Master's thesis, Columbia University.

Witmer, Helen Leland. 1925. Adult Parole with Special Reference to Wisconsin. Ph.D. thesis, University of Wisconsin–Madison (sociology).

——. 1930. The Influence of Old Age Pensions on Public Poor Relief in England and Wales. *Social Service Review* 4(1/4) (March/December): 587–.

——. 1930. Unemployment Insurance in England Today. *Social Forces* 8(3) (March): 433–8.

——. 1930/1. Increasing Research Value of Case Records. *Sociology and Social Research* 15: 116–.

——. 1931. Some Effects of the English Unemployment Insurance Acts on the Number of Unemployed Relieved under the Poor Law. *Quarterly Journal of Economics* 45(2) (February): 262–88.

——. 1931/2. On Demanding the Impossible of Sociology. *Journal of Educational Sociology* 5: 300–.

——. 1932. English Health Insurance and the Poor Law. *Social Service Review* 6(1/4) (March/December): 83–.

——. 1934. Book Review of "The Development of Social Insurance and Minimum Wage Legislation in Great Britain" by Helen Fisher Hohman. *Annals of the American Academy of Political and Social Science* 172 (March): 171–.

——. 1939. Book Review of "The Journal of Social Work Process" by Virginia P. Robinson *et al. American Sociological Review* 4(2) (April): 300.

——. 1939. Book Review of "The Public Assistance Worker: His Responsibility to the Applicant, the Community and Himself" by Russell Kurtz. *American Sociological Review* 4(1/6): 300.

——. 1940. The Diagnostic Significance of Russian Jewish Clients' Attitudes toward Relief. *Smith College Studies in Social Work* 10(4) (June): 285–.

Witt, Marguerite Schlumberger de. *See* Schlumberger, Marguerite de Witt.

Wolfson, Theresa. 1919 People Who Go To Beets. *American Child* (November): 217–39

——. 1922. Posture and Fatigue. *Survey* (April 8): 52–3.

——. 1923. Sweating Survey in the Garment Industry. M.A. thesis, Columbia University.

——. 1925. The Organization of the Woman Worker. Ph.D. thesis, Brookings Institution.

——. 1925. Wages of Organized Women Workers. *American Federationist* 32(7/12) (July/December): 811–.

——. 1925. Where are the Organized Women Workers? *American Federationist* (June): 455–7.

——. 1926. *The Woman Worker and the Trade Unions.* New York: International Pubs.

——. 1926. *The Women's Auxiliary to Trade Unions, and Workers' Education.* Workers' Education Pamphlet Series, no. 8. New York: Workers' Education Bureau of America.

——. 1926. Schools the Miners Keep. *Survey* (June 1).

——. 1929. Trade Union Activities of Women. *Annals of the American Academy of Political and Social Science* 143 (May): 120–31.

——. 1936. The Teaching of Economics in Negro Colleges. *Opportunity* 14(2) (February): 50–.

——. 1937. Industrial Unions in the American Labor Movement. *New Frontiers* (February): 3–52.

——. 1938. The White Collar Worker Asks Questions. *Social Frontier* 4(33) (March): 184–.

Wolfson, Theresa and Alice J. G. Perkins. 1939. *Frances Wright, Free Enquirer: The Study of a Temperament.* New York: Harper and Brothers.

Wolfson, Theresa. Papers at the New York State School of Industrial and Labor Relations, Cornell University, Labor-Management Documentation Center, Martin P. Catherwood Library.

Wollstonecraft, Mary. 1787. *Thoughts on the Education of Daughters, with Reflections on Female Conduct in the More Important Duties of Life.* London: J. Johnson. Reprinted, with a new introduction by Janet Todd, Bristol: Thoemmes, 1995.

——. 1790. *A Vindication of the Rights of Men, in a Letter to the Right Honorable Edmund Burke, Occasioned by His "Reflections on the Revolution in France."* London: J. Johnson.

——. 1792. *A Vindication of the Rights of Woman: With Strictures on Political and Moral Subjects*. London: J. Johnson; Boston: Thomas & Andrews.

——. 1794. *Historical and Moral View of the Origin and Progress of the French Revolution: And the Effect It Has Produced in Europe*. London: J. Johnson.

——. 1798. *Maria: or, The Wrongs of Woman*. London: J. Johnson. Reprinted New York and London: Norton, 1994. [*feminist novel*]

Wolman, Margaret. 1937. Real Property Tax Delinquency in Baltimore. Ph.D. thesis, Johns Hopkins University (economics).

Wolstenholme-Elmy, Elizabeth. *See* Elmy, Elizabeth C. Wolstenholme.

Wood, Edith Elmer. 1914. Four Washington Alleys. *Survey* (December 6): 251–4.

——. 1917. Constructive Housing Legislation and Its Lessons for the United States. M.A. thesis, Columbia University.

——. 1919. *The Housing of the Unskilled Wage Earner. America's Next Problem*. New York: Macmillan.

——. 1920. The Housing of the Unskilled Wage Earner: America's Next Problem. Ph.D. thesis, Columbia University (economics).

——. 1920. Wanted – More Homes. *Journal of the Association of Collegiate Alumnae* 14(2) (November).

——. 1922. Housing and Health through European Eyes. *Journal of the American Association of University Women* 15(5) (October): 132–.

——. 1923. *Housing Progress in Western Europe*. New York: E. P. Dutton.

——. 1926. The Result of the Housing Questionnaires. *Journal of the American Association of University Women* 19(2) (January): 9–.

——. 1931. *Recent Trends in American Housing*. New York: Macmillan Company.

——. 1933. The Economics of the Slums. *Current History (New York)* 39(2) (November): 185–.

——. 1933/4. A Century of the Housing Problem. *Law and Contemporary Problems* 1: 137–.

——. 1934. *The Housing Situation in the United States*. New York: Published for the Committee on the Housing Exhibition by the Museum of Modern Art.

——. 1935. *Slums and Blighted Areas in the United States*. U.S. Federal Emergency Administration of Public Works, Housing Division Bulletin, no. 1. Washington: U.S. Government Printing Office.

——. 1937. Book Review of "The Relation between Housing and Delinquency in New Jersey" by Division of Statistics and Research, N.J. Department of Institutions and Agencies. *American Sociological Review* 2(1/6): 145–.

——. 1937. The Costs of Bad Housing. *Annals of the American Academy of Political and Social Science* 190 (March): 145–.

——. 1938. Book Review of "The Abolition of Poverty" by James Ford and Katherine Morrow Ford. *Political Science Quarterly* 53: 639–.

——. 1938. What Has Kept Costs Down during England's House Building Boom? *Architectural Record* 84(1) (July): 79–82.

——. 1940. *Introduction to Housing; Facts and Principles*. Washington: U.S. Housing Authority.

Wood, Edith Elmer and Elizabeth Ogg. 1940. *The Homes the Public Builds.* Public Affairs Pamphlets, no. 41. New York: Public Affairs Committee.

Wood, Edith Elmer. Papers located in the Architecture Library of Columbia University.

Wood, Elizabeth. 1940. The Role of the Government in Defense Housing. *Land Economics* 16 (November): 382–5.

Wood, Elizabeth Janet. 1931. The Enactment of the Navigation Acts. M.A. thesis, University of California.

Wood, Helen. 1930. A Survey of the Commercial Occupations of Workers Fourteen to Thirty Years of Age in the City of Terre Haute, Indiana. A. M. thesis, Indiana University.

——. 1932. British Imperialism in Africa. M.A. thesis, University of Detroit.

——. 1940. *Young Workers and Their Jobs in 1936: A Survey in Six States.* U.S. Children's Bureau Publication, no. 249. Washington: U.S. Government Printing Office.

Wood, Katherine D. 1939. *The Statistical Adequacy of Employers' Occupational Records.* Social Security Bulletin. Washington: Social Security Board.

Wood, Katherine D[orothy]. Kleuter. 1929. The Question of International Regulation of Migration. Ph.D. thesis, University of Wisconsin–Madison (political science).

——. Coauth. *See* Palmer, Gladys Louise.

Wood-Simons, May. *See* Simons, May Wood.

Woodard, F. M. 1936. *The Town Proprietors in Vermont: The New England Town Proprietorship in Decline.* New York: Columbia University Press.

Woodbridge, Alice L. 1893. Our Working Women. Women Labourers in Factories and Shops. *Social Economist* 5(3) (September): 154–.

——. 1894. Child Slavery in America (Symposium): Child Labor, an Obstacle to Industrial Progress. *Arena* 10(1) (June): 135–43.

——. 1894. Woman's Labor. *American Federationist* 1(4) (June): 66–.

——. 1896. Pay of Women in Mercantile Establishments. *Independent* 48 (July 9): 954.

——. 1897. Woman's View of the Industrial Problem. *American Magazine of Civics* 9 (July): 71–7.

[Woodbury,] Helen L[aura]. Sumner. 1896. *The White Slave: or, "The Cross of Gold."* Chicago: C. H. Kerr. [*novel*]

——. 1905. Chapters in John R. Commons, ed., *Trade Unionism and Labor Problems.* Boston: Ginn and Co.

——. 1908. The Labor Movement in America, 1827–1837. Ph.D. thesis, University of Wisconsin (political economy and American history).

——. 1909. *Equal Suffrage: The Results of an Investigation in Colorado Made for the Collegiate Equal Suffrage League of New York State.* New York and London: Harper & Brothers. Reprinted New York: Arno Press, 1972.

——. 1910. *History of Women in Industry in the United States.* Volume IX of a Bureau of Labor Statistics Report entitled *Report on Condition of Woman and*

Child Wage-earners in the United States. Washington: U.S. Government Printing Office. Reprinted New York: Arno Press, 1974.

——. 1910. Historical Development of Women's Work in the United States. In Helen Marot, ed., *The Economic Position of Women*. New York: Academy of Political Science. Also published in Henry Raymond Mussey, ed., *Proceedings of the Academy of Political Science in the City of New York*. New York: Columbia University, 1910.

——. 1912. *Industrial Courts in France, Germany, and Switzerland*. U.S. Bureau of Labour Bulletin. Washington: U.S. Government Printing Office.

——. 1914. Vocational Education: Its Social Relationships. *Journal of Proceedings and Addresses of the National Education Association of the United States*: 572–7.

——. 1917/1919. *Standards Applicable to Child Labor*. Washington: U.S. Government Printing Office. Also printed in the *Journal of Sociological Medicine* XVIII(2) (April 1917).

——. 1917. Book Review of "Truancy and Non-Attendance in the Chicago Schools: A Study of the Social Aspects of the Compulsory Education and Child Labor Legislation of Illinois." *American Economic Review* 7 (June): 409–11.

——. 1917. What the Federal Government Has Done for Mothers. *Journal of the Association of Collegiate Alumnae* 11(1) (September): 17–.

——. 1917. Working Children of Boston. *Monthly Labor Review* 12 (January/June): 45–59.

Woodbury, Helen L[aura] Sumner. 1918/1936. Citizenship (1827–1833). In John R. Commons, David J. Saposs, Helen L. Sumner, E. B. Mittelman, H. E. Hoagland, John B. Andrews, and Selig Perlman, *History of Labour in the United States*, vol. 1. New York: Macmillan Co.

——. 1924. *Administration of Child Labor Laws, Part 5: Standards Applicable to the Administration of Employment Certificate Systems*. U.S. Children's Bureau Publication, no. 133. Washington: U.S. Government Printing Office.

——. 1930. Book Review of "Victorian Working Women: An Historical and Literary Study of Women in British Industries and Professions." *American Economic Review* 20(1) (March): 88–90.

——. 1930. Book Review of "Women Workers and the Industrial Revolution, 1750–1850." *American Economic Review* 20(4) (December): 720–1.

[Woodbury,] Helen Laura Sumner and Ethel E. Hanks. 1917/1919/1921. *Employment-certificate System*. New York. Washington: U.S. Government Printing Office for the U.S. Children's Bureau.

[Woodbury,] Helen Laura Sumner and Ella Arvilla Merritt. 1915. *Child Labor Legislation in the United States*. Washington: U.S. Government Printing Office.

[Woodbury,] Helen L. Sumner, Ethel E. Hanks, Francis H. Bird, and Ella A. Merritt. 1915–24. *Administration of Child Labor Laws*, part 1: *Employment Certificate System, Connecticut*; part 2: *Employment Certificate System, New York*; part 3: *Employment Certificate System, Maryland*; part 4: *Employment Certificate System, Wisconsin*; part 5: *Standards Applicable to the Administration of Employment-certificate*

Systems. U.S. Children's Bureau Publication, nos. 12, 17, 41, 85, and 133. Washington: U.S. Children's Bureau.

Woodbury, Helen Laura Sumner. Articles and speeches are also published in: *Review of Reviews* (October 1911); *New Republic* (September 18, 1915); the National Education Association's *Journal of Proceedings* (1914): 572–7; *Journal of Sociologic Medicine* (April 1917); and two articles in *Masses* (1912). A collection of her papers may be found at the State Historical Society of Wisconsin, Madison. She made contributions to *Encyclopedia of Social Sciences*, 1926–8.

Woodhouse, Margaret Chase Going. 1916. German War Finance. *Journal of Political Economy* 24 (June): 513–46.

——. 1927. *Planning and Recording Family Expenditures.* Washington: U.S. Department of Agriculture.

——. 1929. *Married College Women in Business and the Professions.* Philadelphia: s.n. Reprinted from Women in the Modern World. *Annals of the American Academy of Political and Social Sciences* cxliii (May).

——. 1929. The Standard of Living at the Professional Level, 1816–17 and 1926–27. *Journal of Political Economy* 37 (October): 552–72.

——. 1931. The Demand for College Trained Women in the United States, a Study of the Employment Situation. *Journal of the American Association of University Women* (January): 61–6.

Woodhouse, Margaret Chase Going and Anne Evans. 1938. *Business Opportunities for the Home Economist: New Jobs in Consumer Service.* New York and London: McGraw-Hill Book Co.

Woodhouse, Margaret Chase Going and Ruth Frances Yeomans Schiffman. 1929. *Occupations for College Women; a Bibliography.* Greensboro, N.C.: North Carolina College for Women.

Woodhouse, Margaret Chase Going and Faith Moors Williams. 1933. *Comparison of Schedule and Account Methods of Collecting Data on Family Living.* Washington: U.S. Department of Agriculture.

Woodhouse, Margaret Chase Going. Coauth. *See* Boehmer, Florence Elsie.

Woodhull [Martin], Victoria C[laflin]. 1871. *The Origin, Tendencies and Principles of Government: or, A Review of the Rise and Fall of Nations from Early Historic Times to the Present; with Special Considerations Regarding the Future of the United States as the Representative Government of the World and the Form of Administration which Will Secure this Consummation. Also, Papers on Human Equality, as Represented by Labor and Its Representative, Money; and the Meaning and Significance of Life from a Scientific Standpoint, with its Prophecies for the Great Future.* New York: Woodhull, Claflin.

——. 1871. *A Speech on the Great Social Problem of Labor & Capital.* Delivered at the Cooper Institute, New York City, Monday, May 8, 1871, before the Labor Reform League. New York: Journeymen Printers' Co-operative Association. Reprinted in *The Victoria Woodhull Reader*, ed. Madeleine B. Stern. Weston, Mass.: M and S Press, 1974.

——. 1871. *A Speech on the Principles of Finance.* Delivered at the Cooper Institute, New York City, Thursday, August 3, 1871. New York: Woodhull, Claflin & Co. Reprinted in *The Victoria Woodhull Reader*, ed. M. Stern.

——. 1872. *Freedom! Equality!! Justice!!! These Three; but the Greatest of These is Justice. A Speech on the Impending Revolution.* Delivered in Music Hall, Boston, Thursday, February 1, 1872, and the Academy of Music, New York, February 20, 1872. New York: Woodhull, Claflin & Co. Reprinted in *The Victoria Woodhull Reader*, ed. M. Stern.

——. 1873. *Reformation or Revolution, Which? or, Behind the Political Scenes.* Speech delivered in the Cooper Institute, New York, October 17, 1873. New York: Woodhull & Claflin. Reprinted in *The Victoria Woodhull Reader*, ed. M. Stern.

——. 1892. *Humanitarian Money: The Unsolved Riddle.* London: Blades, East & Blades, printer. Reprinted in *The Victoria Woodhull Reader*, ed. M. Stern.

——. 1893. *A Lecture by Victoria Claflin Woodhull: The Review of a Century, or, The Fruit of Five Thousand Years.* London: Women's Co-operative Print. Union. Reprinted from the *Boston Times* (October 22, 1876).

——. 1893. *The Scientific Propagation of the Human Race or, Humanitarian Aspects of Finance and Marriage. The Science of Well Being.* Lecture delivered at Carnegie Music Hall, New York City, November 20, 1893, and throughout America from 1870 to 1876. London: Eugenics Society?

——. 1893. The Principles of Finance. *Humanitarian* 3 (September): 161–.

——. 1894. The Evolution of Government. *Humanitarian* 4 (February): 89–.

——. 1895. The Principles of Social Freedom. *Humanitarian* 6 (February): 91–.

——. 1895. Purchasing Power. *Humanitarian* 6 (May): 356–.

——. 1896. The Financial Crisis in America. *Humanitarian* 9 (November): 330–9. Reprinted in *The Victoria Woodhull Reader*, ed. M. Stern.

——. 1896. What of the Future? *The Humanitarian* 8 (February): 90–6. Reprinted in *The Victoria Woodhull Reader*, ed. M. Stern.

——. 1896. Women Suffrage in the United States. *Humanitarian* 9 (July): 1.

——. Edited the *Humanitarian* (monthly), 1892–1901.

Wooding, Marie I. 1895. A Plea for the Working Girl. Chautauquan 21 (August): 625.

Woodruff, Ruth J[ackson]. 1921. A Classification of the Causes of Crime. *Journal of Criminal Law and Criminology and Police Science* 12(1) (May): 105–.

——. 1922/3. A Trade and Its Training (Dental Laboratory Mechanic). *Journal of Personnel Research* 1: 159–.

——. 1926. The Vocational Guidance Association of Philadelphia and Vicinity. *Vocational Guidance Magazine* 5(2) (November): 88–.

——. 1926. The Vocational Guidance Association of Philadelphia and Vicinity, Report for the Year 1925. *Vocational Guidance Magazine* 4(6) (March): 300–.

——. 1929. Every Day Problems in Junior Employment Work. *American Federationist* 36(3) (March): 316–.

——. 1931. The American Hosiery Industry before 1890. Ph.D. thesis, Radcliffe College (economics).

——. 1931. American Hosiery Industry from 1873 to 1895, with Special Reference to the Downward Trend of Prices. *Journal of Economic and Business History* 4 (November): 18–37.

Woods, Kate Tannatt. 1890. Why Some Women Cannot Obtain Employment. *Chautauquan* 11 (August): 618–.

[Woods,] Katharine Pearson. 1890. Queens of the Shop, the Workroom, and the Tenement. *Cosmopolitan* (November): 99–105.

——. 1895. Accidents in Factories and Elsewhere. *Publications of the American Statistical Association* IV(32) (December): 303–21.

——. 1898. Edward Bellamy: Author and Economist. *Bookman* 7 (March/August): 398.

Woods, Katharine Seymour. 1921. *The Rural Industries Round Oxford: A Survey Made on Behalf of the Institute for Research into Agricultural Economics, University of Oxford.* Oxford: Clarendon Press.

Woodward, Emma Hosken. 1885. *Men, Women and Progress.* London: Delau & Co.

Woodward, Florence M. 1936. The Town Proprietors of Vermont: The New England Town Proprietorship in Decline. Ph.D. thesis, Columbia University (economics).

Woodyard, Ella. 1926. The Effect of Time upon Variability. Ph.D. thesis, Columbia University (general psychology).

——. 1940. *Culture at a Price; a Study of Private Correspondence School Offerings.* New York: American Association for Adult Education.

Woolman, Mary Schenck. 1902. Revival of English Handicrafts: The Haslemere Industries. *Craftsman* 1(4) (January): 25–.

——. 1903. Manhattan Trade School for Girls and Board Schools. *Charities; a Weekly Review of Local and General Philanthropy* 10: 29.

——. 1905. Manhattan Trade School for Girls. *Educational Review* 30: 178.

——. 1909. Relative Value and Cost of Various Trades in a Girls' Trade School. *Annals of American Academy of Political and Social Science* 33 (January/June): 127–.

——. 1909. Trade Schools and Culture, *Educational Review* 37 (February).

——. 1910. *The Making of a Trade School.* Boston: Whitcomb and Barrows.

——. 1910. Training the Youngest Girls for Wage Earning. In Helen Marot, ed., *The Economic Position of Women.* New York: Academy of Political Science. Also published in Henry Raymond Mussey, ed., *Proceedings of the Academy of Political Science in the City of New York.* New York: Columbia University.

——. 1917. Training of Girls and Women for Trade and Industry. *Industrial-Arts Magazine* 6 (January/December): 355–.

——. 1920/1922/1923. *Clothing: Choice, Care, Cost.* Philadelphia and London: Lippincott.

Woolman, Mary Raphael Schenk and Ellen B. McGowan. 1913. *Textiles. A Handbook for the Student and the Consumer.* New York: Macmillan.

Woolston, Maxine Bernard Yaple Sweezy. 1936. The Burden of Direct Taxes as Paid by Income Classes. *American Economic Review* 26 (December): 691–710.

——. 1939. Distribution of Wealth and Income under the Nazis. *Review of Economics and Statistics* 21 (November): 178–84.

——. 1940. German Corporate Profits: 1926–1938. *Quarterly Journal of Economics* 54 (May): 384–98.

——. 1940. Nazi Economic Policies. Ph.D. thesis, Radcliffe College (economics).

Wootton, Barbara. 1919/20. Is Progress an Illusion? *Hibbert Journal* 18 (October/July): 18–.

——. 1920. Book Review of "Elementary Economics" by F. T. Carlton. *Economic Journal* 30: 385.

——. 1920. Book Review of "Introduction to Economics" by J. R. Turner. *Economic Journal* 30: 385.

——. 1920. Book Review of "Social Economics" by J. H. Jones. *Economic Journal* 30: 388–.

——. 1920. Classical Principles and Modern Views of Labour. *Economic Journal* 30(117) (March): 46–60.

——. 1921. Book Review of "Economics" by James Cunnison. *Economic Journal* 31: 107.

——. 1921. Book Review of "Economics for Beginners" by M. C. Buer. *Economic Journal* 31(123) (September): 390.

——. 1921. Book Review of "Elementary Economics" by T. N. Carver. *Economic Journal* 31: 391–.

——. 1921. Book Review of "English Political Theory" by Ivor Brown. *Economic Journal* 31: 108–.

——. 1921. Book Review of "Principles and Methods of Industrial Education" by W. H. Dooley. *Economic Journal* 31: 390–.

——. 1921. Book Review of "Wealth: Its Production and Distribution" by A. W. Kirkaldy. *Economic Journal* 31: 105–.

——. 1922. Book Review of "The Industrial State" by M. D. Stocks. *Economic Journal* 32(125) (March): 89–90.

——. 1922. Book Review of "Social Aspects of Industrial Problems" by G. Williams. *Economic Journal* 34(133) (March): 114–15.

——. 1925. Book Review of "The A.B.C.'s of Business" by H. S. McKee. *Economic Journal* 35: 624–.

——. 1925. Book Review of "Elements of Economics" by S. E. Thomas. *Economic Journal* 35(140) (December): 621–2.

——. 1925. Book Review of "Everyone's Economics" by R. Jones. *Economic Journal* 35(140) (December): 621–2.

——. 1925. Book Review of "Labour's Alternative" by E. Fimmen. *Economic Journal* 35: 622–.

——. 1925. Book Review of "The Principles of Business Economics" by J. Stephenson. *Economic Journal* 35(140) (December): 621–2.

——. 1925. Book Review of "A Short Course of Economic Science" by A. Bogdanoff. *Economic Journal* 35: 625–.

——. 1926. Book Review of "Economics of Social Problems" by H. E. A. Silverman. *Economic Journal* 36: 274–.

——. 1927. Book Review of "Descriptive Economics" by R. A. Lehfeldt. *Economic Journal* 37: 634–.

——. 1927. Book Review of "Elements of Economics" by C. R. Fay. *Economic Journal* 37: 635–.
——. 1927. Book Review of "Family Endowment: A Critical Analysis" by A. Gary. *Economic Journal* 37: 629–.
——. 1927. Book Review of "Towards Industrial Recovery" by H. Quigley. *Economic Journal* 37: 649–.
——. 1928. Book Review of "The Economic Theory of the Leisure Class" by N. Bukharin. *Economic Journal* 38: 302–.
——. 1928. Book Review of "Human Nature in Business" by F. Creedy. *Economic Journal* 38: 318–.
——. 1929. Arcadia "versus" London. *Listener* 1(9) (March 13): 317–.
——. 1929. Book Review of "The Intelligent Woman's Guide to Socialism" by Bernard Shaw. *Economic Journal* 39: 71–.
——. 1929. Book Review of "The Unemployed" by R. C. Davison. *Economic Journal* 39: 417–.
——. 1929. The Dream of Equal Wealth. *Listener* 1(8) (March 6): 273–.
——. 1929. A Mid-Victorian Paradise. *Listener* 1(11) (March 27): 393–.
——. 1929. Samuel Butler's Satirical Utopia. *Listener* 1(10) (March 20): 356–.
——. 1929. Shavian Socialism. *Economic Journal* 39(153) (March): 71–7.
——. 1929. Sublime Selfishness. *Listener* 1(12) (April 3): 426–.
——. 1929. Through the Eyes of an Economist. *Listener* 1(14) (April 17): 512–.
——. 1929. The Utopias of H. G. Wells. *Listener* 1(13) (April 10): 464–.
——. 1930. Book Review of "Economics of Inheritance" by J. Wedgwood. *Economic Journal* 40: 278–.
——. 1930. Book Review of "Great Britain from Adam Smith" by C. R. Fay. *Economic Journal* 40: 268–.
——. 1930. Book Review of "Karl Marx" by U. Rühle. *Economic Journal* 40: 323–.
——. 1930. Book Review of "Labour and Internationalism" by L. L. Lorwin. *Economic Journal* 40: 321–.
——. 1930. Unemployment. *Listener* 4(100) (December 10): 965–.
——. 1931. Book Review of "Arbitration Principles and the Industrial Court" by M. T. Rankin. *Economic Journal* 41(164) (December): 613–14.
——. 1931. Book Review of "Gold, Credit and Employment" by G. D. H. Cole. *Economic Journal* 41: 98–.
——. 1931. Book Review of "The National Debt" by E. L. Hargreaves. *Economic Journal* 41: 97–.
——. 1931. Book Review of "Women Workers and the Industrial Revolution" by Ivy Pinchbeck. *Economic Journal* 41(161) (March): 128–9.
——. 1931. Mr. Keynes on Money. *Listener* 5(111) (February 25): 330–.
——. 1932. Book Review of "Poverty in Plenty" by J. A. Hobson. *Economic Journal* 42: 97–.
——. 1932. Book Review of "Tariffs: The Case Examined" by Sir William Beveridge and others. *Economic Journal* 42: 64–.

——. 1932. Book Review of "Women's Place in Industry and Home" by S. Anthony. *Economic Journal* 42(168): 638–9.
——. 1932. Men and Money. *Listener* 8(207) (December 28): 952–.
——. 1932. A Symposium on Gold. *Listener* 7(158) (January 20): 101–.
——. 1933. Book Review of "Democracy, Debts and Disarmament" by Walton Newbold. *Economic Journal* 43: 682.
——. 1933. Book Review of "Honest Doubt" by Ernest Benn. *Economic Journal* 43: 163.
——. 1933. Book Review of "Is Capitalism Doomed?" by Lawrence Dennis. *Economic Journal* 43: 150.
——. 1933. Book Review of "Methods of Social Study" by Sidney and Beatrice Webb. *Economic Journal* 43: 152.
——. 1933. Book Review of "Recovery" by Sir Arthur Salter. *Economic Journal* 43: 272.
——. 1933. Book Review of "The Socialisation of Banking" by Oscar Sachse. *Economic Journal* 43: 682–.
——. 1934. *Plan or No Plan*. London: Victor Gollancz, Ltd. Reprinted New York: Farrar and Rinehart, 1935.
——. 1934. *Taxation under Capitalism*. London: New Fabian Research Bureau.
——. 1934. Book Review of "British Budgets, Third Series, 1921–22 to 1932–33" by Sir Bernard Mallet and George Oswald. *Economic Journal* 44: 123.
——. 1934. Book Review of "British Public Expenditure, 1921–31" by Joseph Sykes. *Economic Journal* 44: 123.
——. 1934. Poverty in Plenty – the Necessity of Planning. *Listener* 12(307) (November 28): 912–.
——. 1935. Book Review of "The Communist Answer to the World's Needs" by J. F. Hecker. *Sociological Review* 27: 362–.
——. 1935. Book Review of "Monographs on the Present Situation in the Soviet Union." *Economic Journal* 45: 759–.
——. 1935. Planning. *New Statesman and Nation* 9(220) (May 11): 686–.
——. 1936. *London's Burning: A Novel for the Decline & Fall of the Liberal Age*. London: G. Allen & Unwin.
——. 1936. Book Review of "Government Control of the Economic Order" by B. E. Lippincott. *Economic Journal* 46: 142–.
——. 1936. Book Review of "The Russian Financial System" by W. B. Reddaway. *Economic Journal* 46: 146–.
——. 1936. Book Review of "South Wales Needs a Plan" by H. A. Marquand. *Sociological Review* 28: 449–.
——. 1936. Some Implications of Anglo-Japanese Competition. *Pacific Affairs* 9(4) (December): 524–.
——. 1937. Book Review of "Mr. Keynes and the Labour Movement" by A. L. Rowse. *Economic Journal* 47: 153–.
——. 1937. Book Review of "Soviet Money and Finance" by L. E. Hubbard. *Economic Journal* 47: 108–.

——. 1938. *Lament for Economics.* New York: Farrar and Rinehart; London: George Allen & Unwin.

——. 1938. Vera Brittain in America. *New Statesman and Nation* 16(398) (October 8): 542–.

——. 1939. Book Review of "The Social Function of Science" by J. D. Bernal. *Economic Journal* 49: 319–.

——. 1939. Book Review of "The Soviet Comes of Age." *Economic Journal* 49: 346–.

——. 1939. Economic Problems of Federal Union. *New Commonwealth Quarterly* 5: 150–.

——. 1940. Book Review of "National Capitalism" by Davies. *Political Quarterly (1930–)* 11: 134–.

——. 1940. Book Review of "Who Shall Pay for the War?" *Political Quarterly (1930–)* 11: 143–.

——. 1940. Book Review of "Workmen's Compensation, Vol. I" by A. Wilson and H. Levy. *Economic Journal* 50: 124–.

Worcester, Daisy Lee Worthington. 1929. The Standard of Living. *Proceedings of the National Conference of Social Work*: 337–53.

Working, Hazel Gertrude Brown. 1932. Allen G. Thurman and Reconstruction. M.A. thesis, University of Chicago (history).

——. 1932. The History of the American Silk Industry. Ph.D. thesis, Radcliffe College (economics).

Wretts-Smith, Mildred. 1920. *The English in Russia During the Second Half of the Sixteenth Century*. Aberdeen: University of Aberdeen Press. Reprinted from *Transactions of the Royal Historical Society*, 4th series, 3(1920): 72–102.

——. 1931. Organization of Farming at Croyland Abbey, 1257–1321. *Journal of Economic and Business History* 4 (November): 168–92.

Wright, Elizabeth Cox. 1927. Common Law in Thirteenth Century English Royal Forests. Ph.D. thesis, University of Pennsylvania (law).

Wright, Esther Clark. 1931. The Genesis of the Civil Engineer in Great Britain, 1760–1830. Ph.D. thesis, Radcliffe College (economics).

Wright [D'Arusmont], Frances [Fanny]. 1821. *Views of Society and Manners in America – in a Series of letters From that Country to a Friend in England During the Years 1818, 1819, 1820, by an Englishwoman.* London: Longman, Hurst, Rees, Orme, and Brown. New ed., ed. Paul Baker, Cambridge, Mass.: Harvard University Press, 1963.

——. 1825. A Plan for the Gradual Abolition of Slavery in the United States without Danger of Loss to Citizens of the South. *New Harmony Gazette* (October 1). Reprinted Baltimore: Printed by Benjamin Lundy.

——. 1828. Explanatory Notes, Respecting the Nature and Objects of the Institution of Nashoba, and of the Principles upon Which It Is Founded. *New Harmony Gazette* (January 30, February 6, February 13).

——. 1829. *Course of Popular Lectures, as Delivered by Frances Wright in New York, Philadelphia and Other Cities of the United States. With Three Addresses on Public Occasions, and a Reply to the Charges against the French Reformers of 1789.* New York:

Office of the *Free Enquirer*. Reprinted in Frances Wright, *Life, Letters and Lectures, 1834/1844*. New York: Arno Press, 1972.

——. 1829. *A Lecture on Existing Evils and Their Remedy: As Delivered in the Arch Street Theatre, to the Citizens of Philadelphia, June 2, 1829*. New York: George H. Evans.

——. 1829. Rights and Wrongs of Women. *Free Enquirer* (April 29): 213.

——. 1830. *An Address to the Industrious Classes: A Sketch of a System of National Education*. New York: Office of the *Free Enquirer*.

——. 1830. *An Address to Young Mechanics*. New York: Office of the *Free Enquirer*.

——. 1830. *Fables*. New York: Office of the *Free Enquirer*.

——. 1834/1844. *Life, Letters and Lectures*. Reprinted New York: Arno Press, 1972.

——. 1835. *Supplement – Course of Lectures, Containing the Last Four Lectures Delivered in the United States*. New York: G. W. & A. J. Matsell. Reprinted in Frances Wright, *Life, Letters and Lectures, 1834/1844*. New York: Arno Press, 1972.

——. 1836. *Course of Popular Lectures, Historical and Political*. Vol. II. Philadelphia: published by the author.

——. 1838. *What is the Matter?* New York: Published for the author.

——. 1848. *England the Civiliser: Her History Developed in Its Principles*. London: Simpkin, Marshall and Co.

Wright, Helen Russell. 1922. The Political Labour Movement in Great Britain, 1880–1914. Ph.D. thesis, University of Chicago (economics).

——. 1931/2. Book Review of "Standards of Living: Proceedings of the Thirteenth American Country Life Conference, Madison, Wisconsin, October 7–10, 1930." *American Journal of Sociology* 37(1/6): 677–.

——. 1932. *Welfare of Children of Maintenance-of-way Employees*. U.S. Children's Bureau Publication, no. 211. Washington: U.S. Government Printing Office.

——. 1932. Expenditures of Railroad Laborers. *Social Service Review* 6(1/4) (March/December): 55–.

——. 1934. The Families of the Unemployed in Chicago. *Social Service Review* 8(1/4) (March/December): 17–.

——. 1934. The Use of Family Expenditures in Cost-of-living Indexes. *Journal of the American Statistical Association* 29, Supplement (March): 118–19.

Wright, Helen Russell and Sophonisba Preston Breckinridge. 1922. *Children of Wage-earning Mothers: A Study of a Selected Group in Chicago*. U.S. Children's Bureau Publication, no. 102. Washington: U.S. Government Printing Office.

Wright, Helen R. and Margaret Cochran Bristol. 1934. Some Aspects of Work-relief in Chicago. *Social Service Review* 8(1/4) (March/December): 628–.

Wright, Icelle Emma and Mary G. Lacy. 1927. *Oklahoma: An Index to the State Official Sources of Agricultural Statistics*. Bureau of Agricultural Economics, no. 21. Washington: U.S. Bureau of Agricultural Economics.

Wright, Julia McNair. 1879. *The Complete Home: An Encyclopædia of Domestic Life and Affairs. The Household in Its Foundation, Order, Economy…A Volume of Practical Experiences Popularly Illustrated*. Philadelphia: J. C. McCurdy.

Wright, Kathryn Robertson. 1939. The Living-wage Principle in Wage Legislation. A.M. thesis, Leland Stanford Junior University.

——. 1940. *Measurement of the Social Performance of Business*. Washington: U.S. Government Printing Office.

Wright, Marie Robinson. 1901. *The New Brazil: Its Resources and Attractions, Historical, Descriptive, and Industrial*. Philadelphia: George Barrie & Son.

——. 1904. *The Republic of Chile: The Growth, Resources, and Industrial Conditions of a Great Nation*. Philadelphia: G. Barrie & Sons/C. D. Cazenove & Son.

——. 1908. *The Old and the New Peru: A Story of the Ancient Inheritance and the Modern Growth and Enterprise of a Great Nation*. Philadelphia: G. Barrie & Sons.

——. 1911. *Mexico: A History of Its Progress and Development in One Hundred Years*. Philadelphia: G. Barrie & Sons.

Wright, Muriel Fanny. 1926. *Periodicals Relating to Dairying Received in the U.S. Department of Agriculture*. Washington: Bureau of Agricultural Economics Library.

Wright, Muriel H[azel]. 1926. First Oklahoma Oil Produced 1859. *Chronicles of Oklahoma* 4(4) (December): 322–.

——. 1930. Early Navigation and Commerce along the Arkansas and Red Rivers in Oklahoma. *Chronicles of Oklahoma* VIII(1) (March): 65–88.

Wulfert, Margaret A. 1925. *Butter and Cheese Markets in the West Indies*. Washington: U.S. Bureau of Foreign and Domestic Commerce.

——. 1926. *Butter and Cheese Markets in South America*. U.S. Bureau of Foreign and Domestic Commerce, Trade Information Bulletin, no. 406. Washington: U.S. Government Printing Office.

——. 1926. *International Trade in Butter and Cheese*. Washington: U.S. Bureau of Foreign and Domestic Commerce.

——. 1928. *Foreign Markets for United States Eggs*. Washington: U.S. Bureau of Foreign and Domestic Commerce.

——. 1936. *Foreign Markets for Wine and Other Grape Products*. Trade Information Bulletin, no. 835. Washington: U.S. Government Printing Office for the U.S. Department of Commerce, Bureau of Foreign and Domestic Commerce.

——. 1940. *Citrus Fruits, World Production and Trade*. Washington: U.S. Bureau of Foreign and Domestic Commerce.

Wunderlich, Frieda. 1915. Hegel und der deutsche Krieg. *Archiv für systematische Philosophie* 21: 127–.

——. 1916. Kapitalistische Philosophie. *Archiv für systematische Philosophie* 22: 219–.

——. 1917. Kapitalistische Philosophie. *Philosophical Review* 26: 447–.

——. 1920. *Hugo Münsterbergs Bedeutung für die Nationalökonomie*. Jena: G. Fischer.

——. 1921. Der Produktivitätsbegriff. *Jahrbücher für Nationalökonomie und Statistik* 116(4) (April): 289–.

——. 1925. *Die Bekämpfung der Arbeitslosigkeit in Deutschland seit Beendigung des Krieges*. Jena: G. Fischer.

——. 1926. *Fabrikpflege: Ein Beitrag zur Betriebspolitik*. Berlin: Springer.

——. 1926. *Produktivität*. Jena: G. Fischer.

——. 1927. Die Arbeitszeit-bestimmungen im Entwurf eines Arbeitsschutzgesetzes. *Archiv für Sozialwissenschaft und Sozialpolitik* 58: 375–.

——. 1928. The German Unemployment Insurance Act of 1927. *Quarterly Journal of Economics* 42 (February): 278–306.

——. 1930. *Der Kampf um die Sozialversicherung*. Berlin: Deutscher Verband der Sozialbeamtinnen.

——. 1931. Sozialpolitik in der Krise. *Diritto del lavoro* 5(1): 406–.

——. 1932. *Social Insurance in Germany*. Frankfurt am Main: German–American Institute.

——. 1932. *Versicherung, Fürsorge und Krisenrisiko*. Leipzig: Kommissions-Verlag von Luhe.

——. 1934. New Aspects of Unemployment in Germany. *Social Research* 1 (February): 97–110.

——. 1935. Book Review of "Conciliation and Arbitration in Industrial Disputes" by International Labour Office. *Social Research* 2(1/4): 252.

——. 1935. Book Review of "Die Frauenfrage in Deutschland. Strömungen und Gegenströmungen 1790–1930" by Hans Sveistrup and Agnes von Zahnharnack. *Social Research* 2(1/4): 249.

——. 1935. Book Review of "International Survey of Legal Decisions on Labour Law, 1932 (Eight Year)" by International Labour Office. *Social Research* 2(1/4): 252.

——. 1935. Book Review of "The Origins of the International Labor Organization" by James T. Shotwell, ed. *Social Research* 2(1/4): 126.

——. 1935. Book Review of "Russia's Iron Age" by William Henry Chamberlin. *Social Research* 2(1/4): 400–.

——. 1935. Insurance or Relief: Some Remarks on the Article of Dr. Colm. *Social Research* 2 (May): 168–75.

——. 1935. Women's Work in Germany. *Social Research* 2 (August): 310–36.

——. 1935/6. Book Review of "Aufstieg durch die Frau – eine grundsatzliche Besinnung und kulturpadagogische Auswertung" by Mina Weber. *American Journal of Sociology* 41(1/6): 133–.

——. 1936. Some Aspects of Social Work in the German Democratic Republic. *Social Research* 3 (February): 19–36.

——. 1937. Education in Nazi Germany. *Social Research* 4(1/4): 347–.

——. 1937. Health Insurance (Note). *Social Research* 4 (November): 509–14.

——. 1938. Deutsch-mann uber Alles. *American Scholar* 7(1) (Winter): 94–.

——. 1938. Germany's Defense Economy and the Decay of Capitalism. *Quarterly Journal of Economics* 52 (May): 401–30.

——. 1938. What Is Next in Unemployment Insurance? *Social Research* 5 (February): 37–54.

——. 1939. Book Review of "The German Universities and National Socialism" by Edward Y. Hartshorne, Jr. *Social Research* 6(1/4): 440–.

——. 1939. Book Review of "Labour Relations in Republican Germany. An Experiment in Industrial Democracy, 1918–1933" by Nathan Reich. *Social Research* 6(1/4): 128–.

——. 1940. Labour under German Democracy, Arbitration, 1918–1933. *Social Research*, Supplement II.

Wunderlich, Frieda Selma. 1925. Attempts to Reorganize the Ministry in France in the Fall of 1789. M.A. thesis, University of Nebraska (Lincoln Campus).

[Wurster], Catherine Krouse Bauer. 1931. An article in *Fortune* (May).

Wurster, Catherine Krouse Bauer. 1934. *Modern Housing.* Boston: Houghton Mifflin.

——. 1937. Now, at Last Housing: The Meaning of the Wagner–Steagall Act. *New Republic*, September 8: 119–21.

——. 1940. *A Citizen's Guide to Public Housing.* Poughkeepsie, N.Y.: Vassar College.

Wyatt, Edith. Coauth. *See* Clark, Sue Ainslie.

Wyman, Lillie B. Chace. 1888–9. Studies of Factory Life. *Atlantic Monthly* 62 (July): 16–29; (September): 315–21; (November): 605–12; 63 (January): 69–79.

——. 1890. Southern Colored Women. *Chautauquan* 11 (April/September): 752–.

——. 1892. Peasant Life in Russia. *Chautauquan* 15 (April): 57–.

——. 1893. Companions of the Cotton Loom. *Chautauquan* 18 (October): 88–.

——. 1896. Girls in a Factory Valley. *Atlantic Monthly* 78 (September): 391–403; (October): 504–17.

——. 1896. Organized Charities of Two Cities. *Lend a Hand* 17(4) (October): 272–.

Y

Yamakawa, Kikue. 1919. *From the Standpoint of Women.* Tokyo: Mita Shobo.
——. 1919. *Modern Life and Women.* Tokyo: Sobunkaku.
——. 1919. *The Victory of Women.* Tokyo: Nihon-Hyoron-sha.
——. 1919. On the Problems of Women at Work. *Kokka-gakkai Zasshi* 33(2–3).
——. 1922. *The Revolt of Women.* Tokyo: Santoku-sha.
——. 1923. *Russian in the Dawn.* Tokyo: Sobunkan.
——. 1925. *Women's Problems and Women's Movement.* Tokyo: Bunka Gakkai.
Yaple, Maxine. *See* Woolston, Maxine Yaple Sweezy.
Yoakley, Ina C. 1932. Wild Plant Industry of the Southern Appalachians. *Economic Geography* 8(3) (July): 311–17.
Yohe, Ethel C. *See* Larson, Ethel C. Yohe.
Yonge, Charlotte F. 1906. Friendly Societies. *Economic Review* (July).
Young, Elva Hulburd. 1902. The Law as a Profession for Women. *Association of Collegiate Alumnae, Publications*, series 3, 5 (February): 15–.
Young, Sadie Gertrude. 1925. Some Historical Evidences of the Repression Theory for the Origins of Revolutions. M.A. thesis. University of Missouri–Columbia.
Youngman, Anna [Prichitt]. 1906. The Growth of Financial Banking. *Journal of Political Economy* 14(7) (July): 435–43.
——. 1907. The Tendency of Modern Combination. Part I. *Journal of Political Economy* 15(4) (April): 193–208.
——. 1907. The Tendency of Modern Combination. Part II. *Journal of Political Economy* 15(5) (May): 284–98.
——. 1908. The Economic Causes of Large Fortunes. Ph.D. thesis, University of Chicago (economics).
——. 1908. The Fortune of John Jacob Astor. Part I. *Journal of Political Economy* 16(6) (June): 345–68.
——. 1908. The Fortune of John Jacob Astor. Part II. *Journal of Political Economy* 16(7) (July): 436–41.
——. 1908. The Fortune of John Jacob Astor. Part III. *Journal of Political Economy* 16(8) (October): 514–30.

——. 1909. *The Economic Causes of Great Fortunes*. New York: Bankers' Publishing Co. Reprinted Freeport, N.Y.: Books for Libraries Press, 1972; New York: Arno Press, 1973.

——. 1910. The Tobacco Pools of Kentucky and Tennessee. *Journal of Political Economy* 18(1) (January): 34–49.

——. 1912. Frankfort-on-the-Main: A Study in Prussian Communal Finance. Part I. *Quarterly Journal of Economics* 27(1) (November): 150–201.

——. 1913. Frankfort-on-the-Main: A Study in Prussian Communal Finance. Part II. *Quarterly Journal of Economics* 27(2) (February): 329–72.

——. 1917. The Revenue System of Kentucky: A Study in State Finance. *Quarterly Journal of Economics* 32(1) (November): 142–205.

——. 1921. The Efficacy of Changes in the Discount Rate of the Federal Reserve Banks. *American Economic Review* 11(3) (September): 466–85.

——. 1922. A Popular Theory of Credit Applied to Credit Policy. *American Economic Review* 12(3) (September): 417–46.

Yudelson, Sophie. 1904. Women's Place in Industry and Labor Organizations *Annals of the American Academy* (September): 343–.

——. 1905. Education and Professional Activities of Women. *Annals of the American Academy of Political and Social Science* 25: 117.

Z

Zakrzewska, Marie E[lizabeth]. and Caroline H. Dall. 1869. *A Practical Illustration of "Woman's Right to Labor": or, A Letter from Marie E. Zakrzewska.* Boston: Walker, Wise and Company .

Zebricov, Mariya. 1884. Russia. In Theodore Stanton, ed., *The Woman Question in Europe.* London: Sampson Low, Marston, Searle.

Zetkin, Clara. 1889. *Die Arbeiterinnen- und Frauenfrage der Gegenwart* [Women workers and the woman question at the present time]. Berlin: Volks Tribune.

——. 1907. *Zur Frage des Frauenwahlrechts.* Berlin: Vorwärts.

Zimmern, Alice. 1894. *Methods of Education in the United States.* London: Swan Sonnenschein.

——. 1895. Women in European Universities. *Forum* 19 (April): 187–99.

——. 1898. *The Renaissance of Girls' Education in England: A Record of Fifty Years' Progress.* London: A. D. Innes.

——. 1899. The Servant Question in America. *Leisure Hour* XLVII (May): 460.

Zimmern, Dorothy M. 1912. Women's Wages. *Women's Industrial News* (July).

——. 1916. The Civil Service and Women. *Political Quarterly (1914–1916)* 8 (September): 79–.

——. 1918. The Wool Trade in War Time. *Economic Journal* 28 (March): 7–29.

——. Coauth. *See* Papworth, Lucy Wyatt.

Zimmern, Helen. 1883. *Maria Edgeworth.* London: W. H. Allen & Co.; Boston: Roberts Brothers.

——. 1893. The Parisian Municipal Refuges for Working Women. *Charities Review* 2(4) (February): 226–.

——. 1895. Female Higher Education in Italy. *Educational Review* (London) 10 (October): 231–.

——. 1896. An Automatic Savings Bank. *Leisure Hour* 45 (April): 364–.

Zink, Norah E. 1938. Dry-farming Adjustments In Utah. Ph.D. thesis, University Of Chicago (geography). .

——. 1939. Dry-farming Regions in Utah. *Economic Geography* 15(4) (October): 421–31.

——. 1940. A Dry-farming Region in Utah. *Economic Geography* 16(3) (July): 281–90.

Zorbaugh, Grace S. McClure. 1926. Lump-sum Compensation. Ph.D. thesis, University of Wisconsin (economics).
——. 1927. Letters of an Industrial Investigator. *American Federationist* 34(1/6) (January/June): 325–.
——. 1928. Recent Tendencies in Administration of Lump Sum Settlements under Workmen's Compensation Laws. *American Labor Legislation Review* 18: 112–.
——. 1929. Lump-sum Compensation. *American Federationist* 36(4) (April): 430.
——. 1930. Credit-union Experience in Iowa. *American Federationist* 37(7) (July): 966–.
——. 1934. The Dean and the Community. *Journal of the American Association of University Women* 28(1) (October): 33–.
——. 1936. Cooperative Employment in Britain. *American Federationist* 43(7) (July): 714–.
——. 1936. General Comment. *Taxbits* 3(4) (February): 5–.
——. 1936. The Total Consumer Problem. *Social Science* 11(4) (October): 360–.
——. 1937. College Grades and the Vocational Motive. *School and Society* 46(1176) (July 10): 62–.
——. 1937. Labor's "Happy End." *American Federationist* 44(10) (October): 1,080–.
——. 1937. Youth Considers Future Problems. *Personnel Journal* 15(8) (February): 300–.
——. 1938. Beginners Guide to Cooperation. *American Federationist* 45(7) (July): 711–.
——. 1939. Consumers' Cooperation in Great Britain. *American Federationist* 46(10) (October): 1,081–.
——. 1939. Vocational Information Conferences at Ohio State University. *Occupations: The Vocational Guidance Magazine* 17(5) (February): 413–.

www.ingramcontent.com/pod-product-compliance
Lightning Source LLC
LaVergne TN
LVHW021003300926
849160LV00007B/235
9780415646079